THE TWO CITIES

RECORDS OF WESTERN CIVILIZATION

RECORDS OF WESTERN CIVILIZATION

Two Renaissance Book Hunters: The Letters of Poggius Bracciolini to Nicolaus de Niccolis. Translated and annotated by Phyllis Walter Goodhart Gordan.

Guillaume d'Orange: Four Twelfth-Century Epics. Translated with an introduction by Joan M. Ferrante.

Visions of the End: Apocalyptic Traditions in the Middle Ages, by Bernard McGinn, with a new preface and expanded bibliography.

The Letters of Saint Boniface. Translated by Ephraim Emerton, with a new introduction and bibliography by Thomas F. X. Noble.

Imperial Lives and Letters of the Eleventh Century. Translated by Theodor E. Mommsen and Karl F. Morrison, with a historical introduction and new suggested readings by Karl F. Morrison.

An Arab-Syrian Gentleman and Warrior in the Period of the Crusades: Memoirs of Usāmah ibn-Munqidh. Translated by Philip K. Hitti, with a new foreword by Richard W. Bulliet.

De expugnatione Lyxbonensi (The Conquest of Lisbon). Edited and translated by Charles Wendell David, with a new foreword and bibliography by Jonathan Phillips.

Defensor pacis. Translated with an introduction by Alan Gewirth, with an afterword and updated bibliography by Cary J. Nederman.

History of the Archbishops of Hamburg-Bremen. Translated with an introduction and notes by Francis J. Tschan, with a new introduction and bibliography by Timothy Reuter.

THE TWO CITIES

A CHRONICLE OF UNIVERSAL
HISTORY TO THE YEAR 1146 A.D.

BY

OTTO, BISHOP OF FREISING

TRANSLATED WITH AN INTRODUCTION AND NOTES BY
Charles Christopher Mierow

WITH A FOREWORD AND UPDATED BIBLIOGRAPHY BY
Karl F. Morrison

EDITED BY
Austin P. Evans and Charles Knapp

COLUMBIA UNIVERSITY PRESS
NEW YORK

Columbia University Press
Publishers Since 1893
New York   Chichester, West Sussex

Copyright © 2002 Columbia University Press
All rights reserved
Library of Congress Cataloging-in-Publication Data
A complete CIP record is available from the Library of Congress.

ISBN: 0–231–12600–X (cloth)
ISBN: 0–231–12601–8 (paper)

RECORDS OF WESTERN CIVILIZATION is a series published under the auspices of the Interdepartmental Committee on Medieval and Renaissance Studies of the Columbia University Graduate School. The Western Records are, in fact, a new incarnation of a venerable series, the Columbia Records of Civilization, which, for more than half a century, published sources and studies concerning great literary and historical landmarks. Many of the volumes of that series retain value, especially for their translations into English of primary sources, and the Medieval and Renaissance Studies Committee is pleased to cooperate with Columbia University Press in reissuing a selection of those works in paperback editions, especially suited for classroom use, and in limited clothbound editions.

Committee for the Records of Western Civilization

Caroline Walker Bynum
Joan M. Ferrante
Carmela Vircillo Franklin
Robert Hanning
Robert Somerville, editor

CONTENTS

FOREWORD: ON TRUTH IN OTTO OF FREISING

Karl F. Morrison

The *Chronicle* of Otto of Freising (*ca*. 1115–1158) has long been recognized as standing in a class of its own. Astonishing as it may seem, those who go to the *Chronicle* as a document of historical information or of developments in the philosophy of history will find only relatively minor adjustments to make in the expert and detailed assessment that Charles Mierow published in 1928. However, since 1928, some scholars have cast all historical narratives in a new light. They study narratives in the light of literary criticism, reasoning that historical narratives are texts constructed by the same kinds of "fictive" or artistic decisions that produce other literary works.[1] Thus, a historical narrative, such as Otto's *Chronicle*, is less a document, valuable as a witness to facts, than an interpretation having little more claim to objective truth, if any, than Shakespeare's plays.

Incompatible Truths

Was Otto not only one of the most distinguished historical writers in the Middle Ages but also a forger? The proposal has been debated and laid aside.[2] However, the production of forgeries was part of the high culture in Otto's day, practiced by dominant orders of church and state. Some forgeries accepted as genuine became cornerstones of the European intellectual tradition and inspirations of its greatest achievements, as did the theological treatises falsely attributed to a follower of the Apostle Paul, Dionysius the Areopagite, which gave Otto the substance of his concluding, apocalyptic sections. In the general culture of Otto's day, the boundaries between factual and fictive, between pious fraud and forensic proof, were fluid.

One compelling fascination of the *Chronicle* is that it displays both sides of the modern critical turn. On the one hand, Otto claimed to deliver truth. On the other, he acknowledged that his own, changeable frame of mind shaped his narrative. "All doctrine," he wrote, "consists in rejection and selection." Writers about the times fled from falsehood and chose truth.[3] And yet, when he sat down to write, the shape he gave the *Chronicle*, by including some materials and excluding others, expressed nothing objective in his data, but rather the "bitterness of mind" that led him to weave his story together "in the fashion of tragedy." Later, in a "joyful mind," he began writing his second great work, *The Deeds of Frederick Barbarossa*, not to lament as in tragedy but to celebrate and rejoice.[4] Between these events, another state of mind had entirely stopped Otto's writing. After some early work on the *Chronicle*, he had found himself so beset by adversity that he fell into a kind of mental torpor, almost like sleep, until an experience he compared with a sudden trumpet blast wakened him and called him back to work.[5]

When not plagued by writer's block, he had no intention of letting facts speak for themselves. He had a lesson to teach, and that lesson required the suppression or slanting of evidence. The purpose of writing history, he said, had always been to provide incentives to virtue and deterrents to vice: to praise the famous works of virtuous men and suppress in silence what base men had done. If the actions of the wicked were to see daylight at all, they were to be presented so as to terrify readers and warn against any kind of imitation.[6] In Otto's view, the purpose of history was not to tell the unvarnished truth but to teach a lesson.

The gloomy theme of the *Chronicle*, that human life's constant instability made it all one great misery, corresponded with what Otto called his "bitterness of mind." He recorded that what put him into that state of mind was a concatenation of local feuds. In one, Otto was a major combatant; in another, he was, by his telling, a bystander caught in crossfire between two magnates in southern Germany. These were dangerous and costly feuds; even the fortifications of Otto's city, Freising, were razed.[7] Still, the *Chronicle* did not pretend to be an objective statement of facts. Otto knew and acknowledged that the interpretive strategy he imposed on universal history derived in great part from local tempests. From them, instructed by traditions of Christian historical writing, he extrapolated an all-encompassing theory of universal history.

Otto was a pioneer in the theological interpretation of history, but his rejection and inclusion of materials in the *Chronicle* set up a field in which all truths were unstable and conflicted. For him, as monk and bishop, the teaching function of history easily turned into preaching — kerygma. Like others of his age and religious duties, Otto believed that the very act of preaching manifested God's plan for the salvation of the world.

The truth Otto thought he found in history was Christ.[8] The events of history were strung together like beads, on a single cord: the biblical revelation on which Christian doctrine rested. Holding firmly to what he considered its Christological center, Otto, the preacher, embraced scripture as the roadmap of the human race's pilgrimage from Creation to Last Judgment and to the eternal destinies of the damned and the saved. Yet a danger had long been obvious in attempting to combine history with theology — that history would subvert religion. Otto of Freising invoked for himself defensive arguments that writers he claimed as kerygmatic "predecessors" — including Augustine of Hippo and Orosius — had constructed against those who impugned the faith in them.[9]

Even in classical antiquity, history had proven to be a formidable enemy of religion, or, more properly, of myths that for believers authenticated religious mysteries. Enlightened minds were hostile to supernatural religion, with the myths and legends that justified it making a closed, or "vicious," circle. History explained how, over time, people had made up myths and legends by telling and retelling stories about the illustrious dead, embellishing the stories at every telling and, in time, instituting religious cults to celebrate them. History provided a way to break out of the vicious circle of myth and cult, to escape the oppressive weight of religion. It allowed an understanding of nature to dispel the fear and darkness that religion cast upon the mind and the acts of moral horror it sanctified.[10]

History was as instrumental in the breakdown of religious tradition among the educated in antiquity as it was during the Enlightenment. Edward Gibbon (1737–1794) looked back on the kerygmatic tradition of monastic histories, in which Otto of Freising stood, as expressing "the dark and implacable genius of superstition," defending, yet vitiating, "the cause of truth by the arms of deceit and falsehood."[11]

Otto called history the realm of the "visible" and theology that of the "invisible." He thought them related as sign and signified. His whole effort was to read history, the visible manifestations of God's work and guidance, as if it encoded and expressed an underlying pattern, God's plan for the salvation of the human race. However, long before Otto's day, the practice of reading history through the lens of Biblical allegory to draw a moral had its critics. It was evidently a way in which human beings could arbitrarily cut and trim historical evidence to fit their own theories about God's unseen hand in human events.

From Otto of Freising's day onward, and irresistibly in the Enlightenment, critics rebuked the Church itself for suppressing authentic biblical history. They charged that the priesthood had usurped a corrupt and corrupting monopoly over reading, interpreting, and preaching, and that the institutional Church and its theology perverted the simplicity of the gospel. Some, indeed, edged into heresy and rejected part or all of scripture as a fraud perpetrated by rulers of the Church, whom they cursed as the harlot of the Apocalypse. Even in the minds of more conservative critics of institutionalized religion, conceptions of history undermined official doctrine.

Otto anticipated that critics would accuse him of emptying his world of every value by mingling difficult and hidden scriptural witnesses with historical accounts. He justified himself by precedent. Not only had his great model, Augustine of Hippo, mingled history with theology in *The City of God*, but authors of books in scripture itself — above all, Christ's beloved disciple — had juxtaposed history with mystic vision. In the work of Creation, had not God himself moved from invisible to visible?[12]

The *Chronicle*, as we have it, took shape over four years (1143–1147) and through at least one major revision of the original version (in or before 1157). In its present form, the text spirals around the theme of human misery, already in Otto's day an age-old theme for preachers. In His perfection, God endured unchangeable; but, like all other creatures, human beings constantly changed, always becoming what they had not been and eventually perishing. Otto looked to the broad sweep of history repeatedly to illustrate that human powers gave no one, even the most eminent, any hope of escaping mutability leading toward extinction. By repeating this simple, familiar theme of human weakness, mutability sweeping all to extinction, Otto hoped to inspire readers with desire for the abiding peace and endless joy of the redeemed in Christ's kingdom, and fear of the eternal, undying death of the damned.[13]

And yet, Otto grasped acutely the instability of the historical truths he affirmed. Without theology's doctrine of redemption, the relentless changefulness of things glared out as banal terror. The shifting powers in the world were like people sick with hectic fevers, tossing themselves restlessly from side to side hoping for a little peace. Human beings were like sea monsters, devouring each other as long as they could, and ending with each one devouring its own flesh. Without theology's truths, there was nothing more to the mutability of the world than the senseless spin of Fortune's wheel. Indeed, Otto began his *Chronicle* with a contrast between those for whom life was a dizzying whirl on Fortune's wheel, and the wise, who rested four-square, immovable in virtue.[14] Otto's story of human misery was a trail of carnage — suicides, murders, and military slaughters, all recorded dispassionately by Otto. He did not dwell on the central event in the story of redemption, the execution of Jesus.[15] But he once paused to ask whether anyone could be saved without bloodshed. Answering his own question, Otto doubted that bloodless redemption was possible. At the same time, he realized that he was incompetent to gauge why God had chosen redemption through blood, or anything else God's boundless power could do.[16]

How did the trail of carnage Otto found in history bear on the truths of theology? Even to ask whether salvation could have been achieved without bloodshed was to indicate one point at which historical data could subvert essential teachings of theology, for it pried into God's reasonings and, if pressed hard, into God's omnipotence. Otto entered many such questions in the *Chronicle*. Why did God delay salvation almost until the end of time? By doing that, He allowed the profane and lost world to go along, cheerfully following its own perverse ways and working out its own damnation; He allowed the greater part of humanity to perish in unbelief. Once the Messiah came, why did God blind the Jews to the redemption they had yearned for, thereby enabling them to compound the severity of their damnation, and why did He allow the early Church to suffer repeated and savage persecution?[17] Why did God allow the kingdom of the Franks, a key agent in the narrative of redemption, to tear itself apart in civil war? Why, in any age, did God permit evil to reign and seem likely in Otto's own day to send Antichrist to vent his cruel malice on the saints?[18]

God's purposes in allowing some evils were evident. For example, God blinded his chosen people, the Jews, so that not one people only, but all nations, might receive the light of truth.[19] Even so, why did He choose that way?

In the Enlightenment, such interrogations of scripture, joined with advances in philology and natural sciences, shattered and discredited age-old theological traditions. Without philology and natural science, Otto was forced time and again to evade the issue by saying that such matters were beyond his powers to sift through, that he did not understand what he read in scripture.[20] God's "just and most secret judgments" were beyond the grasp of human reason. As for His apparent cruelty and that trail of blood, mercy could be a vice even in human judges.[21]

By 1157, when he completed the surviving version of the *Chronicle*, Otto had ventured further to combine the mutually subversive disciplines of history and philosophy. He recognized that those who relied on human reason in philosophy could easily be led by their own reasonings and arguments to deny the faith. Yet, he did not specifically write that the delights of history could lead to the same point. The fact of the matter, however, was that the goal of redemption was to escape history.[22] Toward the end of the *Chronicle*, Otto wrote with admiration of saints in his own day whose holiness mitigated the tribulations announcing the world's impending end. Some lived in monastic orders; others, in solitude without human companionship. In their austerity, Otto wrote, they had transcended human weakness and escaped the hectic spinning of the world. They had already gone beyond history to live in the calm of God's eternal Sabbath. In fleeing falsehood and choosing truth, Otto relied on their prayers to complete his work in the mode of tragedy.[23]

There were, Otto wrote, two ways of knowing. The one was the direct experience of sick persons, actually suffering the ravages of disease. The other was the detached learning of physicians who knew what they learned about disease second hand, by tradition, from medical lore (*per artis notitiam*), or at least by detached observation.[24] This distinction underscores his confidence that apprehending truth was like the direct, life-and-death engagement of someone in the struggle, rather than the expertise relayed by tradition.

Still, those who had passed from visible things and directly apprehended the invisible truth, analogues of the sick person, were exactly those who, even in this life, escaped the turmoil of the ever-changing world. Those who knew it by scholarly tradition continued to suffer the violent shifts of mutability. Religious adepts, monks, and hermits, whom Otto praised as savoring by contemplation the sweetness of Heaven while still alive were withdrawn from the turbulent misery of the world. They were surely among the saints who, physically in the body, fell into the joy of the beatific vision, rapt from their physical senses and gently worked upon by inward sweetness.[25]

With longing for a release that history could not give him, Otto wrote that, in Heaven, when mortality had changed into immortality and animal into spiritual, the redeemed beholding the Creator of the universe in His matchless grace and glory would remember from their earthly lives nothing that would grieve them, but only what would give them joy and stir their gratitude to their Redeemer. Participating in God's own identity, they would know no longer "through the misery of experience." They would know through the One who knows all things; they would know "through the superabundant glory of internal and external Wisdom."[26]

Otto's Results

Despite his questioning, Otto realized that to escape history, human beings would have to escape who they were; for they lived in the medium
of history as surely as fish lived in water. Lacking any notion of evolution,
Otto could not conceive that any other beings, from God down to the
lowest earthworm, had history. While human beings were nothing in
themselves, God had made them alone in His image and likeness. History
was the medium in which human beings realized their nature, their image-
likeness to God and the destiny they were made for. That was true because history was exactly the medium in which human beings encountered
God, their maker and archetype. Despite the quandary at the heart of
his work, Otto preached his great theme that all history was the human
race's pilgrimage into truth, its God-destined redemption from history's
incessant changes and passage into the changeless Being of God himself.

Otto made reason the keystone of his argument. Otto defined "man"
as "a rational and mortal animal." He considered reason, above all, the
faculty that defined being human and, indeed, that characterized human
nature as made in the image of God. Reason was cognate with holiness,
and human beings possessed reason for the purpose of knowing God.
Reason was the means used by the wise to escape the crazily spinning
wheel of Fortune and stand immovable in virtue.[27] The human race's
pilgrimage into truth wakened a latent humanity. In those in whom ra-
tionality expanded, human nature transcended mortality and passed into
immortality, transcended animality and became spiritual.

The world had existed for roughly 6,600 years. Still, for most of that
time, 5,500 years, human reason and capacity for truth by knowing God
had been suppressed. Apart from God's chosen few, the entire human
race lived as brute animals, wandering in error, captivated by demonic
illusions and vain superstition, driven by base, animal cravings. At His
incarnation, Christ recalled the human race to the light of reason; that
is, by enabling it to know God, He recalled the human race to its humanity.[28]

After Christ's incarnation, human beings remained mutable; the un-
redeemed continued alien to reason. And yet, for the 1,100 years after
Christ, vicissitudes of existence became a means of progress toward perfect rest for those called by grace to be "citizens of Christ."[29] This was
so even in Otto's own day, when the "final dissolution" seemed at hand
with the advent of Antichrist and his cruel persecution of the righteous,
a whirlwind of persecution, schism, and destruction, Otto wrote, a reversal

of progress from perfection to failure that was equally, in God's strange
providence, a step toward the everlasting beatitude of the saints.[30] After
the desolations of the present, Otto foresaw Christ's triumphant Last
Judgment and, for the saved, the "eternal day of eternal peace," the direct
vision of God without the mediation of any knowledge.[31]

Human beings, Otto wrote, possessed reason for a second purpose
apart from knowing God: namely, to know themselves, investigating the
matter of truth not only in other creatures but also in themselves. The
two purposes were really halves of the same whole; for knowing themselves
was conditional on knowing God. When they meditated on the constant
turmoil of existence and the rise and fall even of the greatest empires,
reflective minds must be humbled to detect God's hand shifting earthly
power as He willed. They would only realize that, being nothing in themselves, they were what they were by His mercy.[32] When they found wisdom, goodness, or any other virtue in themselves, they recognized that
they derived it by participation in God, who alone was the virtues that
He had, and who was the one font from which all flowed. Moreover, when
they found wisdom or goodness in themselves by loving what they did
well, they recapitulated God's own providence, creating things that had
not existed and loving, governing, and preserving what He created. Looking to eternity, Otto maintained that all the redeemed were incorporated
into the Heavenly Jerusalem by participation, the saints being built into
it as living stones, and participating in God eternally and changelessly.[33]
Even on earth, saints were one by their common participation in Christ,
who was their life.[34]

Otto's reflections on human nature led him to the insufficiency of the
individual. He concluded that, of ourselves, we are nothing and depend
entirely on God's mercy for whatever we are, and that, of ourselves, we
know nothing and depend entirely on God's grace for whatever we have
to say.[35] His conviction of the insufficiency and utter dependence of the
individual is one reason why the actors in his story are names without
faces or characters. Thomas Carlyle's (1795–1881) famous sentence,
"The history of the world is but the biography of great men," is unthink-
able in Otto's frame of reference. Even in the very rare instances in which
Otto gave extended assessments of individual figures, he dropped no hint
of the titanic, individual personality, or of a creative, autonomous will.[36]

To the contrary, Otto's idea of individual insufficiency was part and
parcel of his idea that all human beings derived their existence from the
same source. Just as all wise individuals had wisdom in the degree to
which they participated in the wisdom that was God, and all good indi-

viduals had goodness in the degree to which they participated in the good that was God, so individuals had existence in the degree to which they participated in God as Being. In his *Deeds of Frederick Barbarossa*, Otto quoted Boethius's famous sentence, " A person is the individual substance of rational being," and the absence of creative autonomy implied in this sentence pervades the *Chronicle*. The *persona* was not a unique, self-determining individual but a twig on a vine, one articulation of a universal, infinite Being.[37]

History was the story of humanity in the mass, from a distinctive religious perspective and from hindsight. Frail and dependent as individuals were, Otto recognized access to truth in the collective witness of human experience. This was what drew him to history and, within history, to traditions of wisdom. Otto's conviction that human nature, by virtue of reason, gave access to ultimate truth opened for him a vision of humanity as growing and developing through time, a vision available only by hindsight, at the end of time.

Realizing the vulnerability of his general theme, Otto deployed several tactics to defend it. First, and most important, he claimed for himself the authority of tradition, tacitly disclaiming originality. Reason, the keystone of his great theme, led him to philosophy. He held that pre-Christian philosophers, especially Plato and Aristotle, had investigated the nature of God. They had passed from visible to invisible, he wrote, though, lacking the message of salvation revealed by Christ to the meek of heart, they had only been able to employ natural ability (*naturale ingenium*).[38] Thus, even as God's continuing providence governed the world in the long centuries between Adam and Christ, the search for the objective of reason, innate in human beings, continued imperfectly. Through traditions of wisdom, Christians, enlightened by grace, could profit from historical records of the dark age before grace between Adam and Christ. For, by reflection on proofs of virtue and on miseries of those centuries, they could, by a kind of empathy, feel the full weight of human tragedy and grasp the causes of misfortunes hidden from those who actually lived through past tribulations.[39]

A far purer way to truth than any pagans had known lay open in the Church. God, Otto wrote, had given the spirit of truth to the Church, preserving it from any deception by the spirit of error. Drawing on precedents in Christian historical tradition, supremely represented by Augustine of Hippo and his follower, Orosius, Otto thought he grasped the lessons history had to teach to those who were enduring the agonies of the world's final dissolution. Moreover, he gained assurance from them that, even in the last times, the pursuit of wisdom was accelerated by learning from the experiences of those who had gone before.[40] Christ sustained the faith of the Roman Church, above all, by his prayers for St. Peter. Neither the whole Church nor the see of Rome could be deceived, and whatever the Roman Church believed must be believed; she had authority to settle every controversy. Otto took great care to demonstrate his loyalty to the popes by advocating their side in the major conflicts of his day, and by recording his own attendance at the papal court.[41]

Less theoretically, Otto defended his theme with the simple, direct step of omitting information he found a distraction from his purpose. Thus, he felt able to omit from his accounts the doings of unbelievers, perfidious infidels, whether Jews or gentiles. He suppressed them as lacking in nobility, "hardly worth writing down or relaying to later generations."[42] Less doctrinaire reasons prompted other omissions. Some information he omitted because, he said, it was well known, or to avoid overburdening readers, or simply to make room for information he preferred to include. He justified his omission of information about Christians on the ground that John the Evangelist had omitted much about Christ and His miracles.[43]

Finally, Otto's elitism defended him from the necessity of explaining, or defending, his theme outside his intended audience of very exalted men, including his half-brother, Frederick Barbarossa.

Otto was prepared to think that much of the human race was blind to the truths about human origins, nature, and destiny. To be sure, he wrote that every human being was capable of reason, and that all the wise followed the track of reason through visible to invisible things.[44] However, Otto found reason and its potentials realized only in people like himself. A flint-edged prejudice kept him from recognizing the pursuit of wisdom among Jews, "perfidious" in their stubborn blindness to the revelations of Jesus, among Christian heretics, or among Muslims. A self-congratulatory elitism runs throughout Otto's delight, as an expert, in scholarly techniques of grammar and etymology, and his knowledge of esoteric texts of philosophy, theology, and history, not to mention his deft use of irony and ridicule.

Otto rhetorically identified himself with the ignorance and rusticity of the original apostles, uneducated men of the laboring classes.[45] But this pose carried as little conviction as Marie Antoinette's make-believe as a milkmaid. He classed himself among the wise, distinguished from the simple, who were too weak in mind and heart to be nourished on spiritual milk, instead of on solid food, and who depended on teachers to guide them with rudimentary and carnal figures of speech into the teachings of

Christ. To be worthy of the name, even a heretic could not be one of the uneducated, rustic, and illiterate.[46] Although he included references to numerous female rulers, particularly in antiquity, and to some women paragons of virtue, Otto held to the conventional wisdom that women were frail and given to irrational frenzy. Appropriating an extensive quotation from Augustine, he argued against theologians who considered the female sex a defect of nature, to be corrected in the Resurrection, when all bodies would be re-created male.[47] But, in Otto's account, women impinged on the quest for wisdom only as subverters of men. The veneration of the Blessed Virgin, so marked a feature of religious devotion in Otto's day and, indeed, in his own religious order, left no trace in his history.[48] Otto expressed no sense of companionship in the quest for wisdom with Ethiopians, whose dark color he considered a defect of nature to be rectified at the Resurrection, or with a very great mélange of others, including hermaphrodites, two-headed "monsters," and abortions.[49] Those who were able to extract truth from meditations on history were few, Otto thought, and rather like himself.

An Unresolved Quandary

Despite his formidable argument and rhetorical tactics, Otto realized the fragility of his achievement. He set the quandary of his book in its first lines. The quandary he saw was whether a person should realize that there was no sense in human activities, that anyone's life was a fleck of dust in the senseless, whirling sport of Fortune, or whether those he called wise were on the right track, seeking something eternal but invisible beneath the visible debris of time, something that would make those who found it unshakeable.

Otto's *Chronicle* is the souvenir of Otto's personal effort to apprehend truth: that is, the effort by someone who, by reason, was seeking to escape history but had not yet transcended his mortal or animal state. At every point, Otto had to take into account the facts that neither the seeker nor the arts he employed were adequate to reach the goal. Moreover, human beings could only perceive truth according to their individual capacities and from their place in the flow of revelation, the progress of humanity toward salvation. Even when they saw God directly, the saints in Heaven apprehended him proportionately, according to gifts of grace measured out to each of them rather than as He was.[50]

"But what are we to do?," Otto asked. "If we cannot comprehend [God's judgments], shall we be silent? [If we are,] who will answer gainsayers, who will fight off assailants, who, by reason and the power of words, will refute those who want to destroy the faith that is in us? And so, we cannot comprehend God's secret counsels, and yet we are forced daily to give account of them."[51]

Likewise, reaching always with partial blindness into the mesh of the invisible things that constituted history's infrastructure, human minds could not penetrate beneath the surface wherever they stood in the flow of time, even at the end. Though God had given the spirit of truth to the Church, good and evil people mingled in it, and the Church itself, unable to weigh the hidden merits of individuals, could only judge what was on the surface, what the eyes could see. Any who attempted historical judgments were beset by the same uncertainties that prevailed in human law courts, where litigants threw up clouds of evasions and sophistries, and judges, unable to read their hearts, were often tricked into vindicating criminals who ought to have been condemned.[52]

Thus, Otto recognized that the general interpretation he set down in the extended sermon we call the *Chronicle* reflected his own state of mind. The military and political adversities that he and his family sustained gave him his interpretive key to all human history: nothing lasts, everything perishes. His task was to blend this ascetic, world-despising doctrine with Christian teachings about salvation as he received and interpreted them. He developed his overarching argument that, under God's providence, the center of historical gravity had moved from East to West, in politics, by the succession of empires from Babylon to the Franco-German realm governed by his own dynasty, in wisdom from Babylon and Egypt to the schools of Gaul and Spain (in some of which Otto himself studied), and in religion from the monks of Egypt to those of twelfth-century Gaul and Germany, including members of Otto's own order, the Cistercians.[53] Governed by these movements, Otto held, history had reached its last stage. Dissolution in the terrible reign of Antichrist was at hand, and, after that, God's eternal Sabbath.

A deeply personal truth speaks even through the analogy of patient and physician with two modes of knowing, a truth related moreover to Otto's analogue of historical changes with a sick person tossing from side to side in a hectic fever. About the time Otto completed the revised version of his *Chronicle* and began *The Deeds of Frederick Barbarossa*, he entered months of illness that ended in his death. In the context of Otto's own physical decline, his distinction between a sufferer's immediate experience and an educated observer's knowledge is poignant.

It is evident from these few facts that Otto's overarching interpretive strategy was centered upon his own circumstances, as a member of the ruling dynasty in Germany, as a scholar educated in theology and philosophy in the schools of France, and, a member of one of the most flourishing monastic orders of his day, as a preacher at the end of time. The same self-referential character of his book is indicated by the frequency with which he tells readers that he has seen a place or object mentioned in his story, or that he has built his narrative from word-of-mouth accounts of eyewitnesses, or that he himself was present at an event he relates. He included an exceptionally long and rhapsodic vignette about St. Corbinian, the first bishop of Freising, in the *Chronicle* only because, though unworthy, he himself had succeeded to Corbinian's office.[54]

Since his actual method in rejecting and including materials in the pursuit of truth was decidedly self-referential, was the whole grand interpretive strategy more than a voyage by Otto into his own mind, and perhaps a self-indulgent one? He rejected the satirical judgement that some imagined critic might cast on his qualifications and achievements — the judgment that everyone, untaught and learned alike, was writing poems. But was his history actually a dream palace conjured up by the lying poetic imagination or, more prosaically, a venture in self-discovery, Otto using his work (much as he pictured God delighting in His creation, the world) as a mirror of what, for the moment, he accepted as truth in other creatures and in himself?[55]

Preaching — kerygma — is discourse. As Otto set about writing in a new, joyful frame of mind, he claimed no finality for what, in bitterness of mind, he had chosen as truth and rejected as lies. His interrogations of Christian doctrine are signs of a preaching mission still in progress. Otto insisted that he wrote in the manner of a discussion rather than in that of a debate.[56] And still, he did deliberately challenge other writers. From time to time, Otto indicated points of method or interpretation at which he anticipated criticism, though, he wrote, he would not press his book upon people who were unwilling to receive it or who would scornfully reject it out of hand.[57] But it was exactly against such "gainsayers" and "assailants" that Otto felt called to give account of truths that he could not grasp, which he saw through the changing colors of his own mind, and to which he witnessed with questions.

Even in the debate with himself, Otto could see that there was something fictive in the doctrines he affirmed and something truthful in the unanswerable historical questions that threatened to subvert those doctrines. He could only imagine that resolving the tension between history and religion came when reason opened a mystic's escape from history, here or in Paradise. He could not foresee the time when reason would give another resolution, when what Gibbon called "the bold and sagacious spirit of criticism," meaning history, would open a worldly escape from religion for those who sought it.

Notes

1. A very informative and balanced statement of this position is given by Gabrielle M. Spiegel, *The Past as Text: The Theory and Practice of Medieval Historiography* (Baltimore: Johns Hopkins University Press, 1997), especially, pp. 3–28. I remain partial to the provocative argument of Paul Veyne that neither truth nor history exists. See Paul Veyne, *Did the Greeks Believe in Their Myths? An Essay on the Constitutive Imagination*, trans. Paula Wissing (Chicago: University of Chicago Press, 1988).

2. The hypothesis that Otto of Freising assisted in the forgery of around fifty charters in favor of his city and diocese was set forth by Hans Constantin Faussner, *Die Königsurkundenfälschungen Ottos von Freising aus rechtshistorischer Sicht*, Studien zur Rechts-, Wirtschafts- und Kulturgeschichte, 13. (Sigmaringen: Thorbecke, 1993). A refutation was published by Rudolf Schieffer, "Otto von Freising ein Urkundenfälscher?," in Lothar Kolmer and Peter Segl, eds., *Regensburg, Bayern und Europa: Festschrift für Kurt Reindel zum 70. Geburtstag* (Regensburg: Universitätsverlag, 1995), pp. 245–256.

3. Adolph Hofmeister, ed., *Ottonis Episcopi Frisingensis Chronica sive Historia de Duabus Civitatibus*, letter to Rainald of Dassel, 2d ed. (Hannover: Hahn, 1912), Monumenta Germaniae Historica, *Scriptores Rerum Germanicarum in usum scholarum* [hereafter cited as *Chronicle*], p. 4; in this volume, p. 90.

4. *Chronicle*, letter to Frederick, MGH ed., pp. 2–3 ; in this volume, p. 89. Georg Waitz, *Ottonis et Rahewini Gesta Friderici I. Imperatoris*, I. prol., 3rd ed. (Hannover: Hahn, 1912), Monumenta Germaniae Historica, *Scriptores Rerum Germanicarum in usum Scholarum*, p. 11. Charles Christopher Mierow, trans., *The Deeds of Frederick Barbarossa* (New York: Columbia University Press, 1953), p. 27.

5. *Chronicle*, 8.8 insertion, MGH ed., pp. 300–401; in this volume, pp. 462–463.

6. *The Deeds of Frederick Barbarossa*, I. prol., MGH ed., p. 9; Mierow trans., p. 24.

7. *Chronicle*, 2. prol.; 6.20; 7.26, MGH ed., pp. 68, 282–284, 352; in this volume, pp. 153–154, 381–382, 436.

8. *Chronicle*, 3. prol., MGH ed., p. 130; in this volume, pp. 217–218.

9. *Chronicle*, 2. prol., MGH ed., p. 68; in this volume, p. 154.

10. Lucretius, *De Rerum Natura*, 1.62–65, 95–101, 146–150.

11. Edward Gibbon, *The Decline and Fall of the Roman Empire* (New York: Modern Library, n.d.), chaps. 30, 37.1; vol. 1, p. 650; vol. 2, pp. 353, 363, 650.

12. *Chronicle*, 8. prol., MGH ed., pp. 392–393; in this volume, pp. 455–456.

13. *Chronicle*, 2.43; 8.20, 21, MGH ed., pp. 119, 423, 425; in this volume, pp. 205, 484, 485.

14. *Chronicle*, 1. prol.; 5.36; 6. prol., 9, 17, MGH ed., pp. 7, 260, 261–262, 270–271, 278; in this volume, pp. 94, 358, 360, 370, 377.

15. *Chronicle*, 3.11, MGH ed., pp. 146–147; in this volume, p. 235.

16. *Chronicle*, 4.18, MGH ed., pp. 205–206; in this volume, p. 249.

17. *Chronicle*, 3. prol., 10; 8. prol., MGH ed., pp. 130–131, 146; in this volume, pp. 218–219, 235, 456.

18. *Chronicle*, 3.18; 5.6; 8.3, MGH ed., pp. 157, 260–261, 458–459; in this volume, pp. 240, 358–359, 458–459. Cf. *Chronicle*, 4.4, MGH ed., pp. 189–191; in this volume, pp. 280–283.

19. *Chronicle*, 7. prol., MGH ed., p. 308; in this volume, pp. 403–404.

20. *Chronicle*, 3. prol.; 4. prol.; 7. prol.; 8.26, 32, MGH ed., pp. 131, 182, 309, 433, 451; in this volume, pp. 218, 274, 404, 493, 508. Cf. *Chronicle*, 8.30, MGH ed., p. 442; in this volume, p. 501. Otto is unable to comprehend the nature of supercelestial mysteries but speaks of them on the authority of Dionysius the Areopagite.

21. *Chronicle*, 3. prol., 9, 12, MGH ed., pp. 131, 134–135, 145, 148; in this volume, pp. 218, 222, 233, 237.

22. *Chronicle*, 8.4, MGH ed., p. 398; in this volume, pp. 460–461.

23. *Chronicle*, 7.35, MGH ed., pp. 369–374; in this volume, pp. 445–449.

24. *Chronicle*, 8.28, MGH ed., p. 439; in this volume, p. 498.

25. *Chronicle*, 7.33; 8.33, MGH ed., pp. 372–373, 453; in this volume, pp. 448, 449, 509.

26. *Chronicle*, 8.26, 28, 30, 33, MGH ed., pp. 432–433, 439, 441–442, 452–454; in this volume, pp. 492, 498, 500, 508–511.

27. *Chronicle*, 1. prol.; 7. prol.; 8.3, 12, MGH ed., pp. 6, 180, 307, 396–397, 409; in this volume, pp. 93, 217, 402–403, 459.

28. *Chronicle*, 1.6 (on human bestiality after the Flood, without cities, morals, laws, philosophy, or religion); 3. prol., MGH ed., pp. 44, 130; in this volume, pp. 130, 217.

29. *Chronicle*, 2. prol., MGH ed., p. 68; in this volume, p. 154.

30. *Chronicle*, 5. prol.; 6.36, MGH ed., pp. 227–228, 306; in this volume, pp. 323–324, 401.

31. *Chronicle*, 8. prol., MGH ed., p. 391; in this volume, p. 454.

32. *Chronicle*, 3. prol., MGH ed., pp. 134–135; in this volume, p. 222.

33. *Chronicle*, 7. prol.; 8.29, MGH ed., pp. 307–308, 440; in this volume, pp. 402–403, 499.

34. *Chronicle*, 7.35, MGH ed., pp. 369–370; in this volume, p. 446.

35. *Chronicle*, 3. prol., MGH ed., pp. 134–135; in this volume, p. 222.

36. Otto's most extensive profiles are those of his predecessor as Bishop of Freising, St. Corbinian, Charlemagne, the Emperor Henry IV, Pope Gregory VII, and King Roger II of Sicily.

37. *The Deeds of Frederick Barbarossa*, 1.55, MGH ed., p. 77; in this volume, p. 91. Cf. *Chronicle*, 8.20, MGH ed., p. 423; in this volume, pp. 483–484.

38. *Chronicle*, 2.8, MGH ed., pp. 75, 78; in this volume, p. 163.

39. *Chronicle*, 1. prol.; 5. prol., MGH ed., pp. 7, 226; in this volume, pp. 94, 322–323.

40. *Chronicle*, 5. prol., MGH ed., p. 226; in this volume, p. 337.

41. *Chronicle*, 4. prol.; 7.32–33, MGH ed., pp. 183, 448–454; in this volume, pp. 273–274, 441–444.

42. *Chronicle*, 5. prol., MGH ed., p. 228; in this volume, p. 324.

43. *Chronicle*, 7.21, 23; 8. prol., 26, MGH ed., pp. 343, 347, 392–393, 436; in this volume, pp. 430, 432, 445–446, 496.

44. *Chronicle*, 4. prol.; 7. prol., MGH ed., pp. 180, 307; in this volume, pp. 271, 402.

45. *Chronicle*, 1. prol., MGH ed., pp. 9–10; in this volume, pp. 96–97.

46. *Chronicle*, 8.33, MGH ed., p. 451; in this volume, p. 508. *The Deeds of Frederick Barbarossa*, 1.56 (54)–57 (55), MGH ed., pp. 80–82; in this volume, pp. 94–95.

47. *Chronicle*, 8.12, MGH ed., p. 408; in this volume, p. 469.

48. *Chronicle*, 3.6, 10, MGH ed., pp. 141–143, 146; in this volume, pp. 229, 233–234.

49. *Chronicle*, 8.12, MGH ed., p. 408; in this volume, p. 470.

50. *Chronicle*, 3. prol.; 8.30, 31, MGH ed., pp. 131, 134–135, 441–448; Mierow trans., pp. 218, 222, 501, 505.

51. *Chronicle*, 3. prol., MGH ed., p. 131; in this volume, p. 218–219. See also *Chronicle*, 2. prol., MGH ed., p. 68; in this volume, p. 154.

52. *Chronicle*, 7. prol.; 8.19, MGH ed., pp. 309–310, 418; in this volume, pp. 404–405, 478–479.

53. *Chronicle*, 1. prol.; 5. prol.; 7.35, MGH ed., pp. 7–8, 226–228, 372; in this volume, pp. 94–95, 322–323, 448.

54. *Chronicle*, 5.24, MGH ed., pp. 250–252; in this volume, pp. 347–349.

55. *Chronicle*, 1. prol.; 7. prol., MGH ed., pp. 9–10, 307; in this volume, pp. 96, 402–403.

56. *Chronicle*, 2. prol., MGH ed., p. 68; in this volume, p. 154.

57. For some anticipated objections, see *Chronicle*, letter to Rainald of Dassel, 2. prol.; 5. prol.; 7. prol.; 8. prol., MGH ed., pp. 4–5, 68, 227–228, 308–310, 392–395; in this volume, pp. 89–91, 154, 324, 404–405, 455–456.

A SELECT BIBLIOGRAPHY

By Karl F. Morrison

Brincken, Anna-Dorothée von den. *Studien zur lateinischen Weltchronik bis in das Zeitalter Ottos von Freising*. Düsseldorf: Triltsch, 1957.

Faussner, Hans Constantin. *Die Königsurkundenfälschungen Ottos von Freising aus rechtshistorischer Sicht*. Studien zur Rechts-, Wirtschafts- und Kulturgeschichte, 13. Sigmaringen: Thorbecke, 1993.

Funkenstein, Amos. *Heilsplan und natürliche Entwicklung: Formen der Gegenwartsbestimmung in Geschichtsdenken des hohen Mittelalters*. Munich: Nymphenburger Verlagshandlung, 1965.

Glasser, Hubert. " 'De monte abscissus est sine manibus' (Dan. 2, 45). Die geschichtliche Rolle des Reformpapsttums im Spiegel der Weltchronik Ottos von Freising." In Manfred Weitlauff and Karl Hausberger, eds., *Papsttum und Kirchenreform: Historische Beiträge: Festschrift für Georg Schwaiger zum 65. Geburtstag*, pp. 151–191. St. Ottilien: Eos, 1990.

Goetz, Hans-Werner. *Das Geschichtsbild Ottos von Freising: Ein Beitrag zur historischen Vorstellungswelt und zur Geschichte des 12. Jahrhunderts*. Beihefte zum Archiv für Kulturgeschichte, 19. Cologne and Vienna: Böhlau, 1984.

Grill, Leopold. "Bildung und Wissenschaft im Leben Bischof Ottos von Freising." *Analecta Sacri Ordinis Cisterciensis* 14 (1958): 281–333.

———. "Neues zum Itinerar Ottos von Freising." In Reinhard Härtel, ed., *Geschichte und ihre Quellen. Festschrift für Friedrich Hausmann zum 70. Geburtstag*, pp. 37–46. Graz: Akademische Druck- und Verlagsanstalt, 1987.

Kelly, Henry Ansgar. *Ideas and Forms of Tragedy from Aristotle to the Middle Ages*. Cambridge: Cambridge University Press, 1993.

Kirchner-Feyerabend, Cornelia. *Otto von Freising als Diözesan- und Reichsbischof*. Frankfurt am Main: Lang, 1990.

Klinkenberg, Hans M. "Der Sinn der Chronik Ottos von Freising." In Josef Engel and Hans M. Klinkenberg, eds., *Aus Mittelalter und Neuzeit: Festschrift Gerhard Kallen*, pp. 63–76. Bonn: Hanstein, 1957.

I gratefully acknowledge the assistance of Ms. Amanda Pipkin in compiling this bibliography.

Koch, Josef. "Die Grundlagen der Geschichtsphilosophie Ottos von Freising." In Walther Lammers, ed., *Geschichtsdenken und Geschichtsbild im Mittelalter,* pp. 321–350. Wege der Forschung, 21. Darmstadt: Wissenschaftliche Buchgesellschaft, 1965.

Lammers, Walther. *Weltgeschichte und Zeitgeschichte bei Otto von Freising.* Sitzungsberichte der Wissenschaftlichen Gesellschaft an der Johann-Wolfang-Goethe-Universität Frankfurt am Main, vol. 14, nr. 3. Wiesbaden: Steiner, 1977.

Lhotsky, Alphons. "Das Nachleben Ottos von Freising." In *Europäisches Mittelalter: Das Land Oesterreich. Aufsätze und Vorträge,* Bd. 1, pp. 29–48. Munich: Oldenbourg, 1970.

Mégier, Elisabeth. "*Cives Dei* und *cives mundi* als individuelle Personen in der Chronik Ottos von Freising." In Jan A. Aertsen and Andreas Speer, eds., *Individuum und Individualität im Mittelalter,* pp. 513–529. Berlin: de Gruyter, 1996.

Morrison, Karl F. "Otto of Freising's Quest for the Hermeneutic Circle." *Speculum* 55 (1980): 207–236.

————. "The Exercise of Thoughtful Minds: The Apocalypse in Some German Historical Writings." In Richard K. Emmerson and Bernard McGinn, eds., *The Apocalypse in the Middle Ages,* pp. 352–373. Ithaca, N.Y.: Cornell University Press, 1992.

Müller, Manfred. *Beiträge zur Theologie Ottos von Freising.* St. Gabrieler Studien, 19. Mödling bei Wien: St. Gabriel, 1965.

Munz, Peter. *Frederick Barbarossa: A Study in Medieval Politics.* Ithaca, N.Y.: Cornell University Press, 1969.

Schieffer, Rudolf. "Otto von Freising ein Urkundenfälscher?" In Lothar Kolmer and Peter Segl, eds., *Regensburg, Bayern und Europa. Festschrift für Kurt Reindel zum 70. Geburtstag,* pp. 245–256. Regensburg: Universitätsverlag, 1995).

Schürmann, Brigitte. *Die Rezeption der Werke Ottos von Freising im 15. und frühen 16. Jahrhundert,* Historische Forschungen, 12. Stuttgart: Steiner, 1986.

Spörl, Johannes. "Die 'Civitas Dei' im Geschichtsdenken Ottos von Freising." In Walter Lammers, ed., *Geschichtsdenken und Geschichtsbild im Mittelalter,* pp. 298–320. Wege der Forschung, 21. Darmstadt: Wissenschaftliche Buchgesellschaft, 1965.

Staber, Joseph. "Eschatologie und Geschichte bei Otto von Freising." In J. A. Fischer, ed., *Otto von Freising: Gedenkgabe zu seiner 800. Todesjahr,* pp. 106–126 Sammelblatt des Historischen Vereins Freising, Fasc. 23. Freising: Freisinger Historische Verein, 1958.

EDITOR'S PREFACE

The work which Dr. Mierow here presents in English dress is from the pen of a 'modern' historian, one who in his own day might well have been considered a prophet of the newer history. To a marked degree he possessed the qualities that entitled him to that distinction. He was vitally in touch with the life of his time. A scion of one of the proudest families of Germany, he was half-brother of one emperor and uncle of another; his family connections made it possible for him to observe the actions of the men who made the history of his day; and what is perhaps more significant, those connections compelled him to play a large part in the drama. He was a trusted advisor of emperors. He was, by both taste and training, a part of what was best in the contemplative life of his time. As a student at the new university at Paris during the early years of the twelfth century he brought back to his German home an interest in the newer study of Aristotle. He belonged to one of the earliest Cistercian houses in Germany, later, as bishop of Freising, he became a prelate of the Church. In him were combined the *imperium*, the *studium* and the *sacerdotium*. He was, then, no dry-as-dust historian, but a man of thought and action, filling the intervals of a busy life by interpreting the course of history for his contemporaries in terms which they could understand. He insisted that history must have meaning and purpose. For him it was no mere succession of anecdotes, but the hewing out, through human agencies, of the purposes of a supernatural controller.

In the writing of history the author would begin at the beginning and would carry the story through to his own time. He was not afraid to launch his craft on the turgid stream of contemporary events. Nay, in good modern fashion, in laying down the plan of his work he reserved ample space fully to recount recent and contemporary events; and then, not satisfied to leave the story there, he appended another book as a synthesis of what had gone before and as a prophecy of the future. His is indeed a history of the world from the beginning to modern times, written with a serious purpose.

Finally, he was a 'scientific historian.' He would seek good sources,
study well the evidence, and then tell the truth as he saw it, come
what might, or, if evidence were lacking or conflicting, he would
leave the matter in suspense. "For it is better to fall into the hand
of men than cover up a loathsome sight with colors that distort the
truth." [1]

It is true that the explanation of the beginning and of the course
of history which the reader will find in the pages of the *Chronicle
of the Two Cities* by Otto of Freising differs widely from the synthesis offered by the majority of historians today; it is equally true
that it is borrowed quite largely from Eusebius and Saint Augustine. But for neither of these reasons is it any the less interesting
for one who would understand the time in which Otto wrote, nor
is it for these reasons lacking in sweep and majesty. The world
began with a definite creation at a definite time; for Otto there
were no guesses as to man's relationship with the other anthropoids.
He was not troubled regarding the status of *Pithecanthropus erec-
tus* or at just what point in the Pleistocene (or Pliocene) age
Homo sapiens emerged. Little time is lost in Otto's narrative over
such homely problems as man's gradual and painful acquisition of
the tools with which to master a hostile environment. For him the
course of history is marked by the rush and sweep of empires, each
built to fall, but from the ashes of the last rising yet another; while
above, giving meaning and purpose to the whole, is the struggle
between the two cities — the one of this world and fleshly, the other
in the skies and of the spirit. Let no reader, would he know well the
bishop-historian and his time, neglect to read and to ponder the
eighth and last part of the book, which to the author forms the
climax of and invests with meaning the chapters that precede. To
read Otto for the facts which his book contains on the life and
activities of his own times is good; to read him for the thought which
lies back of his narrative is to get close to the heart of the twelfth
century.

It is curious that a narrative of such significance has waited
until now for a complete translation into a modern tongue. Universally recognized as the outstanding historian of his century,
Otto has none the less been known at first hand only by those who
have taken the trouble to read him in the Latin. In translation there

[1] Otto's preface (Hofmeister's edition), p. 5.

exists only the German rendering of the sixth and seventh books, that part of the whole which is of interest for the light which it throws upon events contemporary, or nearly so, with the author. It is hoped that in thus presenting the work as a whole a real service will be rendered. Those who would come to know the thought and the life of a dynamic period in the history of western civilization, through a first hand reading of its sources, may now have easily accessible this most important work.

A. P. E.

To My Parents

KATHERINE MARIE (CRAMER) MIEROW
CHARLES BERNHARD WILLIAM MIEROW

With Love and Gratitude

PREFACE

This translation of Bishop Otto of Freising's *Chronicle* or *History of the Two Cities*, the first complete version in any modern language, was originally undertaken at the suggestion of Professor James T. Shotwell. It is based upon the text by Hofmeister as published in *Scriptores Rerum Germanicarum in usum scholarum* (Hanover and Leipzig, 1912), and in the preparation of my introduction and commentary I have, of course, availed myself largely of the editor's studies in this field as published in his preface and elsewhere.

I wish to express my grateful appreciation of the generous assistance of the present editor of Records of Civilization, Professor Austin P. Evans, whose many suggestions and criticisms have been invaluable to me. Professor Charles Knapp, as associate editor of this particular volume, has gone over the entire translation with great care and deserves full credit for any felicities of rendering which my version may possess.

Dean Andrew F. West, in whose graduate classes at Princeton I first undertook the study of medieval Latin literature, has shown his constant interest in this as in all of my work, and I feel that I must here acknowledge anew my indebtedness to him for anything that I have been enabled to accomplish in this field.

CHARLES CHRISTOPHER MIEROW

Colorado College
Colorado Springs, Colorado
May 14, 1928

THE TWO CITIES

dum picteritorum temporum calamitatum reminiscimur,
instantis quodammodo pressurae quoquo modo obliviscimur.
Prologue, Book II

melius sit in manus incidere hominum quam tetrae fucatum
superducendo colorem faciei scriptoris amittere officium.
Dedicatory letter to Chancellor Rainald

INTRODUCTION: OTTO OF FREISING AND THE PHILOSOPHY OF HISTORY

1. THE HISTORICAL BACKGROUND [1]

If we wish to comprehend the true significance of *The Two Cities* of Bishop Otto of Freising, it may be well at the outset to review briefly the historical background in relation to which the author and his work must be judged. The development of the Middle Ages in the West is characterized by two ideas: the Roman Empire and the Roman Church. Both are a bequest of antiquity, but as political forces in the form in which they became active they are a creation of the Middle Ages.

The Roman Church sprang into prominence and power at the very time that the Roman Empire in the West was being destroyed. It was the Church that proved to be the real heir of that empire, and her claim was that all which she had increasingly demanded during a long period of development was an ancient possession — the grant of the emperor Constantine.

Likewise when the Western Roman Empire was restored, in 800 A.D., it was commonly believed that the Church had created the new emperor and that Charles traced his authority to her consecration. It was on this assumption that the Church took part in every change in the imperial succession to the end of the Middle Ages.

While the empire of Charles the Great had actually included practically all the Christian peoples of the West, his successors proved to be unable to maintain the material unity of this empire. The *idea* of a Christian Roman Empire — the Holy Roman Empire so-called — persisted, however. In theory the empire of the later ruling houses was just as universal as that of the early Carolingians had been in fact.

Since 800 the Church and State had stood side by side, each claiming supreme authority. In theory at least the Church had the

[1] For the historical background read especially Huber: *Otto von Freising* 38-50; (for fuller titles of books and articles cited in the notes, see Bibliography, pp. 81 *et seq.*) Hofmeister: *Studien* 101-109; Nitsch 334-360; Hauck 4, 206, 325, 342, 345 and in particular 500-503.

1

better position of the two, but she could not maintain her universal status without dependence upon a strong political power; and since the Eastern Roman or Byzantine Empire seemed too distant, as well as unable or unwilling, to afford the needed assistance, the Church decided to lean upon the powerful descendants of Arnulf and Pepin. Then, to avoid submission to the power of a state independent of herself, the Church under Leo III had cleverly maintained her position by making the emperor a successor to the Roman *Augusti*.

The first great conflict between the two powers occurred in the 11th Century — when they were approximately evenly balanced. It revolved about the question of procedure in the installation of the highest ecclesiastical officials. Theoretically the Church was justified in her demand for the free election of bishops and clergy by the people. But on the other hand the king had hitherto actually spoken the decisive word, since it was he who invested the chosen officials with the insignia of office.

Conrad II (1024-1039), a strong emperor, had been succeeded by one still stronger in the person of Henry III (1039-1056), under whom the imperial power was at its highest point. He was able to make and unmake popes at will. Bishop Otto's grandfather, Henry IV (1056-1106), was passionate but weak. In his reign the tremendous conflict between the spiritual and the temporal power began. His great opponent was Pope Gregory VII (Hildebrand), before whom the emperor was obliged to humble himself at Canossa (1077). The emperor's last years were embittered by the revolt of his son, who ultimately forced him to resign. But upon succeeding to the throne, Henry V (1106-1125) renewed the struggle with the Pope. There was a temporary respite secured by the Concordat of Worms, in 1122, whereby it was agreed that the popes should have the right to invest the clergy with spiritual authority (symbolized by the ring and the staff) but that bishops and abbots must be canonically elected in the presence of the emperor, that contested elections were to be decided by him, and that he should invest the clergy with their lands and all civil and judicial functions (symbolized by the sceptre).

Otto of Freising belongs to the succeeding period of tension, when open war was at an end but when the pens and tongues of the two opposing factions were by no means at rest. For Lothar (1125-1137) and Conrad III (1138-1152) were too busy with a stubborn party strife in Germany to continue the conflict against the papal see. And in Conrad's case there was the further distraction of the Second Crusade, in which he was induced to take part. But the emperor Frederick I (1152-1190), being the son of a Hohenstaufen father and a Welf mother, united in his own person the two factions whose incessant strife had occupied the attention of the two preceding rulers. Accordingly Frederick was free to assert with all the more emphasis the claims of the empire. He strove to restore the conditions of the time of the Carolingians and of Otto the First in Italy, and in particular to restore the imperial rights in the northern part of that peninsula. In 1157 a feud arose between the emperor and Pope Hadrian IV because of the Besançon episode, but in the following year through the instrumentality of Bishop Otto they were reconciled. The latter's attitude — not only in this specific instance but in general — is concisely expressed in a sentence by his continuator and pupil Rahewin, who writes that "He felt a poignant sorrow because of the controversy between the State and the Church."[2]

2. BIOGRAPHICAL SKETCH OF THE AUTHOR

With this much by way of orientation, we may now center our attention upon the author and his work. Bishop Otto of Freising stands high among the great and distinguished figures of the remarkable twelfth century as one to whom the consensus of expert opinion, both ancient and modern, accords abundant praise as a careful and critical historian. Acclaimed as early as the sixteenth century [3] as a champion of orthodoxy and a witness to the truth, and recognized today as the author of the most celebrated works of German historical writing of the Middle Ages,[4] Otto is universally

[2] *Gesta* 3. 22.

[3] Huber 125: "Eisengrein, ein Convertit und Katholischer Schriftsteller des 16. Jahrhunderts, zählt Otto in seinem *catalogus testium veritatis* (Diling. 1565. Blatt 99) sogar unter die *'orthodoxae matris ecclesiae doctores.'* Und Convertiten haben in der Regel das beste Talent um Häresieen ausfindig zu machen, wo sie irgend zeigen wollen."

[4] Perdisch: *Der Laubacher Barlaam*, Tübingen 1913, Intro. p. xiii: "Nicht gar zu lange vorher waren in Freising die berühmtesten Werke deutscher mittelalterlicher Geschichtschreibung entstanden, Bischof Ottos I 'Chronik' und 'Taten Friedrichs,' die dann in dem Freisinger Rahewin einen trefflichen fortsetzer fanden."

praised by modern historians as the first to record the leading events
of world history in a smooth and flowing style and at the same time
to attempt to fit them into the eternal scheme.[5] In other words,
his Chronicle is the earliest philosophical treatment of history which
we have,[6] and it has been described as "the first presentation of
universal history that possesses the unity of a work of art."[7]

Before considering his literary activity it may be well to recall
the principal events in his life, for Bishop Otto is an outstanding
figure in the political and religious history of his time: a great
noble and churchman as well as a famous author. Our chief
sources of information — aside from a number of incidental allu-
sions in his own works [8] — are the writings of his pupil and con-

---

[5] Büdinger (Vienna 1881) 365: "Dieser fürstliche Autor ist eben der Erste
gewesen der die Erscheinungen der Universalhistorie, soweit sie seiner Forschung erkennbar waren, in freier Gestaltung wiedergegeben und zugleich in
die ewigen Ordnungen einzufügen gesucht hat."

[6] So Waitz (quoted by Sorgenfrey): "die erste philosophische Behandlung
der Geschichte die wir besitzen."

[7] Hauck (Leipzig 1913) 4. 509: "die erste Darstellung der Universalge-
schichte, welche die Einheitlichkeit eines Kunstwerks besitzt." Elsewhere
(p. 325) Hauck characterizes Otto as "Der erste Geschichtschreiber seiner
Zeit." Other noteworthy testimonies by competent authorities are: *Chronicon
Citizense* (cited by Sorgenfrey, *l.c.*): "*Otto episcopus historicus magnus
et nobilissimus*"; Hashagen 99: "Otto steht als der berühmteste Geschichtschreiber am Eingange der Staufischen Periode"; Wilmans in Vol. 30 of
Scriptores rerum Germanicarum (Hanover, dated 1867), Intro. p. v: "*Ottonis
Frisingensis episcopi chronicon historiae conscribendae artem currente medio
aevo ad summum forsitan provexit fastigium*"; Waitz (Berlin 1844) 110-112:
"ein Werk das immer den besten wird zugeszählt werden müssen"; Schmidlin
(Fulda 1905) 156: "den Schriftsteller, welchen die Historiker als den vol-
lendetsten Geschichtschreiber des Mittelalters, als Typus des medievalen
Geschichtsphilosophen verehren"; Huber, *l.c.*, 199: "Keinem auch nicht dem
besten Geschichtschreiber des deutschen Mittelalters *vor* ihm, für den wir
Lambert von Aschaffenburg halten, steht Otto an Vorzügen nach, keiner
seiner Zeitgenossen kömmt ihm als Historiker gleich, und von wenigen Geschicht-
schreibern des Mittelalters *nach* ihm wird er übertroffen werden." Charles
Homer Haskins ("The Renaissance of the Twelfth Century," Harvard University Press, 1927, p. 238) says: "In Otto of Freising the German historiography
of the Middle Ages reaches its highest point." Perhaps the best tribute to
the importance of Bishop Otto and his work is that of Hofmeister in NA
37. 767, translated on p. 46 of this introduction.

[8] *E.g.*, *Gesta* 1. 8 and 9 (regarding his mother Agnes and her children by
her first husband); *Gesta* 1. 10 and *Chron.* VII 7. 9 (the marriage of his
parents); VII. 17 (the Roman numerals refer to books of the *Chronicle*)

tinuator Rahewin [9] (notably the well-known chapter [10] in which he
records Otto's death and burial) and the *Annals of Austria*.[11]

The high place he occupied by accident of birth will at once be
clear from the statement that he was a grandson of Emperor Henry
IV of Germany (1065-1106), a nephew of Henry V (1106-1125),
half-brother to Conrad III of Hohenstaufen (1138-1152) and ma-
ternal uncle of Frederick I (1152-1190), commonly known as "Barbarossa" — the most famous of the German emperors save only
Charles the Great. Both Conrad III and Frederick I gave Otto
their confidence in matters of state, though he never held the
office of Chancellor.

Otto was born probably between 1111 and 1115. His parents were
Leopold III of Austria and Agnes, the daughter of the emperor
Henry IV, who had formerly been the wife of Frederick the first
duke of Swabia, the grandfather of Barbarossa. Otto thus belonged
to one of the most prominent German ruling houses, that of Babenberg, and at the election of a king in 1125 his father had been one
of the candidates. Otto's brother, Duke Henry "Jasomirgott" (so
named from his favorite oath) of Austria — earlier of Bavaria —

(how his father was once a candidate for the kingship); VII. 21 (concerning
his father and his brother); VII. 34 (his sister Gertrude).

[9] *E.g.*, *Gesta* 3, Prol. (reference to Otto's death and unfinished work);
3. 2 (Otto's sister); 3. 14 (reconciliation between Otto and his brother);
3. 22 (Otto reads and interprets letters from the Pope directed to the emperor
Frederick in 1158).

[10] 3. 4; see also 15.

[11] *Annales Austriae* (Hanover 1851). Hofmeister in NA 37. 109 describes
this important source as "Klosterneuburger Fortsetzung der Melker Annalen,
deren Verfasser 1167 von Ottos Bruder Konrad, Erzbischof von Salzburg, zu
Friesach die Weihe empfing." Wilmans, in the Introduction to his edition of
the *Chronicle*, p. v, says with regard to the date: "*post annum* 1168 *et ante*
1177 *quo schismati finis impositus est opus exaravit.*" The author's source of
information regarding Otto is — according to his own statement — a friend of
his youth named Frederick, one of the fifteen that stopped at Morimund on
their way home from their school days at Paris.

Meichelbeck's *Historia Frisingensis* (1. 1. 339 ff.) contains further source
material, particularly certain of Otto's documents.

Hofmeister, *l.c.* 110, sounds a warning against certain source materials already rejected by Wilmans: "die durch die Hanthalerischen Fälschungen von
1742 und 1747, inbesondere den angeblichen Richard von Klosterneuburg
(Leupold von Lilienfeld) und den falschen Ortilo in die frühere Geschichte
Oesterreiche und der Babenberger und damit auch unseres Ottos einge-
schwärtzten Angaben."

married a Greek princess, Theodora; so the family was related also to the imperial house then ruling in Constantinople. [12]

The betrothal of Agnes, daughter of Henry IV, to Frederick I (Duke of Swabia) of Hohenstaufen — one of her father's most loyal adherents — occurred in 1079.[13] By him she had two sons, Frederick (born 1090) and Conrad (born 1093).[14] It would appear from a passage in the *Chronicle* in which she is referred to as "sister of the king" (that is, Conrad III) that Gertrude, the wife of Duke Vladislav II of Bohemia, was also a child of Agnes and Frederick.[15] On the other hand a statement by Rahewin in his continuation of Bishop Otto's *Gesta Friderici I Imperatoris* tends rather to support the theory that she was the daughter of Agnes by her second husband, Leopold.[16] It seems reasonable however to credit Otto himself, the author of the former passage, with greater accuracy and care than Rahewin in this matter, and to assume that Gertrude was a child of the first union.

In 1106 Agnes was given in marriage to Leopold III, margrave of Austria, by her brother Henry V.[17] Otto says in reference to the motive that actuated him: "Henry the Younger, considering that all his father's strength would lie in Bořivoi, the duke of Bohemia, and in Margrave Leopold, whose sister the aforesaid Duke had to wife, prevailed upon them by many inducements — he offered in

---

[12] See Rahewin's account of Otto's family in *Gesta* 4. 14. These relationships will be made clear at a glance by the following family tree:

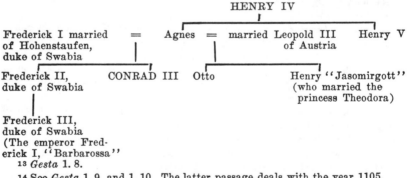

[13] *Gesta* 1. 8.

[14] See *Gesta* 1. 9. and 1. 10. The latter passage deals with the year 1105.

[15] VII. 34: *Gerdrudis sororis regis.*

[16] *Gesta* 4. 14: *cum fratribus suis germanis . . . necnon et sororibus, Gerdruda ducissa Boemiae;* the important word here is *germanis.*

[17] *Annales Austriae, l.c.* See also *Gesta* 1. 10. The previous account referred to in the latter reference is that given in VII. 9 and quoted above in the text.

marriage to the Margrave his own sister (who had recently been left a widow by the death of Frederick, Duke of Swabia) — and persuaded them both to forsake his father." [18] Attention has often been called to the remarkable objectivity shown by the author in referring in this way to the reason for his father's defection — perhaps the decisive factor in the old emperor's downfall.

Otto is proud of his mother's royal lineage [19] through the line of the Salian emperors (regarding whom he is able to amplify from personal knowledge and family tradition the more meagre account given by the literary source he is following for the period),[20] and even traces her line back to Charles the Great through Gisela, her great grandmother, citing two verses from Wipo's *Tetralogus*:

"When to the tenth generation a fourth generation is added,
From the great Charles is descended Gisela, known for her wisdom." [21]

Nor does he fail to celebrate the ancient nobility of his father's family. He refers to his father as "that famous man, the margrave Leopold" [22] and "Leopold, margrave of Austria, a most Christian man and father of the clergy and of the poor," [23] and mentions the fact that he was one of the candidates suggested as successor to

---

[18] VII. 9.

[19] Note the phrase used in *Gesta* 1. 9 (already cited above): *ex nobilissima compare sua Agnete.*

[20] See VI. 20 (of Conrad, duke of Worms; cf. VI. 28 (of Conrad II); VI. 32 (of Henry III).

[21] VI. 28 (see also 32). The line of descent is as follows:

CONRAD II married = Gisela widow of = Ernest I, duke of Swabia
1024-1039

HENRY III   Ernest II   Herman
1039-1056   d. 1030   (Herman IV, d. 1038)

HENRY IV
1065-1106

HENRY V   Agnes
1106-1125

Otto states further (VI. 28 and 32) that Ernest I, duke of Swabia (d. 1015) and the archbishop Poppo of Trèves (1016 — d. 1047) were brothers of Margrave Adalbert of Austria; see family tree below, note 31.

[22] VII. 15.

[23] VII. 21. With this compare *Annales Austriae, l.c.: Hic est ille Liupoldus marchio Austriae, qui cognominabatur Pius nec inmerito, instinctu enim pietatis duo claustra in marchia sua instituit.*

Henry V.[24] Margrave Leopold belonged to the house of Babenberg that had ruled the Bavarian Eastmark since the middle of the tenth century, and Otto regarded as his ancestors those counts of Babenberg who had contended against the family of Conrad of Hesse in the days of Arnulf of Carinthia (887-899) and Ludwig the Child (899-911) until Adalbert of Babenberg was executed as a traitor in 906.[25] In Otto's estimation these ancient representatives of the house of Babenberg — and consequently his own family as well — were Franks. From other evidence [26] it would appear that the Margraves of Austria in the twelfth century were Franks irrespective of their descent from the old Babenberg family: hence Otto's fondness for complimentary epithets in speaking of the invincible valor and noble race of the Franks. In addition to these Otto mentions also his grandmother Itha [27] and his paternal aunt, Gerberga,[28] the wife of Duke Bořivoi of Bohemia; the sons of Gisela by her first marriage to Ernest of Babenberg [29]— Ernest II of Swabia and Duke Herman IV; Margrave Ernest of Austria who fell in battle against the Saxons at the Unstrut in 1075 and his father the margrave Albert or Adalbert;[30] and the latter's eldest son, Leopold II, who with his father had wrested the Eastmark from the hands of the Hungarians.[31] With regard to Bishop Otto's more immediate

---

[24] VII. 17.   [25] VI. 15.

[26] VI. 15: *Ex huius Alberti sanguine Albertus, qui postmodum Marchiam orientalem, id est Pannoniam superiorem, Ungaris ereptam Romano imperio adiecit, originem duxisse traditur* — where Otto is evidently giving his own family tradition. On the plausibility of this statement see K. Uhlirz in *Mitteil. des Inst. für Oesterreich. Geschichtsforschung*, erg. Bd. VI. 57-69, and in *Jahrb. des Deutschen Reichs unter Otto* II 228-231; on the previous statement in this same chapter, *Albertus nobilissimus Francorum comes, Ottonis Saxonum ducis ex filia nepos*, see *Neues Archiv* 37 (1912), 114-115 and B. F. Stein in *Forschungen zur deutschen Gesch.* 24. 141. Furthermore Otto shows an interest in the differences between the various German families and mentions the origin of two bodies of tribal law: Salic Law (IV. 32) and the Law of the Bavarians (V. 9); here we have a strong argument from silence, for if the Austrian Babenberger had lived according to Swabian Law in the twelfth century, the *Lex Alamannorum* would doubtless have been mentioned also in the *Chronicle*. Instead of this we find the statement (IV. 32) that even in his day the most prominent of the Franks still lived in accordance with Salic Law.

[27] VII. 7.   [28] VII. 9.

[29] VI. 28. 29. 31.

[30] VI. 34.

[31] VI. 32. These relationships are shown in the following table:

kin it is perhaps of interest to note that his mother, Agnes, bore Margrave Leopold eighteen children (in addition to five that she bore to Frederick in her previous marriage), seven of whom died in infancy; of the eleven who survived, six were sons and five were daughters. Practically all attained to positions of distinction.[32]

Leopold III of Austria was a devout and kindly man whose de-

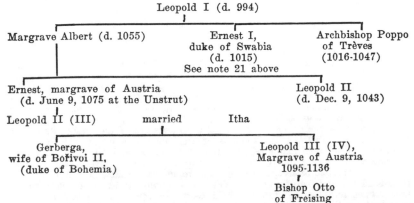

Leopold I (d. 994)

Margrave Albert (d. 1055) — Ernest I, duke of Swabia (d. 1015) See note 21 above — Archbishop Poppo of Trèves (1016-1047)

Ernest, margrave of Austria (d. June 9, 1075 at the Unstrut) — Leopold II (d. Dec. 9, 1043)

Leopold II (III) married Itha

Gerberga, wife of Bořivoi II, (duke of Bohemia) — Leopold III (IV), Margrave of Austria 1095-1136

Bishop Otto of Freising

[32] So the *Annales Austriae*. The following is a brief account of Bishop Otto's brothers and sisters:

ADALBERT or ALBERT, the eldest son, seems not to have been on the best of terms with his father, for he did not succeed him as margrave; we are told (*l.c.*) that he was made *advocatus Niwenburgensis ecclesiae . . . et omnium claustrorum ad advocatiam marchionis pertinentium.* He married the sister of King Bela II of Hungary (VII. 21). Upon his death, which occurred Nov. 9, 1137, Adalbert was buried beside his parents at Klosterneuburg. His father had died only a year before (Nov. 15, 1136; see VII. 21).

Of the second son, HENRY termed "Jasomirgott," it is specifically stated (*Annales Austriae*): *a patre minus diligebatur.* Yet he finally succeeded his father as margrave (upon the death of Leopold's third son and namesake, Oct. 18, 1141; see VII. 25), was made Duke of Bavaria by his half-brother Conrad III (VII. 26) and later first Duke of Austria (1156) by the emperor Frederick (*Gesta* 2. 55). A dispute between Otto and his brother Henry regarding certain Austrian estates belonging to the church of Freising was settled by the emperor, who reconciled the brothers in 1158 at Regensburg (*Gesta* 3. 14). Duke Henry's first wife was Gertrude, the daughter of the emperor Lothar (of Saxony) and widow of Duke Henry the Proud of Bavaria. She died April 18, 1143, and he afterwards married the Greek princess Theodora. Henry was the longest lived of the family.

LEOPOLD, the third son, succeeded his father as Margrave Leopold IV (V) — apparently in accordance with the father's wish. Conrad made him Duke of Bavaria in the year 1139 (see VII. 23: *Conradus rex Baioariam ingressus ducatum Leopoldo iuniori, Leopaldi marchionis filio, fratri suo ex parte matris, tradidit* — to which Otto significantly adds *et exhinc provincia nostra multis malis subiacere cepit*; also VII. 25: *Leopaldus marchio suscepto a rege ducato Norico . . . ducatum . . . potenter habuit ac fortiter rexit.*) Otto records in his chronicle (VII. 25) the damage done by Leopold's soldiers as they passed through Freising on their way to Regensburg in 1141. Leopold died Oct. 18, 1141 (So VII. 25; see also *Annales Austriae*).

Of ERNEST, the fourth son, we have only the statement in *Annales Aus-*

votion to the Church won for him such epithets as "the Pious" and "father of the clergy and of the poor."[33] He founded two monasteries within his domain: Klosterneuburg[34] in 1114 and Holy Cross (near Vienna) in 1136.[35] Moreover upon the death of the first Provost of Klosterneuburg — who was also named Otto — Leopold nominated his son Otto, then a mere child, to succeed him, appointing a certain Canon Opold to act as his substitute until the boy was old enough to assume the duties of this office.[36] The date is

triae: Quartus Ernesto, qui et in eodem loco (i.e., Holy Cross) sepultus iacet. BISHOP OTTO was the fifth son.

CONRAD, the sixth, was Bishop of Passau (Gesta 4. 14) and later Archbishop of Salzburg (Gesta 4, Appendix: Eberhardus Salzburgensis archiepiscopus venerabilis obiit. Conradus Pataviensis episcopus substituitur — in the year 1164). He died in 1168 (Gesta 4, Appendix: Conradus Iuvavensis constanter cum Rolando perseverans defunctus est, eique Adilbertus filius regis Boemici, sororius eius, subrogatur.)

We also know the names of several of Otto's sisters. Rahewin (Gesta 4. 14) states that GERTRUDE was Duchess of Bohemia: this is the wife of Duke Vladislav II of Bohemia, already referred to on page 6 above. Otto's own statement concerning her (VII. 34), predicti Boemorum ducis eiusque consortis Gerdrudis sororis regis, would seem to indicate that she was own sister to Conrad III and therefore not the child of Leopold. It is, of course, possible that Agnes had two daughters named Gertrude (just as she had two sons named Conrad), which might easily account for the confusion. Otto's sister BERTHA was the wife of Burgrave Henry of Regensburg (observe that Rahewin is in error when he calls her ducissa Polanorum in Gesta 4. 14).

AGNES (mistakenly called Gertrude in Gesta 3. 2) was the wife of Duke Vladislav II of Poland. ITA (also called Iuta or Judith) married William, marquess of Montferrat, characterized by Otto (Gesta 2. 16) as Gwilhelmus marchio de Monte-ferrato, vir nobilis et magnus et qui pene solus ex Italiae baronibus civitatum effugere potuit imperium. The fifth sister is nowhere mentioned by name.

Regarding the date of Otto's birth, Wilmans in the preface to his edition of the Chronicle, p. 85 (quoted also by G. Waitz in his preface to the Gesta and cited with approval by later scholars) remarks that. as the marriage of Leopold and Agnes occurred in 1106 (see Gesta 1. 10 and the Annales Austriae on this year), Otto — who was the fifth son — cannot well have been born before 1111; and as one or more of the seven children who died in infancy, or of the five surviving sisters may have been older, we must probably set his birth as late as 1114 or 1115. Furthermore Rahewin (Gesta 4. 14) speaks of him as iuvenis etate at the time of his death in 1158.

It will be evident from the preceding account that the family of Margrave Leopold III did not live very peaceably with one another, and Hofmeister (NA 37. 121) finds the origin of Otto's conviction regarding the transitory nature of all earthly affairs (regarding which subject see also infra, pp. 57-58) and the misery of man's lot in these family relations and in the moving fate that had overtaken his grandfather, the emperor Henry IV.

[33] See note 23 above.

[34] Annales Austriae, l.c.

[35] Ibid.

[36] Ibid. Quem, cum adhuc scholaris esset, mortuo Ottone primo Niwenburgensi ecclesiae preposito, pater suus fecit eidem ecclesiae prepositum, substituens ei vicarium Opoldum nomine. But see Waitz, Ottonis et Rahewini Gesta Friderici I. Imperatoris, editio tertia, Pracfatio p. ix, n. 6: In nullo

uncertain — perhaps 1117.[37] The income derived from this source was used to defray part of the expense of Otto's education at Paris.[38]

There is little definite information about Otto's life as a student [39] but we know of at least one visit which he made to his home. On this occasion he brought with him certain relics for the church at Klosterneuburg.[40] Upon the completion of his studies Otto set out for home with fifteen companions. In the course of his journey he stopped to spend the night at the monastery of Morimund and there with his comrades joined the Cistercian Order [41]— a step of the utmost significance for his future, particularly as regards his endeavors in the field of the philosophy of history.[42] This occurred, in all probability, in 1133,[43] for it was in that year that Leopold, upon the advice of the archbishop of Salzburg and the bishops of

documento quod sciam memoratur, econtra Opoldus saepissime; Fisher, Cod. tradd. Claustron. nr. 20. 23. 25. 32. 117. 206. 224. 249, nusquam vicarius, plerumque canonicus appellatus.

[37] On the whole subject see especially Hofmeister, NA 37. 122-139: Eintritt in den geistlichen Stand. Studium in Paris.

[38] Annales Austriae, l.c.

[39] Waitz, o.c., p. x, is of the opinion that Otto was in Paris during the years 1129-1133; so also Hashagen, o.c.

[40] Annales Austriae, l.c.

[41] Annales Austriae, l.c.: Ibi proposito tempore studii transacto, dum ad propria redire properat, in cenobio Morimundensi, ubi pernoctaverat, se monachum fecit cum aliis quindecim, qui secum venerant, electissimis clericis. Morimund, in Champagne, had been founded in 1115 together with Clairvaux, and was one of the four daughter monasteries of Cîteaux (in Burgundy, near Langres: dép. Haute-Marne).

[42] So Hashagen; but Hofmeister (p. 654) would rather attribute Otto's entrance into the order to the fact that the life at Morimund seemed to him to embody the ideal which the impressions of Paris had aroused to conscious life within him.

[43] Annales Austriae, l.c.: Quo audito, marchio pater eius, cum iam videret locum filii vacare et ecclesiae Niwenburgensem preter se provisorem non habere, sicut vir providus et Deo devotus mittens invitavit in domum suam venerabilis viros, Eberhardum archiepiscopum Salzburgensem, Regimarum episcopum Pataviensem, Romanum Gurcensem, et alias quam plures religiosas personas. Horum ordinatissimum ad Dei voluntatem consilium secutus, canonicos saeculares, qui sibi videbantur divina negligenter et nimis remisse agere, decentissime avertit et regularibus beati Augustini viam regiam et optimam formam vitae tenentibus anno incarnationis Domini 1133, eundem locum perpetuo tenendum potentiva manu tradidit; prepositum eis preponens ex eorundem venerabilium virorum consilio prepositum Chymensem, Hartmannum nomine, virum sanctisssimae vitae, virum Deo et hominibus acceptum, sed peccatis

Passau and Gurk, gave over the monastery of Klosterneuburg (now deprived of its Provost, his son) to the Augustinians.

We learn from Rahewin [44] that Otto became Abbot of Morimund but there is no record of his deeds in this office. In the charter [45] given by Leopold to the monastery of Holy Cross in 1136, mention is made of Otto as a member of the Cistercian Order but not as Abbot of Morimund; it seems reasonable to assume that his father would not have failed to give him the title in this document had he then possessed it. Otto had not long held the dignity of Abbot when he was made Bishop of Freising,[46] succeeding Henry I who died October 9, 1137.[47]

It is natural to conclude [48] that the fifteen "chosen clerics" who came back from Paris with Otto were countrymen of his who had accompanied him as a sort of retinue when he left home to attend school at the great French university. Only one of the number is definitely known to us by name, Abbot Frederick of Baumgartensberg, later bishop in Hungary; it is to him that the author of the first Klosterneuburg continuation of the *Annals of Austria* is

nostris exigentibus post aliquos annos a nobis ablatum, in Brixensem episcopum assumptum.

[44] Rahewin, *Gesta* 4. 14: *Sane vivendi modum iuxta Cisterciensis ordinis religionem instituerat, ibique in monasterio Morimundensi primo abbas, eo usque probatus et electus inventus est, ut merito sibi diceretur: Amice, ascende superius.*

[45] Meiller 1. 1. 22 (quoted by Waitz, *Praefatio*, p. x): *Inde est quod ego Liupoldus D.g. Marchio Austrie . . . Ottone dilecto filio meo, qui se apud Morimundum ordini subiecit Cisterciensi, adhortante, fratres a predicto Morimundensi cenobio evocarim et in loco qui actenus Sattelbach dicebatur, nunc vero . . . ad S. Crucem vocatur, collocaverim.*

[46] Waitz, *o.c.*, p. x, states that he does not believe that Otto was chosen Abbot before the middle of the year 1136 and feels unable to contradict the notice in Albericus (SS. 23. 383) on the year 1146: *Huc usque pertingit narratio episcopi Ottonis, qui fuit vir nobilis et monachus Morimundi, et una die electus in abbatem eiusdem loci, sequenti die factus est in Bavaria episcopus Frisingensis.* On the other hand, Wattenbach, 5th. edition (1885), p. 242 n. 2, feels that the account in *Gesta* 4. 14 indicates that Otto held the office of Abbot for a considerable length of time. See note 44 above. Hofmeister believes that Otto became Abbot in 1137/38.

[47] VII. 21 and Hofmeister's note 5 on p. 340. In the *Annales Austriae, l.c.* we read: *Igitur ipse dominus Otto de Morimundensi cenobio ad episcopatum Frisiensem evocatus est. Ibi qualis eius vita fuerit, et quomodo eius gratia studium floruerit, et quae et quanta scripserit, vel etiam quomodo ecclesia illa per eum profecerit, Rachwynus, notarius eius, plenius omnia scripsit.*

[48] NA 37. 139-149: § 3 *Studiengenossen Ottos.*

indebted for his information about Otto.[49] As regards the others we have Bishop Frederick's assurance that they all reached honorable and dignified stations in life.[50]

The identity of the others has naturally been a favorite subject for surmise and conjecture, but there is not much reliable evidence on which to base a conclusion.[51] Possibly Henry, the son of Duke Engelbert of Carinthia, who was bishop of Troyes when he died in 1169, may have been one of the number.[52] Yet in his case, though he appears to have been a monk of Morimund, there is no proof of his having studied at Paris; and it has been suggested [53] that he may have been older than Otto and that it was perhaps he who occasioned the latter's stay at the Cistercian monastery. Rainald of Dassel, who held the office of chancellor under the emperor Frederick Barbarossa and was one of Otto's most intimate friends,[54] probably studied at Paris and may have been one of Otto's schoolmates there.[55] But in his case there is a likelihood that he was younger than Otto.

It would be a source of even greater satisfaction were we able to learn definitely under what teachers Otto studied during his years at Paris. But owing to the fact that in his *Chronicle* he carefully avoids mention of living authors and scholars, this is a problem difficult if not impossible of solution. He is himself a scholar on the pattern of Gilbert de la Porrée and Hugo of St. Victor, and the influence of these men upon him was clearly very great, but whether he was actually the pupil of either is not known. He does not so much as mention Hugo by name, and in the first book of the

[49] *Annales Austriae, l.c.: Qui etiam, ut ab uno illorum audivi, Friderico nomine, qui et ipse in abbatem Pomkartenperge et deinde in Hungaria in episcopum electus fuerat, omnes in diversas dignitates promoti sunt.*

[50] See previous note.

[51] See especially Budinszky, *Histoire littéraire de la France*, Lüdecke, and Wiedemann. Hofmeister prides himself on having finally cleared away the old baseless suppositions regarding Otto's schoolmates: *e.g.* Popes Eugenius III, Hadrian IV and Alexander III; the German Hardewin; Berengar; Eberhard II, bishop of Bamberg (1146-d. 1170).

[52] So Wiedemann, Lüdecke, and *Hist. litt. de la France.* See also Wattenbach 2. 9, n. 1.

[53] By Hofmeister, NA 37. 139-149: § 3 *Studiengenossen Ottos.*

[54] See especially Otto's letter addressed to him as *Precordiali amico*, p. 3 in Hofmeister's edition of the *Chronicle.*

[55] So Büdinger, *Die Entstehung des achten Buches Ottos von Freising* (1881) 347, who speaks also of Petrus Comestor as a possible schoolmate. See too Hashagen 2, n. 4; Lüdecke 15; Schmidlin 108, n. 3.

Gesta,[56] although he gives a detailed account of the disputes and contentions of the learned men of his day (which is an extremely valuable source for this subject), he never intimates in unmistakable fashion that he heard any one of these famous teachers personally. It seems, however, a fair statement of the facts to say that of the great men of the first half of the twelfth century the three who were of the most significance for Otto's education were Abelard, Gilbert and Hugo.[57] How deeply Gilbert's views had impressed Bishop Otto is seen in the circumstance that he mentions them on his deathbed.[58]

It is furthermore probable, in view of Otto's interest in logic and his acquaintance with the newly translated works of Aristotle, that he was a pupil of Theodoric of Chartres, although definite proof of this is lacking.[59] Bishop Otto appears to have been an ardent student of philosophy in his school days at Paris, and he later made Freising a center for these studies,[60] founding there a school for Aristotle on the hill which was, in consequence, known as *Mons Doctus*.[61] Rahewin states that Otto was a pioneer in the matter of introducing Aristotelian studies into Germany.[62]

As regards travel in foreign lands we know from several refer-

[56] See especially chapters 48-61.

[57] So Hofmeister 161, who believes, however, that only in Hugo's case is there great probability that he was actually Otto's teacher. See especially his article on *Der Bildungsgang Ottos von Freising*, II (§ 5 Abälard, pp. 635-640; § 6 Gilbert von Poitiers, pp. 640-645; § 7 Hugo von St. Viktor, pp. 646-654). But see Hashagen (Dresden 1900) 10-11: *Ansätze zu einem System* 3, a.

[58] *Gesta* 4. 14 (p. 252 Simson): *ut si quid pro sententia magistri Gileberti, ut patet in prioribus* (that is, in chapters 48-61 of the first book of the *Gesta*), *dixisse visus esset, quod quempiam posset offendere, ad ipsorum arbitrium corrigeretur.*

[59] Hofmeister 669, regards this supposition as questionable. Still he calls attention (671) to its likelihood in view of the fact that Otto is so well-informed in regard to Theodoric and his brother Bernhard: *Gesta* 1. 49: *quales fuerunt duo fratres Bernahardus et Theodericus, viri doctissimi.* For Bernhard see also *Gesta* 1. 52.

[60] *Gesta* 4. 14.

[61] Meichelbeck, *Historia Frisingensis* 350.

[62] On "The New Aristotle" and Otto's interest in it, see especially Hofmeister NA 37, § 8 (654-681); J. Schmidlin, *Die Philosophie Ottos von Freising* (1905) 160-175. The most significant passage in the *Chronicle* itself is II. 8. For Otto's position as regards philosophy in general, see Hashagen (Dresden 1900), II (through p. 11); Huber 132-143; Bernheim, *Der Character Ottos von Freising und seiner Werke* (1885) 2-13; Schmidlin, *l.c.* 156-160, 312-323 and 407-423. But see Hofmeister 153.

ences in the *Chronicle* [63] that Otto journeyed to Italy in the latter part of the year 1145, and that he visited Pope Eugenius III on November 18 of that year.[64] Other details of the journey are lacking but he appears to have returned in the middle of the following year. In February of 1147 Bishop Otto was "signed by the cross" at Regensburg [65] and set forth on the ill-fated Second Crusade — then being preached by St. Bernard in consequence of the capture of Edessa by the Turks in 1144. Among the other notable men of the time who were induced to take part in this expedition were King Louis VII of France, Bishop Otto's half-brother the emperor Conrad III, his nephew Frederick Barbarossa and his brother Duke Henry "Jasomirgott." [66] Otto's experiences in connection with the Crusade are perhaps worthy of somewhat detailed recital.

In the latter part of May he embarked with Conrad at Regensburg and set sail down the Danube. Reaching Ardacker, a town on the right bank of the Danube below the river Ensa, on Ascension Day (May 29), they encamped for two or three days to await the arrival of additional troops.[67] Thence they proceeded to the borders of the realm and celebrated Whitsunday (June 8) in a camp not far from the Fischa River. Then crossing the Leitha they pitched their tents in Pannonia. Otto gives a vivid picture of the progress of the Crusaders, some sailing down the Danube, others marching along its banks: "so great a multitude that the streams seemed scarcely large enough for sailing and the expanse of the plains hardly sufficient for the advance on foot." [68]

Unfortunately Otto does not give a like detailed account of the further movements of the Crusaders; he states that the disastrous conclusion of the expedition "for our sins" is known to all, and that it is his purpose to write not a tragedy but a pleasing history.[69] Accordingly he records only a single incident of that perilous and ill-omened advance — the great storm and flood on the night of September 7-8 which caused such havoc in the encampment in the plain of Choroebachica near Constantinople.[70]

[63] VII. 32: *nobis cum aliis multis presentibus*; also 29: *ut ipse vidi* and 33: *vidimus etiam ibi.*

[64] VII. 32 (p. 362 Hofmeister): *in beati Martini octava, quando dedicatio ecclesiae beati Petri celebrari solet*; and in connection with this VII. 29: *ut ipse vidi.*

[65] *Gesta* 1. 42: *Acceperunt eadem hora crucem tres episcopi, videlicet Heinricus Ratisponensis, Otto Frisingensis, Reginbertus Pataviensis.*

[66] V. 18.   [67] *Gesta* 1. 46.   [68] 1. 46.   [69] 1. 47.   [70] 1. 1. 47.

In October the Crusaders reached Nicomedia, and here a controversy arose between Conrad and his princes with regard to the route to be followed in Asia Minor. Otto with 14,000 men separated from his brother's army at Nicaea and started to march along the sea coast, a longer but supposedly safer way into Syria. Both divisions met with disaster. Otto was betrayed by the Greeks and his whole army destroyed by the Turks. The bishop himself, with a few companions who had escaped, embarked on March 21, 1148, and reached a port of Syria.[71] Thence he went to Jerusalem and entered the Holy City on Palm Sunday, April 4.[72] After spending Easter (April 11) there he betook himself to the city of Acre, where he is said to have been on the 24th of June.[73]

Otto's life for the next two years is veiled in obscurity, and it is uncertain whether he returned to Bavaria as early as 1148 or accompanied Conrad on his journey to Constantinople, leaving Acre September 8, 1148, and remaining in the city of Constantinople with the king until February of 1149.

The most valuable part of Bishop Otto's tantalizingly fragmentary account of the Second Crusade consists of a passage in the *Gesta* dealing with the course of events in Syria from March to July 1148 and sketching the itinerary of the pilgrims in brief outline.[74] The conclusions which he draws from the unhappy outcome of the expedition are also worthy of note — particularly by way of contrast with the opinions of his contemporaries regarding the great disaster and more especially with his own general attitude in his *Chronicle*.[75] He says of the Crusade: "Although it was not good for the extension of boundaries or for the advantage of men's bodies, yet it was good for the salvation of many souls. . . ." And again: "If we were to say that that holy Abbot (Bernard of Clairvaux) was inspired by the spirit of God to arouse us, but that we by reason of our pride and wantonness failing to observe his commands deservedly suffered a loss of men and of property, it

---

[71] *Gesta* 1. 57.   [72] *Gesta* 1. 62.

[73] Otto himself says (*Gesta* 1. 63): *Ambo itaque inter Tyrum et Ptolomaidam in loco, qui Palma nomen a re sortitus appellatur, mense Iunio circa nativitatem sancti Iohannis baptistae conveniunt.* With reference to Otto's connection with the Crusade, see especially the introduction to Simson's edition of the *Gesta*, pp. xi and xii, also B. Kugler, *Studien zur Geschichte des zweiten Kreuzzuges*, Stuttgart 1866, 7-10.

[74] *Gesta* 1. 62-63.

[75] See below, pp. 57-59.

would not be at variance from what has been thought and experienced of old."[76]

In 1152 Conrad III died and was succeeded by Frederick Barbarossa, under whom Bishop Otto held a position of influence and honor.[77] He did not accompany the emperor upon his first journey to Rome in 1154.[78] When Frederick was about to set out for Italy again in 1158 he excused his uncle from accompanying him[79] on the plea of ill health, for though not an old man Bishop Otto had for some time past been far from well.[80]

Feeling that the end of his life was near at hand, Otto commended his church to the emperor's gracious care and besought him to guard all its rights and privileges after his own decease.[81] Soon afterwards he set out on a final visit to his beloved monastery of Morimund, and there he died on September 22, 1158.[82] His friend and secretary, Rahewin, gives a full and sympathetic account of his last moments.[83] He states further that although Bishop Otto, shortly before his death, indicated a lowly spot outside the church where he desired to be buried "that he might be trodden upon by the feet of all the brothers," yet his wishes in this one point were disregarded and his body was laid to rest near the high altar and held in due reverence and honor.[84] Only a few months later

[76] *Gesta* 1. 65, especially the opening sentence and the paragraph near the close beginning *ex quo fit.*

[77] Rahewin says of him (*Gesta* 4. 14): *Ob ea et aliarum multarum privilegia gratiarum, fiducia quoque tam secularis prudentiae quam eloquio fretus facundissimae linguae, cum sepius in causis aecclesiae coram regibus et principibus constantissime ageret, et exinde sibi gloria laudem, laus invidiam, ut assolet, non modicam peperisset, laqueos adversantium inperterritus declinavit et obloquentium ora sine lesione probe probus evasit.* For an instance of the respect shown him by Frederick, see *Gesta* 3. 22: *Post haec . . . sacerdotium.* This was in the year 1158.

[78] *Gesta* 2. 16: *ut aiunt.*

[79] *Gesta* 4. 14 (p. 251 Simson).

[80] *Ibid.*

[81] *Gesta* 4. 14 (p. 251 Simson).

[82] *Annales Austriae, l.c.: Ad extremum autem cum iter more solito ad Cisterciense capitulum ageret, et ad cenobium suum Morimundense visendi causa divertisset, gravi infirmitate pressus, in habitu monachili quem numquam in episcopatu deposuerat, omnibus fratribus coram positis et eiulatu maximo perstrepentibus, felicissime in Domino obiit, et ibi sepultus quievit.*

[83] *Gesta* 4. 14, pp. 251-252.

[84] Rahewin's final sentence is interesting: *Ego autem, qui huius operis principium eius ex ore adnotavi finemque eius de principis iussu perficiendum*

(April 5, 1159) his church at Freising was burned to the ground.[85]

3. LITERARY WORK; PERSONAL TRAITS

Before approaching the detailed consideration of Otto's philosophy of history or even attempting a careful investigation of his chronicle, in which that theory is embodied, we may profitably take a hasty preliminary survey of his literary work as a whole and endeavor to find in his writings some indication of the personal traits and characteristics of the author. His extant literary works consist of:

(1) His *Chronicle*,[86] comprising a history of the world from Adam to his own time, compiled between the years 1143 and 1147. The first edition of this book was written at the request of a certain Isingrim [87] and completed by September 11, 1146, or at least before April 9, 1147. No manuscript of this earlier edition has survived. But in 1157 — and after March of that year [88] — Otto sent a second edition to his nephew, the emperor Frederick Barbarossa, at the latter's request.[89] This revised work, transmitted through Raboto, abbot of St. Stephen's of Freising and Rahewin his chaplain, is in general unchanged save for the addition of the introductory and dedicatory letters to the emperor and to his chancellor, Rainald.[90] There are also certain minor additions such as the continuation of

---

suscepi et manu mea ipsius extrema lumina clausi, hoc epithaphium composui et tumulo eius inscribi feci. The epitaph that follows is 54 lines in length.

[85] *Gesta* 4. 15.

[86] On the title, see below, p. 23. For the date of composition, see especially Hofmeister's introduction to his edition of the *Chronicle*, p. XII, and *Gesta* 1, Prologue, page 9 and following (Simson): *Fateor, dum ante aliquot annos priorem hystoriam terminassem, spiritusque peregrini Dei ad sumenda contra gentes quae orientem inhabitant arma totam pene Hesperiam afflasset, pro pacis iocunditate quae orbi momentanee tune arriserat, stilum vertere cogitaram, iamque scribere coeperam, sed, quo instinctu nescio, tamquam animo futura presagiente finemque inspiciente coeptum proieci opus.*

[87] I, Prol (ed. Hofmeister 8): *Quia ergo per haec et huiusmodi mundi probatur versibilitas, necessarium ratus sum ad petitionem tuam, frater karissime Isingrime, historiam texere.* On Isingrim, see F. L. Baumann, *Isingrim, der Freund Ottos von Freising,* in Neues Archiv 6 (1881) 600-602.

[88] See Letter to Frederick, ed. Hofmeister 3, n. 7.

[89] ''*Petivit vestra imperialis maiestas a nostra parvitate, quatenus liber, qui ante aliquot annos de mutatione rerum a nobis ob nubilosa tempora conscriptus est, vestrae transmitteretur serenitati.*'' (ed. Hofmeister 1).

[90] Letter, ed. Hofmeister 2-3.

the list of emperors and popes to bring it down to date. The most important additional material consists of what Otto learned from personal observation or by hearsay from others during his journey to the East on the Second Crusade in 1147-1148.[91] This book will be discussed in greater detail hereafter.

(2) His *Gesta Friderici I Imperatoris,* written between the years 1156 and 1158.[92] In the letter to the emperor accompanying the revision of his chronicle, the author promises to write the history of his nephew's achievements if he may have access to Frederick's official records.[93] In response to this request the emperor gladly sent him — in a letter still extant, and prefixed to the *Gesta* — a resumé of the events of his reign from 1152 to September of 1156. Oddly enough, Bishop Otto was able to bring his work down only to this point by the time of his death, although it is evident that he had planned to continue it still farther.[94] Soon after he died his secretary, Rahewin, undertook the completion of the work in accordance with his friend's express request and with the emperor's sanction,[95] and finished it in 1160,[96] adding two more books to the two completed by Otto.

The first book of Otto's *Gesta Friderici* may be regarded as a second revised and improved edition of the seventh book of his *Chronicle*; for it starts with 1076, the year in which Pope Gregory VII excommunicated Henry IV, briefly recapitulates the reigns of Henry IV, Henry V and Lothar, and then (from chapter 23 to the end of the first book) narrates the life of Conrad III. Having thus given a summary of the deeds of the emperor's grandfather, father and uncle, Otto proceeds in his second book to the history of Frederick's reign. With the eleventh chapter of this book he begins the account of his first expedition to Rome in 1154; in chapters 43-56 he relates the emperor's deeds after his return to Germany to the

[91] For a list of such passages, see Hofmeister's introduction, pp. XIII-XIV.

[92] The best edition is *Ottonis et Rahewini Gesta Friderici I Imperatoris,* B. de Simson, 1912, in *Scriptores rerum Germanicarum in usum scholarum.* For the date of its composition see Simson's introduction, p. XVI, n. 1.

[93] Ed. Hofmeister 3.

[94] *Gesta* 2.56: *Quare huic secundo operi terminus detur, ut ad ea quae dicenda restant tercio locus servetur volumini.*

[95] See Prologue to the third book of the *Gesta* (Simson 162): *eius iussu pariterque serenissimi et divi imperatoris Friderici nutu;* also the epilogue to the fourth book (Simson 346): *nos tamen obedientiae nostrae fructus consolabitur, qua precipienti paruimus.*

[96] *Gesta* 4. 86.

final laying aside of the feud of the Welfs at Regensburg in 1156, when Henry the Lion at last regained Bavaria. The continuation of the work by Rahewin covers the years 1156-1160. There is an appendix, apparently also by Rahewin, consisting of short notes on the years 1160-1170.[97]

(3) A letter of Bishop Otto to Wibald, abbot of Corvey, written after March 9-10 in the year 1152 and containing a discussion of the meaning of Psalms 24.7 and 8, is still preserved.[98]

In the prologue to the first book of his *Gesta* Otto speaks of having started and then discarded a work in the period immediately following the completion of the *Chronicle* (1146-1147); we have no means of discovering what this may have been. Other works attributed to Otto, but of dubious authenticity, are cited in the notes.[99]

[97] Pages 347-351 in Simson's edition. According to Simson's revision of the dates, the events here recorded cover the period between June 24, 1160 and June 8, 1169. For the *Gesta* in general, see the introduction to the excellent edition by Simson already frequently referred to above (*Ottonis et Rahewini Gesta Friderici I Imperatoris, editio tertia, recensuit* G. Waitz, *curavit* B. de Simson, in *Scriptores rerum Germanicarum*, volume 59, Hanover and Leipsic 1912) and the following monographs and journal articles:

Grotefend, Hermann. *Der Wert der Gesta Friderici imperatoris des Bischofs Otto von Freising für die Geschichte des Reichs unter Friedrich I*, dissert. Göttingen (Hanover 1870), pp. 1-70. A detailed examination of Book II.

Hauck, Albert. *Kirchengeschichte Deutschlands*, Leipzig 1913, Vierter Teil, pp. 508-510.

Kohl, Horst. *Beiträge zur Kritik Rahewins*, Chemnitz 1890, pp. 1-24. (In *Jahresbericht des königl. Gymnasiums zu Chemnitz*; I. Die Entlehnungen aus fremden Autoren).

Kugler, B. *Studien zur Geschichte des zweiten Kreuzzuges*, Stuttgart, 1866, pp. 7-10.

Lüdecke, W. *Der historische Wert des ersten Buches von Ottos von Freising Gesta Friderici*, Inaug. diss., Halle a. S. 1884, pp. 1-53; continued as Progr. d. Gymn. Stendal, 1885, pp. 1-32.

Martens, Carl. *Ein Beitrag zur Kritik Ragewins*, Inaug. diss., Greifswald 1877, pp. 1-52.

Ribbeck, Walter. *Kaiser Friedrich I und die römische Curie in den Jahren 1157-1159*, Inaug. diss., Leipzig 1881, pp. 1-70. A sharp attack upon the trustworthiness of Rahewin's account.

Simson, B. v. *Ueber die verschiedenen Rezensionen von Ottos und Rahewins Gesta Friderici I*, in Neues Archiv 36 (1910-1911) 16. 681-716.

Wattenbach, W. *Deutschlands Geschichtsquellen im Mittelalter*, 5th Edition (Berlin 1885), II pp. 247-250.

Wild. *Radevicus und sein Verhältniss zu Otto von Freisingen*, Progr. d. Gymn. Görlitz, 1865, pp. 1-30.

[98] Edited by Ph. Jaffé, Bibliotheca rerum Germanicarum I, nr. 387, pp. 519 *et seq.*

[99] Aside from the writings mentioned above, Otto is said to have written also:

(1) A History of Austria, which Urstisius and Fabricius mention with assurance. (See Hofmeister's preface to his edition of the *Chronicle*, p. VIII:

It is perhaps almost inevitable that, however impersonally a man may strive to write, his character reveals itself to a greater or less degree in his literary work. Thus we are able to see many of the personal traits of Otto the man revealed to us in his historical writings. The pious Christian stands revealed in his abhorrence of Arianism [100] — which was, however, characteristic of his time. Otto's uprightness and personal integrity are indicated by the fact that he misses no opportunity of expressing his sense of pain at sin,[101]

Historiam Austriacam, quam teste Urstisio (Germ, hist. illustr. I, p. 4) *olim Wolphgangum Lazium habuisse ferunt, a Barnaba de Montalbo aliisque laudari Fabricius (Bibl. lat. med. et infimae aetatis,* ed. Mansi V. *Patavii* 1754, p. 187) *dicit.* Wilmans believed that it was to his work that Otto referred in his *Gesta* 1.10, when he said, in speaking of the marriage of his parents: *quod alias a nobis plenius dictum est.* (See *Scriptores rerum Germanicarum in usum scholarum* 30, Intro. pp. xvi-xvii. Wilmans states that nowhere else in the *Chronicle* or the *Gesta* does Otto refer to his parents' marriage, which took place in 1106 A.D.). But Otto is probably alluding to a paragraph in the seventh book of the *Chronicle* (VII. 9: *promissa sorore sua, quae tunc nuper a Friderico Suevorum duce viduata fuerat, in uxorem marchioni — i.e.,* Leopold III, Otto's father; so G. Waitz, *Gesta,* p. XII, n. 1, followed by Hofmeister, *l.c.*). Hence we need not assume the existence of a separate work on Austria.

(2) Roger Wilmans (*Scriptores rerum Germanicarum* 30, Intro. p. xvii) believed that Otto composed a number of works, now lost, on dialectics and philosophy, basing his assumption on a statement of Æneas Silvius (*Historia Friderici* III *imp., ed.* J. Schilter (1702) 10: *In dialectica quoque ac philosophia opuscula nonnulla edidit).* This is questionable, however, for the reference may well be explained by the philosophical digressions so numerous in the *Gesta.* (This is the view of *Hist. litt. de la France* 13.209; Huber, *Otto von Freising* 75; O. Holder-Egger, Hergog-Hauck *Realencyclopädie für protestantische Theologie und Kirche,* 3rd. ed. 14 (1904) 533-437; A. Hofmeister, NA 37 (1912) 153-158, 680-681 and Intro. to his edition of the *Chronicle* p. IX. But Waitz, preface to his edition of the *Gesta* (3rd. ed., Simson) p. XIV, is inclined to agree with Wilmans.)

(3) Schmidlin (*Phil. Jahrb. d. Görres-Ges.* 18.421 ff.) expresses the belief that Otto wrote a work on natural philosophy, arguing from the words *alibi dicta* in VIII. 11 (*Qualiter vero quaedam ex causis sibi reservatis potentialiter creator omnium operetur, alibi dicta presentem locum non flagitant*). Hofmeister, however, holds that this is a mistake, explaining the allusion as a reference to the works of St. Augustine (*De Civitate Dei* 21.7 ff.; *De Genesi ad litteram lib.* 9.17. 32 and 18. 33). *cf.* Hugo of St. Victor, *Summa Sententiarum* 3. 3. See NA 37. 153-156.

(4) Potthast (*Bibl. hist. medii aevi,* II (2) p. 886) mentions a *Fragment concerning Pope Hildebrand* as among the writings of Bishop Otto that have come down to us. This, however, is nothing more than a collection of excerpts from *Gesta* 1. 1 and the *Chronicle* VI. 35 (as pointed out by Huber, *Otto von Freising* 74).

(5) Finally, certain verses once attributed to Bishop Otto are now generally admitted to be the work of another. (See Hofmeister, preface to the *Chronicle,* pp. IX-X).

[100] IV. 6.

[101] I. 19: *Pudet hic inextricabiles flagitiorum recessus pandere,* and later: *parricidium . . . quis non gemens audire poterit?*; II. 3 (Romulus); III. 15 (Nero); II. 9 (Lucretia); III. 7 (Herod); III. 9 (Tiberius); II. 17: *Tedet hic inextricabilem malorum texere cratem.*

and perhaps even more by the lessons which he loves to draw from history: indeed Otto is ahead of his time in regarding history as a teacher of men.[102] Otto is singularly free from the proverbial prelate's pride, tolerant to a marked degree, tactful always, not excessive in praise or blame and not dictatorial. He evidently turned his travels to good advantage in writing his history, as he cites numerous instances of autopsy [103] or information obtained by inquiry in distant lands: this is evidence of his naturally inquiring disposition as well as of his practical cleverness in making the most of his opportunities. He has too a keen sense of justice, and regards it as his function to narrate rather than to pass judgment upon men's deeds.[104] So also with regard to theological questions he is for the most part content to leave decisions to others, merely expressing his opinion.[105]

His local patriotism and love of home are apparent in his chapter on St. Corbinian, with its charming description of the city of Freising, its church and its natural beauties of meadow, stream and woodland.[106] Moreover his works contain passages of rare beauty, clearly revealing his appreciation of nature,[107] and he sees in the beautiful and in the ugly, in the sunny morning and in the night of wind and rain, pictures of progress and of retrogression in the life of the state.[108] It is perhaps significant that he conceives of happiness as consisting of peaceful quiet.[109]

It has been well said that "there is scarcely another individual in whom we see so clearly and so impressively revealed the riches and the variety of the movements that filled the 12th century —

---

[102] Sorgenfrey (Greiz, 1873) 1-19. Among the passages he cites are: II. 24 (modesty); II. 37 (wisdom); Otto's advice to princes in *Gesta* 1. 4 (fear of God).

[103] *E.g.*, IV. 27; VII. 29, 32 and 33.

[104] VI. 23: *Quae omnia utrum licite aut secus acta sint, dicere presentis non est operis. Res enim gestas scribere, non rerum gestarum rationem reddere proposuimus.*

[105] See especially VIII. 35.

[106] V. 24.

[107] *E.g.*, *Gesta* 1. 46.

[108] So Hauck (Leipzig 1913) 503. See Otto's letter to Frederick I, ed. Hofmeister p. 2.

[109] *Chron.*, Prol., p. 10 in Hofmeister's ed. *iocundam tranquillitatem; Gesta, prooemium: unde hoc tempore scribentes quodammodo iudico beatos, dum post turbulentiam preteritorum non solum pacis inaudita reluxit serenitas . . .;* and *Gesta* 1. 34: *de pacis serenitate.*

the complete fulness of the opposing tendencies that live in this time and its people — as in Otto of Freising." [110]

4. THE CHRONICLE OF UNIVERSAL HISTORY

Otto's own designation for his great historical work appears to have been *The History of the Two Cities* [111] — namely, the earthly Babylon and the heavenly Jerusalem. Yet it was often referred to for convenience by the brief title of *Chronicle* [112] by which it is generally known today. The author himself frequently speaks of it merely as "the history." [113] Occasionally he alludes to it as the book in which he deals with "the vicissitudes of the world." [114] Indeed the theory has been held that the title of the book as sent to the emperor Frederick — the second edition — was *De mutatione rerum*. [115] This view however has not found general acceptance, [116] and it is altogether probable that the double title, as given by Hofmeister in his masterly edition of the work, is historically exact: *Ottonis Episcopi Frisingensis Chronica sive Historia De Duabus Civitatibus*.

As Bishop Otto was by no means the first to attempt to give an outline of universal history it is, of course, only to be expected that he should avail himself to a greater or less extent of the works of his predecessors in this field. Indeed he says at the very outset, in the prologue to the first book of the *Chronicle*: "There are extant in this field the famous works of Pompeius Trogus, Justin, Cornelius (*i.e.* Tacitus), Varro, Eusebius, Jerome, Orosius, Jordanes and a great many others." As a matter of fact he makes use of all of these writers. But his chief indebtedness to his predecessors is indicated a little later when he says: "In this work I follow most of all those illustrious lights of the Church, Augustine

[110] Hofmeister, NA 37. 108.

[111] VIII, Prol.: *Hoc opus nostrum, quod de duabus civitatibus intitulavimus*; *cf.* also III, Prol., and VII, Prol.

[112] So in the Emperor's letter: *Cronica, quae tua sapientia digessit*; also Otto himself in his *Gesta* 1. 31: *ut in prioribus cronicis dictum est*.

[113] *E.g.*, in the letter to the Emperor: *qui hanc historiam ex ore nostro subnotavit*; also *Gesta* 1. 11.

[114] *E.g.*, II, Prol.: *promisisse me recolo de rerum mutatione ac miseriis scripturum*.

[115] Büdinger (Vienna 1881) 326-333.

[116] *Cf.*, for example, Hashagen (Dresden 1900), Anhang, p. 34 and Hofmeister's preface, § 2, pp. X-XII.

and Orosius, and have planned to draw from their fountains what is pertinent to my theme and my purpose.'' [117] In his own defense, for treading in the footsteps of such ''illustrious lights,'' he urges the following:

Nor do I think that I shall be justly criticized if, coming after such great men, men so wise and so eloquent, I shall presume in spite of my ignorance to write; since I have both epitomized those things of which they themselves spoke profusely and at length, and have detailed, in however rude a style, the deeds which have been performed by citizens of the world since their time.[118]

In his section on Otto's sources in the *Chronicle* Hofmeister gives an exhaustive list of all the works from which quotations are made in the course of this book.[119] He subdivides these sources as follows:

A. Theologians: among whom the most important are the Bible (in the version of Jerome) and St. Augustine. A total of thirteen, with ten or more mentioned as less certain.
B. Philosophers and grammarians: seven and one doubtful. Aristotle and Cicero are the most important here.
C. Poets: nine in number and a possibility of two others. Vergil, Horace and Ovid are notable in this list.
D. Historians, legends and laws: a list of twenty-eight definite and eleven less certain sources.

He mentions also two lost works and certain letters no longer extant though cited by Otto, and gives a detailed list of passages in which the historian is relating what he has himself seen or heard.[120]

Some of these authorities are perhaps quoted from an intermediate source rather than from the works themselves,[121] others possibly from memory or from notes previously prepared;[122] in the case of many of the more important, Otto doubtless found the manuscripts in his library at Freising,[123] or acquired them for his needs in composing the *Chronicle*.[124]

---

[117] Prologue to Bk. I (Hofmeister's edition p. 9).

[118] *Loc. cit.*

[119] *Praefatio* (§ 7, *De Fontibus Chronicae*) pp. XCI-XCVIII.

[120] *Loc. cit.*, pp. XCV-XCVII.

[121] So, *e.g.*, Hofmeister believes that he quotes Varro at secondhand from Augustine, and Pompeius Trogus, Justin, Suetonius and Tacitus from Orosius.

[122] Especially the poets.

[123] This library had been collected by his predecessors since the ninth century, and two hundred or more MSS from Freising of the time up to the twelfth century are still preserved at Munich.

[124] In Hofmeister's scholarly edition of the *Chronicle* not only are all

In the eleventh chapter of the seventh book of the *Chronicle,*
having now brought his history down to the year 1106, Bishop Otto
bids farewell to his guides in the following terms: "Thus far we
have set down extracts from the books of Orosius, of Eusebius, and
of those who wrote after them, even to our own time. What follows,
since it is still fresh in men's minds, we shall record as it has
been related to us by credible men or seen and heard by ourselves." [125]

It may be well to speak somewhat more in detail of the principal
chronicles and other historical works used by Otto and alluded to
in the sentence just quoted. Chief among them are the *Chronicle*
of Eusebius of Cæsarea (about 260-340), translated and continued
(to the year 378) by Jerome in 382, and the *Chronicle* of Frutolf
of Michelsberg (d. 1103) and its continuation to the year 1106. The
last named work has been published under the name of Ekkehard of
Aura,[126] an older contemporary of Bishop Otto. In many instances
it is impossible to determine whether matter quoted in Otto's
Chronicle comes directly from Eusebius-Jerome or from the later
version of Frutolf-Ekkehard. It will be observed that the year
1106, of which Otto remarks, "Thus far we have set down extracts
from the books of Orosius, of Eusebius, and of those who wrote
after them, even to our own time," is the very year in which the
second edition of Ekkehard's *Chronicle* ends.

Another source of prime importance for Otto's *Chronicle* (especially for the earlier books) is the work of Paulus Orosius, a Spanish
presbyter, who wrote an epitome of universal history from Adam
to the year 417 which he entitled *Seven Books of Histories Directed
Against the Pagans.* His purpose was to defend and exalt the
Church, and to indicate the providence of God as revealed in human
events. This book, like Augustine's *City of God,* was intended as
a reply to the charge that the barbarian invasions and the weakness
of the Roman Empire were punishments sent by the gods for the
abandonment of the ancient religion.

sources carefully indicated in the margins or in footnotes, but by an ingenious
use of various fonts of type the exact indebtedness of the author to each of
his sources is immediately made clearly apparent to the eye.

[125] It will be recalled that the date of Otto's birth is not earlier than 1111,
and probably as late as 1114 or 1115; see note 32 (end) above.

[126] MGH, SS, 6. For a critical discussion of the authorship of this work see
H. Bresslau, NA 21. 197 *et seq.* It is there shown that recension A was
written by Frutolf, the later recensions by Ekkehard.

Several other works used by Otto deserve brief mention. Another book by Eusebius is often quoted. This is the *Ecclesiastical History,* translated and continued by Rufinus of Aquileia (about 345-410). Otto supposed that it had been translated and continued by Jerome.[127] He also refers frequently to the *Tripartite History:* a church history translated at the bidding of Cassiodorus (about 487-583) from Theodoret, Sozomen and Socrates and edited by him. The translator is Epiphanius.[128] For much of the earlier portion of his history Otto draws freely from the works of Flavius Josephus (born in 37 or 38)— particularly his *Antiquities of the Jews* and *The Wars of the Jews.* These he used in the Latin version of Rufinus of Aquileia, together with what the pseudo-Hegesippus [129] records in his history of the Jewish wars.

This may serve as a brief indication of the more important historical works used by our author in the composition of his *Chronicle.* It does not, of course, give any real idea of the breadth and scope of his reading; with regard to this it is interesting to note that a recent critic has estimated that his knowledge of literature is not inferior to that of John of Salisbury.[130]

[127] *E.g.,* IV. 5: *Quae qui plenius scire desiderat, in ecclesiastica Ieronimi historia inveniet.* So also in IV. 6; IV. 14; and especially IV. 21, where he says: *Ieronimus ecclesiasticam hystoriam ab Eusebio scriptam transtulit duobusque libris appositis usque ad mortem Theodorici deduxit.*

[128] Cassiodorus, *divin. lect.* 17. See also Otto, IV. 23.

[129] Apparently a corruption of the Greek author's name: Ἰώσηπος, *Iosippus, Egesippus, Hegesippus.* In this version of the *History of the Jewish Wars* the Greek original is in part abbreviated and in part increased by additions from various sources. The date of composition seems to be after 367. Even Cassiodorus is uncertain as to its authorship, but he says (*divin. lect.* 17) that some attribute the work to Jerome, some to Ambrose and some to Rufinus. In III. 17 Otto makes an accurate statement regarding the works of Josephus; he says: *Extant eius opera: in XX libris Antiquitatum hystoria, de Iudeorum cum Romanis bello libri VII. Liber quoque Machabeorum secundus ab eodem esse compositus a quibusdam dicitur. Alia etiam eius opera preclara Eusebius ponit.* But later he makes the mistake of attributing the Pseudo-Hegesippus version to that *Egesippus qui apostolicae predicationis traditionem simplici sermone V libris conscripsit* (III. 22, quoted from Eusebius-Rufinus 4. 8), saying: *sed et historiam Iudaici belli a Machabeis usque ad excidium Hierosolimarum luculenter ac prudenter contexuit.* On the false Hegesippus see Teuffel's *Römische Literatur* 3 (1913) § 433, 8; Hofmeister, NA 37. 716; Wilmans, introduction to the *Chronicle,* p. XXVII; Sorgenfrey, *o.c.*

[130] See Hofmeister, NA 37. 742-746. For a fuller discussion of Otto's sources in the *Chronicle,* see Büdinger (Vienna 1881) 325-326, 336-357, and (on the eighth book) 357-365; Hofmeister, NA 37. 701-727 (on Otto's knowledge

The *Chronicle* is divided into eight books, the first seven of which deal with the history of the world from the time of Adam to the year 1146, while the eighth is a theological treatise dealing with Antichrist, the Last Judgment and the world to come.[131] This is however, in the author's opinion, an integral part of the whole work: the fitting and necessary climax to the *History of the Two Cities*. To the end of the seventh book is appended a list of Roman emperors and popes.

The first book, while it is the shortest, yet deals with by far the longest period of history — from Creation to the downfall of the Assyrian Empire and the beginnings of Rome. A statement in the fifth chapter of the first book would seem to indicate that Otto subdivides universal history into three great epochs: the first from the reign of Ninus to the founding of Rome, the second to the birth of Christ and the third to his own time.[132] The first book of the *Chronicle*, therefore, covers the first of these grand divisions; the second book in like fashion deals with the second period of history — to the Nativity. The five books devoted to the history of the Christian era deal severally with the following intervals of time:

Book III   To the reign of Constantine and the Christian Roman Empire.
"   IV   To Odoacer and the end of the Roman Empire in the West.
"   V   To the Treaty of Verdun and the division of Charles the Great's empire.
"   VI   To the death of Pope Gregory at Salerno.
"   VII   To the year 1146.

Needless to say, books VI and VII are the most valuable part of the work from a purely factual standpoint. Indeed the entire chronicle might be divided on a different basis into two main parts, the second

of theological and philosophical literature and of the Bible), 727-747 (on his knowledge of other secular writings, particularly ancient literature), also 695, n. 2 (on a life of St. Basil used by Otto); Huber (Munich 1847) 80-90; Sorgenfrey (Greiz 1873); Wilmans, intro., pp. XXVII-XXVIII; and in particular Hofmeister, preface to his edition of the *Chronicle*, § 7, pp. XCI-XCVIII.

131 On the divisions of the *Chronicle* see especially Büdinger 333-335; Hashagen (Leipzig 1900) 34-42; Huber 190-192; Ritter (1911), entire article.
132 *Chron.* I. 5.

being that from Book VII chapter 12 onward, where Otto is no longer dependent upon written sources.[133]

But something further remains to be said in regard to Bishop Otto's selection, arrangement and division of the historical material which forms the subject matter of his work. In the period of classical antiquity Polybius portrayed the interacting politics and wars of the Mediterranean peoples from "the first occasion on which the Romans crossed the sea from Italy" in 264 B.C. down to the subjugation of these peoples beneath the immediate or mediate control of Rome in 146. Following him, and writing under the influence of the completion of the Roman world empire, Pompeius Trogus wrote a historical work on the most comprehensive plan attained in ancient times, for it included all peoples and times of which the learning of his day had any knowledge. We may note in passing that it is to this work, in the Roman Justin's epitome, that Orosius was indebted for his account of pagan antiquity. In Polybius the unifying thought is the gradual subjection of the various states of the known world to the single control of Rome.[134] In the universal history of Trogus (preserved for us, as already stated, in the synopsis by Justin) there are indicated two ideas that seem to the author to control the course of history. First there is the conflict between the opposing impulses of freedom and of might which is forever a cause of warfare and strife between nations. The second principle that Trogus believed he could discover ruling the course of history is that certain states attain to the rank of world empires, and that there is an evident succession according to time and place with a progress from east to west. The order of these is as follows:

EAST	Assyria
	Media
	Persia
WEST	Macedonia
	Rome

In dealing with peoples of the second rank, Trogus treats of them on the occasion of their first conflict with the various world powers. Thus Persian history leads up to an account of Greece and that in

---

133 So Hashagen (Dresden 1900) 26-29.

134 Polybius 3. 1. 4. On Polybius as a historian, see especially Shotwell, *An Introduction to the History of History*, Columbia University Press (1922) 191-201.

turn to the history of Sicily. In like manner Carthage is discussed in connection with Macedonia, a point of contact being found in Pyrrhus. Justin represents the power (*imperium*) or authority which rules the world as being handed over by a failing world empire to its successor. This idea (under the name of *translatio imperii*) plays an important part in the historical views of the Middle Ages, as we shall see.

In the Middle Ages the spirit of historical writing was determined largely by Christianity. So St. Augustine believes that the rise and fall of empires is effected by God in accordance with a plan known only to Himself. And the whole course of history is divided into two main sections: a first in which falls the preparation for the Redemption, and a second in which falls the distribution of the fruits of the Redemption. After the example of Trogus the peoples of antiquity are arranged according to world powers, and the Assyrian and the Roman empires are regarded as the leading states of the heathen world. Furthermore, Jerome in his commentary on the book of Daniel names the world empires, limiting them to four:

Assyrian-Babylonian
Medo-Persian
Macedonian
Roman

And he interprets Daniel's prophecy as indicating that the Roman Empire is destined to last until the end of the world. Orosius too employs a similar theory, substituting Carthage for Persia — for he lived in Spain and in Africa, both formerly ruled by Carthage — and calling attention to the fact that these world empires correspond to the points of the compass.[135]

Hence Otto of Freising also, in his letter to Rainald, says:[136]

Next I shall briefly explain the order in which this history proceeds, that, when this is known, the nature of the work may be the more readily apparent. That there were from the beginning of the world four principal kingdoms which stood out above all the rest, and that they are to endure unto the world's end, succeeding one another in accordance with the law of the universe can be gathered in various ways, in particular from the vision of Daniel.[137] I have therefore set down the rulers of these king-

[135] See Orosius 2. 1. 5.
[136] Page 5 in Hofmeister's edition.
[137] Daniel 7.

doms, listed in chronological sequence, first the Assyrians, next (omitting the Chaldeans, whom the writers of history do not deign to include among the others) the Medes and the Persians, finally the Greeks and the Romans, and I have recorded their names down to the present emperor, speaking of the other kingdoms only incidentally, to make manifest the fluctuations of events.

So we have in Otto's *Chronicle* also a division of the historical material according to world monarchies, namely the Assyrian, the Medo-Persian, the Greek and the Roman — virtually the scheme of Jerome.[138] In certain particulars, however, he is evidently following Orosius, as when he says that the Roman Empire followed the Babylonian "as a son succeeds his father,"[139] the Greeks and Persians being regarded as guardians and guides of the infant kingdom.[140] Yet he avoids Orosius's departure from the general scheme. And like Jerome Otto believes that — in accordance with Daniel's prophecy — the Roman Empire is to last until the end of the world: the Roman Empire, that is, as continued by the Byzantines, by the Franks and finally by the Germans. Otto appears to be the more convinced of his correctness since he is confident of his own sure judgment from his standpoint at the end of the development of the world.[141]

Otto did not find the scheme of Jerome altogether useful as a principle of division, however, for the arrangement of the books does not seem to be based on it.[142] In fact he makes use of the

[138] Huber (191) suggests that the *Chronicle* may be regarded as a drama in four acts, concluding with the *consummatio seculi* (in Book VIII) as the fifth. This thought probably occurred to him in connection with such passages as that in Otto's letter to Frederick (ed. Hofmeister 3) where the writer says he has *non tam rerum gestarum seriem quam earundem miseriam in modum tragediae texuisse*, or in the prologue to the first book (Hofmeister 7) in which he refers to the content of his sources as *non tam historias quam erumpnosas mortalium calamitatum tragedias*. But Otto is thinking of the tragic aspects of life — not attempting to arrange his work in the literary form of an ancient tragedy. How little use he actually made of the world monarchies theory as a basic principle of division will be indicated hereafter.

[139] II. 27. So Orosius 2. 1. 6.

[140] II. 27 and Orosius 2. 1. 6 and 7. 2. 4.

[141] See II. 12, particularly the last sentence: *nos enim circa finem eius positi id, quod de ipso predictum est, experimur futurumque in proximo quod restat timendo expectamus.*

[142] Only the first book corresponds as a whole with the history of the first monarchy (*cf.* I. 32; II, prologue, and II. 1). The second book, it will be remembered, is continued to the death of Cæsar — not at all in accord with

monarchy theory only in the first two books. Moreover, as regards the theory of the continuation of the Roman Empire until the end of the world, Otto is not altogether consistent,[143] and it is in this connection that he avails himself of the *translatio* theory already referred to.[144] The rule of the world was transferred from the Romans to the Greeks,[145] from the Greeks to the Franks.[146] Otto is even inclined to contrast with the *regnum Francorum* a separate *regnum Teutonicorum*.[147] The *translatio* theory is set forth in Books III to V of the *Chronicle*. In the sixth book Otto proposes to relate "How the kingdom of the Franks, so pitifully divided, lost not only the Roman crown of empire, but even part of Francia and in particular of Gaul, together with the palace at Aachen"[148] and remarks at its close: "With so great a transformation, as the times were passing from perfection to overthrow, let us put an end to the sixth book, that, with God's guidance, we may hasten on to the seventh and to that rest of souls which follows the wretchedness

the old world-monarchy scheme. In the course of the same book (II. 25) the end of the second — the Persian — world-kingdom and the beginning of the third — the Greek — is announced. And in this very chapter the end of the third monarchy is stated by anticipation (*loc. cit.*, in speaking of Alexander the Great: *Regni Macedonum monarchia, quae ab ipso cepit, ipso mortuo cum ipso finitur*). And even in the first half of the second book incidents are mentioned which ought properly to be treated in the history of the third monarchy (see, *e.g.*, II. 5; 7 and following; 17). Like confusion is found in the history of the fourth monarchy. At about the middle of the second book (II. 27 and 30; and *cf.* II. 2) Otto remarks that his pen is now to turn to the Roman Empire. But in the third book he feels obliged to return to the end of the third monarchy (III. 2) and here to speak of the downfall of the Greek kingdom (so Hashagen 34-42).

[143] So in IV. 30 ff. he speaks of the destruction of the Roman Empire by Odoacer; in VIII. 2 the view of the eternity of the Roman Empire is mentioned and rejected (*ne videlicet Romano imperio, quod ab ipsis eternum putabatur, calumpniam intulisse videretur*). Yet in other passages the persistence of the Roman Empire is not given up: *e.g.*, in the last words of the letter to Rainald and in the statement made to Isingrim; in VI. 1 and V, prologue. So too Charles the Great is the 69th follower of Augustus.

[144] See page 29 above.

[145] IV. 5; V, Prol; and *cf.* II. 1.

[146] V, Prol. and V. 31 ff. But in V. 16 and 25 there is a *regnum Francorum* aside from the *regnum Romanorum*, one waxing as the other wanes.

[147] VI. 24. The letter to Isingrim mentions the Lombards as intermediate between the two, but Otto calls their kingdom a usurpation: VI. 17 and *cf.* VI. 13.

[148] VI, prologue.

of this present life.'' [149] As a matter of fact he passes beyond his
plan and continues this section of his history to the death of
Gregory VII.[150]

So it may be said that Otto of Freising, while preserving in weakened form the basic ideas introduced into history by Augustine,
has filled in the account of ancient times with a selection of important deeds chosen mainly from sources other than Augustine.
For his sketch of Christian history Otto takes as a framework the
scheme of relations between Church and State originating with
Augustine, but adapts it in original fashion and with somewhat
pessimistic coloring to the interactions of State and Church in the
Middle Ages.[151]

It is evident therefore that Otto developed a plan of division for
himself, and not from a single viewpoint. Even in the first two
books, where he makes some use of the world-monarchies theory,
we find also reminiscences of the old Eusebian synchronistic
treatment of sacred and profane history. Furthermore the gloomy
reflections placed at the ends of these books seem to indicate that
the author's pessimism exercises a far stronger influence than the
monarchy theory.[152] To be sure, it is doubtless true that much of
this seeming pessimism is a deliberate striving for effect, in order
to depict the clear-cut contrast between the miseries of the worldly
city and the joys of the heavenly. But it is worthy of note that
Otto regularly separates the great divisions of his work by long
reflections.[153]

Even more widespread than the arrangement by kingdoms (in
accordance with Daniel) is a division of universal history by epochs
of the world. Here perhaps the most important example is that of
Augustine in the concluding chapter of his *City of God*; his epochs
are:

(1)   From Adam to the Flood
(2)   To Abraham
(3)   To David
(4)   To the Exile
(5)   To the Incarnation

[149] VI. 36.

[150] See VI. 36, and *cf.* the letter to Isingrim, p. 9, ed. Hofmeister: *usque ad
tempus nostrum.*

[151] So Ritter 276.

[152] I. 32 and II. 51. On the subject of his pessimism, see below, pp. 57-59.

[153] See, *e.g.,* IV. 4.

(6) The Present Age
(7) The World to Come [154]

From Augustine this scheme of division passed to Isidore, Bede, Gregory the Great and Ekkehard. Otto of Freising is obviously acquainted with this method of separating the whole course of world history into convenient periods or epochs: in fact there is a distinct reference to it, in Augustinian form, in the eighth book of the *Chronicle*.[155] It may even have been in his thoughts when he spoke of the periods "From Adam to the Flood," [156] "From the Flood to the Confusion of Tongues," [157] and "From the Confusion of Tongues to the Birth of Abraham." [158] But it will be remembered that his own subdivision, as announced in the early part of the first book, is a much simpler threefold arrangement.[159]

In conclusion it will be observed that, although we find in the prologue to the eighth book a statement of the various periods in the development of the Two Cities, we are not justified in taking this from its context and applying it to the preceding books.[160]

In connection with the subject of the divisions of the *Chronicle* it is perhaps of interest to note the various standards employed by the author in the estimate of time. As regards chronology he is open minded to a fault: indeed his lack of precision in dates has almost the appearance of indifference.[161] He often calls attention to discrepancies in the chronological notices of various writers but does not venture a definite opinion of his own. So for the earliest part of his *Chronicle*, the Biblical history, while adopting a scheme of division by epochs (as stated above)[162] he further strives to give some indication of the length of these periods in years; but he cites two differing authorities:

[154] *De civitate Dei* 22. 30.
[155] VIII. 14.
[156] I. 3.
[157] I. 4.
[158] I. 5.
[159] I. 5.
[160] *Hoc opus nostrum, quod de duabus civitatibus intitulavimus, trifarie distinctum invenitur.*
[161] So Huber 94. He cites in substantiation of this statement V. 16: *Hic iuxta quosdam tribus annis regnavit, alii vero scribunt eum uno anno et mensibus tribus, Philippicum vero duobus annis ac VIIII mensibus regnasse. Quam controversiam scriptores viderint.*
[162] See pp. 29-30.

	According to the Seventy	According to Jerome
From Adam to the Flood (I. 3)	2262 years	1666 years
From the Flood to the Confusion of Tongues (I. 4)	531 years	101 years
From the Confusion of Tongues to the Birth of Abraham (I. 5)	541 years	141 years

As is well known, the *Chronicle* of Eusebius of Caesarea, translated and continued by Jerome, begins with the first year of Abraham (the forty-third of the reign of Ninus) ; Otto, on the other hand, mentioning the fact that "the records of the Gentiles begin with the reign of Ninus," continues:

Following them and at the same time comparing our own authors with them, let us begin from Ninus the story of human misery, and let us carry it through, year by year, from Ninus himself down to the founding of the City; from the founding of the City let us relate it in due order as far as the time of Christ, and from Christ, by God's help, likewise down to our own day.[163]

So we find that in the first book of the *Chronicle* and starting with the seventh chapter, dates are expressed in years from the reign of Ninus. But parallel with this scheme Otto uses the synchronistic method of chronology employed by the annalists: he records side-by-side events in Biblical history and the successive rulers of Assyria, of Sicyon,[164] of Argos and of Athens; also, in their proper place, the Judges of Israel and the kings of Italy.[165]

[163] I. 5.

[164] For with the overthrow of Sicyon at the hands of Belus, "the learned Marcus Varro started, as from a far-off date, when he began to write" (I. 6).

[165] The following table may serve to give some idea of Otto's chronology in the first book:

	ASSYRIA	SICYON	ARGOS
The kingdoms of Assyria and Sicyon arose in the days of Terah, about 106 years after the Confusion of Tongues (I. 5)	1. BELUS (I. 5) (Conquers Sicyon in the 45th year of his reign) (I. 6)	1. Agialeus (I. 5)	

The Confusion of Tongues occurred in the days of Peleg (I. 4) ; in order to make the calculation in I. 5 total 141 years it is necessary to assume that it took place when Peleg was 55 years of age (and his son Reu 25). By the arbitrary assumption that Terah was 35 when the kingdoms of Assyria and Sicyon arose (I.5) we may date their origin at approximately 106 years after the Confusion of Tongues. This is according to Jerome. Following the Seventy (I.6) we should set the beginning of the reign of Belus (the founding of Assyria) in the 957th or 958th year after the Confusion of Tongues.

ASSYRIA	SICYON	ARGOS
The death of Belus in the 75th year of his reign (I. 6), in the 1032nd or 1033rd year since the Flood.	NINUS (I. 6) (Builds Nineveh; dies in the 50th year of his reign)	
Abram born in Chaldea (I. 7). 42nd or 43rd year from the reign of Ninus		2. Europs (I. 7)

Hereafter all dates are expressed in years after the reign of Ninus.

SEMIRAMIS

(1. 8) (Van-
quishes Ethiopia
and India; builds
Babylon when her
reign of 42 years
is half over)

ASSYRIA	SICYON	ARGOS	
Abraham (at the age of 75), Sarah and Lot depart from Chaldea to Canaan (I. 9) 113th yeaar.	4. NINUS (I. 9)	5. Telexion (I. 9)	
The Pentapolis (Sodom) destroyed by fire and brimstone. 140th year.			
Ishmael and Isaac begotten by Abraham.	6. ARIUS (I. 10)	(5. Telexion) (I. 10)	
Death of Abraham (at the age of 175).	7. XERXES (I. 11) (or Baleus)	7. Turichus (or Turi- machus) (I. 11)	
The promise made to Isaac.	8. ARMAMI- THRES (I. 11)	8. Leucippus (I. 11)	1. Inachus (I. 11) (In the time of Abra- ham's grandsons)
Covenant made with Jacob.	9. BELOCHUS (I. 11)	(8. Leucippus) (I. 11)	Phoroneus (I. 11) (Son of In- achus, wages war with the Pharphasii against the Telcises and Caratasii. The Telcises settle in Rhodes, (I. 12).

Flood of Ogyges in
Achæa. 260th year.

Death of Isaac (at the age of 180) (Jacob and Esau 120 years old).	10. BALEUS (I. 13)	9. Mesapus (I. 13)	3. Apis (I. 13)

Famine in Egypt in
the reign of Diopolita
(Amases). Joseph
becomes ruler of Egypt.
292nd year.

Jacob dies (at the age of 147).	(10. BALEUS) (I. 16)	Eratus (I. 16)	Argus, son of Apis (I. 16)
Joseph dies in Egypt (at the age of 110).	12. AMINTUS (= Mamirtus) (I. 16)	11. Clemineus (I. 16)	(Argus, I. 16)
Birth of Moses	14. SAPHRUS (I. 16)	Ortopolis (I. 16)	

	ASSYRIA	SICYON	ARGOS	ATHENS	ISRAEL	ITALY
Flood of Deucalion (I.17) 490th year				3. Amphitrion (or Cecrops?) (I. 17)		
The Exodus (Phaëthon) 495th year	Ascathides (I. 18)	Marathus (I.18)	Triophas (I.18)			

Danaüs flees to
Argos (I. 19)
(Busiris; Progne
and Philomela;
Tantalus and
Pelops; Ganymede,
etc.)
535th year

Cretans defeat the
Athenians (I. 21)
(Minotaur; Daedalus;
Lapithæ vs. Thessalians)
640th year
Vesores (= Sesostris),
king of Egypt, declares
war on the Scythians.
(The Amazons)
(I. 22)
820th year

Joshua dies in the land of promise. (I. 24)	18. Aminthas (I. 24)	16. Corax (I. 24)	10. Danaus (I. 24)	4. Erichthonius

ASSYRIA	SICYON	ARGOS	ATHENS	ISRAEL	ITALY
(Cadmus; Orpheus; Musæus; Linus; Apollo) 23. Lampheres		THE KINGDOM OF ARGOS IS TRANSFERRED TO MYCENAE		*JUDGES* 1. Othniel Deborah (I. 24)	*GOLDEN AGE* Laurentian Kingdom arises. Picus, son of Saturn, reigns after his father.
Carmentis invents the Latin alphabet.				Jair (I. 24)	
Helen carried off. The Trojan War. Origin of the Franks. Founding of Patavium. (I. 25) 870th year. Wanderings of Ulysses.				Abdon (or Samson?) (I. 25)	Laurentian Kingdom gives way to Latium. Latinus, son of Faunus, reigns. (I. 25) Æneas wages war in Italy
TAUTENES (I. 27)	Pelasgus (I. 27)			Samson (I. 27)	Æneas rules in Latium. (I. 27)
29. THINEUS (I. 27)	KINGDOM OF SICYON COMES TO AN END. (Aglaleus to Zeuxippus, 945 years)		Mesantus (I. 27)	Eli (I. 27)	Æneas Silvius (For list of succeeding kings see I. 30)
				Samuel (I. 28) For list of 16 Judges, see I. 28.	
DERCILES (I. 28)			Codrus (I. 28)	*KINGS* 1. Saul (I. 28)	
				David (I. 29)	
EUPALES (I. 29)				Solomon (I. 29) (The temple)	Founding of Alba (I. 29)
PIRICIADES (I. 29)				Rehoboam (I. 29) Division of the Kingdom	
36. SARDANAPALUS, (I. 31) The last King.					

At the close of the book Otto remarks: "the kings of the Medes, to whom, as we have said, the authority over the Babylonian kingdom finally passed, begin to be reckoned from this point." [166] Accordingly, in the second book we find events recorded as having happened in the reigns of successive Median kings and then of the rulers of Persia. Next comes an account of Roman history, recorded eventually in years from the founding of the City.[167] There are also references to the kings of Judah and of Israel. At the beginning of the third book dates are still reckoned from the founding of Rome in the first six chapters, but thereafter from the birth of Christ. For as Otto says: "So then with the birth of the new Man who supplanted the old, let us set an end to our annals also, which were reckoned from Ninus to the founding of the City and thence even to this time, and let us begin our annals from His birth." [168] In this book Otto gives lists of the bishops of Rome, Alexandria, Antioch, Constantinople and Jerusalem, and here begins the list of Roman emperors which is continued in the later books by the succession of Frankish and German rulers.

Otto's language and style [169] justly entitle him to be ranked with the best writers of the Middle Ages.[170] In his prologue to the first book, addressed to Isingrim, he expresses his preference for a simple style, remarking of his authorities: "For I should never hold the view that these men are to be held in contempt if certain of them have preserved in their writing the apostolic simplicity; for, as overshrewd subtlety sometimes kindles error, so a devout rusticity is ever the friend of truth." [171]

> THE EMPIRE PASSES TO THE MEDES
> IN THE 1236th YEAR FROM THE
> REIGN OF NINUS, THE 1305th FROM
> BELUS FOUNDING OF BABYLON.
> (For a list of the kings of Assyria, see I. 33).

[166] I. 32.

[167] The first date recorded in years from the founding of the City is that of the institution of the Roman Republic (II. 10), where Otto is apparently following Orosius 2. 5. Further A. V. C. dates are found in chapters 17, 18, 19, 21, 23, 25, 28, 29, 31, 33, 35, 38, 42, 45, 48 and 49.

[168] III. 6, end.

[169] Huber 192-195; Wattenbach (1885) 2. 243 (= 6th edition 2. 273); Hofmeister, NA 37 696-701 (but see E. Norden, *Die antike Kunstprosa* 2. 752, n. 1.).

[170] So Wattenbach (1885) 2. 243.   [171] Page 10 in Hofmeister's edition.

He is admirably clear, concise, and brief in recording events; somewhat more verbose and rhetorical in his frequent "exclamations" at the vicissitudes of human affairs and in his prologues. Yet he is often most impressive despite certain faults of style. His Latin is of course not the classic diction of a Cicero, but is marred to some extent by labored cleverness of expression, picturesque figures of speech and rather dull plays upon words.[172] Furthermore his language is blended with Biblical and ascetic phraseology, scholastic formulas and infrequent Germanisms. Occasionally also there are traces of French and Italian words.[173] And there are, of course, many grammatical usages typical of the Middle Ages.[174] But as already stated, despite minor blemishes Otto's style is marked by clearness, simplicity and beauty of expression. Rahewin makes an interesting remark on attempting to imitate Otto in his continuation of the *Gesta*:[175] "Indeed I admit that my breath is inadequate to play even a tiny flute, to say nothing of filling so glorious and so resonant a trumpet of expression and of speech as that of the author of the preceding book, my venerated master."[176]

Wilmans was of the opinion that Otto's works show many traces of the writer's knowledge of Greek.[177] Other scholars [178] believe that Otto knew Greek writers only in translation or as cited in Roman authorities. Doubtless the truth lies somewhere between these two extreme positions; for while it is inconceivable that a man of Bishop Otto's intellectual ability and scholarly tastes could have taken part in a crusade to Greek-speaking countries without bringing back with him at least some knowledge of the language,[179]

[172] *Cf.*, for example, VI. 13: *non imperatores et augustos sed invasores et angustos*; IV, Prol. (ed. Hofmeister p. 183): *credendaque quae credit, licite possidenda quae possidet credo*; V. 36: *Nonne videtur tibi more, ut dixi, febricitantis mundialis dignitas volvi ac revolvi?* VII. 9: *mundus — vel potius iuxta Augustinum inmundus*; VII. 14: *Hoc privilegium . . . tanquam pravilegium reprobavit*; VII. 28: *Non kalo, id est boni, Iohannis officium agens.*

[173] *E.g., guerra* for *bellum* (VII. 7); *forestus* for *silva* (V. 24).

[174] *E.g.*, the use of *seu* for *et*; and see Hofmeister 697, n. 2.

[175] *Gesta* 3, Prol., Simson p. 163.

[176] Not the least interesting fact in connection with this passage is that Rahewin is borrowing the language as well as the thought of Jordanes in the preface to his *Getica* — just as Jordanes had already borrowed this very sentence from Rufinus! Such slavish imitation is far from being characteristic of Bishop Otto, however.

[177] Archiv. 10. 153.

[178] *E.g.*, Sorgenfrey.

[179] Of course if he learned Greek only on the Second Crusade, we must

we need not assume from the Greek words and expressions used in the *Chronicle* that he was thoroughly conversant with Greek and able to use as sources books written in that tongue.[180] The literary tradition of the Middle Ages knows three principal languages — as Otto himself bears witness when he says: "Hence also three languages are regarded as the most important: the Hebrew, for the worship of God and because of its antiquity; the Greek, for its wisdom and the charm of its expression; the Latin, for power and also for wisdom." [181]

Hofmeister states that Otto's explanations of Hebrew words do not indicate even a casual knowledge of Hebrew; they come from the traditional treasure of ecclesiastical wisdom — and notably from Jerome. Next taking up in detail the list of Greek words and phrases found in Otto's writings, he points out that these are of unequal value, for many drop out at once as being taken over from other writers.[182] The remainder does not seem sufficient to prove

assume that the passages which contain Greek words or phrases appear for the first time in the second edition of the *Chronicle*.

[180] However Schmidlin, *Die Philosophie Ottos von Freising* (Fulda 1905) 171, holds that there is a possibility that Otto had a sufficient mastery of Greek to understand Aristotle in the original, and that he brought back a text from Constantinople. Hofmeister (693) on the contrary says: "Davon, dass er etwa . . . gar Aristotelische Schriften im Urtext hatte lesen können, kann keine Rede sein." The most careful investigation of this question is that made by Hofmeister in NA 37 § 9, *Ottos Sprachkenntnisse*, 681-701.

[181] I. 27, end.

[182] The list as given by Hofmeister (686-688) is as follows:

I.	Prol., ed. Hofmeister p. 7: *monarchia* (III. 3, p. 139; III. 6, p. 142)	
I. 9,	p. 48: *Pentapolin*	
	The next five word for word from	
	Augustine's *De civitate Dei*	
I. 15,	p. 51: *soros*	Augustine 18.15
I. 17,	p. 52: *Minervam*	18.9
I. 26,	p. 60: *licum*	18.17
II. 4,	p. 73: *Theos Sother*	18.23
II. 5,	p. 73: *sophos* (also II. 8, p. 77)	18.24
II. 8,	p. 75: *philosophorum*	
II. 8,	p. 76: *methodis*	
III. 10,	p. 145: *tetrarchas*	
IV. 19,	p. 208: *Chrisostomus*	
V. 4,	p. 233: *sophiam*	
VII. 28,	p. 354: *Kalo*	
VII. 32,	p. 360: *katholicon*	
VIII. 1,	p. 393: *anti*	
VIII. 17,	p. 416: *Eusebiam*	
	Gesta 2. 36 ed. Simson p. 144: *Palologum*	
	2. 41, p. 150: *hysteron*	

that Otto had a real knowledge of Greek, although we may assume a certain vague acquaintance with a number of Greek expressions.[183] There are three short sentences in Greek which appear in Otto's work with a Latin translation appended, and two of these at least are written in Greek letters.[184] But upon examination we find that the first is taken from Jerome, the second from the *Ecclesiastical History* of Eusebius and the third from the liturgy of the Church. The conclusion is, therefore, that Otto did not possess a really comprehensive knowledge of Greek, although he did know the Greek alphabet and a considerable number of Greek words and phrases. But it is out of the question that Otto may have used as sources for the *Chronicle* Greek words in the original.

Though we may be forced by the evidence at our disposal to this negative conclusion respecting Otto's intimate knowledge of Greek, we must not lose sight of the fact that he was a man really distinguished for his great learning. And it must also be remembered that while acquaintance with the Greek language never died out completely, still a comprehensive and intensive knowledge, made possible by a real study of Greek writings, was accessible to but few before the thirteenth century. Mention has already been made of Otto's wide acquaintance with the pagan literature of antiquity,[185] and we have noted that in him we find the first trace of the dissemination of Aristotle's books in Germany.[186] It is evident therefore that he found much pleasure in learned works and learned

---

[183] The blunder in II. 4, where the Greek words have been taken over from Augustine, is perhaps sufficient to indicate how little capable the author was of grasping the significance of a connected group of words: *e.g., Theos = filius Dei!* Huber, however (195), calls attention to Otto's own word *transalpizare* in *Gesta* 2. 12 which is Greek in formation, and regards it as evidence of Otto's knowledge of Greek. So also Büdinger (Vienna 1881) 364; in commenting on Otto's translation of the Greek word *teletarchiam* (in a sentence quoted from the pseudo-Dionysius in VIII. 30) by *perfectionis principem*, he remarks: "Stämmt die Uebertragung von Otto selbst, so beweist sie mehr als alle die einzelnen Wörtchen und Worterklärungen in seinen Schriften, die man anzuführen pflegt, seine gute Kenntniss mindestens des Kirchengriechischen." But as Hofmeister points out in his edition of the *Chronicle* (p. 441, n. 5), the expression goes back to Hugo of St. Victor and even to Scotus.

[184] See III. 12, p. 148 (about Philo); IV. 1, p. 184 (Constantine); IV. 25, p. 216 (earthquake).

[185] See above, p. 26 and note 130.

[186] Page 14 and note 62.

men.[187] Furthermore he often refers his readers to books with which he is himself familiar,[188] and expresses his own judgment of various works.[189] We find him employing the new dialectic method with which his studies at Paris had made him familiar,[190] and there is some evidence to indicate that he was not unfamiliar with Roman Law.[191] He makes no display of his erudition, however, but lets slip many an opportunity of embellishing his works, remarking "this has been fully related by others."[192]

Bishop Otto's deep interest in philosophical studies, originating doubtless in his student days at Paris, is clearly apparent in his writings. In his letter to Chancellor Rainald he says:[193] "I believe, as Boethius says,[194] that the greatest solace in life is to be found in handling and thoroughly learning all the teachings of philosophy." And again he speaks of philosophy together with law as fore-runners of the Messiah.[195] He prizes philosophy because it has given men the capacity to comprehend the higher precepts of life.

It is interesting to note that there are to be found in his works not only the outlines of Church history and the history of dogmas but some attempts at a history of philosophy as well.[196] The *Chronicle* contains many citations of philosophical works,[197] and further-

---

[187] See IV. 8 (about Victorinus and Donatus); IV. 21 (concerning Augustine, Orosius and Jerome).

[188] See V. 32 (biographers of Charles the Great); VIII. 21 (Augustine); IV. 5 (Jerome).

[189] V. 1 (Boethius); V. 8 (Gregory); III. 31 (Origen).

[190] So Hashagen (Dresden 1900) 13 *et seq.*, in reference to VIII. 9: the enumeration of the various meanings of the concept *transire*. In such philosophical and theological attempts and their close dependence on cherished models, says Hashagen (16), Otto affords a lively picture of the learning of the Middle Ages in this period — gladly devoting itself to the new dialectic arts, yet for the most part working on the old traditional foundations.

[191] So Wilmans, p. XXV; he cites Otto's letter to Frederick: *Preterea cum nulla inveniatur persona mundialis quae mundi legibus non subiaceat, subiacendo coerceatur, soli reges, utpote constituti supra leges, divino examini reservati seculi legibus non cohibentur*, with which cf. Digest 1. 3. 31: *Princeps legibus solutus est.*

[192] See I. 21; II. 30; II. 32; III. 19; VIII. 12.

[193] Page 4 in Hofmeister's edition.

[194] Boethius, *De syllogismo hypothetico* 1.

[195] III, Prol., ed. Hofmeister p. 133.

[196] Notably in the *Gesta* 1. 48-61 (concerning Abelard and Gilbert) and 2. 28 (the education of Arnold of Brescia).

[197] So, *e.g.*, Cicero: I. 6. 26; II. 19. 24. 31. 34. 40. 44. 50 and *Gesta* I. 4;

more Otto makes a special point of relating the fates of various philosophers.[198] He often remarks upon the interest in philosophy shown by the saints and the great teachers of the Church.[199] His interest in and his high estimation of pagan philosophy is further indicated by the fact that he alludes to the tradition that Plato was a pupil of Jeremiah [200] — although later in the same chapter he takes occasion to point out the anachronism involved in this theory and evidently believes that Seneca corresponded with St. Paul,[201] referring to him, moreover, as "Lucius Seneca . . . who ought to be called almost a Christian rather than a philosopher." [202] Nor does he scruple to avail himself of heathen testimony to uphold his eschatological views.[203] He believes that Plato knew the entire Christian truth save only the incarnation.[204] Yet Otto emphasizes the subordinate position of the ancient men of genius and criticizes those that treasure philosophy too highly,[205] declaring that a falsely valued philosophy is one of the means that will be used by Antichrist to deceive the more intellectual among the Christians.[206]

We find therefore that Otto, like Gilbert de la Porrée (whose zeal for philosophy he mentions)[207] and Hugo of St. Victor, took the middle ground between Abelard — who had gone so far as to assume for the philosophers of old divine inspiration, and even claimed that they understood the doctrine of the Trinity, and that

Seneca: II. 40 (and see the reference to the spurious correspondence with Paul, III. 15); Plato: I, Prol. (ed. Hofmeister p. 8), I. 17 (and see *Gesta* 1. 5); Aristotle: I. 6, II. 8. (Otto believed that Aristotle's *Categories, On Interpretation, Former and Later Analytics, Topics and Proofs* had all been translated by Boethius (See V. 1, ed. Hofmeister p. 230; however it is probably the translation of Jacobus de Venetia (1128) that Otto used in the *Analytics, Topics* and *Proofs*.); Boethius: V. 1, I, Prol., VI. 9, II. 8, Letter to Rainald, ed. Hofmeister p. 4.

198 *E.g.*, Socrates, Plato and Aristotle (II. 8 and 19); Epaminondas (II. 24); Seneca (III. 15); Julian (IV. 10); Boethius (V. 1). By an error apparently quite general in his time, Otto regards Mercury as a philosopher (I. 16).

199 Moses (I, Prol. to Isingrim, ed. Hofmeister p. 8); Basilius and Gregory of Nazianzus (IV. 10); the Monks (IV. 14).

200 II. 8, with which *cf.* Augustine 8. 11.

201 III. 15.

202 II. 40.

203 *E.g.*, Plato and Josephus (VIII. 8).

204 II. 8.

205 *E.g.*, Origen (III. 27) and Abelard (*Gesta* 1. 49).

206 VIII. 4.

207 *Gesta* 1. 48.

they had attained in their own lives ascetic perfection — and such thinkers as Gerhoh of Reichersberg and St. Bernard, who saw in such claims as this a serious assault upon the originality of Christian truth. And in the philosophy of the twelfth century as well as in his estimate of pagan philosophy, Otto appears to have held an intermediate position between the extremes of nominalism and realism — a middle way which he found in the philosophy of Gilbert de la Porrée.[208] Gilbert neither declares that the universals are the only real and the individuals merely their changing phases, nor does he deny that they have separate existence and declare them to be pure abstractions of the human intellect. He neither so strongly emphasizes the substantial unity between universal and individual that the latter loses its independent existence (realism); nor does he, by too great insistence upon the independence of the individual, completely destroy its connection with the universal (nominalism). His is the standpoint of mediating realism: the universals have indeed a real existence, but it becomes real only in the individuals.

Otto more than the majority of his contemporaries united in himself the realistic inclination with its ecclesiastical faith, and the deep inclination toward contemplative mysticism and the nominalistic tendency to secular philosophy and worldly wisdom.[209] He does not belong to the great systematizers of theology and philosophy, but he is important as an example of how deep and general the spiritual movement which set in at about the middle of the eleventh century had already become in his time, and still more important as an active and successful mediator of the new achievements in subject matter and methods from their French center in Paris to the German southeast.[210] One of Otto's greatest deeds is the transplanting of Aristotelianism to Germany at a time when that land was still plunged in ignorance and Gaul held the undisputed primacy in learning. Gilbert de la Porrée, as already indicated, takes first place among the men whose philosophical teachings Otto studied and accepted, but doubtless the views of all the contemporary thinkers (to whose learning Otto pays unstinted praise) had a fruitful influence upon his intellectual development. The list includes St. Bernard, Abelard, Roscellinus, William of

[208] See Hashagen (Dresden 1900) 11-12.
[209] So Bernheim (1885) 13.
[210] Hofmeister, NA 37. 158.

Champeaux, Anselm of Laon, and Theodoric and Bernard of Chartres.[211] And we must not forget Adam of Petit Pont of whom Otto speaks with respect in another passage.[212]

The chronicle of universal history was brought down to the year 1146, and although Otto afterwards recorded later events he did so in another work, the *Deeds of the emperor Frederick I,* referred to above. But the *Chronicle* was afterwards continued in annalistic form by another Otto, a monk of St. Blaise, a monastery of Swabia in the Black Forest (Baden; Waldshut). This account extends from 1146 to October 4, 1209 — the date of the coronation of Otto IV as emperor at Rome. The opinion has generally been held that the author of this work is that Otto who was elected Abbot of St. Blaise in 1222 and who died on July 21, 1223. The fact that his *Chronicle* breaks off with the year 1209, as already stated, has then been explained on the assumption that the Bishop had reached this point in the narrative when he was cut off by death. This would set the date of composition in the year 1223.[213] Hofmeister, however, in the preface to his edition of Otto's continuation of the *Chronicle* of the Bishop of Freising, believes that it was actually written shortly after the last event recorded — that is, late in 1209 or early in 1210 — and by another Otto of St. Blaise, not the Bishop of that name.[214]

The fact that more than fifty manuscripts of the *Chronicle* of Bishop Otto of Freising are extant or known by report at the present time is in itself evidence that the work was read and re-read during the Middle Ages.[215] Aside from this kind of testimony we find also a large number of writers in the 12th, 13th, 14th, 15th and

[211] *Gesta* 1. 49 (ed. Simson p. 69).

[212] Adam was a native Englishman, who lectured at Paris on the "Little Bridge" which joins the island in the Seine with the left bank. In *Gesta* 1. 53 (on the year 1147) he says of him: *Adam de Parvoponte, vir subtilis et Parisiensis aecclesiae canonicus recenter factus.*

[213] So H. Thomae, *Die Chronik des Otto von St. Blasien kritisch untersucht,* Leipzig (1877) 9; H. Kohl in the preface to his translation, p. VII; Giesebrecht, GDK 6. 294.

[214] For Otto of St. Blaise, see especially Hofmeister's edition in *Scriptores rerum Germanicarum in usum scholarum,* No. 15, Hanover and Leipzig (1912), pp. XXV + 150; the German translation by Horst Kohl in *Die Geschichtschreiber der deutschen Vorzeit,* Vol. 58, Leipzig (1881); H. Thomae in the Inaugural-Dissertation referred to in the preceding note (pp. 1-104).

[215] On this topic see Hofmeister's Introduction, p. XCVIII and pp. XXIII-LXXXVIII.

early 16th centuries who have made use of it in their own writings, sometimes by the actual copying out of extracts, sometimes in a somewhat changed or revised form. A great many of the later excerpts come from an intermediate source rather than directly from Otto. So we find that a large number of his passages have been transmitted to later works through the instrumentality of Godfrey of Viterbo. Both he and Alberic of Trois Fontaines borrowed much from Otto with little or no change. The number of those who used his work as a mine of information or a model of style is so large that it would be wearisome to enumerate the full list.[216]

The first printed edition of the *Chronicle*, that of John Cuspinian, was published in 1515. Two others appeared in the same century: one by Pithoeus in 1569 and the other by Urstisius in 1585. Two editions of the work, not differing essentially from those already mentioned, were published in the seventeenth century. In 1868 Roger Wilmans produced his excellent edition in the *Monumenta Germaniae Historica*. Finally in 1912 Adolph Hofmeister published what will undoubtedly prove to be the definitive edition of the work, indicating in detail, by the use of various fonts of type, the literary sources of each part of the book as we have it today. Hofmeister is also the author of some of the keenest and most valuable studies of the author and his work. His estimate of the historian is as follows:

As for originality, Otto may lay claim to that (aside from his eschatological views) only in the province of his conception of history: and even here he has not pointed out actually new paths. But in that he has used ecclesiastical traditions hoary with age to erect a structure which, in the greatness of its general outlines and in its clarity of execution, has thrown all preceding works into the shade, and in its spirited enlivening of dead material has achieved what none had yet succeeded in accomplishing — he has won for himself forever a place in the history of the spirit of humanity which justifies the detailed investigation of the inception and growth of his world of ideas. His conception of universal history has had the greatest influence upon subsequent ages.[217]

5. BISHOP OTTO, THE HISTORIAN

"The only history of importance to the Christian," says Professor Shotwell, "was that which justified his faith, and it all lay

---

[216] The names are given in Hofmeister's Introduction, pp. XCIX-CII.
[217] NA, 37. 767.

within the sacred writings of the Jews.''[218] So it happens that in the Middle Ages the literature of antiquity was largely superseded by the Hebrew Scriptures, and that there was but one scheme of history which had the sanction of religion. Since the recorded facts could not be questioned without impiety, the only recourse of the Christian historian, when subjected to criticism by the adherents of paganism, lay in comparative history — namely in the attempt to prove the priority of Moses to the Greeks — or in an allegorical interpretation of disputed passages of the Bible. Consequently Christian historiography during the first three centuries of our era followed the lines of comparative chronology on the one hand and of symbolism and allegory on the other.[219] In the field of Christian allegory Origen of Alexandria, who lived in the third century, is easily first. He explains away many a difficulty by denying the literal truth of incidents recorded in the Scriptures, treating them rather as parables or instructive fables.

But the main clue to a proper understanding of Christian historiography in the Middle Ages is to be found in the other tendency already referred to above — Christian chronology.[220] The earliest work in this field is the *Chronographia* of Julius Africanus in the middle of the third century, but the outstanding figure is Eusebius of Caesarea. His chronology of the world is the basis of practically all subsequent historical writings of the Middle Ages.[221] ''For the next thousand years most histories were chronicles, and they were built after the model of Jerome's translation of Eusebius' Canons.''[222] Aside from this sketch of universal history Eusebius wrote the first church history as well; this latter work the author — perhaps influenced by Origen — regards as a chapter in the evolution of a great divine economy. He characterizes the Church — God's own people — as ''a nation confessedly not small and not dwelling in some corner of the earth, but the most numerous and

[218] *An Introduction to the History of History,* by James T. Shotwell, in *Records of Civilization,* Columbia University Press (1922), 284. In connection with this general topic see especially his section on ''Christianity and History'' (278-313).

[219] So Shotwell 288.

[220] Shotwell 301 *et seq.*

[221] Joseph Scaliger (quoted in Shotwell 306, n. 1.) says: *Qui post Eusebium scripserunt, omne scriptum de temporibus aridum esse censuerunt, quod non hujus fontibus irrigatum esset.*

[222] Shotwell 306.

pious of all nations, indestructible and unconquerable, because it always receives assistance from God."[223] "This," says Professor Shotwell, "is the historical prologue to the City of God." For Augustine said: "We must by no means imagine that God willed that the kingdoms of men, their overlordships and their slaveries, should be unresponsive to the laws of His Providence";[224] and this became a premise of historiography in the Middle Ages. The idea of the domination of the multiplicity of historical events by an aim divinely implanted in mankind had a lasting influence upon the view of world history held by writers in succeeding centuries. The highest content of history in Augustine's opinion is the relation of God to mankind, in its progressive development from the creation of Adam and Eve throughout man's earthly destiny to the ultimate consummation in heaven and in hell. As happiness — which Augustine regards as man's chief aim and highest good — is eventually secured (or missed) only in the life to come, the true goal of history is thereby set in that life. In order that the elect may be saved and may attain to the blessedness of eternal life, two things are necessary: first, the content of the true knowledge of God must be revealed to the darkened understanding; and second, the possibility of reconciliation between mankind and God must be earned in another way, namely by Christ's work of redemption, midway in the course of earthly history. Accordingly the whole stream of history is divided into two main branches: a first, in which falls the preparation for the Redemption; and a second, in which falls the distribution of the fruits of the Redemption.

Augustine demands that the historical viewpoint must advance from the outer history of states to a recognition of the moral ideas peculiar to the people. Accordingly, to his mind the highest content of the history of the pagan nations of antiquity appears in their theology: in the idea of divinity at the bottom of polytheism. Moreover he regards empires like the Egyptian, Assyrian and Roman as instruments in God's hand used to try or to punish the Jews.

By virtue of the allegorical interpretations of the Old Testament already referred to — the distinctive contribution of Origen — whereby a deeper, more recondite significance was indicated alongside of the literal sense of the Scriptures, new power had been

[223] *The Church History of Eusebius*, A. C. McGiffert's ed., Book I, Chapter IV, quoted in Shotwell 313.
[224] *De civitate Dei* 5. 11.

gained to answer the most important questions concerning man's being, his relation to God and his destiny in history; and this applied not only to the past and the present but also for the future until the end of the world.

Of all the new thoughts expressed by Augustine, the one that had the most lasting influence upon the view of world history held by later times was, probably, the idea that history is the growing knowledge and realization of an aim in life indicated to mankind — to individuals, to communities, to humanity as a whole — by a higher destiny.

So we find that Otto of Freising takes it for granted that the changing earthly is always to be regarded in relation to the unchanging heavenly. He says:

God does not neglect his world, as some claim, but rather . . . by his omnipotent majesty he created the things that were not, by his all-wise providence guides his creatures, and by his most kindly grace preserves what he guides and controls.

And again:

For we must believe that the author of goodness and the fount of grace permits no evil save that which, however much it may in itself be hurtful, is yet of advantage to the whole. This truth may be seen in the downfall of the Jewish nation, because through the blinding of that people all nations received the light of truth.[225]

For, though separated from Augustine by more than seven hundred years, Otto is deeply indebted to the author of the *De civitate Dei* for his judgment as to the course of history. We find an advance in those parts of Otto's work in which he seeks to indicate more precisely the determination of the course of history by Christ's work of redemption, and therein also follows the course of events through the Christian period up to the present. So in dealing with the pre-Christian era he raises the question whether there may not be some connection between the long delay of Christ's appearing and the history of the heathen peoples — a connection unknown to them.[226] But he has progressed beyond Augustine in other ways as well. Preserving in weakened form the basic ideas introduced into history by his great model, he has filled in the account of ancient history with a selection of important deeds chosen

[225] VII, Prol.
[226] See III, Prol.

mainly from secondary and often gloomy sources; then for his own sketch of Christian history he takes as a framework the scheme of relations between Church and State originating with Augustine, but adapts it in original fashion and with somewhat pessimistic coloring to the relations between the State and the Church of the Middle Ages.

And it must not be forgotten that Otto's *Chronicle* remained for centuries the single notable attempt to apprehend universal history by the standard of higher points of view, as the working out in time, upon the stage of the world, of the conflict of the eternal principles of good and evil.[227]

In the second book of his *Deeds of the emperor Frederick I*, in concluding his account of Frederick's return from Italy in the year 1155, Otto says:

Let it suffice to have told these few incidents out of many regarding the progress and outcome of that expedition. For not all the deeds there bravely performed could be related by me with such accuracy of enumeration and charm of style as though I had seen them with my own eyes. For it is said to have been a custom of men of old that those who had had actual personal experience of events as they took place should be the ones to record these same matters. Whence also it is wont to be called "history" from *hysterein*, which means in Greek "to behold." For each can the more fully relate what he has seen and heard according as he stands in need of no man's favor and is not swayed this way and that, dubiously anxious and anxiously dubious, in his search for the truth. For it is a grievous matter that a writer's mind should depend upon another's judgment as though lacking the power of personal investigation.[228]

Such was his conception of the proper function of a historian. He tells us that he undertook the composition of the *Chronicle* because of sorrow at the misery and change in earthly affairs. "I wrote this history in bitterness of spirit," he says, "led thereto by the turbulence of that unsettled time which preceded your reign, and therefore I did not merely give events in their chronological order, but rather wove together, in the manner of a tragedy, their sadder aspects."[229] It has what might be termed an ascetic tendency:

---

[227] On Christian historical writing in the Middle Ages see especially — in addition to Professor Shotwell's book — M. Ritter 242-276, and Hashagen 70-72 and 97-99.

[228] *Gesta*, 2. 41 (end).

[229] Letter to Frederick, p. 2 in Hofmeister's edition of the *Chronicle*.

he wrote "not to satisfy curiosity, but to display the disasters of failing temporal affairs." [230]

In his letter to the Chancellor, his friend Rainald, Otto very wisely remarks that "all teaching consists of two things: avoidance and selection." [231] Then, proceeding to make the application of this general statement to the field in which he is specifically interested, he goes on: "So also the art of the historian has certain things to clear away and to avoid and others to select and arrange properly; for it avoids lies and selects the truth."

Having thus clearly set forth the whole duty of a historian as he sees it, Otto says further:

Therefore, let not Your Discreet Highness be offended, or (as I have said before) interpret the matter in an unfavorable light in the hearing of the emperor, if it shall appear that in our history certain matters have been spoken in criticism of his predecessors or ancestors, that the truth may be held in esteem, inasmuch as it is better to fall into the hands of men than to lose the function of a historian by covering up a loathsome sight by colors which conceal the truth.[232]

It is of interest in this connection to repeat a modern historian's characterization of his subject:

Impartial, — almost unhuman in its cold impartiality, — weighing documents, accumulating evidence, sorting out the false wherever it can be detected, no matter what venerable belief goes with it, it is piecing together with infinite care the broken mosaic of the past, — not to teach us lessons nor to entertain, but simply to fulfil the imperative demand of the scientific spirit — to find out the truth and set it forth.[233]

To be sure, Otto would not go so far as to deny to the historian the privilege of drawing lessons from the past. He sees God's guiding hand in all the ages. He shows a pure, strong character in the teaching which he seems to find recorded in history. He feels that it is his duty not only to judge events on the basis of truth but also to make a useful application to his own time. He believes that history should be a teacher of men. And in the prologue to the *Gesta* [234] he explicitly distinguishes between the "plain speech of history,"

[230] II. 32.
[231] P. 4 in Hofmeister's edition of the *Chronicle*.
[232] *Op. cit.*, p. 5.
[233] Shotwell 8-9.
[234] P. 12 in Simson's edition.

the smoothly running account of historical events without reflections upon them, and "loftier pinnacles of philosophy" to which his presentation attains. Otto's original treatment of his material, his lively, connected account instead of a mere dry enumeration of events and his philosophical grasp of his subject are worthy of the highest praise.

Perhaps the fundamental characteristic of Otto's philosophy of history is his absolute faith in an ever-active divine will, busying itself with the course of human events. We find also in his works an ethical tendency which has been termed a "Christian pessimism." He emphasizes the vanity of the world in order to distract men's interests from this life and to point to the ethical ideals as the only means of safety. So for example he says:

Does it not seem to you that the world, after the manner of the sea, threatens with destruction by times of storm as the sea does by its waves those who entrust themselves to her? To what else am I to liken men who vie with one another for perishing honors than to creeping things of the sea? In the deep we see the lesser swallowed up by the greater, the weaker by the stronger, and at last the stronger — when they can find no other prey — tear themselves to pieces. Hence springs the saying: "The great fall upon themselves." All these things the prudent reader will be able to find in the course of this history. It is plain therefore that the citizens of Christ ought not, as creeping things of the sea do, to plunge into the salty sea or trust themselves rashly to treacherous gales; they ought rather to sail by faith in a ship, that is, the wood of the cross, and in this present time to busy their hands with works of love, that they may be able by traversing the highways of this life to reach safely the harbor of their true country.[235]

Otto's impartiality and unpartisanship are clearly indicated in the passage from his letter to Chancellor Rainald which has been quoted above.[236] Moreover these characteristics appear repeatedly throughout the course of the *Chronicle*: for example, in his statement that even the popes have no claim upon heaven if they lead sinful lives, and in his remarkably restrained account of heretics.[237] Only in the case of Arius [238] does he use hard words; usually he is

[235] VI, Prol. (ed. Hofmeister 261).

[236] P. 51 and note 232.

[237] VII, Prol. (ed. Hofmeister 310). See also the account of "shameful confusion in the Church of God in the city of Rome" in 1042 (VI. 32).

[238] IV. 5.

content to record the facts and nothing more.[239] He is impartial even in dealing with philosophical questions.

Nor does Otto ever give undue prominence to his ancestors or to his family.[240] He mentions the marriage of his parents merely as a historical fact [241] and gives but a brief and simple notice of his father's death — with no intimation of the relationship.[242] He never deliberately mentions himself, although in a passage in the *Gesta* he refers to himself as one of the bishops whom Pope Eugenius III criticized for advising the emperor against the canons.[243] Furthermore, he relates with marked dissatisfaction the circumstance that his half-brother, Conrad III, cheated Duke Henry out of the treasures of the realm,[244] and narrates freely and openly the story of the defeat which his brother Leopold suffered at the hands of Duke Welf, as also his brother's plundering of the churches.[245]

The one respect in which Otto is not quite unpartisan is in his relations with the house of Wittelsbach. His bitter enmity to the count-palatine appears to have been due in part to the difference in their political attitudes and in part to the fact that the count-palatine, Otto of Wittelsbach, stood on the side of the Welfs against the house of Babenberg. Furthermore, the house of Wittelsbach availed itself of every opportunity that presented itself to take the part of the emperor against the pope. To Bishop Otto this Otto VI appeared to be the evil genius of the emperor Frederick I (with whom he had been brought up), for he was always ready to help secure by violence all supposed or real rights of the emperor. This may serve to explain — though not to excuse — Bishop Otto's attitude. The passage which most strikingly exhibits his feelings is that in which he is recounting the conquest of the Hungarians on the Lechfeld in 955; after relating the treacherous act of the barbarian Count of Scheyern he says of his descendant: "Otto, the count-palatine, heir not unlike his treacherous and iniquitous father, a man who surpasses in malice all his predecessors, even

---

[239] See, *e.g.*, III. 25.

[240] Æneas Silvius well says of Otto: *neque cognationem veritati neque veritatem cognationi offecisse.*

[241] VII. 9.

[242] VII. 21.

[243] *Gesta* 2. 8.

[244] VII. 23.

[245] VII. 25.

to the present day ceases not to persecute the Church of God.'' [246]
As a matter of fact Bishop Otto's opposition to the house of
Wittelsbach goes back to the time of his ancestors — to Duke
Arnulf of Bavaria, whom he characterizes as a person ''without
judgment or justice.'' [247]

Before leaving the consideration of Otto's view of history and
his chief characteristics as a historian there are one or two further
statements of his own on the subject that need to be regarded.
''Let no one expect from me epigrams or moral reflections,'' he
says. ''For it is our intention to set forth, not after the manner of
a disputant, but in the fashion of one telling a story, a history.'' [248]
And again, ''I have undertaken to speak . . . in such a way that
we shall not lose the thread of history, that the devout reader may
observe what is to be avoided in mundane affairs by reason of the
countless miseries wrought by their unstable character, and that the
studious and painstaking investigator may find a record of past
happenings free from all obscurity.'' [249]

His aim then is to give a clear and logical record of events in
orderly sequence, and to yield as little as may be to the temptation
to indulge in rhetorical flourishes and cheap moralizations. But that
he cannot altogether resist the not unnatural desire to comment
somewhat at length on the more striking catastrophes in the long
and pitiful annals of the ages is evidenced by his frequent ''exclamations.'' These can scarcely be listed as anything else than
moral reflections; but they may find excuse as part of that very
philosophy of history which forms the backbone of the whole work
and gives it at once unity and a definite aim.

It may be well in this connection to call particular attention to
a statement found in the sixth book of the *Chronicle*: ''Whether
all these things were done lawfully or otherwise it is not the purpose of the present work to say. For we have undertaken to tell,
in writing, what happened, not to pass judgment on what happened.'' [250] It should be carefully noted that this remark is to be

[246] VI. 20.
[247] VI. 18.
[248] II, Prol. (ed. Hofmeister 68).
[249] I, Prol. (ed. Hofmeister 9).
[250] VI. 23. And *cf.* also VI. 31: *dubium utrum licite an secus* (of the action
taken against the bishops of Piacenza, Vercelli and Cremona, who were convicted of treason and sent into exile in 1037); VII. 11: *Quae omnia utrum
licite an secus acta sint, nos non discernimus* (of the forced abdication of

estimated in the light of the problem before the historian at this point in his account, namely, whether Otto I acted justly or unjustly in deposing Pope John XII. Otto is here desirous of merely recording events, not because the general tendency of his book demands it but because he wishes to withhold judgment.[251]

Otto of Freising noticed especially the tragic in history, and he was a man whose very temperament rendered it impossible for him to make of his history a cold, unfeeling record in the manner of the annalists. Hauck feels that this sensitive, sympathetic nature of Bishop Otto the man colors and molds his style.[252] He says:

> From this quality of Otto's arises the difference of his historical writing from that of his predecessors. It is from one point of view more impartial, more just; from another it is warmer, softer and in particular more thoughtful than that to which men were previously accustomed. The historian's disposition and outlook upon life give his work a characteristic tone. Here too the preëminence of the subjective, to which we have previously alluded, does not fail to reveal itself.[253]

The method of the chroniclers in compiling their historical accounts was to copy out their authorities, even calmly setting down contradictory statements. But Otto was not so credulous, and it is by his critical spirit above all else that he has won his renown as a historian. This manifests itself in different ways. Sometimes his critical method consists solely in setting down various views without deciding which he regards as correct.[254] Sometimes he indicates the untrustworthiness of his account — in much the same fashion as modern newspaper editors in their care to avoid libel suits — by a *fertur, dicitur, asserunt*.[255] He does not believe all the legends.[256] Often, though he believes the stories themselves, he points

---

the emperor Henry IV and the succession of his son); *Gesta* 1. 61 (of the outcome of Gilbert's trial).

[251] So Hashagen (83 and n. 5), who calls attention to the fact that Wilmans (Hanover 1867, Intro., p. XXIX) wrongfully applies this sentence out of its context as illustrating Otto's idea of the function of a historian. See also Wilmans in Archiv 10. 152.

[252] GKD (1913) 4. 504.

[253] On Otto's view of history see especially Huber 163-185; Hashagen 22-34; Hauck, *l.c.*

[254] See Ritter 296, n. 2.

[255] *E.g.*, the story of Prester John (VII. 33).

[256] See, *e.g.*, VI. 11: *Quod utrum ita sit, ipsi viderint.*

out the incredible foundations on which they rest,[257] and he absolutely refuses to accept improbabilities or impossibilities in the legends.[258]

It is perhaps not so surprising that in his treatment of Greek myths he seeks to find sometimes a natural interpretation, sometimes a historical explanation.[259] We may note in passing that his criticism of the legend of the founding of Rome is especially keen.[260] But it is rather remarkable to find, in a writer of the twelfth century, a man so critical and sensible with respect to tales current as fact in his own day — a time when myths were still coming into being in the midst of Europe. Occasionally he prefers to let the reader guess his opinion rather than state it himself in so many words.[261] In general Otto employs every means at his disposal in criticism: sometimes the accurate interpretation and connection of words,[262] often knowledge gained by personal observation.[263] But he is careful not to arouse feelings of doubt in his readers [264] and as a rule does not subject Christian legends to criticism.[265] His judgment and balance are clearly revealed in a statement which he makes with regard to the varying stories of the elevation of Henry I of Germany to the kingship. Otto says:

These conflicting accounts of historians resulted, I think, from the fact that since men's intellectual abilities had begun to grow and to keep pace with the glory of empire, as a result when the imperial authority was transferred to the Franks and men's sympathies were divided upon the physical division of the kingdom, the writers extolled each his own state as much as he could with the aid of his transcendent abilities. But I myself, keeping a middle course in these matters — and, so far as I am able

[257] For an excellent example of Otto's critical spirit, see VII. 7 (regarding Bishop Tiemo). Apparently he does not have implicit faith even in the *Tripartite History*: see IV. 1 (St. Silvester).

[258] So in I. 29 he explains a Biblical incident by interpreting a number figuratively: 700 = "very many"; in II. 25 he says of the legends concerning King Porus: *multa . . . tam mirabilia sunt, ut etiam incredibilia videantur.*

[259] Natural explanations: I. 18 (Phaëthon); I. 21 (Centaurs); historical: I. 15 (Apis); I. 19 (Ganymede); I. 24 (Apollo and the nymph Carmentis).

[260] II. 2.

[261] I. 8: *Quae quanta qualisve fuerit, ex ipsa ruina sui liquido probari poterit.*

[262] III. 2.

[263] IV. 27: *quem ipse vidi.*

[264] See VI. 10.

[265] But note the significant exceptions already indicated above in note 257.

and can conjecture from what they have said, holding fast the thread of
truth — will strive by God's grace to turn aside neither to the right hand
nor to the left.[266]

His criticism sometimes extends also to chronology and he occasionally seeks to correct inaccurate statements made by his predecessors.[267] As Hauck has well said of him: "Thanks to his surpassing natural talent and his broad culture he always preserved
that calm moderation of judgment, which, even in controversy,
recognizes the virtue of restraint." [268]

Surprise has been expressed that a man who had as much as
Otto did, and who was so full of love and peace and good nature,
should take so gloomy a view of the world, and that providence
should usually assume to him the form of an avenging angel.[269]
Huber states that whereas the consolation we find in history today
is the thought of betterment and progress, Otto is cheered by the
constant misery of human existence.[270] As a matter of fact, it appears to some that Otto was so deeply affected by the manifest
misery of this present world that the call to the Second Crusade
appealed to him as a means of release. For he says in a passage of
his *Chronicle* written in the year 1146: "Finally we are oppressed
by so poignant a memory of the past, so violent an onslaught of the
present woes, and so great a fear of future perils that receiving
'the sentence of death within ourselves we despair even of life,'

---

[266] VI. 18.

[267] See I. 6: *Unde apparet Babylonem fuisse ante Ninum, Semiramidemque
uxorem Nini instauratricem eius potius dicendam quam conditricem*; III. 2
(ed. Hofmeister 138): *Diximus secundum quosdam Grecorum monarchiam
usque ad Cesarem extendi. Verisimilius tamen videtur Grecos monarchiam
quidem post mortem Alexandri perdidisse, reges vero preclaros orienti im-
perantes habuisse*; V. 16: *Quam controversiam scriptores viderint.*

[268] KGD (1913) 4. 207.

[269] Huber 154-163. He calls especial attention to the following passages:
I. 7 (Ninus); II. 14 (Cyrus); II. 47 (the Maccabees); IV. 16 (Valens);
IV. 28 (Attila); V. 3 (Theodoric).

[270] Huber (*loc. cit.*) refers to Otto's lamentation for the conquerors of
Troy (I. 26); the death of Cyrus (II. 14); the death of Mithradates (II. 45);
the constant wretchedness of Rome (II. 30); the Punic Wars (II. 32);
Pharsalus (II. 49); the fall of the Western Empire (IV. 31); and the almost
comic paragraph concerning Charles the Fat (VI. 9). Moreover the future
will be no better than the past has been (VII. 34), although the prayers of
the pious, the saints, the monks are a remedy for the manifold misery. (See
VII. 34 and 21; also VII. 35).

particularly since we think that the world cannot long endure.'' [271]

Such a conclusion is scarcely fair to Bishop Otto for, strictly speaking, a man cannot be counted as a pessimist if he asserts that there is no evil which is not of advantage.[272] Otto does say this in no uncertain terms: ''For we must believe that the author of goodness and the fount of grace permits no evil save that which, however much it may in itself be hurtful, is yet of advantage to the whole.'' [273]

It is reasonable to suppose that his somewhat gloomy view of history is due in part to the turbulent state of Germany at the time when he was writing the *Chronicle* [274] — so vividly described to us in a passage at the close of the seventh book [275] — but even more to those unhappy family relations already referred to [276] and to the dire fate that had overtaken his grandfather, the emperor Henry IV. The great opposition between Church and State had caused the bitterest confusion in his own household, and all this must have made a lively impression upon Otto in his youth.[277] It has been well said, therefore, that it was not in hopelessness that his attention was turned toward the course of history, tragic as it sometimes seemed to him.[278] He used black colors with the moral aim of introducing what has been termed a Christian pessimism. He was hurt by the hard and the unreasonable in life because his perceptions and sympathies were so keen. This was true of his personal misfortunes [279] and general experience moved him still more deeply. He was oppressed by the fact that the great sink into insignificance and the strong fall from their power and their pride. And this subjective element in his writing adds much to the vividness and force of his style, rescuing it from dull pedantry and the mere impassive, mechanical recording of events. Moreover we get an interesting sidelight on Otto's character from the admiration which he

[271] VII. 34. So Kugler, *Studien zur Geschichte des zweiten Kreuzzuges* (Stuttgart 1866) 7-10.

[272] So Hauck 503.

[273] VII, Prol.

[274] So Wilmans, p. XIX.

[275] VII. 34.

[276] See note 32.

[277] So Hofmeister 121.

[278] Hashagen 34.

[279] See II, Prol. and *cf.* with this the passage about the house of Wittelsbach in VI. 20.

expresses for the character of a certain Berthold of Zähringen who was apparently a man after his own heart. He says of him:

He is said to have been a most vigorous and valiant man; whence even today it is related of him by our elders that whenever a messenger bearing him some ill-tidings would hesitate, as is natural, he said: "Speak, Speak! For I know that joy always precedes sorrow or sorrow joy: therefore it is as acceptable to me first to hear of storm when I am afterwards to hear of calm as it is when first I have heard of calm to be in expectation of hearing of storm afterwards." A magnificent speech, and worthy of a brave man, who . . . was neither in the day of good things forgetful of evil things and puffed up, nor in the day of evil things forgetful of good things and broken.[280]

It has already been stated that Otto reveals in his *Chronicle* his confident belief in the near approach of the end of the world.[281] So at the very outset he remarks in the prologue addressed to his friend Isingrim: "But we, set down as it were at the end of time, do not so much read of the miseries of mortals in the books of the writers named above as find them for ourselves in consequence of experiences of our own time."[282] And again he says: "For we who live in the closing days of that kingdom are experiencing that which was foretold concerning it, and expect that what we have yet to fear will soon take place."[283] This is not, however, a purely personal opinion but one widely prevalent at the time in which he lived. As early as 1105 a Florentine synod was obliged to declare expressly that Antichrist had not yet appeared. But Pope Lucius II expected his early coming. After Otto's death Gerhoh busied himself with this topic in a remarkable book. St. Bernard looked upon Abelard — the opponent of his beloved Pope Innocent — as a sort of forerunner of Antichrist. Hugo of St. Victor, in his work *De vanitate mundi*, holds that the progress of the world's development is from East to West, and that the West is identical with the end of the world.

It is this last thought that we find reappearing in Otto. He says to Isingrim: "And it is to be observed that all human power or learning had its origin in the East but is coming to an end in the West, that thereby the transitoriness and decay of all things human

---

280 *Gesta* 1. 8.
281 P. 58 and note 271.
282 P. 7 in Hofmeister's edition.
283 II. 13. See also VI. 36; VII. 9; VII. 34.

may be displayed.'' [284] Since then in his time the representatives of wisdom, the *illustres doctores* (theologians like Anselm) lived in the West, Otto is convinced that the world is in its last phases. For there is no farther west.[285]

The demise of Conrad III in 1152 was an event of the utmost significance for Bishop Otto, for his successor, the emperor Frederick I, created for the diocese of Freising the peace he had so long and so ardently desired. The last event Otto mentions in his historical work is the decision of the emperor in the case of Henry ''Jasomirgott,'' brother of the Bishop of Freising, which brought about this result.[286] This was in 1156, only two years before Otto's demise.

But as early as the spring of 1147 Otto had given himself up to hopes for a more glorious future. In writing of the Second Crusade in that year he says:

Suddenly by the right hand of the Most High so great a change was brought about that, all these tumults of wars being lulled to rest, in a short time you might have seen the whole earth at peace and countless numbers from Gaul and from Germany accepting crosses and undertaking military service against the enemies of the Cross.[287]

These hopes, as we have seen, were crushed by the unfortunate result of that ill-omened Crusade. But with the accession of Barbarossa there came a gradual fading of Otto's mournful view of history. Even in the prologue to the second edition of the *Chronicle,* while Otto admits that he had previously written ''in bitterness of spirit,'' [288] it looks almost like a complete change of attitude when he continues: ''I shall not be slow to prosecute this joyous task with joyful mind.'' [289] He goes even farther than this in the prologue of his *Gesta Friderici I Imperatoris*: ''I consider those who write at this time as in a certain manner blessed, because after the turbulence of the past there has dawned the unheard of calm of peace.'' [290]

---

[284] P. 8 in Hofmeister's ed. See also Book V, Prol.

[285] So Hashagen 30-31. And see Hauck 4. 503, n. 2.

[286] *Gesta* 2. 55.

[287] *Gesta* 1. 29. *Cf. Gesta* 1. 44: *repente sic totus pene occidens siluit, ut non solum bella movere, sed et arma quempiam in publico portare nefas haberetur.*

[288] Letter to Frederick, p. 2 in Hofmeister's edition.

[289] *Op. cit.,* page 3.

[290] P. 9 in Simson's ed. And see *Gesta* 1. 65.

To be sure Otto has not altogether lost his feeling for the misery of the world; that was perhaps not to be expected. Particularly when he is narrating again the misfortunes of the realm under Henry IV and Henry V in the first book of the *Gesta* he is moved to the familiar lamentations. But he now likes to mingle the sorrowful and the joyous. And when he becomes deeply interested in the deeds of Barbarossa (in the last chapters of Book I and in Book II of the *Gesta*) he no longer has either the time or the inclination to employ the old dark colors. Perhaps most remarkable of all — especially in view of the judgment of St. Bernard himself regarding the great disaster — is the fact that, in narrating the failure of the Second Crusade, Otto says not a word about the misery of the world.

It would appear that Otto's feeling of happiness and deep satisfaction at the emperor Frederick's accession was based on his conviction that the world's peace was dependent upon the harmonious coöperation of Church and State, and his belief that in Barbarossa the deepest and most profound desires of his heart would find their realization. Hauck says: "Otto's works indicate in their superposition in historical literature the point at which the secular interest demanded its rights beside the theological. Corresponding with this is the fact that, although composed by a theologian, they were not intended solely for theological readers."[291]

6. OTTO'S PHILOSOPHY OF HISTORY

Perhaps the outstanding characteristic of Otto of Freising as a historian is his attempt to discover and to reveal a guiding principle and purpose in the events which he records — a philosophy of history. And he is the first since Augustine to return to this theme. But Otto did not merely take over; he independently worked up anew the philosophy of history of the Middle Ages which Augustine had founded. Moreover he was not influenced in this by Gregory the Great or by his contemporaries, Hugo of St. Victor, Gerhoh or Abelard.

There are, of course, general points of likeness between Augustine and Otto. Neither regards the individual as a principal factor in historical development. Both see the origin, development and end of history in two tendencies or — as they prefer to call them —

[291] On Otto's joy at Frederick's accession see Hashagen 31-33 and Hauck 508-509.

two cities. And these are distinguished from each other on the basis of theological views. In this Augustine and Otto are in complete accord. Another view common to both authors is the strict dualism of the two cities, the impossibility of reconciliation between them. A third general characteristic of the philosophy of history of both these writters — although, of course, by no means confined to their work — is its teleological tendency: everything is judged and explained according to its place in the divine plan of salvation. The City of Earth, in Otto's *Chronicle,* is referred to only insofar as it may serve to set the City of God in clear contrast. But of the two-cities theory we shall take occasion to speak later at greater length and with more details. As a simple record of events the *Chronicle* might perhaps have a heightened value for some historians without the scheme of the two cities. However in that case we should lose a notable spokesman of the spirit of the Middle Ages.

Otto's connection with the Cistercian order is of significance for the underlying plan of his work. For it is, in general, the outcropping of his ascetic thought that gives a certain unified expression to his philosophy of history, which is otherwise rather unsystematic. Indeed, he employs the scheme of the history of the two cities chiefly with the intention of preaching to his readers a turning aside from the *civitas mundi* toward the *civitas dei.* This is of course most clearly apparent in the eighth book. But even in the final chapter of the seventh book, where we might have expected the usual mournful reflections with which Otto is wont to conclude each larger section of this work, we find instead a significant outlook toward the future.

The most notable advance over Augustine is found in those passages of Otto's work in which he attempts to trace the gradual rise of primitive man to a higher stage of civilization.[292] When Otto speaks of the state of the world at the time of the beginning of Christianity he is led to the thought — not, however, original with him — which becomes the guiding principle for his whole conception of post-Christian history, namely, the function of the Roman Empire as protector of the rising Christian Church. After the entrance of Christianity upon the stage of world history the ideal pictures of the two cities gradually fade before the more

---

[292] See, *e.g.*, the important prologue to the third book, particularly pp. 132-133 in Hofmeister.

readily comprehensible powers of the Church and the now Christianized State.

It is perhaps significant also that, as regards political history, from the death of Theodosius to the year 476, Otto narrates the history of the one Roman Empire and interweaves the assaults of the Germanic peoples as though they were nothing very different from the uprisings of governors and of provinces. Then, after the end of Roman rule in the West, he continues his account in much the same way, making due allowance for the newly founded Frankish Empire as a state separated from the dominion of the Romans.[293] Beginning with Clovis he gives in addition to the list of emperors the roll of Frankish kings as well.[294] So the history takes its course, detailing the vicissitudes of the Eastern Roman Empire and finally (after the coronation of Charles the Great as emperor), deals almost exclusively with the destinies of the Franks and then of the Germans, both as bearers of the Roman imperial power.

This is a treatment of history the basal principle of which is that the history of all peoples and kingdoms goes back to the Roman state as to its source, or, more concisely, that the imperial power is the protector of the whole world.[295] And it was to reconcile the identity of the Roman Empire with the unmistakable change of the states that bore its name, that Otto had recourse to the expedient of a repeated *translatio,* or transfer of authority, as already mentioned above.[296] Rome, it is true, merely lent its name to the empire,[297] and the Eternal City had left of its old fame and ancient dignity only a shadow.[298]

This theory of the persistence of the Roman Empire, to which Otto clings, is due to two hypotheses which have been carried over into history. The first of these is the belief, inherited from Augustine, that history must take its course in a series of world empires. The second is the theological view that, in accordance with Daniel, the Roman Empire must inevitably be the last. And aside from this there was further ground for the Roman character of the empire in the circumstance that the emperors since Charles the Great had established the supreme power (though not indeed the seat of

[293] IV. 32.
[294] V. 2. 5. 9. 11. 13 and 16.
[295] So Ritter; and *cf.* V. 29.
[296] Pages 29 and 31 above. *Cf.* IV. 5 and 31.
[297] V. 36.
[298] IV. 31.

their rule) at Rome, where also the crowning of the emperors took place at the hands of the pope.[299]

We find in Otto's *Chronicle* furthermore the conviction that the Church is to grow into an earthly kingdom as well as into a spiritual power — in fact into the greatest of all — but that corresponding to this growth of the Church a progressive decline of the Roman Empire must occur.[300]. Otto traces this decline of the power of Rome and the rise of the temporal power of the Church from the days of Nero,[301] through Constantine's renunciation of the western half of the empire in favor of the Roman Church (the source of grants of landed possessions to the Church), to its climax in popes Leo IX, Alexander II and Gregory VII [302] who began to free the Church from attacks of the empire and to subject kings and emperors to themselves. The authority of the popes to change the dynasties of empires had its source in the act of Pope Zacharias in releasing Pepin and all the Franks from the oath that they had sworn to the Merovingian kings. The temporal power of the Church was notably in evidence when the popes succeeded in forcing Henry IV to be dethroned by excommunication and then wrung from the State renunciation of the investiture, and it reached its climax a century later. The remarkable thing is that Bishop Otto, the ascetically minded historian, is moved by a sort of horror at this temporal power and splendor. When he calls to mind the wars and the misery of war that have been caused by the Church in its effort to attain its aims, he frankly expreses doubt as to whether the present exaltation of the Church is more pleasing than its former humble estate.[303]

But he remarks that the Roman Church regards its acquisitions as justified — and the Church cannot err. And doubtless it is a destiny ordained by God after all.[304]

The full title of Otto's universal history, it will be remembered, is *The Chronicle or The History of the Two Cities*. In these cities, typified by the heavenly Jerusalem and the earthly Babylon, we find running through the entire chronicle of human progress a

[299] See V. 35, and *cf.* V. 32 and VI. 18.

[300] See IV. 4 (ed. Hofmeister 189); IV. 5 (p. 191); IV, Prol. (p. 180).

[301] III. 16.

[302] See VI. 33-34; also VII. 16.

[303] IV, Prol. (ed. Hofmeister 183).

[304] VI. 36. On Otto's philosophy of history see Bernheim (1885) 13-24; Hashagen 16-17; Ritter 264-276.

dualism between those who follow the ruling of God's spirit and those who oppose it. God himself, who separates the light from the darkness, appears to be the original cause of the division.[305] The distinction is clearly drawn between the children of grace and the children of wrath, Jews and Gentiles, sinners and saints.

At various times, especially in Biblical history, the two cities are personified in a pair of individuals who stand forth in sharp contrast with each other. So we read at the very outset of Adam, the first man: "And he begat sons, the first citizens of the two cities of which I have undertaken to treat."[306] And a little later: "After Abel was slain, another son was born to Adam, named Seth, who is a figure of the resurrection: from him the people of God was afterwards begotten." We have therefore in Seth and Cain prototypes of the City of God and the City of Earth. Other notable representatives of each city are pointed out from time to time. So, for example, Enoch[307] and (at least by implication) Noah[308] are mighty citizens of the City of God; Japheth and Ham after the Flood "the first citizens of the cities which constitute the theme of my book."[309] And later Abraham was divinely sent to a land, "which is known to be a type of that city which is our theme, to become a great citizen thereof."[310] His sons Isaac and Ishmael likewise "were the first citizens, after the institution of circumcision, of the two cities I have begun to describe, and the younger suffered persecution at the hands of the elder as a forecast of future events."[311] Here also occurs a sentence of some importance for the later development of the two-cities theory: "Observe that at the beginning of these three generations you will find these citizens begotten of one father, that thereby it might be indicated that the Church in far distant ages was to hold within her single bosom the two peoples, endowed with one faith, sprung from one source."

The succession is continued by Jacob and Esau.[312] Of Jesus (or Joshua) the son of Nun, Otto remarks: "He first, bearing the likeness of the Saviour in office and in name, was privileged to lead the

305 I. 20.
306 I. 2.
307 I. 2.
308 I. 3.
309 I. 4.
310 I. 7.
311 I. 10.
312 I. 10.

people of God into the land of promise, which is a type of that city which is our theme." [313]

David was "a great leader of the City of God, for to him first after the patriarchs was the promise made that of his seed was to be born the Christ, the founder of that city which forms our theme." [314]

When the Jewish people were divided, "each kingdom had citizens of the Kingdom of Christ whose function it was to rebuke the excesses of the sinful people and their deceitful kings." [315] These included, in the kingdom of Israel, Elijah and Elisha; in Judah "Hosea, Isaiah and a great many others whom we shall set down, at the proper place, not only prophesied but also left written memorials that were destined to be of great avail to the City of God." For Otto remarks further: "And that no one may suppose that the City of God at that time was small, hear what was said of Israel alone by the Lord to Elijah: 'I have left for myself seven thousand men'— a number which in the Scriptures is frequently used for an indefinitely large array." [316]

That the heathen are in general to be identified with the other city is implied when Otto says: "I have wished to set down these matters from histories of the Gentiles in order to show that the citizens of Babylon — to their own greater damnation — have known, indeed, how to tell the truth but have not forsaken the deceitfulness of error." [317]

In general therefore in the primitive, cityless time [318] the citizens of the two cities can be distinguished only as the good and the bad. When Babel is founded this city becomes the representative of the Earthly City. Otto says of it: "This is that well-known Babylon, a figure of that city of which all they are citizens who insolently attempt to resist the ordinance of God, and are therefore accounted by the eternal judge as worthy of confusion." [319] And in like manner at the origin of the people of Israel the pious are in a measure crystallized as God's people.[320] However, the City of Earth is not

[313] I. 20.
[314] I. 29.
[315] I. 29.
[316] *L.c.*
[317] I. 18.
[318] I. 6 and III, Prol. (ed. Hofmeister 133).
[319] I. 4.
[320] I. 20 and III, Prol. (ed. Hofmeister 130).

limited to Babylon and the City of God is by no means to be regarded as identical with Israel, for, as Otto expressly states, after
the division of the kingdom: "You can find no one of the kings of
Israel and very few indeed of the kings of Judah that were citizens
of Jerusalem";[321] and again he says: "From Zerubbabel and Jesus
the high priest even to the time of John . . . you will find few
who, because of their words or their deeds, deserved to be counted
among the approved citizens of Jerusalem."[322] Indeed the two
cities are frequently inextricably interwoven one with the other:
there are citizens of Christ living among the citizens of Babylon [323]
and there are also citizens of God's city outside of Israel.[324]

From Babylon the representation of the Earthly City is transferred to the later world monarchies and finally to Rome,[325] and
after Christ's coming the City of God is localized in the Church.
Yet here too it is made clear that those who belong to the Church
are not necessarily citizens of The City of God merely by virtue of
their church membership. There were internal dissensions which
revealed the presence of enemies in the midst.[326] Otto discusses this
somewhat at length in the prologue to the fifth book, as follows:

Furthermore, enough has been said above, I think, regarding the two
cities: how one made progress, first by remaining hidden in the other until
the coming of Christ, after that by advancing gradually to the time of
Constantine. But after Constantine, when troubles from without had
finally ceased, it began to be grievously troubled at the instigation of the
devil by internal strife even to the time of the Elder Theodosius; Arius
was the author of this and the lords of the world, the Augusti, were his
coadjutors. But from that time on, since not only all the people but also
the emperors (except a few) were orthodox Catholics, I seem to myself to
have composed a history not of two cities but virtually of one only, which
I call the Church. For although the elect and the reprobate are in one
household yet I cannot call these cities two, as I did above; I must call
them properly but one — composite, however, as the grain is mixed with
the chaff. Wherefore in the books that follow let us pursue the course of
history which we have begun. Since not only emperors of the Romans but

321 I. 29.

322 II. 16.

323 II, Prol. (ed. Hofmeister 68).

324 III. 14.

325 *Cf.* the quotation from I Peter 5. 13 in II, Prol: "the church that is in
Babylon."

326 III. 22.

also other kings — kings of renowned realms — became Christians, inas-much as the sound of the word of God went out into all the earth and unto the ends of the world, the City of Earth was laid to rest and destined to be utterly exterminated in the end; hence our history is a history of the City of Christ: but that city, so long as it is in the land of sojourn, is "like unto a net, that was cast into the sea," containing the good and the bad. However the faithless city of unbelieving Jews and Gentiles still remains but, since nobler kingdoms have been won by our people, while these unbelieving Jews and Gentiles are insignificant not only in the sight of God but even in that of the world, hardly anything done by these un-believers is found worthy of record or to be handed on to posterity.[327]

We see therefore that the City of God has now actually absorbed the greatest earthly realm, while the representatives of the Earthly City are limited to the extra-Christian territory. That is why Otto feels that he can no longer speak of two cities but really only of one which, to be sure, includes within itself the good and the bad.[328]

In the eighth book Otto, following the New Testament prophecy, traces the final development of both cities and the ultimate goal of each: immortal life for the City of God and an awful doom for the City of Earth.

The City of God, therefore, always consisting of the community of the good, appears under various guises at different times: first it is comprised by the scattered children of God, then by their collection in Israel, later by the Church and eventually by the Christian Empire.

In the prologue to his eighth book Otto makes a statement con-cerning the various periods in the development of the two cities:

This work of ours, which we have entitled *The Two Cities*, is, plainly, divided into three parts. For whereas the City of Christ or the Kingdom of Christ (with reference to its present or its future status) is called the Church, it exists in one form so long as it is seen to hold the good and the bad in one embrace; it will exist in another at that time when it shall cherish only the good in the glory of the heavenly embrace; it existed in yet another while it lived subject to princes of the heathen before "the fulness of the Gentiles" was come in. . . . The evil city likewise we find has three states or stages. Of these the first was before the time of grace,

---

[327] P. 228 in Hofmeister's ed.

[328] See also VII, Prol. (ed. Hofmeister 309-310), and *cf.* IV. 4, where Bishop Otto reviews the progress of the City of God somewhat in detail, dwelling upon its remarkable growth and advancement.

the second was and is during the time of grace, the third will be after this present life.

These divisions, however, seem to be apparent to the author rather in retrospect than in the actual development of his theme in the earlier part of the work.

Augustine, on the other hand, while also making in his *De civitate Dei*, a three fold division of the history of the two cities actually employs this as a framework underlying his entire account: he treats of the Origin (*Exortus*, Books XI-XIV), the Development (*Procursus*, XV-XVII) and the End (*Debiti Fines*, XIX-XXII) of the two cities. In Augustine's view church membership insures salvation: the "City of God" is the "external communion of the sacraments." The "City of the Devil" consists of all heathendom. Still, in a mystic sense, Augustine also conceives of The City of God as the "communion of Saints." [329] This mystic "city" Augustine arbitrarily organizes on the basis of the Catholic Church. When the state becomes Christian the concepts of state and heathendom no longer coincide; yet Augustine persists in claiming that the scheme is valid to the world's end. Hence he speaks of the empirical church as a "mixed body," referring to the invisible mingling of the mystical state within the historical.

General points of likeness between Augustine and Otto have already been indicated,[330] and resemblances in detail are readily apparent in the brief sketch of the *De Civitate Dei* contained in the preceding paragraph. It may be well, therefore, to indicate the chief points of difference:[331]

(1) There is a fundamental difference indicated in the very title, *The Two Cities*. Augustine, on the contrary, deals primarily with the one, *The City of God*.

(2) In keeping with this *historical* aim, Otto does not trace the two cities back before Creation as Augustine does.[332]

This distinction is clearly in Otto's mind when he announces in his dedication to Isingrim that he intends to portray the misery of the City of Earth down to his own day. He refers to Augustine's *mystical* interpretation of the cities when he gives in brief form a synopsis of the *De Civitate Dei*: "the origin and the progress of

329 City of God, 1. 35.
330 See above, pp. 49-50.
331 For this topic see Hashagen 48-69.
332 Books 11-14, *Exortus*.

the glorious City of God and its ordained limits . . . how it has ever spread among the citizens of the world, and . . . which of its citizens or princes stood forth preëminent in the various epochs of the princes or citizens of the world.'' [333] Whereas of his own work Otto says: ''I have undertaken to speak of The Two Cities *in such a way that we shall not lose the thread of history.''*

Otto takes delight in illustrating the moral degeneration of the City of Earth by enumerating the shameful deeds of a Danaüs, a Busiris or a Medea,[334] and he lays particular stress upon the baseness of the City of Earth at times when happy issues are expected from the City of God.[335] And of course this is especially the case when he is speaking of the time of the Incarnation.[336] And with the Incarnation also he reaches an entirely historical conception which is not surrendered in the following books. He says of Rome:

For since that city, founded in treachery, was beyond doubt the city of the world, why did He who was born as the first citizen and founder of the City of God desire to be enrolled in the Roman State, save that he showed thereby that he had come to fashion His own city in strange and inexpressible manner from the city of the world? [337]

After the appearance of the Redeemer there follows a new, formal founding of the City of God with the twelve apostles as its twelve princes. Christ names Peter as leader ''to secure the blessing of unity.'' [338] Hence the City of God is identified with the Catholic Church. Its spread over the entire world is foreshadowed by the definite assignment of a specific portion of the earth to each of the apostles to conquer.[339]

Under Nero we have the first of the ten great persecutions directed against the Church, and besides persecutions there are also heresies whose authors counterbalance the princes of the City of God. Ultimately the Roman Empire becomes Christian and the head of the City of Earth is conquered by the City of God.[340]

Since Otto states that by the close of the fifth century those of

[333] P. 9 in Hofmeister's edition.
[334] I. 19.
[335] I. 20; II. 9; III. 45; VII. 9; VIII, Prol. (ed. Hofmeister 391); VIII. 26 (beginning).
[336] II. 47.
[337] III. 6.
[338] III. 10.
[339] See III. 14 and 22.
[340] III. 45 (end) and IV. 3.

high and low degree alike have turned to the new faith, it seems a necessary consequence to give up the old thought of two states.[341] He will henceforth, he says, speak of but one — the Church.[342] Yet there are references to a City of Earth in the later portions of his work.[343] So we find Otto falling back once more upon a mystical point of view.[344] The sinfulness of the times under Henry IV and Henry V leads him to raise the question as to the means of salvation. He finds two possible ways — the Crusades and Asceticism. This mystic view, it will be observed, is not a mere reproduction of the thought of Augustine but is in strictest accord with the ideals of the Cistercian Order, of which Otto of Freising was a member. The historical state has ceased to portray the City of Earth and the historical church is also no longer the representative of the City of God.

In the description of the last judgment we have further light cast upon Otto's two-cities theory.[345] *Both* cities persist even into the future life, standing on the left hand and on the right, and *both* are to fall into two classes.[346] In the City of God we find a judging class made up of those who have renounced their own will on earth, and a company of those who are to be judged: ''men not so perfect, but yet just, who, lawfully holding their own possessions, have by deeds of mercy earned the right to be placed at His right hand.'' It will be observed that Otto does not go to the extreme view of asceticism in criticizing these. In the City of Earth, at the last judgment, are the unbelievers who have been judged already and the unmerciful and hypocrites who are awaiting judgment.

We may conclude, therefore, that history unfolded before Otto's eyes as a great twofold development. He construed it first in accordance with mystic concepts. Then imperceptibly historical ideas replaced them. Finally these gave way again to the mystic. Nowhere is there any hint that Otto was aware of these modifications; nowhere a clear definition of the two cities. He makes criticism difficult by employing them as general expressions for quite different concepts.[347]

341 V, Prol. (ed. Hofmeister 228), quoted above on pp. 67-68.
342 So also in VIII, Prol.
343 See V, Prol. (end) and VII, Prol.
344 VII. 9.
345 VIII. 15.
346 VIII. 16 and 17.
347 So Hashagen, *loc. cit.* For the two-cities theory in general, see Ritter

Attention has been called to the fact that while both Augustine and Orosius disparaged the Romans, Otto's attitude is far different.[348] He shows his interest in Roman history by the connected account he gives in his *Chronicle*, disturbing its content as little as possible by the synchronistic notices so common in other parts of the work. His ecclesiastical interest in Rome reveals itself in the circumstance that he regards it as a beautiful coincidence that the former head of the world is now the head of the Church.[349] But aside from his high regard for heathen Rome and his altogether natural prejudice for the religious center of his world, Otto evidently has an ethical interest in the ancient Roman character. In commenting upon the Second Punic War he says: "At this point we may reflect not only on the valor but also on the wisdom whereby the Romans made the world their own."[350] Indeed he goes so far as to count the valor of the Romans and the wisdom of the philosophers as together molding the world and making it ready for the coming of the Messiah.[351] The story of Regulus in particular seems to win his admiration, and he lists the separate phases of his valor in terms of the catchwords of ascetic literature: contempt for the present world, renunciation of parents, abnegation of possessions and finally of self.[352]

It is here that we find the clue to his high evaluation of the Romans: it is in consequence of his ascetic ideals, which appear to be so admirably illustrated in the old stories of Rome. And he employs them to emphasize the thought that underlies his philosophy of history:

Accordingly, if even among the nations that were ignorant of God death is regarded as a thing to be held cheap, how shall we that have been called to a knowledge of the truth be excused for our ignorance? . . . It remains for us who are seen to be in the Church to blush for evil works, as an example to the heathen . . . and we should turn away from the love of temporal things and be seized with a longing for the eternal.[353]

242-263 (on Augustine) and 264-286 (on Otto of Freising); Hashagen 44-69; Nitsch 334-360; Hauck 505-508.

[348] Hashagen, *Anhang* 42-44.
[349] III, Prol. (ed. Hofmeister 134).
[350] II. 37.
[351] III, Prol. (ed. Hofmeister 133).
[352] II. 34.
[353] *Loc. cit.*

7. OTTO'S POLITICAL AND THEOLOGICAL VIEWS

Bishop Otto of Freising being at once a servant of the Church and a prince of the realm — a territorial lord — felt in his own person the full force and the relative justification of the claims of both Church and State. To him the empire was a no less necessary member of earthly affairs than the Church: only in their coöperation was that divine peace assured which seemed to him the highest good of this world.

It is possible to gain some indication at least of his personal attitude regarding the conflicting claims of these two mighty powers, partly from his judgment of the ecclesiastical and in particular the papal history of the past, partly from his deliberate discussion of the subject in the prologues to the fourth and the seventh books of the *Chronicle*. Unfortunately in neither can we obtain an absolutely clear-cut expression of opinion; we are led to the conclusion that Otto himself had no absolutely definite views but was swayed this way and that by the anomalies of his own double position. From the historical account it appears that, whenever either Church or State violates the moral considerations demanded by Otto under given circumstances, he ranges himself with its opponent.

In the society of his own time Otto found three distinctly marked circles. There were the monks, who were inclined to strip the clergy of all regalia and to limit them to their purely spiritual functions. This view Otto definitely rejects. In spite of his deeply grounded conviction of the transitory nature of all human affairs, and his praise of those pious men who renounced all earthly goods, he did not choose for himself the practical consequences: he returned from the monastery to the world. A second group was made up of the hierarchy of the secular clergy, who held the theory of the unconditional subordination of the State under the authority of the Church, in accordance with the views of Gregory VII. And finally there was the attitude taken by those who were friendly to the laity, that both Church and State were autonomously justified and that pope and emperor had each his own separate and proper sphere. Otto himself seems to waver between the last two. He expresses himself allegorically when he discusses the question and says that the world is ruled by "two swords." [354] His personal feeling, therefore, appears to be that the means of reconciling the

[354] See **IV**, Prol.

two is inexorable justice towards both — and this seems to be his political creed. Yet he feels called upon to justify the possession of temporal power by the Church on the basis of the presumed grant by Constantine. He adds however:

But you say that to the ecclesiastical rôle powers were given which it is neither seemly nor expedient for it to have, by reason of the sanctity of its office. In answer to this I confess I know no argument in which to take refuge, save that we know that these holy men of apostolic faith and merit — Sylvester, Gregory, Ulric, Boniface, Lambert, Gothard and many others — had these prerogatives. For, to speak as I think myself, I admit that I am absolutely ignorant whether the exaltation of His Church which is so clearly visible today pleases God more than its former humiliation pleased Him. Indeed that former state seems to have been better, this present condition more fortunate." [355]

This passage clearly indicates at once his personal viewpoint and the dilemma in which he was placed. In another part of his work he again treats of the same topic:

However, men are not lacking who say that God desired the State to be brought low, that he might exalt the Church. Forsooth no one questions the fact that the Church was exalted and enriched by the strength of the State and the favor of kings, and it is quite evident that the Church could not have so deeply humiliated the State until the State was enfeebled by its love of the priesthood, and so robbed of its strength that it was pierced and destroyed not only by the sword of the Church — that is, the spiritual weapon — but also by its own weapon, namely the material sword. To settle this point or even to discuss it is beyond our strength. However those priests seem altogether blameworthy who attempt to strike the State with its own sword — a sword which they themselves hold by the king's favor — unless perchance they think to imitate David who by God's grace first struck the Philistine and afterwards slew him with his own sword.[356]

It is perhaps significant that we already find in Otto the basic principles of the absolutism of the Hohenstaufen when he says in his letter to the emperor Frederick: "Kings alone, as being set above the laws and reserved to be weighed in the divine balances only, are not held in restraint by the laws of this world."

So while it is pointless to seek a single guiding thought in Otto's theories regarding the respective status and proper interrelation of Church and State, still Bernheim goes too far in stating that he is

[355] *Loc. cit.*, pp. 182-183 in Hofmeister's edition.
[356] VII, Prol.

through and through a mediating nature and that all his views rest on compromises.[357] Otto had seen in the weak reign of Conrad III how necessary was a strong political power, and accordingly he hailed with joy the beginnings of the rule of Frederick Barbarossa which seemed to promise an end of the internal confusion.[358]

In his philosophical and theological attempts and in their close dependence on cherished models, Otto affords a lively picture of the learning of the Middle Ages, gladly devoting itself to the new dialectic arts, yet for the most part working on the old traditional foundations. So we find that in dogmatic questions he always inclines toward the more orthodox views if they can be justified by reason in scholastic fashion; but that *no human authority has any weight with him in comparison with this scholastic method.*[359] To so great an extent did his studies at Paris influence his later work.[360] Throughout the *Chronicle,* but particularly in the concluding book (because of its subject matter), Otto shows great facility in quoting and applying the Scriptures.[361] That he was recognized as a brilliant student and interpreter of the Bible in his own day is evident from Rahewin's statement concerning his "knowledge of holy writ; in the interpretation of whose secret and hidden statements he excelled."[362]

The material used in theology had remained the same for centuries — Jerome, Augustine, Gregory, etc., — and individuality was shown less in actual novelties than in the selection from this full store of traditional theology. So we find that in general the works of theologians of the Middle Ages consist largely of *extracts,* often copied out from other books made up in the same way.

In the eighth book of the *Chronicle,* in which more than in all the others together Otto's theological views find fullest expression, the Bible forms his point of departure and is continually the foundation of the development of his thought. He often cites the

[357] Bernheim 47-51.

[358] For Otto's political and ecclesiastical views see Huber 143-154; Hashagen 72-97; Bernheim 24-51; Hofmeister 105-109 especially.

[359] For examples of this see VIII. 9 and IV. 18.

[360] Hofmeister (701) remarks that the standpoint which Otto took in the scholarly movement of his time is clear: "die Verbindung philosophischer und theologischer Betrachtungsweise, die vorsichtige Verwertung logischer Begriffe und Methoden für die Auseinanderlegung des Dogmas."

[361] *E.g.,* VIII. 9.

[362] *Gesta* 4. 14 (ed. Simson 250).

Scriptures, however, not from the Vulgate of Jerome (translated from the Hebrew) but from a text resting upon the Greek of the Septuagint.[363] Augustine is a guiding star and Otto never loses sight of him. Yet he is giving us in large measure his own reflections and conclusions, and this part of the work, written under the spiritual excitement of the times immediately preceding the Second Crusade, reveals something of the spirit of Dante and of Milton.[364]

The fact that Otto has no scruples — or but few — about introducing transcendental material into a historical work need not surprise us in a writer of his time. For in the Middle Ages the future life might be subjected to the categories of space and time. Moreover to him the eighth book was no purposeless appendix but the necessary finishing touch. He says:

I must now, I think, make answer to those who will perhaps attempt to belittle this labor of mine as without value, by claiming that I do not properly combine the deep and mystic proofs of the Scriptures with the historical accounts of so many successive misfortunes. In the first place, although I defend myself of this charge by the example of the blessed father Augustine, whom we have undertaken to imitate (he does the same thing in his book on *The City of God*), yet I must assail my critics with the darts of reason and authority. Is not day the more pleasing because it follows night, rest sweeter after toil, sleep after weariness, food after hunger? Why need I speak of the Heptateuch, of the book of the Kingdoms, of the Chronicles? The time would fail me for the telling if I should wish to run through all the pages of sacred Scripture — for example Ruth, Judith, Esdras, Esther, Maccabees — which, though they are full of mystical meaning and sacred wisdom, nevertheless portray divers woes of mortals and tempests of wars. I say nothing of the prophets who, amid the frequent miseries of changing events, sometimes set forth the mysterious prophecies of the Holy Spirit. I leave out of account the Apostles, who often inserted among the most profound secrets of the divine mysteries the impious deeds of this world. Even so Daniel, beginning with a historical narrative, concluded his work with a profound vision. That notable preacher, while discoursing excellently of the most secret miracles of God (being enabled to do this by the wisdom granted him beyond the other apostles) did not blush to mention, for our correction, at the outset of his letters, by way of reproof certain evil works of darkness. Even the disciple that was beloved by Christ, in concluding his narrative of the

[363] *E.g.*, VIII. 30 (ed. Hofmeister 444): *magni consilii . . . angelus;* VIII. 12 (ed. Hofmeister 409).

[364] So Büdinger (360): "Schon kündet sich in diesem 8 Buche etwas von dem Geiste an, aus welchem Dantes und Miltons Werke geboren wurden."

truth of the Gospel which he had begun with that lofty prologue, when he said, "Many other signs therefore did Jesus in the presence of his disciples which are not written in this book: but these are written," and so forth, added thereto a comparison of the Lord foreshadowing the state of the future life in the draught of fishes and in the strength of the net and in the sweetness of the food, saying, "Jesus manifested himself at the sea of Tiberias." So by placing at the very end of his book, in a place of honor, the narrative of this glorious incident, he made the entire compass of his preceding narrative a sort of introduction to his account of this incident. The Lord also, in the beginning "creating the heaven and the earth," produced matter that at first was invisible and without form and afterwards reduced it to order and brought it into the light. We do not think therefore that we are doing amiss if, after enumerating the miseries of this present life, we attempt, insofar as God permits, to treat of the eternal rest of the saints as of light after darkness.[365]

Moreover he is so impressed with the importance of what he is about to say in this concluding section of his *Chronicle* that he inserts within the book a separate preface to his discussion of the future life, in which he reveals the state of mind in which he undertakes this great task:

As I have been lulled by long quiet and was dropping off to sleep, because of manifold occupations, may the trumpet of salvation arouse me as I am about to speak of the final time. For who, even if he were sunk in the slumber of sloth, would not wake up after hearing this trump whereat even the dead arise? I confess that since my understanding had long been distracted by many matters, I felt that I was too little qualified — nay, was absolutely unfit — to discuss such lofty topics and so I placed my finger upon my lips, thinking it better to pass the evil days in silence than to argue rashly about great matters in perturbation of spirit. I know One Who said, "Be still and know." I know perturbation of spirit is always ignorant of a plan, whereas wisdom, the friend of calm, rejects burdensome tasks. While I never earn the privilege of avoiding these completely, at times nevertheless I seem to gain some relief, however slight, and they press upon me less importunately. Accordingly at this Easter season, resting not upon our own strength and might but upon the strength and might of Him "who died for our trespasses and was raised for our justification," let us undertake to speak of the resurrection of the dead and of the end of the world, zealously calling upon Him to give us grace that, being raised from the death of the soul, we may speak worthily of such great mysteries.[366]

[365] VIII, Prol. (ed. Hofmeister 392).
[366] VIII. 8, Preface (ed. Hofmeister 400).

It will be observed that the eschatology of the eighth book does fit in with the proper subject of the *Chronicle* in two respects:

(1) Otto wrote the *Chronicle* under the distinct apprehension of the near approach of the end of the world.

(2) Eschatology is deeply interwoven in the basal concepts of his philosophy of history: the evolution of the Two Cities is to find its culmination in the world to come.[367]

This final section of Otto's work deals in general with the three great subjects of Antichrist, the Resurrection and the end of the two cities. There are, however, two main divisions: first, the end of the world as the concluding act of history (*Interitus*); second, the end of the world as its final status (*Finis*).[368] These are taken up in this order. First the final drama of the cessation of history and its mersion into eternity through the instrumentality of the end of the world is portrayed in four acts:

(1) As Christ occupies the central position in history, even so in the center of the prelude to the universal catastrophe stands Antichrist (*Chronicle* VIII. 1-7).

(2) Next comes the actual end of the world, the collapse of the physical universe (7-9). Here we find that from the eighth chapter on Otto is proceeding on virtually independent views of his own.[369]

(3) This is followed by the resurrection of the dead (10-14).

(4) The picture is concluded by the Last Judgment (15-19).

Then follows the section on the final status of the world, the ultimate fate and condition of the Two Cities — Eternity.

(1) First with painstaking care Otto portrays the place of punishment (20-25).

(2) The work concludes with the glorification of the City of Christ, the eternal Jerusalem (26-34).

In a concluding chapter the author says (35):

Let it suffice to have said this much, in accordance with the capacity of our understanding, concerning the end of the City of Christ. Herein, to use the words of Dionysius, "Taking thought of the limitations of our

[367] So Schmidlin 447.
[368] The following outline of the 8th book is taken from Schmidlin.
[369] So Büdinger, 357-365; and see Schmidlin 454.

powers of speech, we have passed over certain matters, at the same time also honoring with silence the mystery which is above our powers." For "it is the glory of kings to conceal a matter," and so he who divulges mysteries disparages majesty. I am, of course, aware that great things ought to be spoken of in such a way that there shall always remain something to be investigated with care, lest if the whole matter be unfolded promiscuously it may appear of little value. Accordingly, though we devotedly offer to your love these matters which have been set forth, in however rude a style (not out of our own wisdom but in accordance with the teachings of the Scriptures), we do not bestow them upon those who are unwilling to receive or scornfully reject them. For as I have said above of Augustine, some matters are set down in his writings not as assertions but only on the basis of opinion and investigation, and the decision of a final judgment has been left to those who are wiser. It will be your task to supplement what has been said insufficiently, to correct what has been said imperfectly, to prune away the superfluous, and as, laden with sins, I struggle in this wide sea of the world, to aid me by the solace of your prayers.

And so, as Schmidlin has expressed it, "Scholasticism has merged into the mysticism of the seer, conflict into eternal peace, labor into rest, history into changeless, timeless Eternity." [370]

[370] Page 481. For Otto of Freising's theology, see especially Hashagen, 12-16 and 62 and following; Huber 122-132; Büdinger, 357-363, Dernheim 2-13; Hofmeister 701-727 (§ 10 Ottos Kenntnis der theologischen und philosophischen Literatur und der Bibel) and 747-768 (§ 12 Otto von Freising als Cistercienser. Sein Verhältnis zu Bernhard von Clairvaux); Schmidlin (Fulda 1905), 418-423 (cosmological views in the eighth book of the *Chronicle*) and in particular *Die Eschatologie Ottos von Freising* (Innsbruck 1905), 445-481, in Vol. 29 of the *Zeitschrift für katholische Theologie*; Nitsch 334-336.

BIBLIOGRAPHY

I. EDITIONS OF THE CHRONICLE:

(1) Iohannes Cuspinianus, Strasburg, 1515 (Beatus Rhenanus seems to have had some part in this edition).

(2) P. Pithoeus, Basel, 1569.

(3) Christianus Urstisius, Frankfort, 1585.

(4) Urstisius, Frankfort-on-the-Main, 1670 (Reprinted with corrections of typographical errors).

(5) B. Tissier, Paris, 1669 (In *Bibliothecae Patrum Cisterciensium* tomo VIII. Practically identical with (1) above).

(6) Roger Wilmans, Hanover, 1868 (In *Monumenta Germaniae Historica SS.* XX and also in *Scriptores rerum Germanicarum in usum scholarum* under the date 1867).

(7) Adolph Hofmeister, Hanover and Leipsic, 1912 (In *Scriptores rerum Germanicarum in usum scholarum*).

II. TRANSLATION OF THE CHRONICLE:

Horst Kohl, Berlin, 1881; second edition, Leipsic, 1894. A German translation of the letters to the Emperor and the Chancellor, the prologue of the first book, and books six and seven of the Chronicle. (In *Geschichtschreiber der deutschen Vorzeit*, 2. Gesamtausgabe, t. LVII; *saec.* XII, *t.* IX.)

III. SPECIAL ARTICLES:

Annales Austriae, ed. W. Wattenbach, *Continuatio Claustroneoburgensis Prima*: 54 lines on pp. 610-611 of *Monumenta Germaniae Historica Scriptorum Tomus*, IX (Hanover, 1851). The best source for Otto's life.

Bernheim, E. "Der Character Ottos von Freising und seiner Werke," in *Mittheilungen des Instituts für österreichische Geschichtsforschung*, VI (1885), pp. 1-51.

Büdinger, M. "Die Universalhistorie im Mittelalter, II," in *Denkschriften der Wiener Akademie der Wissenschaften, Phil.-hist. Classe*, XLVI (1900 [1898]), pp. 26-41.

Büdinger, M. "Die Entstehung des 8. Buches Ottos von Freising," in *Sitzungsberichte der Wiener Akademie der Wissenschaften, Phil.-hist. Classe*, XCVIII (1881), pp. 325-366.

Gaisser. *Charakteristik des Bischofs und Chronisten Otto von Freising,* Progr. d. Gymn. in Rottweil, Tübingen, 1860.

Giesebrecht, W. de. *Geschichte der deutschen Kaiserzeit,* IV (1875; ed. 2, 1877), pp. 394-399; VI (1895), pp. 291 *et seq.*

Groche, B. *Beiträge zur Geschichte einer Renaissance-bewegung bei deutschen Schriftstellern im XII. Jahrhundert,* dissert., Halle, 1909, pp. 38-48.

Gundlach, W. *Heldenlieder der deutschen Kaiserzeit,* III, Innsbruck, 1899, pp. 256 *et seq.*

Hashagen, Justus. *Otto von Freising als Geschichtsphilosoph und Kirchenpolitiker,* Leipzig, 1900. (Leipziger Studien aus dem Gebiet der Geschichte, VI, 2, pp. 1-101.) Also Dresden, 1900 (Teubner), pp. 1-34.

Hauck, A. *Kirchengeschichte Deutschlands,* IV (1903), pp. 477-485; Dritte und vierte (Doppel-) Auflage, Leipzig, 1913, Vierter Teil, pp. 206; 229, 4; 313, 4; 325; 342; 345; 454; 479; 500-510.

Histoire littéraire de la France, XIII (1814), pp. 268-285.

Hofmeister, A. "Zur Erhebung Eberhards I. auf den Salzburger Erzstuhl 1147," in *Zeitschrift für Kirchengeschichte,* XXIX (1908), pp. 71-78.

Hofmeister, A. "Studien über Otto von Freising," in *Neues Archiv der Gesellschaft für ältere deutsche Geschichtskunde,* XXXVII (1911-1912): "Der Bildungsgang Ottos von Freising," I, pp. 99-161; 633-768. A very important article.

Holder-Egger, O., in Herzog-Hauck, *Realencyclopädie für protestantische Theologie und Kirche,* 3. ed., XIV (1904), pp. 533-537.

Huber, B. *Otto von Freising, sein Character, seine Weltanschauung, sein Verhältnis zu seiner Zeit und seinen Zeitgenossen als ihr Geschichtschreiber,* Munich, 1847.

Lang, L. *Psychologische Characteristik Ottos von Freising,* Diss. inaug., Augsburg, 1852.

Lasch, Berthold. *Das Erwachen und die Entwickelung der historischen Kritik im Mittelalter* (vom VI-XII Jahrhundert), Breslau, 1887, pp. 37-38.

Mone, I. F. *Quellensammlung zur Badischen Landesgeschichte,* I (1848), "Einleitung," pp. 10-12.

Nitzsch, K. W. "Characteristik Ottos von Freising," in Sybels *Historische Zeitschrift*, III, pp. 334-360 (Munich, 1860). Part of an article entitled "Staufische Studien," pp. 322-409.

Ritter, Moriz. "Studien über die Entwicklung der Geschichtswissenschafte." Zweiter Artikel. "Die christlich-mittelalterliche Geschichtschreibung," in *Historische Zeitschrift*, 107 (1911), pp. 237-305.

Schmidlin, Josef. "Die Philosophie Ottos von Freising," in *Philosophisches Jahrbuch der Görres-Gesellschaft*, XVIII (Fulda, 1905), pp. 156-175; 312-323; 407-423.

Schmidlin, J. "Bischof Otto von Freising als Theologe," in *Katholik*, LXXXV, 3. Folge XXXII (1905), pp. 81-112; 161-182.

Schmidlin, J. "Die Eschatologie Ottos von Freising," in *Zeitschrift für katholische Theologie*, XXIX (1905), pp. 445-481.

Schmidlin, J. *Die geschichtsphilosophische und Kirchenpolitische Weltanschauung Ottos von Freising*, Freiburg i. B., 1906 (*Studien und Darstellungen aus dem Gebiete der Geschichte, im Auftrage der Görres-Gesellschaft*, herausgegeben von H. Grauert, IV, 2. 3).

Schmidlin, J. "Albert Hauoks Urteil über Otto von Freising," in *Historisches Jahrbuch*, XXVII (1906), pp. 316-322.

Simonsfeld, H. *Jahrbücher des deutschen Reiches unter Friedrich I*. I (1908), *passim*, but see in particular pp. 650 *et seq.*

Sorgenfrey, T. *Zur Characteristik des Otto von Freising als Geschichtschreiber*, Greiz, 1873.

Waitz, G. "Ueber die Entwicklung der deutschen Historiographie im Mittelalter" (Fortsetzung) 3, in *Zeitschrift für Geschichtswissenchaft* (ed. W. A. Schmidt) II (Berlin, 1844), pp. 110 *et seq.*

Wattenbach, W. in *Archiv für Kunde österreich. Geschichtsquellen*, XIV (1855), pp. 58 *et seq.*

Wattenbach, W. *Deutschlands Geschichtsquellen im Mittelalter*, 5th Edition (Berlin, 1885), I, pp. 2, 5; II, pp. 9, 241-254; 6th Edition (1893-4) I, pp. 2, 5; II, pp. 271-279, 279-284.

Wiedemann, Th. *Otto von Freysingen nach seinem Leben und Wirken*, Passau, 1849.

Wilmans, R. "Über die Chronik Ottos von Freisingen," in Pertz' *Archiv der Gesellschaft für ältere deutsche Geschichtskunde,* X (1851), pp. 131-173.

Wilmans, R. "Zur Geschichte der Handschriften von Ottos von Freisingen Chronik," in Pertz' *Archiv,* XI (1852), pp. 18-64.

Wilmans, R. "Ottos von Freisingen Verhältnis zu den Wittensbachern," in Pertz' *Archiv,* XI (1852), pp. 65-76.

Wyss, Georg von. *Geschichte der Historiographie in der Schweiz,* Zurich, 1895, pp. 62-64.

For a bibliography of Otto's *Gesta Friderici* see note 97.

THE TWO CITIES
A CHRONICLE OF UNIVERSAL HISTORY

DEDICATION

For His Majesty Frederick,[1] victorious, renowned and triumphant, emperor of the Romans, august forever, Otto, by the grace of God <bishop> of the church of Freising, prays for a continuance of the good fortune that now is his,[2] in Him that "giveth salvation unto kings."[3]

Your Imperial Majesty requested of my humble self that the book which several years ago by reason of the beclouded condition of the times I wrote on the vicissitudes of history be now transmitted to your Serene Highness.[4] I have therefore obeyed your command willingly and gladly, so much the more devotedly as I regard it as thoroughly in accord with your royal preëminence that you desire to know what was done in olden times by kings and emperors, and to know this not only for the better protection of the state by arms, but also for its better molding by laws and statutes. Even so that great king of the Persians, Ahasuerus or Artaxerxes,[5] although he had not attained to the knowledge of the true light through the worship of the one God, yet, realizing by reason of the nobility of his soul that this was of profit to royal grandeur, commanded that the yearbooks which had been written during his own reign or under his predecessors be examined,[6] and so he gained glory thereby, his purpose being that the innocent should not be punished as if he were guilty and that the guilty should not escape punishment as though he were blameless.

Furthermore, while no earthly personage is found who is not subject to the laws of the universe and kept under constraint by such subjection, kings alone, as being set above the laws and reserved to be weighed in the divine balances only, are not held in

[1] This letter was written, after March in the year 1157, to the emperor Frederick I, commonly known as Barbarossa (1152-1190). See Intro., § 1.
[2] Otto says *id quod est.*
[3] Ps. 144. 10.
[4] In 1146; see Intro., § 3.
[5] Artaxerxes II, Mnemon (405-362); see II. 20 below.
[6] Esther 6. 1; *cf.* 2. 23.

restraint by the laws of this world.[7] Whence also we have that
testimony of one who was both king and prophet: "Against thee
only have I sinned."[8] It is seemly therefore that a king, who has
not only been ennobled by the loftiness of his spirit but has also
been illumined by divine grace that he might know his Creator
should hold before his mind God, the King of Kings and Lord of
Lords, and that he should take all possible precautions not to fall
into His hands. For inasmuch as it is, according to the apostle,[9]
"a fearful thing" for any man "to fall into the hands of the living
God," yet for kings, who have over them none save Him whom they
need fear, it will be by so much the more fearful to fall into His
hands as they can sin with greater freedom than all others, according to that word of the wise man wherein he says: "Hear, ye
kings, and understand, learn, ye judges of the ends of the earth:
give ear, ye that have dominion over many peoples, and make your
boast over multitudes of nations, because your power was given
you by the Lord, and your strength by the Most High, who shall
search out your works, and shall make inquisition of your counsels.
Because, though ye were officers of his kingdom, ye did not judge
aright, neither kept ye the law of justice nor walked after the will
of God, awfully and swiftly shall he come upon you; because a
stern judgment shall befall them that be in high places."[10] But
you, most glorious Prince, are in deed The Peace Maker,[11] and are
rightly so called, since you have changed the night of mist and
rain into the delightful splendor of morning calm by preserving
for each man what is his, and have restored lovable peace to the
world. Therefore, since God — who was also the beginning [of all
this achievement] — bestowed upon you the power to persevere
therein by grace of divine mercy, you will not fall into the condemnation of this bitter sentence.

The knowledge of history, therefore, will be proper and advantageous to Your Excellency, for thereby, considering the deeds of
brave men and the strength and power of God, who changeth
monarchs and giveth thrones to whomsoever He will, and suffereth

[7] *Cf. Dig.* 1. 3. 31: *Princeps legibus solutus est. Cf.* also Intro., §1.

[8] Ps. 51.4.

[9] Heb. 10.31.

[10] Wisd. of Sol. 6. 1-5.

[11] *Cf.* Giesebrecht, *Gesch. d. Deu. Kaiserzeit,* 5. 99 and 6. 349; Wibald, Epp.
410; *Versus de Friderico,* N. Archiv 15. 394.

changes to come to pass,[12] you shall live ever in His fear, and, advancing in prosperity, shall reign through many circling years. Accordingly, let Your Nobility know that I wrote this history in bitterness of spirit, led thereto by the turbulence of that unsettled time which preceded your reign, and therefore I did not merely give events in their chronological order, but rather wove together, in the manner of a tragedy,[13] their sadder aspects, and so ended with a picture of unhappiness each and every division of the books even down to the seventh and the eighth. In the latter books the rest of souls and the double garment of the resurrection are shadowed forth.[14]

And so, if it shall please Your Majesty to commend to writing to be remembered by posterity the glorious sequence of your exploits, then, if you will arrange the main topics with the aid of the secretaries of Your Highness and transmit them to me,[15] I shall not be slow to prosecute this joyous task with joyful mind, if I have God's grace and if life attend me, expecting nothing as a reward save that Your Imperial Clemency shall be graciously minded to aid in its times of need the church which I serve.[16]

Regarding the expedition which you have planned against the arrogance of the Milanese,[17] I have heard of it with gladness for the honor of the empire and the exaltation of your own person, and have dutifully undertaken the task you have enjoined upon me regarding this matter, a task imposed on my lowly self. I have sent as bearers of these presents the venerable Abbot Raboto of St. Stephen's and our chaplain, Rahewin,[18] who took down this history from my lips, that they may by your grace make suitable response on our behalf concerning this matter.

To the friend of his heart, Rainald,[19] the noble Chancellor of the greatest prince among the princes of the earth, Otto, by the grace

---

[12] *Cf.* Prol., VII.

[13] *Cf.* below, Prol., I, VI. 31; *Gesta* 1. 47. The language is that of Rufinus in his translation of the Ecclesiastical History of Eusebius 1. 8. 4.

[14] *Cf. Augustine*, 22. 30 (end).

[15] See the letter of the emperor to Otto, *Gesta*, ed. de Simson, p. 1.

[16] At Freising.

[17] Announced by the emperor at Fulda, March 24, 1157, and solemnly undertaken by his nobles at Worms a week later; see H. Simonsfeld, *Jahr-bücher des deutschen Reichs unter Friedrich* I, 1. 522.

[18] See Intro., § 3 and *Gesta*, Prol., III, p. 162.

[19] Or Reginald.

of God bishop of the church of Freising, sends greeting and pledge of respectful allegiance.

"Since I believe," as Boethius says,[20] "that the greatest solace in life is to be found in handling and thoroughly learning all the teachings of philosophy," I devote myself to your noble character the more intimately and the more gladly because I know that you have labored zealously hitherto in the pursuit of this very study and that you are preëminently proficient in it.[21] Therefore I write with the more assurance to Your Industrious Highness, not as to a novice but as to a philosopher, regarding the book which I am sending to His Majesty the Emperor, praying that in regard to certain matters therein set down I may find you not an unfavorable but a kindly interpreter. For you know that all teaching consists of two things: avoidance and selection.[22] To begin therefore with that which comes first for those who are approaching philosophy, namely grammar, this study itself is the one which, in accordance with the training it gives, teaches us to select those things which are in harmony with our purpose and to avoid such matters as are a hindrance to our purpose. For example: by bidding us to compare expression with expression by fixed laws under like conditions, it teaches us to clear away and avoid such expressions as do not conform to those laws because they are barbarisms and solecisms. Logic also, the application of which has principally in view the teaching of syllogisms, by clarifying and training the judgment clears away and avoids the admixture of propositions useless for the formation of syllogisms, but selects the useful and arranges them properly. Wherefore, although sixteen combinations of propositions are found to exist, in the first figure, according to Aristotle, only four are discovered to be useful, twelve are found to be useless; in the second in like manner four are useful, twelve useless; in the third six are useful, ten useless. The geometrician also, by employing the *reductio ad absurdum* in the case of part of an incorrect diagram,[23] shows that such a figure is to be avoided, and proves by cogent reasoning that his own demonstration must be accepted. So also the art of the historians has certain things to clear away and to avoid and others to select and arrange properly; for it avoids lies and selects the truth. Therefore let not Your

---

20 *Cf. De consol. philos.* 3, Prose I, (ed. Peiper, Leipsic, 1871).

21 *Cf.* Simonsfeld 423.

22 The text says *fuga et electione.*

23 I translate *falsigraphi.*

Discreet Highness be offended or (as I have said before) interpret the matter in an unfavorable light in the hearing of the emperor, if it shall appear that in our history certain matters have been spoken in criticism of his predecessors or ancestors, that the truth may be held in esteem, inasmuch as it is better to fall into the hands of men than to abandon the function of a historian by covering up a loathsome sight by colors that conceal the truth.[24]

Next, I shall briefly explain the order in which this history proceeds, that, when this is known, the nature of the work may be the more readily apparent. That there were from the beginning of the world four principal kingdoms which stood out above all the rest, and that they are to endure unto the world's end, succeeding one another in accordance with the law of the universe, can be gathered in various ways, in particular from the vision of Daniel.[25] I have therefore set down the rulers of these kingdoms, listed in chronological sequence: first the Assyrians, next (omitting the Chaldeans, whom the writers of history do not deign to include among the others) the Medes and the Persians, finally the Greeks and the Romans, and I have recorded their names down to the present emperor, speaking of the other kingdoms only incidentally, to make manifest the fluctuations of events. I have also discoursed concerning the various orders of holy men, and have given a list of the kings who reigned in Laurentum, Latium and Alba Longa before the founding of the City and after the City was founded, and finally a catalogue of emperors and of the popes of Rome to the time of the present incumbents.[26] And so in the eighth book I have brought my work to a conclusion by speaking of the resurrection of the dead and of the end of The Two Cities. Moreover, I have shown how kingdom was supplanted by kingdom up to the time of the empire of the Romans, believing that the fulfilment of what is said of that empire — that it must be utterly destroyed by a stone cut out from a mountain — must be awaited until the end of the ages,[27] as Methodius states.[28] Farewell.

[24] Note Bishop Otto's lofty conception of the duty of a historian.

[25] Dan. 7; and see Intro., pp. 29-30.

[26] The text reads *qui inpresentiarum est.*

[27] Hofmeister points out that Otto previously thought differently with regard to this: see below, II. 13 *et seq*; VI. 36.

[28] Büdinger has shown that this cannot be referred to any specific passage; but, as Hofmeister points out, Otto had in mind what we read in Pseudo-Methodius (ed. E. Sackur, *Sibyllinische Texte und Forschungen*, Halle a. S., 1898) c. 10 *et seq.*, pp. 78 *et seq.*

BISHOP OTTO'S HISTORY OF THE TWO CITIES

HERE BEGINS THE PROLOGUE OF THE FIRST BOOK

In pondering long and often in my heart upon the changes and vicissitudes of temporal affairs and their varied and irregular issues, even as I hold that a wise man ought by no means to cleave to the things of time, so I find that it is by the faculty of reason alone that one must escape and find release from them. For it is the part of a wise man not to be whirled about after the manner of a revolving wheel, but through the stability of his powers to be firmly fashioned as a thing foursquare. Accordingly, since things are changeable and can never be at rest, what man in his right mind will deny that the wise man ought, as I have said, to depart from them to that city which stays at rest and abides to all eternity? This is the City of God, the heavenly Jerusalem, for which the children of God sigh while they are set in this land of sojourn, oppressed by the turmoil of the things of time as if they were oppressed by the Babylonian captivity. For, inasmuch as there are two cities — the one of time, the other of eternity; the one of the earth, earthy, the other of heaven, heavenly; the one of the devil, the other of Christ — ecclesiastical writers have declared that the former is Babylon, the latter Jerusalem.

But, whereas many of the Gentiles have written much regarding one of these cities, to hand down to posterity the great exploits of men of old (the many evidences of their merits, as they fancied), they have yet left to us the task of setting forth what, in the judgment of our writers, is rather the tale of human miseries. There are extant in this field [1] the famous works of Pompeius Trogus, Justin,[2] Cornelius [*i.e.*, Tacitus], Varro, Eusebius, Jerome, Orosius, Jordanes, and a great many others of our number,[3] as well as of their [3a] array, whom it would take too long to enumerate; in those writings

[1] On Otto's use of these works as sources, see Intro., § 4.
[2] He epitomized the work of Trogus.
[3] *I.e.*, Christian writers.
[3a] The word *their* refers to the Gentiles.

93

the discerning reader will be able to find not so much histories as
pitiful tragedies made up of mortal woes. We believe that this has
come to pass by what is surely a wise and proper dispensation of
the Creator, in order that, whereas men in their folly desire to
cleave to earthly and transitory things, they may be frightened
away from them by their own vicissitudes, if by nothing else, so
as to be directed by the wretchedness of this fleeting life from the
creature to a knowledge of the Creator. But we, set down as it
were at the end of time, do not so much read of the miseries of
mortals in the books of the writers named above as find them for
ourselves in consequence of the experiences of our own time. For,
to pass over other things, the empire of the Romans, which in
Daniel [4] is compared to iron on account of its sole lordship —
monarchy, the Greeks call it — over the whole world, a world subdued by war, has in consequence of so many fluctuations and
changes, particularly in our day, become, instead of the noblest
and the foremost, almost the last. So that, in the words of the poet,
scarcely

"a shadow of its mighty name remains." [5]

For being transferred from the City [6] to the Greeks,[7] from the
Greeks to the Franks, from the Franks to the Lombards, from the
Lombards again to the German Franks, that empire not only became decrepit and senile through lapse of time, but also, like a
once smooth pebble [8] that has been rolled this way and that by the
waters, contracted many a stain and developed many a defect. The
world's misery is exhibited, therefore, even in the case of the chief
power in the world, and Rome's fall foreshadows the dissolution of
the whole structure.

But what wonder if human power is changeable, seeing that
even mortal wisdom is prone to slip? We read that in Egypt there
was so great wisdom that, as Plato states, the Egyptians called
the philosophers of the Greeks childish and immature. Moses also,
the giver of the law, "with whom Jehovah spake as a man speaketh
unto his friend," and whom He filled with wisdom divine, was not
ashamed to be instructed in all the wisdom of Egypt. Did not that

4 Dan. 2. 40; *cf.* below, II. 13.
5 Lucan, Pharsalia 1. 135 (of Pompey).
6 *I.e.*, of course, Rome.
7 The Eastern Roman Empire.
8 *I.e.*, *glarea.*

great patriarch, appointed by God the father of nations, Abraham, a man trained in the learning of the Chaldeans and endowed with wisdom, did he not, when called by God, desert his former manner of life [*i.e.*, go to Egypt] and yet not lay aside his wisdom? And yet Babylon the great, not only renowned for wisdom, but also "the glory of kingdoms, the beauty of the Chaldeans' pride," has become, in the words of the prophecy of Isaiah, without hope of restoration, a shrine of owls, a house of serpents and of ostriches, the lurking-place of creeping things. Egypt too is said to be in large measure uninhabitable and impassable. The careful student of history will find that learning was transferred from Egypt to the Greeks, then to the Romans, and finally to the Gauls and the Spaniards. And so it is to be observed that all human power or learning had its origin in the East, but is coming to an end in the West,[9] that thereby the transitoriness and decay of all things human may be displayed. This, by God's grace, we shall show more fully in what follows.[10]

Since, then, the changeable nature of the world is proved by this and like evidence, I thought it necessary, my dear brother Isingrim,[11] in response to your request, to compose a history whereby through God's favor I might display the miseries of the citizens of Babylon and also the glory of the kingdom of Christ to which the citizens of Jerusalem are to look forward with hope, and of which they are to have a foretaste even in this life. I have undertaken therefore to bring down as far as our own time, according to the ability that God has given me, the record of the conflicts and miseries of the one city, Babylon; and furthermore, not to be silent concerning our hopes regarding that other city, so far as I can gather hints from the Scriptures, but to make mention also of its citizens who are now sojourning in the worldly city. In this work I follow most of all those illustrious lights of the Church, Augustine and Orosius,[12] and have planned to draw from their fountains what is pertinent to my theme and my purpose. The one of these has dis-

---

[9] Hashagen, p. 30, compares this passage with Hugo of St. Victor, *De vanitate mundi* 2 (end).

[10] Prol., V; *cf.* VII. 35.

[11] A monk who was promoted in 1145 to be Abbot of the monastery of Ottenbeuren in Swabia. *Cf. Isingrim, der Freund Ottos von Freising,* F. L. Baumann, Neues Archiv 6 (1881), 600-602.

[12] See Intro., § 4.

coursed most keenly and eloquently [13] on the origin and the progress of the glorious City of God and its ordained limits, setting forth how it has ever spread among the citizens of the world, and showing which of its citizens or princes stood forth preëminent in the various epochs of the princes or citizens of the world. The other, in answer to those who, uttering vain babblings,[14] preferred the former times to Christian times, has composed a very valuable history of the fluctuations and wretched issues of human greatness, the wars and the hazards of wars, and the shifting of thrones, from the foundation of the world down to his own time. Following in their steps I have undertaken to speak of the Two Cities in such a way that we shall not lose the thread of history, that the devout reader may observe what is to be avoided in mundane affairs by reason of the countless miseries wrought by their unstable character, and that the studious and painstaking investigator may find a record of past happenings free from all obscurity.

Nor do I think that I shall be justly criticized if, coming after such great men — men so wise and so eloquent — I shall presume in spite of my ignorance to write, since I have both epitomized those things of which they themselves spoke profusely and at length, and have detailed, in however rude a style, the deeds which have been performed by citizens of the world since their time, whether to the advantage of the Church of God or to its hurt. Nor shall I believe that I ought to be assailed by that verse in which the writer of satire says:

"All of us, taught or untaught, are everywhere writers of poems." [15]

For it is not because of indiscretion or frivolity, but out of devotion, which always knows how to excuse ignorance, that I, though I am without proper training, have ventured to undertake so arduous a task. Nor can anyone rightfully accuse me of falsehood in matters which — compared with the customs of the present time — will appear incredible, since down to the days still fresh in our memory I have recorded nothing save what I found in the writings of trustworthy men, and then only a few instances out of many. For I should never hold the view that these men are to be held in contempt if certain of them have preserved in their writings the

---

[13] *Cf.* for example, Augustine 18. 1; 1. 35; 10. 32 (end); 11. 1.

[14] Orosius, *Adversus Paganos* 1, Prol., 9.

[15] Horace, *Epistles* 2. 1. 117.

apostolic simplicity, for, as overshrewd subtlety sometimes kindles error, so a devout rusticity is ever the friend of truth.

As we are about to speak, then, concerning the sorrow-burdened insecurity of the one city and the blessed permanence of the other, let us call upon God, who endures with patience the turbulence and confusion of this world, and by the vision of himself augments and glorifies the joyous peace of that other city, to the end that by His aid we may be able to say the things which are pleasing to Him.

The first book extends to Arbaces and the transfer of the Babylonian sovereignty to the Medes, and the beginning of the Roman power.

The second extends to the civil war of the Romans, fought with Julius and Pompey as leaders, to the death of Cæsar, and to our Lord's nativity.

The third extends to Constantine and the times of the Christian Empire, and the transfer of sovereignty to the Greeks.

The fourth extends to Odovacar and the invasion of the kingdom by the Rugians.

The fifth extends to Charles and the transfer of sovereignty to the Franks, and the division of the kingdom and the empire under his descendants.

The sixth extends to Henry the Fourth and the schism between the kingly power and the priestly power; it includes the anathema pronounced against the emperor, the expulsion of Pope Gregory VII from the City, and his death at Salerno.

The seventh extends to the uprising of the Roman people and the ninth year of King Conrad.

The eighth is concerned with Antichrist and the resurrection of of the dead and the end of the Two Cities.

HERE BEGIN THE CHAPTERS OF THE FIRST BOOK

1. Preface and the division of the world.

2. How Adam, when expelled from Paradise, begat citizens of both cities, and at what time, according to Josephus, men began to fall away from the laws of their fathers and giants came into being.

3. Of the Flood, as described by Josephus, and the testimonies of the pagans regarding the long life of the Fathers of old; the number of years according to the various narratives; and the heads of families from Adam to Noah.

4. How, after the Flood, the human race was multiplied by the sons of Noah, and in what lands they first began to be dispersed. Of the tower of Babel also and the Confusion of Tongues; the testimony of the Sibyl, moreover, concerning all this; another computation from Noah down to the Confusion of Tongues.

5. A different computation from the Confusion of Tongues to Ninus and Abraham and the beginning of the history.

6. Of the fact that Ninus was the first to take up arms and that, according to the testimony of most writers, men were farmers at that time, and that Ninus founded Nineveh and killed Zoroaster.

7. Of the birth of Abraham and his going out from the land of the Chaldeans, and of the death of Ninus.

8. Of the sovereignty of Semiramis and her founding of the city of Babylon. Also the tradition of the people of Trèves regarding the origin of their own city, and of the death of Semiramis and the beginning of the reign of her son Ninias [*i.e.*, Ninus].

9. Of the dwelling of Abraham with his nephew Lot in the land of Canaan, and of the destruction of the people of Sodom.

10. How Abraham received the sign of circumcision, and in the time of what rulers he begat two sons that were to be citizens of the two cities, and again how Isaac begat two sons as a type of those to come.

11. In the time of what rulers Abraham died, and when the promise was made to his son and to his grandson. Of the laws given to Greece under Phoroneus; of Pheius [*i.e.*, Phegius] and Io the daughter of Inachus.

12.   Of the battle between the Telcisces, the Caratasi, Phoroneus and the Pharphasii, and how people began to live on the island of Rhodes.

13.   Of the flood of Ogyges and the appearance of Minerva, and in the time of what rulers Isaac died.

14.   In the time of what rulers there was a famine in Egypt under Joseph, and the testimonies of the pagans who afford evidence concerning Joseph.

15.   Of the idol Serapis, whence it originated.

16.   Of Argus, from whom the Argives are descended. At what time Jacob died. Of the first bringing of seeds to Greece. Of the death of Joseph and the birth of Moses, and in the time of what rulers this occurred. Of Prometheus and Atlas, and Mercury the grandson of Atlas.

17.   Of the flood of Deucalion and the wasting away of Egypt. Of Bacchus, who is called also Father Liber, and of the origin of Athens.

18.   In the time of what rulers Moses led the children of Israel out of Egypt, and the testimony of Pompeius, Justin and Cornelius — pagan writers — concerning this achievement.

19.   Of Danaüs, of Perseus, and of various abominations of the Gentiles by reason of which one should flee from Babylon and take refuge with our citizens.

20.   For how many years Moses was the leader of the people of God, and at what age he died and left the leadership of the people to Jesus [i.e., Joshua], that he might be a type of the second Jesus, and that it was not without reason that the world then seethed with new and unheard of crimes.

21.   Of the war of the Cretans and the Athenians, and of the Minotaur, and how the fable of the centaurs originated.

22.   Of Vesores [i.e., Sesostris], king of Egypt, and the Scythians, and of the dominion of the Scythians in Asia.

23.   Of the origin of the Amazons and their rule : how they founded Ephesus and the temple of Diana in it, and why they were called Amazons.

24.   In the time of what rulers Jesus [i.e., Joshua] died. Of the Judges who succeeded him. Of Cadmus and the religious teachers. Of the kingdom of Mycenae and of the kingdom of Laurentum in Italy, and of the nymph Carmentis.

25.   Of the rape of Helen and the overthrow of Troy and the be-

ginning of the race of the Romans and that of the Franks, and of the founding of Padua. Of Samson and Hercules and the Golden Age in Italy.

26. Of the beginning of the iron ages under Aeneas and Turnus. Of the wanderings of Ulysses, and the fabulous deeds of Diomedes and likewise of Ulysses. That the statements made concerning Ulysses and Diomedes are reasonable, as is borne out by the writings and experiences of the saints.

27. Of the death of Aeneas and the reign of Silvius. Of the end of the kingdom of the Sicyonians under the judge Eli, and how the Romans and the Greeks began to have kindred customs and languages and became accustomed to call other nations barbarians.

28. Of Samuel and Saul, and of Codrus, the king of the Athenians. The names also of the Judges from Moses to Samuel.

29. Of the times of the Kings and of the Prophets. Of David and Solomon and his son Rehoboam. How under Rehoboam the kingdom was rent in twain in consequence of the sins of his father Solomon and destined soon to be brought to desolation. Of the power of Elijah and Elisha.

30. Of the kings of the Albans to Romulus, and of the Aventine Mount.

31. Of the transfer of the Babylonian kingdom to the Medes.

32. Outcry against Babylon.

33. The names of the kings of the Assyrians from Belus to Sardanapalus.

HERE END THE CHAPTERS OF THE FIRST BOOK

HERE BEGIN THE CHAPTERS OF THE SECOND BOOK

1. Of the kings of the Medes, and in the time of what kings of Judah and of Israel they lived. Of the Chaldeans and of Cyrus. The names of the kings of the Medes.

2. Of Proca and Amulius, and of the genesis of Remus and Romulus.

3. Of the founding of the City of Rome; and of the murder, by Romulus, of his grandfather and his brother, and of the rape of the Sabine women.

4. Of Hosea and Isaiah and the prophecy of the Sibyl.

5. Of Thales, one of the seven wise men, and of the captivity of the ten tribes. Of Phalaris, the Sicilian tyrant.

6. How and by whom the City of Rome was begun. Of Numa. Of the death of Isaiah and of the Samian Sibyl. Of Tullus Hostilius and Ancus Marcius, kings of the Romans.

7. Of the captivity of Judah under T. Priscus, king of the Romans, and of the prophecy of Jeremiah, and of the six other wise men.

8. Of the philosophers, especially Pythagoras, Socrates, Plato and Aristotle.

9. Of Tarquinius Superbus and the violence done to Lucretia.

10. Of the time of the consuls and the expulsion of the kings, and of the zeal of Brutus, the first consul, and the liberation of the City of Rome by Mucius and Delia [*i.e.*, Cloelia].

11. How Babylon was captured by Cyrus. Concerning its site. Of the death of Croesus also.

12. Of the prophecy of Ezekiel, Daniel and Habakkuk.

13. Of the four principal kingdoms which Daniel names in his interpretation of Nebuchadnezzar's dream.

14. How Queen Tomyris killed Cyrus. Lamentation over this and a brief epilogue in praise of Cyrus.

15. Of Cambyses, the son of Cyrus, and the new Babylon founded by him.

16. Of the Magi and Darius, and the complete liberation of the Romans. Of the prophecy of Haggai, Zechariah, Malachi and Esdras. Of the misfortune of Darius in his war with the Athenians, and of his death.

17. Of the misfortune of Xerxes, the son of Darius, who was defeated first by Leonidas, afterwards by the Athenians, and finally was slain by his prefect Artabanus.

18. Of the prodigies seen in the city of Rome, the pestilence and the civil strife that followed in consequence, and of the victory of Q. Cincinnatus Rusticus.

19. Of the wars of various states and especially of the subjugation of the Athenians by the kings of the Persians; of the death of Socrates and the end of Darius, king of the Persians, and of the exile of Dionysius the Sicilian.

20. How the two sons of Darius fought for the throne and how Artaxerxes (under whom the events related in Esther are believed to have occurred) obtained the kingdom upon his brother's death. Of the earthquake and the eruption of Ætna. Of the city of Atlantis and a pestilence among the Athenians.

21. What havoc the Gauls inflicted upon the Romans, and how they withdrew upon receiving money from them.

22. The overthrow of the Lacedaemonians and the rehabilitation of the Athenians under Conon through the agency of Artaxerxes. Of the victory of the Romans and the cavernous opening which M. Curtius, a soldier, closed in an unheard-of fashion, and of the victory over the Gauls.

23. That the Carthaginians and the Romans ratified a treaty through ambassadors, and how a hail of stones actually showered the earth with rocks. Of Artaxerxes, who is also called Ochus, and how he shut up the Jews [in Hyrcania].

24. The beginning of the sovereignty of the Greeks; how Philip by his wisdom and his might made the states of Greece subject to himself, and how he trained his son, Alexander, and what fate he himself met at the last.

25. The reign of Alexander the Great. The end of the kingdom of the Persians and the number of its kings, and the marvellous things which Alexander did and saw. His own end. Outcry, inspired by events, against the cycle of change.

26. Of the associates of Alexander: how they divided the world, and how they killed Olympias, the mother of Alexander, together with her son Hercules, and perished themselves by wounds dealt by each others' hands. Of the Maccabees.

27. That Rome, after the time of Alexander, began to grow as though freed from a guardian.

28. A retrogression, to show how Rome in the days of Alexander, having suffered indignity at the hands of neighboring tribes, did not observe a treaty but renewed the war under the consul Papirius.

29. That Rome after the death of Alexander, as though now secure in her own might, conquered her enemies by the use of wisdom and craft, but was straightway smitten by a pestilence.

30. Of divers vicissitudes of the Romans and of various disasters suffered by them.

31. Of the Tarentines. Of the war waged between Pyrrhus and the Romans. Of the testimony of the Romans themselves to the ability of Pyrrhus, and of the fact that the Tarentines, after his death, sought the aid of the Carthaginians.

32. Of the Carthaginians, and how, on account of the Tarentines, they broke the treaty which they had made with the Romans.

33. The beginning of the Punic War. Of the death of the consul Cornelius and the victory of the Romans.

34. Of the consul Regulus and the serpent which he slew. Of his victory, and how he was at last defeated with great loss and taken captive. How, when he was sent to Rome, he argued against the return of the captives and so was put to death upon his return to Carthage. The testimony of Tullius to his valor and patience. Of the end of the First Punic War, the victory of the Romans, and the closing of the temple of Janus.

35. Of the overflowing of the Tiber and the burning of the City. Of the Transalpine Gauls and the beginning of the Second Punic War.

36. Of the death of Hamilcar, and how his son Hannibal defeated the Romans in various battles so decisively that they even thought of changing their seat of government. Furthermore, how he was driven away from the City by storms. Of the death of the Scipios and the capture of Capua.

37. How Scipio, having been made proconsul, defeated the Carthaginians; how Hannibal killed the consuls Marcellus and Crispinus, but finally, having lost his brother Hasdrubal, retreated to Bruttium.

38. Again of a victory of Scipio and likewise of a victory of Hannibal, and of his return to his native land. Of the final battle between the Romans and the Carthaginians. How Scipio returned, having Terence with him in his retinue, and was received in triumph, and how the Second Punic War was brought to an end.

39. Of the portents which preceded these disasters. Of the destruction of Tarentum. Of the victory of the Macedonians and the Lacedaemonians.

40. Of the defeat of the barbarians by the Romans and the subjugation of King Philip. How Antiochus, to whom Hannibal had fled, was vanquished and begged for peace. Of the death of Hannibal and of Scipio, and the eulogies of Scipio by Tullius and Seneca.

41. Of the site of Carthage, of the Third Punic War, and of the destruction of Carthage. How Scipio divided the kingdom of Numidia.

42. Another calculation of the times in which the Maccabees lived.

43. The overthrow of Corinth. The destruction of Numantia, and a brief digression.

44. Of the Jugurthine War and the various vicissitudes of the Romans in wars with the Cimbri, the Gauls and the Germans. Of the internal troubles in the time of Sulla and of Catiline, and of the Macedonian War. Of the bequest of Asia Minor to the Romans.

45. The stubborn war waged with Mithridates, terminated finally by his defeat. What end the aforesaid king made of his life, both on account of this disaster and because his son was plotting to depose him.

46. That the Romans sent to the East Pompey, who, after conquering the entire Orient, polluted even the temple of the Lord, and having taken Aristobulus captive and cast him into chains, handed over the priesthood to his brother.

47. How and under what rulers of the world Israel lived after the return from Babylon down to this time. Of Herod the alien.

48. Of the victory of Julius Caesar and how he made war against his own citizens when he was not received by them, and broke into the treasury.

49. Of the death of Crassus and the burning of the City. Of the civil war of the Romans, the victory of Caesar and the death of Pompey.

50. How Caesar turned his arms against the Egyptians and gave that kingdom to Cleopatra, and then, coming back to Rome, punished the adherents of Pompey. Of the death of Cato. That Caesar obtained the sole rule and received Tullius and, by his intercession, M. Marcellus into favor, and how he was himself finally murdered with the connivance of the senate.

51. Outcry against the vicissitudes of human events, and the conclusion of the second book.

THE CHAPTERS OF THE THIRD BOOK

1. How Octavian, at first concealing his grief at the death of his uncle, afterwards dealt with his assassins. Of his judgments rendered at Rome. Of his many victories over Antony and Cleopatra, and what end Antony and Cleopatra met.

2. Digression: how the Greeks ruled the Orient from Alexander down to this time, and in what order patriarchal sees came into

existence. The number of the Greek kings, and the abundance at Rome resulting from the subjugation of Alexandria.

3.   How Caesar, having put an end to the sovereignty of the Greeks and having conquered Alexandria together with all Asia, was entitled Augustus. Of his victory in Spain and the closing of the temple of Janus. How he subdued various provinces through the instrumentality of Claudius Drusus. Of the loss of the legions in Germany by Varus.

4.   How, while Augustus tarried in Spain, the entire East voluntarily offered to surrender; how the Parthians, asking for peace, sent back the standards which had been taken from Crassus; and how, after the entire world had been set in order, the temple of Janus was closed. Of the humility of Augustus.

5.   How the census was imposed upon the Jews, as upon all other peoples, under Quirinius, and of Judas of Galilee.

6.   Of the Lord's incarnation, and how those things which took place under Augustus foreshadow Christ's kingdom. The beginning of our reckoning of history from the Lord's incarnation.

7.   How cruel a crime Herod perpetrated upon those of like age with Christ, and what manner of death he suffered on account of this, according to Josephus. Of Archelaus.

8.   Of the famine in the city of Rome and of the opening of the temple of Janus by reason of the uprising of the Dacians and of the Athenians.

9.   Of the death of Augustus and the reign of Tiberius, and Tiberius's triumph over the Germans through the instrumentality of Germanicus the son of Drusus. Of a case of adultery perpetrated craftily by a certain person, and how it was punished by Caesar.

10.   Of the baptism and preaching of John, and afterwards, of the baptism and preaching of the Lord himself. Of John's death. The testimony of Josephus concerning this, and likewise his testimony concerning the Lord.

11.   Of the Lord's passion; what Tiberius decreed at Rome regarding him when he heard of the Lord's miracles; how he dealt with the senate when it opposed him, and what sufferings he inflicted upon the Jews. Of the passion of Stephen and the sufferings of the Jews.

12.   Of the death of Tiberius and the succession of Gaius Caligula; how Gaius persecuted the Jews and, despising Philo, their am-

bassador, profaned the temple. Of the end of Pilate. Of Caesar's victory; of his many abominations and of his own death.

13. Of Tiberius Claudius: that there was a famine in Judea in his reign; that James was killed and Peter placed in chains at the same time. Of the death of Herod the Younger and of Theudas.

14. Of the scattering of the apostles among all nations. Of Peter and Simon Magus. Of Mark the Evangelist and the disciples sent by Peter into the world. Of the victory of Claudius and the uprising of the Jewish people. Of their expulsion from the City and the uprising of the Roman people; of the murder of senators and soldiers. Of the death of Claudius.

15. Of the sinful life of Nero and the persecution directed by him against our people. Of the Egyptian false prophet. Of the death of James and of the writings of the apostles.

16. Of the passion of Peter and Paul, the weakening of the Roman Empire, and the death of Nero.

17. Of the civil discord in the City, the captivity of Josephus, and the reign of Vespasian.

18. Of the destruction of Jerusalem and the captivity of the Jewish people. The statements of Josephus concerning these matters. That Titus and Vespasian because of these achievements were hailed, each of them, as "Imperator," and were received at Rome with a triumph. Of the closing of the temple of Janus and the increase of the Roman Empire. Of an earthquake and a pestilence. Of the death of both emperors, and of the amphitheater.

19. Of the persecution of Domitian, directed against his own people and ours. Of Clement, the successor of Peter. That Domitian sent the apostle John into exile and had the descendants of David sought out. Of his death and of the succession of Nerva, under whom John was recalled from exile.

20. Of Trajan and his victories, and the persecution directed against our people. Of Nero's golden house and the uprising of the Jews. Of the priests of Christ who lived at this time. Of the death of John the Apostle, and the heresies which were then spreading.

21. Of the gentleness and the deeds of Aelius Hadrian, and of the priests who were considered illustrious at that time.

22. Of the heresies and of the citizens of Christ who opposed them. A copy of a letter of Hadrian written in behalf of the Christians.

23. Of the reign of Antoninus, surnamed Pius, and the heresies

that arose in his time. Of the priests and the teachers of Christ who opposed the heresies. A letter also of the emperor in behalf of our people.

24. Of the reign of Antoninus Verus in conjunction with Aurelius Commodus, and of their wars; of our citizens and the terrible persecution, and how the emperor conquered the Germans through the instrumentality of the Christians.

25. Of the reign of Commodus, his lewdness, and his heresies. Of the conflagration at Rome caused by lightning and fire.

26. Of the death of Commodus and the succession of Helvius, who is also called Pertinax, and of his death.

27. Of the reign of Severus, his persecution of our people, and his war against other nations. Of the priests and Fathers of the Church who took their stand in defense of the house of God at that time, and of the controversy which arose between the pope and the eastern bishops concerning the calculation of Easter. Of Judas and Origen. Of the victory of Severus.

28. Of the death of Severus and the succession of Caracalla, and likewise of his death.

29. Of the reign of Marcus Aurelius and his death; of the Roman popes in each period.

30. Of the principate of Aurelius Alexander and his victory. Of the martyrs who suffered under him, of the popes, and of the death of Aurelius.

31. Of the reign of Maximus and his persecution of our people, and of his death.

32. Of the reign of Gordian; the Roman priests and ecclesiastical writers; and of the end of Gordian.

33. Of the reign of Philip, the Christian [emperor], and of his humility.

34. Of the death of Philip and the succession of Decius, and of his persecution of our people.

35. Of the slaying of Decius and the reign of Gallus and Volusianus, and of the death of Origen. Of the question which arose between Cornelius and Cyprian. Of the popes and other priests. Of the passion of Lawrence and the pestilence in the City of Rome.

36. Of the death of Gallus and of Volusianus and the papacy of Sixtus.

37. Of the reign of Valerianus and Gallienus and their persecution of our people, and of the passion of Sixtus. Of the captivity

of Valerianus and the influx of various nations to the detriment of the Roman Empire, and of internal dissensions. Of the death of Gallienus, of the priests of Christ, and of the heretic Manes, leader of the Manichaeans.

38. Of the principate of Claudius, of his triumph, and of his death.

39. Of the reign of Aurelian and his many triumphs, of the city of Rome, which he enlarged, and of that city which he founded in Gaul and named after himself. Of his persecution of our people and of his death.

40. Of the reign of Tacitus and of his death.

41. Of the reign of Probus, his victory and his death.

42. Of the reign of Carus and the wars which he waged in the East, and of his death.

43. Of the reign of Diocletian and his victories; how he chose Maximian as his colleague in the government, and how he persecuted the Christians more than all those who had preceded him; who suffered during his time; of the triumph of Constantine [*i.e.*, Constantius]; how Diocletian and Maximian resigned their royal authority.

44. How Galerius and Constantine divided the empire, and how Constantius upon his death left Constantine as emperor in Gaul.

45. The end of the third book, and a recapitulation of the ten persecutions.

THE CHAPTERS OF THE FOURTH BOOK

1. Of the killing of Maximian and the death of Galerius; of the tyranny of Maximin, Licinius and especially Maxentius, the son of Maximian; how Constantine, in obedience to a vision vouchsafed to him, entered the City after Maxentius was drowned, had the cross set up where the triumphs had been celebrated, and was himself baptized by Sylvester.

2. How Constantine himself and Licinius wrote in behalf of the Church, and how Maximin too did this, but insincerely, and afterwards, being defeated in battle, Maximin died after writing again in behalf of the Christians. Of the end of Licinius also, the husband of Constantine's sister, and, further, of the deaths of Crispus and Licinius, his nephews.[16]

16 Crispus was his son, Licinius his nephew.

3. Of the sole rule of Constantine and the restoration of peace to the churches, and of the bestowal of authority upon the Church — as the Romans claim. Of the transfer of the seat of empire to Byzantium, and the statements of various authorities in regard to this matter.

4. A brief summary from Adam down to this time, concerning the exaltation of the City of God.

5. Of the exaltation of the city of Constantinople. Of the Arian heresy and the Council of Nicaea. Of Paul and Anthony, the first hermits, and the discovery of the Holy Cross. Of the conversion of the Indians and the Hiberi, and of the death of Constantine.

6. Of the reign of the sons of Constantine; how Constantius fell under the power of the Arian heresy. Of the death of Arius, and the priesthood of Athanasius.

7. Of the death of Constantine and the trials of Athanasius.

8. Of the expulsion of Liberius the pope. Of Victorinus and Donatus. Of other renowned priests, and of the barbarity of the persecution.

9. Of the death of Constans and the vengeance exacted by his brother Constantius on account of it. Of the apostasy of Julian and the death of Constantius.

10. Of the wily persecution of Julian. Of the citizens of Christ who manfully resisted him, and how and where Julian was finally overcome.

11. Of the reign of Jovian, the most Christian emperor, and his orthodoxy, and how and where he finally died.

12. Of the reign of Valentinian and of his activity under Julian; of his brother Valens.

13. Of his son Gratian; of Ambrose and the synod of Illyricum.

14. Of the death of Athanasius. Of the Fathers of Egypt, and of the episcopate of Moses. Of the error of Valens. Of the victory and death of Valentinian.

15. Of the reign of Valens and the sons of Valentinian. Of the persecution set in motion by him, and of the victory of Gratian.

16. Of the Goths and the Huns; how the Goths, being made Arians by Valens, afterwards burned him to death.

17. Of the reign of Gratian and Valentinian after the death of their uncle, and of the elevation of Theodosius to the throne [of the East] by Gratian. Of the second synod, held under Damasus. Of

the death of Athalaric, the murder of Valens, and the expulsion of Valentinian.

18. Of the reign of Theodosius and the peace of the Church. Of the priests of Christ. Of his triumphs and his humility, and of his death.

19. Of the reign of Honorius and Arcadius. Of the monk Dirimachius [*i.e.*, Telemachus]. Also of John Chrysostom, of Theophilus and Epiphanius. Further, of the passing of Martin and Ambrose.

20. Of the rebellion of the Goths and the treachery of Rufinus and Gildo; of the fate of Mascezel and the death of Arcadius.

21. Of the reign of Honorius. Of the sedition of the Goths and their invasion of the city of Rome, and their settling in Gaul.

22. Of the deeds of Honorius in Africa. Of the discovery of Stephen, the first martyr. Of the death of Jerome. Of the popes. Of the peace between Augustus and the Goths, and of his death.

23. Of the reign of Theodosius the Younger and of his merits; of the third synod; of the wars which he waged through his generals.

24. Of Valentinian Augustus, the Visogoths, and the Ostrogoths. Of the rivalry between Aetius and Boniface; of the invasion of Africa by the Vandals, and the death of Augustine.

25. Of the earthquake at Constantinople and at Rome; of the beginning of the tyranny of Attila, and of the death of Theodosius.

26. Of the reign of Marcian and Valentinian. Of the fourth synod. Of the tyranny of Attila and the battle between him and the Romans and the Goths.

27. Of the overthrow of Aquileia [by Attila], and of his advance to Ticinum [Pavia], until he turned back in response to the plea of Pope Leo.

28. Of the death of Aetius and Valentinian Augustus, and the invasion of the city of Rome by the Vandals. Of Bishop Paulinus and the death of Attila, and of the emperor Marcian.

29. Of the reign of Leo in the East and the confusion of the Roman Empire in the West. Of the death of Leo.

30. Of the reign of Zeno in the East. Of Romulus Augustulus and the invasion of the city of Rome under Odovacar. Of that man of God, Severinus.

31. Lamentations; and a brief summary of the Roman Empire.

32. How, whence, or by what means the Franks came into Gaul
and began to reign there, after ejecting the Romans.
33. Conclusion of the fourth book.

THE CHAPTERS OF THE FIFTH BOOK

1. How Theodoric, king of the Goths, being sent by Zeno into
Italy, killed Odovacar, and how, living like a tyrant himself, he
cast Boethius into prison; and how he strengthened his kingdom
in its relations with neighboring kings.
2. Of Zeno's death and the succession of Anastasius. Of the
schism in the Roman Church, the exile of the bishops of Africa, and
the death of Anastasius and Clovis.
3. Of the reign of Justin and the recall of the bishops from exile.
Of the persecution by Theodoric, in which Pope John, Symmachus,
and Boethius were put to death. Of the death of the tyrant and
the vision shown in consequence of it, and of the death of Justin.
4. Of the reign of Justinian, his many notable deeds of piety, and
his many triumphs. Of the famous men who lived under him. Of
the tribe of the Lombards, the exaltation of the empire, and his
own death.
5. Of the reign of Justin and of his good works. Of the manner
of dress of the king of the Indians. Of the many victories won
through Narses, the entrance of the Lombards into Italy, and the
death of Augustus.
6. Of the reign of Tiberius Constantine and his giving of alms.
Of the money which he found, and of the Persians whom he conquered through Maurice. Of Gregory, then archdeacon, and of the
death of the emperor.
7. Of the reign of Maurice and of his persecution of the blessed
Gregory, then Pope. Of the man of God Columban and of his
disciples. Of the vision and the experiences of Maurice, and of
his end.
8. Of the reign of Phocas and the passing of the blessed Gregory.
Of the two Bonifaces who came after him, and of Chosroës, king
of the Persians, and of the death of Phocas.
9. Of the reign of Heraclius, his magnificent triumph, and the
bringing back of the Holy Cross. Of the monk Anastasius and of
Mahomet. Of the reign of Dagobert and his victory. Of the fearful end of Heraclius.

10. Of the reign of Heraclius and his murder, and of the punishment wreaked upon those who had done the murder. Of the new heresy of Pyrrhus and Cyrus.

11. Of the reign of Constans and of Pope Martin. Of the victories of Constans and of his journey to the City. Of the sons of Dagobert and the death of Constans.

12. Of the reign of Constantine, of the assembly of a synod, and of the condemnation of the heresy of Cyrus and Pyrrhus. Of Ansegis, mayor of the palace of Francia, of Bishop Lambert, and of the death of Constantine.

13. Of the reign of Justinian; of Kilian; of Pepin, mayor of the palace; of Tiberius and of Leontius. Of the seventh synod.

14. Of the return of Justinian, whom Tiberius and Leontius had expelled, after cutting off his nose, and of his vengeance; how he summoned Pope Constantine and dealt honorably with him, and how, while he was pursuing Philippicus, he was killed by him.

15. Of the reign of Philippicus and of his heresy and death.

16. Of the reign of Anastasius and of the growth and victories of the kingdom of the Franks under Charles the Elder, mayor of the palace, and of the downfall of the empire of the Romans. How Anastasius was made a cleric.

17. That Theodosius, his successor, was also made a cleric and abandoned the empire to Leo. Of the overflowing of the Tiber.

18. Of the reign of Leo the Syrian and of his deeds of impiety. Of Boniface, Pirminius, and Bede; and of the siege of the royal city and the death of Leo.

19. Of the reign of Constantine, the son of Leo; of his evil deeds and his death. Of the death of Charles, the mayor of the palace; and of the succession of his sons.

20. Of the wars of the sons of Charles and of the founding of the monastery of Fulda. How one son became a monk, while the second, rebelling against his brother Pepin, was recalled to peace.

21. That Pepin sent to consult the Pope of Rome regarding the title of king, in the reign of Childeric the Merovingian.

22. That upon the return of the messengers Pepin was chosen as king by the Pope's authority, and that Stephen, the successor of Zacharias, under stress of persecution came to the king.

23. That Pepin with the other nobles of the Franks was absolved from his oath and anointed to be king. Of the citizens of Christ who lived at this time.

24. Of the blessed Corbinian.

25. That Pepin entered Italy at the request of Stephen. Of the death of Boniface and of the second entry of Pepin into Italy. Of the embassy sent by Constantine to Pepin. Of the various wars of Pepin and his death.

26. Of the reign of Charles and his various wars against the Aquitanians and the Saxons. Of his entry into Italy. Of the death of Constantine Augustus.

27. Of the reign of Leo and his death, and likewise of the victories of Charles over the Saxons.

28. Of the reign of Constantine and the patriciate of Charles.

29. Of Duke Tassilo, how he was made a monk. Of the blinding of Constantine and of the reign of his mother Irene.

30. That Pope Leo, being badly treated by the Romans, summoned Charles to the City and voluntarily cleared himself of the charges brought against him.

31. How Charles, having been given the title of Augustus by the Supreme Pontiff, transferred the authority from the Greeks to the Franks in the time of Irene. Of the judgments which he made, and of the embassy of Irene and likewise of the embassy of the emperor Nicephorus, and of the gifts of the king of the Persians.

32. Of the death of Nicephorus and the succession of Michael, and of the renewal of the treaty between the two emperors. Likewise of the deposing of Michael and the death of Charles, and a brief summary of the latter's deeds.

33. Of the reign of Louis and of Pope Leo. Likewise of Stephen, who crowned the emperor. Of the sons of the emperor and of the revolt and death of Bernard.

34. Of the promotion of Lothar by Paschal, and of the messengers of the Bulgarians. Of the death of Louis.

35. Of the civil war between the three brothers and of the division of the kingdom of the Franks.

36. Digression and lamentation over the mutability of events.

THE CHAPTERS OF THE SIXTH BOOK

1. Of the imperial power of Lothar and of Michael and the reign of Charles. The emperor is made a monk and the kingdom is divided among his three sons.

2.   Of the reign of Louis and of Basil, the marriage of Lothar, and the controversy over the kingdom of Charles. Of the victory of Louis and the battle of Charles with the Britons. Of Nomenoë, king of the Britons [*i.e.*, Bretons], and of Erispoë.

3.   Of the case of Lothar, how he was excommunicated by Pope Nicholas for divorcing his lawful wife, and how the bishops who supported him were condemned; and of the entry of Louis into the western kingdoms and the raid by the Northmen.

4.   What fate Lothar met in Italy while he was trying to aid his brother, and how, after his death, his uncles divided the kingdom. Of the craft of Adelchis and the deceiving of the emperor. Of the victories which the emperor [*i.e.*, Louis] won in Campania and Lucania. Of the locusts.

5.   How Charles, King of the West, was deceived into permitting the Northmen to depart after he had trapped them by a siege, and what disasters he suffered afterwards at their hands.

6.   Of the death of the emperor Louis and the reign of his uncle Charles. Likewise of the death of Louis, King of the East, and how Charles, keenly anxious to invade his brother's kingdom, was vanquished by his brother's sons, and how they divided the ancestral kingdom. Also of the entrance of Charles into Italy and of his death. Of Louis the Stammerer and his sons, and of their battle with Boso.

7.   Of the death of Carloman and his son Arnulf; how his brother Louis made the kingdom subject to himself and assigned to Arnulf the duchy of Carinthia.

8.   Of the reign of Charles the Third, the invasion of the Northmen and the death of Louis. Of the return of the emperor Charles into Gaul; how, through the deaths of all of the royal line, he obtained sole rule.

9.   Of the deposing of Charles and the succession of Arnulf. Of the death of Charles and of the upheaval regarding the imperial claim in Italy and Gaul.[17]

10.   Whom the Italians chose as their kings, and whom the West Franks made king over themselves. Of the Hungarians and the invasion of the Northmen.

11.   When Arnulf reigned, what exploits he performed, and his

---

[17] Otto's text reads: *confusione Romani simul et Gallici imperii.* The meaning of the passage seems obvious.

victory over the Northmen. The controversy in the Western Kingdom of the Franks.

12.   What brave deeds Arnulf did upon entering Italy, and what
he bestowed upon Louis, the son of Boso. Of the death of Guido in
Italy, and of his son Lambert, and of Zwentibold, the king's son,
and Odo, king of France.

13.   How Arnulf secured the title of Roman Emperor; likewise
how Louis, the son of Boso, obtained it, and what various writers
think of this. Of the death of Odo and the succession of Charles,
and likewise of the death of Arnulf.

14.   Of the reign of Louis in East Francia and of the death of
Zwentibold and of the raids of the Hungarians.

15.   How Berengar was at first expelled by Louis, but afterwards
blinded Louis and himself gained the throne. How Louis, the king
of East Francia, through a trick of Hatto caused Count Albert to
be beheaded and reduced his domain to an imperial possession. Of
the expedition of the Hungarians and the death of Louis.

16.   Of the reign of Conrad in East Francia, the destruction of the
Hungarians, the flight of Duke Arnulf, the death of the king, and
the succession of Henry the Saxon.

17.   Of the beginning of the reign of the Germans, and various
pronouncements, whether it ought to be called the kingdom of the
Germans or rather be still called the kingdom of the Franks.

18.   Of the reign of Henry in East Francia and of Charles in
West Francia; the decision of the dispute between the two kings
over Lotharingia [Lorraine]. Of the tyranny of Arnulf, duke of
Bavaria, and the victory of Henry over the Hungarians. Of the
Holy Lance and the death of Henry.

19.   Of the reign of Otto and his triumphs over both the Slavs
and the Lotharingians. Of the expulsion of Louis and his restoration through Otto, and of the synod held in the presence of both.
How Otto entered Italy and vanquished Berengar, and afterwards
accepted his submission and that of his son Albert. Of the rebellion
of Otto's son Liudolf and also of their reconciliation.

20.   The triumph of Otto over the Hungarians and the tradition
regarding the Count of Scheyern, and, furthermore the triumph
of Otto over the Slavs.

21.   The complaint of the Romans about the tyranny of Berengar.
On what occasion the king, having first elevated his son to the
throne, entered Italy and rebuilt the palace at Pavia.

22. On what occasion Otto, coming to Rome, obtained the title of Augustus from Pope John and all the people, with the result that the Roman imperial power passed to the Germans or, according to others, to the East Franks. How, when the emperor came to Pavia, Berengar fled.

23. How the emperor, because Pope John had received Albert, deposed him from the papacy and put Leo in his place.

24. On what occasion the emperor captured Berengar and overthrew the Romans who were stirring up rebellion. How, having done this, he turned aside to Spoleto, but returning again to the City besieged it and carried off captive the Pope whom the Romans had chosen. How, returning once more, he hanged some of the Romans and, after his son had first been crowned by the Supreme Pontiff, the emperor died in Saxony.

25. Of the reign of Otto the Second, his experience in Calabria and his death. The tradition of the Romans regarding Saint Bartholomew.

26. Of the reign of Otto the Third; of the martyrdom of Saint Alfred and the death of the emperor.

27. Of the reign of Henry, his triumphs, the founding of Bamberg, and the conversion of the Hungarians. Of Henry's death.

28. Of the reign of King Conrad and his wife Gisela. Of his virtues and his victory over the Poles. Of the rebellion of Dukes Conrad and Ernest, the reconciliation of Ernest, and the king's expedition into Italy.

29. Of the elevation of Conrad to the imperial throne and the riot that arose among the people. Of Conrad's return and also of the rebellion of Duke Ernest and his death.

30. Of the death of Rudolph, king of Burgundy, and the surrender of Burgundy to the emperor's son. A description of Gaul.

31. The rebellion of Odo in Gaul and the expedition of the emperor against him; Odo is forced to surrender. The emperor's expedition into Italy and his victories. The murder of Odo by the emperor's faithful adherents. The captivity of the bishops and the destruction of Parma; the progress of the emperor into Apulia and his victories there; the pestilence that beset him and his army as they were returning [from Apulia], and of the death of his Imperial Highness.

32. Of the reign of Henry and of his virtues. Of his disaster in Bohemia and his triumph in Pannonia. Of his marriage and the

death of Margrave Leopold. Of the schism in the papacy, of the
deposing of Gratian and succession of Clement. What Hildebrand
thought about these events.

33.   Under what circumstances Henry was crowned at Rome by
Clement, and how, passing through Apulia, he returned to his
native land. What men were afterwards placed by him over the
See of Rome, and how Bruno, who is also called Leo, attained to
the papacy. Of the surrender of Dukes Godfrey and Baldwin, and
of the holding of a synod; of the Hungarian expedition. Of the
invasion of Apulia by the Northmen, the passing of Leo, the succession of German popes and the death of the emperor.

34.   Of the reign of Henry and of his mother Agnes; of the liberation of the papacy, and of the rebellion of the Saxons. Of the death
of Alexander and the induction of Gregory the Seventh, and the
schism that arose in consequence between the state and the priesthood. Of the virtues of Gregory and his salutary decrees. Of the
battle between the Saxons and the king.

35.   Of the comet that was seen, and of the conquest of England.
Of the king's marriage and the decree that was promulgated by the
Supreme Pontiff against him. Of the kings raised up against him
but killed within a short time.

36.   Digression regarding the interpretation of what we read in
Daniel, that a stone cut out from a mountain without hands smote
the image upon its feet, that were partly of iron, partly of clay.
The misfortunes of that time, the death of Gregory, and the end of
the book.

THE CHAPTERS OF THE SEVENTH BOOK

1.   Of the election of Victor and his consecration and death.

2.   Of the expedition to Jerusalem in the days of Urban; of the
departure of the expedition and its progress, and of the capture of
Antioch.

3.   The embassy of the Saracens to Duke Godfrey. A description of
ancient Babylon [18] and of modern Babylon.[19]

4.   Likewise the embassy of Godfrey to the Babylonian king. The
treachery of the Saracen. The affliction of the people of God and
the ensuing victory, and after that the famine and the capture of
the city of Jerusalem.

[18] Bagdad.   [19] Memphis, in Egypt.

5. Likewise the strategem of the Babylonian king,[20] the victory of our forces, and the return of the leaders. The appointment of Godfrey as duke over those that remained.

6. How Urban, expelling Gwibert, regained his see, and himself left it vacant by his death at Easter time.

7. Of the death of Godfrey and the reign of his brother Baldwin. Of the death of Gwibert, who had caused the schism, and of Conrad the son of the emperor. Of the second overseas expedition and of its outcome. Of the martyrdom of [Arch-]bishop Thiemo.

8. Of the killing of Sigehard and the civil war between King Henry and his son.

9. How, after many disasters, their armies met on the bank of the river Regen and the father was finally compelled to yield.

10. Of the court which was convoked for the settlement of the strife. Of the victory of King Baldwin and the treachery of the emperor Alexius.

11. How, when the court was held, the father surrendered the royal insignia and the son was elevated to the throne.

12. How the father, crossing over to the Lorrainers, was received by certain persons and still uttered complaint, and how he died at Liége after a battle.

13. Of the siege of Cologne, the restoration of the bishops, and the expedition against the Hungarians.

14. Of the great expedition into Italy, the capture of the Supreme Pontiff and the slaughter of the Romans. Of the privilege extorted by force but afterwards abrogated.

15. Of the capture of Count Reinald, the marriage of the emperor, the schism in the kingdom, the anathema pronounced against the emperor. Of Burdinus and the earthquake, of the raid of the Hungarians, and the vengeance exacted by our people.

16. Of the peace reëstablished under Calixtus and the victory of the emperor over the people of Worms; of the tribute imposed, and of the death of the emperor.

17. Of the reign of King Lothar and the rebellion of Dukes Frederick and Conrad; how Conrad was received by the people of Milan and anointed to be king.

18. Of the schism in the Roman See; how Innocent went to France, held a council, and summoned the king to come to the defence of

[20] The king of Memphis.

the Roman See. Of his expedition into Italy and his elevation to imperial power.

19. How two brothers won the favor of the king. Of the Duke of Poland, the King of Denmark, and the King of the Hungarians. Of the emperor's second expedition and his valiant deeds.

20. Of the flight of Roger and the succession of Reinald. Of the strife between the pope and the emperor and the death of Lothar.

21. Of the illustrious men who died at that time, and of the many disasters which then occurred in various kingdoms.

22. Of the elevation of Conrad to the throne, and the opposition of the Saxons and of Duke Henry. Of the flight of Roger and the death of Pierleoni.

23. How the Saxons were called to peace and Duke Henry was proscribed and expelled. Of the tyranny of Roger. How Leopold became duke, and of the synod held at Rome.

24. Digression concerning the fortunes of King Conrad. Of the revolt of the Saxons.

25. Of the battle of Welf with the duke, and likewise his battle with the king. Of the uprising of the people of Regensburg. Of the expedition of the duke against Welf, and his death.

26. Of the conspiracy of the Bohemians and the king's expedition against them. Of the bestowal of a duchy upon Henry, the brother of Leopold, and the many disasters that in consequence were brought upon the province of Bavaria by Welf and the aforesaid Henry.

27. Of the capture of Tivoli, the uprising of the Roman people, the restoration of the senators, and the death of Pope Innocent. Also of the victory of the people of Verona. Of the Paduans.

28. What fate John of Constantinople met after his Syrian expedition, and how or for what reason his son Manuel entered upon a treaty with our king.

29. Of divers wars waged by the cities of Italy and their varying results.

30. How Edessa was captured and the churches were profaned.

31. Of the persecution of Pope Lucius and his embassy to the king. How the Roman people chose a patrician in addition to the senators, and how for this reason some of them were smitten by the sword of excommunication by Eugenius, the successor of Lucius.

32. Of the messenger of the Armenians, the reason for his coming, and the miracles which he beheld at the Roman court.

33. Of the Bishop of Djebele and the reports which he brought from regions beyond the seas.

34. Of the peace made by the pope with the people of Rome. Of the unrest. Of Boricius and various disturbances throughout the world, and the end of the history.

35. A description of the various religious orders, and the end of the seventh book.

36. A catalogue of the kings and the popes.

THE CHAPTERS OF THE EIGHTH BOOK

1. Of the fourfold persecution of the Church. From what tribe Antichrist is to arise.

2. Of the falling away which is to precede his coming.

3. Of his coming and the persecution which will occur under him.

4. Of his life and teaching.

5. Of Enoch and Elijah.

6. Of the time of the tyranny of Antichrist.

7. What signs are to precede the Lord's coming after the overthrow of Antichrist.

8. Of the destruction of the world by fire.

9. How we are to understand this saying: "Heaven and earth shall pass away."

10. Of the twofold resurrection of the dead.

11. How the resurrection of the dead can be proved by Scriptural authority and by reason.

12. Of what age, of what sex, and with what form the dead are to rise.

13. Whether those who are found alive are to be caught up to meet Christ in that state or are to die that they may rise again.

14. Of the last trump.

15. Of the final judgment and its terrors, and of the appearance of the Judge.

16. Of the ease of the [final] judgment.

17. Of the fourfold classification of those that are to judge and of those that are to be judged.

18. Where the judgment is to take place.

19. Of the speed of the judgment.

20. Of the destruction of the wicked city.

21.   Of the nature of the punishments.

22.   How we are to understand this saying, "With what measure ye mete it shall be measured to you again," if eternal punishments are to be imposed upon those who sin in time.

23.   If those undergoing punishment for their past sins are to repent truly or if they are still to have the desire to sin.

24.   If after the judgment there remains a place for lighter punishments besides the place of the damned.

25.   How the fire burns there and yet does not give light.

26.   Of the glory and the exaltation of the City of God.

27.   What bodies the saints are to have after the resurrection.

28.   In what way they are to have a recollection of the past.

29.   Of the various mansions in the heavenly Palace.

30.   Of the three orders of angels, each itself subdivided into three.

31.   How the saints are according to their merits assigned to the proper orders.

32.   How the statement can stand, that the number of the elect is to be as great as the number of the angels that remains there,[21] if in accordance with the parable of the tenth coin it is supposed that only a tenth part of the angels has fallen and is to be replaced by men.

33.   Of the blessedness of the saints.

34.   How God is to be seen.

35.   Of the end of both cities.

[21] In Paradise.

HERE BEGINS THE FIRST BOOK [22]

1. As I purpose to trace the course of events from Adam, the first man, even down to our own time, let us first, in accordance with the information we have received from our ancestors, briefly take account of the earth itself which the human race inhabits. Writers assert that there are three parts of the world;[23] Asia, Africa and Europe. The first of these they account equal in size to the other two. Yet some have declared that there are only two parts, that is, Asia and Europe; Africa, because of its small size,[24] they join to Europe. Those who called Africa a third part of the world followed the ebb and flow of the seas, not considerations of size. If anyone wishes to know the provinces, the topography and the divisions of these parts of the world, let him read Orosius.[25]

2. Now it was in the East, as can be gathered from the book of Genesis, in the land of Eden, that Paradise is believed to have been established. While the first man dwelt therein, he became disobedient to the word of God, and so by a righteous judgment of God he was cast out into this pilgrimage; he began, first in Asia, to till the ground that had been cursed. And he begat sons, the first citizens of the two cities of which I have undertaken to treat. The elder, incited by envy of the other's good works, murdered his brother and was the first to build a city in this vale of tears. After Abel was slain, another son was born to Adam, named Seth, who is a figure of the resurrection; from him the people of God was afterwards begotten. The sixth in descent from him was Enoch, a

[22] Book I of the Chronicle deals with the period from Adam to the transfer of the kingdom of Babylonia to the Medes. Otto's principal authorities in this part of his work are: Orosius, Book 1; Augustine, *De Civitate Dei* 15-18; and the Frutolf-Ekkehard *Chronicle*. There are also shorter quotations from the Bible, from Josephus, *Antiquitates Iudaicae*, Eusebius-Rufinus, Cicero, Jerome, the *Gesta Treverorum*, the *Annales Hildesheimenses*, and the *Romana* and *Getica* of Jordanes.

[23] Manuscript B2, omitting this clause, adds a passage of about 25 lines on the sphericity of the earth and its five zones. See Hofmeister's edition, 37.

[24] Belief in the small extent of Africa was common in the Middle Ages. (*Cf.* Wright, J. K., *Geographical Lore in the Age of the Crusades*, p. 74.)

[25] The preceding sentences are from Orosius 1. 2.

mighty citizen of the City of God, who so pleased God that he was translated by him and is being kept alive, in a place unknown to all mortals, for the last days of the Church.

But the race of men began to increase and multiply until the sons of God, uniting with the daughters of men, begat giants. Some, attaching less weight to this story — especially because another account has ''angels'' instead of ''sons of God'' — believe that evil spirits in bodily form (whom they call *incubi*) were united with mortal women. Others assert that the sons of God were descended from Seth, the daughters of men from Cain, and claim that these sons, in consequence of their union with these women, were led to forget God — compare the story of Solomon [26] — and hence His wrath was kindled against them all alike.

Of those descendants of Seth who lived righteously even to the seventh generation Josephus speaks as follows in the first book of his *Antiquities*: ''They first devised all the pomp and ceremony of religious observances. And that the matters which had been discovered by them might not slip away from men or perish before they became scarcely known (since Adam had foretold that one destruction of the world was to come through the might of fire, and a second by many waters) they made two columns — one of brick and another of stone — and wrote on both what they had discovered, in order that, if the one built of brick should be ruined by the floods, the column built of stone, which would, of course, survive, might afford mankind a written record. This stone pillar is, in fact, in existence in Syria to this day. Those customs accordingly prevailed for seven generations.'' [27] But of the others he says: ''Then considering their own spirit to be their only lord and ever having regard to might, as time went on they gave up the religious observances of their fathers and turned to iniquity.'' And later:[28] ''For bad angels uniting with women begat sons that worked iniquity. These despised all righteousness because of the confidence they themselves put in their own strength, and are said to have committed deeds like the deeds perpetrated by those who are called giants.''

3. And so when God, because of the increase of their iniquity, had determined to blot out the race of men, he preserved in the

[26] 1 Kings 11.
[27] 1. 2. 3. References are to the translation by Whiston (1883).
[28] *Ibid.*, 1. 3. 1.

ark Noah, a righteous man, the tenth in descent from Adam, with his wife and his sons and their wives, eight souls in all, but he destroyed all the rest by the waters of a flood. Although certain of our people suppose that the period from Adam to Ninus was deliberately passed over by Gentile writers [29] or was wholly unknown to them, "All the authors of secular histories make mention of this flood and of the ark," as Josephus states further.[30] "One of them, Berosus,[31] has spoken as follows: 'Moreover, it is said that some part of that ship which came into Armenia still exists near Mt. Chordeius, and that certain people take from it the pitch which men use particularly for expiatory rites.' Furthermore, Hieronymus the Egyptian, who is known to have written an account of the ancient history of Phoenicia, makes mention of these people. But Manasseas of Damascus [32] too, in the eighty-sixth book of his Histories, speaks thus of them: 'There is also above Miliada [33] in Armenia a lofty mountain called Paris. It is said that many who took refuge there at the time of the Flood were saved and that at the same time a certain man was carried in an ark to Socilem,[34] the summit of a mountain, and that fragments of timbers of the ark were preserved there for a long time'."

Likewise with reference to the Fathers who lived so long before the Flood, Josephus speaks as follows in the first book of his

[29] As distinguished from the Scriptural account or the works of "our people," i.e., Christian authors.

[30] 1. 3. 6.

[31] Or Berossos, a Babylonian priest of Bel, who wrote in Greek an important work in three books on Babylonian history. The first part of his Babyloniaca (or Chaldaica, as it is also called) dealt with the legendary period from Creation to the Flood, the second with the era from the Flood to Nabonassar (747 B.C.) — containing a list of the names of the kings — and the third and most important with the period from Nabonassar to Alexander the Great. Parts of this great work, written perhaps about 280 B.C., are preserved for us by Josephus in his Antiquities of the Jews, and by Eusebius in his Chronicle. Those passages from Berosus that can be checked by native monumental sources are found to be in remarkable agreement with them.

[32] The reference is to Nicolaus, or Nicholas, of Damascus, born about 64 B.C., friend and confidant of Herod the Great. The work here referred to is a universal history, in 144 books, which includes accounts of the Assyrians, Lydians, Greeks, Medes and Persians, though culminating in a flattering account of Herod's reign. This latter part of the work was especially used by Josephus.

[33] Or Miniada.

[34] Or Ocile.

Antiquities:[35] "Let no one, contrasting the life of the men of old with modern times and with the brief span of years that we now live, believe the stories told about the men of old to be false. For because they were holy men and were created by God himself, since there was prepared for them food better adapted to a longer life, they naturally lived through the span of so many years. Furthermore, on account of their merits and the notable useful arts which they continually studied with great care, that is, astrology and geometry, God granted them a longer period of life. For they could not have learned these things thoroughly without living for six hundred years; since it is by the progress of that number of years that one great year is completed. As witnesses, moreover, I have cited all those among the Greeks and the barbarians who preferred to describe ancient times. For Manetho [36] also, who wrote a description of the Egyptians, and Berosus, who first effectively narrated Chaldean history, and Mochus [37] and Estius [38] and Hieronymus the Egyptian besides, who described Phoenicia, agree with my account. Hesiod too, and Hecataeus,[39] and Hellanicus,[40] and Acusilaus,[41] as well as Ephorus [42] and Nicolaus,[43] make mention in their

[35] 1. 3. 9.

[36] An Egyptian scholar and priest of Sebennytos, of the time of Ptolemy I (305-285 B.C.), who wrote in Greek a history of Egypt in three books. He was apparently the first to use the device of grouping the names of the Pharaohs by dynasties. Professor Shotwell, *Introduction to the History of History* p. 64 (Columbia University Press, 1922), characterizes him as "the one historian of Egypt." Fragments of his book are preserved in Josephus. He was epitomized in the chronicles of Julius Africanus and of Eusebius.

[37] A native of Phoenicia. His work on Phoenician history is referred to by Athenaeus 3, p. 126 A.

[38] *I.e.*, Hestiaeus.

[39] The text reads *Eliatheus.* The reference is to Hecataeus of Miletus, traveller, geographer and logographer of the sixth century B.C. He wrote a book of genealogies and an account of his *Travels around the World.* Herodotus names him as a source.

[40] *Ellanecus.* Hellanicus of Mytilene, a contemporary of Thucydides, was the author of a chronicle of Attica from 683-404 B.C.

[41] *Achlansis.* Acusilaus of Argos, about 500 B.C., is the earliest writer of genealogies whose work has come down to us.

[42] *Efforus.* Ephorus, a pupil of Isocrates, wrote in the early 4th century B.C. the first general history of the Hellenic world, from the return of the Heraclidae to the capture of Corinth by Philip in 340 B.C. It was divided into 30 books, and dealt also with Persia and Carthage and other parts of the ancient world in so far as they came in contact with Greece.

[43] Called Manasseas above, see note 32.

histories of men of old who lived a thousand years." Thus far Josephus.

Now the statement I made above, that certain of our people have believed that those times were either unknown to secular writers or were ignored in their accounts, may be thus explained: they either did not deign to count barbarians as writers, or else they considered that only then do books deserve to carry weight, when by the passage of years they have been admitted to the rank of classics. Now from Adam to the Flood there were, according to the Seventy,[44] 2,262 years; according to Jerome, 1,666. There were ten heads of families: Adam, Seth, Enosh, Kenan, Mahalalel, Jared, Enoch, Methusaleh, Lamech, Noah.

4. After the Flood, when Noah planted a vineyard, he drank of the wine and was drunken, and because of his drunkenness he stripped himself naked. One of his sons seeing him thus mocked him; the other [45] covered him. Accordingly these two brothers were, after the Flood, the first citizens of the cities which constitute the theme of my book. From these and a third — namely Shem, Ham and Japheth — because their sons and grandsons were spread abroad everywhere, the whole race of men is descended. Hence Josephus says: "The Galathae were once called Gomeritae.[46] Gomer [47] is founder of their line. Magog gave his name to the Magoges (who are also called Scythians), descended from him. The Medes come from Madai, the son of Japheth; the Ionians and the Elladici come from Japheth's son Javan. Tiras begat the Tyrenses, whose name the Greeks changed to Thracians. Moreover, Kittim [48] held the island of Cethima, which is called Cyprus, and from it all islands and coastlands are called Cethim in Hebrew.

[44] The traditional 70 (or 72) inspired writers who translated the Old Testament into Greek at the bidding of Ptolemy II (285-247 B. C.). The chronology founded upon the dates of the Septuagint gives about 1500 years more from the Creation to Adam than the Hebrew Bible.

[45] In Genesis we read "Shem and Japheth"; so also Josephus and Augustine (16. 10). It would appear from the next sentence that Otto is seeking for two sharply differentiated "citizens" — and two only. For the contrast between the brothers, see also Augustine 16. 1. 2. 10.

[46] *Gamaricae.* These were inhabitants of Galatia, in Asia Minor. The passage is from *Antiquities* 1. 6. 1.

[47] See Gen. 10. 2: "the sons of Japheth: Gomer, and Magog, and Madai, and Javan, and Tubal, and Meshech, and Tiras."

[48] *Cethim.* See Gen. 10. 4.

Hence a certain city of Cyprus also is called Cythis [49] by the Greeks.'' Now all men then had one language and one speech. Therefore, induced by pride, at the suggestion of Nimrod (who was descended from the stock of Ham), they planned to build in the plain of Shinar a tower or city which should reach the heavens. Our [50] Moses sets the matter forth in Genesis after this fashion: ''And the sons of Ham were Cush and Canaan. Cush begat Nimrod: Nimrod began to be a mighty man in the earth and was a powerful hunter, an enemy to Jehovah.[51] The beginning of his kingdom was Babel, and Erech, and Accad, and Calneh, in the land of Shinar.'' But the Lord, the searcher of hearts, the righteous judge, not tolerating the emergence of such arrogance when the world was yet so young, desired to punish it, and so he confounded their languages. Therefore the tower received the name Babel from this confusion. Hence seventy-two tongues were scattered all over the earth. This is that well-known Babylon, a figure of that city of which all they are citizens who insolently attempt to resist the ordinances of God,[52] and are therefore accounted by the eternal judge worthy of confusion. Of this tower and of this confusion, as Josephus likewise declares in his book of *Antiquities*, ''The Sibyl makes mention,[53] saying: 'When all men were of one speech, certain of them built a lofty tower, thinking to climb by it into heaven. But the gods sent winds and overturned the tower, and gave to each a language of his own, and therefore it came to pass that the city was called Babylon.' Estius also speaks of the plain of Shinar in the territory of Babylon, saying: 'But those of the priests who were rescued took the sacred vessels of Jove and came to Shinar of Babylon'.''

Now, according to the Seventy, there were 531 years from the Flood to the time of Nimrod and to the reign of Eber (from him

[49] Perhaps *Citium*, now Larnaka.

[50] So regularly, to distinguish the chosen people — as also the Christians — from the heathen.

[51] Gen. 10. 6. 8-10. But the Vulgate has *coram Domino*, ''before Jehovah,'' whereas Otto's text reads *contra Dominum*, ''an enemy to Jehovah.''

[52] Throughout Otto's Chronicle (as in the book of Revelation) Babylon is taken as a type of the ''City of Earth'' and contrasted with ''New Jerusalem.''

[53] 1. 4. 3. The prophecies of the forged ''Sibylline oracles'' were accepted literally by the early Church. *Cf.* the verse in Thomas a Celano's *Dies Irae:* ''*teste David cum Sybylla.*''

the Hebrews come). But according to the computation of Jerome there were only 101. His reckoning is as follows:[54] Shem begat Arpachshad in the second year after the Flood; Arpachshad in his thirty-fifth year begat Shelah; Shelah in his thirtieth year begat Eber; Eber in his thirty-fourth year begat Peleg, in whose days the world was divided by the Confusion of Tongues. The Seventy place Canaan [55] between Shelah and Arpachshad, and assign to him one hundred and thirty-five years, and besides attribute to those already mentioned and to those to be named hereafter far more years before they begat children than Jerome does. This is why they disagree in their reckoning of the years. The evangelist Luke follows them in his genealogy when he says: "the son of Shelah, the son of Cainan, the son of Arphaxad." [56]

5. Now from the Confusion of Tongues to the birth of Abraham, according to the former authorities, there were 541 years, but according to the reckoning of the latter only 141. The calculation is as follows: Peleg in his thirtieth year begat Reu, in whose time temples, it is said, were first built and men were first worshipped as gods. Reu in his thirty-second year begat Serug; Serug in his thirtieth begat Nahor; Nahor in his thirty-fourth begat Terah, in whose time the kingdom of the Assyrians and that of Sicyon arose, Belus ruling the Assyrians, Agialeus the Sicyonians. Terah in his seventieth year begat Abraham. There are therefore, according to the one set of writers, 1,072 years from the Flood to Abraham.[57] Augustine [58] seems to be following these writers when he says that from the Flood to Ninus was a period of more than a thousand years. But according to the calculation of the other group of authors it was less than three hundred. In their account the reckoning of the years is an absolute tangle in the case of each of the two periods under discussion. All this is according to our own writers. But the records of the Gentiles begin with the reign of Ninus.[59] Following them and at the same time comparing our own authors with them, let us begin from Ninus the story of human

[54] This is from Frutolf, but cf. Gen. 11. 10-16.

[55] According to Gen. 10. 6 a son of Ham.

[56] Luke 3. 35-36.

[57] Namely 531 from the Flood to the Confusion of Tongues (I. 4) and 541 from that event to the birth of Abraham (I. 5). The reference is to the Seventy.

[58] 16. 10 and 18. 22.

[59] Cf. Orosius 2. 2. 4. Eusebius of Caesarea began his chronicle (which was

misery, and let us carry it through, year by year, from Ninus himself down to the founding of the City; from the founding of the City let us relate it in due order as far as the time of Christ, and from the time of Christ, by God's help, likewise down to our own day.[60]

6. Well, then, according to the Seventy, in the year 1032 or 1033 after the Flood, upon the death of Belus, who had held the throne of the Assyrians for seventy-five years in peace, his son Ninus, the first, it is said, who in his lust to extend his sway did not shrink from staining the human race with blood, inflicted upon the world the disquietude of wars and brought practically the entire East under his control. He could do this the more readily because men were as yet simple and rustic, neither protecting themselves by arms nor trained by warfare; they were not yet equipped with knowledge of military matters because they had not united under any laws or regulations up to this time, but, as Eusebius says,[61] "Roaming about more in the fashion of wild animals and beasts, they possessed no cities as the basis of society, no traditions to serve as standards of honor, no laws to bring about uprightness of life. Not even the mere name of the arts and the sciences and of philosophy was known among them — but they wandered about, in the wilderness, rude and nomadic, with no fixed abode." Tullius, too, in the prologue of his first rhetorical treatise, says: "There was a time when men wandered everywhere more in the manner of beasts, and subsisted on the flesh of animals. In what they did, they made no use of reason, but managed everything by bodily strength. There was no regard as yet for holy religion or for duty toward their fellow men; no one had yet seen lawful wedlock, no one had looked on children he knew to be his own or had experienced the advantage that equitable laws convey. And so because of their ignorance and their blundering, greed, a blind and reckless mistress of the soul, took advantage of their strength of body as a pernicious means of satisfying her cravings."[62] Thus far Tullius.

There was also at that time in Europe the kingdom of the Sicyonians, which had begun in the forty-fifth year of Belus's reign, but

translated into Latin by Jerome) with the first year of Abraham — the 43rd of the reign of Ninus.

[60] Otto gives in this sentence the three main divisions of his chronological scheme; see Intro., § 4.

[61] Eus.-Ruf. 1. 2. 19.

[62] Cicero, *De Inventione*, 1. 2.

it was a small kingdom. With this the learned Marcus Varro [63] started, as from a far-off date, when he began to write, in orderly fashion, the history of the Romans; because the transference of power — first to the Athenians, later to the Romans — was, so to say, a beginning, a veritable fountain-source. This explains also the following statement of Cicero: "The control of Greece was in the hands of the Athenians; the Spartans prevailed over the Athenians, the Thebans overcame the Spartans, the Macedonians conquered the Thebans and soon after subdued Asia in war and added it to the empire of Greece." [64] So Cicero. No one who has a knowledge of history can deny that the control of Greece was wrested from the· Macedonians by the Romans.

There was also the kingdom of the Egyptians, which at that time was subject to the Assyrians, together with other kingdoms of Asia. For we read that all Asia, except India, was under the control of Ninus. Semiramis, though a woman, added India to her realm after Ninus's death, since she was not content with the territories that she had received from Ninus, prince of warriors. Accordingly, it is unnecessary to treat of the Egyptians, who were appendages, so to speak, of Ninus's kingdom. Ninus built a very great city which he called, after his own name, Nina or Nineveh, which still exists in Mesopotamia, though its name has been changed: it is called in the tongue of the Mesopotamians Mussa.[65] Our Moses, in the book of Genesis,[66] makes a passing allusion to all this, for, after he had said of Nimrod, as I have stated above, that "the beginning of his kingdom was Babylon in the land of Shinar," he added: "Out of that land went forth Asshur and builded Nineveh." Josephus too says: "Asshur founded the city of Nineveh." [67] Some, however, apply this statement to Asshur, the grandson of Noah. If this is so, it appears that Babylon existed before Ninus, and that Semiramis, the wife of Ninus, must be called its restorer rather than its founder. Ninus put to death Zoroaster, the inventor of the art of

[63] The great encyclopaedist and antiquarian (116-27 B.C.), who wrote over 600 books. The work here referred to is his *De gente populi Romani* (in 4 books) in which he follows the chronology of the Rhodian Castor (60 B.C.). *Cf.* Augustine 18.2 and 16.17.

[64] *Ad Herenn.* 4.25.34.

[65] Now Mosul. But Nineveh appears to have been situated on the left bank of the Tigris while Mosul is on the right bank.

[66] See Gen. 10.10-11.

[67] 1.6.4.

magic. Aristotle says that Zoroaster wrote two million verses.[68] Democritus [69] long afterward glorified his art.

7. In the forty-second or forty-third year after the reign of Ninus, while Europs, the second king, was ruling among the Sicyonians, Abram, it is said, was born in Chaldea. He was summoned by the Lord to be the father of many nations (his name being lengthened by the Lord so that he was called Abraham), and he was commanded to avoid the citizens of Babylon not only as regards mental attitude but also by changing his place of abode, and to enter a land which is known to be a type of that city which is our theme, to become a great citizen thereof. Philo relates that he was cast into the fire by the Chaldeans because he would not worship fire after their custom, but was presently delivered upon prayer to the Lord, even as it is written, "the Lord brought him out of Ur of the Chaldees." In their language, be it noted, fire is called Ur. But Josephus also says: "Berosus makes mention of our father Abraham, not indeed calling him by name but speaking thus: 'In the tenth generation after the Flood there was among the Chaldeans a certain man, great and righteous, skilled in the celestial sciences.' Besides, Nicolaus of Damascus, in the fourth book of his Histories speaks thus: 'Abraham reigned in Damascus, coming from foreign parts, with an army from the land of the Chaldeans which is said to be above Babylon'." [70]

But Ninus, in the fiftieth year of his reign, while winning a bloody victory in the siege of a certain city, raging like a wolf among unprotected sheep, was struck by an arrow and died. And in him truly was the saying fulfilled: "All they that take the sword shall perish with the sword." [71]

8. After Ninus was slain, his wife, Semiramis,[72] a woman of more

---

[68] Aristotle is cited as an authority on Zoroaster by Pliny the Elder (*Nat. Hist.*, 30. 2. 1) and by Diogenes Laertius (*Prooemium* 6, *ed.* Cobet, Paris, 1862), but in neither passage is there an allusion to the number of verses ascribed to him. For a collection of classical passages mentioning Zoroaster's name, see Appendix V in *Zoroaster, the Prophet of Ancient Iran,* by A. V. Williams Jackson, New York (1899).

[69] Of Abdera, in Thrace, a younger contemporary of Socrates, who first developed into a system the atomic theory of Leucippus.

[70] 1. 7. 2.

[71] Matt. 26. 52.

[72] The famous queen referred to by Herodotus (1. 184) as ruling over Babylon, possibly to be identified with Queen Sammuramat, mentioned in the inscription on the statue of Nabu.

than masculine ferocity, ruled the empire of the East and vanquished Ethiopia and India with the sword and brought them under her power. I pass over not only her cruelty but also her delight in detestable passions, because many have spoken at length about these matters. She ruled for forty-two years after her husband's death. When her reign was half over, she built out of baked brick and pitch from the tower of Babel the powerful, renowned and wealthy city of Babylon, the capital of the entire East.

The people of Trèves [73] say that after the death of Ninus Semiramis banished her stepson Trebeta from her kingdom. Trebeta built a fleet and made his way from Asia to Europe, that is, by sea to the Rhine and thence by the Moselle, and settled in a beautiful valley of Gaul. There he founded a prosperous city, abounding in resources and at that time the metropolis of all Gaul, which he called Trèves after his own name. How large it was, and what sort of a town it was, may clearly be proven by its ruins. There they point out a palace [74] of remarkable workmanship, built, as were the walls of Babylon, of baked brick. It still remains so strong that it not only has no fear of any enemy but it cannot even be destroyed by any mechanical device. They exhibit there also a city gate [75] built of stones of incredible size fastened together with iron, which is seen to preserve within its walls the bodies of Saint Simeon and of the venerable archbishop Popio,[76] in a chapel erected by that archbishop. There are in existence there, also, indications of monuments time-honored and splendid, as the inhabitants tell us; one of these, an epitaph cut in stone, found there in our own time, I have set down here:

She who possessed so much, being blessed by marriage to Ninus,
Yet to her realms added more — Semiramis, queen of the Orient!
She, not content with her own, nor yet with the wide world's dominions,
Drove from ancestral throne her stepson, the dear son of Ninus,
Trebeta, who as an exile founded our glorious city,
Trèves,[77] (and so forth).

[73] Or Trier. A similar account is given in the *Gesta Treverorum*, I (*MGH. SS.* 8. 130) — with which, of course, Otto may have been familiar. Yet Hofmeister is inclined to believe that he is here reporting what he has himself seen and heard.

[74] Still extant.

[75] The famous *Portae Nigrae*, still in existence.

[76] Archbishop from 1016-1047. He was of the family of the Babenberg margraves of Austria: see below, VI. 32.

[77] Given in fuller form in *Gesta Treverorum* 2, (*MGH. SS.* 8. 131).

Semiramis was slain, tradition says, by her own son, Ninus or, if you will, Ninias, while she was brazenly tempting him to illicit and incestuous intercourse. This son succeeded to the throne.

9. Now Abraham, in the one hundred and thirteenth year after the reign of Ninus and in the seventy-fifth year of his own life (while Ninus, the fourth ruler, was reigning among the Assyrians, and Telexion, the fifth monarch, among the Sicyonians), Abraham, I say, with Sarah his wife and Lot his nephew, going out from the land of the Chaldeans began to live in the land of Canaan. But Lot (a citizen of Jerusalem, so to speak) dwelling in Sodom, the city of sinners, like a grain of wheat in the midst of chaff, was afflicted in many ways by reason of the evil works of the people of Sodom. Accordingly the Lord, desiring not only to rescue a just man from trial but also to punish the loathsome crimes of the wicked by a new and exquisite kind of punishment, destroyed with fire and brimstone the five cities which the Greeks call the Pentapolis, and saved that righteous man (having first in His mercy warned him through an angel), by leading him forth to a mountain. This was in the one hundred and fortieth year from the reign of Ninus. Even at that time of the early beginnings of the world it was made evident that the citizens of Babylon and lovers of the world, by whom today the Church is oppressed and trodden under foot, would be punished, together with their master, by everlasting fire at the final scrutiny of the judge, and that the righteous, being separated from them, are to be taken up to a habitation in the heavenly kingdom.

10. Now Abraham, who was destined to be the father of many peoples, was the first to receive the sign of circumcision and the hope of the covenant; and begat two sons, Ishmael and Isaac; the one of whom was born after the flesh, the other after the covenant (according to the Apostle)[78] while Arius, their fifth king, was ruling the Assyrians and Telexion was still reigning among the Sicyonians. Because his rule was gentle and prosperous, Telexion began to be worshiped with divine honors by his people after his death. The two brothers I mentioned above were the first citizens, after the institution of circumcision, of the two cities I have begun to describe, and the younger suffered persecution at the hands of the elder as a forecast of future events. Observe that at the beginning of these three generations you will find these citizens begotten of one father, that thereby it might be indicated that the Church in

[78] Gal. 4. 23.

far distant ages was to hold within her single bosom the two peoples, endowed with one faith, sprung from one source.

Now Isaac, as the Scripture relates, begat twins from a single coition, the brothers Esau and Jacob, citizens of the cities I have mentioned so often. Jacob is the man who, beholding the Lord face to face, was called Israel, of whom was begotten after the flesh the carnal Israel, after the spirit the spiritual Israel. These are the three patriarchs, citizens and chief men of the City I have so often named. And because of their preëminent merits and their faith the Lord wished himself to be called their God, saying: "I am the God of Abraham and the God of Isaac and the God of Jacob." [79]

11. Now Abraham died at the age of one hundred and three-score and fifteen years, during which Xerxes (who is also called Baleus) was reigning among the Assyrians and Turichus or Turimachus among the Sicyonians, each the seventh king of his empire. Furthermore, when the eighth kings were in power, Armamithres over the Assyrians, Leucippus over the Sicyonians (among the Argives, whose royal power began at the time of Abraham's grandsons, Inachus, their first king, was on the throne), the promise was made to Isaac as to his father. And when Belochus, the ninth king, was reigning over the Assyrians, and Phoroneus, the son of Inachus, over the Argives (Leucippus was still king among the Sicyonians), the same covenant was made with Jacob. During these days Greece is said to have been instructed, under Phoroneus, for the first time in laws and judgments. His brother Phegius also was worshiped by the Argives as a god after his death. Io [80] too, the daughter of Inachus (afterwards called Isis), and later adored by the Egyptians as a great goddess, lived, we find, in those times. Others say that she was born in Ethiopia, and that, as queen of that people, she ruled justly over a wide territory, and invented the Egyptian writing; for these reasons, they add, she obtained divine honors from the Egyptians.

12. It is said that at about the same time a stubborn combat was carried on by the Telcisces and the Caratasi against Phoroneus, king of the Argives, and the Pharphasii — a combat waged with varying fortune, following which the Telcisces, vanquished and

[79] Exod. 3. 6.

[80] The sister of Phoroneus and Phegius. Observe the frequent intrusion of mythological tales in the midst of what purports to be a historical record (e.g., below I. 19).

put to flight by Phoroneus, settled in the island of Rhodes (then called Offusa) which they regarded as a place of exile, entirely outside the inhabited world. Henceforth that island, in which the city of Colosus [81] was built, began to be populous because it was very convenient for ships.

13. In the two hundred and sixtieth year after the reign of Ninus there was a destructive flood in Achaea in the days of Ogyges [82] (founder and king of Eleusina) [83] which was called, after the king's own name, the flood of Ogyges. At that time Minerva is said to have appeared in the guise of a maiden at Lake Tritonis, whence she is called Tritonia. While Baleus, their tenth king, was ruling over the Assyrians Mesapus, their ninth, over the Sicyonians and Apis, their third, over the Argives, Isaac died at the age of one hundred and eighty years. At that time Jacob and Esau were one hundred and twenty years old.

14. In the two hundred and ninety-second year from the reign of Ninus, when Baleus and Apis, whom I have already mentioned, were in power, and in the reign of Diopolita, king of the Egyptians (whose name was Amases), [84] Pompeius, and Justin (who made an epitome of Pompeius's work) [85] relate that there was first very great plenty in Egypt and afterwards an insufferable famine. This famine Joseph, one of Jacob's twelve sons, who had been sold by his brothers, but by the providence of God was made ruler over all Egypt, relieved by divine direction. These historians say: "The youngest of the brothers was Joseph. Through envy of his superior talents his brothers waylaid him and sold him to foreign merchants. By them he was carried to Egypt. There, after he had by his shrewd wit mastered magic arts, he soon became very dear to the king himself. For he was skilled in portents and was the first to disclose the meaning of dreams, and it was plain that nothing of divine or human law was unknown to him, so much so that he even foresaw many years in advance that there would be a barrenness of the fields and had in consequence stored up grain; and so

---

[81] Apparently Rhodes, the city of the Colossus, is meant.

[82] He was in Attic legend the father of the hero Eleusis.

[83] *I.e.,* Eleusis.

[84] Ahmose I, 1580-1557 B.C.

[85] The universal history of Pompeius Trogus, a contemporary of the historian Livy, is known to us today only in the abridged edition of *M. Iunianus Iustinus,* or Justin. This particular passage is quoted by Otto from Orosius 1. 8.

great was his skill that his replies seemed to come not from a man but from God." Thus far Justin. But how the people of God went down into Egypt and sojourned there our own Moses (to whom also the Gentiles themselves bear witness as a wise and learned man, as we shall point out hereafter) [86] has recorded in writing.

15. At that time Serapis, the great idol of the Egyptians which the *Ecclesiastical History* states [87] was destroyed in Christian times under the emperor Theodosius, was made by the Egyptians for Apis, the king of the Argives. He had sailed to Egypt in his fleet, and had died there. But why the idol was called after his death not Apis but Serapis, Varro explains as follows: [88] "For because the coffin in which a dead man is placed, which everybody calls a sarcophagus, is named in Greek *soros* and it was only after he was buried and before his temple had been built that they began to worship him there, he was called at first Sorapis (from *soros* and Apis) and then — by the change of a single letter, as frequently happens — Serapis." Some say, though, that this image was made for our Joseph because he saved the Egyptians from famine.

16. Upon the death of Apis, his son Argus, from whom the Argives get their name, succeeded his father on the throne. In his day, while Eratus reigned among the Sicyonians, and Baleus was still living as king among the Assyrians, Jacob died at the age of one hundred and forty-seven years. At that time also, through importation of seeds from other lands, Greece for the first time began to have fields of grain. Observe that Greece, which excels all other nations in wisdom, received grain from other lands, but developed laws in and from herself (as is clear from the preceding account); she was instructed in judgments and laws before she had abundance of bread.

While Amintus,[89] the twelfth king, ruled the Assyrians, Clemineus, their eleventh king, the Sicyonians, and Argus was yet alive among the Argives, Joseph died in Egypt at the age of one hundred and ten years. After his death the people of God began to increase and multiply in Egypt, and, after the death of those who had known Joseph, began to be grievously oppressed by the Egyptians.

---

[86] I. 18 below.

[87] Eus. Ruf., *Eccl. hist.* 11. 23.

[88] Quoted by Augustine 18. 5, the basis for this chapter.

[89] *Mamytho,* according to Augustine and Jerome; *Maminthus* in Jordanes and in Frutolf; Otto himself, in I. 33, has *Mamirtus.*

Accordingly Moses, destined to be the liberator of this people, was born when Saphrus, the fourteenth king, ruled over the Assyrians, Ortopolis among the Sicyonians. It is said that it was in these same times that Prometheus lived, who, they claim, through his great wisdom made men out of clay, and also his brother Atlas, who is said — because of his knowledge of astronomy — to support the heavens. Mercury, a grandson of Atlas by his daughter Maia, who is also called Hermes Egyptius or Trimegister,[90] was a great philosopher who wrote remarkably profound philosophical works.

17. In the four hundred and nintieth year from the reign of Ninus, when Amphitrion, the third in line from Cecrops — or, according to others,[91] Cecrops himself — was king at Athens, a memorable flood (Deucalion's flood) took place. Because he saved from their boats those who came to him in the region of Mount Parnassus, cared for them, and supported them, we read in fables that he restored the human race. Plato states that at this time also Ethiopia seethed with dread diseases and a deadly pestilence. During these days, too, Father Liber drenched with blood a straightforward folk that had never harmed any one, but was content with its own territories: he defiled India with passions.

But, since we have made mention of Athens, let us tell how and by whom it was founded, and why it obtained this name. Well, then, Varro relates that, when it was founded and builded by Cecrops, an olive tree appeared in one place and a fountain burst forth in another. When the king, alarmed by these portents, had sent to Delphic Apollo to inquire about them, the oracle, it is said, replied that the olive was a sign of Minerva, the water a sign of Neptune, and that it was within the power of the citizens to call their city by the name of either of the two deities, as they preferred. The king, calling together the people of both sexes, placed the men on one side and the women on the other, and since the women outnumbered the men by one, they decided, on the basis of this omen, that the city should be dedicated to Minerva. So the city was called *Athenae*, a feminine plural word which in the singular number is the Greek name of Minerva. Because their lands, not long afterwards, were devastated by a raging sea, they ascribed this calamity

[90] Augustine 18. 39 says that Mercurius Trismegistus was the grandson of the elder Mercury, who in turn was the grandson of Atlas by his daughter Maia. *Cf.* also Augustine 8. 23.

[91] *I.e.,* Eusebius and Jerome, as we learn from Augustine 18. 10.

to Neptune as god of the sea, and decided to placate him by never again appealing to the votes of women. And so that city, destined to be the most renowned nurse of the liberal arts and of the greatest philosophers, at its first founding was inaugurated by the sport of demons.[92]

18. In the four hundred and ninety-fifth year from the reign of Ninus, while Ascathides [93] was king among the Assyrians, Marathus among the Sicyonians, Triophus among the Argives — Moses, the man of God, after Egypt had first been smitten with ten plagues, freed Israel from its slavery and led it forth [from Egypt]. Justin (or Pompeius) and Cornelius [94] bear witness to this, but in different ways. For Pompeius (or Justin) says: "Moses, the son of Joseph, was commended by the beauty of his person and by his inheritance of his father's wisdom. But when the Egyptians suffered from boils and eruptions, in accordance with the advice of an oracle they drove him forth with the sick from the bounds of Egypt that the plague might not spread to more victims. Therefore, becoming the leader of the exiles, he carried off by stealth the sacred vessels of the Egyptians, and when the Egyptians sought to regain them by force of arms they were compelled by storms to return home." But Cornelius speaks as follows of the same event: "Many authorities agree that, when a pestilence arose in Egypt which defiled men's bodies, King Bochoris, after consulting the oracle of Ammon in search of a remedy, was bidden to purge his kingdom and to transport this race of men into other lands, as a people hated by the gods. Thus that rabble was sought out and collected. After they were left in the wilderness, though the rest were disheartened and in tears, Moses, one of the exiles, advised them to expect no aid from the gods or from men but to put their trust in him as a heaven-sent leader, by whose aid they should first of all dispel their present sorrows." And so both those writers, although they have maliciously concealed many of his notable deeds, have yet involuntarily paid tribute to that great leader, our Moses. I have wished to set down these matters from histories of the Gentiles in order to show that the citizens of Babylon — to their own greater damnation — have known, indeed, how to tell the truth, but have not forsaken the deceitfulness of error.

[92] It was a tenet of Neoplatonism that there were powers known as *daemons*, intermediate between gods and human beings. *Cf.* I. 26 below.

[93] Or *Acchatades*, as the name appears in the list in I. 33 below.

[94] *I.e.*, Tacitus.

At that time an intolerable heat parched the earth, because the sun wandered from its course. Hence the heathen, deluded by a misguided error, invented that absurd fable of Phaethon.

19. In the five hundred and thirty-fifth year from the reign of Ninus, fifty murders are said to have been committed on one night among the children of Aegytus and Danaüs, two brothers. But Danaüs, the instigator of this horrid crime, withdrew to Argos and was kindly received by Sthenelus, their king; afterwards Danaüs treacherously drove Sthenelus out of his kingdom and himself reigned in his stead. It is from him, I think, that the race of the Danaï is descended, and from him the crime of perfidy was disseminated among them. Whence comes Vergil's well-known line :[95]

"Hear now the Danaäns' snares, and thus from one wicked action
Learn all,"

and again this :[96]

"Danaäns ever I fear, even with gifts in their hands."

During these days Perseus, sailing from Greece to Asia, conquered the barbarous tribes and called them, from his own name, Persians.

I am ashamed to lay open here the tangled ways of crime. For it was then that the wickedness of Busiris flourished, a man who sacrificed his guests to his gods. As for the murderous deed of Procne and Philomela, and the serving by a wife of her son as food to her husband, who will be able to hear of that without a groan? I pass over the shameful deeds of Tantalus and Pelops, and the story of Ganymede, the son of King Tros, who was most shamefully carried off by Tantalus, king of the Phrygians, under cover of the name of his god Jupiter, and of the tale of the very great war that was aroused thereby. Why should I speak of the disgraceful deeds of the Limniades, of Oedipus who murdered his father and married his mother — becoming the brother of his sons and his own stepfather, of the poisons administered by Medea and of her cruel passion? Were not the crimes of this age so dreadful and so unheard of that even the stars are said by the very citizens of the world to have fled?[97] What else, then, can I say at this point than

[95] Aeneid 2. 65-66.

[96] Aeneid 2. 49.

[97] Electra, one of the Pleiads, is said to have left her place in the heavens that she might not be forced to see the downfall of Troy, founded by her son Dardanus. She became a comet.

that we must flee out of the midst of Babylon and from the companionship of its most accursed citizens and pass over to our own fellow citizens?

20. When Moses had brought forth the people of God out of Egypt, he gave them the law on Mount Sinai, and, after he had been their ruler in the wilderness for forty years, he died at the age of one hundred and twenty years, and left the leadership of the people to Jesus [*i.e.*, Joshua], the son of Nun. He first, bearing the likeness of the Savior in office and in name, was privileged to lead the people of God into the land of promise, which is a type of that city which is our theme.

I think it must be ascribed not to mere accident, but to the providence of God who divideth the light from the darkness, that at about the time of the going out of the children of Israel from Egypt — or, according to others, during the time of their sojourn in the land of promise — the world seethed with new and unheard-of crimes (as I have just related). For even as we read that Herod, a king of this world, was troubled when Christ, the King of Heaven, was born, so quite naturally, when the Lord descended into Egypt and led his people forth from that country, the devil was disturbed, and incited to iniquitous ventures and most vile deeds the city that had been entrusted to him. For the same reason to this day we frequently see the world shaken and disturbed when the Lord calls his servants from the Egypt of the world to his own kingdom. For a like cause therefore, such events took place at the time of the entrance of the people of God into the land of promise and of the ejection of the tribes that had dwelt there.

21. They say that in the six hundred and fortieth year from the reign of Ninus there was a monstrous war between the Cretans and the Athenians, that the victory fell to the Cretans, and that some vanquished Athenians were exposed to the Minotaur, who was either a wild man or a human beast. We need not pursue this story, since it is a very familiar one, not only in consequence of this war but also in fables because of the ingenious devices of Daedalus, and is a theme worn threadbare by boys in the schools.[98] At that time the Lapithae, battling desperately with the Thessalians and from a distance seeing them riding about on horseback, thought

[98] An interesting incidental witness to the persistence of pagan culture in Christian times. The story is from Orosius 1.13, as is also the rationalization of the myth of the centaurs.

they were part of their horses; hence arose the myth of the centaurs.

22. In the eight hundred and twentieth year from the reign of Ninus, Vesores,[99] king of Egypt, declared war upon the Scythians.[100] The Scythians jeeringly retorted that it was to no purpose that a most wealthy monarch had undertaken a war against paupers. Moreover, they added that he need not come to them, since they were ready to meet him of their own initiative. Deeds followed the words. A battle was fought, and, when Vesores fled and was forsaken by his army, great booty was captured. The Scythians would even have devastated Egypt had they not been checked by the marshes of the Nile. Returning thence they ravaged Asia and made practically that entire land tributary. Since they stayed there for fifteen years, their wives declared that unless they came back they would have children by their neighbors. So they were obliged to return.

23. In the meantime two young princes, Plinius and Scolopecius, who had been driven out of Scythia with a great following, settled in the territories of Pontus and Cappadocia, near the river Thermodon.[101] While they were pillaging all the surrounding country they were destroyed by an ambuscade of the neighboring tribes. Their wives, deeply moved at once by exile and by this bereavement, and forgetting the frailty of their sex, killed the males that survived, took up arms, and, seeking marriage with their neighbors, put to death their boy babies but kept the girls. In this way the race of the Amazons was derived. These women, strange to say, became so powerful that they ruled almost all Asia and Europe. It is said that they founded Ephesus at that time and erected to Diana as to a goddess of war a temple renowned for many centuries to come. Furthermore, from the fact that they burned off their right breasts that they might not interfere with the aim of their arrows, they were called Amazons, as being without breasts.[102]

24. Now Jesus [i.e., Joshua] died in the land of promise while

---

[99] I.e., Sesostris. Herodotus (2. 102-110) gives an account of his reign that is much colored by myth. Many of the exploits attributed to him seem to be founded upon stories of the deeds of Ramses II.

[100] Cf. Justin 2. 3. 8 and Herodotus 2. 103. With the Scythian reply as here reported, cf. Herodotus 4. 127, where a similar answer is made to Darius.

[101] A river of Pontus, now the Termetschai.

[102] This story is from Orosius 1. 15. With it cf. Jordanes, Getica 7. 49 and 51, 8. 56, 20. 107.

Aminthas, their eighteenth king, was ruling among the Assyrians, Erichthonius, their fourth king, among the Athenians, Corax, their sixteenth king, among the Sicyonians, and Danaüs, their tenth king, among the Argives. From this time on there began to be Judges among the people of God; the Judges continued to the time of Saul. When the first of these, Othniel, was Judge, Cadmus invented the Greek alphabet. During this time there were religious teachers who spoke concerning false gods: Orpheus, Musaeus and Linus. Furthermore, the kingdom of the Argives came to an end, and its power was transferred to Mycenae, the home of Agamemnon. In Italy also the Laurentian kingdom arose, where the father of Faunus, namely Picus, the son of Saturn (who was also called Sterces because he first caused fields to be fertilized with manure), reigned after his father. This was while Deborah, a wise woman and a prophetess, was Judge of Israel, and Lampheres, their twenty-third king, ruled the Assyrians. Apollo invented the lyre and the art of medicine. Not long after, while Jair was Judge of Israel, the nymph Carmentis invented the Latin alphabet.

25. In the eight hundred and seventieth year from the reign of Ninus, Helen, they say, was carried off, and in consequence an alliance was formed against Troy. Then followed that ten-year siege and that famous destruction of Troy. Let him who desires to know of this read Homer and his imitators, Pindar [103] and Vergil. That in consequence of all this the race of the Romans had its origin from Aeneas, an exile, and, as he says in his own praise, a brave man — but according to others a betrayer of his country and a necromancer, inasmuch as he even sacrificed his own wife to his gods — is related by Vergil.

Writers say also that the race of the Franks had its beginning from the Trojans. For, while the leaders of the Trojans were roaming about with no fixed abodes, a great many of them settled in Scythia and chose a king to reign over them. At first they were called Sicambri; [104] afterwards, as time went on, under the emperor Valentinian, setting before themselves the prize of freedom, when they had made the neighboring tribes subject to their sway,

[103] The reference is to the Latin Iliad, strangely associated — since the 12th century — with the name of Pindar of Thebes. Orosius (1. 17) refers merely to Homer as his authority.

[104] Or Sugambri, a German tribe forming one division of the Frankish people and tracing their name to the Sigamber who is mentioned by Gregory of Tours 2. 31 (p. 41 in Brehaut's translation).

they were called Franks by the aforesaid emperor in the Attic tongue, from their ferocity — or Franks from their nobility, since in their language *franco* is the word for *noble*. However, some say that they were called Franks after a certain Franco, a leader of the Trojans who settled near the Rhine. For proof they point to a city still in existence which, they claim, he built and called by the ancestral name of Troy; he named its river, they add, Xanthus. This city was afterwards destroyed by the Saracens,[105] but was rebuilt by the Christians; it is called Xantis [106] even to this day. But how they came into France, which they now inhabit, we shall state at the proper place [107] and time, with God's help. Let these words concerning the origin of the race of the Franks suffice for the present.

Since the Trojans were scattered far and wide over the earth, Antenor also became the founder of a city — Patavium. This is why Vergil writes thus:[108]

"Then did Antenor escape through the midst of hostile Achaeans,
Reaching the Illyrian bays and the distant realms of Liburnia,
Safely passing beyond the source of the river Timavus." [109]

And again:

"Yet he founded here the city and homes of Patavium."

And Lucan speaks of "the savage Patavi." Some think that their city is Poitiers in Gaul, others that it is Passau in Bavaria, but others that it is Padua in Venetia, which is also called Patavium. The last is most probable and most in keeping with Vergil's account.

Now this most celebrated catastrophe occurred when the Laurentian kingdom had already given way to Latium, and when Latinus, the son of Faunus, was on the throne, and Abdon (or, according to others, Samson, the strongest of men) was Judge of the Hebrews. Men even thought him to be Hercules because of his remarkable strength: whether they were right in thinking him to be Hercules

[105] Not by the Saracens but by the Northmen, in the year 863, as Hofmeister points out.

[106] Xanten in Rhenish Prussia.

[107] See IV. 32.

[108] Aeneid 1. 242-244.

[109] Near the head of the Adriatic. The Timavus rises in springs a few miles northwest of Trieste.

is not for me to say. Yet that Samson and Hercules were contemporaries is indicated by the fact that they lived at about the time of the overthrow of Troy.[110]

These beginnings of the Roman kingdom had their inception in the Golden Age, that is, in the period that was free from idle luxury and from the tumult of wars, at Laurentum, under Saturn. But next succeeded the age of iron.

26. For Aeneas, crossing by ship from Phrygia to Italy, received in marriage the daughter of King Latinus, and, since a very dangerous war arose on this account between Turnus and himself, taught the Golden Age to transform itself to iron by the shedding of human blood. This matter Vergil, whether truthfully or falsely (with the gloss of adulation), treats of in the course of his beautiful poem. Let these words suffice concerning the exiles from Troy.

But such great disasters pursued the victors that in connection with so pitiful a revolution of fortune there is room for doubt as to which side succumbed to an evil fate. For to say nothing of those who met death in the long conflict (the Phrygian Dares declares [111] that the slain numbered eight hundred and eighty-three thousand of the Argives, six hundred and sixty-six thousand of the Trojans) how great were the perils of Ulysses, how great the weariness of his long wanderings!

These gave rise to the poet's well-known lines:[112]

"Tell me, O Muse, of the man who, after Troy had been captured,
Saw the cities and customs of other men without number."

For traversing almost the entire world, not so much by journeying through it as by wandering about in it, he had a share in all the misfortunes of land and sea. Hence that notable orator, in his book *On Duties* says: "How much Ulysses suffered in those long wanderings, when he was a slave to women — if Circe and Calypso were women — and in every conversation endeavored to be affable to all! How many insults he endured, of slaves, male and female, that he might at last attain his heart's desire. Ajax — of such a temper is this soldier reputed to have been — would have pre-

110 On the time of Hercules, see Frutolf, p. 44.1; on the other hand, the *Annales Hildesheimenses* clearly state that Hercules died before the beginning of the Trojan War, while Samson ruled the Hebrews only after the city had been captured (when Abdon was Judge).

111 In Chapter 44; but his figures are 886 and 676 thousand.

112 Horace, *Epistles* 2.3.141-142.

ferred to seek death rather than endure such things."[113] Ulysses is said to have been the first to found Lisbon in Spain, which was recently[114] taken by our people from the Saracens, and Troy in France, of which mention was made above. For this reason also the tradition about Franco appears to be false. But what am I to say about those hardships of Ulysses and others, famed in story, which almost exceed belief? Finally, not only are the legends in accord, but even the histories are full of the tale that the companions of Diomedes were changed into birds,[115] and that, since he himself was transformed into a god, they flit about his temple, which is situated on the island of Diomedia, not far from Monte Gargano,[116] and serve as water carriers. Varro, according to Augustine, appears to substantiate this to the extent, at least, that he says that these birds recognize as fellow citizens those that come from Greece, but repel strangers by viciously pecking at them. To win further credence for the tale, Varro makes mention also of that notorious Circe who changed the comrades of Ulysses into beasts, and of the Arcadians who, as they swam across a pool, were transformed into wolves; if they did not feed on human flesh, they were to return to the form of men after eight years by recrossing the stream. He even names a certain Demenutus, who tasted of a sacrifice that the Arcadians were offering and, being transformed into a wolf, did not return to his own shape until the tenth year. For this reason he says their god was called Lycaeus,[117] for the Greeks call a wolf *licus*. He says that the *luperci*[118] of the Romans, too, had their origin from them. Whether they invent all these stories out of love for their gods, or such things can really be brought to pass by the mocking action of demons and certain hidden forces of nature, does not concern the present work. However, Augustine says[119] that in his time a certain Praestantius told of his own father the tale that he took a drug in cheese, and as a result lay for many days in

[113] Cicero, *De Officiis* 1. 31. 113.

[114] October 24, 1147. Hofmeister points out that this is a statement evidently added in the second edition of the Chronicle.

[115] See Aeneid 11. 271 and Augustine 18. 16.

[116] In Apulia.

[117] An epithet of Pan, who was worshiped on Mt. Lycaeus in Arcadia.

[118] Perhaps from *lupus* and *arceo*: "warders off of wolves." The *Luperci* were priests who participated in the great festival of the *Lupercalia,* celebrated in ancient Rome on Feb. 15th. See Fowler, *The Roman Festivals,* pp. 310-321.

[119] Augustine 18. 18.

his bed as though asleep, but when he woke he stated that he had become a horse and had carried provisions. That same Father relates that, when he was in Italy, he heard of certain women who made a practice of giving wayfarers devilish concoctions in cheese, by reason of which they fancied that they had been changed into pack animals; when they came to themselves after the lapse of time, they testified that they had retained all the while their reasoning faculties. You find this account of the hermit Macarius also: that there was brought to him a girl who, so her friends said, had been changed by sorcery into a mare; he gazed upon her and said that he saw a maiden, not a mare. So she who seemed to her friends to be a mare was to the man of God a maiden. Thereupon, pouring forth prayers to God, he freed the girl and her friends from the legerdemain of the demons. Now, from these and similar accounts it is evident that demons cannot, indeed, change the nature of men, but that, by taking possession of those parts of the body through which reason usually operates, they dull a man's mind and the eyes of those that look on him, and by occult arts and hidden forces of nature bewitch them all, so that they believe that a change has occurred. Hence Paul says to the Galatians: "O foolish Galatians, who did bewitch you?" For demons, by God's dispensation, have great knowledge and power, both because of the cunning of their nature and because of their great age and experience, so that they not only deceive the citizens of the world, but would injure even the citizens of Christ were they not prevented by Him. This can be shown clearly by the fact that Balaam, who was, to be sure, a Gentile and a prophet, had so much power in consequence of the devices of demons that he would even have been able to curse the people of God if he had not been forbidden by Him. For he did not worship the Lord, that is, the true God (some think he did, inasmuch as he is reported to have said, "I will speak to the Lord"), but, when he thought he was talking to the demon whom he called lord, the Lord in his wisdom interposed to prevent what he had wickedly planned; hence he spoke words not, as he had willed, harmful to his people, but, in accordance with the ordinance of the Lord, beneficial. Another circumstance that gives credence to this interpretation is the fact that Balaam tried by frequent sacrifices and offerings to turn him from his purpose: to have such a thought or presumption regarding the Divine Majesty, whose nature is unchangeable, would be absurd.

27. While Tautenes reigned among the Assyrians, Pelasgus among the Sicyonians, and Samson was Judge of Israel, Aeneas, upon the death of Latinus, ruled in Latium for three years. When he was dead he was deified by his people because he was no longer visible. When their twenty-ninth king Oneus [120] was ruling the Assyrians, Mesantus the Athenians, and the fourth Latin king, Aeneas Silvius (born to Aeneas not by Creusa but by the daughter of King Latinus), was in power, and while Eli was Judge of the Hebrews, the kingdom of the Sicyonians, which had endured for five hundred and fifty or more years,[121] came to an end. Hence comes the following statement of the chronographer Castor:[122] "We shall mention also the kings of the Sicyonians from Agialeus even to Zeuxippus, who reigned altogether nine hundred and forty-five years, and six priests of the flesh who were in office thirty-two years. After them Caridemus was appointed priest, but he, since he could not stand the expense, fled." Hereafter the state of the Athenians began to have prestige in Europe. The Aeneas I have mentioned was called Silvius from *silva*, because, when he was still a lad, his mother, going into hiding through fear of Ascanius, hid him in the woods.

From this time on the Greeks and the Latins, uniting as into one seed, so to say, began to have a certain kinship of customs and language, and they were wont to call other races barbarians on the ground that they lacked keenness of intellect and elegance of language. That the Greeks do in fact excel all other peoples in intellectual power as well as in charm of speech the poet declares when he says:

"Greeks have the gift of keenness, Greeks speak with smooth-
      flowing diction,
Thanks to the Muse." [123]

And elsewhere:

"Greece, an eloquent nation, but by no means courageous in battle." [124]

---

[120] Also called *Thineus;* see I. 33 below.

[121] *Per annos nongentos quinquaginta et novem*, Augustine 18. 19; DCCCC-LXII, Frutolf and Jerome. The statement in Otto is obviously a slip, as the next sentence indicates.

[122] Jerome, *Chron.* 885.

[123] Horace, *Epistles* 2. 3. 323-324.

[124] Ovid, *Fasti* 3. 102.

Hence also three languages are regarded as the most important: the Hebrew, for the worship of God and because of its antiquity; the Greek, for wisdom and the charm of its expression; the Latin, for power and also for wisdom.

28. After the death of Eli, Samuel was made Judge of the Hebrews. When the Hebrews asked him for a king they received Saul at the time when Derciles was reigning among the Assyrians. About the same time Codrus, king of the Athenians, thrust himself in disguise in the way of his enemies, the Peloponnesians, and by starting a dispute provoked them to kill him. He did so because the Peloponnesians had received an oracle saying that they would not be conquered by the Athenians unless they should first slay the king of the Athenians. Hence Vergil says: "And Codrus's quarrelsome words"; and again, "Let them burst [with rage] even as did the sides of Codrus." For this the Athenians voted to reverence him, and from that time forth they began to have, instead of kings, magistrates to govern their state as a republic.

Tradition states that these were the Judges among the people of God, after the patriarchs: Moses, Jesus [i.e., Joshua], Othniel, Ehud, Deborah, Gideon, Abimelech, Tola, Jair, Jephthah, Ibzan, Elon, Abdon, Samson, Eli, Samuel.

29. From this point are reckoned the kings and the times of the Prophets. The first of these, after the rejection of Saul, was David, a great leader of the City of God, for to him first after the patriarchs was the promise made that of his seed was to be born the Christ, the founder of that City which forms our theme. His son Solomon, while Eupales was ruling the Assyrians, erected a temple most renowned alike for its sanctity and for its workmanship, at the time when Alba [125] was founded in Italy. Furthermore, lest on account of his power and his celebrated wisdom, in which he surpassed all mortals, he might be thought to be that seed which had been promised to David, described by God's messengers, destined to possess all nations, Solomon was permitted by the Lord to fall. For, since he was a most ardent lover of women — he is said to have had as many as a thousand wives, almost all foreign-born — he was dragged by them into the abyss of idolatry. Therefore it came to pass that, though the Lord spared him because of the merits of his father David, he rent the kingdom out of the hands of his son Rehoboam, in the days when Piriciades was ruling the As-

[125] *I.e.*, *Alba Longa*, the city founded by Ascanius. See Livy 1. 3.

syrians, and left him only two tribes, namely Judah and Benjamin. Forthwith that once famous kingdom, divided now against itself, in accordance with the word of truth [126] was doomed to be brought to desolation, so completely that you can find no one of the kings of Israel and very few indeed of the kings of Judah that were citizens of Jerusalem. And — to use words of authority — "from David unto the carrying away to Babylon" all, except Hezekiah and Josiah, committed trespass, yet not all the rest were reprobate. Accordingly, as the sins of each kingdom demanded, first Israel, later Judah too, was led into captivity. Yet each kingdom had citizens of the Kingdom of Christ whose function it was to rebuke the excesses of the sinful people and their deceitful kings. Prominent among these in the Kingdom of Israel were Elijah and Elisha, who because of their notably virtuous lives were endowed with grace by the Lord to shut up heaven and open it again, to raise the dead, to give orders to kings, and to perform countless miraculous prodigies and display marvellous signs. The former of these was carried alive into the air in a fiery chariot and is believed to be alive still,[127] while the other, even after his death, is known to have raised a dead man. And that no one may suppose that the City of God at that time was small, hear what was said of Israel alone by the Lord to Elijah: "I have left for myself seven thousand men" — a number which in the Scriptures is frequently used for an indefinitely large array. In Judah, moreover, Hosea, Isaiah and a great many others whom we shall set down at the proper place not only prophesied, but also left written memorials that were destined to be of great avail to the City of God. But now let us return to the citizens of the world.

30. When Alba was founded by Æneas Silvius, the kings of the Latins established the seat of their sovereignty there. Æneas Silvius was succeeded by Latinus, the latter by Alba. After Alba in turn came Egyptus, and Capys,[128] and Tiberinus. From Tiberinus the Tiber (which was previously called the Albula) received its name. After Tiberinus his son Agrippa reigned, then Aremulus, and in due course Aventinus. All of these were called Silvii after

---

[126] Matt. 12. 25 and Luke 11. 17.

[127] See below, VIII. 5.

[128] Between Capys and Tiberinus Otto here has omitted *Carpentus* (or more correctly *Capetus*), whom both Ovid and Frutolf (following Jerome) mention, but he has included him in his list of kings at the end of Book VII.

the first Silvius, just as in later times the Caesars were named after Julius Caesar. When Aventinus died and had been buried on the mount called from his name the Aventine, he was worshiped by the people as a god. Others say that this hill was called the Aventine because the birds flocked to it.[129] Between Aventinus and Romulus there are said to have been only two kings, Proca and Amulius. When, therefore, the kingdom of the Romans was, so to speak, about to be born, the famous and powerful kingdom of the Babylonians began to wane through the decay of old age.

31. Accordingly, in the year one thousand two hundred and thirty-six from the reign of Ninus, and in the year one thousand three hundred and five [130] after the sway of his father Belus, and in the year one thousand one hundred and sixty-four from the founding or the restoration, under Semiramis, of Babylon, their last king and the most corrupt, Sardanapalus,[131] their thirty-sixth king, reigned among the Assyrians. He was discovered by his prime minister, Arbaces the Mede,[132] in woman's apparel, twirling the distaff amid the troops of his mistresses. And, because his people were aroused against him by Arbaces, Sardanapalus threw himself into a blazing funeral pile. Thus that powerful and flourishing empire passed to the Medes.

32. It is not necessary at this point to enlarge upon the miseries of temporal affairs. For mark you, that mighty kingdom, although not yet utterly destroyed, still by its change gives to itself premonition in divers ways of its own utter ruin! What then shall we say, who think to cleave to transitory things, when we see them change, then when they have changed begin to degenerate, and finally perish utterly? This indeed, with God's help, we shall show fulfilled in the case of Babylonia, and we expect from many passages of Scripture and the clearest evidences that it must beyond all doubt be brought to pass in the case of the whole world also.

Now after this the kingdom of the Babylonians continued in Babylon because of the high position the city had once had, but it

129 Certain MSS insert at this point a paragraph on the founding of Rome; see Hofmeister's edition, p. 65.

130 Hofmeister points out that Otto took this number from Augustine 18. 21 although it does not agree with his own words in I. 6 above.

131 Or Asshurbanapal, 668-626, the last great Assyrian emperor. The fall of Assyria and the destruction of Nineveh did not occur until 606 B.C.

132 This story, which is here taken over from Orosius 1. 19, apparently goes back to Ctesias, whose account is cited in Diodorus Siculus 2. 21-28.

continued in name only; in point of fact the kingdom was in the hands of the Chaldeans till the authority passed to the Medes. For they had from this time on kings of the Chaldeans, strong in might but not famous enough to be added to the list of their predecessors. Whence it is evident that Nebuchadnezzar [133] and the other kings from Sardanapalus down to the time of Cyrus [134] were not of the muster roll of illustrious monarchs. From this one can gather how great had been the prestige and the power of that kingdom under the earlier line, since it was of such fame and influence even in the time of the later rulers. Furthermore, the kings of the Medes, to whom, as we have said, the authority over the Babylonian kingdom finally passed, begin to be reckoned from this point. So with our account of this great change that occurred in that mighty kingdom and of the changes in lesser realms, their decreases in power and the other disasters wrought by changing conditions, let us bring the first book to a close, that we may come to those vicissitudes which befell the kingdoms of the Medes, the Persians, the Greeks, and especially the Romans.

33. Now these are the kings of the Assyrians:[135] Belus; Ninus; Semiramis; Zammeis, who is also called Ninias [*i.e.*, Ninus], the son of Ninus and Semiramis; Arius; Aralius; Xerxes, also called Baleus; Armamithres; Belochus; Baleus; Althadas; Mamirtus; Machaleus; Sperus; Mammilus; Sparetus; Acchatades; Aminthas; Bellepares; Lamprides; Sophares; Lampheres; Paminas; Sosar; Mitreus; Tautenes; Teuteus; Thineus, or Oneus; Derciles; Eupales; Laostenes; Piriciades; Offraticus; Ofratenes; Vacrazenes; Thonos Concoleros, who is also called Sardanapalus.

<h3 style="text-align:center">HERE ENDS THE FIRST BOOK</h3>

[133] Or Nebuchadrezzar II, the greatest of the Chaldean emperors, 604-561 B.C.

[134] Cyrus the Great of Persia, 558-528.

[135] The names of the kings of the Assyrians, from Jerome, are found in their proper order in Jordanes and Frutolf. Although Otto, with Frutolf and Augustine 16. 17 and 18. 21, begins with Belus, yet by omitting Belochus between Aminthas and Bellepares he agrees more closely with Jerome and Jordanes in his total; moreover he is not always consistent with himself.

HERE BEGINS THE PROLOGUE OF THE SECOND BOOK [1]

I recall that in the preceding book I promised that I would write about the instability and the sorrows of the world. And, by God's help, I have indeed brought down this history — in some fashion — as far as the fall of the first Babylon and the beginning of the second, I mean Rome. For that these are related empires may be inferred not only from the words of writers of history — who have stated that the sovereignty of the latter city succeeded that of the former as a son succeeds his father; the short-lived empires of the Medes and the Persians and of the Macedonians intervening (like the guardians of a little child) not by right of permanent inheritance but by mere temporary succession — but also from the epistle of the chief of the apostles, who, writing from Rome, calls that city Babylon, saying, "The church that is in Babylon saluteth you." [2] Then too, when we call to mind the disasters of bygone times, we almost forget the pressure of the present time that in a way weights us down. For example, but lately an uproar has been heard everywhere throughout the world, but particularly in our province [3] which that nobleman Welf [4] recently invaded in hostile fashion, devastating the farmlands and plundering the property of the churches of God; [5] and — what is worse — we are in danger of our lives, and our very souls are imperilled. For as there is a controversy concerning the dukedom between him and Henry, duke of Bavaria, [6] both of them estimable young men and of ardent

1 Book II covers the period from the fall of Babylon and the beginnings of Rome to the end of the Roman Republic (44 B.C.). Otto's chief authorities for this section of his work are: Orosius, especially Books 2, 3, 4, and 6; Augustine De Civitate Dei 18; and Frutolf. There are shorter quotations from the Bible, the Romana of Jordanes, from the Antiquitates Iudaicae and the De bello Iudaico of Josephus, and from Aristotle, Cicero, Boëthius, the expository works of Jerome, Ennius, Seneca's letters to Lucilius and Lucan's Pharsalia.

2 I Pet. 5. 13.

3 I.e., Bavaria.

4 In 1143. This is Welf VI, a brother of Henry the Proud.

5 Cf. VII. 26 below.

6 I.e., Otto's brother, Henry "Jasomirgott." See Intro., p. 9.

spirit, what else can be expected at the hands of either than the ruin of the poor and the desolation of the churches, as the famous verse has it:

"Whene'er their rulers rage 'tis ever the Achaeans who suffer." [7]

Therefore let us leave this to the judgment of God and to the prayers of the Church, and let us rather, with God's help, advance the work we have undertaken. But let no one expect from me epigrams or moral reflections. For it is our intention to set forth, not after the manner of a disputant, but in the fashion of one telling a story, a history in which on the one hand the varying experiences of the citizens of Babylon and their sufferings and, on the other hand, the progress and achievements of the citizens of Christ, their progress through and beyond those sufferings, shall be interwoven. A sufficient reply has been made, I think, by our predecessors [8] to those who assail the faith that is in us.

HERE BEGINS THE SECOND BOOK

1. When the kingdom of the Assyrians had been transferred to the Medes, Arbaces, who had been the cause of this change, seized the throne and held it for twenty-eight years, while Uzziah was reigning in Judah, and Shallum or Menahem in Israel. Sosarmus succeeded Arbaces, while Ahaz was reigning in Judah and Pekah in Israel. In the fifteenth year of the reign of Sosarmus fell the first Olympiad,[9] so called. Thereafter an Olympiad was regularly marked by a contest and games at Elis, a city of Greece,[10] every fifth year — four years intervening between two Olympiads. Sosarmus left as his successor Madidus,[11] while Ahaz was reigning in Judah, Hoshea or Pekah the Second in Israel. Cardices followed him, while Hezekiah reigned in Judah, Israel having been led into captivity.[12] After him came Dioces, while Manasseh reigned in Judah. After him Phraortes ruled for twenty-two years and pol-

[7] Horace, *Epistles* 1. 2. 14.

[8] Augustine and Orosius. On the word *maiores,* which Otto here employs, *cf.* VIII. 13 below.

[9] 776 B.C.

[10] Otto gives *apud Helidem Greciae urbem* in the text. The reference is to Olympia, of course.

[11] *I.e.,* Medius; Jordanes, *Romana* 52.

[12] Samaria fell late in 722 B.C., and Sargon, king of Assyria, carried away its inhabitants into captivity in 721.

luted his reign by many — yes, by incessant — wars. This was while that most righteous king Josiah reigned in Judah. Then came Dyocles who greatly enlarged the kingdom, since he was very proficient in warfare. He was succeeded by Astyages,[13] a cruel, inhuman man, who killed the only son of a certain Harpagus [14] and served him to his father as food, and then taunted the father with his unhallowed meal by displaying the head and hands of the boy. His grandson, Cyrus the Persian, when he became of age, presently declared war against his grandsire. Therefore Astyages, forgetting his evil deed, placed Harpagus in command of the army. While the latter was handing over the entire army to Cyrus, Astyages went back to the Medes and assembled an army. After a second conflict, when the Persians were in flight, their wives and mothers taunted them so shamelessly that they turned back and won the victory, taking Astyages prisoner. When he had captured his grandfather, Cyrus made him ruler of the Hyrcanians and brought to an end the kingdom of the Medes, which, we find, endured for two hundred and fifty-eight years. The above account is according to Orosius. This is the Cyrus by whom Babylon was afterwards destroyed. His uncle was Darius, king of the Medes,[15] who, as we read in Daniel, overthrew Belshazzar. Hence, according to others, he obtained the throne of the Medes not by war but by right of inheritance, after the death of his grandfather Astyages and his son Darius, just as you have the account in Daniel: "King Astyages was gathered to his fathers and Cyrus the Persian reigned in his stead." But I recall that elsewhere in Daniel [16] the Darius who overthrew Belshazzar is called not the son of Astyages but the son of Ahasuerus. Now it may well be that he had two names. Hence Josephus, in the tenth book of his Antiquities,[17] says: "Darius, the son of Astyages, who with his kinsman Cyrus destroyed the empire of the Babylonians, but was called by the Greeks by another name." Mean-

---

[13] The last king of Media. For the story here alluded to, see Herodotus 1. 119.

[14] The text reads *Arpalo*.

[15] "Darius the Mede" is unknown to history. Attempts have been made to identify him with Cyaxares II, the father of Cyrus, with Astyages himself, or with the satrap Gobryas. Farrar says (*The Book of Daniel*, p. 217): " 'Darius the Mede' probably owes his existence to a literal understanding of the prophecies of Isaiah 13.17 and Jeremiah 51.11 and 28."

[16] Dan. 9. 1.

[17] *Cf. Antiquities* 10. 11. 4.

while the Chaldeans, of whose number were Nebuchadnezzar [18] and his successors, invaded Babylon and afflicted the City of God with many evils. Yet they were not of the number of the preceding kings, as has been said above,[19] since the Medes held the authority. Now these were the kings of the Medes:[20] Arbaces, Sosarmus, Madidus, Cardices, Dioces, Phraortes, Dyocles, Astyages, Darius, Cyrus. From this point are reckoned the kings of the Persians.

2. I think it is time for us to apply our pen to the beginnings of the rule of the Romans. For although the kingdom of Babylon, stripped of its glory and under a special prefect, still continued intact under the overlordship of the Medes down to the time of Cyrus, and was by him totally destroyed (as will appear in the sequel),[21] yet upon its decline I may properly narrate the rise of the Roman Empire, which, as I have said, succeeded it as a son succeeds his father. Well, then, it passed into the hands of the Medes at the time when Procas was king in Italy; it was utterly overthrown by Cyrus at the time when Rome, freed from the tyrannical rule of the Tarquins, began to stand firmly established in its own authority.

Amulius succeeded Procas. Amulius's brother Numitor, when he learned that his daughter Rhea Silvia, whom he had made a vestal virgin, was guilty of unchastity from the fact that she bore children, ordered the twins whom she had brought forth to be exposed and cast into the water. These are the twin brothers Remus and Romulus, founders and builders of the city that was destined to be the capital of the world. The writers of Rome,[22] assuming that Rome was destined to gain the rule of the whole world by martial prowess, claim that they were also the sons of Mars, and in proof of this assert that they were nursed and nurtured, contrary to nature, by a she-wolf — the beast, at any rate, of Mars. But whether they were really nourished by a wolf, as those writers say, or (as others have it)[23] by some harlot or other called "Wolf" on account of her vile manner of living — as we call the houses of such women

[18] Or Nebuchadrezzar, 604-561. His reign "was the high-water mark of Chaldean civilization" (Breasted).

[19] I. 32; cf. III. 2 below.

[20] This list of kings is most in accord with Jordanes.

[21] II. 11.

[22] E.g., Livy.

[23] quamvis non desint qui dicant, Augustine 18. 21; this is also the opinion of Jordanes, Romana 51 and Frutolf; the latter says that the other tradition was an invention of the poets.

lupanaria, after that same word, *lupa, wolf* — is no concern of mine. I merely make this statement, that they were the sons not of Mars but of some man and, according to certain reliable authorities, a priestess.

3. In the year one thousand three hundred from the reign of Ninus, the four hundred and fourteenth year after the fall of Troy, in the sixth Olympiad, when four thousand four hundred and eighty-four years [24] had elapsed since Adam's time, while Ahaz reigned in Judah (or, according to Augustine, his most righteous son King Hezekiah) and Hoshea or Pekah the Second reigned in Israel — Rome, the greatest and most famous of cities, was founded on the Palatine Hill. The twins Remus and Romulus were its builders, while their grandfather Numitor was still alive. Presently Romulus stained this kingdom by murder, killing his grandfather [Amulius] and his brother, and polluted it also by the rape of the Sabine women. He slew their husbands and parents and unlawfully and cruelly joined them in sinful union with himself and his followers.

4. At about this same time, it is generally agreed, those renowned men whom I mentioned above,[25] Hosea and Isaiah, prophesied and left their prophecies behind them in writing. One of these, we see, foretold the calling of the Gentiles not only by his words, but by his deeds as well, in that he took a harlot to wife.[26] This is why he says also:[27] "I will call that my people which was not my people." The other, moreover, spoke concerning the coming of Christ, his passion, his resurrection and the spread of his kingdom (which is the Church) in this life, its glorification hereafter when the city of the wicked shall have been eternally damned, and its continuance with Christ its founder forever, setting all this forth in language so clear, so polished, and so felicitous that he seems to have composed not a prophecy but the actual record of the good tidings.

At that time too, some say, the Sibyl Ericthea prophesied.[28] Be-

---

[24] This number is not in agreement with those given in I. 3 and I. 6 above; Jordanes, *Romana* 52, has 4650th year from the beginning of the world; Frutolf, p. 50, 25, has 3211th year.

[25] I. 29 end.

[26] Hos. 1. 2-3. With what follows *cf.* Augustine 18. 28.

[27] So Paul in his epistle to the Romans 9. 25. Hofmeister remarks (p. 71, n. 18): *cum Osea* 1, 9 *longe aliis verbis utatur;* but see Hos. 2. 23.

[28] Augustine (18. 23), from whom this sentence is taken, has *Sibyllam Erythraeam,* "the Erythraean Sibyl."

cause of the testimony afforded by her writings Augustine seems to hold [29] that she belonged to the City of God, as did Job and many others of the Gentiles. To prove this that same Father quotes in his book *The City of God* her very clear prophecy regarding the incarnation, passion, and second coming of Christ, which I have inserted below:[30]

*J*udgment's sign upon earth: with sweat shall the dry land be dripping,
*E*verlasting the king who shall come to reign from the heavens
*S*urely to judge the world, in the flesh appearing in person.
*O*n that day shall believers see God, yea! also the faithless;
*U*p with the saints on high, when the age has now reached its conclusion,
*S*ouls and bodies alike shall be there for His judgment upon them.

*C*hoked with thick brambles the earth then all untilled shall lie fallow.
*R*iches and idols together shall men then put from them forever.
*E*arth shall the fire consume, consume too the sea and the heavens,
*I*t shall seek out and destroy the portals of loathsome Avernus.
*S*aints in the flesh shall obtain the freedom and light of salvation;
*T*hen shall the guilty be burned with fire that dies not forever.
*O*n that day shall no secrets be hid: each shall speak of the actions
*S*ealed in his innermost heart; to the light shall God then reveal them.

*T*here shall be gnashing of teeth and all shall be sorrow and wailing;
*E*ven the light of the sun shall be dimmed, and the stars lulled to silence;
*O*pen sky like a scroll shall be rolled, the moon's splendor be darkened;
*U*p from the depths shall the vales be exalted, the hills be downtrodden;

*U*tterly level the whole, no longer things high or exalted,
*I*nto the plains shall the mountains sink down, and all the blue waters
*O*ver the world shall cease, the land disrupted shall perish.
*S*o shall the fountains and rivers alike flow in torrents of fire.

*S*ending down from on high a sorrowful sound, shall the trumpet
*O*ver the land peal forth, to bemoan sad and varied affliction;
*T*artarus' depth shall the earth reveal, bursting open;
*E*very king shall be sent to stand in God's holy presence;
*R*eeking sulphurous streams and flames shall flow down from the heavens.

In the initials of these verses,[31] in the Greek, he says there is

---

[29] 18. 23: . . . *ut in eorum numero deputanda videatur, qui pertinent ad civitatem Dei.*

[30] The poem is taken from Augustine 18. 23.

[31] The poem is an acrostic whose initials in the original (according to Augustine, *l.c.*) spell Ἰησοῦς Χρειστὸς Θεοῦ υἱὸς σωτήρ, which Otto here renders correctly as "*Iesus Christus filius Dei salvator,*" though he trans-

found the phrase *Iesus Christus Theos Sother,* which means "Jesus
Christ, the Son of God, the Saviour." He relates, moreover, that
Lactantius [32] gives another prophecy of the Sibyl concerning Christ,
which runs as follows: "Afterwards he shall fall into the hands
of unbelievers. And they will give God buffets with their unholy
hands and from their unclean lips will spue forth their venomous
spittle. But he will present to their stripes his pure and holy back,
and will receive the blows of their fists in silence, that none may
know whence the word comes or whither it is directed, that he may
talk with them that are below and be crowned with a crown of
thorns. For his thirst they gave him vinegar, and for his food gall;
this was the table of inhospitality they spread for their Lord. For
thou thyself in thy folly didst not recognize thy God, who baffled
the understanding of mortals, but crowned him with thorns and
mixed the bitter gall. But the veil of the temple shall be rent in
twain and at midday there shall be utter murky night for three
hours, and he shall die the death, undergoing sleep. And then returning from the world below he shall be the first to come to the
light, displaying, to those recalled, the beginning of the resurrection." However there are not wanting those who claim that this
Sibyl made her prophecies at the time of the Trojan War.

5. In the reign of Romulus, after the theological poets whom I
mentioned above,[33] there lived, men say, Thales of Miletus, one of
the seven wise men whom they called *sophoi.*[34] In those days also
the ten tribes were conquered by the Chaldeans in Samaria and
led into captivity, and a Chaldean people was settled in Samaria
who, according to the book of Kings, feared God and yet did not
desert their idols.[35] But the reason why they feared God was that,
when they first came into Samaria, the Lord had sent his lions

literates the Greek as *Iesus Christus Theos Sother."* (For a discussion of
Otto's knowledge of Greek, see Introduction, pp. 39-41). The initials of the
Latin poem as Otto records it spell: IESOUS CREISTOS TEV DNIOS
SOTER; in my metrical translation: JESOUS ChREISTOS ThEOU UIOS
SOTER.

[32] Caecilius Firmianus Lactantius, the pupil of Arnobius and (in his old
age) tutor of the young prince Crispus, the son of Constantine. The quotation
occurs also in Augustine 18. 23.

[33] I. 24.

[34] The seven were: Solon, Periander, Chilon of Sparta, Pittacus, Bias,
Thales, and Cleobulus of Lindus; see II. 7 below. It will be remembered that
Thales predicted an eclipse of the sun in 585 B.C.

[35] II Kings 17; 24-29.

against them. It is clear, then, that what they wished to accept
of the law they accepted, what they did not wish to accept they
rejected, after the manner of aliens. Hence you have the statement in the Gospel [36] that the Jews had no dealings with them.

At about this time when Phalaris, the Sicilian tyrant, was tor-
menting innocent people with many varied forms of torture, a
certain Perillus, a worker in bronze, desiring to please his prince
and to offer him an instrument for his cruelty thoroughly suited to
him, made a brazen bull in whose side he fitted a door, to the end
that, when those to be tortured had been admitted by this door and
were in agony from the fires set underneath the bull, they might
appear to give voice not to the groan of a human being but to the
bellowing of a beast. The tyrant graciously accepted this image,
and placing its inventor himself inside it punished him with his
own device.

6. Romulus, collecting from all sides companies of shepherds,
brigands, and robbers — for whom he even opened a place of
refuge [37] — cruelly inaugurated the kingdom that was to be the
capital of the whole world. This is why Juvenal says: [38]

Yet, howe'er far back you go in tracing your lineage and station,
Surely your name you derive from that most disgraceful asylum:
Whoe'er the first of your line, your ancestor was doubtless a shepherd —
Were he anything else 'twould be what I prefer not to mention.

He also selected a thousand youths from the plebs and named them
milites, and called a hundred of the elders "senators." From these
sources the military class and the senatorial dignity had their
beginning. Romulus was succeeded by Numa, a man who brought
into the City the worship — nay, rather the sacrilege — of many
gods and built the capitol from its foundations. In his days, while
that most evil king Manasseh — by whom Isaiah, it is said, was
killed — reigned among the Hebrews, men declare the Samian
Sibyl lived. Numa was succeeded by Tullus Hostilius, who was the
first of the Roman kings to use royal crimson and the *fasces.* He
enlarged the City by adding the Caelian Hill. After him, Ancus
Marcius added the Aventine Hill and the Janiculum to the City,
and founded Ostia on the seashore, sixteen miles from the City. [39]

[36] John 4. 9.
[37] The *asylum* of which Livy speaks (1. 9).
[38] *Satires* 8. 272-275.
[39] The well-known port of Rome, at the mouth of the Tiber.

7. During the reign of the next king, Tarquinius Priscus, who built the Circus and increased the number of the senators, Judah too was led into captivity by the Chaldeans,[40] together with her king Zedekiah. In these days there were very many citizens of Christ's kingdom, and especially prophets, who denounced the people of God for their evil works and prophesied disasters to come. Some of them were led into captivity along with the guilty people; others were left even by the enemy to their own inclinations and devices. In these days, moreover, that man of God Jeremiah prophesied and left in writing a work exceedingly helpful to the Church of God. He set down therein the sins of the iniquitous people and the captivity from which they were to be delivered after seventy years, and made many predictions concerning the state of the Church and the coming of Christ. They say that Pittacus of Mytilene,[41] one of the seven sages, lived at that time. Eusebius declares that the other five, namely Solon of Athens, Chilon of Lacedaemon, Periander of Corinth, Cleobulus of Lindus, and Bias of Priene, lived at the time when the people were being held in captivity. None of these, however, has left any memorials in the form of books except Thales, who wrote "On Physics,"[42] and Solon, who gave the Athenians their laws.[43]

8. After the theological poets and those whom I have called the sages there arose the philosophers, men who preferred to be called by the modest name "philosophers," that is "lovers of wisdom," rather than by the name "wisemen." Pythagoras, the first of these, discovered the seven intervals of musical sounds through the various sounds caused by the blows of mallets, and was very famous and of great service in many other ways. After him Socrates trained Plato and Aristotle,[44] the most renowned of all the philosophers, and with a keenness proportioned to their youth, since they sur-

[40] The destruction of Jerusalem and the final Captivity occurred in 586 B.C.

[41] In whose days lived the famous Lesbian poets, Alcaeus and Sappho.

[42] Although the founder of the Milesian school of cosmologists deserves the title of the first man of science he does not appear to have written anything.

[43] Archon in 594 B.C., "the first great Greek statesman of whom we obtain an authentic picture, chiefly through his surviving poems" (Breasted).

[44] The Greek life circulating under the name of Ammonius makes Aristotle a pupil of Socrates, though he was born fifteen years after the elder philosopher's death. Hofmeister believes that the Latin version of this Life was known to Otto or his teachers, disagreeing with Rose, who assigns the translation to the 13th Century.

passed their very teachers in understanding. The one of these discusses the power, wisdom and goodness of the Creator, and the
creation of the world and of man, with as much clearness as wisdom, and so near is he to the truth that on this account he is believed by some of our people to have heard Jeremiah in Egypt and
to have been instructed by him in our faith.[45] The other developed
Logic in six books, namely: Categories, On Interpretation, Former
Analytics, Topics, Later Analytics, Proofs. The first of these treats
of simple terms; the second of propositions; the third of the combinations of propositions useful for forming syllogisms, and thereby
clarifies and instructs the judgment; the fourth of methods, that is,
the way to use syllogisms; the fifth of the need of demonstration;
the sixth of avoiding the fallacies of the sophists, so that thus he
completely trains the finished philosopher not only to know how
to recognize truth but how to avoid falsity. Finally at the close
of his Refutations he boasts that he must be called the pioneer and
inventor of this art or power. His words are as follows: "Moreover we must not let escape us what happens in a case like this.
For of all the things that are discovered, such indeed as are borrowed from others, having been previously worked out, are elab-
orated in detail by those who afterwards take them up. But those
matters which are discovered entirely from the very foundations
usually gain but small development at first. Yet that increase is
far more useful than the additions that are made to such matters
later from those beginnings. For perhaps the beginning is the most
important thing of all, as they say; wherefore it is also the most
difficult. For it is very difficult for a thing as diminutive in size
as it is important in essence to be comprehended. But when this
has been discovered, it is easy to add to and develop what we
have."[46] Later in the same passage he testifies that he was the
first to set forth the combinations necessary for syllogisms; necessary, I mean, both in matter and in form, by reason of which the
science of logic has its beginning, saying: "Moreover in regard
to syllogisms in general we have nothing else to say than that we
struggle for a long time in the wearing effort of seeking them.
Now if it seems to us, basing our conclusion as it were upon those
things which are from the beginning, that this art is considerably
in advance of other matters that have been augmented by tradition,

[45] See Augustine 8. 11: and *cf.* his *De doctrina Christiana* 2. 28 and 43.
[46] Aristotle, *Elenchi* 2. 9. *Cf.* Bk. V. note 16.

the task left for all of you, or for those who shall hear you, will be to show indulgence, to be sure, for those parts of the art that are not yet developed, but to be very grateful for what has been discovered.''

Hence it comes about that, although syllogisms were made before Aristotle's time, yet they were not made according to strict rule, but were expressed in a haphazard manner, so to speak: that is, not as invariably so and so, but as sometimes so and so and sometimes not. Hence we have that syllogism of Plato's which Boëthius quotes in his commentary upon the book *On Interpretation*:[47] ''The senses,'' he says, ''do not grasp the nature of substance. Whatsoever does not grasp the nature of substance does not grasp the conception of truth itself. Sense therefore does not grasp the conception of truth.'' That this cannot stand in this form is proved by compelling arguments in the Former Analytics.[48] So much for Aristotle.

That Plato, who was not only a fellow pupil of the aforesaid Aristotle under Socrates, but also his teacher [49] after the death of Socrates, lived long after Jeremiah [50] is indicated by the fact that the *sophoi* (that is, the Wise Men)[51] who preceded the philosophers lived at about the time of the captivity. Not amiss, therefore, is the judgment of those who have said [52] that he and the other philosophers by natural keenness comprehended the invisible as it were by means of the visible. For all things that could be discovered by human wisdom regarding the nature of God they found out, all except those matters on which ultimate salvation depends. These things are learned through the grace of Jesus Christ by the gentle of heart. Hence Augustine says [53] that he found this in Plato: ''In the beginning was the word,'' and all that the evangelist sets forth in that most profound discourse, up to the point where he begins to speak of the mystery of the incarnation.

9. At the time at which the people of God were in captivity in Babylonia, the kingdom of the Romans too was oppressed by the might of Tarquinius Superbus and his unrighteous tyranny. After

[47] Commentary on *Peri Hermenias*, 2nd ed., 4. 10 (*ed.* Meiser, 2. 316).
[48] 1. 13, where Plato's syllogism is not cited.
[49] This statement is taken from the Life of Aristotle mentioned above.
[50] So Augustine 8. 11.
[51] σοφοὶ . . . *quod est sapientes,* Augustine 18. 24.
[52] *Cf.* Augustine 8. 10, an exposition of Paul's words in Rom. 1. 20.
[53] *Confessions* 7. 9.

he had committed other cruel acts, that most vile deed against Lucretia, purest of women, a deed basely performed by Tarquinius's son and wickedly concealed by the father, was the wholly adequate cause for his overthrow. It was no small proof of her chastity that she turned her own hand against herself because she could not escape the violence of the tyrant. Hence one has beautifully said:

> "When with the cruel steel Lucretia her pure heart was piercing,
> Spake she, addressing the life issuing forth from her breast:
> 'Go now and bear me witness I did not encourage the tyrant,
> Blood, to the souls of the dead, Spirit, before the gods'." [54]

10. After Tarquinius had been banished from his kingdom, the Romans, abjuring the name of king, chose for themselves consuls who were to advise the State rather than to rule it. So, then, in the two hundred and forty-fourth year after the founding of the City they selected Brutus as the first consul. He imitated the wickedness of the kings of the earlier days by putting to death his sons and the brothers of his wife, the Vitellii. Yet some say that he did this in his passion for impartial justice, that he might seem, forsooth, to love not his own household but the state. Hence also he is said to have adopted the Roman people in place of his sons. Tarquinius beleaguered the City for three years with the aid of Porsenna, king of the Etruscans, and would have taken it or have subjected it again to his sway had not the aforesaid king raised the siege, because he was moved by the fortitude of Mucius who let his hand burn off, or the courage of Delia,[55] the maiden who swam across the Tiber. Mucius together with other Romans had sworn that he

---

[54] Godfrey of Viterbo, *Speculum regum*, 1. 670 *et seq.*, has inserted these verses under Ovid's name, but they are not to be found in Ovid where he speaks of Lucretia's deed (*Fasti* 2. 788). They are found also in Conradus de Mure in his *Repertorium vocabulorum exquisitorum* (1273) and in *Codex Valentianensis* 145 (12th Century), and in others of apparently more recent date, often differing from the version given by Otto and agreeing rather with Godfrey. Aldus, Fabricius and others have published them under Ovid's name; most recently A. Riese, *Anthologia Latina* 1, *fasc.* 2 (1870), p. 254, n. 787, and E. Bährens, *Poetae Latini minores*, 4. (1882) p. 443, n. 549. These same verses are also found in fuller form in many MSS under the name of *Hildebertus Cenomanensis*; whether they are really to be attributed to him is still a subject for investigation. *Cf.* B. Hauréau, *Les Mélanges poetiques d'Hildebert de Lavardin*, Paris 1882, pp. 158 *et seq.*

[55] *I.e.,* Cloelia; see Livy 2. 13.

would kill the king, but, when he had reached the king's camp and was unable to fulfil his vow because he had been taken captive by the soldiers, in the presence of the king he burned his hand in the flames, saying, "See now what manner of man you have escaped. Three hundred of us have taken the same oath." [56] Delia, although she was one of the hostages, escaped by stealth from the camp and swam across the Tiber. Therefore the king, as I have said, moved alike by the man's fortitude and by the maiden's bravery, withdrew from the City. This first period was the infancy, so to speak, of the Roman people.

11. In the meantime, while Tarquinius was assailing the City with violence and war, Cyrus, whom I mentioned above, roaming far and wide over the empire of the East, made war on Babylon as its capital. But when one of his soldiers, too impetuous to be a man of discretion, tried to swim across the Ganges river [57] (which under another name is said to be one of the four rivers of paradise), not being able to withstand its current he was drowned. The king, deciding to punish the river because of his love for the young man, drew it off into four hundred and sixty channels and made it passable even by old women on foot. By that clever device too he turned aside from its usual course the Euphrates, which flowed through the midst of Babylon, and thus, marvellous to relate, took that very great and prosperous city, in the one thousand four hundredth year after it was founded. I wish to quote below the words of Orosius regarding the appearance as well as the overthrow of Babylon. He says: "Cyrus captured a city which it was almost too much for mortals to believe could be built by human workmanship or destroyed by human power." [58] And further on he says: "The capture of Babylon proves that whatever has been made by the toil of men's hands falls into decay and is destroyed by time." Regarding its appearance he speaks also as follows: "It is conspicuous from all sides because of the flatness of the country, and is of great extent on account of the nature of the ground; it is built in the form of a square, like a camp, with walls of equal length. Scarce believable is the tale of the strength and the size

---

[56] *Romana* 121-122.

[57] The Gyndes, probably the modern Diyalah, is meant. See Herodotus 1. 189 for the story here referred to. Note, however, that the Greek historian speaks of the loss of one of the sacred horses — not one of the soldiers.

[58] See Orosius 2. 6.

of its walls, namely, that they were fifty cubits in thickness, and four times that in height. Its circuit measured four hundred and eighty *stadia*; its wall was built of baked bricks cemented with bitumen; a wide moat outside flowed by like a river. In the face of the walls there were a hundred brazen gates. Moreover its width accommodated twenty four-horse chariots in the space between the outer and inner walls, the stations of the defenders being distributed equally on both sides where the towers were built. The houses inside were arranged for eight families and were remarkable for their menacing height.'' When Cyrus had taken this great city he pursued Croesus, the great and famous king of Lydia who had come to its aid, but had fled in terror. Cyrus conquered him and deprived him of his kingdom and of his life.[59]

12. No long time before this Ezekiel and Daniel prophesied in Babylon. The former wrote a very deep and obscure prophecy of the spiritual temple, which is the Church, and of the vision of the four living creatures. The other, a man of notable wisdom, in consequence of which he was called ''the man of our desires,'' [60] wrote with prophetic inspiration a most magnificent revelation concerning the changing of kingdoms. Both have revealed many things as useful to us as they are spiritual in their mystic and prophetic sense, things regarding the times of Antichrist and the resurrection of the dead, as well as of the last judgment and of the kingdom of Christ that is to endure forever. Habakkuk also is known from Daniel's history to have written in Judea at the time at which Ezekiel and Daniel prophesied in Babylon. Because he saw the people of God unjustly oppressed, living in misery in a strange land, whereas their oppressors, he saw, were prosperous and in power, he burst forth in such bold utterance, even against the Lord, as to say in effect that He either cared nothing about human affairs or else did not weigh them with even balances. It may be, rather, that he marvelled at His patience in these matters, for he did not doubt His omnipotence or His justice. For this reason he was called the Wrestler.[61] He also composed a very fine song in which he declared

---

[59] *captumque et vita et patrimonio donavit,* says Orosius 2. 6. 12 and Frutolf, p. 55, 40. Hofmeister suggests that Otto may have misunderstood what Cicero says about the funeral pyre erected by Cyrus (*De finibus* 2. 22 and 76).

[60] Jerome, *Ep.,* 22. 9, *ad Eustochium.*

[61] Jerome, *Ep.,* 53. 8, *ad Paulinum;* cf. also the prologue to his commentary on Habakkuk.

that he was smitten with horror at the thought of the incarnation, the passion, the second coming of the Lord, and the rejection of the Jewish people and the calling of the Gentiles, saying, "Jehovah, I have heard." [62]

13. But since, as I have said, Daniel wrote a prophetic account of the changes of kingdoms, it seems worth while to comment a little on this account. While he was interpreting the dream of the king of the Babylonians he said, "You yourself, O King, are the head of gold that you saw. After you shall arise another kingdom inferior to yours, after that yet another, after that a fourth which, because it shall be very strong, is compared to iron that breaks in pieces all things." [63] See how the prophet in citing four kingdoms named the first, because of its magnificence, from gold; the fourth he called iron on account of its power and the subjection to it of the world by war. Two intermediate kingdoms intervened. The first and the fourth, which I mentioned above, are the mighty kingdoms of the Babylonians and the Romans, one of which fell in the East, the other, as I have often remarked already,[64] arose in the West.[65] The empires of the Persians and the Greeks existed in the interval between them. Some, however, including the kingdom of the Persians as well as that of the Medes and the Chaldeans with the Babylonians, have put the African kingdom in the second place among the four chief empires of the world. Thus they locate the four kingdoms of the world according to the four points of the compass: the Babylonian in the East, the African in the South, the Macedonian in the North, and the Roman in the West. Of the same prophet's statement, that the kingdom which he compared to iron had feet (a part which, being the extremity of the human body, commonly signifies the end) that were partly of iron, partly of potters' clay, until it was smitten and utterly destroyed by the stone cut out from the mountain without hands, we shall, with God's help, speak in the proper place. For we who live in the closing days of that kingdom are experiencing that which was foretold

---

[62] Hab. 3. 2; *cf.* Augustine 18. 32.

[63] Dan. 2. 37-40. The prophet's words are summarized and abbreviated.

[64] I. 30 (end) and 32; Prol., II.; II. 2.

[65] Orosius 2. 2 in speaking of the relationship between the kingdom of the Assyrians (or Babylonia) and the Roman Empire says, among other things: *tunc orientis occidit et ortum est occidentis imperium.* There is a similar statement in Augustine 18. 27, except for the remark regarding the agreement in time.

concerning it, and expect that what we have yet to fear will soon take place.[66]

14. Cyrus, swollen with pride by so many triumphs, set out with an army of two hundred thousand men against Scythia, over which Queen Tomyris reigned at that time. When he had crossed the Araxes river he pitched camp, cleverly enticed the Scythians from their country, and killed a third of the queen's army together with her son. Because of this the woman shrewdly lured Cyrus into a trap and destroyed him and his entire army, so that, it is said, not one man survived to announce this great disaster. It is even said that the queen, unmindful of her sex, plunged his head into a skin filled with human blood, saying: "Glut yourself with the blood for which you thirsted." A strange and pitiful thing this, not to be attributed to chance occurrence but to the secret judgments of God. Who that hears these things would not be amazed? Or whose heart, even though it be made of stone, would not a deed so astonishing and so deplorable move to love of God and contempt of the world? For behold, the man who had triumphed over the entire East and over Babylon itself, whom Isaiah had addressed,[67] long before, on account of his notable valor, as the Anointed — to whom, according to that same prophet, the Lord had subdued nations and had loosed the loins of kings; had broken in pieces the doors of brass and cut in sunder the bars of iron — this man, I say, an object of terror not only to the lands but also to the waters, is deceived by a weak and frail woman and blotted out and destroyed along with such a countless host of soldiers. What shall we say to this, we that desire to cleave to the world? We can, I shall not merely say see, we can even feel how wretched is the lot of mortals; and yet we cling to frail and transitory things as though they were strong and abiding. I should say that this ought to be attributed not to the hardness but to the goodness and mercy of the Creator, who has desired this misery to be inherent in mortal affairs that He may draw us to love Him and may bring us to enduring abodes in the Heavenly City. This is the Cyrus who, when he had seen the

[66] Otto changed his mind with regard to this when he wrote his letter to the Chancellor Reinald (p. 91, n. 27). With the view here expressed cf. VI. 36. A similar opinion is found in the preface of *Petri monachi in translationem Methodii* (E. Sackur, *Sibyllinische Texte und Forschungen*, Halle a S., 1898, pp. 59 et seq.) ; cf. also VII. 9 below and Hashagen, p. 30.

[67] Isa. 45. 1. For the story of the struggle between Cyrus and Queen Tomyris see Herodotus 1. 205-214.

testimony of Isaiah (which we have set down) brought to him by the Jews, relaxed somewhat, as Jerome says, the captivity of the Jews; the forty years from the first captivity of Judah under Jeconiah — according to the computation of the aforesaid Jerome from the prophecy of Ezekiel [68] — had been completed. This was in the thirtieth year after the despoiling of the Temple.

15. Cyrus was succeeded by his son Cambyses,[69] who profaned the religion, nay rather the sacrilegious ceremonies of the Egyptians. Some say that he was a second Nebuchadnezzar, and that the events recorded in the book of Judith took place under him, especially as the history of the Romans [70] states that Holofernes was slain by Judith, that embodiment of purity, in the times of Tarquinius Superbus, and men say that the first year of the reign of Cambyses was the eighteenth of Tarquinius. Hence these two chaste maidens, Judith and Lucretia, are found to have been contemporaries.

But a question arises which those who hold this view cannot resolve, namely, how these events can have application to Cambyses who reigned only eight years; for in the book of Judith the expedition [against Holofernes] is said to have been undertaken in the twelfth year of the reign of Nebuchadnezzar. Moreover, who was that king of the Medes, Arfaxat,[71] who, as the same book states, was conquered in war by the aforesaid king? We should by no means put credence in these stories were it not for Josephus who in the eleventh book of his *Antiquities* calls him malevolent.[72] In that passage Josephus also relates that he sent a letter against Jerusalem in which he forbade that its building should proceed further, claiming that it was a seditious city and an enemy to kings. But Augustine, on the other hand, says in his book *The City of God* [73] that those things "that are recorded in the book of Judith" occurred under Cyrus. Although here the number of years causes no difficulty, and there is no obscurity regarding the victory over the Medes (if only the name of their king is changed), yet it is more probable that these things took place under his son Cambyses, who is said by Josephus to have been the enemy of the

[68] See Jerome on Ezekiel 4. 4-6.
[69] He reigned from 529-522 B.C.
[70] *I.e., Historia miscella* 1. 13, not used by Otto.
[71] Or Arphaxad.
[72] *Antiquities* 11. 2. Josephus, however, is speaking of Cambyses.
[73] 18. 26.

Jewish people, rather than under Cyrus who, by mitigating their captivity, not only did not display cruelty toward the people of God but even showed that people very great kindness. Besides, the difficulty I have mentioned may be solved thus: the three years of the rule of the Magi which ensued, according to Josephus [74] (other accounts say that they were in power for only seven months),[75] may be credited to Cambyses, and thus the above mentioned expedition under Judith took place at about the beginning of his twelfth year. Cambyses is said to have restored as New Babylon in Egypt the city which, previously founded by Apis,[76] the king of the Argives, had been called Memphis.

16. Upon the death of Cambyses, when the Magi were appropriating his kingdom, Darius,[77] one of those who checked the audacity of the Magi, was made king by common consent. Josephus, in the eleventh book of his *Antiquities*,[78] says that these Magi were called the Seven Lords and that they reigned for three years; Eusebius declares that they ruled three years and seven months.[79] Now because Darius had as a private citizen made a vow to the true God that, if he should be elevated to the throne by His aid, he would send back His people to their native land, he fully loosed the captivity of the Jews and allowed the Temple to be restored.

At that time the Romans too were completely set free from the tyrannical [80] rule of the Tarquins. The last of the prophets —

[74] Otto is here mistaken since Josephus does not assign three years to the Magi (*Antiquities* 11. 3).

[75] Frutolf p. 56. 55: *regnaverunt secundum quosdam septem mensibus, iuxta Iosephum vero anno uno.*

[76] Frutolf, p. 38. 25, following Jerome, states that Memphis was founded by Apis, king of the Argives; Bede draws from the same source. Furthermore Bede states — following Josephus — that *Babylonem in Aegypto* was built by Cambyses. Hofmeister remarks that he finds these two traditions united nowhere before Otto.

[77] He reigned from 521-485 B.C.

[78] *Antiquities* 11. 3: *Post Magorum vero interitum, qui defuncto Cambyse principatum Persarum anno tenuerunt, hi qui septem domini nuncupabantur apud Persas filium Histaspis Darium regem ordinaverunt.* Otto either completely misunderstood this or used a very corrupt text.

[79] Jerome's Chronicle on the year of Abraham 1496: *Ideo secundus annus in Magorum fratrum VII mensibus conputatur.* Hofmeister thinks that Otto's III (*tres*) arises from the word *in* whether misread or corrupt. He points out moreover that this passage (like I. 27 above) proves that Otto sometimes used the Chronicle of Jerome itself.

[80] *iniusta*; so also in II. 2 above.

Haggai, Zechariah and Malachi — uttered their prophecies. Since one of these had said of the Church, "The latter glory of this house shall be greater than the former," the Jews, imagining that this had been spoken concerning the material temple, were deceived by a mistaken hope. Esdras the Scribe also, whom some hold to be one of those called prophets, a man who did good in the restoration of the books of the Law and the titles of the Psalms, lived, it appears, in these same times. Finally, from that time (that is, from Zerubbabel and Jesus the high priest even to the time of John)[81] no prophets spoke nor did the kingdom prosper; and except for Jesus the son of Sirach[82] who, imitating the work of Solomon,[83] wrote the book which they call Wisdom, and the Maccabees,[84] some of whom made a brave stand for the law of God by their endurance, others by their fortitude, you will find few who, because of their words or their deeds, deserved to be counted among the approved citizens of Jerusalem. Yet they had kings even after this, whom we shall set down at the proper place, but not so renowned that they deserved to be listed with the kings of earlier times.

Darius first suppressed the Babylonians, who wished to throw off the yoke of Persian domination, and then, because Anthyrus, the king of the Scythians, was unwilling to give him his daughter in marriage, he declared war against Anthyrus, thus jeopardizing seven hundred thousand armed men for the love of one mere woman. After losing eighty thousand men there he moved his force against the Athenians, because they had sent the Ionians[85] to aid the Scythians. The Athenians with only ten thousand men met on the plains of Marathon[86] the great army that was still left of the seven hundred thousand (only eighty thousand had been lost in Scythia), and after killing two hundred thousand of them,

---

[81] *I.e.*, the Baptist.

[82] The writer of the book known as *Ecclesiasticus* or *The Wisdom of Jesus the son of Sirach*, composed (as he tells us) by his grandfather, of the same name; see the Prologue and also 50. 27.

[83] *I.e.*, the apocryphal book, *The Wisdom of Solomon.*

[84] Mattathias and his five sons: John the Holy, Simon the Guide, Judas the Hammer, Eleazar the Beast-Sticker and Jonathan the Cunning; their family name was "Asmonaeans" but during the long struggle for Jewish Independence (secured in 142 B.C.) these leaders were given the title of "Maccabaeans."

[85] Orosius 2. 8. 7: *cur Ionas adversum se auxilio iuvissent.* Otto has confused this.

[86] 490 B.C.

strange to say, put the rest to flight. After this, while he was again making preparations for war against the Athenians, Darius died on the march [87] and his son Xerxes succeeded him.

17. In the two hundred and seventy-fifth year from the founding of the City, when the vestal virgin Popilia was buried alive for unchastity, Xerxes,[88] succeeding to his father's throne, made preparations for war against the Athenians. It is wearisome to weave together here the tangled net work of woes,[89] yet I wish to touch upon them briefly to point out the miseries of mortals. For at that time Xerxes with an incredibly large host — for there are said to have been a million armed men and twelve hundred ships of war and three thousand transports — was met in the pass of Thermopylae [90] by Leonidas, king of the Spartans, with a mere handful of men (that is, only four thousand) and the battle continued for three days. On the fourth day, when Leonidas saw that the enemy was surrounding him on all sides, he dismissed his allies and dared to attack the great Persian army with only his own troops (who amounted to but six hundred), inspiring them with those famous words: "Take your morning meal now: you shall sup with the dead." For an entire night and half of the following day he slaughtered the enemy, so much so that, utterly exhausted by their own efforts and not by the Persians' blows — for the enemy made no attempt at defense and even succumbed to wounds inflicted by their own men — they that were victorious died not smitten but smiting. Thus perished Leonidas and his men. Xerxes after two defeats prepared for a naval combat. But, dismayed by the strategy of the Athenians and the other Greeks no less than by their valor, he turned over his army to Mardonius, and embarking in a small boat at Abydus he returned to Persia, accompanied by a single attendant. Mardonius encountered the Greeks in battle in Boeotia;[91] his troops were destroyed, his camp — filled with the royal treasures — was taken, and he was compelled to flee with a few survivors like a man escaping naked from shipwreck. And, strange to say, the army of the Persians which was fighting in Asia on that

---

[87] Otto here misread his sources, Orosius 2. 8. 13 and Frutolf, p. 57. 30.

[88] Xerxes I, 485-465 B.C.

[89] *Cf.* I. 19 above and Orosius 3. 2. 9: *contexui indigestae historiae inextricabilem cratem.*

[90] 480 B.C.

[91] At Plataea in 479 B.C.

same day under the command of Monimical [92] was able to hear at noon on that very day about this great disaster of their allies, even at that distance; seized with despair at the tidings the Persians turned and fled. And in this way under this king and the two that preceded him, one million nine hundred thousand men were, you will find, torn from the vitals of that kingdom alone in three wars. Greece too won the victory at the price of the death of her sons and the greatest peril. Xerxes, after so many luckless wars, was held in contempt even by his own people and was murdered by his prefect Artabanus. A Xerxes [93] likewise succeeded Artabanus when he had completed his reign, and again after him came a Xerxes, [94] and then Sogdianus, [95] and so in due course Darius surnamed Nothus. [96]

18. In the two hundred and sixtieth year after the founding of the City, when wars had ceased for a brief period, a very great plague in the City destroyed not so much the lower classes as the men of consular rank and the soldiers. They say that a prodigy preceded this pestilence, for the sky appeared to be on fire. At that time two ex-consuls, Aebutius [97] and Servilius, perished. This epidemic had devastated the City in like manner four years before. This calamity was followed by another the following year. For the slaves threw off the yoke and attacked their masters under the leadership of Herdonius, a Sabine [98] — exiles against citizens — and set fire to the Capitol. While the consul Valerius, a most valiant man, strove to hold them in check, he triumphed pitiably over his slaves at the cost of his life.

The next year there was a disastrous war with the Aequi and the Volsci. For the consul Minicius was defeated in a battle with them and was besieged with his army that suffered from cold [99] and hunger. Thereupon Quinctius Cincinnatus, summoned from the

---

[92] Otto has *sub Monimicale duce*; Orosius has *sub monte Mycale navali praelio*. Otto's mistake appears to be due to a poor MS (*e.g., cod. Bob.* of Orosius has *mone mycale* for *monte Mycale*).

[93] Frutolf has the proper form: *Artaxerxes Longimanus* (465-424 B.C.).

[94] Xerxes II, in 424.

[95] Also in 424.

[96] Darius II, 424-405; *cf.* II. 25 below.

[97] *Butius* in the text.

[98] In 460; see Livy 3. 15.

[99] Orosius and Frutolf say *ferro*. Hofmeister remarks that Otto's account probably rests upon a misunderstanding of the name Mt. Algidus.

furrows to the *fasces,* overwhelmed the enemy and raised the siege;
and placing his ox-yoke upon the Aequi [100] entered the City in
triumph, clad as he was like a farmer, and driving the vanquished
before him. Even at that time, amid the beginnings of that City
which was to gain the sovereignty of the whole world, it was pointed
out that "God chose the weak things of the world that he might put
to shame the things that are strong." [101]

19. In the three hundred and thirty-fifth year from the founding of the City there were perilous hazards of war in Sicily as well
as in Greece — in Sicily between the inhabitants of Catina and
those of Syracuse; [102] in Greece between the Lacedaemonians and
the Thebans, the Spartans and the Athenians. Xerxes, [103] Darius
Nothus and Artaxerxes [104] — of whom we shall speak hereafter —
the kings of the Persians, on account of their hatred of the Athenians incited against them the other cities [105] that I have mentioned.
And to such an extent did this mischief begin to spread that the
city of Athens, that great and glorious city which had flourished no
less through the wisdom than through the valor of its citizens, was
almost totally destroyed, [106] so that its people even thought of changing its site. Tullius, the greatest example of Roman eloquence, bears
witness to this as follows in his book *On Duties*: [107] "When the
Athenians could in no wise withstand the attack of the Persians
and were planning to abandon the city, transport their wives and
children to Troezen [108] and embark on their ships to defend the
liberty of Greece by their fleet, they stoned to death a certain
Cyrsilus who counselled them to remain in the city and receive
Xerxes." And again he says, [109] commending their valor when they

[100] There is perhaps a play upon the proper noun in the Latin, which cannot
be adequately rendered in translation: *iugumque boum Equis imponens.*

[101] I Cor. 1. 27.

[102] The reference is to the time of the renowned Athenian expedition against
Syracuse (415-413).

[103] This is Artaxerxes I, Longimanus, whose name is not mentioned by
Orosius.

[104] *I.e.,* Artaxerxes II, Mnemon (405-362), of whom Orosius makes mention
in 3. 1 (but says nothing of this sort). This is the Artaxerxes of the Anabasis.

[105] Otto has again fallen into error by abbreviating Orosius too much.

[106] The walls of the Piraeus and the long walls between the city and the
harbors were torn down in 404.

[107] Cicero, *De officiis* 3. 11. 48.

[108] Across the Saronic Gulf, in Argolis.

[109] *De officiis* 3. 11. 49.

were involved in the extremest danger: "Themistocles, after the victory in the war against the Persians, said in the assembly that he had a plan that was advantageous to the state but there was no need of its being generally known; he asked that the people should appoint some one to whom he might communicate it. Aristides was chosen. Themistocles told him that the fleet of the Lacedaemonians, which had been beached at Gytheum,[110] could be secretly set on fire; if this should be done, the power of the Lacedaemonians would inevitably be broken. When Artistides had heard this, he came to the assembly, which was eagerly waiting, and said that the plan which Themistocles suggested was exceedingly advantageous, but by no means honorable. Therefore the Athenians decided that what was dishonorable was not even advantageous and, accepting the opinion of Aristides, rejected the whole plan without even hearing it. And so the Athenians, the wisest of all men, taught by their own misfortunes finally learned that, just as small states grow by harmony, so the very greatest fall through discord. Whence it is evident that even the wisest sometimes profit more by experience than by the precepts of the learned. As this story has been related at length by others, I have merely epitomized it for the sake of brevity. Socrates, the chief of the philosophers, moved by these calamities, is said to have killed himself by poison.[111] We find that he handed down no books as a memorial of himself;[112] hence the following is still commonly reported as a saying of his: "I prefer to write upon the hearts of men rather than on the skins of dead animals."

These times are notable for the fall of Athens,[113] for the death of Darius[114] king of the Persians and for the exile of Dionysius [115] the Sicilian tyrant. For Sicily is said to have been the nurse first of the Cyclopes and afterwards of tyrants, even down to the present day;[116] the former always fed upon the flesh of men, the latter upon

---

[110] Or Gythium, on the Laconian Gulf.

[111] So Orosius 2. 17. 16. Augustine, on the other hand, has the correct account (8. 3).

[112] Cicero, *De oratore* 3. 16. 60, Jerome, *Contra Rufinum* 3. 40, and Augustine *De consensu evangelistarum* 1. 7 record that Socrates wrote no books, but they do not quote the saying here adduced by Otto.

[113] In 404, after the defeat at Aegospotami. See note 106.

[114] *I.e.*, Darius II (Nothus), in 405.   [115] Dionysius I.

[116] The reference is to Roger of Sicily; see VII. 23 below.

their sufferings. Tullius says [117] of this Dionysius that because of
his monstrous cruelty toward his people he kept faith with none
and expected no good from anyone: "through fear of the razors of
the barbers he used to singe his hair himself with a glowing coal."

20. When Darius died he left two sons, Artaxerxes and Cyrus.[118]
When they fought for the throne, after many had been slain on both
sides Artaxerxes, though severely wounded, was saved by the speed
of his horse but Cyrus was killed by his brother's soldiers.[119]
This brought the conflict to an end. And so Artaxerxes, having
won the victory, strengthened his hold on the throne by murder.
This is the Artaxerxes who is called Ahasuerus.[120] In his reign
belongs the story that is related of Esther and Mordecai, in the
days when all the people of Israel, being freed from peril of death,
were restored to their former freedom, two hundred and ninety
years having elapsed from the first captivity — according to the
computation of Jerome based upon Ezekiel's prophecy.

At that time Sicily was shaken by an earthquake and fields and
houses were destroyed by an eruption of Ætna. Then too the city
of Atlantis,[121] breaking away from the dry land, was converted into
an island. The remnant of the Athenians was miserably destroyed
by a plague. Behold the times filled with every misery!

21. In the three hundred and sixty-fourth year from the founding of the City the Senones, a tribe of Gauls, under the leadership
of Brennus moved their forces against Rome and, scorning the
ambassadors whom [the Romans][122] had sent to secure peace,
raised the siege of the town of Glusinum [123] (which is now called
Tuscia) and hastened to overwhelm the Romans. When Fabius, the
consul of the Romans, had met them he fled with great loss [124] —

[117] Cicero, *De officiis* 2. 7. 25.

[118] *I.e.*, Artaxerxes II (Mnemon) and Cyrus the Younger.

[119] At Cunaxa, in 401.

[120] See Jerome on Ezekiel 4. 4-6.

[121] Orosius (2. 18. 7) further locates it as *Locris adhaerens terrae contigua*.
The story of Atlantis is as old as Plato.

[122] The sense requires that these words (not in the text) be supplied as the
subject of *miserant*.

[123] *I.e.*, Clusium: *urbem Clusini, quae nunc Tuscia dicitur*, Orosius 2. 19. 5;
now Chiusi.

[124] Neither Orosius nor Jordanes says anything with regard to his death
although Frutolf (p. 59. 40) mistakenly reports that he was killed. Hofmeister
will not express an opinion whether Otto used some other author or made a
prudent guess at the truth.

as the river Allia [125] bears witness. Nor was this the end of the troubles of the Romans. For the Gauls entered the city and had no scruples either about setting it on fire or burying in the ruins of their houses the old men who sat in their homes motionless as images.[126] The young men also, only a thousand of whom had survived, they pursued (as they fled) to the Capitol, and would not cease besieging it until, having received a thousand talents of gold, they withdrew by agreement. The Romans, exhausted by these defeats, thought of changing their place of abode.

22. During these days Artaxerxes,[127] the king of the Persians, ordered all Greece to forsake warfare and to be quiet, adding that any who broke the peace would be chastised with the sword. He could do this the more easily because all were wearied by the varying results of so many wars and full of loathing for them, and desired to recover by the aid of peace. The Lacedaemonians, being the most restless and avaricious of the Greeks and swollen with insolence because they had previously defeated the Athenians in war, had attempted to throw the entire East into confusion by war. King Artaxerxes wished to check their insolence. He entrusted his army to Conon, an Athenian who was in exile at his court, and sent him with the Persian troops against the Lacedaemonians. The latter, seeking and obtaining aid from Hercinio, the king of Egypt, and collecting from all sides the forces of their allies, prepared for war — selecting Agesilaus, a lame man, as their leader. Accordingly Conon and Agesilaus, men of tried valor, meeting in battle fought most bitterly and for a very long time with much bloodshed on the part of both armies; when they parted from each other both were unsubdued, though exhausted. Conon, again drawing up the forces of the Persians in battle array, devastated the fields and houses of the Lacedaemonians. Not to delay you with many words, after many varied campaigns and hazards of war with victory vacillating between the two combatants, finally the state of the Lacedaemonians, so prosperous and so eager for glory, was reduced to such straits that all her young men were destroyed and scarcely a hundred graybeards were to be found in her. Conon, returning to Athens, was received with the greatest rejoicing on the part of his countrymen; he himself, however, was sad because of the desolation

---

[125] The little stream that joins the Tiber some eleven miles north of Rome.
[126] For the story, see Livy 5. 41.
[127] *I.e.*, II, Mnemon (405-362). See note 118.

of the city. And so he filled again with spoils taken from the Lacedaemonians the city that had been emptied by them, and the city which had in days gone by been burned by the Persians was rebuilt again by these at his request.[128] When no long time had elapsed after this the Romans, who for seventy years had suffered many reverses at the hands of the Volsci, the Falisci, the Aequi and the Sutriones, finally under the leadership of Camillus [129] put an end to the struggle by capturing many of their towns. By the generalship of Titus Quinctius they conquered in battle near the river Allia the people of Praeneste,[130] who had often come as far as the gates of Rome. At about the same time Rome was again devasted by pestilence and a great prodigy followed in the next year: for an insatiate gulf and crevasse in the earth appeared in the very midst of the forum and waited for a living man to cast himself into it as a sacrifice to the gods that had been consulted. A soldier, Marcus Curtius, appeased this ominous chasm for, when he had cast himself in, fully armed, he closed the awful gulf by his death. It was at this time that games at which plays were produced were established at Rome, on the advice of the priests, to placate the gods. At that time the Gauls, desiring to destroy Rome again, encamped with a mighty host at the fourth milestone from the City. Titus Quinctius [131] met them with an army of the Romans, conquered the barbarians, put them to flight and forced them to return to their own country. When they came back again with fresh troops they were vanquished anew by the Romans.

23. In the four hundred and second year from the founding of the City, ambassadors of the Carthaginians — a city that was the metropolis of all Africa and held sway far and wide — came to Rome and these two states ratified a treaty each with the other. At that time also there was a night that continued beyond its due length and a hailstorm pelted the land of Rome with real stones. In these days Artaxerxes, who is also called Ochus,[132] after making Sidon, Egypt and Syria subject to his sway, compelled many of the Jews to dwell in Hyrcania near the Caspian Sea. These are said to have

---

[128] Conon rebuilt the long walls of Athens with money furnished by the Persians after the victories at Cnidus and Coronea in 394.

[129] M. Furius Camillus, who had captured and destroyed Veii in 396.

[130] Palestrina.

[131] *I.e.,* Cincinnatus.

[132] This is Artaxerxes III (362-338).

multiplied and to have become by this time a great people, and it is believed that in the days of Antichrist they will burst forth from that place.

24. I think it is time for us to come to the eras of the Greeks. Well, then, at this period Philip the son of Amyntas, the father of Alexander the Great, held the throne of the Macedonians for twenty-five years. Reared at the court of Epaminondas,[133] king of the Thebans, a man of great energy and of surpassing wisdom, Philip himself developed such qualities of valor and of tact that he united and subordinated to his own control the states of the Greeks which in their lust for power had severally planned to rule. For by instigating the weaker to fight against the stronger he shrewdly aroused them all in succession and was finally established as lord and master of them all. So that flourishing land of Greece, a land that had enjoyed its own freedom, he deprived of liberty and when the city of Byzantium offered resistance he invested it with a blockade. This city, founded by Pausanias, king of the Spartans[134] (and subsequently increased in fame and wealth by Constantine, and called Constantinople after his name), is known to have been until recently the capital of the entire East. Since his supplies were exhausted in the siege, Philip had recourse to piracy and seized the spoils of a hundred and seventy ships and gave them to his soldiers. Abandoning the siege he hastened against the Scythians with his son Alexander on a plundering expedition. Overcoming them by craft rather than by valor he made many of them captive and though he found no gold or silver he carried off a vast amount of booty consisting solely of flocks. After this he declared war on the Athenians. And they, earnestly appealing to all the states of Greece through ambassadors, besought even the Lacedaemonians[135] and the Thebans to repel by their united strength the common enemy of them all. But they strove in vain against the onrush of the torrent. For they were not merely conquered by Philip but were even delivered up to slavery with other states of Greece and sold under the wreath, since some were made captives while others were destroyed.

Philip also rebuked his son Alexander for seeking to obtain the

---

[133] See Orosius 3. 12. 2. This was from 368 to 365.

[134] The victor at Plataea in 479.

[135] So the MSS of Orosius; Justin 9. 3. 5 quite properly mentions the Thebans only.

good will of the Macedonians by bribery, saying in a letter: "What flaw in your reasoning powers has induced you to think that men whom you had corrupted with money would be faithful to you? Or are you doing this that the Macedonians may regard you not as their king but as their quartermaster and commissary?" Although Philip was thought to be surpassed by his son in achievements and in fame, yet he is said by Tullius to have been superior to his son in affability and kindliness. Tullius says:[136] "Accordingly the one was always great, the other frequently most despicable, so that they seem to give prudent counsel who advise that the more exalted we are, the more humbly we conduct ourselves." They say of Philip that he was a most zealous opponent of false gods and that he destroyed their altars and temples. And when, on many different occasions, he was asked by his men what death was preferably to be chosen by a wise and valiant man, he is said to have replied, "The death which would suddenly end a man's life with the sword, when he was at the height of his authority and fame, having subdued and put down all movements of wars and uprisings against him." Men say that such was in fact his own fate, and that those false gods whom he had persecuted would not prevent it. For while he was giving his daughter in marriage to Alexander, the brother of his wife Olympias, and was celebrating the nuptials in magnificent style, he was killed[137] through craft by Pausanias, a young Macedonian noble, between the two Alexanders, his son-in-law and son.

25. In the four hundred and twenty-sixth year from the founding of the City, upon the death of Philip, Alexander succeeded to the throne. It is related of him that he was the son, not of Philip, but of a certain Magian, Nectanabis, king of the Egyptians. When Alexander assumed royal power, since he was unable to keep back the impulse to valor within him and was not content with the territories left him by his father, although that father had been a great warrior and a most valiant man, he planned to enlarge his empire. Therefore, having settled and arranged matters in Greece, he took with him but few men, that is, thirty-two thousand foot soldiers, seven thousand five hundred horse, and one hundred and eighty ships; and I am not sure whether it was more daring to attack the entire East with so small a force or more remarkable that he was able to conquer it with so small a force. Now he wished

[136] *De officiis* 1. 26. 90; quotation repeated in Otto's *Gesta Friderici* 1. 4.
[137] In 336.

to attack Darius, the son of Arsamus,[138] king of the Persians, who
was the fourteenth from Cyrus to hold sole sway over the whole
Orient, principally because he had demanded tribute from his
father Philip. And when Darius, first sending an insolent embassy
by which he called himself king of kings and blood kinsman of the
gods (whereas he termed Alexander his slave), had met Alexander
with an army of six hundred thousand, he was defeated by Alexander's strategy no less than by his might. Darius, recruiting another army, again prepared for war. In this conflict not only was
he conquered,[139] but his mother, his sister and his wife as well, with
his little sons were taken captive. His courage broken at this,
Darius was willing to hand over to Alexander the half of his kingdom to redeem the captives, but was utterly unable to obtain his
wish. When Alexander had gained his victory over the Persians,
he sent Parmenio with a force to attack their fleet. He himself
marched with his army into Syria, and when the kings there came
to meet him of their own accord and submitted to his sway he received certain of them into favor, certain he supplanted, others he
put to death. He captured Tyre also, that famous and wealthy city,
which resisted him because it relied on the Carthaginians. Then
passing through Cilicia, Rhodes and Egypt, he allowed all these
lands to surrender to him. At that time also he founded Alexandria
in Egypt. After this he came to Jerusalem and was received by the
Jews with great honor. Entering the temple he offered sacrifice to
the true God and reverenced the High Priest with the greatest
deference, according to Josephus. When all marvelled at this,
Alexander declared that this was the priest of the Most High God,
who was making the earth subject to him [Alexander], and by
whose revelation he had recognized the priest. Darius, giving up
hope of peace, again undertook to fight a battle. In this battle
victory long remained doubtful, for Darius, who had frequently
been defeated before, was prepared to die if he did not conquer,
whereas by his former victory Alexander was the more emboldened
to fight. Finally, when the Persians were forced to retreat, Darius,
though he desired to die, was removed from the battle by his friends.
In this last war the strength of the Persian empire, it is said, failed
so utterly that thereafter that once renowned and mighty kingdom

---

138 Darius III, Codomannus (336-330).
139 At Issus in Cilicia, in 333.

patiently bore the yoke of slavery. In these three wars a million and a half Persians are said to have fallen.

And these are the kings of the Persians: Cyrus; Cambyses; the Magi; Darius; Xerxes; Artabanus; Artaxerxes, also called Longianus; Xerxes; Sogdianus; Darius Nothus; Artaxerxes, also called Mnemon or Ahasuerus, the son of Darius and Parysatis; Artaxerxes, also called Ochus; his son Arses; and Darius the son of Arsamus. Together these kings ruled the East for two hundred and twenty years or more.[140] From this point [141] is reckoned the empire of the Greeks or Macedonians.

Alexander, having spent thirty-three days estimating his booty, entered the city of Persepolis, the capital of the Persian Empire, as victor. When Darius, giving up the contest, trusted to flight, his followers (to win Alexander's favor) treacherously bound him, pierced him with many wounds and left him in the road breathing his last. Alexander coming upon him was moved with compassion and ordered that he be borne to the tomb of his fathers. The following notable incident too is related of him. Desiring to learn who the traitors were that had betrayed their lord, he promised under oath that he would raise aloft and make conspicuous any who should confess himself the slayer of Darius. Allured by this hope those evil men came forward and betrayed themselves, and Alexander straightway gave orders that they should be nailed to a lofty cross. And so, as he had promised, he made them of high estate on the cross and notorious in every age for their treachery.

Meanwhile Alexander, king of the people of Epirus (an uncle of Alexander the Great), while he was striving to imitate Alexander was killed by the Bruttii and the Lucani. Now Alexander the Great, after the death of Darius, added the Hyrcani and the Mardi to his empire, and when Alestra, the queen of the Amazons, brazenly came to him with gifts to bear him children, he received her. It is too long a story to enumerate all Alexander's tribes and kingdoms, for he made the entire Orient, from Scythia to the boundaries of his own land,[142] subject to his authority. Nearer India is proof of this, for, although it forms the boundary of the world, being

---

[140] per annos 240, says Frutolf, p. 61. 25; per ann. pl. m. CCXXX, Jordanes, Romana 57; 233, Augustine 12. 11.

[141] Namely 330, when Darius was murdered.

[142] The text reads ad finem terrae suae; cf. I Macc. 1. 3: usque ad fines terrae.

situated in the ocean at the farthest East, and appears impassable to men and habitable only by beasts and serpents, yet it was made subject to Alexander and so accessible. In India he took by storm a remarkably high and rugged cliff to which many peoples had flocked together; this place Hercules had found impregnable, so that even he seemed to be surpassed in power by Alexander. In India too he defeated in single combat Porus,[143] king of the Indi, a man of enormous wealth and unusual spirit and courage, and to signalize his victory restored him to his throne and had him as his guide in viewing the farthest bounds of that land. If anyone desires to know about Porus's golden house and the silver-and-gold vine with clusters of grapes made of precious stones, let him read the letter of Alexander to his teacher, Aristotle the philosopher. Therein the careful student of events will find the perils he endured, and the phases of the sun and moon that foretold his death, and many matters so strange that they seem actually beyond belief.

After Alexander had won the victory over the entire East, and while he was preparing to make Rome also with all the West subject to himself, he returned from India to Babylon. There ambassadors met him from the foreign tribes of almost the entire world, including even the remotest West — namely from Spain, Gaul, Germany, Africa and practically all Italy — so that one would see that legates had come to him from lands to which you would scarcely have believed even rumors about him had spread in so short a time. And strange to say, so great fear had taken hold of all the earth that when he had reigned only twelve years, though he had established himself in the farthest East, the peoples of the remotest West, moved with terror of him, sent ambassadors to him to seek peace. Now Alexander, while tarrying at Babylon, died [144] by poison through the treachery of an attendant, at the day, the hour and the place predetermined [145] by the phases of the sun and the moon in India.

How pitiful the lot of mortals! How blind, how wretched their minds! Is not this the Alexander who brought low the proud and glorious kingdom of the Persians and transferred their power to the Macedonians? Is he not the man before whom the whole world trembled though it had not seen him and, not daring to await his

[143] In 326 at the battle of the Hydaspes.
[144] In 323.
[145] *Cf.* Frutolf, p. 74.

coming, voluntarily gave itself over to slavery? And yet so great and so fine a man is destroyed by draining a single cup, by the treachery of a single attendant, and the whole world is shaken by one man's death. The dominion of the Macedonian empire which had its beginning in him came to an end [146] with him at his death. But we who love the world, who desire to cleave to it as though it were something eternal and abiding, do not consider such things as this. We fall with the falling, slip with the slipping, roll with the rolling, in a word, perish with the perishing. The City of Christ, however, founded upon a firm rock, is not shaken by the misfortunes and tempests of the world, but, continuing immovable and unshaken, gains an eternal kingdom and an eternal crown.

26. Now upon the death of Alexander, who for twelve years had kept the world in subjection to himself by the sword, his generals, like a lion's whelps tearing limb from limb the great prey secured for them by the mighty beast, for fourteen years greedily tore asunder the body of the empire united by Alexander, choosing each for himself a separate province; and they held the sovereignty of the East in their control long after this. Accordingly Ptolemy [147] seized Egypt, Antipater [148] Greece, Seleucus [149] (from whom Seleucia [150] is named), the father of Antiochus,[151] took Syria and Babylonia, Asander [152] Lycia and Pamphylia,[153] Antigonus Greater Phrygia and others a province apiece, and according to the book of the Maccabees [154] "they did all put diadems upon themselves." And while they were dividing provinces and kingdoms they conceived so great a hatred for one another that at last all perished by wounds mutually inflicted. For in order that they might be able to revel more unrestrainedly, Asander [155] and Antigonus killed Olympias, the mother of Alexander, together with her son Hercules who was fourteen years old.

---

[146] *Cf.* III. 2 below.

[147] Ptolemaeus I, known as Soter, 323-285.

[148] He died in 319.

[149] The First, Nicator, 312-281.

[150] On the Tigris, the first capital of Syria.

[151] The First, likewise known as Soter, 281-261.

[152] *Cassander* in the text; Hofmeister points out that Asander is here meant.

[153] *Lyciam et Pamphyliam Nearchus, Cariam Cassander . . . accipit,* says Orosius 3. 23; Otto has confused this.

[154] I Macc. 1. 9.

[155] The son of Antipater III.

Some time later there lived those most valiant citizens of Christ whom I mentioned above,[156] the Maccabees. Some of them were made perfect through martyrdom by King Antiochus, in defense of the covenant of God, as the first martyrs of the ancient law; wherefore also they alone of the Fathers of old time are worshipped by the Church among the martyrs. Others, Judas and his brothers, by fighting manfully and defending their country by warfare, after the slaughter of countless enemies were themselves also slain in war.

27. But now let us direct our account to the empire of the Romans. For (as I have often said already) the kingdom of the Romans succeeded the kingdom of the Babylonians as a son succeeds a father. So then while it continued in its youthful period — its infancy, as it were — the two empires we have just mentioned (namely, those of the Persians and of the Greeks) were its guardians, so to speak, and its guides. Accordingly when they fell and, if I may say it, died, the kingdom of the Romans, which had now arrived at a robust age, shaking off the teacher's yoke, began to reign for itself, without restraint, and to take cognizance of the domain belonging to it by right of inheritance.

28. So then, in the four hundred and twenty-sixth year from the founding of the City — namely, the year in which Alexander succeeded Philip, while her keeper was still alive, so to speak, Rome was greatly humbled. For after the Romans had harried the Samnites with war and many of them — to wit, twenty thousand — had fallen, the Samnites, aroused by the loss of their men, lured the Roman soldiers into a narrow pass [157] and so completely overwhelmed them that they had it in their power to choose whether they should kill the Romans or rather take them prisoners and reduce their captives to slavery. For up to that time it had been possible to kill Romans but not to take them prisoners. And so, being ignominiously captured and stripped of their garments and weapons and, besides, compelled to give hostages, the Romans returned in disgrace. And as Orosius says, "there would either be no Romans at all today or they would be slaves to a Samnite lord, if they, when made subject to the Samnites, had kept the terms of the treaty as they expect treaties to be kept by their subjects." [158] In

156 In II. 16.
157 The Caudine Forks, 321 B.C.
158 Orosius 3. 15.

the following year the Romans broke the compact and renewed the war with the Samnites under the leadership of their consul Papirius.[159] He was a man of such courage and ardor, they say, that they would have ventured to oppose him even to Alexander the Great had the latter come against them.

29. In the four hundred and fiftieth year from the founding of the City, when Alexander was dead and his kingdom had been divided against itself by his associates and thereby was doomed to desolation, when now the kingdom of the Romans had begun to stand of its own authority and in freedom, as though its keeper were dead, in the consulship of Quintus [160] Decius Mus and Fabius Maximus (the latter was then consul for the fourth time) four very valiant tribes, the Etruscans, the Umbrians, the Samnites and the Gauls entered into an alliance against it. The Romans, having as I said above reached a vigorous estate, attempted to divide their enemies by employing craft and cunning. Accordingly, while they compelled the Etruscans and the Umbrians to turn back by setting fire to their crops, they entered upon combat with the Samnites and the Gauls. Amid the most bitter fighting on both sides Decius fell [161] with seven thousand of his army, but Fabius emerged victorious, having slain fifty thousand of the opposing force. But as the Romans were returning from this victory a great plague broke out in the City and so their joy was turned to mourning.

30. In the following year the Romans were again defeated by the Samnites. But when the consul Papirius was sent against them he came out victorious. Then in the next year Fabius Gurges fought with them but was worsted and driven back into the City. When the senate voted to depose him from the consulship because of this disgrace his father, Fabius Maximus, volunteered and joining battle with the enemy, captured their leader Pontius,[162] killed many thousand men and by his triumph at last brought the Samnite War to a close after it had dragged on for fifty-nine years with much bloodshed on both sides.[163] However the Samnites, planning to call

[159] L. Papirius Cursor.

[160] Orosius (*loc. cit.*) has: *Fabio Maximo V, Decio Mure IIII consulibus,* which Otto seems to have misunderstood.

[161] At Sentinum in 295; see Livy 10. 28.

[162] The renowned Samnite who so signally defeated the Romans at the Caudine Forks.

[163] The dates ordinarily assigned to the Samnite Wars are as follows:
    First   343-341   Second   326-304   Third   298-290

the old struggle to life again, entered upon an alliance with the Lucanians, the Bruttians, the Etruscans and the Gauls against the Romans.[164] Thereupon a battle was fought most valiantly with great loss to both sides,[165] as the Gauls, fighting manfully according to their custom, cruelly slaughtered the Romans.

I have recorded the hazards of many wars and woven into my account changes in sovereignty as tragic as they were numerous. But inasmuch as, after a cursory survey of the achievements of the Babylonians, the Medes, the Persians and the Greeks we have finally come to the history of the Romans, let us for the sake of brevity touch only lightly upon the deeds performed, whether valorously or otherwise; only lightly, I say, because they have been related eloquently and at length by many writers. I wish the reader to observe just this one point: that Rome was practically never free from wars abroad or from secret plots or pestilences at home. Hence Orosius, in directing attention to the malevolence of a plague that raged at Rome on one occasion, said,[166] "A census was announced which should investigate not how many had perished but how many had survived." A little farther on he says again: "See now what manner of deeds I have continuously recorded, and how many that took place each year. There are exceeding many years in scarcely any one of which nothing occurred that was not sad, for this reason, because those same writers, having undertaken the task rather of eulogizing, passed over numerous disasters, lest they should offend the persons for whom and about whom they were writing these things, and should appear to be trying rather to terrify than to instruct their hearers by examples from the past. Now we who live at the end of the ages cannot know the calamities of the Romans except through those who have praised the Romans. Hence it may be imagined how serious those were which have purposely been suppressed to save their reputation, when those that could barely emerge amid the flatteries are found to be so significant."

When the Samnite War had not yet been brought to a conclusion the great and famous struggle with Pyrrhus ensued. He traced his descent from the line of the great Achilles and held the kingdom

---

[164] The war of 285-282.

[165] Orosius, who is Otto's source for this, speaks only of the loss of the Romans.

[166] Orosius 4. 5.

of Epirus. Now the men of Tarentum were responsible for this war.

31. In the four hundred and sixty-fourth year from the founding of the City the people of Tarentum made an attack upon a fleet of the Romans that was passing by, pressing to the assault from a spectacle in the theater. Although certain of the Romans slipped away in flight the Tarentines caught some and killed others. When the Romans, sending an embassy, had complained of this without accomplishing anything, they invaded the territories of the Tarentines under the leadership of Aemilius,[167] devastating them with fire and sword. The Tarentines, inasmuch as they were descended from the Lacedaemonians, importuned Pyrrhus, king of the Epirotes, by an embassy and secured his assistance. While he was starting out for the war against the Romans he consulted that most deceitful and futile [168] Apollo of Delphi and, as was usual, received from him an equivocal response. For he said:

"You, O descendant of Æacus, surely the Romans shall conquer."

Accordingly in the consulship of Laevinus,[169] Pyrrhus and the Romans joining battle (not for any material advantage but for glory and the defence of liberty) near Heraclea,[170] a city of Campania, and the river Liris, contended long and bitterly — for fifty days, it is said [171] — both sides choosing to die rather than to yield. Finally the Romans, overcome by fear — particularly of the elephants, which they saw then for the first time — are said to have been turned in flight. Of their number fourteen thousand eight hundred and seventy infantrymen are said to have been killed, ten thousand taken captive; and of the cavalry two hundred and fifty-six were killed, eight hundred and two captured and twenty-two standards lost. How great were the losses which Pyrrhus also sustained in winning the victory he himself disclosed. For when he had returned to Tarentum and there set up a trophy to Jupiter he is reported to have said,

"The Romans,
Hitherto ever unconquered, all powerful Sire of Olympus,
These have I conquered in fight — and myself by them have
been conquered." [172]

---

[167] Consul in 280.
[168] This characterization is from Orosius 4. 1. 7.
[169] P. Valerius Laevinus, consul in 279.
[170] The battle was fought in 280.
[171] Otto's source for the duration of this battle is not known.
[172] See Orosius 4. 1. 14.

When criticized by his followers for saying that he, the victor, had been conquered he replied, "In truth if I conquer once more in this fashion I shall return to Epirus without any soldiers." As the Romans fled another catastrophe befell them. For their foragers, violently lashed by the hail, were found lying by the road, some lifeless and others at the point of death. When they took up the warfare a second time within the limits of Apulia and fought for a long time, Pyrrhus was defeated.[173] Of the Romans five thousand fell, of the army of Pyrrhus twenty thousand. Pyrrhus himself was severely wounded in the arm. In a third combat that was waged between them in Lucania [174] with great loss to both armies,[175] Pyrrhus was finally vanquished and so at last in the fifth year was obliged to flee from Italy. But he is said to have carried on this war with such courage and nobility that he was highly praised even by the Romans themselves. This can be perceived in his famous remark about restoring captives. For he says:

"I do not ask for gold; there is no reward you should give me;
Let us not barter like hucksters but carry on warfare like warriors,
Both of us risking our lives — with the sword, not money, contending.
Let us through valor discover the outcome by fortune established,
Whether 'tis I or you whom she wishes to reign. And moreover,
Hear my decision: the brave who were spared by the fortune of battle,
These I shall freely set free; as a gift receive them and take them.
For to the gods above, the gracious and mighty, I give them." [176]

These words, written by a certain ancient writer,[177] Tullius quotes in the book *On Duties* as evidence of Pyrrhus's fineness of character. Again he says of the same man,[178] "For when King Pyrrhus had taken the field against the Roman people, and a struggle for empire was in progress between the Romans and that noble and mighty king, a deserter came from him to the camp of Fabricius and promised him that, if Fabricius would set a reward, he would secretly return to the camp of Pyrrhus, even as he had come by stealth into the Roman camp, and would kill him by poison. Fabri-

---

[173] At Asculum in 279.

[174] At Beneventum in 275. But this is in Samnium, not in Lucania. Orosius (4. 2. 3) locates the third battle *apud Lucaniam in Arusinis campis*; Jordanes (*Romana* 156) says: *Lucaniae suprema pugna Sybarusinis quos vocant campis.*

[175] Orosius mentions only the soldiers of Pyrrhus that were slain.

[176] Cicero, *De officiis* 1. 12. 38.

[177] Ennius, whom Cicero does not mention.

[178] Cicero, *De officiis* 3. 22. 86.

cius had him brought back to Pyrrhus, and this deed of his was applauded by the senate.'' Pyrrhus afterwards successfully waged many wars in Greece, and finally died at Argos, a city of Achaea, being wounded by a stone. Upon his death the Tarentines asked aid of the Carthaginians and received it.

32. Inasmuch as we have made mention of Carthage, we think it not out of place to say a few words about it. This city, we find, was founded by Elissa [179] seventy-two years before Rome. It traced its origin to Tyre. Moreover, being the metropolis of all Africa, it had very powerful kings who extended its authority so far that it was even set by some among the four principal empires.[180] But how this city, ''the glory of kingdoms'' [181] and abounding in wealth, began to decline I shall explain in a few words. Pompeius or Justin [182] speaks in this fashion: ''The Carthaginians always had discord as an inherent and internal affliction. So deplorably did they suffer from this that they never enjoyed true prosperity abroad or real peace at home. When amid other misfortunes they suffered from pestilence as well, they employed murder as a remedy. For they used to offer up human beings as victims and would sacrifice children on their altars — though children arouse the compassion even of enemies.'' And so, because the gods were estranged, as they themselves put it (but, as we may rightly explain it, because the true God was offended at sacrilege of this sort), they fought with disastrous results both in Sicily and in Sardinia and were afflicted by many pitiful calamities from the times of Cyrus, Darius, Philip and Alexander down to the period of which we are now speaking. Accordingly, while they were making ready to aid the Tarentines they were reminded by Rome of their agreement and of a treaty that had been made. But they had no scruples about breaking it; indeed they made matters worse by perjury. This was the source of disasters and of a very great war. The Romans never experienced a greater war than that which now ensued with Africa, a war as famous as it is notable for its extent and duration, and one whose

179 *I.e.*, Dido.

180 Orosius 2. 1; 7. 2. *Cf.* II. 13 above.

181 So Isa. 13. 19 (of Babylon).

182 Hofmeister points out that although the following statements are in accord with Justin — sometimes almost word for word — yet Orosius sets them down as his own work, having previously made mention of his authority. Apparently Otto has incautiously united two passages in his hasty resumé of Orosius.

disasters were so many and so varied that by itself it suffices to illustrate the vicissitudes of human woe. But inasmuch as others have given a satisfactory account of it in detail, in order to be brief we desire to touch only lightly upon its history, particularly as we are writing not to satisfy curiosity but to display the disasters of failing temporal affairs.[183] For we have composed this account of wars and tottering kingdoms, not to arouse others to war by the example of those who considered that they had played the man, but to reveal the miseries in wars and in the various hazards of changing, unstable events.

33. So then, in the four hundred and eighty-third year from the founding of the City, the Romans undertook the African war under the leadership of Appius Claudius,[184] who was then consul with Quintus Fabius,[185] and prepared first to vanquish Hiero, king of the Syracusans, who was on friendly terms with the Carthaginians. When they had conquered him without serious effort they granted his plea for peace upon his promise to pay an indemnity. After that they laid siege to Agrigentum,[186] a city of Sicily, where there were Carthaginian troops and a garrison under the command of Hannibal.[187] When this general had been reduced to the greatest straits the city was at last taken. A few, including the king, made their escape by secret flight, the rest were sold as slaves. Then, in the consulship of Gnaeus Cornelius Asina[188] and Gaius Duilius, when the Carthaginians were making ready for a naval battle, they were met by the aforesaid consuls with a Roman fleet. After Cornelius Asina had been invited by Hannibal to a conference on peace and treacherously slain, Duilius fought a naval battle with the Carthaginians and came out victorious, killing or capturing many thousands of the foe.[189] When the Carthaginians renewed the war again under their king Hanno they were put to flight, with great loss, by Lucius Cornelius Scipio[190] who was then consul with Gaius Aquilius Florus.

183 Cf. Orosius 3, Praef.: scriptores autem, etsi non easdem causas, easdem tamen res habuere propositas, quippe cum illi bella, nos bellorum miserias evolvamus. Cf. II. 51 (beginning) below.
184 Surnamed Caudex. He was consul in 264 B.C.
185 This should be Marcus Fulvius. The error is copied from Orosius 4. 7.
186 Captured in 262.
187 The elder.
188 Consul in 260 B.C.
189 The great victory of Duilius at Mylae.
190 Consul in 259 B.C.

34. After this Regulus [191] assumed direction of the Punic War and pitched his camp near the river Bagrada.[192] There a serpent of marvelous size (for its skin was a hundred and twenty feet long) devoured many of the soldiers, but it was slain by Regulus no less by craft than by valor. Its hide was taken to Rome as a curiosity. Regulus engaged in battle with three commanders, namely with the two Hasdrubals from Africa and with Hamilcar, who had been summoned from Sicily. After killing seventeen thousand of their troops and taking five thousand men and seventeen elephants captive, he put the rest to flight and received eighty-two towns in surrender. Therefore the Carthaginians, dismayed by so many defeats and stripped of their resources, sued for peace. But when they had heard the hard terms of peace — preferring to die as free men rather than, having been made slaves, to live in misfortune and misery — they summoned help from their allies, the Spaniards and the Gauls, secured by the payment of money the help of Xanthippus, king of the Lacedaemonians, and renewed the war. The Romans, though they fought furiously, were defeated everywhere, and so at last in the tenth year the Carthaginians won a glorious victory. There thirty thousand Romans were killed; Regulus with five hundred men was taken prisoner and cast into chains. After winning the victory Xanthippus, fearing a reversal of fortune, returned to Greece. When the Romans learned of this disaster of their troops they declared war anew upon the Carthaginians under their consuls Aemilius Paulus and Lucius Metellus.[193] And so, not to delay you with many words, the Carthaginians, after countless hosts of theirs had been everywhere overwhelmed and routed both in naval and land battles, were again compelled to seek peace. When they sent Regulus, whom with others they held as captive, for this purpose but failed to obtain their desire, they cut off his eyelids and killed him by keeping him awake. Tullius, in his book *On Duties*,[194] relates the story as an evidence that death is to be held cheap in the cause of honor and justice. He writes in this

[191] M. Atilius Regulus, consul in 257.

[192] In Numidia.

[193] Hofmeister remarks that by compressing too much the too profuse account of Orosius and carelessly combining it with Jordanes, *Romana* 172 *et seq.*, Otto has been betrayed into the mistake of thinking that L. Caecilius Metellus, consul 251 B.C., was the colleague of Aemilius Paulus in 255 B.C. Paulus's colleague was Fulvius Nobilior.

[194] Cicero, *De officiis* 3. 26. 99.

fashion: "When Marcus Regulus in his second consulship had been ambushed in Africa and taken captive (the Lacedaemonian Xanthippus was the leader in the field, but Hamilcar, the father of Hannibal, was commander-in-chief), he was sent to the senate on parole, bound by oath to return to Carthage himself unless certain noble captives should be restored to the Carthaginians. When he had come to Rome he saw a specious semblance but, as the event proves, judged it to be deception. I mean this: he had the opportunity to remain in his own country, to be with his wife, with his children, and to retain his consular rank and dignity. Who would deny that these are, as you consider them to be, advantageous? Who? Greatness of soul and true strength deny it. For it is characteristic of these virtues to fear nothing and to hold all temporal things in contempt." And farther on he says: "He came into the senate, discharged his commission, but refused to express an opinion, declaring that so long as he was bound by an oath to the enemy he was no senator. He said that the restoration of the captives was not to their advantage, for they were young and good leaders while he himself was already exhausted by old age. Because his influence prevailed, the captives were retained. He himself returned to Carthage and neither love of country nor love of his dear ones held him back. Yet he was not unaware at the time that he was setting out to face a most cruel foe and to meet exquisite tortures, but he thought his oath ought to be kept. And so even when he was being killed by being kept awake, he was in better case than if he had remained at home, an aged captive, a consul forsworn." [195] Likewise he says elsewhere: "But I have never considered Marcus Regulus sorrow burdened or unfortunate, or deserving of pity. For it was not his greatness of soul that was racked by the Carthaginians; not his real worth, not his faithfulness, not his firmness, not any other virtue — not, in short, his soul itself. For surely, being bulwarked and surrounded by so many virtues, it could not be affected at all, however deeply his body was affected." [196] Thus Tullius.

Do you see in how many ways we are incited in these words to follow a pattern of endurance and through love of virtue to despise death and pain? For what else is the declaration that it is characteristic of valor to fear nothing, to hold all things in contempt,

[195] *Op. cit.*, 3. 27. 100.
[196] Cicero, *Paradoxa* 2. 16.

and the fact that neither love of country nor love of his dear ones or even torture, the racking of his body, diverted Regulus from his promise — what else is this than contempt for the present world, renunciation of parents, of possessions, and finally of one's very own self? This threefold renunciation we often find in Holy Scripture.[197] Accordingly, if even among the nations that were ignorant of God death is regarded as a thing to be held cheap, how shall we that have been called to a knowledge of the truth be excused for our ignorance? But will anyone say that, though in harmony with the philosophers death is to be held cheap in comparison with virtue, yet the world with its lusts is not to be scorned (in harmony with the Gospel) in comparison with love for the heavenly country? What is more stupid than this, what more silly, more mad? As though all worldly pleasure were not brought to a close, ended, snuffed out by death. Hence comes the well-known maxim of the wise man: "Dead flies ruin the fine scent of a perfumer."[198] It remains for us who are seen to be in the Church to blush for evil works, as an example to the heathen, even as the prophet says, "Be ashamed, O Sidon, saith the sea";[199] and we should turn away from the love of temporal things and be seized with a longing for the eternal. But enough of this.

In the consulship of Atilius Regulus and Lutatius [200] the Romans, after what has just been set forth, again inflicted so many defeats upon the Carthaginians that at last they accepted peace on the terms laid down by the Romans. These terms were that for twenty years they should pay every year as indemnity the weight of three thousand talents, and that they should withdraw from Sicily and Sardinia, which they were then holding. This treaty was made in the twenty-third year from the beginning of the Punic War. No one would have power to enumerate the kings, the consuls and the senators [201] that perished in the course of it, or tell how great car-

---

[197] *E.g.*, Matt. 10. 37, 16. 24, 19. 29; Luke 9. 23, 14. 26-33.

[198] Eccles. 10. 1.

[199] Isa. 23. 4.

[200] Orosius speaks of this Atilius Regulus (consul 250 B.C.) in 4. 10; Otto has again fallen into a serious error by abridging too much. The Lutatius (C. Lutatius Catulus) mentioned by Orosius in the same passage was consul in 242. It was in the following year that he gained the decisive victory over the Carthaginians at the Aegates Islands.

[201] Otto adds the senators, whom his sources do not mention.

nage was wrought among both peoples. Then the gate of the temple of Janus was closed for the first time since the days of Numa.

35. In the five hundred and seventh year from the founding of the City a great disaster put a stop to the rejoicing over this victory. For the City was afflicted by an overflow of the Tiber and by a fire, and was laid waste with pitiful havoc both among houses and among men. During these days, as the Romans were fighting with the Cisalpine Gauls, they were defeated in the first contest but were victorious in the second. Then, too, the Carthaginians broke the truce. It is from this time that the Second Punic War is reckoned.

36. Now it sorely irked the Carthaginians that their renowned city, which had previously been accustomed to rule lands and islands and to exact tribute therefrom, should now be obliged to submit to the control of the Romans and be forced to give tribute to them. While Hamilcar, the leader of the Carthaginians, was in consequence plotting war against the Romans, he was killed by the Spaniards. But Hannibal, who to please his father had taken an oath against the Romans at the altar, strove with all his might for vengeance. And so, finding meet opportunity, he besieged Saguntum,[202] a city of Spain friendly to the Romans. Spurning the ambassadors of the Romans and treating them most shamefully, he stormed and took the city in the eighth month. Then for the destruction of the Romans he pressed forward through Gaul. He first opened a way through the Pyrenean Alps [203] by fire and sword, and conquered the Alpine Gauls who offered resistance to him. After he had crossed the Alps he fought a battle at the river Ticinus in the consulship of P. Cornelius Scipio and P. Sempronius Longus. Now after Scipio had been wounded but had been saved from death by his son Scipio, who was afterwards called Africanus, practically the entire army of the Romans was annihilated. A second time they made ready to fight and a second time were conquered. When the Romans renewed the struggle they were driven in flight again. In this last battle Hannibal was wounded. Afterwards, while he was crossing over into Etruria in early spring, he lost an eye in the Apennines because of the excessive cold. In a

202 Taken and destroyed in 219.

203 On the medieval conception of the Pyrenees, cf. H. Thomae, Die Chronik des Otto von St. Blasien (Leipzig 1877), p. 12, n. 1. Otto often refers to the Alps under this name: cf., for example II. 37; VII. 14 (beginning) and 17, and in many places in the Gesta Friderici. The expression Pyreneae Alpes is found in Gesta Friderici II. 13 (p. 92, ed. Simson).

word, the Romans were so utterly overwhelmed by Hannibal's valor and skill in these and other battles, and especially in the battle at Cannae — where he killed or captured almost the whole Roman army, particularly the men of consular rank, so that three pecks of rings stripped from the hands of dead nobles are said to have been sent to Carthage as a token of victory — the Romans were, I say, so overwhelmed by these disasters and a prey to such utter despair that they even planned to desert the City and change their place of abode. According to Orosius there is no doubt that all would have been reduced to slavery or utterly exterminated if Hannibal had, after so many victories, moved forward to take the City. But Hannibal shortsightedly lingered in Apulia, in the neighborhood of Tarentum, and lost many of his soldiers in consequence of the heat and the noisome odors of that land.[204] Accordingly in the consulship of Sempronius Gracchus and Quintus Fabius Maximus, Claudius,[205] an ex-praetor, having been made proconsul, was the first to defeat Hannibal's army, which was weakened more by the nature of the country than by the strength of the Romans, and Claudius thus gave the rest of the Romans hope of conquering Hannibal. Meanwhile the Scipios in a decisive battle overwhelmed Hasdrubal,[206] a Carthaginian general who was raising an army against Italy. In the consulship of Gnaeus Fulvius and Sulpicius, Hannibal moved his camp from Campania and attempted to assail the City. But while men and women alike flocked to the walls in their terror and prepared to defend it, Hannibal was twice prevented by hail and rainstorms from attacking the City. They say that at that time Hannibal superstitiously remarked that sometimes the will, sometimes the opportunity to take Rome was denied him. What the Romans attributed to their gods as defenders of the City, that we indeed may ascribe to the secret and awful judgments of God,[207] without whose nod not a leaf falls to the ground. He desired to preserve this City amid so many perils and dangers and wished it gradually to increase and grow until it should rule the

[204] Hofmeister remarks that Otto apparently invented this story through a misunderstanding of Jordanes, *Romana* 191.

[205] M. Claudius Marcellus, who defeated Hannibal at Nola in 215.

[206] In the Spanish campaign, 218-211.

[207] Orosius (4.17) argues that Rome was defended from Hannibal not by its own valor but by the compassion and judgment of the true God. But Augustine says (3.20) that it is ridiculous to attribute the safety of the City to the protection of its false gods. See note 208.

whole world.[208] The reason for this — insofar as human frailty can measure it — we shall, by God's grace, set forth hereafter when we shall have come to the principate of Augustus Caesar.

This happened in the tenth year after Hannibal came into Italy. Meanwhile the two Scipios were killed in Spain by Hannibal's brother Hasdrubal. At that time when Capua, a city of Campania, was captured by the consul Quintus Fulvius,[209] its leading citizens killed themselves by poison.

37. And so when, after the Scipios had been killed, all were dismayed and terror-stricken and there was greatest lack of money, Scipio,[210] though a mere stripling, voluntarily came forward, in the consulship of Marcus Claudius and Valerius Livianus,[211] to avenge his father and his uncle. Accordingly Scipio, having obtained the office of proconsul at the age of twenty-four, crossed the Pyrenees with an army and there captured New Carthage and greatly increased the soldiers' pay from the booty of the city. He sent Hannibal's brother Mago to Rome along with other captives, conquered Hasdrubal [212] king of the Carthaginians and either destroyed eighty cities or accepted their surrender.

At this point we may reflect not only on the valor but also on the wisdom whereby the Romans made the world their own. For when they found themselves unable to vanquish Hannibal, who lingered on in Italy with African troops, they invaded and devastated his home kingdom, regarding it as drained of military forces and so defenseless; their purpose was thereby at least to compel their foe to return to his native land. From all this it appears (as a wise man has said)[213] that in war wisdom is the dominant factor.

Meanwhile, in Italy, Hannibal destroyed the consul Marcellus and his army, and in like manner killed Crispinus by shrewdly leading him into a trap. In the consulship of Claudius Nero and M.

[208] Augustine (especially in books 4 and 5) argues that it was by God's will that the Roman Empire was saved from so many perils and made so great and so enduring; cf. Orosius 7. 1.

[209] Then proconsul.

[210] P. Cornelius Scipio, the victor at Zama, son and nephew of the brothers who were killed in Spain.

[211] Livianus, i.e., Laevinus. These men were consuls in 210.

[212] But Scipio failed to prevent him from crossing the Pyrenees to join his brother Hannibal.

[213] Sallust, Catiline 2. 2: conpertum est in bello plurimum ingenium posse.

Livius Salinator, Hannibal's brother Hasdrubal (who had been sent by the Carthaginians to aid his brother) was caught by an ambuscade set by the Romans.[214] For after crossing the Pyrenees [215] he came face to face with Roman troops, and joining battle with them was killed with practically his entire army. Roman captives who were present to the number of four thousand were released. Of the Romans eight thousand fell in this battle, but of the Africans fifty-eight thousand were killed and five thousand four hundred and four were taken prisoners. Hasdrubal's head was thrown down before the camp of his brother Hannibal. When he saw it and learned of the slaughter of his countrymen, Hannibal, in the thirteenth year after he had entered Italy, withdrew to the land of the Bruttii. In consequence the following year was spent without the excitement of warfare between him and the Romans, since both sides were exhausted.

38. Meanwhile Scipio ranged through the whole of Spain from the Pyrenees to the ocean and made it a Roman province. But Hannibal, strange to say, though his entire army was almost annihilated — not only by battles but also by the ravages of disease — conquered the consul Sempronius, who opposed him with a Roman army, and compelled him to flee to the City. But, since by this time almost all Africa had been harried by Scipio with fire and sword, Hannibal was recalled by his countrymen; and so, after killing all the Italian soldiers who were unwilling to follow him, he left Italy in tears. When he was drawing near to the African coast he ordered a lookout to climb the mast; story says that this lookout reported that he saw a tomb in ruins. When Hannibal reached Carthage he asked for an interview with Scipio. But though these two famous warriors admired each other as they talked together there, they separated leaving the question of peace undecided and once more joined in battle.[216] This battle was fought with great skill and courage on the part of both leaders but it finally brought complete victory to the Romans. Twenty thousand of the Carthaginians were slain and eighty elephants were killed or captured. Hannibal, advising the Carthaginians to set their hopes on peace, escaped by stealth with four soldiers and made his way to Hadrumetum.[217]

---

[214] Near the Metaurus river in Umbria.
[215] *I.e.*, the Alps. See note 203.
[216] At Zama in Africa, in 202.
[217] A seaport south of Carthage and east of Zama.

Accordingly peace was granted the Carthaginians by Scipio, with the consent of the senate, in the consulship of Gaius Cornelius Lentulus and Publius Aelius Paetus. More than five hundred ships of the Carthaginians were towed out to sea and burned within sight of the city. Scipio, who gained the name Africanus from his conquest of Africa, was received with a triumph when he entered Rome. The comic poet Terence, wearing a liberty cap in token of the freedom granted him, accompanied him in his triumph. Hereby the Second Punic War, which had lasted for eighteen years, was brought to an end in the five hundred and forty-sixth year from the founding of the City.

39. Dire portents preceded this battle. The sun seemed smaller and there were round shields in the heavens. Orosius relates [218] that the sun fought with the moon, that two moons rose simultaneously, that two shields sweated blood and that ears of grain dripped with blood as they fell into baskets. Tarentum too was destroyed in these days, that famous and wealthy city of Campania to which the war with Pyrrhus as well as that with the Carthaginians was due. From this time on the Romans began to enrich themselves with the booty from the cities I have mentioned — gold, jewels, silver and precious goods. In previous wars they had carried off only cattle and other insignificant things.

After the African war came the Macedonian. [219] This ended in the defeat of the foe, though with great loss to the Romans, and the consul Quinctius Flamininus made peace with Philip. [220] After this he conquered the Lacedaemonians in war and received from them men of the highest birth as hostages — Demetrius the son of Philip and Armenes the son of Nabis — and led them in triumph before his chariot. The Roman captives who had been sold by Hannibal were sent back with their heads shaved as a sign that their servitude was at an end.

40. At that time Lucius Fulvius [221] in a very difficult war conquered the Insubres, the Boii and the Cenomanni, who had advanced as far as Cremona and were devastating both that city and Placentia. Flamininus, the proconsul, defeated King Philip, who

[218] See Orosius 4.15. But Orosius places these between the battles of the Trebia and Lake Trasumenus.

[219] The Second Macedonian War, 200-197 B.C.

[220] Philip V of Macedonia.

[221] L. Furius, the praetor, is meant; the error is copied Orosius 4. 20. 4.

was moving against him with the Thracians, Macedonians and Illyrians, and slew many thousands of the Macedonians. Hannibal went in search of Antiochus,[222] king of Syria, and when he had found him at Ephesus incited him against the Romans, but in vain. For by this time the Republic had made so great headway that the efforts even of so great a king were impotent and made no progress against the Romans. For Hannibal, who had been put in command of the fleet of Antiochus, was defeated by Scipio in a naval battle.[223] Under these circumstances peace was sought and obtained by Antiochus. Then, not long after, Hannibal fled to Prusias, king of Bithynia, and ended his life by taking poison because the Romans demanded that he be given up to them. In this way then the Romans, little by little, sought to deprive of their sovereignty the Macedonians or the Greeks, who had ruled over almost the whole of Asia from the time of Alexander onward, until under Caesar Octavian they reduced them completely to their sway. These matters will by God's grace be spoken of at greater length when we shall come to that period.

During these days Scipio Africanus, a man worthy of all praise among his countrymen, was banished from the City by his ungrateful fellow citizens and fell sick and died at the town of Liternum. On his sepulcher he had inscribed these words: "Ungrateful land of mine, thou hast not even my bones." Of this man Tullius speaks thus in the prologue to the fourth book of his work *On Duties*:[224] "My dear son Marcus, Cato, who was of the same age as Scipio, the first who was called Africanus, has recorded that Scipio used to say that he was never less at leisure than when he was at leisure, nor less alone than when he was alone. Truly a magnificent saying, and worthy of a great and wise man, for it indicates that on the one hand in times of leisure he was wont to think about his employments, and that on the other when he was alone he used to hold converse with himself, so that he never was idle and at times had no need of speech with another. And so the two things that bring feebleness to others, namely, leisure and solitude, were a stimulus to him." Lucius Seneca too, who ought to be called almost a Christian rather than a philosopher, commending Scipio's manliness and his admirable endurance says,

---

[222] Antiochus III, of Syria, with whom the Romans contended from 192-189.
[223] In 190, near the mouth of the Eurymedon.
[224] Cicero, *De officiis* 3. 1. 1. Otto's text says "fourth book."

in his letters to Lucilius: "I write these words to you as I lie in the villa of Scipio Africanus, venerating his spirit and the altar which I suspect to be that great man's tomb. I am persuading myself that his soul has indeed returned to heaven whence it came, not because he led great armies — for these Cambyses, a madman, and a madman who successfully used his frenzy, also had — but on account of his surpassing self-control and righteousness, which I regard as all the more worthy of admiration in him at the time when he left his country than it was when he defended that country. Scipio ought either to have failed Rome or Rome should have been free. 'I desire,' he said, 'in no wise to infringe upon the laws or the established practices: let there be equal rights for all citizens. Enjoy without me, my Country, the service I have done. I was the source of your freedom, I shall also be a proof of it: I depart if I have grown greater than is of advantage to you.' Why should I not marvel at this great-heartedness by reason of which he withdrew into voluntary exile and relieved the state? Matters had reached such a pass that either freedom must do harm to Scipio or Scipio must do harm to freedom. Neither was right in the sight of heaven. Therefore he yielded to the laws and retired to Liternum, being destined to make the Republic accountable for his own exile as well as indebted to him for Hannibal's exile." [225]

41. Now when the Romans had vanquished the Greeks and the Syrians, the Spaniards and the Africans, they determined to destroy Carthage utterly because they thought it a rival of the city of Rome. Its site, as Orosius remarks, is said to be as follows: "Enclosed by a wall twenty miles in circuit, practically the entire city was surrounded by the sea and its inlets, which extended a distance of three miles. The city had a wall of hewn stone thirty feet thick and forty cubits in height. Its citadel, which was called Byrsa, occupied slightly more than two miles. On one side the city and the Byrsa have a wall in common, which overhangs that sea which they call the Lagoon, because it is shut off by the interposition of a projecting tongue of land." [226]

Hence the Third African War began, in the consulship of L. Censorinus and M. Mallius,[227] in the fiftieth year [228] after the Sec-

---

[225] Seneca, Epistle 86.
[226] Orosius 4. 22. 4.
[227] *I.e.*, Manilius. They were consuls in 149.
[228] From Orosius 4. 23. 1. But according to Otto's own statement in 4. 20. 1 it

ond War, or even later. Accordingly Scipio Minor, who was at that time military tribune, leading a Roman army into Africa in company with the consuls, pitched camp near Utica and, summoning the Carthaginians into his presence, bade them give up their arms and their ships. This they set out to do without delay. But, when they were also ordered to retire from their city to a distance of ten miles from the sea, they went back, repenting of their acquiescence, and made ready to defend the city. Choosing the two Hasdrubals as their leaders, they tried in vain to fashion new weapons, supplying the lack of bronze with gold and silver. The Romans began a vigorous assault upon Carthage. The Carthaginians, being brought to the utmost extremity, first killed Hasdrubal because they had become suspicious of him, and finally all surrendered to the Romans. And so Carthage was utterly destroyed by the Romans; the stones of its walls were ground to powder and the city itself was burned, affording a pitiful spectacle of human woe. It is said to have burned continuously for seventeen days. The entire number of captives, except a few of the chief men, was sold. The queen, Hasdrubal's wife, by reason of these calamities, in womanish frenzy cast herself and her two sons into the flames. And so the last queen and the first (I mean Dido) had a similar fate and a like exit from life. The destruction of this most powerful city took place more than seven hundred years [229] after its establishment, and in the six hundred and third year from the founding of the City, when Gnaeus Cornelius Lentulus and Lucius Mummius were consuls. And so the Third Punic War was brought to an end in the fourth year after it started. Orosius states that he is absolutely ignorant of its cause. Meanwhile, upon the death of Masinissa, Scipio divided the kingdom of Numidia among his sons.

42. That Simon, the last of the Maccabees,[230] was the leader of the Hebrews at about the same time may be inferred both from a computation of the dynasties of the Greeks and from the consul-

would be the sixtieth. It should be the fifty-second, which is perhaps what Otto had in mind when he added to the statement of Orosius the words *vel amplius*.

[229] This does not agree with II. 32 (beginning).

[230] Hofmeister remarks that Otto has here overlooked John Hyrcanus, Simon's son, of whom Frutolf p. 84. 60 and p. 85. 49 *et seq.* speaks at considerable length, whereas in II. 47 below he states that Simon's sons succeeded him. The first book of the Maccabees ends with the death of Simon and his elder sons.

ship of the aforesaid Lucius.[231] For since a golden shield is found
to have been sent by Simon to Rome in the one hundred and seventy-
second year of the rule of the Greeks, and the same book testifies
that a message was sent by Lucius the consul to Ptolemy, king of
the Egyptians, the discerning reader will find that the treaty of
friendship between Simon, the high priest, and the Romans was
ratified in the fourth year before the destruction of Carthage, which
took place in the one hundred and seventy-seventh year of the kingdom of the Greeks.[232] And that what I have said may become more
evident, I will add that in the four hundred and twenty-sixth year
from the founding of the City, Alexander, who is said in the history
of the Maccabees to have been the first to reign in Greece, succeeded Philip on the throne. But you will find that Carthage was
destroyed in the six hundred and third year from the founding of
the City. So then, the number of years from the beginning of the
rule of the Greeks — that is, from the time when Alexander began
to reign down to the destruction of Carthage — amounts to one
hundred and seventy-seven. You will find, however, that an ambassador was sent by Lucius to Ptolemy, king of the Egyptians, in
behalf of the Jews in the one hundred and seventy-fourth year,[233]
that is, the third year before Carthage was destroyed. But if the
beginning of the kingdom of the Greeks is reckoned from the sixth
year of the reign of Alexander, that is, from the time when he subdued the Medes and the Persians upon the death of Darius — and
it was then that the Greeks began to have authority — you will
find that it was in the third year after the destruction of Carthage
and the close of the Third Punic War that this embassy, or rather
this injunction, was directed to Ptolemy and Antiochus, the most

[231] *I.e.*, Mummius.

[232] Hofmeister remarks that, from the year 426 A.U.C., the time at which
(according to II. 25) Alexander succeeded his father on the throne, to 603
A.U.C., the date just given for the conclusion of the Third Punic War, is 177
years. But since, according to Frutolf (p. 84. 45) Carthage was destroyed in
the 32nd year of Phylometor, and this is found to be the 177th from the first
year of the first Ptolemy (according to the years assigned by Frutolf to the
preceding Ptolemies as kings of Alexandria), there is a question whether Otto
may not have read in some author "the 177th year of the kingdom of the
Greeks" and been led thereby to change "the 606th year" found in Orosius
and Frutolf to "603rd year" (in II. 41 end), mistakenly starting his computation with the first year of Alexander the Great.

[233] I Macc. 15. 10, where, however, there is no mention of an ambassador
being sent to Ptolemy.

powerful monarchs of the East. Nor is it strange that the Romans had now learned to command even the kings of the East, seeing that they had gained the victory over so great a city — a city which had subdued to itself not only Africa but also Sardinia, Sicily and almost all of Spain. If, however, the calculation of the rule of the Greeks is started not with Alexander but with Seleucus,[234] his successor in Syria, this embassy is known to have been undertaken by the Romans in behalf of Simon and the people of the Jews in the twenty-first year after the destruction of Carthage, and Judas and Jonathan are believed to have lived before the destruction of Carthage. And so not inappropriately the Maccabees, those notable zealots in behalf of the law of God, and the Scipios, the renowned defenders of the city of Rome and of the laws of their native land, are found to have been contemporaries. For Jerome in his commentary on Daniel seems to indicate that, according to Maccabees, the reckoning of the rule of the Greeks begins with Seleucus. This he does when he says, "After the death of Iaddi,[235] the priest who presided over the temple under Alexander, Omas[236] assumed the high priesthood. At this time Seleucus, having conquered Babylon, placed upon his head the diadem of all Asia in the twelfth year after the death of Alexander. From this time the writings of the Maccabees reckon the rule of the Greeks." Add, therefore, to the previous calculation the six years of Alexander (during which, after the death of Darius, he ruled all Asia) and the twelve of Seleucus and you will obtain eighteen. If to these should be added the three years by which the former reckoning went beyond the destruction of Carthage, you will make up the total of twenty-one years, as has been said. But whether this or that shall prove to be right, it is indicated by either computation that it was after the victory over Pyrrhus and the triumphant close of the second African war that the Romans first became famous and first extended their sway over foreign lands.

43. When Carthage was overthrown, under the consuls I have named, Corinth — the workshop, so to speak, of all the artisans and the richest of all the cities of Macedonia and Achaea — was destroyed by the Romans with fire and sword. Thus the pitiful and lamentable conflagration of two most famous cities blazed forth

[234] Seleucus I founded the kingdom of Syria in 312 B.C.
[235] Or Jaddua. The passage is in Daniel 9. 34.
[236] *Onias* in the text.

upon the world in a single year. It was from this that the Corinthian metal, or Corinthian ware, took its name and origin because metals of different kinds were fused in consequence of the fire. A misfortune that ensued clouded this great victory. For not long after, in the consulship of Mancinus, a disastrous battle was fought with the Numantines in Spain, and a very disgraceful treaty was agreed upon for the sake of ransoming the captured soldiers, as had previously been done by Pompey.[237] By a decree of the senate, therefore, the treaty was abrogated and Mancinus, its author, was sent in chains to the Numantines. Scipio Africanus, being by general consent elected consul, led an army to take Numantia by storm. And so when the Numantines saw that they were being defeated by the courage and the shrewdness of the Roman leader, since they were ready to die rather than be slaves, they first made themselves drunken with a barbarous potion [238] and then rushed into the Roman camp, and would undoubtedly have routed the enemy had not Scipio come to the rescue. Finally, utterly broken by profoundest despair, they chose to give themselves and all their belongings to the flames rather than serve the Romans, that Rome might not witness a triumph there over a single man or over a single piece of property.

The misfortunes that we have set down are sufficient to prove the mutability of human affairs. Hence since much has been said concerning the citizens of the world I think we should hurry on to the citizens of Christ and to Christian times. For I desire the reader to remember that, in accordance with my promise, I ought to record the conflicts of this world in order to demonstrate the wretchedness of changing events; that by pondering upon such events we may be led to pass by the eye of reason to the peace of Christ's kingdom and the joy that abides without end.[239]

44. Although the Romans now possessed the sovereignty of almost the whole world, yet they still had wars abroad, since the nations were not yet fully subdued. They had too an abundance of internal misfortunes at home. Out of this situation sprang the Jugurthine War, that was brought to a conclusion under Metellus

237 Obviously not Pompey the Great but Quintus Pompey, who as consul in 141 B.C., led an army into Spain and was forced by the Numantines to make peace.

238 Otto says *barbara*; but Orosius and Frutolf have *larga*.

239 *Cf.* Prol., I (beginning); II. 51; IV. 33; V. 36 (end); VI. 9; VI. 17 (end); also VIII. 34.

and Marius,[240] and the war of the Cimbrians and the Teutons, a
most bitter war waged by Gauls and Germans, and conducted in so
deplorable and inhuman a fashion that, you will find, eighty thousand Romans and forty thousand camp followers and soldiers'
servants were routed by the aforesaid tribes in one battle, besides
Gaius Mallius the consul, Quintus Caepio the proconsul and the
consul's two sons. How great their loss was when they were defeated in the fifth consulship of Marius it is unnecessary to relate,
since such grievous disasters to the victors preceded.

After this disaster there followed a very great calamity, suffered
by the Romans in consequence of civil war for which Sulla and
Gaius Marius were responsible. This dragged on for ten years and
one hundred and fifty thousand Romans are found to have been
killed. That in consequence the Republic of the Romans was not
merely enfeebled but almost ruined Tullius bears witness, speaking
as follows in his work *On Duties*: "Nevertheless, so long as the
sovereignty of the Roman people was maintained by acts of kindness, not by acts of injustice, wars were waged either in defense
of allies or for sovereignty and the consequences of the wars were
either temperate or necessary. The senate was a haven of refuge
for kings, peoples and nations. Our magistrates and our commanders were eager to obtain praise for this one thing — the defense of the allies with fairness and with good faith. Accordingly
such a policy might truthfully be called maintaining a protectorate
over the world rather than overlordship. But even before Sulla's
victory we were gradually weakening this custom and this rule of
procedure, and thereafter we abandoned it completely. For when
so great cruelty had been exercised against citizens no action against
allies could seem unfair. In Sulla's case, therefore, a dishonorable
victory followed an honorable cause. For when, having set up a
spear, he was selling in the forum the property of men who were
upright and rich and at all events citizens, he had the audacity to
say he was selling his own plunder."[241] And farther on Tullius
says, "We have seen Marseilles carried in a triumph as evidence of
her lost power, and a triumph celebrated over that city without
whose help our generals never celebrated a triumph in connection

---

[240] Q. Metellus defeated Jugurtha in 109; Marius and Sulla captured the
Numidian king in 105.

[241] Cicero, *De officiis* 2. 8. 26 and 27.

with Transalpine wars."[242] And a little later: "Never will the seeds and the causes of civil wars be lacking so long as profligate wretches shall remember that bloody spear and cherish the hopes thereby suggested."[243] Whence it appears that among the Romans there was an increase, indeed, in wealth and in power but a decrease in truth and justice from the time they became avaricious. So we have again the following statement of Tullius:[244] " 'Would that fortune had reserved me,' said Gaius Pontius the Samnite,[245] 'until those times when the Romans begin to accept bribes, and that I had been born then; I should not have allowed them to continue to rule.' Verily he would have been obliged to wait for many generations, for this vice has crept into the state but recently."

The aforesaid Sulla instituted the proscription lists and, after putting to death many ex-consuls, he also deprived Marcus Marius of his life by putting out his eyes and by cutting him limb from limb. Of him Tullius says in his *Paradoxes*: "I saw Marcus Marius, who seemed to me in prosperity one of the fortunate men, in adversity one of the greatest men; no mortal can be happier than that."[246] Gaius Marius, when he saw the head of his comrade, was seized with despair and bared his throat to the slave.

Then followed the civil war of Catiline, which Sallust has brilliantly and very clearly set forth,[247] as also the war with Jugurtha. During these days there is said to have been a serious struggle with Macedonia also.[248] It was then too that Attalus, king of Asia, died and bequeathed his kingdom to the Romans in his will.[249]

45. Amid these calamities that I have mentioned the disastrous Mithradatic War,[250] greater than all the wars that preceded it except the African, continued for forty years — or as others say for thirty. It began to rage in the six hundred and sixtieth year after

242 *Ibid.*, 2. 8. 28.

243 *Ibid.*, 2. 8. 29.

244 *Ibid.*, 2. 21. 75.

245 The hero of the battle of the Caudine Forks.

246 Cicero, *Paradoxa* 2. 16.

247 Frutolf (p. 87. 3) mentions Sallust as authority for the Jugurthine War and the Conspiracy of Catiline (p. 89. 20; also Orosius 6. 6. 6); but Hofmeister does not believe that the actual works were well known to Otto.

248 Four separate wars with Macedonia are usually listed, and the dates given are I 214-205; II 200-197; III 171-168; IV 148-146. Macedonia became a Roman province in 146.

249 In 133.

250 Against Mithradates VI. It started in the year 88.

the founding of the City, a year in which civil war as well had started, and was brought to a conclusion in the consulship of Cicero and Antonius. As Lucan says, [it was]

"Scarcely at length concluded by means of barbarian poison." [251]

For when Mithradates, king of Pontus and Armenia, tried to despoil Nicomedes, king of Bithynia (a friend of the Roman people) of his kingdom, he was warned by the senate not to do so; threats were added in case he should not cease. Thereupon Mithradates was aroused and not only expelled Nicomedes from his kingdom but also harried Cappadocia with fire and sword, driving out from it another king, namely Ariobarzarnes.[252] Besides, he came to Ephesus and ordered all Roman citizens to be put to death upon a given signal. Then, sending his general Archelaus into Greece, he received in surrender not only Athens but all Greece. Sulla, sent against him with an army, killed a hundred thousand of the men of Archelaus and recaptured the city of the Athenians at last after a long siege. When Mithradates learned of the slaughter of his troops he sent an army of eighty-three thousand picked men to aid Archelaus. Fifty thousand of these are said to have been slain. In a third combat with Sulla, Archelaus was again defeated;[253] on this occasion all his forces were routed. By these and countless other disasters, which it would take too long to enumerate, that most powerful king, who had brought under his yoke almost the entire East, was finally reduced to such a pass that he who had previously ruled not only nations but even their kings and feared only poison, not the sword, and had fortified his constitution against poison by many antidotes, was reduced, I say, both by his luckless wars and the grief caused by a son who was plotting to depose him from his throne, to such extremities that he wished to kill himself with poison but could not, since his nature had previously been made proof against it by drugs. And so, after killing his wives and his daughters, since he himself could not perish by any kind of poison (as I have said), he bared his throat to a soldier and so departed this life, being seventy-two years of age. He has left us an example of the wretched lot of mortals. They say of him that, when he was being deposed

[251] Lucan, *Pharsalia* 1. 337.

[252] *Barzane* is given in the text.

[253] Sulla defeated Archelaus in Boeotia in 87, driving him to the Piraeus; a second time in the battle of Chaeronea in 86; and a third time in the battle of Orchomenus in 85. Otto is following Orosius 6. 2. 5-7.

from the throne by his son, he looked down from a very high wall and made entreaties to him but was not heard. And he said: "Inasmuch as Pharnaces bids me die, O ye gods of my fathers — if any such there are — let him, I pray, at some time hear this same command from his own children." In saying "gods of my fathers — if any such there are" he expressed his disbelief that they were true gods.

46. Now when the Mithradatic War was ended, and the troubles with the allies as well as the civil strife had quieted down, and after the conspiracy of Catiline had been completely suppressed, the Romans, unable to contain themselves and not content with the bounds of the empire that they had now begun to have, were eager to reduce the whole world to the status of a province. For this reason Pompey, their most famous leader, undertook to guide an army into Asia and in a short time subjected almost the entire East to the control of the Romans, replacing some kings and subduing others. He came to Jerusalem among other kingdoms of the East and, having captured the city, profaned the Temple by offering victims in that structure in which only the people of God were permitted to sacrifice; and he sent their king, Aristobulus,[254] in bonds to Rome and conferred the high priesthood upon his brother Hyrcanus.[255]

But, since we have made mention of the Jews, among whom alone (if we except a few men such as Job) according to the prophet God is believed to have been known at that time, I shall indicate in a few words how matters were with the City of God after the time of the prophets and the release from the Captivity even down to the present day.

47. After the death of Alexander, when his generals were dividing the various provinces, Egypt fell to the lot of Ptolemy the son of Lagus. He took captive many of the Jews. After him came Ptolemy Philadelphus, who not only out of respect for their religion released the captives but even bestowed royal gifts upon the temple and demanded from Eleazar, the priest, the books of the Law. When he had received them and had placed them in the famous library,[256] he sought for interpreters of them to translate them from the Hebrew into the Greek tongue. Accordingly there were given him presbyters to the number of seventy, one from each

[254] Aristobulus II, the son of Alexander; see Augustine 18. 45.
[255] Josephus, *Antiquities* 14. 8; *Jewish War* 1. 5.
[256] Which he founded at Alexandria.

tribe. These men, being skilled in both languages, dwelling each in a cell by himself, produced by the inspiration of the Holy Spirit a uniform version of great use to the City of God. Jerome, however, states that they made the translation in one and the same house at Alexandria, conferring with one another.[257] After this the Jews were taken captive by Ptolemy, king of Alexandria, who is also called Epiphanes,[258] and were then afflicted with many persecutions by Antiochus [259] and forced into idolatry. That most valiant man Judas [260] with his brothers very boldly resisted him. Jonathan succeeded Judas, Simon followed him and after Simon came his sons.

Now since all the canonical histories are brought to an end in the book called *The Maccabees,* we can learn only from the histories of the pagans what the status of the kingdom of the Hebrews was after this down to the time of Christ. The custom of anointing did not cease during the Babylonian captivity, as they themselves guilefully claim, but according to their own writers of history the Hebrew people had not only high priests but kings as well [261] after that time. The first of these kings, after Simon and his sons, was Aristobulus. He was succeeded by Alexander, himself both king and priest. Because of the excessive cruelty with which he treated his people, he was told, when he inquired how he might be reconciled to them, "By dying." After him his wife Alexandria [262] reigned. Her sons were Hyrcanus and Aristobulus. While one of them, Aristobulus, was on the throne, Pompey the general of the Romans was appealed to by Hyrcanus, and when Aristobulus had been taken captive (as I have said above) and had been cast into chains Hyrcanus was put in his brother's place. Thus, whether they like it or not, the Jews are confuted by their own testimony that when Herod, the first alien, reigned over them and when Christ was born, that prophecy was fulfilled which says [263] "The sceptre shall not depart from Judah, nor a lawgiver from between his feet, until He come who is to be sent," and so forth.[264]

[257] Jerome, *Praefationes in Pentateuchum.*

[258] Ptolemaeus V, 205-181. Otto has skipped over Ptolemy III, Euergetes (247-221) and Ptolemy IV, Philopater (221-205).

[259] Antiochus IV, king of Syria. The Jews were subject to the Seleucidae from 198-167.

[260] The greatest of the Maccabees.

[261] *Cf.* the prologue of Hegesippus; Augustine 18. 45.

[262] Or Alexandra.

[263] Gen. 49. 10.

[264] Augustine, *loc. cit.,* cites the same passage but not in the same words.

Precisely who were citizens of Christ in these days cannot easily be estimated. For by those days the prophets had become mute and there were, as it is written,[265] deep silence and most profound night. This very stillness and this darkness of night presaged the word that was soon to come from the royal throne of the Omnipotent. As the night is rendered the more intense by the approaching light of day, and as, when all are sunk in deep slumber, everything is held in the grip of silence, so when the Word of God was about to appear in the flesh and to illumine the whole world with His light, not only did swirling mists of evil befog and plunge in darkness the city of this world, but the shadows veiled the very City of God; it was plunged in silence, that men might exult so much the more as they caught sight of the Light coming in the flesh, proportioned to the eagerness with which they had awaited Him before when they were plunged in darkness and exhausted with woes. But that there were even at that time citizens of Christ (although they are not mentioned because of the silence of writers) we are given to understand principally from the fact that we believe that the seven thousand men who lived in the time of Elijah should be ever present for the City of God even to the end of the world.

Hyrcanus associated with himself in the administration of the affairs of the kingdom a foreigner, Herod the son of Antipater. And he, playing the part of a wicked and treacherous vassal, deprived Hyrcanus of his kingdom and of his life, usurped the throne, and finally kept his hold on it by permission of the Romans. Further, that he might be under less restraint in his possession of the kingdom, he abolished not only the anointing of kings but even that of priests, and in profane and sacrilegious fashion he adopted for his own use the sacred robe which only priests had been permitted to wear, to the end that when the anointing of kings and priests had deservedly ceased it might be known that the Holy of Holies was soon to come, to be anointed by an invisible oil as true king and true priest. If any would learn of Herod's further wickedness and of the manifold subtlety that he used in his dealings with the Roman empire, let him read Josephus.

48. In the six hundred and ninety-third year from the founding of the City, when Pompey had returned from the East and because of his many victories had been welcomed with a mighty triumph,[266]

---

[265] Wisdom 18. 14-15.
[266] This was in 61 B.C.

Gaius Julius Caesar, in the year when he himself and Lucius Bibulus were consuls, was sent by the senate to the West to subdue Cisalpine Gaul, Transalpine Gaul and Illyricum. And so he reduced to a province the bravest peoples in the world by the expenditure of much Roman blood and, having crossed the Rhine, conquered the Germans, the most ferocious and warlike of all peoples, not only by a bitter and perilous war but also by bribes and by the exercise of great practiced wisdom. If anyone desires to know the virtues and the valor of the Germans, let him read the life story of Caesar as written by Suetonius.[267] Josephus also, or Hegesippus, in a speech in which Agrippa exhorts the Jews to submit to the Roman empire by instituting a comparison with the Germans, makes mention of their valor and describes them as such utter strangers to fear that they scarcely fear death itself. Furthermore, when Julius tarried [268] beyond the appointed period, namely five years, in reducing these tribes to subjection, upon his return to Rome the triumph and the second consulship that were his due were refused him by the senate, through the advice of Pompey and the influence of Marcellus, then consul.[269] This circumstance was the cause of a grievous war, and not only of civil strife but also of internal disaster. For when Caesar heard of this action he hastened to Ravenna. Setting out from that town to Ariminum and tearfully relating his wrongs to his allies, he hastened to the City with his army. And when the citizens fled in terror along with Pompey, first to Brundisium and then to Dyrrachium,[270] a city of Greece, Caesar entered the City as victor and, breaking down the doors of the treasury, carried thence seven thousand one hundred and thirty-five pounds of gold and nearly nine hundred thousand pounds of silver. Then returning to his legions, which he had left in Ariminum, he crossed the Alps and there, bestowing munificent gifts upon both the Gauls and the Germans, whom he had conquered shortly before, he complained of the insults imposed upon him by his fellow citizens and

---

[267] This is a mistake which apparently is due to Orosius (6. 7. 2). Frutolf makes the same blunder (p. 89. 35). "But observe," says Hofmeister, "*secundum viros doctos esse codices commentariorum Caesaris, quorum inscriptiones Suetonii nomen exhibeant.*"

[268] Hofmeister states that he cannot find this in Orosius or in Frutolf, but calls attention to Annolied, 399 *et seq.*; Kaiserchronik, 455 *et seq.*

[269] C. Claudius Marcellus, in 49 B.C.

[270] Or Epidamnus; now Durazzo.

demanded and obtained their help.[271] Of the Gauls only the people of Marseilles, who are called also Phocaeans, refused to bring help to Caesar because they came into Gaul from Greece. Accordingly they were conquered in a desperate and wearisome conflict. At that time too Petreius and Afranius were forced by the bitter pangs of thirst to surrender to Caesar.[272]

49. In the six hundred and ninety-seventh year [273] from the founding of the City, Crassus,[274] colleague of Pompey in the consulship, a man on fire with the flames of avarice, was despatched to Asia. He went to Jerusalem for the sake of the Temple treasures, which Pompey had left untouched, and plundered them. Then directing his march through Mesopotamia, because he again failed to chasten his greed and coveted too much the gold of the Parthians, he was ignominiously slain [275] by them with the loss of much of his army. In the second year after this the City suffered from an unusually severe conflagration; fourteen regions, including the Vicus Iugarius, were consumed. After these disasters there ensued a civil war set in motion by the greatest discord and turmoil. When Caesar came with the flower of the Gauls and the Germans, Pompey, desiring to defend his country, called to his aid through his son the nations and the kings he had subdued in the East. The leading Romans and the senate together with Lentulus, the consul, visited Pompeius Magnus, who was tarrying in Greece at about the time at which there was wont to be a change of consuls and, removing Lentulus from the consulship, appointed Magnus leader of the army with universal approval. But Caesar, undismayed by the winter storms, rashly ventured upon the sea against the wishes of his soldiers, set out for Epirus, and there pitched a camp not far from Magnus. Here, impatient of delay, he dressed himself in a poor cloak and in order to meet Antony risked the treacherous squalls; but because as the winds arose he almost suffered shipwreck, he was obliged to return to his troops. So then strong forces were assembled from every part of the world, and nations con-

---

271 A similar statement is found in the *Gesta Treverorum* 13; Annolied, 405 *et seq.*; Kaiserchronik, 461 *et seq.*; *cf.* what Orosius (6. 15. 3) and in particular Lucan (Pharsalia 1. 296 *et seq.*, 392 *et seq.*) say with regard to Caesar's address to his soldiers at Ariminum after crossing the Rubicon.

272 Pompey's legates surrendered at Ilerda in the summer of 49.

273 Orosius 6. 13. Crassus went to Syria in 54.

274 M. Licinius Crassus, the wealthiest man of his time.

275 At Carrhae, in 53.

quered at the cost of much Roman blood were now forced to fight each other merely at the call of the Romans. For by this time the growth of the Republic had reached such a stage that it could go no further. And as it could not be destroyed from without it must needs collapse upon itself, as the poet says.[276] And so the two armies met on the plains of Pharsalus,[277] eighty-eight cohorts being drawn up in triple line on each side. You might have seen a lamentable and heart-rending combat: the citizens who were lords of the wide, wide world [278] divided against each other, aided by the resources of the whole earth, and, (so to speak) the sons of one mother, desiring to disembowel one another with their own hands. Though both armies gave way and the outcome was long in doubt, Pompey was finally forced by the ferocity of the Julian soldiery to flee with his followers, and so the victory fell to Caesar. There were slain in this battle fifteen thousand Pompeians, among them thirty-three centurions. Pompey, making his escape by flight, embarked upon a merchant ship. Having sailed to Egypt by way of Cyprus, by the order of Ptolemy he was killed as a favor to Caesar as soon as he set foot on shore. Pompey's wife fled with her sons but the fleet was destroyed and many were killed. Pompeius the Bithynian was slain there. The ex-consul Lentulus was killed at Pelusium.[279]

50. After Caesar had put all things in order he came to Alexandria. When Pompey's head and armlet were presented to him there he wept. Having a premonition of treachery he turned his arms against the Egyptians. After conquering them he gave over the throne of Alexandria to Cleopatra. For Ptolemy, after he had been defeated in a naval battle, had embarked in a small boat. But since many kept crowding on board he was drowned, and being washed ashore had been recognized through the evidence supplied by a golden coat of mail. After this Caesar went to Rome and was named by the citizens dictator and consul. He carried the war over into Africa and, joining battle with Juba and Scipio at Thapsus, caused great slaughter of Romans and of barbarians. Juba bade a soldier cut his throat; Scipio killed himself. The unyielding Cato committed suicide at Utica [280] by drinking poison. Caesar ordered

---

[276] Lucan, *Pharsalia* 1. 81: *In se magna ruunt; cf.* Augustine 18. 45.

[277] In 48.

[278] *Cf.* Vergil, *Aeneid* 1. 282: *Romanos rerum dominos;* also V. 1 below.

[279] The city at the most easterly mouth of the Nile.

[280] Whence he is known as *Cato Uticensis,* as distinguished from *Cato Maior* (the Censor).

Pompey's nephews and his daughter Pompeia to be killed. Then he entered the City in four triumphs. Presently setting out for Spain against the Pompeian troops, he carried on a desperate conflict with them there. After they had been conquered by mighty efforts he returned to the City in the third year after the civil war had started. He now held the whole City in his power and, since all the offices that existed in the City were vacant, Caesar alone was everything in the City. At that time Marcus Tullius Cicero was received into favor by him, and through Cicero's intervention Marcus Marcellus, in whose behalf Cicero delivered an eloquent and brilliant speech which begins thus, "Of the long silence, Conscript Fathers, that I have observed during these days. . . . " [281] He says in this speech that above all those qualities of Caesar whereby he subdued diverse nations was the fact that he had conquered his own spirit and received into favor Marcus Marcellus, previously his enemy. He continues thus, "To conquer one's spirit, to restrain one's wrath, to be restrained in victory, not only to raise up a prostrate adversary notable for high position, intellect and valor, but even to enhance his former dignity — one who should do these things I do not compare with the greatest men; I regard him as like as can be to a god." [282] While Caesar was occupying the highest station he was killed in the senate house upon the instigation of Brutus and Cassius, with the complicity of the senate, for planning to inaugurate a form of government at variance with the customs of the fathers. Now this narrative that I have epitomized is set forth by Lucan [283] in a fine and beautiful series of verses.

51. At this point we are constrained to cry out against the wretchedness of life's vicissitudes.[284] For lo! we see at what cost, not only to its enemies but even to its own citizens, the Roman Republic grew. For by alternating changes, after the manner of the sea — which is now uplifted by the increases that replenish it, now lowered by natural loss and waste — the republic of the Romans seemed now exalted to the heavens by oppressing nations and kingdoms with war and by subduing them; now in turn was thought to be going down again into the depths when assailed by those

[281] Cicero, *Pro Marcello* 1. 1.

[282] *Op. cit.* 3. 8.

[283] Not so, for he stops in the midst of the Alexandrine War.

[284] So likewise below, IV. 31 (beginning); and *cf.*, for example, Orosius 5. 5 (beginning): *exclamare hoc loco dolor exigit. Cf.* also I. 32 above.

nations and kingdoms or overwhelmed by pestilence and sickness, and — what is more significant even than such matters — after they had arranged everything else well and had set it in fine order, they were miserably disemboweled by falling upon one another in internal civil strife. All these calamities springing out of unstable events and (so to speak) the daily deaths of mortal beings should have had the power to direct men to the true and abiding life of eternity. But as we have said above,[285] when the city of the world was afflicted by these and like misfortunes the rising of the true Light [286] was drawing nigh as though following the darkness of murky night. And so, since after hurrying over the instances of fluctuating disasters that affected the Medes and the Persians, as well as the Greeks and the Romans, we are now approaching the coming of Him who, being truly the peacemaker, pacified all things ''whether things upon the earth, or things in the heavens,'' [287] even Christ Jesus himself, let us set an end to this second book, inasmuch as we are hastening on to speak of that peace which was secured to the whole world under Augustus at the coming of Christ's nativity.

HERE ENDS THE SECOND BOOK

[285] II. 47.
[286] *Cf.* below, III. 45 (beginning).
[287] Col. 1. 20.

THE PROLOGUE OF THE THIRD BOOK [1]

Not unmindful of my promise,[2] beloved brother, I shall not hesitate to complete the discussion of the Two Cities, already brought down to the times of Caesar Octavianus with such style as I had at my command, particularly since we have now come to Christian times, and by God's grace I shall speak the more willingly as I shall now be able, because of growing faith, to speak more fully of the City of God. For heretofore, though I had at my command much regarding the citizens of the world, I was in position to say but little about the citizens of Christ, because from the time of the first man to Christ almost the whole world (except a few of the Israelitish race), led astray by error, given over to empty superstitions, ensnared by the mocking devices of demons [3] and caught in the toils of the world, is found to have fought under the leadership of the devil, the prince of this world. "But when the fulness of the time came, God sent forth his Son" [4] into the world to lead back into the highway mortal men, who were wandering like the brutes [5] through trackless and devious places. By taking upon himself the form of a man He proferred mortal men a highway; to recall those who were utterly astray from the error of falsehood to the light of reason, He revealed Himself as the truth; to make over anew the perishing He showed Himself as the true life, saying, "I am the way, and the truth, and the life," [6] as though He were saying, "You

[1] The third book, starting with the events that followed the assassination of Julius Caesar, carries on the account of the history of Rome to the death of Constantius and the accession of Constantine in 306 A.D. Otto's chief authorities for this period are: Orosius, Books 6 and 7; the *Ecclesiastical History* of Eusebius, translated and continued by Rufinus, Books 1-8; Frutolf's *Chronicle*. There are also quotations from the Bible and passages in which Otto has made use of Jerome's *De viris illustribus,* of the *Annales Hildesheimenses,* and of Regino's Chronicle.

[2] *Cf.* above, Prol., I, pp. 95 *et seq.* The beloved brother whom he addresses in the passage here referred to is Isingrim.

[3] The gods of the pagan world.

[4] Gal. 4. 4.

[5] The text reads *more pecudum; cf.* Orosius 1. 1. 3: *ritu pecudum.*

[6] John 14. 6.

are wandering astray; come therefore to me who am the way. That you may tread this way undismayed, learn that I am the truth. And if you have no provision for the journey, realize that I am the life." For many seek the way but, not finding the true way, wander about instead of walking in the right path. Again many tread a way which seems the true way, but do not thereby attain life. Of these methinks it was said: "There are ways which seem right unto men, but their ends lead to destruction." [7] But the Saviour, coming into the world, says, "I am the way, the truth, and the life," that is, "Through me alone one walks safely, with me alone one reaches truth, in me alone one continues in true life."

But at the very outset the question may properly be raised why the Saviour of all men was willing to be born at the end of the ages which Paul calls "the fulness of the time"; and why He permitted the whole Gentile world to perish [8] in the sin of unbelief in so many past ages. Who that is circumscribed by the corruptible flesh of mortals would venture to inquire into the cause of this dispensation set away in the most profound and righteous treasures of the judgments of God; who, I say, would venture, seeing that the apostle says, "O the depth of the riches both of the wisdom and the knowledge of God! how unsearchable are his judgments, and his ways past finding out!" [9] and so forth? What then shall we do? If we cannot understand we are not to be silent, are we? In that case who will reply to the defamers, stay the assailants and above all confute those who seek by argument and by the force of words to destroy the faith that is in us? Accordingly we cannot comprehend the secret counsels of God and yet we are frequently obliged to attempt an explanation of them. What? Are we to attempt an explanation of things which we are unable to understand? We can render explanations, human explanations to be sure, though we may still be unable to comprehend God's own explanations. And so it comes to pass that while we speak of theological matters, since we lack the language appropriate to these matters, we who are but men use our own terms and in speaking of the great God employ mortal expressions with the more assurance because we have no doubt that

---

[7] *Cf. Prov.* 14. 12: *Est via, quae videtur homini iusta, novissima autem eius deducunt ad mortem.*

[8] *Cf.* Eusebius-Rufinus, *Historia ecclesiastica* 1. 2. 17. On the other hand Orosius 7. 1 differs radically both in language and in thought.

[9] Rom. 11. 33.

He understands the formulas we devise. For who understands better than He who created? Hence it follows that, although God is called ineffable, He yet desires us to say much in His praise. Therefore, since He is called ineffable, after a certain fashion He is seen to be effable. As Augustine says,[10] this contradiction in terms can better be resolved by silent faith than by wordy disputation. And another has said: "Let what is beyond words be revered through the agency of silence."[11]

So then "If God," as the Apostle says, "endured with much long-suffering vessels of wrath fitted unto destruction,"[12] if, desiring to reveal unto His Church the riches of His goodness, He permitted the city of the world to have long temporal prosperity in the free exercise of its own will, He is not to be blamed either because He abandoned that city to its own devices or because to His chosen people — chastised by contrast with that city of the world — He revealed the riches of His goodness. For on the one hand if He permits men to do what they themselves at all events desire to do, He cannot justly be accused by them; and on the other hand He should be greatly praised and revered by those whom, as He bestows on them His grace without price, He deters from such things as they wish to do to their own hurt and prevents from bringing such intentions to accomplishment. He cannot be said to be acting unjustly if in accordance with justice He does not bestow His grace, even as He must be believed to be acting only in mercy when He imparts it without price to whom He will. And so, if He abandoned so many ages of the past, not by forcing them into sin but by not giving them what was His own — with this purpose, that by the example of those that had gone before He might reveal to future generations what must be avoided by them, that they might render thanks unto their Saviour — if, I say, with this purpose He abandoned them to their own will, both that they might learn what they could do by themselves without Him and that when redeemed they might learn in addition what they possessed by their Saviour's mercy, then as He could not justly be blamed by the former, even so He gave the latter abundant reason whereby He ought rightly to be loved by them.

There is besides a reason why Christ wished to be born at this

10 Augustine, *De doctrina Christiana* 1. 6; *cf.* his *Sermo* 117. 5. 7.
11 *Verba Euagrii in Monachico libro, Hist. Trip.* 6. 21, says Hofmeister.
12 Rom. 9. 22.

time rather than at any other, namely in the sixth age [13] and when the world was united under the sway of the Romans and organized as a whole under Augustus Caesar. For inasmuch as he willed to be made flesh in order to atone for the sin of our first parent, who, putting away the delights of paradise, preferred to inhabit the land of the curse at the caprice of his own will, it was most fitting that this be done in the sixth age rather than in any other, because He also created that first man on the sixth day. Nor ought He to have been made flesh in an early age of men. For the men that were descended from these sinful parents, men whose nature, marred by disobedience, made them more inclined and prone to evil, who as yet were making no use of their reasoning powers, and were roaming about rather in the manner of wild, brute beasts — the natural goodness within them being obscured, — these men, I say, had not learned to live companionably with one another, to be moulded by laws, to be adorned with virtues, and to be lighted by the power of reason to the knowledge of the truth. Hence we have most shameful stories and even more shameful deeds, most monstrous recitals and still more monstrous acts, regarding all of which I think I have said enough in what has preceded. Since men were thus devoid of reason, incapable of receiving the truth, unacquainted with justice and with laws, how could they receive, how understand, how comprehend the laws and the most lofty precepts about life that were to be given by Christ? And so the Law was given first that it might be suited to their feeble intellects and might support the infancy of the world not with solid food but with milk. Then as this age gradually grew and made progress — partly through the association of men dwelling together, partly through the putting together of their wisdom for the purpose of establishing laws, and partly through the agency of the wisdom and of the teachings of the philosophers — it was fitting that the Saviour of all should appear in the flesh and establish new laws for the world at the time when, as I have said, the whole world had now bowed before the power of the Romans, and had been moulded by the wisdom of the philosophers, and the minds of men were suited to grasp more lofty precepts about right living.

Now at this point I think I ought to answer the question that I

---

[13] See Augustine 22. 30, and *cf.* Intro. § 4 for the seven ages as Augustine enumerates them.

put off above,[14] why the Lord of the universe wished the whole world to be subject to the dominion of one city, the whole world to be moulded by the laws of one city. In the first place He wished it, as I have said, that the minds of men might be more ready to understand, more capable of understanding great matters. Secondly, He wished it that unity of faith might be recommended to them after they had been united in this way, in order that all men, being constrained by their fear of a single city to revere one man, might learn also that they ought to hold to one faith, and through that faith might learn that God must be revered and adored not merely as a celestial being but as the Creator of all. Hence upon His coming a census of the whole world was ordered, doubtless that men might learn that One was come who would enroll all who came to Him as citizens in the Eternal City. Hence at His birth throughout the entire circuit of the universe the world, exhausted by calamities and wearied by its own dissensions, willed to be at peace and to serve the emperor of the Romans rather than to rebel, that understanding might be vouchsafed of the fact that He had come in the flesh who said in mercy to those weighed down and wearied by the weight of earthly burdens, ''Come unto me, all ye that labor and are heavy laden, and I will give you rest.''[15] For this reason peace, at that time a new thing, was granted to the world in order that the servants of the new king might be able to journey more freely over the whole world and implant health-bringing precepts about right living. It is not therefore to accidental causes, nor to the worship of false gods, but to the true God who forms the light and creates the darkness that, in my judgment, we must ascribe the fact that the commonwealth of the Romans expanded from a poor and lowly estate to such heights and to a great sovereignty under the primacy of one man. But why He bestowed this boon upon that people or that city rather than on others we cannot even discuss; unless perhaps I should say it was done because of the merits of the chief of the apostles who, He foresaw, would have His seat there, upon whom as upon a foundation He also promised that He would build His Church, namely, that the place which was to be the head of the Church universal (on account of the seat of the chief of the apostles) might beforehand attain to sole rule over the Gentiles

[14] II. 36.
[15] Matt. 11. 28.

also, from whom true believers were to be gathered.[16] Most fittingly, therefore, that city was in earlier days the head of the world which was afterwards to be the head of the Church. But if any man is contentious, let him hear that it is "in the power of the potter to make one vessel unto honor and another unto dishonor."[17] Let him hear that it is in the power of the judge to put down whom He will and to lift up whom He will. Finally, if the Lord, who is the judge and arbiter of the world, holding a cup in His hand,[18] first making Babylon drunken humiliated it at last at the hands of the Medes and, when the Medes had been brought low by the Persians, the Persians in turn by the Greeks, and the Greeks finally by the Romans, wished for a time to exalt Rome, which was also in its turn to be put down, if, weighing in balanced scales all human events, He weaves such changes as those, will it be possible for the Creator to be blamed by His creature? And so let us humble ourselves under the mighty hand of the Lord who changes thrones[19] and according to His will has mercy on whom he pleases, and let us, ascribing it to His compassion if we are anything (who of ourselves are nothing), and attributing to His grace what we say (who of ourselves know nothing), pursue the work we have begun.

HERE BEGINS THE THIRD BOOK

1. In the seven hundred and tenth year[20] from the founding of the City, after the assassination of Gaius Julius Caesar, Octavianus — who by his uncle's will had received his uncle's name and had been made his heir — at first concealing his grief at Caesar's death, [later] entered upon a struggle with Antony and put him to flight. Antony had besieged Brutus and Cassius at Mutina to avenge Caesar[21] and had been declared an enemy by the senate. When Antony was afterwards received back into favor, Octavianus

16 Augustine 15. 12, solves the problem in a far different way.

17 Rom. 9. 21.

18 *Cf.* Jer. 51. 7; Ps. 75. 8.

19 *Cf.* p. 88 (end); below, VI. 9; Prol., VII; Dan. 2. 21: *mutat tempora et aetates, transfert regna atque constituit.*

20 44 B.C.

21 Orosius and Frutolf correctly record that D. Brutus was besieged at Mutina. Otto, confusing him with M. Brutus, added Cassius on his own account.

in company with him undertook a civil war, and after fighting many battles finally killed Pompey, the son of Gnaeus Pompey, and drove Brutus and Cassius to kill themselves. Then coming to Rome after many triumphs he discharged twenty thousand soldiers from service, restored thirty thousand slaves to their masters and crucified six thousand whose masters were not found. Antony, however, divorcing Octavia the sister of Caesar, withdrew to Egypt and there, making Cleopatra the queen of Egypt his wife,[22] attempted to rebel against Caesar. After Caesar had subdued everyone else and made all subject to himself, planning a naval battle against Antony also he set out from Brundisium for Epirus. And so they met and fought long and bitterly, namely from the fifth hour of the day even to the seventh, with loss to both forces and with victory hanging in the balance. The rest of the day and the following night brought victory to Caesar. Cleopatra with her troops was the first to flee from the battle and Antony followed her as she fled. Twelve thousand of Antony's army are said to have been slain there and six thousand wounded. Then Caesar, having been called [by his troops] *Imperator*, was consul for the fourth time,[23] with Marcus Licinius.[24] Antony, being defeated in the naval battle, prepared to fight on land; when this conflict occurred he was again vanquished. And when he once more ventured forth on the first of August to put his fleet in battle array, all deserted to Caesar; forsaken by his men he took refuge in the city of Alexandria. There, when he saw that Caesar was close upon him, he killed himself with his sword. And Cleopatra is said to have killed herself by applying asps to her breasts.

2. And so Caesar, by gaining possession of Alexandria, the richest of all cities, put an end to the kingdom of the Greeks. For in this city (founded by Alexander in Egypt) kings of the Greeks, we find, reigned up to this time. Hence some make the rule of the Greeks extend as far as the time of Caesar. For after the death of Alexander the Great, when his associates [25] divided up that part of Asia which had been conquered by him, four kingdoms came

---

[22] This is from Jordanes, *Romana* 251. Orosius and Frutolf give a different account.

[23] In 30 B.C.

[24] *I.e.*, Crassus.

[25] The text gives *commilitones*; this is the word used by Orosius 3. 23 (end). Augustine (18. 42) says *comites*. *Cf.* above, II. 26.

into being in the four quarters of the globe. Of these two were pre-
eminent: to the south that of Egypt, whose principal city was
Alexandria; to the east and north [26] that of Syria and Mesopotamia,
whose capital was Antioch, which Seleucus the Great (of whom
mention was made above)[27] is said to have founded. He called it,
men say, by the name of his father Antiochus, and established the
seat of his power there instead of at Babylon. For it was previously
called Reblatha [28] (so men say) and then, according to the prophet,
"the head of Syria, Damascus."[29] Now in these cities dwelt very
powerful kings, the Ptolemies and the Antiochi; in their lust for
power they raged against each other and seized the control of the
East in turn. However, the greater authority ultimately fell to the
Ptolemies. All these matters are known not only from secular histories but also from the vision of Daniel, wherein he speaks of the
kingdoms of the south and of the north, and still better from the
commentary of Jerome on that prophet.[30] Accordingly, when in the
course of time the Church was organized by the early Fathers on
the basis of the distribution of the nations, these two cities, as
being the most worthy after the city of Rome, were alone deemed
worthy to have patriarchal sees [31] as Rome itself had a see. Later
to be sure, as the Church grew, Constantinople and Jerusalem obtained patriarchal sees by permission of the Fathers — one because
it was a seat of empire, the other on account of the Holy Sepulcher
and that temple of the Lord, so ancient, so deeply reverenced by
the whole world.[32] Accordingly we read in the Council of Nicaea
regarding the Church at Jerusalem: [33] "Let the Bishop of Ælia
be honored by all, with due recognition of the jurisdiction of his
metropolitan."[34] Some refer this to Caesarea in Palestine because,

[26] *I.e., aquilonem*: *cf.*, for example, Dan. 11. 6. 7. 8. 11, *etc.*

[27] II. 26; II. 42.

[28] Jerome, on Isa. 13. 1.

[29] Isa. 7. 8.

[30] Jerome, on Dan. 11. 4 *et seq.*

[31] For a discussion of the special position of the churches of Rome, Alexandria and Antioch, see *e.g.*, Cambridge Medieval History, Vol. I, pp. 171
et seq., for that of the church of Jerusalem, see pp. 174 *et seq.*

[32] *Cf. Decr. Grat.*, *c.* 3 and *c.* 6 *et seq.*, *d.* 22 *ed.* Friedberg, *col.* 75 *et seq.*,
from the first, sixth and eighth synods of Constantinople.

[33] *Cf.*, for example, *Decr. Grat.*, *c.* 7, *d.* 65, *ed.* Friedberg, *col.* 251; *Rufinus,
Historia ecclesiastica* 10. 6 (*can.* 8); *interpret. Dionys. Exig.*, Mansi, *Ampl.
coll. conc.*, II, *col.* 680 (*can.* 7). They do not agree verbatim with Otto.

[34] By "metropolitan" is meant the bishop of the metropolis or capital of
the province.

when Jerusalem was destroyed by Titus and Vespasian, Caesarea was made the metropolis of Palestine and thus continued without interruption to be the metropolis of that province in accordance with ecclesiastical law. For where under the rulers of the heathen there were flamens, there bishops were afterwards stationed by our Church. Where they had archflamens, we established archbishops; where they had protoflamens, we began to have primates or patriarchs,[35] all indeed of one order, but of varying dignity according to the differences between the cities. Others give the text of the aforesaid sentence as "Obtaining the rights of a metropolitan," and interpret it thus: after the statement, "Let the Bishop of Ælia [36] (that is, Jerusalem) be honored by all," then, to prevent anyone from thinking that he should be honored by all as the highest pontiff (that is to say the Roman pontiff), the statement was added "obtaining the rights of a metropolitan," that is, "we declare that he should be honored, not as chief pontiff, but as a metropolitan." But whether it be this way or that it is apparent, nevertheless, that he was not yet a patriarch. But enough of this.

I have said that according to some authorities the monarchy of the Greeks continued to the time of Caesar. But it seems more reasonable to say that the Greeks lost their monarchy indeed after the death of Alexander, but had famous kings who governed the East. This is why Daniel, in speaking of the empire of Alexander, says:[37] "It shall be scattered to the four winds of heaven, but not to his posterity, nor according to his dominion wherewith he ruled." And again we read of Antiochus that during the siege of Alexandria he received an ambassador of the Romans. When the latter had found him walking on the beach and had vainly summoned him to desist from his siege of the city, baffled he described a circle about him on the ground with a staff that he happened to be carrying and said, "So speaks the senate and the Roman people that before you step out from that circle you are to depart from the city." Upon hearing this the king was terrified and soon raised the siege. From these and other stories we learn that, even before the Romans had kings, they yet had authority over the greatest kings. Why then do we credit the Greeks with a monarchy, unless it be that Rome

[35] An interesting example of how the Christian church availed itself of the institutions of the pagans.

[36] *Aelia Capitolina* was the name of the Gentile city founded by Hadrian on the ruins of Jerusalem; see III. 21 (end) below.

[37] Dan. 11. 4.

had not yet concentrated the authority in one person, and that our city, continuing in Judaea down to the time of Caesar, was under their authority? The prophet [38] calls Nebuchadnezzar also king of kings: yet as the Medes had control of the empire at that time he was not king of kings, save insofar as the prophet judged him worthy of this name, both by reason of the fame of the city which he had assailed and because of the entreaties of the people of God whom he held captive.

Now from Alexander to Cleopatra all the kings named Ptolemy numbered eleven. And Caesar found so great a supply of money at Alexandria that the prices of slaves at Rome were doubled in consequence.

3. In the seven hundred and thirty-fifth year [39] from the founding of the city of Rome, Caesar, having won the victory over the Alexandrines and subjugated all Asia and even fully quieted all civil discord, returned as victor from the East on the sixth of January, in his fifth consulship, which he held with Lucius Apuleius as colleague.[40] He entered the City in a threefold triumph, closed the Gates of Janus and was hailed by all with the name Augustus. This name, unknown to all the ages up to this time and signifying the most exalted sovereignty,[41] is the prerogative of kings of the Romans alone. Under these circumstances you find the temple of Janus closed for but the third time since the founding of the City: the first occasion was under Numa, the second after the First Punic War. Augustus, who had governed the state for twelve years with these consuls whom I have named, from this day forth ruled alone,[42] and thus the powers formerly wielded by several yielded to the primacy of one man — which the Greeks call monarchy. Henceforth the Romans began to have kings instead of their consuls, who, because they held sole rule over the whole world, were called *Imperatores* and *Augusti*.

[38] Dan. 2. 37.

[39] Orosius 6. 20 says 725 *A.V.C.*, *i.e.*, 29 B.C., the correct date.

[40] What Otto actually says is *ipso et Lucio Pelogio* (sic) *quinquies consulibus;* he appears to have missed the exact meaning of Orosius 6. 20. 1: *ipso imperatore Caesare Augusto quinquies et L. Apuleio consulibus.* The consul's praenomen was Sextus (not Lucius).

[41] Otto's phrase is: *apicem declarans imperii.* Orosius 6. 20. 2 says: *Quod nomen cunctis antea inviolatum et usque ad nunc ceteris inausum dominis tantum orbis licite usurpatum apicem declarat imperii.*

[42] Frutolf (p. 93. 40) says that Octavian reigned first for twelve years with Antony and Lepidus, and then for forty-four years alone.

After this Caesar, opening the Gates of Janus, declared war upon the Cantabri and Astures, valiant tribes of Spain, and when he had subdued them in the course of five years in a stern and arduous conflict, he returned victorious to the City and closed the Gates of Janus again. Then through the instrumentality of Claudius [and] Drusus [43] he reduced Gaul and Rhaetia [44] to a province; the peoples of Noricum, Illyricum, Pannonia, Dalmatia, Moesia, Dacia and Thrace he either subdued through his generals or segregated within the barriers formed by those mighty streams, the Rhine and the Danube. At this time Drusus is said to have founded Mainz [45] in Gaul and to have founded or restored Augusta in Rhaetia, so called from the name Augustus [46] and previously known as Vindelica. His monument is pointed out to this day at Mainz in the shape of a pyre.[47]

At that time Varus, while acting insolently and avariciously — as was the habit of the Romans — toward the vanquished, was annihilated by the Germans, together with three legions.[48] Augustus is said to have taken this disaster to the Roman arms so to heart that he very frequently dashed his head against a wall and repeatedly said, in the extremity of his grief, "Quintilius Varus, give me back my legions." Suetonius records that this war between the Romans and the Germans — 'a very serious and bitter contest, the greatest since the African wars — was waged for three years by fifteen legions. Hence we may infer how great was the strength of the aforesaid tribe of Germans, since at the time of the greatest power of the Roman Empire it wrought such great havoc with the Roman army. The inhabitants of Augsburg have a tradition that this massacre occurred there, and as proof point to a hill formed

[43] Otto actually says per Claudium Drusum.

[44] In 15 B.C.

[45] Hofmeister remarks that scholars of the present day believe that Drusus pitched a Roman camp at Mainz; cf. E. Hübner in Jahrbücher des Vereins von Altertumsfreunden im Rheinlande 80 (Bonn, 1885), pp. 85 et seq. The Annolied 505 and Kaiserchronik 385 have Caesar in place of Drusus.

[46] The Annolied 483 et seq. states that Augusta was founded by Drusus. Mommsen (Corpus Inscript. Lat. 3. 2, p. 711) is among those that favor this common belief.

[47] Still extant and now called Eigelstein: see Stein in Pauly-Wissowa, Realencyclopädie der class. Altertumswissenschaft 3. 2, col. 2715 et seq. (s. v. Claudius, n. 139). Cf. Frutolf p. 98. 25: Drusi . . . , qui apud Mogontiam habet monumentum.

[48] At the famous battle of the Teutoberg Forest, in 9 A.D.

from the bones of the dead which in the vernacular they call Per-leich even to this day, because a legion perished there.[49] They point out also a village named after Varus.[50]

4. Meanwhile as Augustus was tarrying at Tarragona, a city of Hither Spain, ambassadors of the Indians and the Scythians came with gifts, asking for peace. And just as of old, while Alexander tarried in Babylon, the nations of the remotest West came to him of their own accord as suppliants and pledged their fealty, so now the nations of the remotest East came to the farthest West to Caesar. Even the Parthians, restoring standards which they had taken from the Romans when they killed Crassus, and giving hos-tages, demanded peace. And so when all the world had been made subject to the Romans and had been divided into provinces, the Gates of Janus were closed by Augustus for the third time and they remained closed for twelve years. But Augustus himself, although now master of all the world, yet never permitted himself to be called master either in earnest or in jest. In this he really avoids our arrogance: for we, though Christians and priests, greatly seek after the very thing which the heathen with natural insight refused.

5. It was at this time, when a census was decreed by Augustus for the Jews as well as for all other nations, while Cyrinus [51] was governor, that Judas of Galilee, who is mentioned in the Acts of the Apostles,[52] is found to have lived. Of him Josephus speaks as follows in the second [book of his] history of the Jewish War: ''At this time a man of Galilee, Judas by name, induced the people to revolt, persuading them that it would be a very bad thing for them to submit to pay tribute to the Romans and in addition to the sovereignty of God to accept the overlordship of men.'' [53] Of Cyrinus he speaks thus: ''Cyrinus, a man advancing with the con-sent of the senate through the various offices even to the rank of consul but distinguished in other ways, came with a few companions to Syria, being sent by Caesar to administer justice to the na-tions.'' [54]

[49] Cf. Excerptum de Gallica historia, MGH, SS. 23, pp. 389 et seq.

[50] ''Pfersee,'' to the west of Augsburg. On the other hand the Exc. de Gall. hist. states that the lake ''Verrisse'' received its name from Verres, a tribune of the soldiers.

[51] Quirinius.

[52] Acts 5. 37.

[53] 2. 8. 1.

[54] Antiquities 18. 1. 1.

6. And so when all the strife of sedition was at last allayed, a hitherto unknown peace was restored to the world and the whole earth divided into provinces in accordance with the census held by the Romans. This was in the forty-second year [55] of the reign of Caesar Augustus and the seven hundred and fifty-second year [56] from the founding of the City, in the one hundred and ninety-third Olympiad, when five thousand five hundred years had elapsed since Adam, and an alien, Herod the son of Antipater, was ruling in Judaea, in the sixty-sixth week according to Daniel.[57] At this time Jesus Christ, the Son of God, but according to the flesh a son of David, was born of the Virgin Mary in Bethlehem of Judaea. And that he might be pointed out as the light of the world and the true peace, on the night on which he was born an angel appeared to shepherds amid a great light, announcing the joy due to him that had been born. And a multitude of the heavenly host sang, in unison with him, GLORY TO GOD IN THE HIGHEST, and proclaimed that peace had come on earth to men of good will.

Observe that, as I said above,[58] the kingdoms of the Babylonians and the Romans had an origin and a development in many ways alike. For while their first king, Ninus, reigned among the Babylonians, in the forty-second year of his reign, Abraham, to whom the promise about Christ was first made, was born. And again when the first Caesar, Augustus, was reigning among the Romans, it was likewise in the forty-second year of his reign that the Christ promised to Abraham and desired by all the nations was born. It is to be observed furthermore that the reign of Augustus was in many ways a prophecy of the reign of Christ who was born in his times. For Augustus, returning from the East on the sixth of January, after he had made kings subject to himself and put down civil strife, was received in the City with a threefold triumph and was called Augustus. And Christ, being born and veiling his majesty

---

[55] Frutolf, p. 95.5; Jordanes, *Romana* 85. Jordanes, who says that Augustus reigned for 56 years, appears to date the beginning of his rule by the battle of Philippi. This computation accordingly makes the birth of our Lord coincide exactly with the beginning of the Christian Era. But see the next note.

[56] This would be 2 B.C. So Orosius, 6.22.1 and 7.3.1; Frutolf says the 751st; Jordanes the 755th.

[57] *Cf.* Jerome on Daniel 9.24.

[58] Not so, but see below, IV.21 and 31. In VI.22 (*cf.* IV.5) Otto makes the same statement *iuxta maiores nostros, i.e.*, Orosius. *Cf.* Prol., II.

humbly in the flesh, was in like manner on that same day (that is, the sixth of January, which we call the Epiphany) worshipped with three sets of gifts, a star serving as guide for the Three Wise Men from the East; and he who had previously been hidden was revealed and hailed as August and King of Kings. At that time indeed this was only foreshadowed, but it is seen more clearly than light itself that by this time it has been brought to accomplishment, namely, that Christ not only reigns in heaven but also governs all kings on the earth. Whence the Church with beautiful fitness sings to his praise on that day on which, as we have said, this was foreshadowed, "Behold the Lord, the Conqueror, comes, and in his hand are the majesty and power and dominion." [59] And in the offertory, "And all the kings of the earth shall worship him, all nations shall serve him." [60] For in that he is called "the Lord, the Conqueror," the name August is ascribed to Him; and in that the "majesty" and "dominion" are said to be "in His hand," imperial dignity is attributed to Him; and in that kings are said to worship Him and all nations to serve Him, the most exalted sovereignty — that is, sole authority over all the earth — is declared to be His.

We find that during these days an abundant stream of oil flowed in the Trastevere district of the City, that it might be made evident that He was to be born in the flesh who was destined to be anointed above all kings with the oil of gladness and exultation through the Holy Spirit. But regarding peace and the subjugation of the world, I gave an account, I remember, in the Prologue. To that account this should be added, I think, that the Son of God, coming in the flesh, desired to be enrolled as a citizen of the Roman state. For since that city, founded in treachery, was beyond doubt the city of the world, why did He who was born as the first citizen and founder of the City of God desire to be enrolled in the Roman state, save that He showed thereby that He had come to fashion His own City in strange and inexpressible manner from the city of the world? And, to speak more plainly, though born among the Jews, He was enrolled among the Gentiles, that in this way He might clearly make it known that grace was to be transferred from that people to the Gentiles. So then, with the birth of the new Man who supplanted the old, let us set an end to our annals also, which were

---

[59] See the *Missale Romanum* (Milan, 1474), *ed.* R. Lippe, I, London, 1889 (Henry Bradshaw Society, 17), p. 31, *in epiphania Domini, Introitus.*

[60] See *l.c.,* p. 32, *in epiph. Dom., Offertorium.*

reckoned from Ninus to the founding of the City and thence even to this time, and let us begin our annals from His birth.[61]

7. In the third year from the incarnation of the Lord, Herod, the king of the Jews, hearing from the Magi that the Christ had been born, committed a most monstrous crime. For fearing — since he was a foreigner — that a child had been born of the seed of David who would demand the throne of his father by right of inheritance, he had made careful inquiries concerning the place and the time, and then ordered that male children of two years of age and under in the vicinity of Bethlehem should be put to death. But Christ's foster-father was warned beforehand by an angel, and the child was taken to Egypt. The Lord, in punishment for this crime, afflicted Herod severely with a most awful and loathsome visitation of disease. This is why Josephus, in the seventeenth book of his *Antiquities,* speaks of him as follows: "Moreover a disease that grew worse from day to day tormented Herod, exacting punishment for a sin committed long before. For without, on the surface of his body, he was burned by a slow fire, but inside a mighty conflagration was concealed. He always had an insatiate desire for food; yet his gluttony, stimulated by his greedy jaws, could never be appeased. For his intestines were streaming with ulcers."[62] A little farther on he says· "But he had also to fear that they were welling up with worms and rotting away: he was also puffed up beyond belief by pride." Later he adds: "Now those who have skill in divination said that these were penalties imposed by God's will on account of his many impious and cruel acts." He relates also that, when Herod had begun to despair of recovery, he summoned to himself the nobles and chief men from each of the villages or castles and cast them into prison. And calling to him his sister Salome and her husband Alexander he said, "I know that the Jews will rejoice at my death but, if you will obey my injunctions, I shall be able to have mourners and a funeral notable for the great number of those that lament. Accordingly, as soon as I breathe my last, put to death all whom I have under guard, that Judaea everywhere — every house in it — may grieve at my death." And not long after, when he perceived that the end of his life was at hand, he asked for a small knife to cut an apple; having received it he directed its stroke against himself. The same writer adds that be-

---

[61] *Cf.* above I. 5.

[62] *Cf.* Eusebius-Rufinus 1. 8. 5, and see *Antiquities* 17. 6. 5.

fore he died he murdered his third son,[63] having killed two before. And so he ended his life in accursed fashion, both because of his very great bodily pains and because of his sinful deeds of murder. It is believed that this atonement was exacted of him beyond question on account of his sacrilege toward Christ and the deed committed upon the children of equal age with Christ. Upon the death of Herod his son Archelaus succeeded to the throne.

8. In the sixth year [64] from the incarnation of our Lord there was a very great famine in the city of Rome. This is said to have grown so serious that Augustus ordered the schools of gladiators, and foreigners, and even the slaves (except physicians and teachers) to be sent out of the city. At that time, when Augustus was already an old man, the Gates of Janus, which had become rusty from long disuse, were opened on account of an uprising of the Athenians and the Dacians. They were not closed until the time of Vespasian. Yet, although the soldiers were under arms, there was never din of war for any long period. Doubtless we must believe that it was due to the advent of a new king that uprisings so serious were brought to an end without grave disasters of war. Thus far Cornelius Tacitus.[65]

9. In the fifteenth year from the incarnation of our Lord, Augustus died in the fifty-eighth year of his reign and Tiberius, his stepson, succeeded to the throne. He governed the state with great moderation and neither injured the citizens at home nor provoked a storm of war abroad. In the fourth year of his reign — that is,

[63] Antipater; not the third in point of age, but the third that Herod killed.

[64] The number may be computed from Orosius 7. 3. 6; Frutolf (p. 95. 35) has A.D. 7.

[65] This is an obvious error, as Wilmans observed. Otto was probably led into this by incautiously abbreviating the account of Orosius in 7. 3. 7. In the course of his Chronicle he indicates the endings of his various authorities, namely:

Cornelius Tacitus (an error)	III. 8
Luke (The Acts)	III. 15
Jerome (Ecclesiastical History)	IV. 18
Really Eusebius-Rufinus; see Frutolf, *a*. 398.	
Orosius (Frutolf, *a*. 426)	IV. 22
Theodoret, Socrates, and Sozomen	IV. 23
(*Historia Tripartita*)	
Jordanes (*Getica* and *Romana*)	V. 4
Victor, Bishop of Tours (Chronicle)	V. 4
Really Bishop of Tunnuna	
Isidore's Chronicle	V. 9
All previous chronicles	VII. 11
(with the year 1106)	

in the nineteenth year from the incarnation of our Lord — Germanicus, the son of Drusus and father of Caligula, triumphed over the Germans. At that time, furthermore, Tiberius is said to have been so kind-hearted that, when those in charge [of the taxes] tried to persuade him to increase the tribute, he replied that it was the duty of a good shepherd to shear his flock, not to eat it up.

During these days a certain villain, Mundus by name, very craftily deceived a certain pious matron, Paulina. For when he had often tempted her without avail to commit adultery, he induced the priests of a temple by a bribe to announce that one of the gods wished to have intercourse with her. The woman reported the matter to her husband; the husband approved. And so, coming by night to the temple, the woman awaited the god. Mundus accordingly came and gained his desire in the guise of a god. After this he taunted the woman with what he had done. She again informed her husband. When Caesar had learned of the crime from the husband he destroyed the temple as a due punishment; the priests he crucified but, moved by a foolish compassion, he spared the young man as one deluded by a great passion, and persuaded him to leave the city. These facts I wanted to set down to show that Tiberius was indeed merciful but lax in his punishment of evildoers, a fault of almost all clement judges.

10. In the thirtieth year from the incarnation of our Lord and the fifteenth of Tiberius Caesar, when now four princes, whom the Greeks call tetrarchs, ruled in Judaea (Archelaus having died),[66] John began to preach in the desert the baptism of repentance. To his baptism the Lord also came to be baptized, that he might bless the waters. And after this He began to preach and work miracles. He chose twelve leading men of His country, whom He called apostles; He appointed one of them as the leader to secure the blessing of unity — Peter.[67] After these He appointed seventy-two [68] men of inferior rank, disciples. When only a short time had elapsed after this, John, the greatest citizen of the City of God (as The Truth Himself said in bearing witness to him: "Among them that are born of women there hath not arisen a greater than John the

---

66 A mistake on Otto's part. Archelaus had previously been banished for his cruelty. The date of his death is unknown.

67 Cf. below, III. 14 (beginning).

68 So Luke 10. 1 (but the American Revision has "seventy" in the text); Eusebius-Rufinus too has seventy.

Baptist''), accused Herod of incestuous marriage. On account of
this he was imprisoned by him and on Herod's birthday, as you
have the account in greater detail in the Gospel,[69] he was brought
out and shamefully murdered during the feast. Josephus records
this and the great war that ensued in consequence between Herod
and Arethas, king of Arabia,[70] because that country sought vengeance for a daughter's disgrace. In this war, he states, Herod's
army was destroyed. Now Josephus speaks as follows: ''Certain
of the Jews were of the opinion that Herod's army had perished
because in his case divine vengeance was quite justly set in motion
to avenge John, who was called the Baptist, whom Herod had punished, a very good man who taught the Jews to give heed to righteousness, to observe justice in their dealings with one another, to
maintain a spirit of reverence toward God, and to unite in one
through baptism. For thus only, he said, would baptism be acceptable, if it were not merely received to wash away sins, but also
retained as a means to chastity of the body and justice and purification of the soul, and regarded as the sign and trustworthy proof
of all the virtues together. When he was teaching through precepts
of this sort, and a very great multitude was flocking together to
him, Herod, fearing that the people, won over by John's teaching,
might perhaps fail to support his own rule — for he saw that the
people were ready to obey John's admonitions and warnings in all
things — believed it better that the man should be put to death before any disturbance occurred than that he should himself repent
too late after an uprising had occurred. Because Herod entertained
these mere suspicions, John was arrested and taken to the fortress
of Machaerus [71] and was beheaded there.'' So much concerning
John. Of the Saviour [Josephus] tells as follows: ''In these same
times lived Jesus, a wise man, if indeed it is proper to call him a
man. For he was the doer of marvellous deeds, and the teacher of
such men as gladly hear the truth, and he won as his followers
many of the Jews and many even of the Gentiles, and he was believed to be the Christ. When Pilate, upon the accusation of the
chief men of our race, had decreed that he should be crucified, those
who had loved him from the beginning did not desert him. He ap-

[69] Matt. 14. 3.

[70] The King of Arabia Petraea, whose daughter Herod had married and
then discarded for Herodias.

[71] In Peraea.

peared to them on the third day, alive again, even as divinely inspired prophets had foretold regarding him that these and countless other miracles would come to pass. Even to this day both the name and the sect of Christians, who were so called from him, persist." [72] This testimony of a very learned man, but a Jew, concerning our religion, I wished to set down that I might make it clear that the Jews are not ignorant of the coming of Christ, but are blinded by their hostility and are unwilling to believe, so that their damnation is the greater.

11. In the thirty-fourth year from His incarnation, while Tiberius was still reigning, and Pontius Pilate was governing in Jerusalem, the Lord deigned to come to His passion and to be crucified at the sixth hour in the place called Calvary, outside the gate, at the Preparation, being handed over by the Jews to the Gentiles. From that hour until the hour at which he breathed his last, the ninth, there was darkness not only in Judaea but also over the whole world. And, as it is written,

"Then did an impious age fear the coming of darkness eternal." [73]

The fourteenth moon,[74] which then shone, has proved even to the unbelievers that this darkness occurred in consequence not of an eclipse of the sun but of a miracle. An earthquake also at that time destroyed certain cities of Asia; on this account Tiberius freed them from tribute and gave them their independence. Men say that at this time one of the philosophers, who, they think, was Dionysius the Areopagite,[75] said: "The God of Nature suffers." After the resurrection and ascension of the Lord, Pilate wrote [76] to Tiberius Caesar concerning His life, His miracles, His passion and His resurrection also. Upon hearing this Tiberius brought a proposal before the senate recommending that he should be worshipped among the gods. But the senate refused to ratify Caesar's edict

[72] It is now quite generally believed that this passage in Josephus is a later interpolation. *Cf.* Hastings, *Encyclopaedia of Religion and Ethics*, article on "Josephus."

[73] Vergil, *Georgics* 1. 468; Orosius 7. 4. 14 quotes the verse.

[74] Orosius 7. 4. 15. *Cf.* also below, III. 27. The Passover of the Jews was celebrated on the fourteenth day of the first month, that is, of the lunar month whose fourteenth day falls on or next follows the day of the vernal equinox. The point which Otto is trying to make here is that an eclipse at such a time would be impossible.

[75] The supposed disciple of St. Paul.

[76] *Cf.* Frutolf, p. 97. 25.

because the case had not been laid before them first; they even voted that all adherents of this name should be extirpated from the City. For this reason the emperor was transformed from a very mild prince into a most savage beast, and ordered a great many of the senators and nobles to be put to death. And so it came to pass that, because they were unwilling to accept Christ as king, they found their king Caesar an avenger. However, men believed that all this came to pass by the will of God, to prevent faith in Christ from seeming to have won credence from a man who was an unbeliever, and authority from an earthly ruler.

In the same year Stephen, a great ruler of the City of God, was stoned by those who killed his Lord also. Tiberius banished the Jews who had been persecutors of Christ to provinces of more rigorous climate; those who had remained in the City he put out of the way, condemning them to perpetual slavery. These are the beginnings of travail. By what kinds of trials they were afterwards afflicted by the Romans in accordance with the prophecy of the Lord, because they had not known the time of their visitation, we shall tell when we shall reach that period.[77]

12. In the thirty-ninth year from the incarnation of the Lord, Tiberius died by poison, in the twenty-third year of his reign. Gaius Caligula, the third in line from Augustus, succeeded him on the throne. He was a man infamous above all who preceded him, and one who really seemed to have been employed to punish the Roman blasphemers and the Jewish persecutors. In his time, because the Jews in Alexandria were being crushed under the weight of many misfortunes, Philo Judaeus,[78] a leader among the leading philosophers, was sent by them to Caesar to present their complaint. This is the Philo who wrote among many famous works, a book in which he highly commends the Christians.[79] The Book of Wisdom [80] also, which begins thus, "Love righteousness," is believed by some to have been written by him, because it is redolent of Greek eloquence. As evidence of this you will find set down there certain statements about Christ in the style not of prophets, but of historians, not of those foretelling the future, but of those recording

[77] III. 17 and 18; cf. 21.

[78] Of Alexandria. He flourished about 40 A.D.

[79] Jerome, De viris illustribus 11, who has greatly abridged the profuse account of Eusebius-Rufinus, Historia ecclesiastica 2. 17.

[80] Called "The Wisdom of Solomon" in the Apocrypha.

the past, as for example: "The wicked said: 'Let us unjustly oppress this just man'." [81] And again: "He professeth to have knowledge of God, he nameth himself the son of God." [82] And likewise: "Let us condemn him to a shameful death." [83] Jerome relates that this Philo was so ardent a follower of Plato that it was said of him by the Greeks in an epigram: "*y Philon platanon, y Platon philanon,*" that is, "Either Philo is Plato's disciple or Plato is Philo's." [84] Now when he undertook the embassy from the Jews to Caesar, not only was he despised by the emperor on account of his race, but it was also commanded by Augustus [85] that the temple should be profaned and that he himself should be worshipped there as a god. Pilate, too, was treated with such indignities by Caesar that he is said to have killed himself with his own sword. Behold the most just and mysterious judgments of God: he avenges himself on his foes through the instrumentality of a most sinful man, and, without bestirring himself at all, triumphs over his enemies by the efforts and the frenzy of the citizens of the world. There are some who say that he [Pilate] was sent out into exile to Vienne, a city of Gaul, and was afterwards drowned in the Rhone. Whence the inhabitants claim even today that ships are endangered there.

During these days Caesar, hurrying through Germany and Gaul, proceeded to Britain.[86] When he had received there in submission Bellinus,[87] the son of the king of the Britons, he returned to Rome. But his cruelty was as great toward his own people as it had been toward the enemy. For his own sisters, whom he first debauched, he afterwards condemned to exile. After committing these and many other crimes, as shameful as they were cruel, he was killed by his own bodyguard in the fourth year of his reign. After his death two little books were found, one of which was entitled *The Dagger* and the other *The Sword,* in which the names of illustrious Romans destined to death are said to have been written. A casket, too, full of various poisons was found at his house. These poisons, when poured into the sea, even killed many of the fish. There is no

[81] Wisd. of Sol. 2. 10; *cf.* 1. 16 and 2. 1.
[82] Wisd. of Sol. 2. 13.
[83] Wisd. of Sol. 2. 20.
[84] Jerome, *De viris illustribus* 11. The passage which Otto thus transliterates reads as follows: ἢ Πλάτων φιλωνίζει ἢ Φίλων πλατωνίζει.
[85] *I.e.,* Caligula.
[86] But got no further than the shores of the ocean.
[87] *Cf.* Suetonius, *Caligula* 44.

doubt that the Lord took so monstrous a tyrant from this life because the times of the Christians were germinating. How great
slaughter of the people he was on the point of causing, and would
have caused if he had lived, we may learn from the death of the
fishes.

13. In the forty-third year from the incarnation of the Lord,
upon the murder of Gaius, Tiberius Claudius, the fourth in line
from Augustus, took over the government. Luke relates that in his
days there was a famine in Judaea, the famine which Agabus had
foretold; he adds that alms were sent from Antioch through Paul
and Barnabas to the brethren who dwelt in Judaea.[88] Josephus also
states that Helena, the queen of the Adiabeni, contributed very
very large sums to relieve the necessities of the poor in these days.[89]
Luke adds the further statement that, at this time (which Eusebius
establishes beyond doubt as the reign of Claudius), Herod killed
James and imprisoned Peter, who was, however, freed by an angel.[90]
Divine vengeance punished this crime committed by the king, as
Luke records in this fashion: "When," says he, "Herod had gone
down to Caesarea, and on the day of a feast had, clad in striking
royal apparel, taken his seat on the throne, and was making an
oration to the people from his tribunal and the people were ac-
claiming him by crying, 'The words of a God and not of a man,'
immediately an angel of the Lord smote him because he gave not
God the glory, and he was eaten of worms and gave up the ghost."[91]
You will find the same story recorded by Josephus also, at greater
length. Josephus likewise states that in these days lived Theudas
of whom Luke represents Gamaliel as speaking in this wise: "A
certain Theudas arose giving himself out to be somebody, but he
was slain, and all who followed him were dispersed."[92]

14. Now when the City of Christ and the Empire, which before
his nativity was restricted almost solely to Judaea, were to be
spread abroad to all nations, the apostles, as princes and builders
of this city, went forth into every land to preach the word of life,
and were scattered into the uttermost limits of the earth. Hereupon
Peter, who led the others, received as his jurisdiction Rome, mis-

[88] For the incident referred to see Acts 11. 27-30.
[89] *Antiquities* 20. 2. 5.
[90] Acts 11. 3-19 and 12. 2.
[91] *Cf.* Acts 12. 21-23.
[92] See Acts 5. 36.

tress of the whole world. Paul, who excelled the rest in wisdom, journeyed to Greece, the most learned of all lands, and the fountain of all philosophy; John to Asia; Andrew to Achaea; Matthew to Ethiopia; Thomas and Bartholomew to the two Indias; Simon and Thaddaeus to Egypt and Mesopotamia and to farthest Persia, and Scythia; Philip to Hierapolis; James, remaining in Judaea, ruled the church of Jerusalem. The other James [93] had been beheaded by Herod; yet he had before that preached to the Spaniards, it is said, and his tomb is still held in honor in that land.[94] These men, attacking the world not with arms but (far more effectually) by the word of God, triumphed over the whole earth much more gloriously than the Romans by shedding not their own blood, but that of others, had triumphed.

So Peter, having come to Rome, found Simon, an arch-heretic, the most skilled of all men in magic arts, a man most vile, leading the City astray. This man had been baptized some time before by Philip in Samaria. But, because he sought from the apostles the power of working miracles without getting it, though he offered them money, he fell away again and turned aside after Satan, and, performing miracles by many acts of legerdemain due to demons, he did not blush to call himself a god. But Peter began to teach in the city of Rome the saving words of life, and what he taught by word of mouth he confirmed by the power of his signs. From this time forth there began to be Christians at Rome.

During these days Mark, who was the first to rule the church at Alexandria, wrote down in Italy, at Peter's dictation, the gospel in the Latin tongue.[95] Matthew had previously written his Gospel in Judaea in the Hebrew speech. The other two — that is, Luke and John — composed their Gospels later in the Greek language. After that Peter, receiving the see of Rome and striving by precept and example to build the City of God out of living stones, adorned the noblest cities of the earth with citizens and priests of Christ. For he sent Saint Apollinaris to Ravenna, Saint Clement to Metz, and

---

[93] The son of Zebedee.

[94] *Cf.* among others the *Miracula S. Iacobi apostoli,* whose author is reputed to be Pope Calixtus II, *Acta SS. Boll.* 25 Iul. t. VI, pp. 46 *et seq.* For the legends regarding these missions mentioned by Otto *cf.* Lipsius, R. A., *Die apokryphen Apostelgeschichten und Apostellegenden.*

[95] Hofmeister remarks that Otto may have imagined that he could infer this from the words of Eusebius and Jerome; it is often expressly stated that Mark wrote in Greek, *e.g.,* by Hugo of St. Victor, *Erud. Didasc.* 4. 6.

to Trèves,[96] that most flourishing city of Gaul, three leaders at once — Valerius, Eucharius and Maternus. After they had crossed the Alps, Maternus died on the way as they journeyed; his associates, alarmed by this catastrophe, returned to Rome. Thereupon, according to the tradition, the blessed apostle sent his pastoral staff to restore Maternus to life through their instrumentality. When they came to the place of the sepulcher, they found that he had been thirty-three days in the tomb. And yet, being full of faith and good works, the men of God, in obedience to their master, touched him with a rod and aroused their comrade from death. It is said that after Eucharius and Valerius he ruled the church of Trèves and Cologne for as many years as he had lain days in the sepulcher. Moreover, in proof of the event that I have mentioned, that same rod is still displayed at Trèves and at Cologne, in such wise that the people of Trèves have the upper part of it and the people of Cologne the lower.

At that time Claudius attacked the Britons with an armed force because they had not restored deserters, and accepted the submission of this most ferocious nation without bloodshed or a battle.[97] He also added to his empire the Orkneys, islands situated at the very end of the ocean, and — marvellous to relate — returned to the city in the sixth month from the time at which he had begun his progress. In the seventh year of his reign so great an uprising occurred at Jerusalem at the feast of the Passover that of those who, on account of the crowding of the people in the courts of the Temple, were crushed to death, thirty thousand were found to have been Jews. In the ninth year of his reign he ordered the Jews to be expelled from the City. Not only Josephus but Suetonius records this fact: "Claudius," says Suetonius, "expelled from Rome the Jews, who were always causing a disturbance at the instigation of Christ." In the following year there was so great a famine in the City that, when the emperor was insulted by being struck with crusts of bread in the midst of the forum, he escaped the fury of the angry mob only by fleeing into the palace. Not long after this he put to death for trifling causes thirty-five senators and three hundred knights. And he himself died by poison in the fourteenth year of his reign.

15. In the fifty-seventh year [98] from the incarnation of our Lord,

96 Or Trier.
97 In 43 A.D. See Tacitus, *Agricola* 13 and 14; *Annals* 12. 31-40.
98 So Frutolf; actually in 54 A.D.

Nero, the fifth in line from Augustus, came to the throne. He was the most shameful of all, for he even surpassed in worthlessness his uncle,[99] Gaius Caligula. He was a man of such wantonness that he disgraced himself by putting on various costumes and making the rounds of the cities and the theaters of Greece as well as of Italy, outdoing even the actors themselves in buffoonery. He was of such unbridled luxury that he used golden nets for fishing and is said never to have had less than a thousand state coaches in his retinue. In his utter wantonness he even ordered the City to be set on fire. While it was burning — for six days and seven nights continuously — he stood on the loftiest tower of the palace of Maecenas, delighted by the beauty of the conflagration, and, clad in tragic costume, declaimed the Iliad. I shrink to speak of his lusts, because he left neither his mother nor his sister untouched and did not hesitate to sin even against nature. What is more wicked than the fact that he did not save from death even his teacher Seneca? Seneca was famed for his life and for his learning; he cultivated the pursuit of philosophy, and showed that he would be friendly to the Christian religion by sending many letters to Paul the Apostle and receiving replies from him.[100] Whence also he is placed by Jerome in his book of illustrious men,[101] in the roll of our own citizens. Besides, when Nero had killed many senators, he revealed himself as murderous, and as incestuous in his dealings with his mother, his brothers, his sisters and his wives. He was furthermore of such insatiate avarice that, in addition to an incalculable treasure of money which he had extorted by violence from merchants, he decreed that ten million sesterces be given him by the senate every year. To these disgraceful deeds he added impiety towards God: he was the first to institute a persecution of the Christians. This we believe was not done without the design of God, namely that His City might first have a foe of this sort, a foe whom even the city of earth would abhor on account of the crimes involved in his monstrously wicked deeds, a foe to whom nothing seemed dishonorable save honor.[102]

In the first year of Nero's reign, Anianus became Bishop of

[99] The emperor Gaius was the youngest son of Germanicus; Nero (L. Domitius) was the son of Cn. Domitius and of Agrippina, the daughter of Germanicus.

[100] Otto may have read the extant letters which are falsely attributed to him.

[101] Chapter 12.

[102] *Cf.* the famous statement of Tertullian (*Apolog.* 5) quoted by Eusebius-

Alexandria, succeeding Mark the Evangelist. During this same time the Jews were greatly troubled by a false prophet, a certain Egyptian who, by his magic art, had speedily won the reputation of a prophet, so much so that he had gathered about him thirty thousand men and seized the Mount of Olives, and was ready to invade the city [of Jerusalem] from this point and to subject it to his autocratic power. But Felix encountered him and put him to flight, and by putting the others to death or taking them captive easily put an end to all that he had begun. Hence, in the Acts of the Apostles, Felix says to Paul:[103] "Art thou not the Egyptian who before these days stirred up the people?" After Felix, Festus was set by Nero in authority over the Jews. While Paul's case was being aired before him at the insistence of the Jews, Paul appealed to Caesar, as the Acts of the Apostles relates.[104] He was sent in bonds to Rome and upon his arrival there preached the word of life without cessation. Thus far Luke brought his book of the Acts of the Apostles.

But after the Jews saw that the snare which they had stretched to trip up Paul was frustrated, they turned the enormity of their wickedness against James, the brother of the Lord, who was termed "The Just," the Bishop of Jerusalem, and called upon him to deny his faith in Christ. The scribes and the Pharisees placed him upon a pinnacle of the Temple, and cried out in a loud voice, saying to him: "Most just of men, to whom we ought all to give heed, since the people go astray after Jesus who was crucified, proclaim to us what is the way of approach to Jesus." But he while declaring with resolute voice and fearless spirit that Christ sits in heaven at the right hand of the highest virtue, cast himself down from the pinnacle of the Temple, remaining, however, utterly unscathed. But he was struck by a fuller's pole, and so his martyrdom was accomplished. He was believed by the Jews themselves to have been a man of such sanctity and justice that Josephus will have it that it was because of his death that the city was presently destroyed by the Romans. He not only moulded the City of God by his deeds, but also wrote one of the seven canonical epistles, so called,[105] a letter

Rufinus, *Historia ecclesiastica* 2.25.4: *non nisi grande aliquod bonum a Nerone damnatum.*

[103] According to Rufinus the spokesman was "*sub Felice tribunus*"; cf. Acts 21.37-38.

[104] Acts 25.11.

[105] *Cf.* Eusebius-Rufinus 2.23-24. The General Epistles are meant.

very useful and seasoned with the salt of wisdom. The writings of the other apostles, except the epistles of Peter and of Paul, of John and of Jude, and the gospels of John and of Matthew are not included in the canon.[106] James was succeeded by Simeon, the son of Cleopas, who is mentioned in the gospel. Hegesippus states that, after the flesh, he was the cousin of the Lord.

16. Now while Nero endeavored to destroy the City of God by persecuting the Christians, directing that the most blessed leaders of the apostles, Peter and Paul, be punished, — Peter on the cross with feet upwards, Paul by the sword, — he crowned both with blessed martyrdom. The following year the wretched City paid the penalty for this. For a pestilence devastated it so grievously that the dead numbered thirty thousand. In that persecution Processus and Martinianus [107] and many others were killed. At Rome Linus succeeded Peter,[108] at Antioch Euodius. During these days two towns in Britain were taken with very great slaughter of citizens and allies. At the same time Roman soldiers came ignominiously under the yoke of the Parthians, many provinces in the East being lost. Three cities in Asia, namely Laodicea, Hierapolis and Colossae [109] were overthrown by an earthquake. Observe that when the apostles were crowned with martyrdom in Rome, the secular prestige of that city began to diminish.

When Nero heard that Galba had been made emperor by the army in Spain [110] he strove in his depression of spirit to throw the state into utter confusion, and was declared by the senate a public enemy. And so, perceiving that he could not bring his evil designs to accomplishment, he fled to the fourth milestone from the City and killed himself in the fourteenth year of his reign. In him the family of the Caesars came to an end. Yet there were not lacking men to say [111] that this which is contained in the writings of the apostle,[112] "And now, ye know that which restraineth, to the end that he may be revealed in his own season," and also, "He that

---

[106] Cf. Eusebius-Rufinus 3. 24.

[107] According to the Acts of Linus these were the two soldiers who guarded Peter and who were converted by him; see Lipsius, *Petrus-Sage,* pp. 137 ff.

[108] For a list of the Popes as recorded by Bishop Otto, see the Catalogue following Book VII of the Chronicle, and notes.

[109] Cities of Phrygia.

[110] The aged governor of Hispania Citerior, proclaimed *imperator* by his soldiers in 68 A.D.

[111] Cf. Augustine 20. 19.

[112] II. Thess. 2. 6 and 7.

restraineth, let him restrain until he be taken out of the way," was spoken of Nero, under whom Paul wrote; and they thought that Nero was not dead but had been withdrawn alive from human affairs until the last day, to appear in that generation which then was, and that he himself would be Antichrist.[113] But now let us return to the regular sequence of our history.

17. Galba, the sixth in line from Augustus, came to Rome when he learned of the death of Nero. Since he here adopted a certain Piso, a noble, as his son, both were killed by Otho [114] in the seventh month of his reign. And so, while Otho was usurping the power at Rome and Vitellius [115] likewise was attempting to seize it in Germany, in Syria Vespasian [116] was declared Emperor by his army on the report of Nero's death. He had been sent by Nero against the Jews, and had oppressed them with many afflictions, and he was holding as prisoner Josephus, their bravest and wisest priest. Doubtless it was on account of the crime committed against the leaders of the apostles that Rome suffered this civil discord and the dismemberment of its most glorious empire.

Josephus, the son of Mathias, was afterwards of so great authority, not only among the Jews but also among the Romans, that a statue was erected in the City in his honor, and his books too were placed in the library. His works are extant: *An Account of Antiquities,* in twenty books, and seven books concerning the war of the Jews with the Romans. The second book of the Maccabees also is said by some [117] to have been written by him. Eusebius mentions other famous works of his.[118]

Otho prepared to make war against Vitellius. In the course of this war he had come off victorious, first in the Alps, a second time near Placentia,[119] and a third time in the neighborhood of a place which is called Castor's; but when in the fourth battle, at Bed-

---

[113] *Cf.* also Jerome on Dan. 11. 29, and below VIII. 2.

[114] Marcus Salvius Otho Titianus, emperor from January to April, 69.

[115] Aulus Vitellius was proclaimed emperor by his legions on the Rhine. He defeated Otho near Cremona and reigned from April to December in the Year of the Four Emperors.

[116] Titus Flavius Vespasianus, 69-79.

[117] Hofmeister declares that he is unable to decide whether Otto himself or some earlier writer has so corrupted the statement of Eusebius-Rufinus, *l.c.* 3. 10. 6 (repeated by Jerome, *De viris illustribus* 13); *cf.* Jerome, *Dial. adv. Pelag.* 2. 6: *Iosephus Machabaeorum scriptor historiae.*

[118] Eusebius-Rufinus, *l.c.,* 3. 9. 4.

[119] Now Piacenza.

riacum,[120] he saw his forces defeated, he committed suicide in the third month from the time that he had begun to reign. Vitellius, coming to Rome, usurped the throne and did many cruel and wicked acts there. When he heard about Vespasian, at first indeed he thought of laying down his authority; but afterwards, being encouraged by his adherents, he drove Sabinus, Vespasian's brother, in flight to the Capitol with his troops, and there consigned all amid flame and ruin to a common pyre. Thereupon Vespasian left his son Titus to besiege Jerusalem and set out for Rome by way of Alexandria. He had assumed the imperial title after the death of Nero, at the urgent advice of the leading men and particularly of Josephus who, when cast into chains, had persistently maintained that he must be released by this same Vespasian, but as emperor. In the meantime Vitellius was taken prisoner by his own men and, being ignominiously dragged by a hook along the Sacred Way and through the Forum, was drowned in the Tiber and deprived even of ordinary burial. Meanwhile many cruelties had been practiced by his soldiers [121] even upon the senate. When Vespasian learned of the death of Vitellius he stopped at Alexandria.

18. Now since the Jews were unwilling to repent of their crime committed against the Saviour, after forty years [122] from the Lord's passion (which they had received as a period in which to repent) — nay, had heaped sin upon sin in putting to death Stephen and the two Jameses — the vengeance of heaven, which had been foretold them by the Lord, was now destined to burst forth upon an impious people. But the citizens of Christ were forewarned by a divine oracle to depart from the wicked city and its most sacrilegious people — even as Lot from Sodom [123] — into a town named Pella, across the Jordan. The faithless city was beset by Titus with a siege at the very time of the Passover feast, when all the people were flocking together from every quarter for the festival, and was finally taken at the cost of much Roman blood. But Titus was kept away from the Temple, which a multitude of priests and chief men guarded. When he took it by a great effort on the part of his men, he destroyed it utterly, with the city itself, as though it had been annihilated by the budding church of God

120 The text reads *Briacum*. Bedriacum is located on a tributary of the Po not far from Cremona.

121 By Vespasian's soldiers, according to Orosius 7. 8. 9.

122 *I.e.*, A.D. 70.

123 *Cf.* above, I. 9.

and, in accordance with the Lord's prophecy,[124] he left there not one stone upon another. Eleven hundred years had elapsed from its first founding. Cornelius [125] and Suetonius record that six hundred thousand Jews were killed at that time. But whosoever desires to know to the full the heartrending destruction of all the Jews, let him read Josephus,[126] their own historian, who relates that at that very season of the Passover feast there were three million men shut up in the city as in a single prison house. The same writer narrates that one million, one hundred thousand of these perished, partly by famine, partly by fire and by sword, in this one city alone, exclusive of those who died in other cities and other fortresses. He says, among other things, this: "I think that, even if the warfare of the Romans against these impious citizens had ceased for a little while, the city would have paid the penalty either by earthquake or the waters of a flood or by the fires of Sodom and lightnings hurled from heaven, because Jerusalem had begotten this present generation of men, far more accursed and iniquitous than those who suffered these penalties; wherefore also the entire race equally deserved to be blotted out." The rest of the Jews, who are said to have numbered nine hundred thousand,[127] are scattered abroad throughout the whole world even to the present day. After so magnificent an achievement Titus was hailed by his army as "Imperator." Vespasian then entered the City with his son Titus, sitting with his son in one chariot, and was there received with the greatest jubilation and an unheard-of triumph, the Jewish captives and their library [128] being paraded before him. This is believed to have taken place by a righteous judgment of God, to the end that they who had sinned against God, Father and Son, should be punished by men, father and son.[129] And so, when all the

---

[124] Matt. 24. 2.

[125] *I.e.,* Tacitus.

[126] Namely, the fifth and sixth books of his *Jewish War.*

[127] Rufinus and Orosius have *nonaginta milia.* One variant reading gives *nongenta milia; cod. Monac.* 6380, once at Freising, has $\overline{CCCC}$.

[128] From Josephus, *Jewish War* 7. 5. 4.

[129] *Cf.* Eusebius-Rufinus, *Historia ecclesiastica* 3. 5. 5: *Iusto scilicet Dei iudicio,* etc., who differs, however, from Otto in that he thinks the reader should be reminded of the fact that both the Saviour's death and the destruction of Jerusalem occurred at the Passover season. On the contrary Orosius 7. 9. 8 speaks of the glorious spectacle, *patrem et filium uno triumphali curru vectos gloriosissimam ab his, qui Patrem et Filium offenderant, victoriam*

tumult of war had been allayed, the emperors closed the Gates of Janus for the sixth time since the founding of the City.

During these days the empire of the Romans was greatly increased, for Achaea, Lycia, Rhodes, Byzantium, Samothrace, Cilicia and Commogene were reduced to provinces and became obedient to Roman laws and Roman jurisdiction. In the ninth year of their reign cities of Cyprus were destroyed by an earthquake and the City itself was swept by a pestilence.

In that same year or, according to others,[130] in the tenth [of his reign], Vespasian died of dysentery in his own villa in the Sabine country. His son Titus [131] succeeded him, the eighth in line from Augustus — if we exclude Otho and Vitellius from the number of the emperors — a man of greater restraint than all emperors before him, so much so that he was called The Delight of Mankind. He used to say that a day on which he had done no good was lost. There were no wars in his reign but Rome was in large measure consumed by a conflagration. He built the amphitheater at Rome and dedicated it with five thousand beasts. In the second year of his reign, in the same villa in which his father had died, he too died lamented by all. Eusebius relates [132] that in the same year Linus, after twelve years passed in the holy office, handed over the bishopric of the city of Rome to Anacletus.

19. In the eighty-third year from the incarnation of the Lord, Domitian,[133] the ninth in line from Augustus, succeeded his brother Titus. He not only began to practice savage cruelty upon his own people, putting some to death and sending some into exile, but even brought great calamity upon the state by recklessly exposing his army to the Germans and the Dacians. He even developed madness so desperate that he had himself addressed and worshipped as god and lord. He too brought persecution upon the Christians, being second here to Nero.

In the fourth year of his reign Anianus, who had ruled the Church of God at Alexandria for twenty-two years, died. Habilius succeeded him. Anacletus also, who according to Eusebius had held the

reportasse, but makes no mention of a just judgment of God as revealed in the event.

130 Jordanes, *Romana* 263.
131 Titus Flavius Vespasianus, 79-81.
132 Eusebius-Rufinus 3. 13.
133 Titus Flavius Domitianus, 81-96.

priesthood in the city of Rome for twelve years, departed this life and left the see to Clement. But others call this man Cletus and place Anacletus after Clement.[134] This is the Clement of whom Paul makes mention [135] as his fellow worker when he says, ''With Clement and the rest of my fellow workers.'' This great prince of the City of God, a man endowed with wisdom and so amiable that he was beloved by Jews and by Gentiles, not only molded the Church of God by word and by deed but also left memorials in the form of books destined to benefit the City of God. There is extant, besides other works of his, a letter to the Corinthians which he dictated in the name of the Roman church. This is, clearly, so similar to that which Paul wrote to the Hebrews that the letter I have mentioned is, in consequence, thought by many to be not Paul's but Clement's. Upon this Clement Peter bestowed the power of binding and loosing which had been bestowed upon Peter by the Lord, and appointed him as his successor in the priesthood. But why two are found to be intermediate between him and Peter we think has been sufficiently set forth in the record made by others.[136]

When Domitian set out to persecute the City of God he ordered that John, the only survivor of the apostles (for all the rest had been crowned with martyrdom), should be banished to the island of Patmos; and there, by divine revelation, John composed the Apocalypse. Domitian also ordered descendants from the stock of David to be sought out. These he summoned to his presence, but when he learned that they were poor, and upon questioning them concerning the kingdom of Christ heard that it was a heavenly, not an earthly kingdom, he let them go free. He even, issuing another proclamation, stopped the persecution which he had ordered to be directed against the churches. But in the fifteenth year of his reign he was murdered in his palace and was buried in shameful fashion. Nerva [137] succeeded him on the throne in the one hundred and forty-ninth year [138] from the incarnation of the Lord. He ordered the exiles to be recalled. In consequence John also was permitted to return from Patmos to Ephesus.

[134] *Cf.* Frutolf, p. 101. 50; 103. 20. So, *e.g.*, Regino in his list of Roman popes, *Chron.*, ed. Kurze, p. 38, and Otto himself in the catalogue subjoined to Book VII below.

[135] Phil. 4. 3.

[136] Frutolf, pp. 99 *et seq.*

[137] Marcus Cocceius Nerva, 96-98.

[138] Note the chronological error perpetuated in the best MSS.

20. Nerva died in the first year of his reign, and Trajan,[139] the eleventh in line from Augustus, reigned in his stead. Nerva in his lifetime had adopted him as his son and as heir to the throne. Trajan took the helm of state at Cologne, a city of Gaul. Crossing the Rhine he reduced Germany to its former status and subdued many tribes beyond the Danube. In the East also he conquered Babylon and the regions beyond the Euphrates. Hence comes the saying,[140] ''When Trajan fought, the Parthians were defeated.'' He was the second emperor after Nero to persecute the Christians, but he was made more lenient by the official report and advice of Pliny, the judge.[141] During his time the Golden House of Nero was struck by lightning and burned. The Jews at this time too by many uprisings threw the East into confusion. At that time Ignatius, the third since Peter, ruled the Church at Antioch, succeeding Euodius. At Rome, Euaristus had succeeded Clement, who had ruled the church for nine years. At Jerusalem, Justus ruled the church, succeeding Simeon. Polycarp governed the see of Smyrna, Papias that of Hierapolis; both were disciples of John. Papias is said to have written five books which were called *Of the Lord's Words*.[142] John, after many notable exhibitions of his miraculous powers at Ephesus, was the only one of the apostles who departed to the Lord in peace without the shedding of his blood.

At that time there arose after Simon a heretic named Menandor. Then flourished the heresy of Cherintus, who said that Christ's kingdom was to be of the earth and that the demands of the fleshly appetites must be fully satisfied by food, drink and wedlock. There were also the Hebiones, that is, ''The Poor''— so called from the poverty of their intellect — who thought Christ merely a man. The heresy of the Nicolaitans also raged at that time. They were men who without any regard for the proprieties or any respect for public opinion declared that promiscuous and illicit unions were permissible. They maintain that they have as authority for such an attitude Nicolaus, one of the seven who were appointed deacons

---

[139] Marcus Ulpius Traianus, 98-117.

[140] Which has the true ring of a copy-book maxim! It is not found in Otto's sources.

[141] *I.e.*, the younger Pliny, whose famous letter to Trajan regarding the treatment of Christians in his province of Bithynia is here referred to.

[142] Otto has omitted the word *explanatio*: ''An exposition of the Lord's words'' is the full title.

with Stephen;[143] they maintained this because he made accessible to all his own wife, whom he considered very beautiful. Clement of Alexandria, however, makes excuse for him by saying, among other things, "I have ascertained that Nicolaus knew no woman at all save her whom he had received in marriage, and that his children continued in spotless virginity and in the holiness of unviolated bodies even to extreme old age. Since this is the case, it is evident that the fact that he led forth his wife into the midst of the apostles, because of a suspicion of excess of passion, resulted from contempt for vice or lust, that he might thereby show that he was himself temperate in that which he was thought to seek too eagerly. For he was constantly rebuked by the apostles for loving her too tenderly." So Clement writes.

In the twelfth year of Trajan, Primus, the fourth in line from the Apostles, governed the church at Alexandria, succeeding Cerdo. The Church at Rome was governed by Alexander after Euaristus. After Ignatius, Heros presided over the church of Antioch.

21. In the one hundred and eighteenth year [144] from the incarnation of the Lord, Trajan died, in the nineteenth year of his reign of dysentery at Seleucia,[145] a city of Isauria,[146] it is said; and his cousin's son Aelius Hadrianus [147] succeeded him on the throne, the twelfth in line from Augustus. He gave orders at the suggestion of Quadratus, a disciple of the Apostles, and of Aristides the Athenian, a man full of faith and wisdom, that Christians should not be punished without having charges presented against them. He also was given the title of Father of his Country for governing the state with great justice; his wife was called Augusta. He checked the Sarmatians in war and restrained the Jews when they rebelled and tried to return to Palestine, ordaining that they should no longer have the right to enter Jerusalem. The Christians, on the other hand, he permitted to dwell there.

In the third year of his reign Alexander, pontiff of the city of Rome, died and Sixtus succeeded him. At Alexandria Primus too died and Justus was chosen in his place. The city of Jerusalem was in large measure rebuilt by the emperor Aelius Hadrianus, who drove out the Jews. It was called after his name Aelia and was

---

143 Acts 6. 5.
144 So Frutolf and Orosius (7. 12); actually in 117.
145 Now Selefke.   146 In Asia Minor.
147 Publius Aelius Hadrianus, 117-138.

inhabited by the Gentiles. So the City of God, after having fifteen priests according to the covenant of circumcision (from the apostle James even to that time) now began to have priests according to the other covenant [148] of believers. The first of these was Mark; Sixtus had died, Telesphorus was governing the Church of Rome and Eumenes was guiding the church at Alexandria in succession to Justus.

22. Therefore since the City of God, which is the Church, was being extended far and wide throughout the whole world, its old enemy strove the more craftily to attack it; and he who before had assailed the Church by persecutions from without now craftily sought to pollute it with internal strife — that is, with the poison of heresies. Hence after Menander two most vile heretics arose, Saturninus of Antioch and Basilides of Alexandria. Basilides required his followers to keep silence for five years, after the Pythagorean custom, and asserted that in time of persecution faith in Christ ought to be denied. Irenaeus [149] records that Carpocrates the heretic also lived at that time. But the City of Christ, being founded upon a firm rock,[150] could be shaken neither by storms without nor by dissensions within; and not only had illustrious priests who instructed it by word and example, but also did not lack famous men, endowed with the greatest wisdom, to defend it, not only by their words but by their writings as well, from the attacks of the wicked. Among these Hegesippus [151] was considered the most renowned; the tradition of the apostolic preaching he wrote out in simple style in five books. He also wove together in a clear and sensible account the history of the Jewish War from the time of the Maccabees even to the destruction of Jerusalem. Justin also, a man full of our wisdom as well as of that of the philosophers, makes mention of these matters in writing to Antoninus [152] his defense of our religion. He writes also regarding Caesar Hadrian that he sent a letter of this sort in behalf of the Christians: "I have received a letter written to me by a famous man, your predecessor Serenus Granius, and it is not my pleasure to pass over

[148] Otto says *ex alio pariete*. The reference seems to be to the Gentiles and the covenant of faith.

[149] Bishop of Lyons.   [150] Matt. 7. 25; Luke 6. 48.

[151] See Introduction, note 129. The pseudo-Hegesippus version of the History of the Jewish Wars is not by the author of "the tradition of the apostolic preaching . . . in five books" (quoted from Eusebius-Rufinus 4. 8).

[152] Antoninus Pius, 138-161.

his report in silence lest the innocent too be troubled and an occasion for robbery be afforded slanderers. Therefore if the provincials are in a position to support this petition of theirs against the Christians, so clearly as to accuse them of aught before a court of law, I do not forbid them to take that procedure. But I do not allow them to employ mere entreaties and mere outcry in this matter. For it is much more just, if anyone shall wish to bring accusation, that you should have knowledge of the charges. Accordingly, if anyone makes accusation and proves that the aforesaid men are doing anything contrary to law, you will set penalties also in proportion to the offenses. And, by Hercules, you will make it your especial care that, if anyone shall, merely to set scandal afloat, summon anyone of these men to trial, you shall punish him with severe penalties for his wickedness."

23. In the one hundred and thirty-ninth year from the incarnation of our Lord, Hadrian died in the twenty-first year of his principate. Antoninus surnamed Pius, the thirteenth in line from Augustus, succeeded him on the throne. He governed the state so peacefully that he was in consequence called Father of his Country. In his times Hermes wrote *The Shepherd's Book*. In the first year of the reign of Antoninus, Telesphorus died after holding his priesthood for eleven years; Hyginus was chosen in his stead. During his time Valentinus and Cerdon, whom Marcion afterwards followed, were leaders of heresies. Cerdon's doctrine was that He who in the law and the prophets is called God was not himself the Father of our Lord Jesus Christ, because God indeed is known but Jesus unknown, God is just, but Jesus only good.

At that time the philosopher Justin, of whom I made mention above, a man born of a noble family of Neapolis in Palestine,[153] wrote among other very famous works an Apology concerning our faith; he addressed it to the emperor and made him well disposed to the Christians. Consequently the emperor promulgated the following decree regarding those who were suffering wrongs in Asia: "The Emperor Caesar Augustus Marcus Aurelius Antoninus, Armenicus, Pontifex Maximus, holding the Tribunician Power for the fifteenth time, Consul the third time, to all the peoples of Asia, Greeting. I doubt not that even the gods are concerned that no guilty person shall lie hid. For it is much more fitting that they themselves should punish those who are unwilling to sacrifice to

153 Sichem, now Nabulus.

them than that you should do so.'' [154] A little farther on he said: ''You disregard all the other gods but banish the worship of the immortal God whom the Christians worship. But I, following my father's policy, decree with like moderation that, if anyone persists in troubling men of this sort without any accusation at all, he who shall be reported on this account shall be absolved, even if it be proved that he is what he is accused of being, a Christian. Let him, however, who brings the accusation be subject to the very penalty to which he exposed the Christian.''

Pius succeeded Hyginus. After Eumenides,[155] Marcus had the see at Alexandria. Pius left his see to Anicetus; Marcus put Celadion in his own place. Hegesippus, whom I mentioned above, relates that in the days of Anicetus he came to Rome and was there until the time of Eleutherius.[156]

24. In the twenty-second year of his reign Antoninus brought the last day of his life to a close at the twelfth milestone from the City. After him Marcus Antoninus Verus,[157] the fourteenth in line from Augustus, took the helm of state with his brother Aurelius Commodus [158] as associate in the one hundred and sixty-second year from the incarnation of the Lord. They overwhelmed in hard-fought conflict Vologesus, king of the Parthians, because he was devastating Armenia, Cappadocia and Syria.

In the days of these emperors, when many citizens of Christ were battling bravely for their faith everywhere in the world, Polycarp, bishop of Smyrna and a disciple of the Apostles, was crowned by a most glorious martyrdom for the Lord. It is said of him that he imitated his teacher John who, on entering the baths at Ephesus to bathe, had caught sight of Cherintus there and dashed out exclaiming: ''Let us flee, lest the very baths fall upon us wherein Cherintus, the enemy of truth, is bathing.'' So likewise Polycarp, on meeting Marcion and being asked by him if he recognized him, replied, ''I recognize, I recognize the firstborn of Satan.'' When many were crowned with martyrdom together with Polycarp, a certain Metrodorus, a presbyter of the heresy of Marcion, was given to the flames.

[154] Quoted from Eusebius-Rufinus, 4. 13.

[155] In 21 above we read of Eumenes (= *Neumene* of the text) as bishop of Alexandria.

[156] The year of accession of Anicetus was 157; of Eleutherius 177.

[157] Or Marcus Aurelius Antoninus, 161-180.

[158] *I.e.*, Lucius Verus, with whom he reigned until 169.

During these days Soter succeeded Anicetus at Rome, and at Alexandria Agrippinus had been put into Celadion's place. At Antioch Cornelius had been chosen in the stead of Heron and had died, and Theophilus, the sixth in line from the Apostles, held the see. He molded the City of God not only by his deeds but also by his writings, and left useful memorials in the form of books. During this same time Dionysius, bishop of Corinth, Melito, bishop of Sardis, and Apollinaris, bishop of Hierapolis were distinguished princes of the City of God. Of these Dionysius, who left many writings useful to the Church, relates of Dionysius the Areopagite [159] that he was ordained by Paul as bishop of the Athenians. The other two, among other notable books, wrote an Apology for our faith addressed to the emperor. In the seventeenth year of Antoninus, who was the third after Nero to start a persecution of the Christians, Soter died and Eleutherius succeeded him.

At that time a very serious persecution was oppressing the City of Christ in Gaul. This affliction raged especially at the most famous cities of Gaul, Lyons and Vienne. But while many were crowned with martyrdom during this time of trial, Photinus too, the bishop of Lyons, burdened with the feebleness of years and with sickness [160] was made perfect by the most glorious suffering for the Lord. He was succeeded by Irenaeus the pupil of Polycarp. (I made mention of them both above.) Irenaeus was a man very useful to the City of God, not only by his preaching but also by the publication of writings. There are extant from these times letters sent by martyrs in Gaul to the Christians in Asia which you will be able to find in the History by Eusebius,[161] the History which they call Ecclesiastical. At that time there were terrible plagues in many provinces of the Romans.

During these days also the emperor was making preparations to join battle with the Germans, a valiant nation. When his army had been utterly exhausted by thirst and filled with terror not only by the numbers of the foe but even more by their bravery, in answer to the prayers of the Christians who were in the armed forces rain suddenly poured down in abundance to relieve the Romans; and the barbarians, who were already drawing dangerously near, were frightened off by incessant flashes of lightning. Thus the

---

[159] See Acts 17. 34.
[160] The text has *moribus* — an evident misprint for *morbibus*.
[161] See Eusebius-Rufinus 5. 1.

enemy were put to flight by the prayers of the saints and the Romans won the victory not by their own strength but by the strength of God. Letters of the emperor are said to have been sent to many persons acknowledging that the victory had been bestowed upon him through the prayers of the Christians.[162]

25. In the one hundred and eighty-first year from the incarnation of the Lord, Antoninus died in Pannonia [163] in the nineteenth year of his reign. His son Marcus [164] Antoninus Commodus, the fifteenth in line from Augustus, succeeded him. He was given over to luxury and wantonness and put many of the senators to death. This Commodus — "The Pleasant" — was in all respects unpleasant [165] to the state, save that he waged successful war against the Germans.

During the same time countless heresies bloomed. One, the heresy of the Encratites which possessed a certain author, Tatian, was especially pernicious. They taught that men should abstain from animals, thereby showing themselves ungrateful to God who created these for man's use. They also opposed marriage, thus accusing Him who from the beginning made them male and female for the renewal of the human race. Clement,[166] of whom I made mention above, in writing against them says, among other things, "Do they condemn the Apostles also? For Peter and Philip had wives and also gave their maiden [167] daughters in marriage. Paul the Apostle, too, is not averse to making mention of his spouse or to sending his greetings to her in a certain letter of his. He says that the reason for not taking her about with him is that he may be freer for the preaching of the Gospel."

At that time the Capitol at Rome was struck by lightning, and a library collected with great care on the part of older generations was destroyed by fire. Another fire also that started at Rome con-

---

[162] Orosius 7. 15. 11: *exstare etiam nunc apud plerosque dicuntur litterae imperatoris*; Eusebius-Rufinus 5. 5. 5: *Tertullianus . . . imperatoris epistulas etiam nunc haberi dicit.*

[163] At Vienna.

[164] L. Aurelius Commodus, 180-192. Orosius and Frutolf have the correct *praenomen*, Lucius.

[165] *incommodus*; the pun on the Emperor's name is difficult to reproduce in English.

[166] Of Alexandria.

[167] Otto has *virgines* corresponding to *viris* in Eusebius-Rufinus, but MS Clm. 6375, once at Freising, has *virgines*.

sumed the Temple of Vesta and the Palace and many sections of the City. During these days Eleutherius died and left his seat to Victor.

26. Commodus, after perpetrating many disgraceful deeds, is said to have been strangled in the thirteenth year of his reign, in the house of Vestilianus. After him an old man, Helvius,[168] reigned, the sixteenth in line from Augustus, called Pertinax because when he was chosen to the throne he pertinaciously resisted. In the fifth month [169] after he had begun to reign Julian,[170] a man learned in the law, killed him in the palace. While [Julian] tried to seize the throne he was deprived of his life by Severus near the Mulvian bridge,[171] in the seventh month from the time at which he had usurped the imperial power.

27. In the one hundred and ninety-fifth year from the incarnation of the Lord, Severus, an African by nationality, called Pertinax because he had avenged that emperor, gained control of the world. He was seventeenth from Augustus. A naturally brutal man, he set in motion a persecution of the Christians, the fourth after Nero's; he also overwhelmed in war the Jews and the Samaritans, the Parthians, the Arabs and the people of Adiabene,[172] and killed Pescennius [173] who was starting from Egypt and Syria to set up a tyranny.

In his time, when persecution was raging everywhere in the world against the citizens of Christ, at Alexandria Leonidas the father of Origen received the palm of martyrdom even as did many others. Origen,[174] though still a boy, yet strove earnestly for martyrdom. At this time there were not only martyrs to inspire by their example the citizens of Christ to endurance, but there were also teachers and most eloquent authors to guide them to wisdom by their teaching and their writing.[175] Of these Demetrius was selected to succeed Julian at Alexandria and Serapion was ordained bishop at Antioch, the eighth in line from the Apostles. Theophilus governed the church at Caesarea in Palestine and Narcissus that at

---

[168] He reigned for three months in 193.

[169] So, among other MSS of Orosius, Clm. 6380, once at Freising.

[170] Didius Julianus, 193.   [171] Now Ponte Molle.

[172] In Assyria.   [173] = *Fescenninum* of the text. He was called Niger.

[174] He published in 246 or 248 his eight books *Against Celsus* (the Greek scholar who had attacked Christianity in a book called *A True Account*).

[175] After enumerating the bishops that follow, Eusebius-Rufinus 5. 22 states that mention has been made only of those *quorum fidem et scientiam ex proprii operis indiciis possumus habere compertam.*

Jerusalem. There were many notable priests in other places also. Thus Victor still ruled the see of the Church at Rome.

While these men presided over the Church there arose in the provinces of Asia a question concerning the day of Easter. Some claimed that, on whatever day of the week the fourteenth of the month [176] had come, the fast ought to be celebrated on that day, although this custom was not observed anywhere in the Church. For this reason assemblies of bishops and councils were called not only throughout the separate provinces but also in the city of Rome (Victor was in charge of that city), and it was established by a general decree that it should not be permissible to celebrate the mystery of Easter at any time other than the Lord's Day. The bishops of the region of Asia, however, sought to confirm the custom handed down by the men of old. Among them Policrates,[177] writing — because he was thought to have especially weighty authority — to Victor, the bishop of the city of Rome, says among other things, "Accordingly we observe the day of Easter inviolate, neither adding anything nor taking anything away. For certain great lights of the Church have fallen asleep in Asia — great and chosen men. Among them are Philip the Evangelist and his two daughters; yes, and John also, who lay on the breast of the Lord; Polycarp too, and other saints who await the coming of the Lord from the heavens that they may arise from the dead. Now all these observed the day of Easter on the fourteenth day of the month, according to the Gospel. I also, the least of you all, Policrates, according to the tradition of my fathers, seven of whom in succession were bishops, have observed this day that it might coincide with that on which the Jewish people banish leaven. Hence, most beloved brethren, I, who am carrying sixty-five years in the name of the Lord, who have acquaintance too with many bishops throughout the world and am a devout student of the Holy Scriptures, shall not be disturbed by the things which are being pressed to cause terror, because my ancestors said,[178] 'We ought to obey God rather than men,' steadfast because we have not grown gray in idleness but have ever been busied with the teachings of Christ." But Victor, in consequence of these representations, only became still more firmly fixed in his resolve; and so he strove to cut off

176 The text reads: XIIIIa *luna*; see note 74, Bk. III.
177 Bishop of Ephesus.
178 So Peter and the apostles, as reported in Acts 5. 29.

from communion the churches of all Asia, together with the neighboring provinces. This did not please all the bishops. Indeed, on the contrary they wrote to him bidding him rather to employ peaceable measures and strive for harmony. The letters are extant wherein they sharply rebuke Victor on the ground that he was taking counsel injurious to the best interests of the Church.

At that time Judas discoursed learnedly of the weeks of Daniel.[179] Origen too was then being educated in the house of Clement, the scholarly presbyter of Alexandria, who himself composed valuable books.[180] After Origen grew to young manhood he not only received from Bishop Demetrius [181] a commission to teach at Alexandria, but began to preach the word of God everywhere. Since he was preaching to women and to men alike, fearing the temptations of a hazardous period of life and having zeal for God, but not according to knowledge, he laid hands on himself and made himself a eunuch in the conviction that he must literally fulfil the gospel statement that there are eunuchs who have made themselves eunuchs for the sake of the kingdom of God.[182] This is the Origen who lived from the days of Severus even to the time of the second Gallus,[183] and wrote many useful commentaries on the Holy Scriptures.[184] But since he placed too much confidence in human strength and rashly relied on earthly wisdom, he brought utter confusion upon his work and his religion by intermingling, as some claim, good teaching with error. Hence you have this judgment concerning him: "When he did well, none did better; when he did ill, none did worse." [185]

After Julian and Pescennius had been killed, Severus equipped an army against Albinus,[186] Julian's colleague, who was plotting war in

---

[179] See Dan. 9. 24.

[180] *Cf.* especially Eusebius-Rufinus 6. 13.   [181] Of Alexandria.

[182] Matt. 19. 12.

[183] The text here reads *usque ad Galli secundi tempora.* Just what Otto means by "the second Gallus" is not apparent. He may possibly have confused this Gallus (who ruled 251-253) with Gallus (Secundus), the nephew of Constantine, who was associated with Constantius in the government from 351 to 354 and who would be much better known to Christian writers.

[184] Eusebius-Rufinus 6 discourses at great length on the books composed by Origen; the passage is abridged by Jerome, *De viris illustribus* 54.

[185] *Cf.* for example Sulpicius Severus, *Dialogues* 1. 6, *Vitae Patrum,* 4. 2, Migne, *Patrologia Latina* 73, *col.* 817; Pseudo-Hier., *De lumin. eccl.* 4 (of Origen): *Melior omnibus in bonis, peior in malis.*

[186] Clodius Albinus, Caesar in Gaul.

Gaul. This war was brought to a conclusion by the shedding of much blood on both sides and Albinus was finally slain at Lyons. After this Severus declared war on the Britons. After he had with great difficulty subdued them he girdled part of the island by a wall.[187]

28. Antoninus Severus brought his days to a close at the town of York [188] in the fifteenth year [189] of his reign. Aurelius Antoninus Bassianus, who is called also Caracalla, the eighteenth in line from Augustus, succeeded him in the two hundred and thirteenth year [190] from the incarnation of the Lord. Upon the death of Victor, Zephyrinus succeeded. Now Caracalla was more cruel than his father and utterly without restraint in his lusts, for he even took his stepmother to wife. While he was undertaking a war against the Parthians he was killed by the enemy between Edissa [191] and Carrhae. Upon his death Macer [192] Opilius, or Macrinus, the praetorian prefect, usurped the throne [193] becoming thus the nineteenth in line from Augustus. In the first year of his reign he lost his life in an uprising of the soldiers.

29. In the two hundred and twenty-first year from the incarnation of the Lord, Marcus Aurelius, priest of the temple of Elagabalus,[194] obtained the imperial power, the twentieth in line from Augustus. He is said to have lived a most immoral life. In his time, upon the death of Zephyrinus, Calixtus undertook the government of the Church of Rome. Aurelius was killed, with his mother, during an uprising of the soldiers in the fourth year of his reign.

30. In the two hundred and twenty-fifth year from the incarnation of the Lord, Aurelius Alexander,[195] the twenty-first in line from Augustus, was chosen emperor by universal consent. He was

187 He restored the Roman wall which had been partly destroyed.

188 Then called *Eboracum*, in Britain.

189 We read 18 in Frutolf and Jerome, with whom Orosius and Jordanes agree. Regino and Bede attribute 17 years to Severus. He reigned 193-211.

190 Hofmeister expresses uncertainty as to whether he is correct in joining this date to the preceding account, remarking however that if it refers to the following statement it arose from Frutolf's 203 through some one's mistake in writing or reading; in any case, the death of Pope Victor is incorrectly inserted at this point.

191 Or Edessa: Urfa, in Mesopotamia.

192 So the two MSS of Orosius: *Monac. Lat.* 6380 (once at Freising) and Bern. 160.   193 217.

194 He reigned from 218-222.

195 Or Alexander Severus, 222-235.

the son of Mammaea,[196] a Christian woman. He governed the state justly; he also conquered Xerxes,[197] the king of the Persians, in a very great war. Moreover on the advice of Ulpian [198] he showed great moderation and self-restraint towards the state. Yet Gordian and Epimachus suffered under him; and Palmatius, the consul, with his wife and sons and forty-two others of both sexes were beheaded. Furthermore Simplicius, a senator whom Pope Calixtus had baptized, suffered with many others. In his time Urban succeeded Calixtus at Rome. As Urban lived but a short time, Pontianus undertook the guidance of the Church of Rome. Alexander was killed at Mainz during an uprising of the soldiers in the thirteenth year of his reign.

31. In the two hundred and thirty-eighth year from the incarnation of the Lord, Julius Maximus, or Maximinus [199] (a Thracian by race, the twenty-second in line from Augustus) was made king by the army, without the senate's consent, because he had waged war successfully in Germany. Because he hated his predecessor Alexander, who was the son of a Christian mother, he persecuted the City of God; this was the fifth persecution since Nero's time. During these days, while the tribulation of persecution was at its height, Origen wrote a much needed and excellent book about martyrdom. But in the third year of his reign Maximus was killed at Aquileia by Pupienus.[200] Pupienus however and his brother Balbinus [201] lost their lives in the palace while they were striving to usurp the throne.

32. In the two hundred and forty-first year from the incarnation of the Lord, Gordian,[202] the twenty-third in line from Augustus, was made emperor in succession to Maximus. Upon the death of Pontianus, Anteros succeeded him. Upon his death Fabianus, so tradition says, was adjudged worthy of the bishopric because of a dove which glided down from the heavens and hovered over his

---

[196] Or Mammea.

[197] Artaxerxes I or Ardeshîr, 226-240, first ruler of the new Persian empire of the Sassanidae.

[198] The great jurist, Domitius Ulpianus, one of the emperor's advisers.

[199] The emperor Maximin (235-238), whom Jordanes (*Getica* 15. 83-88) extols as the Goth who became ruler of the Roman Empire.

[200] After Gordian I, Gordian II, Pupienus Maximus and Caelius Balbinus had in turn held the imperial title for a brief period.

[201] Otto is in error regarding the relationship.

[202] The third Gordian, 238-244.

head. Others state that it was Zephyrinus who had had this experience. Then also Bishop Zebennus died at Antioch and Babylas assumed the primacy of the Church there. At Alexandria Heracles succeeded Demetrius.[203] At that time there were many who gave lustre to the City of God by their writings. Of these Africanus, a man of note among ecclesiastical writers, left many books as memorials of himself. Gordian, when yet a mere youth, declared war on the Parthians. When he had overwhelmed them by his successes he was killed in the sixth year of his reign by the treachery of his own men, near the Euphrates.

33. In the two hundred and forty-seventh year from the incarnation of the Lord, Marcus Julius Philippus,[204] the twenty-fourth in line from Augustus, obtained the throne in conjunction with his son Philip. This is the first of the emperors who was a Christian. In the third year of his reign the completion of the one thousandth year[205] from the founding of the City was celebrated by the emperor by magnificent games amid universal rejoicing. There is a story that, when he desired to be present at the sacraments of the Church at an Easter vigil, he was not admitted by the bishop of the City until he should take his position with the penitents and make atonement for the sins that current reports ascribed to him. They say that he submitted to this with great humility.

34. In the sixth year of his reign he was killed, with his son, in an uprising of the soldiers, through the treachery of Decius;[206] and Decius, the twenty-fifth in line from Augustus, reigned in his stead in the two hundred and fifty-third year from the incarnation of the Lord. Because he hated Philip he instituted a most cruel persecution of the City of God, the seventh persecution since Nero. In the course of this persecution Fabianus, bishop of Rome, was crowned with martyrdom and Cornelius assumed the bishop's seat there. At Jerusalem Alexander, a great prince of the City of God, was crowned with martyrdom. At Alexandria Dionysius had succeeded Heracles in the bishopric shortly before this time.

35. In the third year of his reign Decius and his son were killed by barbarians. Gallus, with his son Volusianus,[207] succeeded him on the throne, the twenty-sixth in line from Augustus. In his time

---

[203] This was while Alexander still ruled; see Eusebius-Rufinus 6. 26 (19); cf. Frutolf on the year 234.

[204] Philippus Arabs, 244-249.   [205] In the year 248 A.D.

[206] 249-251.   [207] 251-253.

Origen died in the seventieth year of his age. Then also a trouble-
some question arose between Cyprian, bishop of Carthage, and
Cornelius the pope at Rome — both men of notable sanctity and
wisdom. Cyprian, supported by the African bishops, asserted that
heretics who return to communion with the Church ought to be
rebaptized; but Cornelius, upheld by the priests that had been
ordained throughout Italy, insisted that they were to be cleansed
by the laying on of hands only, and that the sacrament of baptism
must by no means be repeated. Cyprian wrote books of notable wisdom and abounding eloquence concerning our faith.

When Cornelius was crowned with martyrdom at Rome, Lucius
received his see. He held it for only eight months and was succeeded by Stephen. In his time Dionysius, the most renowned of the
bishops of Alexandria, ruled the church there. Among other evidences of his unusual powers he wrote to Stephen, the pontiff at
Rome, with regard to suppression of the arrogance of Novatus and
the restoration of peace to the Church of God, saying among other
things, "Know, my Brother, that all the Churches in the East,
which before were in confusion, have now become harmonious again,
and all, with one mind, are rejoicing and exulting over the peace
which, beyond their hopes, has been restored to the Church."

(36.)[208] In these days, or in the time of his predecessor Decius,
when everywhere in the world the citizens of Christ were being
sought out to be subjected to exquisite methods of torture, Saint
Lawrence was, according to some authorities, crowned with martyrdom at Rome on a gridiron.[209] We find that under Gallienus and
Valerianus,[210] the rulers who succeeded Gallus, Sixtus (whose deacon
Lawrence was) was made perfect by martyrdom. It may, however,
well be that all these rulers were called Decii,[211] or that the order
of the pontiffs has been confused through the carelessness of

---

[208] From this point until the end of Book III there are variant chapter
numbers, this paragraph being chapter (36) in Hofmeister. The latter's
numbering is followed in the translation, with the variant numbers in
parentheses in the margin.

[209] This account agrees more closely with Bede and Usuardus than with
Adonis martyrologium Aug. 10; they all place the martyrdom of Lawrence
and of Sixtus under Decius (Aug. 6).

[210] 253-260.   [211] Otto's critical tendency may here be noted.

writers.[212] At this time a plague spread over all the provinces of the Romans.

(37.) 36. Gallus and Volusianus were killed in the second year of their reign, while they were making preparations for a civil war against Aemilianus. Aemilianus lost his life in the third month from the time at which he had usurped the imperial power. Upon the death of Stephen, Sixtus became Pope at Rome.

(38.) 37. In the two hundred and fifty-ninth year from the incarnation of the Lord,[213] and in the twenty-seventh place after Augustus, Valerianus was chosen Caesar in Rhaetia, Gallienus in Rome, by the senate. They set in motion against the City of God the eighth persecution since the time of Nero. During these days two brilliant luminaries of the City of God were made perfect by a glorious martyrdom, Sixtus at Rome, Cyprian at Carthage. Dionysius succeeded Sixtus. Valerianus was taken captive by Sapor,[214] king of the Persians. Bereft of his sight, he grew to old age in disgraceful slavery to the Persians. For he received as his lot this service at the king's court, that whenever the king sought to mount his horse he stooped and assisted him, not with his hand but with his back. Gallicnus, moved by so distressing a warning in the case of his associate, became more lenient toward the Christians and by published decrees ordained that each man should, in whatever way he thought best, worship the divine.

(39.) In those days the Germans crossed the Alps and, after devastating Rhaetia and [northern] Italy, came as far as Ravenna. The Alemanni, marching through the Gauls, laid Italy waste.[215] The Goths roved through Greece, Macedonia, Pontus and Asia. The Quadi and the Sarmatians took arms and entered the Pannonias. Spain was being blotted out by a flood of the more distant Germans. The Parthians gained possession of Mesopotamia and Syria. Since, over and above these disasters, the whole world was suffering from a grievous pestilence and a terrible misfortune, the empire of the Romans was not only assailed by foes from without but also torn by civil discord within. For Ingenuus[216] was killed

---

212 Frutolf in discussing this matter (p. 100. 15 and 108. 35) conjectures that the order of the popes has been confused *vitio scriptorum pro similitudine nominum.*

213 Frutolf and Orosius 7. 22. It was in 253.   214 Sapor I, 240-271.

215 They were checked at Mediolanum, now Milan.

216 *Genuus* in the text. These were the days of the so-called "Thirty Tyrants."

at Zmirna [217] while he was attempting to seize the throne; and Postumus,[218] who had usurped imperial power in the Gauls — though to the great advantage of the state — lost his life in an uprising of the soldiers in the tenth year. Aemilianus was slain [219] at Mainz for a like reason. Marius, who had assumed royal power in the Gauls in succession to Postumus, was put to death. When Victorinus was making ready to succeed him he in turn was bereft of life. While all this was happening in the Gauls, Odenatus [220] collected a band of country folk in the East, checked the Persians, recovered Mesopotamia and came with his rustics as far as Ctesiphon, victor over Syria. Gallienus who, forsaking the state, tarried at Milan and gave himself over to voluptuousness, was put to death. Felix succeeded Dionysius. At Antioch, Timeus followed Domnus and Cyrillus followed Timeus. Dorotheus succeeded Cyrillus who in turn was followed by Anatholius.

At that time a certain Manes,[221] a Persian by race, a barbarian in habits and in life, taught a monstrous heresy. For at one time he wished it to be believed that he himself was Christ, and at another he declared that he was the Paraclete. Carried away by mad frenzy he chose twelve disciples, in imitation of Christ, and sent them to preach impious doctrines borrowed from former heretics. His followers are called Manichaeans even today.[222]

(40.) 38. In the two hundred and seventy-fourth year from the incarnation of the Lord, Claudius [223] was chosen emperor with the consent of the senate, the twenty-eighth in line from Augustus. He overwhelmed in war the Goths, who for fifteen years had roved through Illyricum and Macedonia and had ravaged them with incredible slaughter. For this reason a golden shield in the senate house and a golden equestrian statue were awarded him by the senate. But in the second year of his reign he fell sick and died at

[217] Orosius has *Myrsam*; Mursa on the river Dravus, in Pannonia.

[218] The text gives *Postumius*.   [219] See 36 (37) above.

[220] Or Odenathus of Palmyra; his wife Zenobia ruled after his death in 267.

[221] Or Mani (215-277). He is said to have been of Iranian descent, but born in Babylonia. He first appeared in public as the herald of a new religion in 242 A.D., and taught an extreme form of dualism, Light and Darkness being the opposing principles.

[222] For almost a thousand years Manichaeism maintained itself as a powerful rival of Christianity. It gained a foothold in the West as far as Spain, and the Catharists or Albigenses of France in the 12th and 13th centuries held many of the same doctrines.

[223] This is Claudius II, 268-270.

Sirmium.[224] His brother Quintilius was put into his place by the army, but died on the seventeenth day of his reign.

(41.) 39. In the two hundred and seventy-sixth year from the incarnation of the Lord, Aurelian,[225] the twenty-ninth in line from Augustus, became emperor. Since he was a warlike man he moved his troops to the Danube and there overwhelmed the Goths in many desperate battles, and restored the frontiers of the Roman empire.[226] Departing thence he journeyed to the East and reduced to subjection Zenobia[227] who, after the murder of her husband Odenatus, had been usurping the throne of Syria. In Gaul too he conquered, without great difficulty, Tetricus,[228] who was unable to check a mutiny of his own army. These things done he entered the City in triumph, victor over the East as well as over the North. Subsequently he graced Rome with a stronger circuit of walls.[229] In Gaul he founded a very beautiful city on the river Loire which he called Aurelianis[230] after his own name. He was the eighth emperor after Nero to afflict the City of God, though at the outset he had been distinctly lenient towards it. A flash of lightning crashed down before his eyes to the very great terror of all, and not long after he was killed in the sixth year of his reign.

(42.) 40. In the two hundred and eighty-first year[231] from the incarnation of the Lord, Tacitus, the thirtieth in line from Augustus, was made emperor; he was killed in Pontus in the sixth month thereafter. After him Florian,[232] while seizing control of part of the empire, lost his life at Tarsus, in the third month from the time at which his usurpation began.

(43.) 41. In the two hundred and eighty-first year from the in-

---

[224] Near Mitrovitza, on the river Save. [225] He reigned from 270-275.

[226] As a matter of fact he sacrificed Dacia, and the Danube became the boundary of the Empire.

[227] Defeated at Antiochia and at Edessa.

[228] Defeated at Chalons in 274.

[229] The famous rampart still called by his name.

[230] Now Orléans; see Orosius, l.c.; Eusebius-Rufinus 7. 30, 18 et seq. (26). This account of the founding of Orléans is accepted by scholars today. In the 14th C. the University of Orléans (universitas Aurelianensis) boasted that it had been founded tempore gloriosissimi Aurelii imperatoris; cf. dipl. Hugonis episc. Aurelianensis, a. 1367, Oct. 4, in M. Fournier, Les statuts et priviléges des universités françaises, 1. 125.

[231] Frutolf and Orosius 7. 24. Tacitus reigned in 275. The dates for the succeeding reigns are taken from the same sources.

[232] Or Florianus.

carnation of the Lord, Probus,[233] the thirty-first in line from Augustus, secured the throne and by many gallant wars conquered the barbarians, who had seized the Gauls. Then in civil wars he put down Saturninus in the East and Proculus and Bonosus at Cologne. But he was slain by his soldiers in an iron tower at Sirmium in the seventh year of his reign.

(44.) 42. In the two hundred and eighty-eighth year from the incarnation of the Lord, Carus of Narbonne,[234] the thirty-second in line from Augustus, obtained imperial power. Having associated his two sons, Carinus and Numerian, with him in imperial authority he waged war with the Parthians, and in their country besieged two very famous cities, Chote [235] and Ctesiphon.[236] But he was struck by lightning near the Tigris and died in the second year of his reign. His son Numerian also was deprived of his life by Aper, his father-in-law.

(45.) 43. In the two hundred and nintieth year from the incarnation of the Lord, Diocletian,[237] the thirty-third in line from Augustus, was chosen emperor by the army. When he first assumed office he slew Aper, the murderer of Numerian, with his own hand. In a hazardous and difficult war he conquered Carinus, whom his father had sent to Dalmatia as Caesar, and who was living a sinful life. Presently, when Amandus and Aelian with a host of rustics were setting on foot seditious uprisings in the Gauls, he appointed Maximian Herculius as Caesar and sent him into the Gauls. By the valor and discipline of his soldiers he easily overcame the band of untrained country folk. A certain Carausius — a man ignoble in birth but not ignoble in dexterity of hand and brain — while he was already an object of suspicion to Maximian, invaded Britain and assumed the purple. At that time Achilleus turned traitor in Egypt, the Quingentiani attacked Africa, and Narses, king of the Persians, devastated the East. Accordingly Diocletian, moved by these disasters, promoted Maximian Herculius from the rank of Caesar to that of Augustus and made Constantius and Galerius Maximianus Caesars. This is the Constantius who had six sons by Theodora the step-daughter of Maximian Herculeus, and a son, Constantine, by Helena a concubine. They say that this Helena was a native of a canton of the Treveri. Carausius was treacherous-

---

[233] He reigned from 276-282.   [234] He reigned from 282-283.
[235] In Mesopotamia.   [236] On the Tigris; *Ictesifontem* in the text.
[237] He reigned from 284-305.

ly put to death by his associate Allectus in the seventh year from the time he had usurped the purple. Allectus was killed two years later by Asclepiodotus the prefect.

Then the emperors started a persecution against the Church of God — the ninth since Nero's — which, we find, was not only the last [238] but was also far more severe than all that had preceded it, because of the craftiness of the ancient foe, who now had but a short time and on this account burned with the greater frenzy. This persecution was prolonged for ten years and was prosecuted ceaselessly by proscriptions of the faithful, the slaughter of martyrs and the burning of churches. Hence no one can count how many thousands of the saints the City of God in these days did not indeed (as the emperors fancied) lose, but in all truth gathered into her bosom to live forever. For the City of Christ is but refined by buffetings and oppressions of this sort and is tried like gold in a furnace, to the end that, since it is built of living stones, it may receive none save those that have been tested and polished.

During these days, while Augustus was preparing war against the aforesaid tyrants, Amandus and Aelian, Mauricius came with a Christian legion to Rome, to Marcellinus — the pope who had succeeded Caius — and after receiving a benediction from him set out with the emperor against the foes of the empire. When they had crossed the Alps and had encamped at Octodurum [239] it became known that they were Christians, and Mauricius, as their chief and the leader of the rest, was summoned to worship idols. But this most valiant wrestler of Christ and bearer of His standard, who had duly obeyed an impious and sacrilegious king in warring against the foes of that monarch's realm, refused to render obedience when he gave commands in opposition to the King of Heaven. Herein we are reminded that we ought indeed be subject to kings in lawful matters, but that, if they order anything contrary to God and to our souls' salvation, we should learn to say with Peter, "We must obey God rather than men." [240] Mauricius, with his

---

[238] *Cf.* Orosius 7. 25. 13 and 27. 13. But Otto speaks differently below, III. 45 (end). The persecutions as listed by Otto are as follows:

1. Nero	(III. 15)	6. Maximin	(III. 31)
2. Domitian	(III. 19)	7. Decius	(III. 34)
3. Trajan	(III. 20)	8. Valerian and Gallienus	(III. 37)
4. M. Aurelius	(III. 24)	9. Aurelian	(III. 39)
5. Septimius Severus	(III. 27)	10. Diocletian and Maximian	(III. 43)

[239] Now Martigny.   [240] Acts 5. 29.

companions — who are said to have numbered six thousand six hundred and sixty-six — was crowned with martyrdom at Agaunum, a town situated on the Rhone. A considerable number of that company, however, slipped out of the town. The Romans, pursuing them, killed nine at Bonn, a town of Gaul, called also Verona.[241] Gereon with three hundred and thirty of his followers they put to death in a suburb of the city of Cologne. Victor also with three hundred and sixty they slew in the city of Troy, which is now called Xanten. Nor should the reader be shocked if he hears that the saints sought to escape martyrdom, since Peter was told, "Another shall gird thee, and carry thee whither thou wouldest not."[242] For, because the saints are not able to hate their own flesh, they love life but they set above it the heavenly life and the love of God. I think it a not unreasonable belief to say that the Lord wished his martyrs to flee, to the end that so great a treasure should not be left to one place or to one city, but that they should rather be divided among different places and provinces.

At the same time the Blessed Vitus, a mere boy in years — for he is said to have been only seven years old — but a man in bearing, was first scourged by his father Hyla, who is said to have been of the order of patricians, and afterwards crowned with martyrdom by Diocletian through various kinds of torments. Afra too, with her mother Hilaria and certain girls — named Digna, Eumenia [or Eunomia], Eutropia and many others — was given over to the flames by Gaius, sitting as judge at Augsburg,[243] and received the palm of martyrdom. She was at first a sinner but was afterwards converted by Bishop Narcissus and baptized; having been slain by fire and having obtained a crown of everlasting glory she has given sinners great confidence of obtaining grace from the Lord. But let us now return to the citizens of the world.

Constantius declared war on the Alemanni. At first he was defeated by them; but afterwards he came forth victorious with incredible slaughter of the barbarians, putting seventy thousand to death. Besides, Augustus Maximian overwhelmed the Quingentiani by war in Africa. Diocletian besieged Achilleus in Alexandria.

---

[241] C. and Cuspinian omit *quae et Verona.* With regard to this name, common in the XI-XIV centuries, see K. Simrock, Bonna-Verona, in *Bonn, Beiträge zu seiner Geschichte und seinen Denkmälern, Festschrift für den Internationalen Congress für Altertumskunde und Geschichte,* Bonn, 1868.

[242] John 21. 18.　　　　[243] The text is *apud Vindelicam Augustam.*

When after eight months he took the city he destroyed it, proscribed all Egypt and put Achilleus himself to death. But while Maximian was preparing to attack Narses, the king of the Persians, he was defeated in an engagement that occurred between Callinicum [244] and Carrhae and upon his defeat fled to Diocletian. The emperor, stirred with anger thereby, let Maximian in his purple robes run ignominiously before his chariot for several miles. Maximian was inflamed with rage at this and collecting his troops from all sides fell upon the enemy, conquered Narses and put him to flight; he captured too his wives, his sisters and his children. Then he came with great booty to the emperor in Mesopotamia and was received with the highest honors. Now because Diocletian and Maximian had afflicted the Church with many persecutions, and by their cruel punishments had disturbed the status of the City of Christ, the avenging right hand of God, which had permitted his citizens to be chastised by a few, gave Diocletian and Maximian over to such madness and change that both of them (Maximian, indeed, was loathe to do so, but he was constrained by his love of his associate) resigned the imperial power and assumed the dress of private citizens — aye, even of plebeians — Diocletian at Nicomedia, Maximian at Milan in the twentieth year from Diocletian's accession.

During these days Marcellus replaced Marcellinus, and was succeeded in turn by Eusebius. After Eusebius, Melchiades undertook the government of the Church of Rome.

(46.) 44. After the abdication of the emperors, Galerius and Constantius, who had been chosen by them as Caesars, shared the imperial power. Galerius Maximianus obtained Illyricum, Asia and the East; Italy, Africa and Gaul fell to the lot of Constantius. Constantius, a most amiable man, was however content with Gaul and Spain and left the other lands to Galerius. This Constantius showed great mercy to men and the greatest reverence toward God, and held God's worshippers in honor and respect. Galerius appointed two Caesars, Maximin in the East, Severus in Italy. However, he himself kept Illyricum. Constantius, dying in Britain,[245] left Constantine [246] the son of Helena as emperor in Gaul.

(47.) 45. So then, because the persecutions being now at an end a much coveted peace — like the dawn after the darkness of night — illumined the Church of God under the emperor Constantine, let us,

---

[244] In Mesopotamia; *Gallienicum* in the text.
[245] In 306.   [246] The Great, sole ruler 323-337.

who have long since been exhausted by the many whirlwinds of disaster, bring our third book to a conclusion, that we may come to those times in which the Lord willed to exalt his abased and humiliated Church. For you will find ten persecutions from Nero to this time. Our ancestors have handed down as a tradition and have recorded in writing the statement that the earthly city, too, was afflicted by ten plagues under the emperors who set in motion the persecutions which we have mentioned. The diligent student of history will be able to find all of them. Accordingly, just as Egypt when smitten with ten plagues let the people of God go free, so the earthly city when smitten by ten plagues in the course of the ten persecutions permitted the people of God (that is, the Church) to have peace. Moreover, even as when Pharaoh was utterly destroyed, together with his army, while he was pursuing the people of God to the Red Sea (this was the eleventh persecution), so the earthly city, which was recently smitten by divine vengeance in many ways and is now, with Antichrist its head, being smitten, shall set in motion an eleventh persecution (that is, the last and most perilous of all) and therein shall Antichrist be smitten and the earthly city shall be utterly destroyed. But the City of Christ shall be magnified and exalted and shall be brought to a glorious consummation [247] to reign with Him forever.

HERE ENDS THE THIRD BOOK

[247] The thought is virtually that of Orosius, but the words with very few exceptions are Otto's.

THE PROLOGUE OF THE FOURTH BOOK [1]

I think there is now no wise man who does not consider the works of God — no wise man who, having considered them, does not stand amazed and is not led through the visible to the invisible.[2] For the Lord had wished His City, though foreordained before the foundation of the world, to lie hid until the appointed time and made ready to exalt it at the proper time. Therefore at the time of its humiliation He graciously consoled it, by foretelling through His prophet the time of exaltation: "Stretch forth thy tents," He said, "and strengthen the curtains of thy habitations. Lengthen thy cords."[3] And again: "Whereas thou hast been forsaken, I will make thee a joy of many generations."[4] When therefore the Lord willed to exalt His Church, which had been exhausted by many trials and persecutions, He chose, in preference to all others, a personage through whom He might the more readily accomplish this exaltation. Accordingly He commissioned the emperor of the Romans,[5] to whom the whole world at that time paid honor, to effect it; and gave him not only faith whereby, departing from the darkness of error, he might come to know the true light, but also love whereby he might exalt His city with many honors and enrich it with many treasures and possessions. And that you may know that all this was brought to pass not by chance, at haphazard, but through the profound and righteous judgments of God, behold a man who but yesterday was skulking in hiding and fleeing from

---

[1] The fourth book of the Chronicle, beginning with the reign of Constantine, brings the story of Rome down to the times of Romulus Augustulus and Odoacer (476 A.D.). In conclusion Otto gives a brief sketch of the origins of the Franks and their early history. The principal sources for this book are Frutolf, Orosius 7, Eusebius-Rufinus 8-10, Rufinus (the continuation of the Ecclesiastical History of Eusebius) 10-11, the Tripartite History 1, 6-11, the *Getica* of Jordanes (especially chapters 24-25, 30, 35-42). There are, as usual, frequent quotations from the Bible, and the *Romana* of Jordanes is occasionally used.

[2] Hofmeister calls this a commonplace remark and refers the reader to a list contained in Hashagen's *Otto von Freising* 34, and to Augustine 10.14; etc. See below, VIII. 33.

[3] Isa. 54. 2.   [4] Isa. 60. 15.   [5] *I.e.*, Constantine the Great.

every man (of even the lowest condition) become speedily of so great authority that he rules kings, judges kings; behold him held in so great veneration by the world that the lords of the earth come to bow before him and worship the soles of his feet as he sits upon the throne.[6]

But here a serious question arises and a great argument regarding the justification of kingship and of priesthood. For some under color of religion,[7] others out of regard for secular dignity — since by such dignity the authority of the kingship is seen to have been diminished — claim that this temporal glory and honor are not permissible to priests of Christ, to whom the glory of the heavenly kingdom is promised, and they point out many arguments in support of this contention. Two rôles, they say, have been established by God in the Church: the priestly and the kingly. Of these the priest ought to administer the sacraments of Christ and to render ecclesiastical judgments with the sword of the spirit. The other bears a material sword, for the exercise of secular judgments against the enemies of the Church, by defending the poor and the churches of God from the assaults of evil men, and by punishing the wicked. These are the two swords which we read about in the story of the passion of the Lord.[8] But Peter is found to have used only one.[9] Therefore, as spiritual gifts also pertain to the spiritual sword — that is tithes, first fruits, oblations of the faithful and other things of this sort — so all earthly dignities, dukedoms, counties and matters of that kind belong to the material sword. These things God has desired to exist in his Church in orderly fashion, not confusedly, that is, not together in one person but separately in the two I have mentioned. Accordingly, just as it is not permissible for the person who bears the material sword to deal with those things that are spiritual, so it is not fitting that the other should usurp those powers which are not properly his.[10] Men adduce many passages of Scripture to establish what I have just said. In fact they adduce the example of our Lord himself and of the saints, as for instance the well-known gospel command: "Render unto Caesar the things that are Caesar's, and unto God the things that are

[6] It is interesting to note that "the practice of kissing the Pope's foot was adopted by the Papal in imitation of the ancient imperial court" (Bryce).

[7] It appears from *Gesta Friderici* 2. 28 that Otto has here in mind Arnold of Brescia.

[8] Luke 22. 38. [9] John 18. 10.

[10] The Latin puts it in the positive form: *ea quae huius sunt.*

God's." [11] And even as the Lord declared this in His words, so He showed it forth in His deeds, on that occasion when, recognizing the principle "to whom tribute, tribute" [12] — He paid the tribute for Himself and for Peter. [13] Paul too, understanding that honor must be paid to whom honor is due, and believing that all authority is of God — Paul, I say, when brought to trial appealed not to Peter (who then presided over the Roman See) but to Nero, a most vile and impious man who by God's will had been appointed king over the whole world. [14] This much regarding the honoring of kings. But that every possession is of the grace of kings men prove from Augustine, who says: "By what right do you possess villas? divine or human? By divine: 'The earth is the Lord's and the fulness thereof.' By human, that is from kings: this is why we say 'This land is mine, this estate is mine.' Likewise if you say, 'What have I to do with a king?' 'Tell me, what have you to do with possessions?' " [15] To all this the reply is made that the Lord wished those powers which are called royal to honor His Church with earthly dignity. For the explanation that we have made above indicates that this was done by God's ordering. Finally, it is not to be believed that Christ permitted His Church, His bride, His body, to which He is believed to have given His life's breath as an earnest, to be deceived by the spirit of error; upon it, as I have said, He had bestowed the spirit of truth. Besides, men of established sanctity are found who are believed to have had kingly honors, to have won the kingdom of God in addition to those kingly honors. By these arguments, therefore, and by others which it would take too long to recount, it is shown that Constantine properly bestowed royal powers upon the Church, and that the Church legitimately accepted them. For when we inquire of kings by what sanction they have their powers, they are accustomed to reply, 'By the ordination of God and election by the people.' If, therefore, God did not act unrighteously in ordaining that the aforesaid honor should be conferred upon kings, how much more surely is He not to be called unrighteous for ordaining this also, that the honor should be transferred from that rôle to the ecclesiastical authority? Finally, if in addition to the fact that He Himself had ordained it, He wished that in this latter case, as in the former, election by the people (and furthermore, in this specific

---

[11] Luke 20. 25.   [12] Rom. 13. 7.   [13] Matt. 17. 24-27.   [14] Acts 25. 10-11.
[15] Augustine on John 6. 25 *et seq*. Otto has made some changes in abbreviating this famous passage.

instance, the nomination of a successor) should be in harmony with His own will, then we must believe that neither did He Himself arrange matters unjustly, nor did the emperor wrongfully designate a successor, nor did the Church receive these honors illegitimately.

But you say that, to the ecclesiastical rôle, powers were given which it is neither seemly nor expedient for it to have by reason of the sanctity of its office. In answer to this I confess I know no argument in which to take refuge save that we know that those holy men of apostolic faith and merit — Sylvester,[16] Gregory,[17] Ulric,[18] Boniface,[19] Lambert,[20] Gothard [21] and many others — had these prerogatives. For, to speak as I think myself, I admit that I am absolutely ignorant whether the exaltation of His Church which is so clearly visible today pleases God more than its former humiliation pleased Him. Indeed, that former state seems to have been better, this present condition more fortunate. However I agree with the holy Roman Church, which, I doubt not, was built upon a firm rock, and I believe that what she believes must be believed and that what she possesses can legitimately be possessed. For that she can be deceived by no error can be proved by this: "And the gates of hell shall not prevail against it." [22] Moreover, that her faith is to abide forever we may know from what was said to Peter: "I made supplication for thee, Peter, that thy faith fail not." [23] But that every least point of controversy may be solved by its own authority and example is again implicitly intimated by what is said to Peter: "Put out into the deep, and let down your nets for a draught."[24] Let what has been said concerning the righteousness of the priesthood and of the kingship suffice. But if anyone wishes to reason about it more subtly and profoundly, he will by no means submit to having the matter prejudged by me.

[16] Sylvester I, pope in 314, the builder of St. Peter's.

[17] Gregory I, the Great, 590, who sent Augustine to Britain. See *Cambridge Medieval History* 2. 236, 262.

[18] Bishop of Augsburg, 923-973.

[19] St. Boniface (Winfrith), first archbishop of Mainz (in 748), the Anglo-Saxon missionary to Germany.

[20] The text has *Lanpertum*; he was bishop of Liége, in Belgium, about 700.

[21] Abbot of the monastery of Nieder-Alteich on the Danube (in lower Bavaria), afterwards bishop of Hildesheim (in Hannover) 1022-1038, canonized by Pope Innocent II (1130) at the Council of Rheims.

[22] Matt. 16. 18. *Cf.* below, VI. 23 (end).

[23] Luke 22. 32.

[24] Luke 5. 4.

HERE BEGINS THE FOURTH BOOK

1. Now in the three hundred and eleventh year from the incarnation of the Lord,[25] Constantine, the thirty-fourth in line from Augustus, succeeded his father on the throne, the more pious heir of a pious father. Meanwhile the praetorian guard chose Maxentius, the son of Herculeus, as Augustus. Caesar Severus was sent against him by Augustus Galerius but was driven in flight to Ravenna and killed there. When Maximian Herculeus heard that Constantine had been proclaimed emperor in the Gauls,[26] laying aside the garb of a private citizen [27] he planned to trap Constantine through treachery. But when he had come into the Gauls for this purpose he was betrayed by his daughter, Constantine's wife, forced to flee and killed at Marseilles. When Severus had been killed Galerius made Licinius emperor. After he had cruelly carried on a persecution of the Christians for ten years,[28] Galerius was smitten with a divine punishment by the Lord and paid the penalty. For his vital organs decomposed within him and he reached so horrible a state that he belched forth worms. When he had been despaired of by physicians and realized that his was the vengeance of heaven he ceased from his persecution; but finding the violence of his malady beyond endurance he died.

When Constantine had been appointed emperor in the Gauls by his father, as I have said above,[29] Maximin and Licinius aspired to the throne. They practiced cruelty and lust without measure upon those of our faith. Besides, Maxentius oppressed the citizens of Rome with many afflictions. Finally, among other deeds of his this tale is told of him, that he ordered the wives of the senators and the chief nobles to be promiscuously carried off to satisfy his

[25] Galerius died in that year but Constantine's reign as sole ruler did not start until 323. His father, Constantius, had died in Britain in 306, and the army had thereupon hailed Constantine Augustus. When he first assumed the title there were five Augusti in the empire: Galerius, Maxentius, Maximin, Licinius and Constantine.

[26] The news that impelled Maximian to resume his former rank was that his son Maxentius had been declared emperor at Rome; see Orosius 7. 28. 5, Frutolf, p. 111. 30. Otto has apparently fallen into error by abbreviating the account in Eusebius-Rufinus 8. 13. 15 (16).

[27] Maximian had been compelled to resign his office also when Diocletian abdicated in 305.

[28] Starting with the edict of Nicomedia, Feb. 23, 303.

[29] III. 44 (end).

lust; the senators themselves, being overwhelmed with terror, submitted in silence, groaning. The senators too, or if you will those who appeared to be rather prominent in the senate house, he contrived to have proscribed, trumping up false charges against them. To these crimes he added the infamous chicanery of the art of magic, putting to death pregnant women and examining their viscera and making predictions of what was to happen through incantations composed by diabolic art. And so while the emperor Constantine, who was a religious man and by this time a supporter of the Christian faith, was preparing war against this most impious tyrant, he was troubled in many ways and frequently raised his eyes to heaven. By night, as he was buried in sleep, he saw the sign of the cross gleaming with fiery radiance in the eastern sky. When he inquired what it meant, he heard angels saying to him, "Constantine_ΘΟΥΘΩ ΝΥΚΑ" [= ἐν τούτῳ νικήσεις?], which is to say, "In this sign thou shalt conquer." In the morning when he awoke he summoned to him the soldiers who were Christians and, learning from them with regard to what he had seen that it was the sign of the Christian faith, happy now and carefree about the vision he fortified his brow with the sign of the cross and promised that he would be a Christian if success should be his portion. Now this most serene prince was sorely distressed because he could not overcome the tyrant [30] without much shedding of the blood of the citizens. Therefore the Lord, being minded to reward the devotion of the emperor as well as to come to the rescue of His afflicted Church, destroyed the tyrant in marvellous wise, without danger either to the emperor or to the Roman people. The tyrant had assembled ships in the manner of a mousetrap near the Mulvian bridge that he might take his enemy at unawares as he came up in ignorance of the trap. Augustus was in fact already approaching, already the pennons were flying at close quarters, and lo! the tyrant was himself by God's will swept by a fiendish spirit into the devices which he had prepared for his enemy — even as it is written, "He is fallen into the ditch which he made" [31] — and unaccompanied by any associate, alone, according to the desire of the emperor, without danger to either army he perished. When Constantine, having won the longed-for victory, had entered the city he was received with great rejoicing by the citizens. But when, according to custom, a

30 *I.e.*, Maxentius.
31 Ps. 7. 16.

triumph was being prepared for him, he declared that this victory must be attributed not to him but to Christ. The cross, through whose might the enemy had been conquered, he had put in the place of a triumph and caused it to be worshipped.

Upon the death of Melchiades, Sylvester had succeeded. According to traditional practice of the Romans, Constantine was baptized by him in the Church which is called St. John's.[32] The cause of his conversion is as stated above. Accordingly what we read in the Life of Saint Sylvester about his leprosy and his conversion is seen to be apocryphal.[33] However, the Tripartite History states that he was baptized in Nicomedia toward the end of his life.[34]

2. When Constantine became a Christian he restored peace to the churches. In fact, even Licinius gave his assent to this policy. Therefore both emperors by passing decrees ordained that Christ, Who had freed the State from the tyrant, must be worshipped as God; and after entering upon this policy they wrote about it to Maximinus, who held authority over the East. When he learned of it Maximinus ordained by an edict that the Christians should no longer suffer persecution for their faith. He even gave this as a reason: "the more they seem to be held in check, the more they grow." Therefore he affirmed that no one should be forced to worship the [pagan] gods unless he be drawn thereto by his own inclination. Although Maximinus was doing this out of fear of the Augusti, he pretended that he was doing it of his own authority. For though he was the most self-willed of men, he desired not only to be placed on an equality with the most moderate princes but even to be preferred to them. After the lapse of a short interval Licinius broke the treaty and prepared to take the offensive. And so after harrying many cities and provinces he finally, relying on the aid of demons and responding to their promptings, went forth to war and ventured on a battle. But when he saw his army routed in that battle he took off the imperial insignia and, mingling in the throng of camp followers, fled from the fight, disgraced as he deserved to be. Then, returning to his own country, he at first indeed put to death his priests on the ground that they had deceived him. But when he saw himself smitten by God with the most fearful maladies, and realized that a very terrible death was drawing

[32] The church of St. John Lateran is meant. *"Fabula notissima,"* says Hofmeister.
[33] Note Otto's open-mindedness. *Cf.* C. M. H. 1. 8.   [34] 3. 12.

near, moved by penitence (though too late) he confessed the God of the Christians and wrote in their behalf in this fashion:[35] "The Emperor Caesar Galerius Maximus, Germanicus, Sarmaticus, pious, blessed, invincible, august. Exercising care without ceasing for our provincials and taking thought for their best interests, we never cease to provide those things which look to the good of the state. Hence I doubt not that it is well known to all men, and a matter clearly understood, that many raids and plundering expeditions have been made by the officials, the incentive being that it had been commanded by our fathers, Diocletian and Maximian, of blessed memory, to forbid meetings of Christians." And below: "Therefore that all fear or misunderstanding may be removed for the future, we solemnly ordain by the force of this our edict that it shall be known to all to be permissible, by the bounty of this our indulgence, to those who hold in reverence the Christian doctrine and religion, to observe, each one, this religion and ritual as he will and according as it pleases his inclination. We also permit them to build as they wish houses of prayer — that is, their churches. And indeed, that this grant of ours may be regarded as in all respects more ample, we also ordain formally by this law that if any houses, fields or estates whatsoever have hitherto been taken from the property of Christians by the commands of our parents and confiscated to the uses of the imperial treasury, and moreover if any have been coveted by anyone or if they have been divided up or bestowed upon anyone as a gift, we command, I say, that all these be restored as before to the legal control of the Christians and all be given back to their proper owners."

Who would not wonder at this change wrought by the right hand of the Most High, whereby a most godless man, who had proscribed our people in tablets of brass, meant to endure as it were forever, wrote so suddenly in their behalf against his will, when touched by the hand of God. Presently Maximinus, being afflicted by the most bitter ravages of disease, which began with the loss of his eyes, put an end to his life. Licinius, who had previously afforded Con-

[35] The source for this is Eusebius-Rufinus 9.10 (9). In this rather confusing account Otto is referring to the rescripts of Licinius, published at Nicomedia in June 363, carrying out the policy upon which he and Constantine had agreed at Milan. It will be remembered that Galerius had previously issued an Edict of Toleration at Nicomedia in 311, just before the close of his life.

stantine generous assistance respecting the City of God, now driven
to madness by the instigation of demons, drove the Christians out
from the palace and strained all his energies to persecute them.
Constantine moved his fighting forces against him, defeated him —
first in Pannonia, afterwards at Cybalae — and finally, when he
was venturing frequent battles on land and on sea, compelled him
to surrender. Fearing what had been done by Maximian Herculeus
he stripped him of his rank and put him to death. His sons, Constantine and Crispus, and the sons of his sister by the aforesaid
Licinius — namely Constantius [36] and Licinius — he made Caesars.
Of these he afterwards killed Crispus and Licinius, from what
motive I know not.

3. Therefore, when his associates had reached the end of their
reign, and in consequence Constantine was now ruling alone and
held the sole power over the empire, the longed-for peace was restored in full to the long afflicted Church, even as it is written:[37]
"I have seen the wicked in great power, and exalted, and I passed
by, and, lo, he was not." Since wicked men and persecutors had been
removed from the earth and the righteous had been set free from
distress, therefore, as though a cloud had been dissipated, a joyful
day began to gleam forth upon the City of God all over the world.
You might have seen the peoples that had been in hiding rush
forth now from all sides to join other peoples and unite with them,
unified into one body as members of a single organism. You might
have seen also, now that sorrow was turned to joy, festivals and
dedications of churches in every city, stronghold and village attended by the greatest rejoicing of our people. For the Christian
emperor, out of his devotion to his faith, wished with all his
heart that these things should be done. Then for the first time
edicts were promulgated that churches should be built; then for
the first time the Catholics were permitted to enrich their churches
with their estates. And, as the history of the Romans has it, his
Most Serene Highness [38] not only granted his consent to these
things but also, setting an example to others, so greatly exalted the
Roman Church that he handed over the imperial insignia to Saint
Sylvester, pope of that city, and withdrew to Byzantium and there
established the seat of his realm.[39] This is why the Church of

---

[36] Hofmeister remarks that this son of Licinius never existed.

[37] Ps. 37. 35-36.   [38] Constantine, of course, is meant.

[39] New Rome, or Constantinople, became the capital of the empire in 330.

Rome claims that the Western realms are under its jurisdiction, on the ground that they had been transferred to it by Constantine, and in evidence thereof does not hesitate to exact tribute to this day — except from the two kingdoms of the Franks. But the advocates of empire affirm that Constantine did not hand over his kingdom in this way to the Roman pontiffs, but out of reverence for the Lord accepted them as fathers — thinking of them as priests of the most high God — and consented that he and his successors should be blessed by them and sustained by the protection of their prayers. And to prove this they adduce the fact that Constantine himself, when he divided the kingdom among his sons, handed over the West to one,[40] the East to the other;[41] and thus Rome with the West fell by lot to Theodosius [42] and to others in succession, not merely to heretics but also to religious princes. They say that never would so devout a ruler have left to his sons what he had previously handed over to the Church, nor would so Catholic an emperor as Theodosius have appropriated what was not his, if it belonged to the Church. To settle definitely all these matters is not the purpose of the present work.

4. But it is pleasing to contemplate in how marvelous a way — a way past all expression — the City of Christ, making its gradual progress among the citizens of the world, grew to such heights. For to go rather far back, when the first man had been created and had fallen from the delights of paradise, a merciful God left him a guide for learning the truth in this vale of tears. Because the sons of men were constantly led away therefrom (though some few continued in the knowledge of the truth yet the majority went astray) God preserved his own people but destroyed the rest by the waters of the Flood. Then when the human race was propagated anew from those thus preserved, gradually the knowledge of the truth was [again] blotted out in them and error began to increase to such an extent that at about the time of Abraham, the tenth in line from Noah, you would find few citizens of Jerusalem save himself and his wife. From him also you will find citizens of both cities descended,[43] and from his son Isaac the two peoples whom I have mentioned. But by Jacob (who is known also as Israel), the third

---

[40] Constantine II received the prefectures of Italy, Gaul and a part of Africa.

[41] Constantius obtained the prefecture known as *Oriens*.

[42] Who became a Christian.   [43] *Cf.* I. 10 above.

generation, you will find that there were begotten twelve princes of the people of God, which was called after him Israel. This people went down into Egypt and, after it had wandered long among the citizens of the world and in that very pilgrimage had grown into a great people, was led back by signs and wonders to the land of its fathers, receiving on the way the Law as a provision, so to say, for its journey, and there it received many temporal blessings. Yet although, as time went on, it had very powerful kings, it never held sole sway over its realm. But when the Lord wished His city to spread abroad and to be extended from that people to all nations, He permitted the realm to be weakened under pressure of the people's sins, and the people itself to be led into captivity. But among the nations which He was to summon to faith in himself, He established the sovereignty of the Romans to rule over the rest. When this had reached its fullest development and the pinnacle of power, He willed that His Son Christ should appear in the flesh. When, as the Gospel says, He had come unto His own and was not received by them that were His — nay was even despitefully entreated by them and nailed to a cross — by a righteous judgment the chosen were taken out from that people and the rest were blinded; and when, though reconciliation was offered them, they did not return to their senses, they were miserably scattered into captivity among all nations. So then the Lord, transferring His city from that people to the Gentiles, willed that they should first be humbled, despised and afflicted by many misfortunes — even as it is written, "He scourgeth every son whom He receiveth." [44] But because scourgings, when they exceed due measure, break the spirit rather than heal it (as medicines taken to excess), at the proper time, as I have said before, He exalted His forsaken and humbled Church. That it might therefore become more tranquil with respect to the promised heavenly kingdom, He bestowed upon it the greatest temporal power possessed by any realm. And thus as I have said the City of God, increasing gradually, reached its pinnacle and undivided authority. And observe that before His incarnation His city was not honored to the full, but that afterwards, when He had risen to the skies with the body He had assumed and had, so to say, accepted His throne, [then] according to the parable He exalted His kingdom, which is the Church, to the highest dignity — than which there is nothing loftier on earth — that hereby He might re-

[44] Heb. 12. 6.

veal Himself to the citizens of the world as not only the God of heaven but also as Lord of the earth, and that through the prosperity of this land of our sojourn He might teach His citizens that the delights of their own country were eagerly to be sought.

Nor ought it perplex you that we said above [45] that sorrows and changes in our estate were the way to our country, whereas now we affirm that prosperity constitutes that way. For while the variety and prosperity of the way draw the fool the more to self love, on the other hand both of these withdraw the wise man through that contemplation of which we have spoken, and kindle his love for the heavenly country. This is why, I think, the wise man, in the book which is called Ecclesiastes (that is to say, the Preacher), alike when the misfortunes and when the successes of our mortal lot are portrayed, preaches about both in such a way as to show more clearly than light that he is induced by the consideration of either state to despise the world and to love the heavenly country. Hence when he has spoken at sufficient length regarding each topic, he terminates the argument with that conclusion to which all things tend: "Let us hear the conclusion of the whole matter," he says. "Fear God, and keep his commandments; for this is the whole duty of man." [46] And that you may know that one and the same thing draws the fool to the abyss of sin and inspires the wise with a desire for the heavenly life, hear the prophet: "For thou, Jehovah, hast made me glad through thy work," he says, "and I will triumph in the works of thy hands." [47] And he adds: "A brutish man shall not know this, nor shall a fool understand." [48] It is as though he were to say, "Thy work, which is not apprehended by a fool, why or for what it is made, and draws him beyond all measure to a destructive love of self, inflames *me* to know Thee, who, being Thyself most fair and sweet, hast made that work fair and pleasing."

So then the City of Christ is seen to have received already, at the present time, practically all that was promised it — all, indeed, except immortality. Then, that through those things which you see fulfilled already you may know that all the other things also which are promised must indubitably be fulfilled, mark that the cross of Christ, His shame, His punishment — and the very mention of

---

[45] II. 43 (end), and 51.

[46] Eccles. 12. 13. I have given the version of the American Revision instead of translating the text of Otto accurately.

[47] Ps. 92. 4.   [48] *Loc. cit.* 6.

crucifixion was once abhorrent to the whole world — has now attained to so great glory that the cross is now worshipped by kings and has become to almost all men the object of love and veneration. Note that kings now glory in having their insignia adorned with that whereby, previously, punishment was meted out to sinners and to men utterly debauched. If therefore God has so honored His punishment, how will He honor His body, His saints, His likeness? Therefore the seasons of prosperity and of present peace are to the minds of the wise an evidence of future blessedness. But let us now return to the sequence of history.

5. Constantine, as I have said, transferred the seat of empire to Byzantium and, having enriched it by the treasures of almost all other cities, called it after his own name Constantinople. Hereafter, for this reason, it was known as The Royal City or New Rome. Having obtained a patriarchal see [49] it won a place next to that held by the Church of Rome itself, the place which the church of Alexandria had previously held. From this time on we find the sovereignty of the Romans transferred to the Greeks. On account of the one-time exalted position of the City, sovereignty remained with it in name, though in fact power went to the Greeks. The situation, then, was like that of Babylon. Note that as the kingdom of Christ expands the worldly kingdom is constantly diminishing.

So when the City of Christ was prospering in many ways and had peace without from its foes, the devil, the enemy of the human race, sought to assail it from within. After Peter had been crowned with martyrdom in the time of persecution, Achillas had undertaken the direction of the Alexandrine patriarchate; when he died with the church at peace, Alexander ruled that church. In his time the presbyter Arius,[50] the vilest of all men, devised his most impious heresy regarding the inequality of the persons of the Trinity. To answer him that very famous Council of Nicaea was assembled, and there Arius with his adherents was condemned and the Catholic faith was strengthened in the presence of the emperor.

In these days lived those most renowned princes of Christ, Paul and Antonius,[51] the first hermits. The former, fleeing from persecu-

---

[49] Cf. III. 2 above and note 32.

[50] For a convenient account of this controversy and the famous Council held at Nicaea in 325, see C. M. H., 1. Chapter V (Arianism).

[51] For Antonius (St. Anthony), one of the earliest of Christian monks, see C. M. H., 1. 521-522. Cf. IV. 14 below.

tion by Decius and desiring to hide in desert places, changed a matter of compulsion into one of inclination; he lived in the desert most abstemiously and died full of days. And while his soul was being received among the companies of prophets and apostles it was seen by Antonius. The other, Antonius, likewise a man of most holy and simple life, after inspiring many to the zeal for a stricter life rested in peace.

About the same time Helena, the mother of Constantine, found at Jerusalem the cross of the Lord.[52] Leaving half of it there she removed the other half to the Royal City. She also caused one of the sacred nails to be worked over and had fashioned therefrom a bridle for her son Augustus. Herein men claim the prophecy was fulfilled which says, "And it shall be that what is on the bridle shall be called holy unto the Lord." [53]

At the same time farther India received the seeds of the word of God, thanks to two boys, one of whom was called Edisius, the other Frumentius.[54] Frumentius was afterwards ordained bishop there and won fame through his many virtues. The nation of the Hiberi also, which is situated in the region about the Black Sea, received the faith through a captive woman. Whoever desires to know these matters more fully will find them in the Ecclesiastical History of Jerome.[55]

Constantine destroyed the Goths, a very savage people, in the country of the Sarmatians. His cousin Dalmatius,[56] the brother of Gallus and Julian, he made Caesar. Constantine died in the thirtieth year of his reign, on the highroad near Nicomedia, when he was planning to march against the Persians. He left the state in good order and handed it down to his sons.

[52] See, *e.g.*, *Legendarium Teutonicum saec.* XII *in.*, ed. Buch, *Zeitschrift für deutsche Philologie* 10, pp. 155, 588 *et seq.*, and Rufinus 10. 7.

[53] Zech. 14. 20. The American Revision translates: "In that day shall there be upon the bells of the horses, HOLY UNTO JEHOVAH."

[54] *Frumenticius* in the text.

[55] Otto thought that the Ecclesiastical History of Eusebius, translated and continued by Rufinus, had been translated and continued by Jerome. *Cf.* IV. 6 (end), 14, 18, 21. Possibly the error was due to some MS. used by Otto. The source of this paragraph is Rufinus 10. 9 and 11.

[56] Otto is in error when he calls him the brother of Gallus and Julian; see the Tripartite History 6. 1 for a correct statement. Gallus and Julian were the sons of Constantine's younger brother, Julius Constantius. Dalmatius (or Delmatius), the son and namesake of Constantine's half-brother, was made Caesar in 335.

6. In the three hundred and forty-first year from the incarnation of the Lord, Constantius his son, the thirty-fifth in line from Augustus, with his two brothers (Constans and Constantine) succeeded Constantine. He was led astray by a certain presbyter who was a disciple of Arius and fell a victim to the Arian heresy. Now the cause of his error was as follows. The sister of his august father had, upon her deathbed, with the greatest earnestness commended the aforesaid presbyter to her brother. When he too was dying in his suburban villa at Nicomedia, and was dividing the empire among his sons, Constantius, to whom the sovereignty of the East chanced to fall, happened to be absent. His father sent him his last will and testament by that follower of Arius, whom he charged to deliver it to no one else. The presbyter, delivering the sovereignty to Constantius along with the will, became so intimate with the emperor that he readily infected him with the poison of his most pernicious doctrine and won him over to his own sect. Eusebius, bishop of Nicomedia,[57] a man contaminated by the same poison, urged that Arius (who on account of his poisonous treachery had been banished from Alexandria by the venerable bishop Alexander) should be recalled and that a council should be convoked. And so, at the bidding of the emperor, Alexander as well as Arius was summoned to Constantinople for a hearing. All night long the man of God, Alexander, lay prostrate in prayer, commending the cause of the Church to the Lord. When day broke Eusebius called Arius to the church. On the way, while he stepped aside in obedience to human necessities, by a righteous judgment of God his bowels gushed forth and he died in a foul and filthy place, and thus he paid the penalty for his blasphemous and fetid soul. His followers fled, full of shame and confusion. But, concealing what had occurred, they inflamed the emperor, through his eunuchs, all the more against the teachers of the orthodox faith. Not many days later Alexander died and Athanasius[58] was chosen in his stead. He was a man of ardent spirit and most vigilant in ecclesiastical matters, and was not only very shrewd in combating the craftiness of heretics but stood forth also as a most valiant champion against the power of the emperors. If anyone desires to know his virtues, his struggles and his labors

---

[57] Constantine's chief Eastern adviser, afterwards bishop of Constantinople.
[58] Born about 297, died in 373. For an account of his life-work, see C. M. H. 1. 127 *et seq.*

let him read the Tripartite History, or the Ecclesiastical History written by Jerome.[59]

7. While Constantine was waging war against his brother Constans he was killed by his generals, not far from Aquileia [60] near the river Alsa. Upon the death of Constantine, Constantius alone held the East; Constans ruled the West, for Caesar Dalmatius, their cousin, had previously been slain by his soldiers. Now the heretics, fearing that if Athanasius should have an opportunity of approaching the emperor he would steep him in the Catholic faith, having first hoodwinked Augustus, lyingly declared that Athanasius was an evil and debauched man, and displayed as proof the forearm of a certain Arsenius, which they said had been cut off by Athanasius by means of his skill in magic. They did this because it was not known where the aforesaid Arsenius was; he had been expelled from the Church by Athanasius for definite reasons. Therefore, at the bidding of the emperor a council was assembled at Tyre.[61] When Athanasius was put on trial there, Arsenius was brought forth into the council. Since he had both his hands the lie of the calumniators was revealed. Into that same council a harlot was brought who claimed that she had been seduced by Athanasius. The priest of Christ urged his presbyter Timothy to speak for him. Now when Timothy inquired of her if he himself had committed this sin, she said, "You, you did it, in such and such a place." Then shame at being made ridiculous began to lay hold on all. And yet the emperor's persecution of Athanasius did not on this account cease, but he even compelled him — after facing many perils — to flee to the West where Constantius's brother held sway. By him Athanasius was kindly received, honorably entreated and afterwards sent back with full authority to his own see. While he was living there in the church of the Treveri, under Maximin, priest of that church, he is said by some to have published "Whosoever Will." [62]

8. At that time Liberius, the pontiff of Rome, after a dispute with the emperor — in the course of which Constantius thought at

[59] The Ecclesiastical History of Eusebius, translated by Rufinus, is meant. See note 55 above. Otto is here referring to Rufinus 10. 12-15.

[60] In Rhaetia, now Aalen. This was in 340.

[61] In 335; see C. M. H. 1. 128.

[62] See *Gesta Treverorum* 19. The Tripartite History 3. 8 speaks of the sojourn of Athanasius at Trèves, and Frutolf on the year 359 as well as Jerome states that it was in the days of Bishop Maximin.

first that Liberius ought to be reminded that he was [only] a bishop of his Empire, afterwards that he ought to be reprimanded — was driven into exile and Felix, his deacon, was chosen by the heretics in his stead. Between this Liberius and Sylvester, Julius held the see.[63]

In these same days Victorinus [64] the rhetorician and Donatus [65] the grammarian were regarded as famous men at Rome. In those days there flourished, as princes of the City of God, certain bishops: Paulinus of Trèves,[66] who had succeeded Maximin; Dionysius of Milan; Eusebius of Vercelli and Hilarius of Poitiers. All these are said to have been sent into exile because of their testimony to the Catholic faith. Of these men Hilarius not only instructed the Church of God by word and by example, but also left as memorials many writings that are redolent of Gallic subtlety and eloquence.[67]

After Athanasius had been thrust from his rightful seat [68] George shamelessly claimed the episcopate for himself. The church of Antioch and that of Jerusalem suffered greatly from these evils. Indeed not they alone but the City of Christ spread abroad all over the world suffered from evils from within.

9. Now Constans fought nine battles, with varying success, against Sapor king of the Persians who had invaded Mesopotamia.[69] Finally, while he was thinking of attempting another battle though without any clearly definite plan, he was himself defeated by night and fled. Afterwards he was killed by the craft of Magnentius in the town of Helena on the borders of Spain. Magnentius usurped imperial power at Autun.[70] In Illyricum the soldiers proclaim a certain old man named Veteranio [71] as emperor. Nepotianus,

[63] Otto (as also the Tripartite History) here omits Mark, who was bishop of Rome between Sylvester and Julius (see Rufinus, *Historia ecclesiastica* 10. 23) but includes his name in the list at the end of Book VII below.

[64] Commentator on Cicero and translator of Neoplatonic works. In his old age he became a Christian.

[65] Aelius Donatus, the teacher of Jerome; see Teuffel's *Römische Literatur,* 6th ed., 3, § 409 (1913).

[66] Exiled at the Council of Arles in 353. For brief sketches of these men see C. M. H. 1. 131, 532.

[67] That Otto was well acquainted with the works of Hilary is apparent from *Gesta Friderici* 1. 55 *et seq.* and 58.   [68] At Alexandria.

[69] It was not Constans but Constantius who fought with Sapor II.

[70] In 350. He was a barbarian, the son of a former slave.

[71] Or Vetranio. On these various claimants for the throne, see C. M. H. 1. 59 *et seq.*

the son of Constantine's sister, assumed imperial authority but was crushed by the Magnentian leaders. When Constantius determined to avenge his brother he first compelled Veteranio to lay aside the purple; then he declared war on Magnentius. A dreadful battle ensued with very great loss to the Romans. But Magnentius was defeated and killed himself, not long afterwards, at Lyons. His brother Decentius, whom he had made Caesar in the Gauls, hanged himself at Sens. Constantius executed his cousin Gallus, who had been made Caesar, for conducting himself like a tyrant, and killed Silvanus also for his cruelties in the Gauls. Presently he chose Julian,[72] the brother of Gallus, as Caesar and sent him to the Gauls. Julian had been made a priest [73] by the Augusti and had been ordained as reader but, having been led astray by evil men, he had entered upon a military career. Julian restored to its former status the Gauls, which had been overrun by the enemy; he put the Alemanni and the Germans to flight and drove them across the Rhine. When, elated by these successes, he came to a certain temple, a crown suddenly fell upon his head. On seeing this his soldiers declared that the imperial authority was by this portent presaged for him by the gods. Unbalanced by the experience and by the prosperity he first enjoyed, Julian usurped the title of Augustus and renounced his faith in Christ. Meanwhile Constantius had moved his military forces against the Parthians but, upon learning of Julian's treachery, he started to return to face. civil war, but died on the way in the twenty-fourth year of his reign.

10. In the three hundred and sixty-fourth year from the incarnation of the Lord, upon the death of Constantius, Julian, the thirty-sixth in line from Augustus, assumed imperial power. He at first, as though censuring the deeds of his predecessor, ordered the bishops to be recalled from exile, but afterwards he set out to persecute the Church of God — by craft, however, rather than by violence. Then, as though swayed by religious scruples, he decreed that Christians must be excluded from the games, must be kept from taking the oath of military service, and finally that they must be stripped of every earthly possession, inasmuch as their own law declares, "So therefore whosoever he be of you that renounceth not all that he hath, he cannot be my disciple." [74] He ordered the tem-

---

[72] Famed as "the Apostate" for his reversion to pagan beliefs. Emperor 361-363. See Sihler, *From Augustus to Augustine* (1923) 191-217.

[73] At Macellum in Cappadocia.   [74] Luke 14. 33.

ples of the heathen to be opened; the imperial prerogatives — such as cooks, eunuchs, barbers, a public race course for horses and mules — he dispensed with, as a philosopher; he devoted himself to study, staying awake by night and writing, and by day reading in the senate what he had written. In consequence he esteemed the philosophers above all other men; he alone [75] of the emperors since Julius Caesar cultivated the study of philosophy. But in his writings he assailed not only the emperors who preceded him but also the Christians. Hence Socrates,[76] in the Tripartite History, speaks thus of him: "In that he expelled the cooks and the barbers he acted the part of a philosopher but not of an emperor; but to belittle and to abuse was in keeping neither with a philosopher nor with an emperor." [77]

At that time lived very famous citizens of the City of God, certain bishops, Meletius [78] of Antioch, Maris of Chalcedon, Basil of [79] Caesarea and Gregory of Nazianzus.[80] Of these Maris alone, who was advanced in age and of feeble health and failing vision, resisted Julian to his face once while he was sacrificing to Fortune in the Royal City, and was not afraid to call him impious and godless and an apostate, as Sozomen relates in the Tripartite History. When Julian, posing as a man of philosophic calm, had reproached him for nothing save his blindness, saying, "Nor is your Galilean god able to cure you," he is said to have replied, "I thank my God for blindness, because this has been done to keep me from seeing you stripped of your piety." Basil and Gregory, being removed from the life of philosophers and hermits to the highest priesthood, not only resisted this tyrant and the heretic Valens [81] by their priestly authority, but also left for the Church of God very useful and profound writings as memorials.

Julian, desiring, as I have said, in consequence of the subtlety of his intellect to follow the philosophers, was raised out of himself

[75] It is strange that Otto has overlooked Marcus Aurelius.

[76] Co-author with Theodoret and Sozomen of the Ecclesiastical History translated by Epiphanius at the bidding of Cassiodorus and commonly known as the Tripartite History. [77] 6. 1.

[78] The text has *Miletus*; see C. M. H. 1. 134 *et seq.*, 138, 141. He presided at the Council of Constantinople in 381.

[79] St. Basil, bishop of Caesarea in Cappadocia, who has been characterized as "the real father of Greek monachism"; see C. M. H. 1. 527 *et seq.*

[80] Bishop of Constantinople in 381.

[81] The emperor Valens (364-378) was an Arian.

into such folly that, following the example of Pythagoras, he said that the spirit of Alexander rested in him and he was preparing — in imitation of him — to make the whole world subject to himself. While to achieve this purpose he was moving his army against the Persians, he was enticed into an ambush by a certain man. And there, when the soldiers were losing their strength because of the barrenness of the place, he was struck by a missile hurled at random and died in the thirty-first year of his age, one year and eight months from the time at which he had become emperor, and in the seventh year from the time when he had been ordained Caesar.

It is related of him that when he saw the spear coming toward him he realized that this was the act of divine vengeance; yet he was not moved to repentance but only rendered the more obstinate, and that he cried with blasphemous lips, "Thou hast conquered, O Galilean." For this was the name he had been wont to use of Christ. Thus then did the Lord fully free His City from a most impious tyrant who had devoted the blood of the Christians to his own gods. We read in the Life of Saint Basil that it was in consequence of the prayers of this holy man Basil (for Julian had then determined that on his return he would utterly destroy Caesarea in Cappadocia, over which Basil presided) that this weapon had been sent from heaven by the blessed martyr Mercurius; by way of proof it is declared that a spearhead, which lay near the tomb of the martyr, was found to be bloody in the morning.

But because Porphyry and Kalistus and other adherents of his eulogize the wisdom and the piety of Julian, I shall briefly disclose what sort of effigies were found after his death to have been provided by him for the practice of his magic art. Socrates, in the Tripartite History, speaks in this fashion: "And when he was dead, and a righteous man had succeeded the unrighteous on the throne, those who entered a certain temple saw a woman suspended by her hair, with her arms outstretched; her abdomen he had opened that he might make inquiries in her liver about a victory over the Persians. This crime was discovered at Carrhae. In Antioch, men say, there were found in the palace a great many chests full of human heads and countless dead bodies sunk in wells." [82] In that city, so the aforesaid author relates, when the fact of his death was learned not only our people in their churches but also the heathen

[82] 6. 48.

in their theaters danced for joy and cried, "You great fool, where are now your prophecies? God and his Christ have conquered."

11. In the three hundred and sixty-sixth year from the incarnation of the Lord, after the death of Julian, when the soldiers were in the greatest disorder, Jovian,[83] a Pannonian by race and a most earnest Christian, was desired by all [as emperor]. When he said that he could not govern the heathen because he was a Christian they declared themselves Christians. Thereupon Jovian was chosen as emperor, the thirty-seventh in line from Augustus. Because of the peril of his army he made a treaty with Sapor, king of the Persians, which was, to be sure, humiliating to the Romans [84] but was rendered necessary by the critical situation: he ransomed his army by surrendering to Sapor a certain town together with the upper part of Mesopotamia. Since he was an orthodox Catholic he recalled to their own sees the bishops who had been driven into exile by Constantius; he caused the temples of the heathen gods to be closed and put their priests to flight. He asked Athanasius, the defender of the orthodox Catholic faith, to instruct him in writing regarding the faith. Athanasius, associating with himself the best of the bishops, wrote back in this fashion: "Athanasius and the other bishops, assembled to represent all the bishops of the Egyptians, of the Thebaid and of Libya, to the most holy and clement victor, Augustus Jovian. It is seemly that a prince pleasing to God should have a desire for knowledge and a longing for heavenly things. For thus dost thou truly have thy heart in God's keeping and so shalt thou govern the Empire in peace for many cycles of years. Since therefore Thy Piety desires to learn from us the creed of the Catholic Church, we, returning thanks for this to the Lord, have taken pains to the end that we might make known to Thy Piety the creed that was promulgated by all the fathers in Nicaea. For it was this that certain men repudiated, frequently, indeed, plotting against us because we did not acquiesce in the Arian madness. For a certain Arius and his followers tried to break away from this faith and to introduce an impiety in opposition to it, declaring that the Son of God was fashioned of previously non-existing elements — that He was a created being, a product, and as a result changeable. By such statements they led many astray so that even men who were regarded as persons of consequence were

[83] He reigned from 363-364.
[84] He ceded the greater part of Mesopotamia to the Persians.

influenced by such blasphemy.'' And a little later: ''Considering
the injury which is inevitably done the people in a case of this sort,
we have taken pains to present to Thy Piety the confession of the
Council of Nicaea. And this is the creed of the Council of Nicaea:
'We believe in one God, the Father Almighty,' and so forth. Those
who say, 'There was a time when He was not, and He did not exist
before He was born,' and declare that, because He was made out of
elements previously non-existent, the Son of God is either of another
substance or essence [from that of which God the Father is com-
posed] or was created, or changeable or variable, these men, we
declare, the Holy Catholic and Apostolic Church anathematizes.'' [85]

Upon reading this letter the emperor gratefully accepted it and
supported by edicts the orthodox Catholic faith. He even promulgated a law whereby death was fixed as the punishment not only
of ravishers and violaters of holy nuns but even of those who merely
cast lewd glances upon them. Furthermore, Athanasius came to
the emperor while the latter was staying at Antioch and, in intimate converse, instructed him regarding the orthodox Catholic
faith. The most Christian emperor himself came from Antioch to
Tarsus and there, after giving honorable burial to the body of his
predecessor Julian, he received the title of Consul. Thence he departed for Illyricum. As he was journeying through Galatia he
perished by a premature death in a certain house that had recently
been plastered: when live coals were brought into it he was suffocated by the heat of the coals and the fumes from the walls. Thus in
the thirty-third year of his age, and in the eighth month of his reign,
he finished both his rule and his life.

12. In the three hundred and sixty-seventh year from the incarnation of the Lord, Valentinian,[86] also a native of Pannonia, a
man of lowly birth but notable for strength of mind and body, an
urbane man, assumed imperial power at Nicaea with the consent of
the soldiers, the thirty-eighth in line from Augustus. This man had
been appointed Commander of a Thousand under Augustus Julian
and had his post of duty at the palace on a certain day when the
emperor entered the temple of Fortune. Now the temple attendants
desired to purify by a heathen rite those who were coming in. As
he preceded the emperor, Valentinian chanced to have on his cloak
a drop from the sprinkling. Insulted at this, as if he had been not

---

[85] This is from the Tripartite History 7. 3 et seq.
[86] This is Valentinian I, who reigned from 364-375.

cleansed but polluted by expiatory rites of this kind, he performed the act of a truly brave and zealous soldier by striking the temple attendant with his fist. For this reason he was discharged from military service by Julian and was thrown into prison. After Julian's death he was rewarded, according to the Lord's promise, a hundredfold, for he obtained imperial power in place of the status of a soldier. He chose his brother Valens [87] as his associate in the imperial power. He put to death the tyrant Procopius [88] together with his accomplices. During these days a very severe earthquake stirred the sea also, so much so that it affected many islands and cities.

13. In the fourth year of his reign he made his son Gratian [89] emperor. At that time real wool, mixed with rain, is said to have descended at Arras. Upon the death of Auxentius, bishop of Milan, Valentinian summoned a council of bishops and, after delivering a word of exhortation, persuaded them to chose a bishop. An uproar followed, since some favored this man, others that,[90] but finally Ambrose [91] the presiding officer and a catechumen [92] was demanded by all as Bishop. The emperor, therefore, seeing that the wishes of all were fixed upon him, directed that after receiving the rite of baptism he should be ordained priest. Thus Ambrose, who afterwards greatly enriched the Church of God not only by his deeds but by his words and writings also, received at one and the same time the gift of baptism and the gift of priesthood. The emperor assembled a synod in Illyricum and there, after confirming the Council of Nicaea, he and the Augusti associated with him in the imperial power wrote in this fashion :[93] "The Emperors — the Mighty, the Righteous, the Victorious, the August — Valentinian, Valens and Gratian; to the Bishops of the dioceses of Asia, Phrygia, Caro-Phrygia and Pacatiana, Greetings in the Lord. When the great council was held in Illyricum and a careful examination was made there of the Word of Life, the thrice-blessed bishops made clear the consubstantial trinity of Father and Son and Holy Spirit.

[87] Who governed the East from Constantinople.

[88] The kinsman and general of Julian, executed in 366.

[89] He reigned from 367-383.

[90] The uproar was caused not by the bishops, but by the *civitatis habitatores*, as we learn from the Tripartite History.

[91] Bishop of Milan from 374-397.

[92] *I.e.*, he was still receiving elementary instruction in religion.

[93] Tripartite History 7. 9.

Deviating in no wise from this doctrine, they perform today the proper rites prescribed by the religion of the great King. Accordingly, Our Majesty has decided to have this doctrine taught, yet in such a way that none may say, 'We follow the religious observance prescribed by the emperor who governs this land of ours,' instead of rendering obedience to Him who delivered unto us His counsels of life. For the Gospel of our Christ reads thus:[94] 'Render unto Caesar the things that are Caesar's; and unto God the things that are God's'.''

14. In these days when Damasus following Liberius held the see of Rome, Athanasius after many trials found rest in a peaceful death in the forty-sixth year of his episcopate.[95] He had caused to be appointed in his stead Peter, the sharer of his trials. But Lucius, an Arian, usurping the see drove Peter in flight to Rome.

During the same time Egypt possessed many thousands of saints, pupils of Antonius,[96] who were applying themselves to philosophy in the desert: of these the two Macarii, Isidore, Pambos, Moses and Benjamin, Skirion, Elijah and Paul, Hilarion, Pachomius, John and very many others won fame above other mortals by signs and apostolic miracles. If anyone is eager to know their virtues, their continence and their labors (which transcend the powers of human frailty) let him read Jerome [97] and that History which is called Tripartite, and the Lives of the Fathers. When one of these men, Moses, was being forced into a bishopric and was being presented to Lucius, as patriarch of the Alexandrians, for consecration, he publicly called Lucius a heretic and refused to have placed on his own head the sin-stained, bloody hands with which Lucius had sent holy and orthodox men into exile for their orthodox Catholic faith. Moses received the bishopric rather from the bishops who were in exile.

Meanwhile the emperor Valens, who had at first been an orthodox Catholic, later, ensnared by his love for his wife (another Eve) and deceived by the trickery of Eudoxius, the Arian bishop of Constantinople, became a victim of the Arian heresy and was baptized by Eudoxius and, to make his misfortune complete, bound himself by a most wretched oath to protect this impious dogma. Valentinian crushed in war the Saxons, a very valiant people, who were raiding the borders of the Franks. The Burgundians — who at the time

---

[94] Matt. 22. 21.   [95] He died in 373.
[96] See IV. 5 and note 51 above.   [97] *I.e.*, Rufinus 11. 2. 8.

when, long before, the interior of Germany was subdued by Drusus [and] Tiberius [98] had departed thence and had taken possession of Gaul — he conquered in a desperate battle.[99] But while he was preparing a campaign against the Sarmatians, who had seized Pannonia, he died at the town of Brigetio in the eleventh year of his reign.

15. In the three hundred and seventy-eighth year from the incarnation of the Lord, Valens, the thirty-ninth in line from Augustus, ruled in the East; Gratian and Valentinian,[100] the sons of Valentinian, governed in the West. Valens — deceived, as I said above, by the trickery of the Arians — then made a law that monks should be forced into military service. Hence many soldiers of Christ in Egypt were crowned with martyrdom for refusing to be the soldiers of an earthly king. Meanwhile he sought to discover by necromantic arts who was to reign after him. Because four letters Θ. E. D. A. [= θεοδ?][101] were revealed to him he caused all those men to be put to death who, he learned, had these letters at the beginning of their names. In harmony with this plan he ordered the death of Count Theodosius,[102] the father of the Theodosius who afterwards became emperor; although Theodosius, when sent by Valens against Firmus,[103] had destroyed not only Firmus himself but also the tribes of the Moors that he had stirred to rebellion. Theodosius, first receiving the sacrament of baptism at Carthage, voluntarily bared his neck to the executioner. Meanwhile Gratian, relying upon the aid of Christ, routed more than thirty thousand of the Alemanni at Strassbourg, a town of Gaul, with small loss to the Roman troops.

16. At about the same time a controversy which arose in the kingdom of the Goths between Fritigern [104] and Athalarich compelled Fritigern, because he had the weaker case, to ask for the aid

---

[98] Otto says *a Druso Tyberio.*

[99] There appears to be no contemporary authority for this statement. Valentinian was allied with them against the Alemanni, an alliance which was not too comfortable but apparently did not come to open rupture.

[100] This is Valentinian II, 375-392.

[101] Otto's text has Θ. E. D. α.; we find in Pierre Pithou the reasonable reading: θ. ε. ο. δ.

[102] He was executed at Carthage (A.D. 375-376).

[103] A Moorish prince who had set himself up as emperor.

[104] His conflict with Athalarich (or Athanarich) occurred about 370; see C. M. H. 1. 214.

of the Romans. When he had come to Valens he received soldiers from him and drove Athalarich in flight. Accordingly, desiring to repay the emperor for his kindness, he embraced his pernicious dogma and in consequence the Goths became Arians. Ulfila,[105] the bishop of the Goths, then invented a Gothic alphabet, and when he had translated the Holy Scriptures into Gothic and begun to preach in the kingdom of Athalarich, the latter, because he was a pagan, inflicted punishments upon many of the Goths whom the Arians hold in reverence as martyrs.

Not long afterwards, when the Goths were now at peace among themselves, the Huns — a horrible race (for they derive their origin, as Jordanes relates,[106] from evil spirits and harlots) — guided by a deer, made their way out of the swamps of Lake Maeotis and so greatly terrified the Goths (a very valiant race) together with Hermanric, their king, that the aforesaid king — who had previously conquered many nations — died in the one hundred and tenth year of his life, as much from dread of this race as from a wound treacherously inflicted upon him by a certain soldier. Jordanes records that Hermanric was king of the Ostrogoths. The aforesaid writer, who was himself a Goth, relates that the Goths had two kingdoms, the one that of the Visigoths, the other that of the Ostrogoths.

After the death of Hermanric the Goths, broken in spirit, again sent to Valens and asked him for a place to dwell in. Valens permitted them to settle among the Thracians. When, because of the hatred and envy of their neighbors, they were suffering there from an unbelievably severe famine, they were treacherously invited by a certain leader to a banquet. But they first guarded themselves against the trap by slaying those who had invited them, and afterwards, scattering everywhere, devastated the whole country with fire and sword. Valens, moving his army from Antioch against them, was moved by a late repentance and ordered the orthodox Catholic bishops to be recalled from exile. Yet on account of his oath he himself did not abjure his own heresy. A battle was fought

---

[105] Or Ulfilas. The text has Gulfilas. The renowned apostle of the Goths was made bishop about 341. See C. M. H. 1. 212 *et seq.*

[106] See *Getica*, chapter 24. Jordanes, the author of the *Romana* and the *Getica*, is often quoted, but not always accurately, in Otto's Chronicle; he wrote in 551 A.D. For an English translation of the *Getica* see *The Gothic History of Jordanes* by Charles C. Mierow (Princeton University Press, 1915).

in Thrace.[107] When the Roman army was put to flight the emperor, wounded by an arrow, fled and wished to hide in the shelter of a certain little hut. The Goths, pursuing him, burned him and the hut together in the fifteenth year of his reign and the fourth year after his brother's death. This is believed to have happened through a righteous judgment of God; he who had consumed the Goths with the fire of faithlessness when they were seeking the true faith was himself burned by them with actual fire and lacked even ordinary burial.

17. In the three hundred and eighty-third year from the incarnation of the Lord, Gratian,[108] the fortieth in line from Augustus, obtained with his brother Valentinian the imperial power. He had previously held it in company with Valens. Desiring to aid the state, Gratian made Theodosius,[109] a Spaniard by race (a brave and God-fearing soldier) Emperor of the East, investing him with the purple at Sirmium.

In his time a second synod, of one hundred and fifty bishops, was assembled in the Royal City under Pope Damasus to oppose Macedonius and Sabellius.[110] The former was maintaining that the Holy Spirit had been created by the Son, the other was asserting that the Holy Spirit was indistinguishable from the Father; indeed he asserted that the Father was the Son too. When these heresies had been condemned and anathematized together with the Arian heresy, the orthodox Catholic faith was strengthened.

Now Theodosius conquered the Gothic tribes not only by valor but also by wisdom. Entering upon a truce with Athalarich their king he invited him to visit him in Constantinople. When Athalarich had come to that city he brought his last day to a close. But the tribes of the Goths, noting the courage and the gentleness of the emperor, subjected themselves to the sway of the Romans. Theodosius chose Arcadius,[111] his son, as his associate in the imperial government. Meanwhile Maximus,[112] seizing the rule in Britain by making himself tyrant, killed Gratian in Gaul [113] in the

---

[107] Adrianople, in 378.

[108] He became emperor as a boy of nineteen immediately after the death of Valens in 378.

[109] He reigned from 379-395.

[110] This is the Council of Constantinople, which was convened in 381. See C. M. H. 1. 141.

[111] He became emperor at eighteen, in 395.

[112] Clemens Maximus, 383-388.   [113] At Lyons, in 383.

sixth year of his reign after the death of Valens [114] and expelled his brother Valentinian from Italy. Valentinian fled to Theodosius and was received by him like a son.

18. In the three hundred and eighty-eighth year from the incarnation of the Lord, after Gratian was slain, Theodosius, the forty-first in line from Augustus, obtained the sole rule of the Roman empire.

During these days the City of Christ began to have full joy and perfect peace, since troubles from abroad and from within the state were ended. There flourished at that time men of renown influential because of their characters, their manner of life and their wisdom: Martin [115] bishop of Tours, Ambrose [116] ecclesiastical head of Milan, Severinus [117] prelate of Cologne and Jerome [118] the presbyter. We find that Augustine too as catechumen was baptized by Ambrose at that time.

Accordingly, this most Christian prince, trusting in God more than in man, moved his army against Maximus to avenge the dead and restore the exile. He attacked Maximus in the territory of Aquileia and put him to death. Seeing this Count Andragathius, who had been his supporter, drowned himself. When the victory was won Theodosius came to Rome with his little son Honorius. After setting the state in good order there and leaving to Valentinian the government of the West, he returned to Constantinople. Valentinian, while he was on his way back, was (so some say) hanged by treachery of Arbogast [119] and Eugenius.[120] Eugenius was made emperor by Arbogast. But others claim that out of grief by his own hands he brought death on himself in this way.

This is the Valentinian who, though he was made a catechumen by Ambrose, was prevented by a death of this sort from receiving the sacrament of baptism. The aforesaid bishop wrote a mournful

---

[114] *I.e.,* of his sole reign.

[115] With whom the beginnings of Gallic monachism are associated. He became bishop in 372. *Cf.* C. M. H. 1. 534.

[116] See IV. 13 above and note 91.

[117] He succeeded Euphrates as bishop of Cologne in 346.

[118] *I.e.,* St. Jerome, the most learned representative of Christianity, about 342-420, translator of the Bible into Latin and author of many other valuable books.

[119] The Frank who held the title of count and was virtually ruler of Gaul at this time.

[120] Valentinian II was strangled in 392; Eugenius reigned from 392-394.

letter with regard to this matter which begins thus: "My anguish, my anguish!" [121] And therein we find written by the same man: "Because I have lost him whom I was about to regenerate in Christ; but he has not lost the grace which he asked for." With this utterance as authority certain theologians of our time reason, even after the explicit statement of the Gospel wherein it is said, "Except one be born of water and the Spirit, he cannot enter into the kingdom of God," [122] that one may be saved without the sacrament of baptism, whether by the pouring out of blood for a witness to Christ's passion or, it may be, by the Lord's declaration. They argue thus, because, "God did not limit his power by the sacraments." They do not consider with proper care under what circumstances authors speak: what it is they say merely by way of opinion, what by way of assertion, what by way of consoling themselves in the extremity of their grief. But, although it be true that God's power is not restrained by ecclesiastical rules or by sacraments, it will yet be necessary for me, who am bound by the Christian rule, to believe that no one can be saved except by such things. Wherefore, although it may be possible for God on His own express testimony, as was said above — for God, I say, who is omnipotent — to save Jew or Gentile or unbaptized person without the pouring forth of blood, yet it will be impossible for me to believe this. And so in such matters the divine power is limited, not for Him but for me. [123] Now if they say all this out of pity it is strange that they do not out of the same pity have the same feeling in the case of infants. But if they retort that the former, being adults, can believe and that the latter cannot, let them hear by way of answer that the latter are held bound only by original sin while the former are not. It remains therefore that we should marvel with them and they with us at the divine power in such cases, and not investigate it, exclaiming with the apostle, "O the depth," [124] and

[121] See Hugo of St. Victor, *Summa Sententiarum* 5. 5 and Jer. 4. 19. Hofmeister points out that this biblical quotation is not the beginning of the letter referred to. Otto has been using Hugo's work (*l. c.*) instead of that of Ambrose.

[122] John 3. 5.

[123] This very revealing passage should be carefully noted. It is an excellent illustration of Otto's attitude on questions of faith, and of the authoritarian point of view in general. But Otto could criticize the Church freely enough on questions not involving the faith.

[124] Rom. 11. 33.

with the prophet, "Thy judgments are a great deep."[125]   But enough of this.

Upon learning of Valentinian's death, Theodosius, while he was making ready an army against the tyrants, sent Eutropius[126] a eunuch to John, a monk of Egypt, and inquired of the man of God the outcome of his plans. John, with spirit of prophecy, of which he was full, promised Theodosius complete victory over the tyrants. Therefore this most God-fearing emperor, armed with faith rather than with military strength, moved his army against the tyrants. He sent the Goths ahead, ten thousand of whom are said to have been put to flight by Arbogast, and he himself with the others proceeded on his way. When they had come face to face in the Alps[127] and the tyrants, on the higher ground, had a better opportunity for fighting, Augustus spent the whole night in wakefulness with tears and prayers, committing himself to God. When day broke, battle was joined; the tyrants were defeated and Eugenius was taken captive and put to death. Arbogast laid hands on himself and put an end to his life. That this victory was obtained from the Lord through the merits of a most pious emperor and the prayers of the Church is proved by a rainstorm sent from heaven and driven by the wind into the faces of the enemy. Even a certain pagan poet,[128] judging that all this was brought to pass by God's grace, celebrated it to the honor of the emperor in this fashion:

> "Greatly beloved of God, for whom the elements battle;
> Even the winds conspire to answer his trumpet calls."

When all was thus quiet and in good order, Theodosius found rest in a peaceful death at Milan in the eleventh year of his reign after the death of Valens.[129] To this point Jerome carried his ecclesiastical history.[130] This is the Theodosius who was prevented by Am-

[125] Ps. 36. 6.

[126] Eunuch of the palace in 395, later high chamberlain, patrician and consul. See IV. 19 below.

[127] On the Frigidus, a tributary of the Isonza, in 394.

[128] Claudian, *De tertio consulatu Honorii*, verses 96 and 98. These lines are quoted by Orosius 7. 35. 21 and Augustine 5. 26, as well as by Frutolf, p. 132. 20.

[129] Frutolf says "after the death of *Gratian*," and it is evident from IV. 19 (beginning) that this is what Otto meant to write. *Cf.* IV. 18 (beginning) and IV. 20 and 21. Theodosius died in 395.

[130] Otto means the Ecclesiastical History by Eusebius, translated and continued by Rufinus; *cf.* Frutolf on the year 398.

brose from entering the doors of the Church because, through human frailty, he had punished the inhabitants of Thessalonica without restraint and without judgment.[131] To this he submitted with humility and absented himself from communion until, his penance having been accomplished by tears and by good works, he was reinstated by the aforesaid bishop. For so glorious a deed that priest is held in the greatest veneration in the aforesaid city [132] even today among all Roman Catholic priests.

19. In the three hundred and ninety-ninth year from the incarnation of the Lord, upon the death of their father,[133] Honorius obtained the government of the West, Arcadius that of the East, in the forty-second place from Augustus. Damasus was still bishop at Rome, Theophilus at Alexandria, John at Jerusalem, Flavian at Antioch and Nectarius in the Royal City.[134] During these days a certain monk, Dirimachius,[135] coming to Rome from the East, because he tried — out of respect for religion — to stop a gladiatorial exhibition (or rather, madness) was overwhelmed with stones by the bystanders and killed. Upon hearing of this Honorius ruled that Dirimachius should be counted among the martyrs and, because of what had happened, he put an end to a sinful exhibition. Not long afterwards, upon the death of Nectarius, Theophilus, the bishop of Alexandria, was summoned by the emperor with other bishops to ordain a bishop of the Royal City. Although the emperor had planned to place his presbyter Isidore in the aforesaid see, John of Antioch [136] was demanded by all as bishop and, having been elected despite the wishes of Theophilus, was finally ordained by him. Hence Theophilus always strove to have him deposed.

This John — who was also, on account of his eloquence, called Chrysostom, as though he had a mouth of gold — was first ordained deacon by Meletius, prelate of Antioch, in that church; after the

131 For the penance imposed by the bishop upon the emperor after the massacre of Thessalonica in 390, see C. M. H. 1. 244-245.

132 *I.e.*, Thessalonica, now Saloniki. Hofmeister thinks that Otto learned this while on the Crusade of 1148 and there added the sentence to his Chronicle.

133 *I.e.*, Theodosius. Upon his death the Roman Empire was permanently divided into an Eastern and a Western realm. Arcadius obtained the eastern half, Honorius (395-423) the rule in the West.

134 *I.e.*, Constantinople.

135 The name as given in the text is *Dirimachius*; the Tripartite History says *Telemachus*. The date, as usually given, was 404.

136 St. John Chrysostom came into prominence at Antioch in 387, after

death of Meletius, John departed into the desert and there for
three years devoted himself wholly to God. He had then been ordained presbyter by Evagrius. He was "mighty in deed and
word," successful in reforming character, but lacking in tact in
his immoderate severity and zeal for God, and of such excessive
outspokenness that by those who were unacquainted with him he
was thought to be vainglorious and verbose. Hence after he attained to the episcopate he became so odious to his priests, whose
characters he was always seeking to improve, that they formed a
conspiracy against him, defaming him in many ways. They slandered him greatly, calling him mad and insolent and (so to say)
headstrong. The fact that he suffered no one to eat with him seemed
to lend credence to these charges. But he is said to have done this
on account of his excessive fasting, in consequence of which he
frequently had headaches. He was greatly beloved by the people,
however, on account of the sermons which he delivered. What they
were like may be inferred from his books which are extant in the
Church even to this day. To cap the climax of his unpopularity was
the fact that he not only was harsh to his priests but in his zeal for
justice he did not hesitate to contradict even the nobles themselves.
So it came to pass that, when a certain Eutropius — a eunuch, a
consul and the friend of the emperor — by whose advice a law was
passed that those who fled to a church should be dragged thence,
himself fleeing from the emperor's wrath lay beneath an altar not
long afterwards, John publicly assailed him from the pulpit and
preached a denunciatory sermon against him. Therefore Theophilus, having found his opportunity, strove by every means to
depose John, thinking him deserted by his friends. Thereby he not
only arrayed his own flock against him but also incited the bishops
to oppose him, communicating with the bishops in the vicinity by
word of mouth and with the more distant bishops by letters. Hence
it came to pass that he met Epiphanius,[137] bishop of Salamis in
Cyprus — a man of great piety, to be sure, but rather unsophis-
ticated, as might be expected in one brought up in the desert — and
associated Epiphanius with himself to depose John through the
instrumentality of Origen's books. And so the priest I have men-

the riot. He was chosen bishop of Constantinople ten years later. For an
account of the controversy between Theophilus and Chrysostom see C. M. H.
1. 489-494.

[137] Not to be confused with the bishop of Pavia. (V. 1 below).

tioned, bearing the denunciation of Origen, came to the Royal City and, declining John's invitation (because of Theophilus) went to his own house. When John sent a messenger to him and asked him to come to him and stay with the other bishops, Epiphanius replied that he wished neither to stay with him nor to have John pray with him unless he subscribed to the denunciation of Origen's books. Since John delayed doing this his enemies persuaded Epiphanius to come into the Church of the Apostles on the following day, when the people had assembled, to denounce the books of Origen, and to brand John, in the presence of the people, a defender of Origen. Upon learning of this John sent a message to Epiphanius in these words: "You have done many things, Epiphanius, contrary to the rules: in the first place you have officiated at an ordination in a church established under my jurisdiction; then without my bidding you have celebrated the sacraments on your own authority; again, you made excuses when invited and now you again take too much upon yourself. Wherefore take care lest a disturbance arise among the people and you yourself incur the responsibility for this thing." Upon hearing this Epiphanius withdrew and, as some say, sent back this message to John: "I hope that you do not die a bishop." To which he is said to have replied: "I hope that you do not get back to your native city." Each wish was fulfilled. For Epiphanius died on his journey and John was deposed not long after. After this John, in order to reprove the empress Eudoxia [138] because she had aroused Epiphanius against him, according to his custom preached to the people a sermon full of vilification of all women. Eudoxia, greatly incensed at this, complained to her husband. Therefore Theophilus, since he thought that John had now become odious not only to his associates but to the rulers as well, planned to depose him. Convoking the bishops in a suburb of Chalcedon, he brought forward accusers and called him to the hearing to answer the charges which were being made against him. But John maintained that a general synod should be held for this purpose. When Theophilus, supported by the other bishops, summoned him again and again to appear and John persisted in his determination, they voted that he should be deposed from his episcopate as disobedient. The people cried out against it, rising in revolt, but the emperor confirmed the decision of the bishops and John was deposed and car-

[138] Daughter of Bauto the Frank, whom Eutropius had induced Arcadius to marry.

ried off into exile. Upon seeing this many even of those who had hated him were moved with compassion, and said that John had been slandered, especially since it now became apparent to all that he had been condemned in consequence of the ill will of Theophilus.

At that time Innocent had the see in the city of Rome after Siricius and Anastasius had held that priesthood. John, who had afterwards been recalled by the emperor and people on account of an earthquake which had occurred while he was deposed — a rather unusual thing in the City — was again furtively casting aspersions on the empress. When she was again seeking to lay a trap for him he delivered that famous sermon which begins, ''Again Herodias rages and again is thrown into a frenzy; once more she dances, once more she longs to receive the head of John in a basket.'' Therefore Eudoxia, enraged all the more, had him deposed and driven into exile again. When Innocent heard of this act he condemned it and gave notice to the clergy in writing that they were not to elect a successor. But presently John's death put an end to the controversy. Theophilus also departed this life not long after and left his see to Cyril. This Theophilus, although he was blamable in John's case, yet stood forth as a brave champion against the Arians and the Anthropomorphites — whose heretical doctrine, recently arisen, taught that God was limited by his bodily form. This heresy had so infected the more guileless monks and hermits of Egypt that they came to Alexandria and started an insurrection against Theophilus to secure a profession of true faith; and if the aforesaid bishop had not had the presence of mind to say, ''I see you as one seeth the face of God,'' [139] he would not have escaped the frenzy of the excited populace. At about the same time, during the reign of Honorius and Arcadius, the most blessed prelates Martin and Ambrose, priests of highest worth to the City of God, departed to the Lord. But let us now return to the orderly course of our history.

20. So then the Goths, after the death of Theodosius, since they did not receive from his sons the customary grants, chose a king for themselves upon the advice of the patrician Rufinus [140] and withdrew from the senate. But Rufinus was afterwards found out and beheaded before the gates of the city of Constantinople. His head

---

[139] Cf. Gen. 33. 10.

[140] Rufinus of Aquitaine, praetorian prefect and adviser to both Theodosius and Arcadius.

and his right hand were carried about the city in mockery. Gildo [141] also, Count of Africa, with unheard of daring began to lop off Africa from the sovereignty of the Romans. His own brother Mascezel, whose two sons Gildo had killed, was sent against him with an army. Mascezel conquered his foe more by God's grace than through the valor of his soldiers. Routing seventy thousand men with a small force (five thousand men) he put the tyrant to flight. Gildo died not many days later, being strangled. Then Mascezel, elated by his success — as often happens — began to persecute the churches of God. Therefore by a righteous judgment of God this man, who had previously been exalted in confessing Him, was now deservedly brought low for despising Him. For he died not long after. The emperor Arcadius too, a mild and quiet man, reached the end of his life in the fourteenth year of his reign after the death of his father, and left the Empire of the East to his son Theodosius,[142] an eight-year-old boy. His prefect Anthemius,[143] who had enclosed the Royal City with a huge wall, assumed charge of everything.

21. In the four hundred and twelfth year from the incarnation of the Lord, upon the death of Arcadius, Honorius,[144] the forty-third in line from Augustus, became Western Emperor. But the Goths, incited by Rufinus and Stilicho,[145] with their king Alaric [146] (called in their tongue Baltha, that is "The Bold"; he was of the family of the Balti, and so next in nobility to the Amali),[147] moved through Dalmatia and Venetia and pitched camp on the borders of Aemilia.[148] Having sent an embassy to the emperor — who, as it chanced, was at that time stopping in Ravenna [149] — they haughtily demanded a country to dwell in, adding that if they

[141] A Moorish prince who revolted in 394, seeking to secure the north coast of Africa for himself.

[142] Theodosius II acceded to the throne upon the death of Arcadius in 408. He died in 450.

[143] The praetorian prefect was the grandfather of the emperor Anthemius (467-472).

[144] Western Emperor from 395 to 423.

[145] The Vandal who acted as guardian and regent for the boy emperor. He was eminent both as a soldier and as a statesman.

[146] This is Alaric I, king of the Visigoths from 395 to 410.

[147] The royal family of the Ostrogoths; see *Getica*, 252 *et seq*.

[148] The province in upper Italy.

[149] Since 402 the imperial residence for the western half of the empire, though Rome was still the capital.

could not obtain it as a gift they would seize it themselves. Accordingly the emperor upon advice handed over to them a district in the country of Spain, land which had rebelled against him. When the Goths were on their way to take possession of it, Stilicho, a patrician and the father-in-law of Honorius, treacherously followed them and joining battle with them lost his army and was himself put to flight. The barbarians, aroused by this action, returned to Aemilia, their starting point, and laying waste the whole province with fire and sword moved on towards the City. They even forced their way into the terror-stricken town and, after giving instructions that no holy places should be violated, burned several regions of the City and carried off an incalculable amount of booty. Pope Innocent, like that just man Lot, stayed at Ravenna that he might not behold the punishment of the wicked City.

During these days, when the pagans were murmuring against our faith and saying that Rome had been preserved by *their* gods in the highest honor, but had been dishonored in Christian times, Augustine wrote his book entitled *The City of God*,[150] Orosius compiled his *History*,[151] Jerome translated the *Ecclesiastical History* written by Eusebius [152] and by adding two books brought it down as far as the death of Theodosius.

Now this invasion of the City by Alaric, as notorious as it was presumptuous, took place in the one thousand, one hundred and sixty-fourth year from the founding of the City, and in the four hundred and fifteenth from the incarnation of the Lord. As I have said above [153] the empire of the Romans, which had an origin and a progress in many respects similar to those of the kingdom of the Babylonians, was (according to the calculation of our elders) dishonored by Alaric in a year as far removed from its founding as the year in which Babylon was brought low by Arbatus was removed from the founding of that city. In this invasion [of Rome] Placidia, the sister of Honorius, was captured along with other booty. Afterwards Ataulf [154] obtained her in marriage.

[150] The *De civitate Dei*, in 22 books, was not completed until about 426, although begun in the days of Alaric's invasion.

[151] The title of his work is *Pauli Orosii presbyteri historiarum adversum paganos libri VII*, and it consists of a chronicle of universal history from Adam to the year 417 A.D.

[152] Otto is mistaken in this: it was Rufinus who translated and continued Eusebius; *cf.* above IV. 5 (end); 6 (end); and 14.

[153] III. 6; *cf.* also IV. 5 and below IV. 31 and VI. 22.

[154] Alaric's brother-in-law and successor, king of the Visigoths 410-415.

Meanwhile Constantine,[155] seizing Gaul, made his son from a monk into a Caesar. No long time afterwards both were deprived of life and throne alike — the father at Arles, the son at Vienne. The Goths, after gaining their victory over the City of Rome, planned to go through Apulia and Campania into Sicily and Africa. But when they recklessly put out to sea on the shores of Bruttium they lost many of their number. Alaric, too, brought the last day of his life to a close. The barbarians loved him so much that they turned the river Busento from its course near the city of Cosenza and, having buried him there together with many treasures, killed all the captives who had knowledge of what had been done and then turned the river back into its proper channel. Upon his death the Goths, disheartened both by this and by the former disaster, chose Ataulf as their king and decided to return. As they retraced their way through Rome they laid waste what they had spared before. But Ataulf, for love of his wife Placidia, withdrew from the territory of the Romans and settled in Gaul, near the province of Narbonne, where the man of God Egidius afterwards dwelt, a man who permitted the metropolis to be called after his own name, "The City of St. Egidius," [156] in a place which even to this day is called the Palace of the Goths. Later, driven out by Count Constantius,[157] he settled with the Goths in Spain. Wallia, the third in succession after him, who followed Segeric, waged war upon neighboring tribes and particularly the Vandals [158] who were themselves at that time newcomers in Spain.

22. Tonorius, through Count Marinus, vanquished Heraclian, count of Africa, as he was coming against Rome and drove him to Carthage where he was afterwards killed. By the aid of Constantius (who had crushed Constantine and Constans in Gaul), Honorius restored complete peace to the Church of God in Africa.

During these days under Pope Innocent the bodies of certain saints — Stephen the first martyr and others — were revealed to Lucian, a priest, while John was bishop of Jerusalem. Not many days later, under Boniface (who had been chosen in the place of

---

[155] According to Orosius a common soldier, who was proclaimed in Britain in 407. His son's name was Constans. Both were killed in 411.

[156] St. Gilles, near the mouth of the Rhone.

[157] General of Honorius. In 418 he settled the Visigoths in southwestern Gaul. See C. M. H. 1. 404; also 287.

[158] Against whom he fought for Rome, receiving a grant in southern Gaul. See C. M. H. 1. 404.

Zosimus,.the successor of Innocent), Jerome the presbyter departed to the Lord in Bethlehem, in the ninety-first year of his age. Upon the death of Boniface, Celestine held the see in the City.

Wallia made a treaty with Augustus and restored to him his sister Placidia.[159] To this point Orosius carried his chronicles. Honorius died [160] at Rome in the thirty-first year of his reign — two years of which he had ruled under his father, thirteen with his brother and the rest with his brother's son.

23. In the four hundred and twenty-seventh year from the incarnation of the Lord, Theodosius the Younger, the forty-fourth in line from Augustus, reigned alone upon the death of his uncle. In the Tripartite History his virtues are extolled above those of all his predecessors. Among those virtues this too is recorded: that like Alexander the Great, while he was with his army and was suffering from thirst, exhausted by the heat of the sun and stained with dust, when a very welcome drink was brought to him he refused it, that he alone might not be relieved before the others.

In his time lived John Cassian, a hermit, who compiled the Collations [161] of the Fathers, and Germanus, bishop of Auxerre. Moreover, under Pope Celestine, or his successor Sixtus, while Juvenal was bishop of the royal city, through the efforts of Cyril of Alexandria and Arcadius (a bishop sent from Italy) a third synod, consisting of two hundred bishops, was summoned to meet at Ephesus to oppose Nestorius [162] who was asserting that there are two persons in Christ. It was shown at the council that there was one person in the two natures of Christ, and Nestorius with his followers was condemned by a just anathema.

Theodosius sent Valentinian,[163] the son of his aunt Placidia and Constantius, with his mother into Italy to oppose John,[164] who had

---

[159] The emperor's sister had an adventurous life; made a hostage by Alaric, married by Ataulf, mistreated by Sigerich (Segeric), she was now returned to the Romans by Wallia (in accordance with the treaty made with Constantius) and became the wife of the Roman general Constantius. Upon his elevation to the rank of Augustus in 421 she received the title of Augusta.

[160] In 423. The relatives here referred to are his father Theodosius, his brother Arcadius (the Eastern Emperor), his brother's son Theodosius II.

[161] They contain the most complete exposition of the philosophy of primitive Christian monachism; see C. M. H. 1. 525.

[162] Bishop of Constantinople in 428. For the Nestorian controversy see C. M. H., 1. 494-503.

[163] This is Valentinian III, 425-455.

[164] A usurper, proclaimed emperor upon the death of Honorius in 423, overthrown in 424.

seized the rule of the West. With them he sent Aspar and Ardaburius as associates. John was killed at Ravenna, according to some by the craft of Aspar and Ardaburius; others, however, say it was by the intervention of an angel. Thus through the merits of a righteous prince the state was freed from a tyrant.

To this point Bishop Theodoret and Socrates and Sozomen, most eloquent men, brought their Histories. These were afterwards condensed into one volume and translated into Latin by Cassiodorus Senator, who employed in the work the lawyer Epiphanius. From the fact that this volume had had three authors, it received the name *Tripartite History*.

24. After the tyrant had been put to death, Theodosius, considering that Valentinian (by whose aid a civil war had been settled) deserved a reward, chose him as his associate in the government and decided that he should have the title of Augustus.[165] During these days the Visigoths dwelt in the Gauls. The Ostrogoths and the Gepidae, from whom the Avars and the Lombards are descended, crossed the Danube. The Gepidae made their home near Belgrade and Sirmium; the Ostrogoths, who had previously stayed in Pannonia, thereafter lived in Thrace. After remaining there for forty-eight years they migrated toward the West. The Vandals, having as allies the Germans with their leader Godigisel,[166] had seized Spain. At that time there were two notable generals, Aëtius and Boniface; of these Boniface received from the emperor the rank of count of Africa. But because Boniface was unjustly accused before Placidia, the emperor's mother, by a treacherous denunciation made by Aëtius, Dukes Mavortius and Galbio were sent against him. When they were killed by Boniface, Count Sigisvult was despatched against him. Boniface, crossing over into Spain, called in the Vandals and handed over the whole of Africa to them. They soon spread everywhere, devastating the land with sword and flame. Among other outrages they invested by siege the city of Hippo over which the blessed Augustine then presided. But the blessed bishop departed to the Lord in the third month of the

[165] Manuscript C₄ adds at this point in the margin (in the same hand):
This Valentinian was the last of the Augusti in the city of Rome. After him no one was called Augustus in Rome until Charles the Great, king of the Franks. That after him the Roman Empire on this side of the sea [*i.e.*, the west] was handed over to the kings of the Franks with the name of Caesar Emperor Augustus is not unreasonable, since Romans and Franks spring from the same fount of Trojan blood.

[166] Slain in battle in 406. Otto's text gives his name as Modigisilus; he is also called Godegiskl.

siege and in the seventy-sixth year of his life,[167] that he might not witness the destruction of his city. When no long time had elapsed after this it became evident to Placidia that Boniface had been falsely accused before her, and so she summoned him and appointed him Master of the Soldiery. But the Romans granted the Vandals peace, handing over to them part of Africa. During these days Gaiseric, king of the Vandals, since he was an Arian, persecuted the Christians and drove bishops into exile. He invaded Carthage and despoiled it of many treasures and ecclesiastical ornaments.

25. In the thirtieth year of the reign of Theodosius there was a dreadful earthquake at Constantinople. But when because of this the people, with Proclus their bishop, sang by divine admonition "ayoc . otheoc . ayoc . yckyrωc . ayoc . aϑanaϑωc . eleyſon . ymas," that is, "Holy God, God holy and strong, holy and immortal, have mercy upon us," the earthquake ceased.[168] Therefore it was commanded by the emperor and by his sister Pulcheria that this chant should be sung all over the world. At this time Rome also fell in ruins, in many of its wards, in consequence of an earthquake. In these days Attila,[169] king of the Huns, having put to death his brother Bleda, wielded the power of a tyrant and began to devastate Thrace and Illyricum. Theodosius persuaded him to go out from his territories by giving him six thousand pounds and promising him in addition a thousand pounds per year. Not many days later Theodosius died at Constantinople in the forty-first year of his reign and in the twenty-sixth year after the death of his uncle.

26. In the four hundred and fifty-third year from the incarnation of the Lord, upon the advice of Pulcheria, Marcian,[170] the forty-sixth in line from Augustus, obtained control of the Empire in the East, and Valentinian, the forty-fifth in line, control in the West. In the latter's time, under Pope Leo, when Juvenal was bishop of Jerusalem and Anatolius bishop of Constantinople, a fourth synod, of six hundred and thirty priests, was assembled at Chalcedon [171]

---

[167] Augustine died Aug. 28, 430. For an account of his life see especially *Sancti Augustini Vita Scripta a Possidio Episcopo*, by H. T. Weiskotten (Princeton University Press, 1919).

[168] Manuscript B₂, in a more recent hand in the margin, adds this canny remark: *Bonus cantus tempore terre motus!*

[169] For a vivid description of this terrible conqueror read Jordanes, *Getica* 178-183.

[170] He reigned 450-457.

[171] For the Monophysite or Eutychian controversy and the Council of Chalcedon (449), see C. M. H. 1. 503-512.

to oppose Eutyches, an abbot of the Royal City, and his defender Dioscurus, formerly bishop of Alexandria, who were maintaining that the Word of God and the flesh had one nature. When these heresies had been condemned, together with the Nestorian heresy, the orthodox Catholic faith was strengthened in its teaching that there are in Christ a divine nature and a human nature but only one person. These are the four synods [172] which — so Saint Gregory, bishop of the city of Rome, testifies — are to be held in equal veneration with the four gospels.

Now during the reign of Marcian and Valentinian, Attila, king of the Huns, made subject to himself very valiant tribes — the Ostrogoths and the Gepidae and many other peoples — and overran Macedonia, Moesia, Achaea and Thrace. Since he was planning to conquer the Romans and the Visigoths as well (the former of whom he envied on account of the time-honored dignity of their city, the others because of the strength they owed to their bravery), and feared that these two peoples might unite against him, he endeavored to separate them from each other by craft — for he was very shrewd. Sending an embassy both to Valentinian, Augustus of the Romans, and to Theodoric,[173] king of the Goths, he addressed to each individually a message of peace. Announcing to the Romans that he was preparing war not against them but against the Goths, and to the Goths the same thing about the Romans, he strove to incite them each against the other. But Aëtius, who was at that time patrician of the Romans, saw through the trick of Attila and, writing a letter to Theodoric, king of the Goths, in Valentinian's name, urged in the most friendly terms that the two peoples should unite against a most cruel tyrant and the invader of the whole world. Thereupon Attila, since he could make no progress in this fashion, openly declared war on the Goths. As the Romans had been aroused by ambassadors, the Goths secured Patrician Aëtius as an ally. He came to the rescue of the Goths, joining to himself Franks, Sarmatians, Armatiani, Burgundians, Saxons, Ripariolii, Briones and many other tribes of the Celtic country and of Germany. But Attila, with Ardaric king of the Gepidae, and Walimir

[172] Namely, The Council of Nicaea in 325 (IV. 5 above); The Second Council, that of Constantinople in 381 (IV. 17); the Council of Ephesus in 431 (IV. 23); the Council of Chalcedon in 451 (IV. 26).

[173] Not Theodoric the Great, but the first Visigothic king of this name, 419-451. Mommsen introduced the custom of referring to him as ''Theodoric I'' to avoid confusion.

king of the Ostrogoths, and countless throngs of kings and of peoples, set his troops in motion. The armies took up positions in the Catalaunian Plains. [174] Attila sought to learn the outcome of the struggle through the entrails of cattle, and learned by these most disgusting auguries that he must be defeated, but that the most powerful of all in the opposing army would fall. Troubled at this, but elated by the fact that the mightiest man on the other side (who, he supposed, was Aëtius) must perish, he addressed his troops and, proclaiming that they must find encouragement in the previous successes that had attended upon their valor, he started the battle. The Romans held the higher ground. From the ninth hour of the day the combat was waged by those most valiant races who fought very bitterly even until nightfall. Theodoric, king of the Goths, according to the prophecy made to Attila, fell while hurrying hither and thither to encourage his men. Attila confessed himself vanquished by turning in flight, but thanks to the darkness this could be concealed. When day broke the Goths sought their king but found only his dead body. They then wished to charge against the foe under Thorismud, the king's son. Thereupon Aëtius, fearing that the Goths, swollen with pride by the destruction of the Huns, might menace Rome, called Thorismud to him and said: "Your brothers who have remained at home will seize the throne when they learn of your father's death. Do you therefore return, to keep them from forestalling you." Thus Aëtius, shrewdly deceiving the young man, persuaded him to decline battle for the reason I have mentioned and to return to his own home. It is told of Attila that he had built a pyre of benches upon which he had determined to cast himself if the enemy should force their way in. There perished in this most famous battle, as Jordanes relates,[175] on both sides one hundred and sixty-five thousand men besides fifteen thousand who had fallen in the encounter between the Franks and the Gepidae the night before. Thorismud,[176] being chosen king by his men, returned to his own country as Aëtius advised and entered Toulouse.

27. Attila, made safe by the withdrawal of the Goths, turned aside against the Romans and invested with a siege Aquileia, the

---

[174] In 451. The site of this great battle is usually placed at Châlons-sur-Marne, but von Wietersheim and Hodgkin believe it was fought near Mery-sur-Seine; see Hodgkin 2. 143-145 and C. M. H. 1. 416, note 2.

[175] *Getica* 41. 217.

[176] King of the Visigoths 451-453.

metropolis of Venetia, which is situated on the Adriatic Sea. Since
he was unable to capture it after carrying on the siege for a long
time, and since his army was already making ready to withdraw,
Attila, as he was walking alone near the walls and debating in his
mind what to do, observed that the storks were carrying their
young out of the city. Upon seeing this he inflamed his men the
more to overwhelm the city. "This," said he, "is an omen for us.
These birds, I say, forseeing the coming disaster are deserting a city
destined to fall." This said he got ready his engines and bringing
to bear all manner of catapults attacked the city, captured it and
destroyed it utterly, so that scarcely a trace remains. Some say
that he found the city without an inhabitant. For having escaped
by sea without Attila's knowledge, they began to take up their
habitation on an island (henceforth called Venice, because the
Veneti dwelt there). They took with them the remnant of their
possessions, including the patriarchal chair of the blessed Her-
machoras, first bishop of that city. Hence even today — as is well
known — there is a dispute between the Gradenses and the Aquilei-
enses regarding the office of patriarch. Now so long a time was
spent in the siege of this city, and so large a number of troops was
involved, that the inhabitants even today affirm that a hill of remarkable size called Udine [177] was transported thither by the army
to serve as a siege rampart. This hill I myself have seen.[178] Others
however assert that this hill was constructed by Julius Caesar.
Attila, elated at these successes, roved through the other cities of
Venetia and razed them to the ground, with cruel visitation devastating Milan, the capital of Liguria and Ticinum, also called
Pavia. When presently he was planning to go to Rome, Pope Leo
came to meet him. Attila, influenced by the authority and the entreaties of the pontiff, and terrified as well by the example of
Alaric — who had not lived long after capturing the City — returned to his own country.

28. In the meantime Valentinian, jealous of the abilities of
Aëtius, ordered that he and the senator Boëthius [179] should be put
to death. On this account he was himself deprived of his life,[180]

---

[177] *Utinum* in the text.

[178] This is only one of a number of instances of personal observation
recorded in the *Chronicle*.

[179] Not the famous author of the *De consolatione philosophiae*.

[180] Valentinian III was murdered in March, 455.

not long afterwards, by the friends of Aëtius in the thirtieth year of his reign. For twenty-five years he had ruled with his father-in-law Theodosius and the rest of the time with Marcian. Upon his death Maximus [181] usurped the throne, taking also Valentinian's wife Eudoxia the daughter of Theodosius. Because of this indignity Eudoxia called in Gaiseric, king of the Vandals. When the Romans learned he was coming they tore Maximus limb from limb as being the cause of this calamity, in the third month from the time when he had usurped the imperial power. Then forgetting their ancient nobility and valor they fled in all directions. After this when Gaiseric wished to burst into the City as though it were empty of inhibitants, Pope Leo went to meet him at the gate and besought him to refrain from killing the citizens and burning the City. Accordingly, though the barbarian did indeed invade the City, seize booty and roam through it for fourteen days — carrying off among other captives Eudoxia and her two daughters — still, in accordance with the priest's admonition, he refrained at least from burning and from the murder of citizens. This second invasion of the City by the Vandals — Alaric's was the first — occurred in the one thousand two hundred and fourth year from its founding. After capturing the City the Vandals scattered throughout Campania and, devastating the whole of it with fire and sword, stormed Naples and Nola, the most famous cities of that province. Paulinus, the most holy bishop of Nola, gave himself up to the barbarians to redeem its captives: you have a fuller account of this in Gregory's *Dialogue*.[182] Then Gaiseric, enriched by the treasures of Italy, united the daughter of the emperor Valentinian in marriage with his son Thrasamund.[183] His son Hilderic,[184] following the admonitions of his mother, was a Catholic.

Now when Attila, as he was departing from Italy, had asked that Honoria, the sister of the emperor Valentinian, be given him and had not gained his request, he returned in indignation to his own land and married there a very beautiful maiden. While he was giv-

[181] Petronius Maximus, 455. He, together with the eunuch Heraclius, had instigated the murder of Aëtius.

[182] Gregory, *Dialogue* 3. 1; but Otto has cited Gregory following Frutolf.

[183] It was Huneric, not Thrasamund, who married Eudoxia the daughter of Valentinian III. Huneric succeeded his father as king of the Vandals (477-484).

[184] Or Ilderich. He did not become king of the Vandals until 523; Huneric was succeeded by Gunthamund (484-496) and he in turn by his brother Thrasamund (496-523). Previous to Hilderich the Vandals were Arians.

ing a luxurious banquet to celebrate his love for her he became intoxicated and the following night as he lay on his back at the girl's side he was choked by a flow of blood from the nose. When day broke he was found dead by his followers. This occurred, I think, through a righteous judgment of God, to the end that he who had ever thirsted for human blood should perish suffocated by his own blood. On that same night Marcian, as he slept, had a vision of the bow of Attila broken. This is the Attila who, as a certain writer [185] says, was "born into the world to shake the nations, the scourge of all lands, haughty in his walk, rolling his eyes; a lover of war, yet restrained in action; mighty in counsel, gracious to suppliants and lenient to those who were once received into his protection. He was short of stature with a broad chest and a large head; his eyes were small, his beard thin and sprinkled with gray; and he had a flat nose and a swarthy complexion." Jordanes writes that he had five hundred thousand men in his army. While he was marching to and fro all over the world he also crowned with martyrdom eleven thousand maidens at Cologne. He also made Saint Nicasius, bishop of Rheims, a martyr, slaying him in the service of the Lord. Not long afterwards Marcian was killed at Constantinople by the treachery of his courtiers in the seventh year of his reign.

29. In the four hundred and sixtieth year from the incarnation of the Lord, Leo,[186] who had been born at Bissa [187] and was formerly tribune of the soldiers, was the forty-seventh in line from Augustus to receive the government of the East, being crowned by the patriarch [188] Anatolius. He chose his son Leo [189] as his associate in the government. Majorian,[190] however, had received the government of the West at Ravenna. When he was killed in the fourth year of his reign near the city of Tortona, Severus,[191] again at Ravenna and without the authorization of Augustus, usurped the throne. After

---

[185] *I.e.*, Jordanes: see *Getica* 35. 182.

[186] Leo I, 457-474.   [187] In Thrace.

[188] *I.e.*, of Constantinople. This became a precedent.

[189] Leo II (474) was the infant son of Zeno the Isaurian (not of Leo I). At the conclusion of his reign of nine months he was succeeded by his father.

[190] He succeeded Avitus as Western Emperor in 457 and abdicated in 461. His death occurred that same year.

[191] Libius Severus, nominally Emperor of the West from 461 to 465. Upon his death there was a vacancy in the West until Anthemius, a son-in-law of the emperor Marcian, was appointed in 467. Meanwhile the entire empire was once more united (in name at least) under Leo I. *Cf. Getica* 45. 236.

holding it illegally for four years he died at Rome. When he was dead, Augustus sent Anthemius to Rome, making him Caesar (he had formerly been a Patrician). He drove into exile Arvandus, prefect of the Gauls, who was minded to usurp the throne, and commanded that a Patrician of the Romans [192] should be put to death for plotting the same thing. Leo appointed Zeno, his son-in-law, to rule the East and put Basiliscus, brother of his wife Verina, in charge of Africa. Making peace moreover with the Ostrogoths he received as hostage Theodoric [193] the son of Theodemir (the latter was the brother of King Walamir), a boy eight years of age. Yet he afterwards sent him back to his father with honor. Meanwhile Patrician Ricimer killed Anthemius in the fourth year of his reign. Ricimer himself brought the last day of his life to a close three months later. While Anthemius was still alive Leo had sent Olybrius to the City. The latter assumed the title of emperor and received as his wife Placidia the daughter of the emperor Valentinian. After seven months however he brought both his life and his reign to a close at the same time. After his death Glycerius took up the imperial authority at Ravenna. When he was deposed in the following year and ordained bishop in Salona, a city of Dalmatia, Patrician Nepos,[194] son of Nepotianus, ruled the West. Leo therefore made Leo, the son of Zeno by his daughter, emperor. Leo himself brought his life to a close in the eleventh year of his reign. Leo [i.e., the Younger Leo], after ruling for a few months, made his father Zeno emperor and died. Basiliscus, the ruler of Africa, made his wife Zenobia empress. When Zeno came to the Royal City and was received with rejoicing by the senate and the people, Basiliscus laid down the insignia of his office and fled to a church.

30. In the four hundred and seventy-sixth year from the incarnation of the Lord, Zeno, an Isaurian by race, obtained the government of the East as forty-eighth in line. Nepos held the government of the West — that is, the Roman government. When he was driven from the throne Patrician Orestes [195] made his son (to be termed now not Augustus, but Augustulus)[196] Emperor of

---

[192] The text reads: *patricium Romanorum*. But his name was Romanus.

[193] This is Theodoric the Great, King of the Ostrogoths (475-526).

[194] He became emperor in 474, fled to Dalmatia the following year, and lived in exile until his death in 480.

[195] A Roman of Pannonia, formerly secretary to Attila; see C. M. H. 1. 429.

[196] *I.e.*, Romulus Augustulus, 475-476. See *Getica* 241-243.

the West. Now when the Roman Empire which, after all the other kingdoms of the world had been beclouded, seemed to be holding sway alone, must have meted out to it the same measure which it had meted out to other tribes — since their sins demanded such a fate, according to a righteous judgment of God — then Odovacar, a Rugian by nationality, moved his army from the farthest bounds of Pannonia, together with the Turcilingi, Sciri and Heruli, to invade the realm of Rome. When Patrician Orestes met him at the borders of Liguria, terrified at the sight of his troops he fled, betaking himself to Ticinum.[197] Odovacar followed him, captured the city and put him to death; then, distributing his soldiers over all Italy he usurped the imperial title.[198] When Odovacar had left his own country and was passing through the lower parts of Noricum (or perhaps Upper Pannonia) he visited Severinus,[199] bishop of Ravenna — the man of God who, as he preached the word of God, had built a cell near the foothills of Comagenis — and consulted him regarding the outcome of his plans. With prophetic inspiration, with which he was filled, Severinus truthfully foretold to him everything, as the sequel afterwards made plain. Augustulus, beholding his father slain and his city taken by the enemy, was utterly dismayed at heart and voluntarily laid down the purple together with his kingdom in the eleventh month of his reign. Odovacar accordingly entered the City as victor, a foe with none to resist him, and, making it subject to himself, ruled it as king; finally as its master he oppressed it with burdensome servitude; indeed he enslaved too all Italy, which was delivered over into bondage to him for fourteen years.

31. We are obliged to cry out against the miseries of life's vicissitudes, for the time and the place demand it. For behold! that great and powerful kingdom which once terrified the peoples by its mere name and shook the earth, already began to diminish little by little from the time of the first invasion, which took place under Alaric, until finally, fallen from its high estate, it lay open to the barbarians to be trodden under foot by them. To make my meaning clearer I will say that the hapless City was merely captured and plundered the first time by Alaric, the second time by Gaiseric;

---

[197] Now Pavia.   [198] He ruled in Italy from 476 to 493.

[199] For the interesting tale of his life see *Eugippii Vita Sancti Severini*, written in the year 511 (English translation by G. W. Robinson, Cambridge, Mass., 1914). But Severinus was not bishop of Ravenna.

but now we find it was not only captured by Odovacar but for fourteen years was subjected, to its bitter sorrow, to his power and sway in strict accordance with the rights of a master. Note that (as I said before) not only its origin but also its end is evidently similar to that of the Babylonian Empire. That empire not many years after it was founded began to make peoples subject to itself. Rome in like manner, when it reached a sturdy maturity, by growing gradually — at first by conquering the neighboring cities, afterwards by spreading out to more distant regions — came, a step at a time, to the pinnacle of the world. But as no one becomes supreme suddenly or falls precipitately from the highest to the lowest place, so the aforesaid City, when it was, as I have said, at the very summit and could go no higher on earth, but deserved now to be brought low, began gradually to lose its strength and, as though it were now in its declining years, to suffer a diminution of the honor to which it had attained in its sturdy maturity. There was added, moreover, to crown its woes the change of the seat of government effected under Constantine (this is always the doom of transitory things). Just as, in the former case, when the seat of government was transferred to the Medes, the empire continued in name only, so too, when the power of the City had been diverted to the Greeks or to the Franks, barely a trace of its ancient dignity and name remained. The former empire was brought low by the prefect Arbaces and was afterwards conquered by Cyrus. Rome likewise was first dishonored by Alaric and afterwards taken possession of by Odovacar, who had all the rights of a master. But inasmuch as I have undertaken to write about the vicissitudes of history and the fall of empires to illustrate human misfortunes and the fluctuations of our unstable world, I will note this: just as Babylonia came to an end while Rome was being born (as, I remember, I said above), so now, while the kingdom of the Franks was, so to speak, being planted, Rome in its extreme old age under Augustulus — that is, in the one thousand two hundred and twenty-seventh year from its founding — was given over to the barbarians and threatend to fall.

32. At this point I think I must tell, as I promised above,[200] how the Franks, of whom I have made mention, came into the Gauls and by what means they severed themselves from the control of the Romans and began to be independent. They started, as

[200] I. 25.

I have said, from Troy. When they had established for themselves a home in Scythia they were called Sicambri. When the world had been made into a Roman province, and they too along with everyone else had been made subject to Rome, in the course of time they were called Franks by Valentinian for the reason which we have given above, and for ten years were left free to govern themselves. Upon the completion of this period, when the Romans demanded the customary tribute, the Franks — made imperious by liberty, as regularly happens — refused to give tribute. Now they had among them princes of ancient name and valor, Priam and Antenor. Wherefore when a war was made upon them by the Romans and Priam their king, together with many others, was killed, the remainder, effecting their escape, settled in the regions of Germany near Thuringia, with their princes, the sons of Priam and Antenor, Marcomir [201] and Sunno. Upon the death of Sunno they took counsel together and made Pharamond the son of Marcomir their king. From this time on they also began to have laws that were drawn up by Wisogastaldus and Salagastus. They say that the law which even today is called Salic, after his name, was framed by this Salagastus. This law the noblest of the Franks, who are called Salian, still use. Upon the death of Pharamond his son Clodion, who wore his hair long, succeeded him; from him the kings of the Franks were called "the longhaired." During these days, as I said above, when Francia was, so to speak, in process of being sown, Rome began gradually to decline. By this time the peoples that before had inhabited provinces of the Romans — not kingdoms — were learning to chose kings; now they were learning to break loose from the power of the Romans and to stand in the authority set up by their own discretion. After this the Goths, when they had plundered even the City itself, settled, as I have said, in the province of Gaul beyond the Loire. The Burgundians also lived near the Rhone and they too began to have kings not long after. So the Franks, crossing the Rhine, drove out the Romans who dwelt there and afterwards, having captured Tournai [202] and Cambrai (cities of Gaul) and having advanced little by little from those places, subjugated Rheims, Soissons, Orleans, Cologne,

[201] *Marcomede* in the text. For Marcomir and Sunno see C. M. H. 1. 256; for ''The Franks before Clovis,'' 1. 292-303.

[202] On the Scheldt, the capital of the Salian Franks in the middle of the fifth century.

Trèves and almost the whole of Gaul and Germany from Aquitania as far as Bavaria.

Upon the death of Clodion his son Merovech, from whom the Franks were called Merovingians, succeeded him. After him Childeric obtained the royal power; he was driven out by his people for living a licentious life and Aegidius, a Roman, was chosen in his place. But Childeric, being recalled after eight years, assailed Agrippina and, driving out the Romans who were adherents of Aegidius and settling his own followers there, called the place Colonia because the Franks colonized it. When Aegidius was dead his son Syagrius reigned in the city of Soissons. Childeric, departing this life, left the throne to his son Clovis.[203] This is the Clovis who was baptized by Saint Remigius and was the first Christian king of the Franks. But Syagrius, being unequal to fighting with Clovis, fled to Alaric who was then governing the kingdom of the Goths, the ninth in line from Alaric the Great. When Clovis demanded that he be given up, he was given up and put to death. The Romans who lived in the Gauls were exterminated so that no remnant of them is to be found there. It seems to me, therefore, that the Franks who dwell in the Gauls borrowed from the Romans the language which they still use today. For others who remained near the Rhine and in Germany use the Teutonic speech. What was previously their native tongue is unknown.

Clovis, after conquering the Alemanni, declared war upon the Goths also and the Aquitanians, when he had already become a Christian. While on his way to this war he vowed a vow to Saint Martin [204] and when he came back, after vanquishing the Goths and killing Alaric, he enriched the Church of Saint Martin. He desired then to redeem from the chamberlains his horse (which he had turned over to them) at the cost of one hundred *solidi*, but Martin remained obdurate. When he had recovered it by the additional payment of another hundred *solidi* he is said to have remarked: "Martin's a valuable aid, but dear at a trade."

33. Since we have touched briefly upon the period from Constantine down to the decline of this mighty empire, and to the weakening of the valiant Gothic race also, and more especially since we have come to the beginnings of the Franks, upon whom the sole rule afterwards devolved — because as Rome fell Francia arose

203 The founder of the Frankish state, 481-511; see C. M. H. 2. 109-116.
204 Bishop of Tours; his biography was composed by Sulpicius Severus.

to receive her crown — since, I say, we have written all this, being drawn away from the enticements of the present life by this remarkable newness and mutability of temporal affairs, and being drawn away even against our will from the contemplation of our present woes to the quest of the unchanging heavenly country, let us set an end to this fourth book that we may the more readily relate what is to follow.

HERE ENDS THE FOURTH BOOK

THE PROLOGUE OF THE FIFTH BOOK [1]

As part of the fundamentals, like the alphabet and the rules of the art of grammar, children are usually told that the younger they are so much the more observant they are. This I think is not inaptly said, since we are on the one hand trained by the writings and institutions of our ancestors, who devoted themselves to wisdom before us, and by the passage of time and the resultant experience in life, yes, trained the more quickly the more advanced the age of the world is in which we are set; on the other hand, after mastering for ourselves the things that were discovered before us, we can devise new things with the same inspiration as those of old.[2] The prophet foresaw that, in the old age of the world (for the reasons which I have mentioned), wisdom must be multiplied; and so he said: "Many shall run to and fro, and knowledge shall be increased."[3] That is why, though our ancestors were men renowned for wisdom and of notable ability, the causes of many things lay hidden from them which have begun to be revealed to us through the lapse of time and the course of events. And so all now see to what the Roman Empire came — that Empire which, because of its preëminence, was thought by the pagans to be eternal and even by our people to be almost divine.

As I said above, all human power or wisdom, originating in the East, began to reach its limits in the West. Regarding human power — how it passed from the Babylonians to the Medes and the Persians and from them to the Macedonians, and after that to the Romans and then again to the Greeks under the Roman name — I think enough has been said. How it was transferred from the Greeks to the Franks, who dwell in the West, remains to be told in the present book. That wisdom was found first in the East (that

[1] In Book V, Otto brings his account of universal history down from the days of Theodoric the Great (493) to the division of the kingdom of the Franks by the Treaty of Verdun in 843. His chief source for this period is Frutolf's *Chronicle,* but there are also many paragraphs based upon Regino. The *Getica* of Jordanes is still followed in the opening chapters, and there are Scriptural citations throughout the book.

[2] *Cf.* what Otto adduced from Aristotle in II. 8 above.

[3] Dan. 12. 4.

is, in Babylonia) and was carried thence into Egypt, because Abraham went down to Egypt in a time of famine, Josephus makes clear in the first book of his *Antiquities,* speaking as follows concerning Abraham: "He bestowed on them a knowledge of arithmetic and himself delivered over to them also all the lore of astronomy. For before Abraham the Egyptians were absolutely ignorant of these things."[4] That wisdom passed from Egypt to the Greeks in the time of the philosophers the same author indicates in these words: "For these are known to have been implanted by the Chaldeans in Egypt, whence also they are said to have made their way to the Greeks." Thus far Josephus. From the Greeks it appears to have been carried to the Romans, under the Scipios, Cato and Tullius, and especially in the times of the Caesars, when a group of poets sang songs of many kinds, and afterwards to the extreme West — that is, to the Gauls and the Spains — very recently, in the days of those illustrious scholars Berengar,[5] Manegold[6] and Anselm.[7] Men divinely inspired were able to foresee and as it were to have a vision of these things. But we are in position not merely to believe but also actually to see the things which were predicted, since we behold the world (which, they predicted, was to be despised for its changeableness) already failing and, so to speak, drawing the last breath of extremest old age.

Furthermore, enough has been said above, I think, regarding the two cities: how one made progress, first by remaining hidden in the other until the coming of Christ, after that by advancing gradually to the time of Constantine. But after Constantine, when troubles from without had finally ceased, it began to be grievously troubled at the instigation of the devil by internal strife even to the time of the Elder Theodosius; Arius was the author of this and the lords of the world, the Augusti, were his coadjutors. But from that time on, since not only all the people but also the emperors (except a few) were orthodox Catholics, I seem to myself to have

[4] 1.8.2 (Whiston).

[5] Berengar of Tours, 999-1088.

[6] Of Lautenbach, d. after 1103; *cf.* Endres, *Histor. Jahrbuch* 25 (1905), pp. 168 *et seq.*

[7] Hofmeister is undoubtedly correct in thinking that Anselm of Laon (d. 1117) rather than Anselm, archbishop of Canterbury, is meant. *Cf.* v. G. Lefèvre, *De Anselmo Laudunensi scolastico,* (1895), and see *Gesta Friderici* 1.49 and 52.

composed a history not of two cities but virtually of one only, which I call the Church. For although the elect and the reprobate are in one household, yet I cannot call these cities two as I did above; I must call them properly but one — composite, however, as the grain is mixed with the chaff.[8] Wherefore in the books that follow let us pursue the course of history which we have begun. Since not only emperors of the Romans but also other kings (kings of renowned realms) became Christians, inasmuch as the sound of the word of God went out into all the earth and unto the ends of the world, the City of Earth was laid to rest and destined to be utterly exterminated in the end; hence our history is a history of the City of Christ, but that city, so long as it is in the land of sojourn,[9] is "like unto a net, that was cast into the sea,"[10] containing the good and the bad.[11] However, the faithless city of unbelieving Jews and Gentiles still remains, but, since nobler kingdoms have been won by our people, while these unbelieving Jews and Gentiles are insignificant not only in the sight of God but even in that of the world, hardly anything done by these unbelievers is found to be worthy of record or to be handed on to posterity.

Here Begins the Fifth Book

1. When the empire of the Romans had been seized by the barbarians, Zeno Augustus entrusted the government of the West to Theodoric, king of the Ostrogoths, the twelfth[12] in line from Ermanarich, earnestly commending to his keeping the senate and the Roman people. When Theodoric was proceeding on his way toward Italy with the forces of the Goths and had encamped near the river Isonzo, in the territory of the Aquileians, Odovacar met him with a great army but was put to flight. After that, when Theodoric had taken up a position near Verona, Odovacar again ventured a battle and was again forced to flee. Broken in spirit by these defeats, Odovacar directed his course toward the City. But the gates were closed against him and an entrance was denied him; however, having devastated the whole surrounding country with fire and sword, he withdrew to Ravenna. Theodoric followed him

---

[8] *Cf.* below, Prol., VII (end); Prol., VIII (beginning).

[9] *Cf.*, for example, Augustine 5. 16; Hashagen, *Otto von Freising* 51, note 1.

[10] Matt. 13. 47.

[11] *Cf.* Prol., VII (end) and Prol., VIII (beginning) below.

[12] The seventh, according to Jordanes and Frutolf.

and for three years besieged him; and when he finally received his submission,[13] though he had pledged his word to spare him, he treacherously murdered him. But the Rugians, the allies of Odovacar, were devastating Ticinum (over which Saint Epiphanius then presided) and the surrounding country as well. This bishop was a man of such holy life that, when he was sent by Theodoric to Gundobad, king of Burgundy, to redeem captives, six thousand captives are said to have been restored to him by the king solely out of reverence for his piety. After killing Odovacar, Theodoric turned aside to the City and was received with great joy on the part of the citizens.

Behold a state miserably overthrown; see a people that once, because of its wisdom and its strength, was master of the world reduced to such weakness that, when trodden underfoot by a tyranny of the barbarians and enslaved under a grievous despotism, it cannot be freed save by a barbarian; mark how it receives a tyrant with submission and with gratitude in order to escape the overlordship of another tyrant!

Theodoric, having gained the sovereignty over the Romans, was unmindful of the charge imposed upon him by Augustus and, confusing right and wrong (after the manner of a barbarian) and insolently inflicting divers injuries upon the people, turned his rule into a tyranny.[14] Anicius Manlius Boëthius,[15] a most illustrious man of the consular order, noting this and considering it thoughtfully, planned to thwart his tyranny but was driven into exile by Theodoric and imprisoned at Pavia. There he wrote a very valuable philosophical work on contempt for the world. There are extant besides this other famous writings of his. Among these he has left a work as useful to the Church of God as it is subtle, directed against Sabellius and Arius with regard to the rules of faith in the Holy Trinity, and against the Nestorian and the Eutychian heresies. He also translated books of Aristotle [16] from the Greek into

---

13 Theodoric's conquest of Italy was achieved between 490 and 493.

14 Other medieval chroniclers agree in this picture of Theodoric's reign. *Cf*. Frutolf, p. 129, and Regino, p. 20.

15 Consul in 510 and author of the well-known work *De consolatione philosophiae*, which he wrote in prison. He was put to death in 524.

16 The question of the translation of Aristotle's logical treatises by Boëthius is the subject of much dispute. Only the *Categories* and *De Interpretatione* were known prior to the twelfth century. The *Prior* and *Posterior Analytics*, the *Topics* and the *Elenchi* were translated, probably in 1128, by

the Latin tongue, and either translated or composed a great many
commentaries to aid in their study. As an introduction to Aristotle's *Topics,* furthermore, he wrote a book about the topics and
species.

Theodoric, recognizing the fact that he was an alien and desiring
to strengthen his sovereignty — acquired in such a questionable
way — took in marriage a daughter of Clovis, king of the Franks,[17]
and married his sister Amalafrida to the king of the Vandals. His
two daughters he bestowed, the one upon Sigismund king of the
Burgundians, the other upon Alaric king of the Visigoths. This is
the Alaric who (as we said by anticipation in the preceding book)
was afterwards killed by Clovis when the Goths were defeated.

2. In the four hundred and ninety-first year from the incarnation of the Lord, in the reign of Clovis, the sixth king of the
Franks in line from Pharamond, Zeno died in the seventeenth year
of his reign. When his brother Longinus was preparing to succeed
him he was repulsed by Ariadne, and by her advice Anastasius, the
forty-ninth in line from Augustus, obtained the throne with the
consent of all and chose Ariadne as his wife. Now when Anastasius,
a Eutychian, was reigning in the East and Theodoric, an Arian,
was oppressing Rome, a great controversy arose in the Church of
God since Symmachus and Laurentius contended for the pontiff's
chair in the City. When this dispute had been protracted for three
years without cessation and the blood of many priests and laymen
had been shed, Theodoric put an end to it by convoking a synod.
For he established Symmachus in the see as having been elected
by the wiser counsel. He deposed Laurentius but made him bishop
in Luceria.[18] Later, when Laurentius caused a popular disturbance,
Symmachus relegated him by banishment to Dalmatia. In this
schism Paschasius,[19] a deacon — a man who had the zeal of the

one James of Venice. This has led some students to deny that Boëthius ever
translated the latter works. In his *Studies in the History of Medieval Science*
Professor C. H. Haskins throws new light on the subject from MS sources.
The gist of his argument is that both Boëthius and James translated the
works in question. *Vide* Chap. XI, esp. pp. 225-233.

[17] It was not Clovis's daughter but his sister, Audefleda, whom Theodoric
married. See Gregory of Tours, *Historia Francorum* 2. 31.

[18] This is an error; it should be Nuceria.

[19] See Gregory, *Dialogue* 4.40. We still have a letter from Paschasius to
Eugippius, the author of the Life of St. Severinus, protesting his inability to
improve upon this work and urging the writer to publish it without change.

Lord but not according to wisdom — upheld Laurentius; for this, as Saint Gregory states in his Dialogue, he paid the penalty after his death, even though he was a man of such holiness that, when he was dead, a blind man obtained his sight by placing his woolen undergarment on his bier. In these days Thrasamund, the son of Gaiseric king of the Vandals, sent two hundred and twenty bishops into exile to the island of Sardinia for their adherence to the Catholic faith. At that time Bishop Fulgentius was considered notable and renowned for his life and wisdom. Throughout this same time also, while in Africa a certain Arian named Olimpius was uttering shameful and blasphemous words about God, he was struck by a fiery sword from heaven while he was bathing. When a certain person wished to be baptized by a bishop of this same heresy, as the heretic said, "I baptize thee in the name of the Father, through the Son, in the Holy Spirit," suddenly the water was no longer visible. Upon seeing this the man who was to have been baptized fled to a church and received baptism according to the rule of the Catholic Church. Anastasius offered the dignity of the consulship to King Clovis by a letter. In spite of the admonition of Pope Hormisdas, Anastasius did not withdraw from the Eutychian heresy but stubbornly persisted in it. He died in the twenty-eighth year of his reign, struck by lightning some say. Clovis also reached the end of his life and reign in the thirtieth year, and left four sons, one of whom was named Chlotar,[20] who divided the government among them.

3. In the five hundred and nineteenth year from the incarnation of the Lord, while Chlotar was reigning with his brothers in Francia, Justin,[21] an old man — by race an Isaurian or an Illyrian, the fiftieth in line from Augustus — obtained the imperial power with the consent of the senate. In his time Hilderic, the son of Thrasamund by Eudoxia, obtained the throne. Since he was a Catholic he recalled all the bishops who had been sent away into exile by his father. Moreover, Augustus Justin persecuted the heretics with the zeal of faith. Theodoric the Arian sent to him Pope John, with a threat that if he did not cease from the persecution of the Arians, he [Theodoric] would bring affliction upon the Christians; but after

20 He succeeded to the throne with his three brothers, Theodoric (Thierry), Clodomir and Childebert, in 511.

21 Justin I, Emperor of the East (518-527), the uncle of Justinian, who succeeded him.

the emperor, moved to compassion by the entreaties of the priest, granted this and dismissed him honorably, even as he had received him with honor, Theodoric placed John in chains on his return and sacrilegiously let him die of starvation. Before this he had cruelly killed Symmachus the Patrician and Boëthius, a most noble senator, of whom I made mention above. For these deeds he was carried off by sudden death not many days later, in the thirtieth year of his reign. According to the Dialogue of Gregory he was seen by a certain man of God to be cast into Etna by John and Symmachus. This story is, I think, the source of that tale which is current generally, that Theodoric descended to the world of shades alive, seated on his horse.[22] However, another statement that men make, that he was a contemporary of Ermanarich [23] and Attila, cannot be true at all, for it is an established fact that Attila wielded his power as tyrant long after Ermanarich; and Theodoric, after the death of Attila, was handed over by his father to Augustus Leo as a hostage when he was but a boy eight years old. Upon the death of Theodoric, Athalarich [24] the son of Theodoric's daughter Amalasuntha, a boy of ten, took the helm of state. His father, while he yet lived,[25] had commended this boy to the princes of the Goths, exhorting them to love the senate and the people of Rome, and to strive to keep the Emperor of the East well-disposed. Justin reached the end of his life in the eighth year of his reign, after designating Justinian, his sister's son, as his successor on the throne.

4. In the five hundred and twenty-seventh year from the incarnation of the Lord, Justinian, the fifty-first in line from Augustus, obtained the imperial power while the sons of Clovis were still reigning in Francia. This most zealous and Christian monarch resurrected his domain, as it were, from the dead. The state, which had been in large part overthrown, he reëstablished and among other brave and valiant deeds triumphed gloriously, through Patrician Belisarius, over the Persians who had invaded the Roman territories. The laws published before his time had been put together in loose fashion with no semblance of order. Justinian made a compendium of all these laws. This he reduced to order and published

[22] Cf. Müllenhoff, *Zeitschrift für deutsches Altertum* 12 (1865), 330 et seq.; O. L. Jiriczek, *Deutsche Heldensagen* 1 (1898), 268 et seq.

[23] Or Hermanaric. He ruled over the Ostrogoths from 351 to 376.

[24] Or Athalaric. He ruled from 526 to 534. *Cf.* the *Romana* 367 and *Getica* 59. 304.

[25] Jordanes and Frutolf tell this story of his grandfather, Theodoric.

in a single volume, a volume which to this day is called after Justinian the *Leges Justinianae*. He adorned the Church of God also with many beautiful basilicas throughout the length and breadth of his domain: among others was one in the Royal City, a basilica preëminent for its material and its workmanship, in honor of wisdom divine, called by the Greeks *Sophia*. He also caused the king of the Heruli, Grates by name, who came to him at Constantinople, to be baptized at the festival of the Epiphany of the Lord. At that time also Garda, king of the Huns, and a certain widow woman of the Huns with a hundred thousand of their race are said to have accepted the faith and to have received the sacrament of baptism.

Now Athalarich, entrusting himself (still a young man) and his mother, a widow, to Augustus, in accordance with his father's behest, was taken under his care by that most considerate prince. But when Athalarich was killed not long after by his own people, his mother associated Theodahad with herself in the government. Theodahad (acting the part, I will not say of an ingrate but of a disloyal, treacherous soldier) strangled her in the bath. Therefore Justinian despatched Patrician Belisarius first into Africa and after destroying the Vandals freed that province from the barbarians and restored it to Roman control. Afterwards, when he sent Belisarius against Theodahad as a traitor and an assailant of the empire, the tyrant, losing heart, sent Pope Agapetus to him to seek peace. Agapetus won back to the Catholic faith the emperor, who had been deceived by the folly of Eutyches. Besides this, Agapetus excommunicated Anthemius, bishop of the Royal City, for defending the same heresy. He then brought his life to a close there and departed to the Lord. This pope [26] was a man of such holiness that he gave sight to a blind man in the gateway of the Royal City just as he was entering it on his way to see the emperor. Meanwhile, Belisarius put Theodahad to death,[27] compelling him to pay the penalty for his perfidy. He sent as a prisoner to Constantinople Witigis, who usurped the throne after the death of Theodahad, and brought to an end the kingdom of the Goths which, so Jordanes records, had endured for two thousand years or more. And so,

26 Otto has mistakenly transferred to Agapetus what we read in Frutolf, on the year 524, concerning Pope Joan.

27 Hofmeister thinks that this error of Bishop Otto may have arisen from Frutolf's words on p. 140. 5. It was Vitiges, armor-bearer of Theodahad, who slew him, when made king by the Goths themselves. Vitiges (or Witigis) reigned from 536 to 540.

having rooted out the Vandals from Africa and the Goths from Italy, he restored both provinces to their former status. To this point Bishop Jordanes,[28] a Goth by nationality (as he himself records), carried his history of the Goths and his Chronicles.

Belisarius engaged in battle with Theodebert, king of the Franks, the brother of Chlotar,[29] who had invaded Italy with two hundred thousand men. When the Franks asked for peace he granted it, and without the loss of a Roman soldier persuaded them to depart from the borders of Italy. Meanwhile the Parthians, devastating Syria and Neo-Caesarea with an army, were marching on Antioch. Since Patrician Germanus and his son, the consul Justin, were not strong enough to fight it out with them, they abandoned the city and withdrew to the region of Cilicia. The Persians burst into Antioch as easily as if it were empty, carried off booty, devastated the neighboring cities, and within a year's time destroyed the property of all Coele Syria. Belisarius, who had conquered Goths and Vandals, gathering an army checked them and forced them to depart from the territories of the Romans. But since the Goths under their king, Totila,[30] were breaking out again and causing a disturbance, he had not time to remain there and so turned back to Italy.

In these days the Lombard tribes — who had come, as had the Goths, from the island of Scandza [31] — dwelt in Pannonia with Alboin, their king. Not long after they seized Italy, which they still inhabit, as will be told hereafter.

Belisarius, remaining in Italy, unwillingly sent into exile Pope Silverius upon testimony of lying witnesses. He did this at the advice of Augusta Theodora, because he was unwilling to free from excommunication the heretic Anthemius who had been excommunicated by Belisarius's predecessor, Agapetus. Belisarius did a like thing to Silverius's successor Vigilius, under whom the fifth general synod had been convoked at Constantinople.[32]

Under this pope, Arator, a sub-deacon, composed in verse an anthology of the Acts of the Apostles. During the same time Cas-

[28] On the ecclesiastical condition of Jordanes, see *The Gothic History of Jordanes*, by Charles C. Mierow (1915), Introduction, pp. 5-10.

[29] He was his brother's son; *cf.* Frutolf, p. 115. 35. But Jordanes (*Getica* 57. 296) mistakenly includes him among the sons of Clovis. See also Gregory of Tours 3. 1.

[30] He reigned from 541 to 552.

[31] *I.e.*, the Scandinavian peninsula.

[32] The Fifth Œcumenical Council, held at Constantinople in 553.

siodorus Senator [33] and the Abbot Dionysius flourished. The former wrote a brilliant exposition of the Psalms, the latter subtly composed the Easter Cycles. By way of showing his devotion to Julian, Priscian [34] of Caesarea dedicated to him as Consul and Patrician his books on the art of grammar, a toilsome work, prolix but useful. In these days also Saint Benedict, at first a hermit but afterwards an abbot, was held in esteem for his signs and wonders and his abstemious life. He instructed many by word and by example, and aroused in them a desire for the way of a more rigorous life, composing, as Gregory says, ''a rule for the monks clear in expression and rare in discretion.'' [35] This is known to be still in great repute in the Church. If anyone desires to know what other princes or citizens of the City of Christ were at that time renowned for their manner of life and their wisdom, let him read the *Dialogue* of Gregory.

The body of Saint Antonius was found and buried at Alexandria. The emperor Justinian, an illustrious ruler, having exalted the state as greatly as the times allowed, brought his life to a close in the thirty-ninth year of his reign. To this point Victor, bishop of Tours,[36] carried his Chronicles.

5. In the five hundred and sixty-seventh year from the incarnation of the Lord — while Chilperic, the son of Chlotar, was reigning with his three brothers in Francia — Justin the Younger,[37] a nephew of Justinian and a Thracian by race, was the fifty-second in line from Augustus to obtain the imperial power. The Patriarch Eutychius crowned him. Since he was a Catholic he enriched with priceless treasures and abounding possessions the churches of God which his predecessor had built. In his time the peace between the Romans and the Persians was broken. The emperor sent Julian to Arethas,[38] king of India. Julian reported that he had found

[33] He lived from about 487 to about 583, and was one of the most eminent men of his time.

[34] Author of the most complete work on Latin Grammar which we possess: *Institutio de arte grammatica,* in 18 books. Otto made use of this authority himself: *cf.* above, II. 8 and Prol., V (beginning).

[35] *Dialogue* 2. 36.

[36] Not of Tours but of Tunnuna in Africa. Mommsen (*MG., Auct. Ant.* 11. 175) has shown that Otto's source here is the preface of Isidore's *Chronica maiora* (or of the *Annales Hildesheimenses,* which contain a transcription of Isidore's *Chronica*).

[37] Justin II, 565-578.

[38] To persuade Arethas, who reigned in Abyssinia (not India) over the

Arethas almost naked, having about his loins only a girdle and linen cloths inwrought with gold, and over his stomach a tenuous garment held together by precious pearls; he wore on each of his arms five circlets and armlets of gold, on his head a cloth adorned with jewels, about his neck a golden necklace; he stood in a high four-wheeled car supported by four elephants and held a diminutive gilded shield and two small golden darts. When Julian had armed him against the king of the Persians he returned. Julian sent Narses [39] against Totila, king of the Goths, and with the aid of the Lombards killed him and utterly extirpated that tribe from Italy. Narses slew Bucelin [40] who had been sent by the king of the Franks to devastate Italy. Sindoaldus, king of the Brendi, who was the sole survivor of Odovacar's Counts in Italy, he hanged. And so when Patrician Narses, by destroying the barbarians, had restored Italy to her former condition, the Romans — as was usually the case — grew jealous of his success and sent a deputation to the emperor and to his wife Sophia, accusing him of many things. The emperor, troubled thereby, sent Longinus to Italy to take his place. Augusta Sophia too, in the manner of a woman taunting Narses, who was a eunuch, declared that she would put him in her seraglio among the women. Narses, greatly enraged at all this, withdrew to Naples and sent an embassy to call the Lombards from Pannonia into Italy. Extraordinary portents preceded their coming; as Saint Gregory testifies, fiery battle lines were seen in the heavens, together with the blood which was presently to be shed. Thereafter Rome lost not only the Transalpine territory but also the part of Italy itself which from that time down to the present day has been called Lombardy, after the barbarians who settled there. Justin adopted Count Tiberius as his son and appointed him Caesar. When Justin lay in bed suffering from the gout and realized that he was going to die, summoning into his presence the pontiff Eutychius and the senate he advanced Tiberius from the rank of Caesar to that of Augustus. Justin died in the eleventh year of his reign.

6. In the five hundred and seventy-sixth year from the incarnation of the Lord, Tiberius Constantine, a Thracian by race, was

Axumite kingdom, to break faith with his Persian overlord. This was in 572. See C. M. H. 2. 271.

[39] The successor of Belisarius. The defeat of the Ostrogoths and the death of Totila occurred in 552.

[40] The chiefs of the Alemanni, Leutharis and Bucelin, invaded Italy in 553. Bucelin was defeated the following year near Capua.

crowned by the patriarch Eutychius and became the fifty-third emperor in line from Augustus. Since he styled his wife Anastasia "Augusta," Sophia, the wife of his predecessor, became very indignant because she had expected to be united in marriage with him, and so she persuaded Justinian to aspire to the throne. But when the plot proved incapable of accomplishment the emperor took Justinian, indeed, back into favor because he had been bribed by him; but he compelled Sophia to live as an ordinary subject, taking from her all the prerogatives of sovereignty. The ill-gotten treasures which Justin had stored away he bestowed lavishly upon the poor. The story is told of him that, while he was walking about in his palace and saw a cross graven in the pavement, he ordered it to be removed, reverently saying: "We ought to wear the cross of the Lord on our brows, not to trample it under our feet." When after this cross was removed a second appeared, and after the second in its turn had been taken out a third had been found, he is said to have discovered a vast treasure of gold. It is also recorded that, upon the death of Patrician Narses, he found a great deal of gold and silver in a well. All of this, according to his custom, he lavished upon the poor. In him is seen fulfilled the saying of the Lord, "To him that hath shall be given," for while he was bountifully distributing his substance in the service of Christ he ever received from Him bountiful supplies. Again, when Italy had been devastated by the Lombards, under Pope Benedict, and Rome was suffering severely from famine, he bestowed many thousands of bushels of grain upon the citizens, sending ships from Egypt. Through Duke Maurice he gloriously defeated the Persians,[41] who were overrunning the boundaries of his empire, and afterwards gave him his daughter in marriage and bestowed upon him the rank of Caesar. To Chilperic, king of the Franks, he sent magnificent gifts. In these days Saint Gregory,[42] archdeacon of the church at Rome, having been sent to Constantinople by Pope Pelagius, wrote and dedicated to Leander his *Moralia*, a commentary on Job, and in the presence of the emperor convinced Eutychius, bishop of that city, that he had erred in his belief regarding the resurrection. The most Christian emperor Tiberius rested in peace in the seventh year

[41] In 578 Maurice invaded Arzanene and captured the fortress of Aphoumon. He was made Caesar in 582.

[42] Afterwards Pope Gregory I. The work here referred to is *Expositio in librum b. Iob, sive Moralium libri XXXV*. It was dedicated to Leander of Seville.

of his reign, after choosing, by the advice of Sophia, his son-in-law Maurice as emperor in his stead.

7. In the five hundred and eighty-third year from the incarnation of the Lord, Maurice, a Cappadocian — the first emperor who was a Greek by race and the fifty-fourth in line from Augustus — obtained the throne. In his time Saint Gregory, a true citizen of the City of God, with the consent of the emperor of Rome was chosen pope by the clergy and the people and ordained. However, the emperor, being a man of insatiate avarice, persecuted him grievously in his quest of money.

At that time the man of God Columban, of the race of the Irish and Abbot of Luxeuil, because in his zeal for God he had taxed Brunhild, the queen of the Burgundians, with very evil and vicious deeds, was compelled to leave his monastery and go into Italy to a place which is called Bobbio and to remain there to the day of his death, even as the just Elijah suffered grievous persecution at the hands of Jezebel. His pupils were most illustrious citizens of the kingdom of Christ: Leodegar [Léger],[43] who afterwards, while he was bishop of the church at Autun,[44] was crowned with martyrdom; Romaricus, who founded a celebrated convent for consecrated virgins on a mountain which is called from his own name Remiremont; Gallus [45] who, dwelling in Suevia in the territory of Constance, holds a church famous by the power of his name and which, as we have seen, has only recently been enriched by many honors and treasures; and many others. Tradition has it that the aforesaid man of God [Léger] became the father of three hundred monks. All of them, following the admonitions of their father (all except Ebroin)[46] are believed to have been enrolled among the citizens of Christ. Ebroin was the only one of them all who was enticed by Brunhild by means of transitory honors; he alone turned back and entered military service. He was made Mayor of the Palace, afflicted the aforesaid servants of God with many evils, and made the blessed Leodegar [Léger] a martyr. But Brunhild, paying the penalty for her crimes, was afterwards tied by King Chlotar to the tails of

[43] Hofmeister points out that Otto is confused in his dates; Léger had not yet been born when Columban died in 615.

[44] Not of Auxerre (*Autisiodorensem*) as Otto states.

[45] Founder of the monastery of St. Gall on the shores of the Lake of Constance.

[46] See C. M. H. 2. 126. Otto is in error when he says that Ebroin was "enticed by Brunhild by transitory honors." He lived long after her time.

wild horses and ended her life most wretchedly, leaving to us a warning that we should shrink from cruelty.

But Maurice, since he persisted in persecuting the most blessed Pope Gregory, in the nineteenth year of his reign saw in his sleep a man clad in the garb of a monk, and with a sword in his hand, advancing menacingly upon him and declaring unmistakably that he must die. Terror-struck at the sight, he reviewed his crimes and humbly wrote both to Pope Gregory and to other bishops, abbots and hermits begging them to implore God, on his behalf, that he might be allowed to pay the penalty for his sins in this present life, not in the life to come, and to win God over by their entreaties. He himself, with many tears, proffered the same request to God. When therefore God, at the petition of the Church, wished the emperor to give heed, Maurice in his sleep beheld himself standing in the presence of the Crucified at the brazen gate of his palace and listening to a terrible voice, "Bring me Maurice," and again, "When do you wish that I should punish you for the evils you have done, in this life or in the life to come?" And when Maurice replied, "Not in the life to come," the voice gave command that Maurice with his wife and children and all his kin should be given over to Phocas. When day broke Maurice summoned into his presence his son-in-law Philippicus and, after narrating his dream, inquired if he knew Phocas. After deliberating a little in silence Philippicus said, "He is a young man, and rash." The messengers also whom he had sent to men of God on their return brought like answers to his vision. Moreover an army which had been sent out by Maurice mutinied because of its sufferings from hunger as a result of his avarice, and proclaimed Phocas emperor. Maurice fled on hearing this, since he had a presentiment that the things pointed out to him in the vision would be fulfilled. Phocas followed him and in accordance with the prediction of the vision beheaded him as he humbly admitted his guilt, near Chalcedon, with his wife and sons. This was in the twenty-first year of his reign. It is said that, when he was beheaded, milk flowed out with the blood, a sign that is interpreted as a token of pardon obtained from the Lord.

8. In the six hundred and third year from the incarnation of the Lord, Phocas, the fifty-fifth in line from Augustus, obtained the throne. He had a wife named Leontia. He was originally the groom of a certain Patrician; afterwards he was a soldier and finally emperor. In the second year of his reign the most blessed Pope Greg-

ory, who had brightly illumined the City of God by precept and example, departed to the Lord leaving his writings as most delightful memorials. Boniface, the third pope to succeed him, pressed successfully upon Phocas a plea that by his authority the Roman Church should be called the head over all the Churches. He made this plea because the Church at Constantinople kept writing that it was the first in rank, I suppose because the seat of government had been transferred to that place. After this Boniface another Boniface, the fourth in line from the blessed Gregory, by his entreaties prevailed on the same Augustus to allow the temple that had been built by the emperor Domitian, a temple called the Pantheon,[47] to be given to the Church of God and dedicated in honor of all the saints. During these days Chosroes [48] king of the Persians, roving through the East, robbed the Romans of many provinces and, carrying off from Jerusalem the standard of the life-giving Cross, set it up in his own land where he had compelled his subjects to worship him as a god. Phocas, after perpetrating many crimes and murders, was put to death in the eighth year of his reign by Heraclius the son of Patrician Heraclius, exarch [49] of Africa, at the instigation of Patrician Priscus his own son-in-law.

9. In the six hundred and twelfth year from the incarnation of the Lord, after Phocas had been slain, Heraclius, the fifty-sixth in line from Augustus, obtained the throne. He was crowned by the patriarch Sergius while Chlotar, the son of Chilperic, was reigning in Francia. In the second year of his reign he had by Eudocia a son called Heraclius, or perhaps Constantine. But upon the death of Eudocia he had an incestuous union with Martina, his own sister's daughter, and by her became the father of Heraclonas. It was to this point that Bishop Isidore carried his history. Inasmuch as in the eighth year of his reign he asked for peace from Chosroes, king of the Persians, and did not obtain it, in the fourth year thereafter — in the twelfth year of Heraclius reign — he moved his forces against Persia and, having killed the son of Chosroes in single combat on a bridge over the Danube, he laid Persia waste and killed Chosroes, taking also from his profane hands the wood of the Holy Cross. Finally, in the seventh year from the time he

---

[47] The Pantheon — originally built by Agrippa in 27 B.C. — was burned in 80 A.D. and restored by Domitian.

[48] The second of that name, 589-628.

[49] The text reads *pretoris*.

had set out, he returned as victor to the Royal City and not long afterwards restored to Jerusalem the Wood, bringer of Salvation. From this time forth the elevation of the Holy Cross began to be celebrated in the Church of God.

During these days the Persian Anastasius, who was at first a Magian but afterwards accepted the faith and became a monk, suffered a glorious martyrdom for Christ at the hands of the Persians, together with seventy others. Marzabonas acted then as judge. A man possessed of a demon presently put on the tunic of Anastasius and so was cured. Heraclius brought back Anastasius's body with the captives from Persia, and gave it honorable burial in the monastery of Saint Paul which is called *Aquae Salviae*. At this monastery, as is well known,[50] there is now a group of holy monks called after Anastasius. About the same time Mahomet,[51] whom the Saracens hold in reverence to this day, is said to have lived. He was of the stock of Ishmael by a Gentile father and a Jewish mother.

During these days, upon the death of Chlotar, Dagobert, still a mere boy, who had been brought up by the blessed Arnulf,[52] Mayor of the Palace (who was afterwards Bishop of Metz), obtained the sole rule in Francia except that he entrusted to his brother Charibert certain cities and villages along the Loire. From Clovis's time even to this time the kingdom of the Franks had been divided into many parts among sons and sons' sons, with the result that its government was in great confusion.[53] The territory of the Franks by this time extended from Spain even to Pannonia; it included two very famous dukedoms, Aquitaine and Bavaria — Aquitaine

---

[50] It was in 1140 that Pope Innocent II offered the monastery of Saints Vincent and Anastasius, at *Aquae Salviae*, to Bernard of Clairvaux of the order of Cistercians. He made Bernard of Pisa (who afterwards became Pope Eugenius III) its Abbot; *cf.* P. F. Kehr, *Italia pontificia* 1. 170. *Aquae Salviae* is near Rome.

[51] Or Muhammad, 570-632. See Chapter X (pp. 302-328) in C. M. H. 2. With reference to the statement in the text that his mother was a Jewess, Hofmeister declares that he is able to find this nowhere else save in authors who have borrowed it from Otto's Chronicle.

[52] Joint founder, with Pepin I, of the Carolingian dynasty. From 687 until 751 the Mayors of the Palace (an office which had become hereditary in this family) were the real rulers of the Frankish kingdom.

[53] See, *e.g.*, the *History of the Franks* by Gregory of Tours, translated in part by Ernest Brehaut in *Records of Civilization*, or the account in C. M. H. 2. 116-125.

to the west, Bavaria to the east. Since Dagobert held imperial sway over the whole kingdom he gave laws to the Bavarians. When, during the lifetime of his father Chlotar, he had entered upon a battle with the Saxons and had been severely wounded, he sent a messenger to his father and upon receiving aid from him again took up the struggle. Having conquered the Saxons and put them to flight he brought the whole province under his jurisdiction. It is said that he put to death all the males of that race whose stature exceeded the length of the sword which he happened to be wearing at the moment. At that time the blessed Cunibert governed the Church at Cologne.

Now Heraclius, led astray by the patriarch Sergius, became a Eutychian heretic. He also became a mathematician and an astrologer. Since he foresaw in the stars that "the circumcised" would lay waste his empire, he supposed that the Jews were meant and so he sent messengers to Dagobert, king of the Franks, demanding that all the Jews in his kingdom should be baptized. He was successful in this plan and did the same thing in his own kingdom. Not long afterwards the Saracens, a circumcised race, laid waste his empire. When Heraclius sent an army and tried to hold them in check he lost one hundred and fifty thousand men. When on this account he opened the Caspian Gates [54] and led forth through them that most savage race [55] which, on account of its cruelty, Alexander the Great had shut up north of the Caspian Sea, and so renewed the war, in one night fifty-two thousand men of his army, it is said, were smitten by an angel of the Lord. The emperor was brokenhearted at this calamity and fell into frenzy in his grief. Becoming dropsical he brought his life to a close in the twenty-seventh year of his reign. Mark the righteous judgments of God. The emperor who at first, by the virtue of the Cross, triumphed over the most powerful king of the Persians, afterwards, when he lost his soldiers at the hands of the Saracens, reft of reason because of his grief and forgetful of that sign by which he had before conquered, thoughtlessly led forth a most cruel race — a race which even a pagan had shut up — and was therefore justly punished by the Lord, in order that a place for repentance might be left for him and that he might become a warning and a reproof to posterity.

[54] At the foot of the Caucasus on the boundary of the two empires.

[55] The reference here is to the Avars, one of the great waves of Asiatic nomads that periodically broke over Europe during ancient and medieval times.

All these things ought to incite us to contempt for the world and to love of God, for God rewards those that hope in Him and condemns those that hold Him lightly.

10. In the six hundred and thirty-ninth year from the incarnation of the Lord, while Dagobert was reigning in Francia, Constantine Heraclius,[56] the son of Heraclius, the fifty-seventh in line from Augustus, obtained the throne. In the fourth month of his reign he was killed by poison through the treachery of his stepmother Martina and the patriarch Pyrrhus; Martina herself, aided by her son Heraclonas,[57] usurped the throne and held it for two years. Then Constans,[58] the son of Constantine, the son of Heraclius, mutilated the nose of the son and cut out the tongue of the mother and was made emperor by the senate. Further, Pyrrhus the patriarch, the instigator of the crime, was driven into exile and Paul was chosen to fill his place. This is the Pyrrhus who, in conjunction with Cyrus bishop of Alexandria, founded the heresy which denied the two wills in Christ.

11. In the six hundred and forty-second year from the incarnation of the Lord, after Heraclonas and his mother had been driven out, Constans the son of Constantine reigned, the fifty-eighth in line from Augustus. Since he had fallen into the same heresy as his grandfather Heraclius he sent Pope Martin into exile at Cherson because, having held a synod, he had excommunicated the patriarch Paul, Pyrrhus and Cyrus. At Cherson Martin departed to the Lord, a man renowned for many signs and wonders. Thereupon Constans, summoning a synod under the charge of Pope Vitalian, abjured his heresy and sent to the blessed Peter copies of the gospels, of remarkable size, covered with gold and adorned with jewels. Not many days later, wishing to rescue Italy from the power of the Lombards, he sailed over the seas and made port at Taranto. Afterwards coming to Benevento he took practically all the cities in which the Lombards lived; Luceria he razed to the ground. Then accepting as a hostage the sister of Romuald, a daughter of King Grimoald, he directed his march to Naples. As he hastened from Naples toward the City he met Pope Vitalian, together with the clergy and laity at the sixth milestone and, entering Rome [59] in this

[56] Or Constantine III, the colleague of Heraclius since 613. Died 641.

[57] Or Heraclius, crowned in 638; see C. M. H. 2. 391.

[58] Constans II, who became emperor in 641.

[59] In the spring of 663. E. W. Brooks (C. M. H. 2. 394) remarks that he was the first emperor who had been seen in the ancient capital for 190 years.

fashion, with every mark of respect he bestowed upon the blessed
Peter a cloak woven of gold thread. Moreover he was planning to
restore the seat of empire to the City because he hated the people
of Constantinople as supporters of heretics (they had been his advisers with respect to the sacrilege against Pope Martin).[60] In his
time the blessed maiden Gertrude, the daughter of Pepin, found
rest in a happy death. Dagobert too died and was succeeded by his
son Clovis; for while he was yet alive he had left Austrasia to his
other son, namely Sigebert, and had entrusted him to the regency
of Cunibert, bishop of Cologne, and Pepin. Constans, leaving the
City, made his way into Sicily. There he remained for six years.
Then by the treachery of his own troops he was murdered in the
bath in the twenty-eighth year of his reign. Upon his death the
soldiers made a certain Mzhezh,[61] an Armenian, emperor. Upon
learning of this Constantine, the son of Constans, entered Sicily,
put Mzhezh and his father's murderers to death, and after restoring
order in Italy returned to the royal city.

12. In the six hundred and seventieth year from the incarnation
of the Lord, Constantine [62] the son of Constans, with his two brothers Heraclius and Tiberius, obtained the imperial power, being the
fifty-ninth in line from Augustus, while the sons of Dagobert were
reigning in Francia. In his time legates were sent by Pope Agatho
and there was assembled in the presence of the emperor a synod,
the sixth,[63] consisting of a hundred and fifty, or according to others
two hundred and eighty-nine, bishops. The presidents of this synod
were George, the patriarch of the city, and Macarius of Antioch,
who, as Sergius, Cyrus, Pyrrhus and others of his predecessors had
done, claimed that there is in Christ but one will and but one opera-
tion. After George had been recalled to the Catholic faith by the
legates of the Apostolic See, Macarius and his followers were
anathematized and Theophanes, an abbot of Sicily, was appointed
in his stead. In the same synod, after the heresy had been condemned, such huge spider webs fell down in the sight of all that
every one perceived that by this deed all the filthiness of false doc-

[60] Otto has confused the meaning of Frutolf who wrote: *quia odiosus factus
est Byzantiis, eo quod Martinum papam ignominiose tractans exiliavit.*

[61] *Mitium* in the text. He reigned for about half a year: 668-669.

[62] Constantine IV, Pogonatus, the legitimate ruler from 668 to 685. He had
been crowned by his father Constans in 654.

[63] At the Sixth General Council, which was held at Constantinople in 680,
the Monothelete doctrine was condemned.

trines had been swept away. During these days the blessed Arnulf, who had been Mayor of the Palace, renounced the world and, as we have said, was afterwards made bishop in the church at Metz. His son Ansegis [64] held the position of Mayor of the Palace. The blessed Lambert governed the church at Maastricht which was afterwards moved to Liège. Constantine brought the last day of his life to a close in the seventeenth year of his reign.

13. In the six hundred and eighty-seventh year from the incarnation of the Lord, Justinian [65] the son of Constantine, the sixty-first in line from Augustus, became emperor. He made peace with the Saracens and freed Africa from them, subjecting it to Roman dominion. He also sent an imperial commissioner,[66] Zacharias, and ordered that Pope Sergius, who was unwilling to subscribe to his heretical synod [67] held in the royal city, should be brought to him as a prisoner. But the soldiery of Ravenna, taking the pope by force out of his hands, drove Zacharias from the City. At that time Saint Kilian,[68] together with his supporters, was crowned with martyrdom. Pepin,[69] the son of Ansegis, being made Mayor of the Palace, administered the kingdom of the Franks; and the years of the Mayor of the Palace are henceforth set down in sequence in the catalogue of the kings. For from this time on the kings reigned in name only, being stripped of all share in the kingdom and of all honor, and the Mayors of the Palace had the management of the kingdom.

In the tenth year of his reign Justinian, after first having his nose cut off,[70] was driven into exile by Leontius the Patrician whom he had kept in chains for three years. Leo (or Leontius) held the imperial power for three years. At the end of this period Tiberius, who is also called Apsimar, after cutting off the nose of Leontius thrust him into a monastery and held for seven years the throne he

[64] He governed, together with Cunibert bishop of Cologne, in the name of Sigebert, the child who had received the title of King of Austrasia in 634.

[65] Justinian II, Rhinotmetus, 685-711.

[66] The text gives *protospatiario*. The *spatharius* was a military chamberlain (C. M. H. 2. 413).

[67] Of 692 — the Trullan or Quinisext; *cf.* C. M. H. 2. 408 *et seq.*

[68] He preached in Franconia on the banks of the Main.

[69] This is Pepin II, of Heristal, undisputed master of all Gaul from 687 to 714. He was the son of Ansegis (Arnulf's son) and a daughter of Pepin of Landen.

[70] Hence "*Rhinotmetus.*"

had usurped. During these days the seventh synod was convoked at Aquileia by the blessed Pope Sergius.

14. In the six hundred and eighty-seventh year from the incarnation of the Lord, Justinian, who had been banished by Leo, captured the royal city with the aid of Tervel, king of the Bulgars, and regained the imperial power, holding it for six years. He made Tiberius and Leontius prisoners and dragged them in chains through the streets, and afterwards, while all the people shouted, "Thou shalt tread upon the asp and the basilisk and shalt trample on the lion and the dragon," [71] he trod upon their necks with his feet and finally beheaded them. Those who were of the faction that had perpetrated the cruelty upon him he caused to be tortured with various torments, and almost every time that he wiped a drop of moisture from his mutilated nostrils he ordered some one of them to be put to death. He dug out the eyes of Callinicus the patriarch [72] and sent him into exile to Rome; in his place he put Cyrus, an abbot of Pontus, who had ministered to his necessities when he was an exile, and made his own son Tiberius his associate on the throne. He also summoned Pope Constantine, received him with respect and, after humbly confessing his sins, sent him back with honor, having renewed all the privileges of the holy Roman Church. Furthermore he collected an army and sought to arrest Philippicus whom he had banished to Pontus. But Philippicus was proclaimed emperor by the army and killed Justinian, having met him in battle at the sixth milestone from the royal city. The loyal adherents of Philippicus slew Justinian's son also.

15. In the seven hundred and thirteenth year from the incarnation of the Lord, Philippicus,[73] the sixty-third in line from Augustus (after striking out from the list of kings Leontius and Tiberius[74] who had usurped the throne in the lifetime of Justinian) reigned. Dagobert the Younger reigned in Francia — in name only, however, for Pepin, the mayor of the palace, held all that made the throne worth while. Out of his affection for a certain monk who was a hermit and a heretic, who had predicted that he would be

[71] Ps. 91. 13. Otto gives the quotation exactly, whereas in Frutolf a few words are changed. There is, of course, a play upon the names "Leontius" and "Apsimar," and "basilisk" is to be interpreted as a contemptuous diminutive of "basileus"—"Kinglet."

[72] Of Constantinople.

[73] Or Vardan, 711-713.

[74] Yet Otto himself seems to count them; but see V. 27 and 28.

emperor, he called a synod of pseudo-bishops and condemned the holy general synod, the sixth. Cyrus too he deposed and thrust into a monastery, and ordained as patriarch in the royal city John, his associate in heresy. He also sent to Pope Constantine a letter regarding his faith, but Constantine refused to accept the letter. Furthermore, the Roman people decreed that neither the writings nor the pictures of Philippicus should be received and that his name, being the name of a heretic, should not be read when masses were solemnized. When on the holy sabbath of Pentecost Philippicus, having left the bath at about midday, was reclining on a couch, he was seized by Rufinus and Patrician Theodore — who entered through the Golden Gate — and was blinded, a year and six months from the time he had begun to reign.

16. In the seven hundred and fourteenth year from the incarnation of the Lord, Artemius, who changed his name and had himself called Anastasius, was chosen emperor, the sixty-fourth in line from Augustus, on the holy day of Pentecost. According to some authorities he reigned for three years. Others write that he reigned only one year and three months, and that Philippicus had ruled for two years and nine months. Let the historians settle this controversy.[75] So then Anastasius, having secured the throne, in a letter sent to Rome declared himself a defender of the Catholic faith and a supporter of the sixth council [synod]. In his time Dagobert king of the Franks died. When Pepin, the Mayor of the Palace, also died his son Charles [76] administered the kingdom of the Franks for twenty-seven years, during which there were kings, but kings without honor or power. Charles, grandfather of Charles the Great, overwhelmed in many stubborn battles Raginfrid, who wished to invade his kingdom, and at last shut him up in his own country, leaving him only the city of Angers to live in. Charles also conquered the Bavarians and subjugated Alemannia too (men call this country Suevia) and their duke, Lantfrid. He subdued Gascony and Eudes, duke of Aquitaine. In Saxony and Frisia he waged valiant wars. He put to flight three hundred and eighty-five thousand of the Saracens who had entered the boundaries of Aquitaine with their wives and sons. In so doing Charles lost only fifteen hundred of the Franks, as Eudes, the duke of Aquitaine, testifies in a letter which he wrote to the blessed Pope Gregory II. Charles en-

75 A typical attitude of Otto on disputed points.
76 This is Charles Martel (714-740), the victor at Tours in 732.

tered Gascony again in the twentieth year of his reign and killed Eudes, and in the following year began a war against the sons of Eudes. When the Saracens sought to enter Gaul again he destroyed them near Narbonne. When they were laying Provençe waste a second time and had captured Arles, they were compelled by Liutprand, king of the Lombards, to flee from Charles's territories. Liutprand had given aid in answer to an appeal from Charles. Liutprand had adopted Charles's son Pepin, who had accepted the tonsure. While the kingdom of the Franks was being enlarged thus in many ways under Charles, its very warlike prince, the empire of the Romans, whose seat had been transferred to the royal city, was not only being made smaller by its foes through the loss of provinces but was being dashed to pieces by internal troubles. For at about the beginning of the reign of Charles the soldiers, having formed a conspiracy against Anastasius, made Theodosius emperor against his will. Upon learning of this Anastasius withdrew to Nicaea. Theodosius defeated him in a pitched battle and making him a cleric afterwards even had him ordained priest.

17. In the seven hundred and seventeenth year from the incarnation of the Lord, Theodosius,[77] the sixty-fifth in line from Augustus, obtained the imperial power but he reigned for one year only. For Leo, commander of the East, making preparations for civil war, seized Theodosius's son — also called Theodosius — in Nicomedia. Broken-hearted at this, Theodosius voluntarily resigned the purple at the advice of the patriarch Germanus and the senate and became a cleric. During these days the Tiber overflowed and submerged many buildings at Rome. The flood continued for seven days but when the citizens offered litanies it finally subsided upon the eighth day.

18. In the seven hundred and eighteenth year from the incarnation of the Lord, Leo,[78] a Syrian by birth, became emperor, the sixty-sixth in line from Augustus, while the elder Charles was still living in Francia. Leo ordered the images of the Lord and of the saints to be burned; he also had many who resisted his impiety beheaded. Among others Theodosia, a virgin of Christ, suffered martyrdom. She is still held in the deepest veneration in the royal city. At her burial her body showed no signs of decay; indeed it is preserved in that state now in the Church of the Nuns, and is

[77] The third of this name, 716-717.
[78] Leo III, the Isaurian, 717-741.

displayed to all strangers, being throught of as a divine physician. Carried in the hands of maidens it is regarded as a good omen whenever she makes herself feel heavy to those upon whom she presses. I myself also, together with many others, learned this fact by personal experience recently [79] when the crusade to Jerusalem was sent out under Conrad king of the Romans and Louis king of the Franks.

Leo, moreover, expelled the patriarch Germanus from his see and put Anastasius in his place. For this reason Gregory the pope,[80] having often warned the emperor by letter and found him obdurate, persuaded Italy to withdraw from his jurisdiction. In this same period Boniface,[81] who was sent into Germany by Pope Gregory, and the blessed Pirminius, who was the founder of many monasteries, were accounted notable men. The remains of St. Augustine were transported by Liutprand, king of the Lombards, from Sardinia to Ticinum.[82] Moreover the Venerable Bede, priest of the Angles, rested in peace leaving many writings as memorials. During these days the Saracens invested the royal city with a siege for three years and at last, as the citizens cried out to the Lord, were smitten with famine, cold and pestilence and withdrew. In the City three hundred thousand perished, it is said, of the pestilence. Leo, that wicked emperor, died in the twenty-fourth year of his reign.

19. In the seven hundred and forty-second year from the incarnation of the Lord, Constantine,[83] Leo's son, succeeded his father on the throne, the sixty-seventh in line from Augustus. In all respects he surpassed his father in wickedness, being a slave to enchantments and bloody sacrifices and invocations of demons, to luxury also and to impurity; further, in the manner of the tyrants of old, he persecuted the Church of God. He was so cruel and wicked that by a righteous judgment of God that most famous kingdom seems to have been made smaller on account of his sins — in part too on account of the sins of his father. In the first year of Constantine's reign Charles, the son of Pepin, died leaving three

---

[79] As Hofmeister remarks, this statement was not included in the first edition of the Chronicle, which was sent to Isingrim. Apparently the life of Saint Theodosia was not read in the West.

[80] Gregory II (715-731).

[81] Or Winfrid (680-754), the missionary statesman; see C. M. H. 2. 536-542.

[82] Or Pavia.

[83] Constantine V (Copronymus), 741-775. He is characterized by Frutolf (p. 157. 57) as *impius et anticristi precursor*.

sons — Carloman, Pepin [84] and Grifo. Of these Grifo, who was the youngest, declared war upon his brothers at the advice of his wife, Suanihilda,[85] a kinswoman of Odilo, duke of the Bavarians, and seized Laon. The brothers collected an army and beseiged Laon. When Grifo surrendered they imprisoned him in a castle near Alverna.[86]

20. In the seven hundred and forty-third year from the incarnation of the Lord, Pepin and Carloman moved their troops at first into Aquitaine against Hunald, the duke of that province, and having captured a stronghold which is called Loches in a place known as Vetus Pictavis they divided the kingdom. Carloman obtained Austrasia, Alemannia and Thuringia, Pepin Burgundy, Neustria and Provençe. Then after fighting many battles, in the seven hundred and forty-sixth year from the incarnation of the Lord, after the monastery of Fulda had been founded, Carloman revealed to his brother his desire to renounce the world. This purpose he realized in the following year. Going to Zacharias, the Roman pontiff, he was by him made a cleric. Presently he assumed the garb of a monk in the monastery of St. Sylvester, which is situated on Mt. Soracte.[87] But since he could not enjoy the peace and quiet he had hoped for because many came from Francia to see him, he went to the monastery of Saint Benedict, situate on Monte Cassino, and there lived happily during his remaining days. But Grifo, rebelling against his brother, seized Bavaria and drove Duke Tassilo out of that country. But Pepin restored Tassilo to his dukedom and granted his brother twelve counties. Not content with these Grifo fled to Waifar, duke of Aquitaine.

21. In the seven hundred and fifty-first year from the incarnation of the Lord — when, as I have often said, the mayors of the palace had entire administrative control of the government and the kings of the Franks reigned in name only — Pepin, who had received the office of Mayor by order of succession, sent Burchard [88] bishop of Würzburg and his chaplain Fulrad to Zacharias to pro-

---

[84] Pepin III, "the Short," mayor of the palace from 741 to 751 and king from 751 to 768.

[85] Frutolf (p. 158. 31 and 32) correctly records that she was Grifo's mother.

[86] In the Forest of Ardennes.

[87] *Sorapte* in the text. It was here, on the mountain familiar to all readers of the Odes of Horace (1. 9), that Pope Sylvester I (in the time of Constantine) is said to have lain in hiding while persecution raged.

[88] This statement seems to conflict with that in Chapter 22 below. Otto here

pound to him a question. The pontiff accordingly sent back decision to the effect that he who had charge of all matters should be called king rather than he who merely bore the name of king. At that time Childeric, who was descended from the blood of the ancient kings of the Franks (who were called Merovingians after Merovech, the son of Clovis), held the royal name — a mere empty title, however, as I said above.

22. Accordingly in the seven hundred and fifty-second year from the incarnation of the Lord, after the messengers returned from Rome, Pepin was, by the authority of Pope Zacharias, elevated to the throne by Saint Boniface, bishop of Mainz, and other princes of the realm. This was done in the city of Soissons. In the following year, upon the death of Zacharias, Pope Stephen succeeded him. Since Stephen was suffering many outrages at the hands of Aistulf, the king of the Lombards, he met Pepin as the latter was returning from his expedition against the Saxons in a village which is called Quierzy (here also he received news of his brother Grifo's death) and besought Pepin to come to the aid of the holy Roman Church.

23. In the seven hundred and fifty-fourth year from the incarnation of the Lord, Pepin, with other nobles of the kingdom of the Franks, was first absolved by Pope Stephen from the oath of allegiance which he had sworn to Childeric (Childeric was tonsured and thrust into a monastery) and afterwards was anointed king. Here the rule of the Merovingians was brought to an end and that of the Carolingians, by which even the power of Constantinople was to be diminished, began. (From this the Roman pontiffs draw their authority for changing the kingdoms.) Pepin, who had at first governed the kingdom of the Franks in actual fact, governed it from this time on both in name and in fact. In his time flourished those very famous princes of Christ's kingdom: Boniface, the aforesaid archbishop of Mainz; Rupert, the archbishop of Salzburg; Corbinian, bishop of the church of Freising and very many others.[89]

24. Since I have made mention of the blessed Corbinian,[90]

alludes to the visit of Pope Stephen to Frankland and the reanointing of Pepin by his hand.

[89] Otto is in error regarding Rupert ("Robertus") and Corbinian; the former flourished c. 700, the latter in the time of Pepin of Heristal and of Charles Martel.

[90] In the account as here given Otto appears to be writing from memory, though following in the main the *Life of Corbinian* as given in *Acta SS. Boll.*,

whose place I unworthily hold,[91] I think it unbecoming to pass over altogether in silence the achievements of so great a man. He was the son of Waldegisus and Corbiniana, parents distinguished in worldly affairs. Even in his childhood he had a foretaste of that divine favor which he was afterwards to receive so fully. For he was not ensnared by the temptations of the world, was content with food and clothing alone, out of all his parents' possessions, and lived in a little cell which he had built for himself. Moreover, when at the vintage season a certain man had offered him the first drawings of the new-made wine, the pressure of the effervescing must broke the bottom out of the vessel. But the man of God, unwilling to break the silence prescribed by the Rule,[92] forbore to direct the attention of the servants to this happening; yet by his prayers he prevented the wine from flowing uselessly away. Since he was worthy, on account of his faith and virtue, to be advanced to higher station he was ordained bishop by the blessed Gregory, pontiff of the city of Rome, and sent out to the heathen. By and by, as he was coming back through the Tridentine valley and was entering Bavaria, he was welcomed in a friendy spirit by Duke Tassilo and his son Theodo,[93] and received from them the mountain of Freising. There in honor of Saint Benedict he built, at first, the church which is still visible in our day and there he subsequently gathered together a holy company of monks. This mountain is situated in a very fair and pleasant spot, notable for its streams of limpid waters and particularly for that swiftly flowing river, the Isère. It views as in a mirror the whole expanse of that district, far and wide; from its southern slope it looks out upon a broad and level plain. In those days it was hemmed in, it is said, by forests as is a lookout for hunters. There still remain traces of the woods in the plain, amid the thickets, in the form of ancient tree-trunks, and even today there is a plentiful supply of deer and of wild goats. But on the northern side there is still to be seen surviving a wood of no mean size (what is commonly called a forest), very valuable to the city for building material for houses, and for firewood. The land adjoining the mountain is bounded on the south by the river Isère,

8 Sept. 3. 281 *et seq.; cf.* Riezler *Abhandl. der k. bair. Akad. der Wiss., hist. Cl.* 18. 1 (1888), pp. 217 *et seq.*

[91] As bishop of Freising.

[92] Rule of St. Benedict, *c.* 42.

[93] Otto is in error, as Wilmans has pointed out. The *Life* mentions Duke Theodo and his son Grimoald in *c.* 3, Grimoald alone in *c.* 4 and thereafter.

on the north by the Amper. A very fertile valley is thus formed which extends four German miles.[94] At its farther limit, where the rivers I have mentioned flow together, there is situated (as everyone knows) a place called Moosburg, very beautiful and delightful, having a company of clerics in the church of Saint Castulus. Saint Corbinian enriched the church of Freising with many honors and possessions, and inspired it by the example of a most saintly life. It is told of him that on one occasion, when he was on his way to Rome to satisfy the needs of his church, a bear killed his packhorse. The man of God caught the bear, placed his packsaddle upon the beast, and ordered him to carry it; and the word of the Lord, rendered "sharper than any sword," [95] compelled that wild animal to obey the behests of the man of God. On that same journey, while his companions were suffering from hunger in a desert place, an eagle suddenly brought them a fish. All that were present ate of the fish and were, in consequence, both amazingly refreshed and greatly exalted. At another time, while he was making a journey to King Pepin,[96] he protected by the sign of the cross a robber who had been sentenced to be hanged — inasmuch as he could not prevail upon the judge to liberate him in answer to his entreaties. Continuing his journey to the king he asked that the accused (who had by that time been hanged) be given to him whether dead or alive. His request was granted. Quickly making his way back to the place he found the robber, who by that time had hung for two days on the scaffold, still alive; he took him down unhurt and having admonished him suffered him to depart. By these and other virtues and by miracles wrought in consequence of his virtues — which it would take too long to recount — that man of God brought fame upon the aforesaid church as its first supervisor.

25. In the seven hundred and fifty-fifth year from the incarnation of the Lord, King Pepin, at the request of Pope Stephen, moved his troops against Aistulf, king of the Lombards, and prepared to invade Italy. Though the Lombards opposed him in the narrow mountain passes, after slaying many he penetrated the fastnesses with enormous effort and encamped in a plain. Aistulf withdrew to Pavia. This city Pepin invested for a long time, in fact until he had received forty hostages and assurance upon oath

94 *I.e.*, about twenty English miles.
95 Heb. 4. 12.
96 He is called *maiordomus* or *princeps* in the *Life*.

that the Lombards would molest the Roman Church no more. Thereupon Pepin raised the siege and having, with the soldiery of the Franks, escorted Pope Stephen with every mark of honor to his own see, returned to his own land. In this year the blessed archbishop Boniface — who, men say, marked out the limits of the dioceses of Bavaria just as they remain today, and founded the monastery of Fulda, and performed many deeds that were to be of service to the Church of God, in Gaul as well as in Germany — was crowned with martyrdom by the Frisians while he was preaching the word of life. In the following year, because Aistulf was disregarding all his promises, Pepin again besieged him in Pavia and compelled him to carry out fully his promises. He also relinquished Ravenna, together with many other cities of Italy, to the blessed Peter and returned to the Gauls.

In the next year when (as I have often said) the Roman Empire was waning as that of the Franks was increasing, envoys of the emperor Constantine came to Pepin at Compiègne, bearing him gifts. Tassilo also, duke of Bavaria, made his way to that place with the elders of his people and pledged loyalty to the king and his sons under oath. In the following year the king conquered the Saxons in a war hazardous and stubbornly fought and made them tributary to himself. Not long afterwards he set in motion his troops against Waifar [97] duke of Aquitaine because the latter was molesting the churches under Pepin's jurisdiction; however, upon receiving hostages from him he returned home. During these days the blessed Othmar,[98] who had been banished to Stein, an island of the Rhine, departed to the Lord. Pepin in many hard-fought battles overwhelmed Waifar who was still making war on him. Tassilo duke of Bavaria disregarded his oath and again attempted to make war upon his uncle Pepin. These days were difficult and perilous because two very valiant men, the dukes of Aquitaine and Bavaria, were in arms against the king. At that time the Turks, issuing by the Caspian Gates, clashed with the Avars; many were destroyed on both sides. Now Pepin, after waging many battles of varying outcome, finally slew Waifar. Not long afterwards on his journey home he was taken sick at Tours and conveyed thence to Paris. In the fourteenth year from the time that he was anointed king, but the twenty-sixth since he had begun to assume kingly powers

97 The war with Aquitaine lasted from 760 to 768.
98 Abbot of St. Gall.

after his father's death, he died, leaving two sons, Charles and Carloman.

26. In the seven hundred and sixty-ninth year from the incarnation of the Lord, while Constantine was still ruling, Charles began to reign, dividing the kingdom with his brother. First he drove Runald — who upon the death of Waifar was renewing the war in Aquitaine — in flight to Lupus, duke of Gascony, and afterwards received his submission and that of Lupus. In the following year — while he was holding a general assembly at Worms — he determined to visit the tombs of the apostles to pray there.[99] In the third year of his reign, after his brother Carloman had died and Carloman's wife and sons were in flight to Desiderius king of the Lombards, Charles as sole king entered Saxony with an army but, after laying waste the whole land with fire and sword, he accepted hostages and returned. Later, at the request of Pope Hadrian, he entered Italy and beseiged Desiderius king of the Lombards at Ticinum [100] and, leaving his army there, went to Rome to pray. On his return from Rome he compelled the exhausted city to surrender and led the king away captive. Meanwhile the Saxons, emboldened by the king's absence, had forgotten their oath and were laying waste the lands adjoining their own.

The king, having subdued Italy, returned to Francia; presently, having arranged his forces in three divisions, he entered Saxony,[101] laid the land waste by fires and carried off an enormous quantity of booty. Not long afterwards he withdrew after again receiving hostages from them. During these days Constantine, the persecutor, died in the thirty-fifth year of his reign; his son Leo succeeded him.

27. In the seven hundred and seventy-sixth year from the incarnation of the Lord, Leo, the sixty-sixth [102] in line from Augustus, received the imperial power. At first he seemed too lenient and therefore the chief nobles demanded his son as emperor. During the same time the Saxons, as was their custom, made false promises — not once but many times; Charles overwhelmed them in a number of battles and persuaded many of them to accept the

[99] Frutolf (on the year 770) makes this statement concerning the mother of Charles the Great, as does Regino.

[100] Or Pavia. Charles began the siege in 773; the city fell the following year.

[101] In 775. The first campaign against the Saxons had started in 772, before Charles left for Italy. They were not finally crushed until 804.

[102] On the discrepancies in the numbering of the emperors cf. above, V. 19 and V. 15, and note 74. This is Leo IV, 775-780.

Christian faith. The emperor Leo died in the fifth year of his reign.

28. In the seven hundred and eighty-first year from the incarnation of the Lord, Constantine the son of Leo, the sixty-seventh in line from Augustus, succeeded his father on the throne. A daughter of Charles,[103] who had been betrothed to Constantine, was given in marriage to another by her mother. In the first year of his reign [104] King Charles went to Rome and was honorably received there by Pope Hadrian. And there, while Holy Easter was being observed, Charles's son Pepin was anointed king of Italy and another son, namely Louis, as king of Aquitaine, by that same pontiff. Charles himself was saluted as a Roman patrician amid the acclaim of all the people. Furthermore Pope Hadrian sent envoys to Tassilo to enjoin him to be faithful to his king.

29. At about the same time, while the king was celebrating the Lord's Eastertide, Tassilo came to Ingelheim with the chief men of his nation. When he was accused there by the Bavarians with failure to keep faith with his king — nay even charged with bringing in the Avars to lay waste the kingdom — he was convicted on these and other like charges and was condemned, as guilty of treason, to be visited with capital punishment. The king, however, moved with compassion, permitted him to assume the garb of a monk in the monastery at Lorsch, which he had built himself,[105] and there to do penance for his sins. Now Constantine, having been blinded — at the suggestion, it is said, of his own mother Irene — died not long afterwards in the fourteenth year of his reign. His mother reigned [106] after him for five years. She deserved to have the rule over the world, which had passed into her woman's hands in no honorable fashion, transferred [as it was] in her day to the Franks.

30. In the seven hundred and ninety-ninth year from the incarnation of the Lord, Pope Leo, who had succeeded Hadrian, was most shamefully treated by the Romans at the celebration of the Greater Litany; indeed it would seem that his eyes were dug out. He came to King Charles and complained of what had happened. According-

---

[103] Rotrud. The betrothal was arranged at the instance of the empress Irene, regent for her young son.

[104] *I.e.*, of Constantine's reign, 780-781.

[105] The monastery of Lorsch was founded in 764, but not by Tassilo; *cf.* Hauck, *Kirchengeschichte Deutschlands* 2. 56 (second edition). Tassilo seems to have been immured in a monastery at Jumièges rather than at Lorsch.

[106] Irene was empress of the Eastern Empire from 797 to 802.

ly Charles, flushed with victory (he had already greatly extended
the kingdom of the Franks by subjecting to himself the Bavarians,
Aquitainians, Saxons, Danes,[107] Northmen,[108] Britons, Pannonians
and many other provinces), and deserving further advancement,
set out for Rome to avenge the pope. The day before he entered the
City, Leo met him at the twelfth milestone and welcomed him with
all honor. When the day broke Charles entered the City, was welcomed by the pontiff and by all the people, and escorted to the
Church of Saint Peter. After seven days had elapsed the king
called an assembly and set forth the reason for his coming. Leo
too, whose rivals had brought a serious charge against him, of his
own free will and accord — out of a good conscience — cleared
himself, by an oath taken upon the most sacred gospels and in the
presence of all, from the charge that had been preferred against
him.

31. In the eight hundred and first year [109] from the incarnation
of the Lord, and the one thousand, five hundred and fifty-second
year from the founding of the City, Charles, in the thirty-third
year of his reign, was relieved by the supreme pontiff of the title of
patrician and was called Emperor and Augustus, the sixty-ninth
in line from Augustus. As he was being crowned all the people
shouted thrice, "To Charles Augustus, crowned by God, the great
and peace-bringing emperor of the Romans, long life and victory!"
Hence the government of the Romans, which from Constantine
down to this time was centered in the royal city — that is, Constantinople — was transferred to the Franks.[110] Augustus called
the citizens together and, after conducting a trial of those who
had been guilty of sacrilege toward the pontiff, condemned them to
death; but, upon the intercession of the aforesaid pope, merely
drove them into exile, sparing them that they might have a chance
to repent. Irene, the empress of Constantinople, sent ambassadors
to Charles and asked that peace be established between the Greeks
and the Franks. The emperor sent messengers back with the ambassadors and asked Irene to be his wife. When she had consented

---

[107] *Cf.* Frutolf p. 162. 50. But on p. 170 he correctly places the war with
the Danes long after Charles's coronation as emperor.   [108] See preceding note.

[109] On Christmas Day in the year 800. Otto's year began on December 25.

[110] MS C$_4$, in the same hand and the same ink, adds in the margin: *Regnum
Romanorum cis mare Francorum regibus amministrandum cum cesaris imperatoris augusti nomine commissum est.* The same marginal note is found
above on IV. 24.

the patrician Aëtius, defeating the queen's desires, made his brother Nicephorus emperor while the ambassadors of Charles were still in the royal city, and thrust Irene into a monastery. Nicephorus, having become king, sent his deputies with the ambassadors of the emperor; and he and the emperor made a treaty with each other, through letters and messengers. The king of the Persians also honored the emperor with gifts.

32. In the eight hundred and twelfth year from the incarnation of the Lord, the emperor Nicephorus was killed by the Bulgarians in a conflict between the two states and his son-in-law Michael was set on the throne in his stead. He dismissed with honor the messengers sent by Charles to his predecessor, and despatching his own representatives with them to Augustus, renewed the compact of peace with him. But when without success he had led his army against the Bulgarians, he resigned the throne and became a monk. Leo [111] the son of the patrician Bardus succeeded him.

Now after Charles had transferred the government of the Romans to the Franks, and while he was waging many wars with valor and good fortune and was greatly extending his kingdom, in the forty-sixth year of his reign — the forty-third since Italy was made subject and the fourteenth of his rule as emperor — he died, in the seventy-second year of his age, at Aachen. There he had built a church of marvellous workmanship in honor of St. Mary, ever Virgin, and he had established there the seat of his power. In this church he was buried. But if anyone desires to know his deeds and the wars which he waged, and to hear also about the bridge which he had built across the Rhine at Mainz, and about the palaces too which he had constructed with regal magnificence at Nimwegen, Ingelheim and other places in his kingdom, let him read his biography and the story of his achievements, which has been related by many.[112] He was, as a certain writer says of him, of large and sturdy frame and of imposing stature. His head was well rounded on top, his eyes very large and bright and his nose a little larger than normal. He had beautiful white hair. His expression was cheerful and jovial; in speech he was voluble and exuberant; in

---

[111] Leo V, the Armenian, *strategus* of the Anatolics, 813-820. It was he who concluded the treaty with the Empire of the West and delivered it to Louis after Charles's death.

[112] Frutolf, following Einhard, has inserted in his Chronicle a continuous account of the deeds of Charles the Great (pp. 161 *et seq.*). Otto, in what follows, has drawn upon Frutolf, not upon Einhard himself.

food and drink he was temperate, especially so in drink. By his valor the kingdom of the Franks was greatly augmented and the mightiest of all kingdoms — that is, the Roman — was transferred from the East to the West. His single sway stretched from the land of the Bulgarians or Illyricum to the land of the Spaniards, and from the land of the Danes to that of the Calabrians — besides outlying regions, to wit, Bohemia, Poland, Dalmatia, Istria, Venetia, Brittany and certain others. With the exception of Pannonia all this territory is included today, as everyone knows, in two realms: that of the Romans and that of the Franks.[113]

33. In the eight hundred and fifteenth year from the incarnation of the Lord, Louis [114] son of Charles, whom Charles had himself in his lifetime selected to be his successor and had called Augustus, upon learning of his father's death made his way from Aquitaine to the palace at Aachen and, having been made king by universal consent, ruled as the seventieth in line from Augustus. In the first year of his reign he learned from information lodged by certain persons that the chief nobles of the kingdom had been put to death at the command of Pope Leo for conspiring against the pope. Summoning into his presence his nephew Bernard,[115] king of Italy, he sent him to Rome to investigate the matter. Bernard was taken sick in the City and reported the result of his mission to the emperor through Count Heroldus. Leo also sent envoys to the emperor and cleared himself of the charges that had been brought against him. Not long after this Leo died and Stephen was chosen in his place. Immediately after his consecration Stephen sent envoys to the emperor to mollify him and to announce that the pope would come to him; and he followed his envoys into Gaul. The emperor, meeting him at Rheims, received him with all honor. Accordingly the

---

[113] Otto's language here is rather obscure. The passage reads: *Regni vero terminus a Bulgaris seu Illirico usque ad Hyspanos, a Danis usque ad Calabros, exceptis adiacentibus regionibus, utpote Boemia, Polonia, Dalmatia, Histria, Venetia, Brittannia aliisque provinciis, quae modo duo regna Romanorum et Francorum, excepta Pannonia, esse noscuntur, fuit.* I have taken the *exceptis . . . provinciis* to mean the territories which Charles had not fully incorporated into his realm but over which he exercised a considerable measure of influence. But it is difficult to bring the passage into conformity with anything approaching accurate geographical knowledge.

[114] Or Ludwig "the Pious," 814-840.

[115] Otto calls him *nepotem.* Bernard, or Bernhard, was the son of the emperor Charles's dead son Pepin and was appointed under-king of Italy in 813 at the same time that Louis was raised to the position of emperor.

pope — having, according to custom, celebrated solemn mass — crowned Louis with a diadem and pronounced him emperor of the Romans. This year, the year in which he was crowned by the Roman pontiff was, so some claim, the second of his reign; others make it the seventh. Presently the emperor, holding a general assembly at Aachen, chose his firstborn son Lothar as his associate in the government. His other two sons, Charles [116] and Louis, he entitled kings; the one he placed over Aquitaine, the other over Bavaria. Not long afterwards he learned that Bernard, the king of Italy, with the cities of his realm had conspired against him. While he was moving an army against Bernard, the latter, losing courage, surrendered to the emperor at Châlon-sur-Saône. The emperor, coming to his palace at Aachen and there observing Holy Easter, conducted the trial of those who had been guilty of conspiracy and, when they had been condemned to death by vote of the court, he merely had them, as well as their king, deprived of their eyesight. Yet there are those who claim that the emperor captured Bernard by craft and deprived him first of his eyes and afterwards of his life.[117]

34. In the eight hundred and twenty-second year from the incarnation of the Lord, the emperor despatched his son Lothar into Italy. But while he was himself holding court in the town of Frankfort, various envoys from the barbarians — among them two brothers — came to him, contending for the right to rule the Wiltzi. The emperor, having decided their dispute, sent them home as his subjects and bound to him by pledges of loyalty. When Lothar had set matters in Italy in order and was preparing to return to his father, he was invited to the City by Pope Paschal. Here he was welcomed with all honor and on the holy Easter day was crowned by the pope himself, and obtained the title of Augustus. During these days, while the emperor was holding an assembly at Aachen, messengers of the Bulgarians came to him to have their boundaries established. The emperor Louis, who was, it is said, expelled from the kingdom on account of the evil deeds of his wife, but was afterwards restored,[118] completed the last day of his life in the twenty-sixth year of his reign.

---

[116] This should be Pepin. Frutolf does not give the names in speaking of the year 817 but later (on the year 822) has the correct name *Pippinum*.

[117] Bernard was blinded April 17, 818 and died a few days later.

[118] He was deserted by his troops on ''The Field of Lies'' in 833 and restored to the throne the next year.

35. In the eight hundred and forty-first year from the incarnation of the Lord, when Lothar had returned from Italy and was intent upon ruling as king, Charles and Louis, his brothers,[119] taking it amiss that they should be deprived of their father's kingdom now that their father was dead, declared war upon their brother. Accordingly since God, the creator of all things, was unwilling that even the kingdom of the Franks — into which, after the countless changes which I have mentioned above, the kingdom of the Romans had been merged — should remain in the state to which it had advanced, His purpose being to reveal the wretchedness of men and the instability of the world with its revolutions, He permitted that kingdom to be wretchedly divided against itself and thereby brought to desolation and destruction. So, then, the brothers I have named brought together from all sides the flower of the kingdom and, meeting Lothar at Fontenoy-en-Puisaye,[120] fought most bitterly. The strength of the empire on both sides was so grievously shattered — so it is said — in this conflict that henceforth the Franks, the bravest of all peoples, not only could not widen their domain but could scarcely defend what they had acquired. When the lamentable battle between the brothers was at an end, a bloody victory finally fell to the lot of Charles and Louis, and therefore they made a compact with each other and shared the empire. By this division [121] the western part of the realm (that is, from the British Channel to the Meuse) fell to Charles; the eastern (that is, all Germany to the Rhine) fell to Louis; the central portion (that is, Belgic Gaul) was allotted to Lothar — and from his name it is called Lotharingia even to this day — together with the title of Roman Emperor. Thereafter, since the kingdom had been divided there were, we find, two kingdoms, an eastern and a western; one of them comprises the share of Louis and Lothar and the seat of government of the Franks, the palace of Aachen, and the rule over the city of Rome; the other (the western, which is still called the Kingdom of the Franks, whereas the other is known as the Kingdom of the Romans) consists of the share of Charles.

36. We are compelled even against our will to ponder upon the judgments of God and the instability of the world. For behold! as I

[119] Charles the Bald, half-brother to Lothar, and Louis (the German) are meant. Pepin of Aquitaine (called Charles in V. 33 above) had died in 838.

[120] *Fontoniacum* in the text. This was in June, 841.

[121] The Treaty of Verdun, 843.

have said above,[122] we see earthly pomp and power departing with time, even as the heavens revolve from east to west. And to keep us from supposing that mortal life has achieved permanence in any part of the universe, but that even there men suffer loss after the manner of a man in a fever — even as you read in Job, "They have changed the night into day, and again after the darkness I hope for the light" [123] — wherever they turn they have no permanence and we perceive that they have found only labor and sorrow. Does it not seem to you that earthly honors come and go, as I have said, as a man's fever comes and goes? For men that have a fever place their hope of peace in a change of their present condition, and therefore, when they are suffering, they toss themselves this way and that in frequent changes of position. It was in this way that, clearly enough, earthly power passed from Babylon to the Medes, from them to the Persians, afterwards to the Greeks, finally to the Romans, and under the Roman name was transferred to the Franks. And when it appeared that it would continue there, as if it had firmly established for itself a permanent abiding place, it began to be subject to so many woes (as is evident in what was said above) that one might well say with Job, "When I come to the dawn, wearied by the torments of the night, I wait for the darkness; and when I have obtained it I suffer still greater pains and long again for the daylight." [124]

So when the Franks, who were most proficient in warfare,[125] had greatly extended the bounds of their kingdom and had brought Rome, the capital of the world, under their sway, when they had become objects of dread to all nations and were to all appearances invincible, at that time becoming divided against one another in a struggle not only between fellow citizens but even between members of the same household (since brothers were its authors) they foreshadowed the final outcome — that the earthly power which, fleeing so to speak from the east to the west, had at last, so men fancied, found stability and peace, must in accordance with the saying of the Evangelist be brought to desolation. From all the facts, then, it is clear that no trust is ever to be reposed in powers that are doomed to perish, and that no one who is himself slipping can sup-

---

[122] Prol., I; Prol., V. [123] Job 17. 12.

[124] *Cf.* Job 7. 3 *et seq.* This is not a quotation but a paraphrase.

[125] Otto evidences a strong admiration for the Franks. *Cf.* above, V. 35; below, VI. 2; VII. 4 (beginning).

port another who wishes to lean upon him. Hence the saying of the Prophet is pertinent: "Cursed is the man that trusteth in man, and maketh flesh his arm."[126] For how will he sustain you who cannot stand himself? Or how will he strengthen you who is in himself weak? Since therefore the world passeth away and the lust thereof, who will doubt that we must depart from it to the living God who cannot be moved and remains unchangeable, and to his blessed and eternal city? Accordingly, since all the kingdoms of the earth have suffered overthrow, and since even the kingdom of the Franks, who were the last that were privileged to possess Rome, was, as we see, diminished from the time it was divided — let us who are writing a history to display the changes and chances of this world, let us, absolved by this shift in earthly authority as by a sufficient argument for the immutability of the heavenly kingdom, now bring this fifth book to an end.

HERE ENDS THE FIFTH BOOK

[126] Jer. 17. 5.

THE PROLOGUE OF THE SIXTH BOOK [1]

The blessed prophet, contemplating the unstable and pitifully fluctuating changes of the world and judging that they might most fittingly be compared with the sea, said, "Yonder is the sea, great and wide, wherein are things creeping innumerable." [2] Does it not seem to you that the world, after the manner of the sea, threatens with destruction by times of storm as the sea does by its waves those who entrust themselves to her? To what else am I to liken men who vie with one another for perishing honors than to creeping things of the sea? In the deep we see the lesser swallowed up by the greater, the weaker by the stronger, and at last the stronger — when they can find no other prey — tear themselves to pieces. Hence springs the saying: "The great fall upon themselves." [3] All these things the prudent reader will be able to find in the course of this history. It is plain therefore that the citizens of Christ ought not, as do creeping things of the sea, to plunge into the salty sea or trust themselves rashly to treacherous gales; they ought rather to sail by faith in a ship — that is, the wood of the Cross — and in this present time to busy their hands with works of love, that they may be able by traversing the highways of this life to reach safely the harbor of their true country.

How the kingdom of the Franks, so pitifully divided, lost not

[1] The sixth book of the *Chronicle* begins with the Treaty of Verdun (843) and the reign of Lothar, whom Otto counts as the seventy-first Roman emperor in the line started by Augustus, and concludes with the Norman conquest of England (1066), the humbling of Henry IV before Pope Gregory VII (Hildebrand) at Canossa in 1077 and Pope Gregory's death at Salerno in 1085. Otto's chief authorities here are Frutolf, Regino (from 853 to 967) and Wipo (from 1024 to 1085). In the latter part of the book he has also employed the *Annales Hildesheimenses* and a certain "*libellus*" of Herimannus Contractus (on Conrad II and Henry III). There are the customary quotations from Scripture.

It will be remembered that Books VI and VII of the *Chronicle* have been translated before (into German, by Horst Kohl, Leipzig, 1894). I have availed myself of this version and have — as usual — taken full advantage of Hofmeister's very complete and useful notes as also of the chronology which he has provided in the margins of his edition of the text.

[2] Ps. 104. 25.   [3] Lucan, *Pharsalia* 1. 81.

only the Roman crown of empire but even part of Francia (and in particular of Gaul), together with the palace at Aachen, remains to be told in this work.

HERE BEGINS THE SIXTH BOOK

1. After the division of the kingdom of the Franks, Lothar — to whom, as I have said, had fallen the title of emperor of the Romans as well as Lotharingia — was ruler, as the seventy-first in line from Augustus. Theophilus [4] was by now gone and his son Michael [5] was reigning over the Greeks in the royal city. The Norsemen, sailing up the Loire from the sea, burst into the city of Nantes,[6] and on the holy Easter Sunday killed the bishop, while he was administering general baptism according to custom, together with his clerics; then, scattering over the surrounding country, they laid waste the entire province with sword and flame. Indeed they seized the cities of Angers and Tours also and did not shrink from burning the Church of the blessed Martin. At that time Charles — to whom, as I said above, the western realms had fallen in the division — took Pepin the king of Aquitaine and, upon the advice of the bishops, gave him the tonsure and made him a monk in the monastery of St. Medard at Soissons. The emperor Lothar divided among his three sons the kingdom which had been allotted to him, giving to Louis Italy and the title of emperor, to Lothar Lotharingia and to Charles Provence. Having set everything in order he himself became a monk in the monastery of Prüm, in the sixteenth year of his reign after the death of his father. See how greatly the Roman Empire had fallen! When the kingdom of the Franks was divided into three parts it became a third part of a third part!

2. In the eight hundred and fifty-fifth year from the incarnation of the Lord, Lothar having laid down the garb of military life and assumed the dress of private life, his son Louis — His Most Serene Highness, the seventy-third in line from Augustus — obtained the throne. Basil, who had already killed Michael,[7] was then reigning in the royal city. Lothar, to whose control the kingdom of Lothar-

---

[4] Eastern Emperor (829-842) succeeding Michael II, the Stammerer.

[5] Michael III (known as the Drunkard), 842-867.

[6] This was in 843. For a brief discussion of these Viking raids, see C. M. H. 3, Chapter XIII, pp. 309-339.

[7] Otto is in error, since Michael was not murdered until 867.

ingia had fallen, married Theutberga the sister of Hubert the abbot. Not many days later Charles, who had received Provence in the division of the kingdom, died. Hence a dispute arose between his brother Lothar and his uncle Charles. Lothar bestowed upon Hubert the abbot, brother of the queen, the duchy that lay between the Jura Mountains and the Great St. Bernard.[8] Louis the Elder, king of East Francia, valiantly waged many wars against the Slavs, and having taken captive their leader Rastiz, put out his eyes.

During these days, while the princes within the kingdom of Charles were falling by wounds dealt them by one another, the Bretons invaded the land as though it were deserted [9] and, crossing the Loire, moved on as far as Poitiers laying everything waste with fire and sword; having thus enriched themselves with booty won from the Franks they returned home. Accordingly Charles, hiring Saxons for money, made war on the Bretons. But as soon as the battle started the Saxons, who had been stationed in the first line, terrified at the darts of the enemy turned and fled. The Bretons made charges from this side and from that, and the Franks fought manfully in keeping with their native quality of ancient valor; but after many had been slain and wounded on both sides, the battle was interrupted by the intervention of night. When, after day broke, the battle was taken up anew, Charles fled and thus set the bad example of flight to his men. At this sight the Bretons with a shout burst into the camp of the Franks and, having killed and captured many and carried off their tents together with much other booty, they departed. Because of this disaster Charles gave to Robert,[10] a valiant man, the duchy between the Loire and the Seine, that he might subdue the Bretons.

During these days while Nomenoë,[11] the king of the Bretons, was persecuting the Church of God in many ways, he saw in a vision the blessed Maurelio, bishop of Angers, coming to meet him and declaring that he was striking him with his staff to make him cease to oppress the churches. Nor was he deceived by the vision, for he straightway fell to the ground, was carried home by his attendants and by a manifest judgment of God ended at once his tyranny and

[8] His duchy corresponded roughly to French Switzerland of today.

[9] The Bretons under Nomenoë were victorious over the forces of Charles on the plain of Ballon in 845.

[10] Known as Robert the Strong, Marquess of Neustria.

[11] *Noemeticius* in the text.

his life. His son Erispoë [12] succeeded to the throne. Charles again undertook a war against the Bretons but had little success; indeed his only accomplishment was an agreement that hostages should be given by both sides and that both sides should maintain peace. Presently, however, Erispoë king of the Bretons voluntarily came to Charles submitting himself to his authority.[13] Charles bestowed many gifts upon him and sent him back to his own kingdom.

3. At that time, when the Church was gaining influence in the greatly divided kingdom of the Franks while Nicholas was pope, Lothar, out of love for Waldrada his concubine, sought in many ways an occasion for divorcing his wife, queen Theutberga. Therefore he enticed Gunther, archbishop of Cologne, who was at that time a man of preëminent authority in the kingdom, to accomplish for him the thing which he purposed in his heart; he won Gunther over by raising in him false hopes, by the promise that if he should be freed from Theutberga he would marry the archbishop's granddaughter. Gunther, associating with himself Theutgaud, the archbishop of Trèves, called together a council at Metz. Into this council he summoned the queen and by producing false witnesses convicted her not only of other sinful practices but also of incest. Accordingly a decree of divorce was granted, in conformity with the king's wish, and penance was enjoined upon the queen for the crime she had committed. Therefore the king, having obtained the desired pretext, held an assembly at Aachen at which he produced in written form the condemnation of Theutberga and declared that he could not contain himself. At the suggestion of Gunther all exclaimed, "It is better to marry than to burn" [14]; Waldrada was led forth and, arrayed in royal apparel and attended by a retinue of servants, obtained the name of queen. In this way, while the king brought to accomplishment the purposes he had formulated in his mind, he craftily deceived Gunther whom he by his false promises had made the partner of his wickedness. When these matters had come to the attention of His Highness Nicholas the pope, the latter, being a holy man and full of zeal for God, sending legates to the king rebuked him for the crime he had committed and invited him to do suitable penance. The legates however,

[12] *Herispeius* in the text.

[13] Charles recognized Erispoë as king of Brittany, after an unsuccessful expedition directed against the young ruler.

[14] I Cor. 7. 9.

corrupted by a bribe, took no steps at all to carry their commission into effect but came back enriched by many gifts, saying they had found scarcely anyone in the aforesaid kingdom who was acquainted with the ecclesiastical laws. The bishops of Trèves and Cologne followed them but, when they were compelled by the supreme pontiff to justify the judgment they had expressed, were found guilty and deposed; while they were striving in many ways to secure their reinstatement they died in Italy as exiles, being granted only the communion of the laity. Lothar, after repeated warnings, upon violating the oath which he had sworn in the presence of Bishop Arsenius, legate [15] of the holy Roman Church, was excommunicated by the pope.[16] In consequence of this the gravest danger threatened him personally and his whole kingdom. A great many letters sent by both parties with regard to this matter are still extant. Observe now that as the State declined the Church became so powerful that it even judged kings.

At this same time Louis, the king of the eastern realms, entered the western kingdoms at the invitation of certain nobles and, seizing the frontiers of the country, moved on as far as Sens. But when, leaving an army in the West, he had returned to his own land and the nobles who had invited him had been received back into favor by Charles, such of Louis's followers as had remained were obliged to depart from those territories. During these days Hubert the abbot, the brother of Theutberga, having long resisted Lothar was finally killed by Count Conrad. At the same time the Norsemen, laying waste by way of the Loire the country about Nantes, Tours and Angers, killed Duke Robert when he went out to meet them.

4. During these days the Saracens came from Africa and laid waste the region about Benevento, the region which was formerly called Samnium.[17] When the emperor Louis began to gather forces from all sides to withstand them he called his brother Lothar to his aid. The latter collected an army and, having entered Italy, paid a heavy penalty for his evil deeds, for he lost many of his army

[15] The text gives *apocrisiarius.*

[16] Nicholas I. He died in 867 and was succeeded by Hadrian II, who took a less firm stand.

[17] They had gained a foothold in Sicily in 827 and since 837 had frequently been invited to serve as mercenaries in Italy. Lothar I and Louis II organized a fruitless expedition against them in 847. In 867 they plundered the abbeys of Monte Cassino and St. Vincent of Volturno. It is this raid which is referred to in the present passage.

both on account of the unaccustomed heat and from the bites of spiders. After this Lothar went to Rome and was received with all honor by Pope Hadrian, who had succeeded Nicholas, and was asked outright by him if he had obeyed the admonitions of his predecessor Nicholas. When Lothar and all the princes who had come with him falsely affirmed that he had well observed Nicholas's injunctions, the Pope handed the Lord's body to him and to his retinue with an appeal to their consciences.[18] It is said that after their return everyone who had approached the Lord's table with a false heart and a defiled conscience died within a year. Lothar himself was smitten with disease on the journey home and departed this life at Piacenza. When Charles heard of the death of his nephew he invaded his kingdom.[19] Because his brother Louis [20] attempted to prevent this they came to an agreement and divided the kingdom in question equally at Meersen. Louis obtained the palace at Aachen. After no long time had elapsed Adelchis, duke of Benevento, relying upon the Greeks and associating with himself the Samnites, Lucanians and Campanians, prepared to rebel against the emperor Louis. The emperor [21] collected his forces and assailed Benevento in war. Adelchis met him, overreached him by guile, won him over by presents and persuaded him to leave his borders. Then the emperor, in his progress through Campania and Lucania, took all their cities except Capua without great difficulty. Since he could not easily take this by storm (because it was built of squared stones), he besieged it and laid waste the country round about. The Capuans, in utter despair, opened the gates of their city and came in tears to the emperor's feet with their bishop, who bore the body of the blessed Germanus; begging for pardon they committed themselves to his mercy. The emperor, who was a very pious man, received the citizens into his favor, and having expelled the Greeks, restored all the cities of Lucania and Campania to the authority of Rome. Meanwhile Adelchis endeavored to ensnare the king a second time with his artifices: he met him and persuaded him to disband his army and to spare the country, adding that it was not necessary for a king to destroy needlessly a people subject

18 For the judgment of God invoked by this communion see C. M. H. 3. 44.

19 Charles the Bald entered Lorraine and was there crowned king at Metz on Sept. 9, 869.

20 *I.e.*, of course, Louis the German, not the emperor Louis II.

21 *Augustus* in the text.

to him. The king, in response to the duke's request, sent home all but a few of his soldiers and, suspecting no harm, entered Benevento. At about midday, as he lay on his couch, the citizens of Benevento suddenly rushed in and he was forced to arm himself. But since the citizens with their duke Adelchis threatened to set fire to the palace, they compelled the emperor to seek peace and to promise upon oath that he would never again enter their territories without their consent. After making this ignominious compact the emperor went to Rome and there, in the presence of Pope John (who had succeeded Hadrian) and of the entire senate, set forth his case. Accordingly Adelchis was declared an enemy and a tyrant by the senate; and the emperor was then, on the authority of God and the blessed Peter, absolved by the Pope from the oath which he had sworn against his will and to save his life. But although the emperor was believed to have been justly freed from his oath, yet to avoid criticism he refused to go in person to crush the tyrant; he collected an army, however, and sent the queen thither. When Adelchis heard this he was panic-stricken and fled to the island of Corsica, thus avoiding the emperor's anger. After no long time had elapsed innumerable locusts, larger than all other locusts and having six wings apiece, came from the east and covered Gaul; having consumed the grain crops everywhere they finally settled down on the English ocean. They were carried off by the wind and drowned in the salt sea, and afterwards, being piled up by the waves upon the shore in an enormous heap, they tainted the air of the neighboring regions by their offensive smell.

5. At that time Charles, the king of West Francia, by the aid of the Bretons trapped the Norsemen who, after killing Robert [22] and other nobles of the kingdom, were making wild raids in all directions. Charles besieged the city of Angers of which the Norsemen had taken possession. The Bretons, seeing that all the hope of the enemy would lie in the river, tried to divert it from its channel. Upon seeing this the Norsemen begged for peace, and by promising the king money persuaded him to raise the siege dishonorably. But according to their custom — for they are a very restless race — they by no means kept their promises but entered Francia by way of the Loire and did the king far greater harm than before. How much damage the aforesaid people did to the kingdom of the Franks has been sufficiently recounted, I find, by others. For they

[22] Marquess Robert fell at Brissarthe in 866.

are a very fickle and inconstant race, not content with their own
territories yet making friends wherever they go and very courteous.
As I have said they always harried the western kingdom while the
Saxons, who also are fickle but ferocious, constantly attacked the
eastern.[23]

6. In the eight hundred and seventy-fourth year from the incarnation of the Lord, Louis, that most courteous emperor, brought
his days to a close in the nineteenth year of his reign.[24] In the same
year his uncle, the elder Charles, king of West Francia, went to
Rome and received the title of emperor from John, the supreme
pontiff, and from the citizens — for money, it is said — and reigned
as the seventy-fourth in line from Augustus. Not long after, his
brother, Louis the Elder (the Eastern King), died at Frankfort,
leaving three sons — Carloman, Louis and Charles. The emperor
Charles, upon hearing of his brother's death, prepared to invade
the kingdom of Lotharingia;[25] collecting an army he first seized
the palace at Aachen and moved forward as far as Cologne. Meanwhile Carloman, the firstborn son of Louis, entered Italy and attempted to seize the imperial power. But Louis, who had attended
his father's funeral, had been elected King of the East by his nobles
and had already begun to reign. On hearing that his uncle Charles
had entered the borders of his kingdom he sent an embassy to him
and warned him to depart from his realm. When Charles refused
to agree to this, Louis collected an army and set out to do battle
with him. Without delay the conflict took place, in the district of
Maifeld not far from Andernach, near the Rhine. After many on
both sides had been slain Charles was finally compelled to flee. The
sons of Louis made an agreement and divided their father's kingdom: Carloman received Bavaria, Pannonia, Kärnten, Bohemia and
Moravia; Louis, East Franconia, Thuringia, Saxony, Frisia and
Lotharingia; Charles, Alemannia and certain cities of Lotharingia
(the latter he accepted because they contained an abundance of
wine).[26] Charles the Second, now as emperor, a second time hastened to Rome. While he was returning from Rome and journey-

---

[23] Hofmeister points out that this is an error and cites V. 27, VII. 8, and
Gesta Friderici 1. 4, as well as Isidore, *Origines* 9. 2. 100 and a letter Otto
wrote to the Abbot Wibald (Jaffé, *Bibl. rerum Germanarum, nr.* 387, p. 520).

[24] He died on August 12, 875.   [25] Or Lorraine.

[26] Regino (on the year 842) makes this statement concerning the cities
across the Rhine ceded to Louis the Elder.

ing through Lombardy, he went to Pavia. When he heard there that Carloman, the son of his brother Louis, had entered Italy with a great army, he wished to return to Francia but died on the way — of poison, it is said — in the third year of his reign. In the following year Louis, the son of the younger Charles,[27] who was called the Stammerer, ended his days, leaving two sons, Louis and Carloman. The third son, who was afterwards called Charles, had not yet been born. His domain was Provençe, which his father Charles,[28] the son of the emperor Lothar, had obtained in the division. Boso, to whom the emperor Charles had given that land, was eager to invade it and so came to Lyons. There he was anointed [29] king of Burgundy by the bishop of Lyons; but he was kept out of it by the young men I have mentioned, Louis and Carloman.

7. In the eight hundred and eightieth year from the incarnation of the Lord, Carloman the son of Louis, to whom Bavaria had fallen by lot, after many triumphs which he had enjoyed in his father's time and after his father's death — and by which he had greatly extended his country's bounds — died of a stroke of paralysis and was buried in a place in Bavaria called Ötting. He left a son by a lady who was of high rank but was not his lawful wife. This son he had called Arnulf, from the name of the blessed Arnulf, whom he regarded as the founder of the Carolingian house. This is the Arnulf to whom the sole rule afterwards fell.[30] But Louis, the king of East Franconia, learning of his brother's death came to Regensburg, the metropolis of Bavaria, and subjected all the princes of that land to his sway. He also bestowed upon Arnulf the duchy of Carinthia together with the fortified town of Moosburg.

8. In the eight hundred and eighty-first year from the incarnation of the Lord, Charles, who in the division had obtained Alemannia, moved his army into Italy and, having accepted the surrender of all Lombardy, pressed on as far as the City. There he obtained from Pope John and from all the people the title of Emperor and

---

[27] Hofmeister calls attention to Otto's mistake. Having just called Charles the Bald ''the Elder,'' Otto is here referring to Charles, king of Provençe, the son of the emperor Lothar I (see VI. 1 *et seq.*, above), as the Younger. But Louis the Stammerer was the son of Charles the Bald.

[28] Otto means the father of Louis the Stammerer. But see note 27.

[29] Boso was crowned at Lyons in the autumn of 879. He was the son-in-law of Louis II.

[30] Arnulf ruled from 888 to 899.

Augustus, and reigned as the seventy-fifth in line from Augustus.[31]

At that time the Norsemen invaded the kingdom of Louis by way of the river Waal, burned the palace at Nimwegen and then, scattering over the surrounding country, laid waste Cologne, Bonn and Aachen, as well as the adjacent regions, fortresses and villages. Meanwhile King Louis died at Frankfort and was buried by his father's side in the monastery at Lorsch. The Norsemen, feeling secure when they heard of the king's death, burst into Trèves (the most famous city of Gaul, once destroyed by Julius Caesar), on the very day of the Lord's Supper, and remaining there until Easter wasted with fire both the city itself and the surrounding regions. When the bishop of this city and Count Bertolf went forth to meet them a battle followed. The bishop lost his life and the rest were put to flight. The Norsemen returned to their ships laden with the booty of the Franks.

While this was going on in Gaul the emperor Charles the Third tarried in Italy. Therefore the princes both of Gaul and of Germany all pressed him hard with entreaties, importuning him to return and take up his father's kingdom now that his brother was dead, and to free his country from invasion by its foes. Returning without delay he took as allies the Lombards, Bavarians, Saxons, Frisians, Alemanni, Thuringians and many others to oppose the Norsemen, who were still tarrying in the kingdom, and set his force in motion against them. He made Godefrid the king of the Norsemen a Christian, giving him in marriage Gisila the daughter of Lothar,[32] together with the province of Frisia, and raised him from the sacred font.[33] By such means he persuaded him to depart with his followers from the borders of the kingdom. In the following year Louis, the son of the son of Charles the western king, died[34] and was buried in the monastery of St. Denis, leaving his brother Carloman as heir to the kingdom. Besides other valiant deeds Carloman performed this noteworthy exploit: he routed eight thousand Norsemen in battle. Not long afterwards Carloman, while he was on a hunting expedition, was gored by a boar and died. Therefore the West Franks, having lost their princes, of their own initiative

[31] Charles III (the Fat) was crowned by Pope John VIII in February, 881.
[32] *I.e.*, of Lothar II, king of Lorraine.
[33] Thus apparently becoming his godfather; *cf.* 11 below (Zwentibold).
[34] In 882. This is Louis III, the son of Louis II (the Stammerer) and grandson of Charles II (the Bald).

called in the emperor Charles, who was accounted the sole survivor of the Carolingian line at that time, and when he came subjected themselves to him. Thereupon he waged many wars of varying outcome with the Norsemen.

9. In the eight hundred and eighty-seventh year from the incarnation of the Lord, since the emperor Charles had commenced to fail in body and in mind, the princes of the kingdom brought to the throne Arnulf [35] the son of Carloman; this they did at Tribur upon the anniversary of the death of St. Martin. And strange to say, you might have seen the emperor who after Charles the Great had the fullest power among all kings of the Franks, in a brief space of time reduced to such insignificance that, in need even of bread, he was pitifully begging a stipend from Arnulf, who had by this time become king, and gratefully receiving from him a few sources of revenue in Alemannia. Behold the wretched condition of our mortal lot! The king who, in the division of the Eastern realm among the brothers had received the smallest share at first, attained to such heights that he received both the Eastern and the Western Kingdoms, together with the title of Roman Emperor, but finally fell so low that he was in need even of bread. He might have said with Job, ''Thou hast lifted me above the clouds and hast cast me down mightily,'' [36] and with the Psalmist, ''For thou hast taken me up and cast me down.'' [37] To what may I liken worldly prosperity but to a cloud which by quickly passing deceives him who relies upon it, and by reason of its unsubstantial nature cannot sustain him who leans upon it? The higher, therefore, a man is raised above the clouds the more mightily is he dashed down upon the earth and crushed. This sport — a sport most pitiable, a sport described by the philosophers as the sport of fortune, that after the manner of a wheel makes the highest lowest and the lowest highest, but in real fact a state of things made uncertain in accordance with the nod of a God who exchanges kingdoms — might challenge us to forsake worldly misery and to seek the true life.

It is said of this Charles that he was a very earnest Christian. Wherefore this trial is believed to have come to him at the last to test him. For he died in the course of the year after he was expelled from his kingdom, and was buried in the monastery of

---

[35] This is Arnulf of Carinthia (887-899) ; see VI. 7 above. Charles the Fat was deposed at Tribur, near Darmstadt, toward the close of the year 887.

[36] Job 30. 22.   [37] Ps. 102. 10.

Reichenau. From this time on there was confusion,[38] we find, with respect to the title of Roman Emperor, a confusion which continued even to the time of Otto.[39] For upon the death of Charles, who had reigned for six years and had lived a seventh as a private citizen, the empire was split into different parts, since the separate provinces wished to select each their own king. However, the largest share fell to Arnulf.

10. The Italians set two kings over them — Berengar duke of Friuli and Guido duke of Spoleto. Of these Berengar was expelled from his native land by Guido and came to Arnulf as a fugitive. The western Franks, with Arnulf's consent, chose Odo the son of Robert (a valiant man) as their king. He manfully waged many battles against the Norsemen.

During these days the tribe of the Hungarians, setting out from Scythia and ousted by the Patzinaks,[40] drove out the Avars from Pannonia and commenced to live there themselves. This people was at that time — it is said — so savage and bestial that they ate raw meat and even drank human blood. That this may not seem to any man beyond belief, let all hear that the Patzinaks and those who are called Falones [41] even today eat raw and unclean flesh, such as that of horses and cats. Furthermore they are very proficient in the use of bows and arrows and are accustomed to inflict injury with them even as they flee. They differ then from the Bretons or from the Frisians in that these two peoples inflict injuries with missiles, the Hungarians do so with arrows. During this same time the Norsemen were roving about through Gaul in the neighborhood of Sens, Paris and Troyes.

11. Arnulf ruled the whole of East Franconia, the district which is called at the present time the Teutonic Kingdom — that is, Bavaria, Suevia, Saxony, Thuringia, Frisia and Lotharingia; with his consent Odo held the western country. Arnulf bestowed upon Zwentibold [42] king of the Moravians the duchy of Bohemia; indeed he named his own son Zwentibold after the king of the Moravians and permitted the boy to be raised by the king from the sacred font.

---

38 *Cf.* below, VI. 13.

39 Otto I, the Great, 936-973. He was emperor 962-973.

40 *Pezenati* in the text. They are also called "Petchenegs."

41 Hofmeister identifies these as the "*Cumani*" called by the Slavs "Polowcos." See Zeuss, pp. 743 *et seq.*; also Müllenhoff, in *Zeitschrift für Deutsches Altertum* 10 (1856), 165; *Gesta Friderici* 1. 32.

42 He is also called Svátopluk.

But above all other places in his kingdom he loved Regensburg [43] the metropolis of Bavaria. Therefore he enlarged its walls, and adorned the monastery of the blessed Emmeram with many ornaments and enriched it with large possessions. They have a tradition there and exhibit a written document [44] which declares that the king I have mentioned [Arnulf] transferred St. Denis [45] from Gaul to the aforesaid monastery. Whether it be so or not I leave to them to determine. Not long after, while Arnulf was staying in Bavaria to quiet the Slavs, the Norsemen invaded his kingdom of Lotharingia; they routed the nobles who had come out to meet them and killed many. Upon hearing of this Arnulf collected an army and attacked the enemy, and in the battle that ensued he displayed so great valor and might in defeating them that only a bare handful slipped away in flight and returned to their fleet, saving their lives but nothing else. The victory won, Arnulf returned to Bavaria. At that time a serious controversy over the kingship arose in the western kingdom between Charles, the son of Louis,[46] and Odo — a controversy which compelled Charles, on account of the weakness of his cause, to go to Arnulf as a suppliant and beg aid of him.

12. In the eight hundred and ninety-fourth year from the incarnation of the Lord, King Arnulf, having set everything in good order in Germany, invaded Lombardy with his army. Having captured the very strong city of Bergamo he hanged Count Ambrose on a gibbet. All the cities of Italy, smitten with terror at this deed, dared not fight any longer but of their own act submitted to his sway. The king also pressed on as far as Piacenza. Having returned to Gaul by the Greater St. Bernard he held an assembly at Worms, and, in the monastery of Lorsch — which was close to that city — granted to Louis the son of Boso [47] certain cities and districts near the mountains. At that time Guido,[48] who had usurped the kingdom of Italy, died. His son Lambert went to Rome and had himself

[43] Or Ratisbon.

[44] Hofmeister is convinced that Otto saw a "*translatio s. Dionysii*," whether the one written in 1049 and edited by L. de Heinemann (N. Archiv 15. 331), or another. See MGH. SS. 11. 343; N. Archiv 29. 641.

[45] Or St. Dionysius.

[46] Charles the Simple; *cf.* C. M. H. 3. 71.

[47] Louis the Blind; he was proclaimed king of Provence in an assembly held at Valence in 890.

[48] Or Guy, who was consecrated as emperor by Pope Stephen V in 891. He died in 895.

proclaimed emperor. The king again held an assembly at Worms and with the consent of the nobles handed over Lothar's kingdom to his own son Zwentibold. Odo also, the king of [West] Francia, came to Arnulf with many gifts and, having been received with honor, returned in possession of all the things for which he had come.

13. In the eight hundred and ninety-sixth year from the incarnation of the Lord and the seventh of his own reign, Arnulf, the victorious king, on this occasion at the request of Pope Formosus — who was suffering grievous persecution at the hands of the citizens — entered Italy a second time and moved on as far as the City. Having taken it by force of arms he was crowned by the aforesaid pope and, according to some authorities, obtained the title of emperor and Augustus. He commanded that those who had started the uprising against the pope should be beheaded. After Arnulf had returned from the City, Lambert, who had unlawfully usurped imperial authority, died and Louis the son of Boso was invited by the Lombards to accept the imperial power.

I have found that in certain histories of the Romans no mention is made of Arnulf in the list of emperors after Charles III, as if the imperial power had been transferred from the Franks to the Lombards, and as if Louis and those others who succeeded him are counted in the number of the emperors.[49] Others place Arnulf in the list, and have been wont to call those that reigned in the period of confusion, down to the time of Otto, not emperors and Augusti but usurpers and *angusti*.[50] Not long afterwards, when Odo king of the Franks died and was buried in the monastery of St. Denis, Charles [51] was elected king by common consent. Arnulf died in the twelfth year of his reign but, as has been explained before, in the fifth year of his imperial power, and was buried beside his father in the place called Ötting, as Regino relates. However, his sepulcher is pointed out in the monastery of the blessed Emmeram at Regensburg.[52] Of course it is possible that he was buried at Ötting and afterwards moved to Regensburg.

14. In the nine hundred and first year from the incarnation of

49 *Cf.* VI. 22 below.

50 It is impossible to bring out in English the play on the words *Augustus* and *angustus*.

51 Charles the Simple, who had already been crowned at Rheims in 893 in Odo's absence.

52 Or Ratisbon. Arnulf's tomb, destroyed by fire in 1642, was restored in

the Lord, Louis the son of Arnulf was made king at a place called
Forchheim,[53] and was invited by the nobles of Lotharingia to rule
over Belgica [54] because they were hostile to Zwentibold. When
Zwentibold, having learned of this, was perpetrating many evil
deeds and greatly disgracing his rule by pillage, murder and burning, he was finally put to death in formal open war by Counts
Stephen, Gebhard [55] and Matfrid. In this way Louis, unhindered,
obtained his kingdom. During these days the Hungarians, roving
about in Lombardy,[56] slew with their arrows such natives of that
country as withstood them and after cruelly devastating the province returned to their own homes.[57]

15. In the nine hundred and fifth year from the incarnation of
the Lord, Louis the son of Boso, obtaining the title of Emperor,[58]
drove out Berengar. And when he held the entire Italian kingdom
subject to his will, he disbanded his army and went with a few followers to Verona. There he was betrayed by the citizens, taken captive and deprived of his eyesight after Berengar, who was in exile
in Bavaria, had been recalled. Henceforth Berengar held the kingdom of Italy together with the title of Roman Emperor.

At about the same time Albert,[59] a most distinguished count of
the Franks (and through his daughter, grandson of Otto duke of
the Saxons), killed Conrad, who is believed by some to have been
the brother of King Louis. On this account the king made war on
the aforesaid knight, who was in the fortified city of Bamberg [60]
where now, one sees, a famous bishop's seat is established. But when
the king saw that he could accomplish nothing by force, he had
recourse (by the advice of Hatto, archbishop of Mainz) to guile.
Accordingly as we find in the histories of the deeds of the kings, and

1786; see H. Graf v. Walderdorff, *Regensburg in seiner Vergangenheit und
Gegenwart*, 4th ed. (1896), pp. 396 et seq.

[53] Louis IV (the Child) was proclaimed King on Feb. 4, 900.

[54] *I.e.*, Lotharingia.   [55] Duke of Lorraine.

[56] It was in 900 that a band of Hungarians ravaged Bavaria on their return
from an expedition into Italy. They devastated Carinthia in 901.

[57] On the banks of the Theiss.

[58] Louis received the imperial crown in 901 from Pope Benedict IV.

[59] Or Adalbert, the head of the house of Babenberg. Conrad the Old — not
a brother of Louis IV, as Otto says "was believed by some": see Frutolf,
p. 175, on the year 912 — was the head of the rival Franconian house of the
Conradins. He was slain by Albert in 906.

[60] So Frutolf (and Ekkehard *Sangallensis*), agreeing with Liudprand; but
they are wrong.

even to this day hear in common talk on the street corners and in the gossip of palaces, Hatto went to Albert in his city of Bamberg and conferred with him, as though from friendly motives, regarding the possibility of securing the favor of the king. Albert devoutly obeyed his admonitions and humbly sought safe conduct. Not to delay you with a long story, after the aforesaid priest had pledged his honor they set out upon their journey. They had already gone out from the town and were now drawing near to the neighboring village, which is still called Teurstat,[61] when the bishop said, "It will be hard for us to endure fasting; if it please you, let us turn aside here for breakfast before we present ourselves before the king." Then Albert, ingenuously, after the manner of princes of old, believing all that he heard and without any suspicions of treachery at all, gladly took the bishop back to breakfast in the town from which they had set out. After they had refreshed themselves they went on to the court. The prince was placed on trial and sentenced to death as guilty of treason. He reminded the bishop of the pledge he had given. Thereupon the bishop retorted that he had scrupulously kept his word [62] in that he had brought him back safe and unhurt to the town. So Albert was beheaded and his possessions — out of which the Church of Bamberg was, it is said, afterwards enriched — were confiscated by the state. To this Albert, the Albert [63] who afterwards added to the Roman Empire the Eastern March — that is, Upper Pannonia, which he had taken from the Hungarians — is said to have traced his descent. Let others judge this deed of the bishop as they will and defend it as committed for the advantage of the kingdom: *I* believe that not only should a bishop not have ensnared a Christian by guile — certainly he should not have done so for the sake of any gain — but he ought not even to have spoken with a double heart [64] in a case involving capital punishment.

Not long afterwards, the Hungarians made war upon the Bavarians, killed their leader Leopold,[65] the father of Duke Arnulf,[66] and then, scattering over the whole kingdom, roved through Ale-

[61] Still a suburb of Bamberg, to the south.

[62] This is found only in Liudprand, whom Otto has followed here and in several other passages; cf. VI. 23 below.

[63] Margave Adalbert of Babenberg (died 1055), the founder of the Austrian House and an ancestor of Bishop Otto himself; see VI. 32 below.

[64] The text reads *in corde et corde*; see Ps. 12. 2.

[65] Or Liutpold, killed in 907.   [66] Arnulf the Bad, of Bavaria.

mania, Franconia, Saxony and Thuringia. Louis the king of East
Francia died in the twelfth year of his reign without leaving an
heir. In his person and that of his brother Zwentibold, according
to some authorities, the line of the Carolingians failed for the time
in the Eastern kingdom.[67] Whence a certain modern historian says,
''The last of the Augusti was Augustulus, and the last of the
Carolingians was Zwentibold.'' Upon the death of Louis, Otto
duke of the Saxons was demanded by all as king. But that most
renowned prince, being burdened with years, refused to be made
king.

16. In the nine hundred and thirteenth year from the incarnation of the Lord, Conrad [68] the son of the Conrad who had been
slain by Albert was, upon the advice of the aforesaid Duke Otto,
made king of East Francia by general consent. Some say that he
was the son of a brother of Louis, and accordingly count him as the
last of the Carolingians. In the first year of his reign the Hungarians again streamed forth to lay waste the land.[69] They were,
however, defeated by the Suevi and the Bavarians near the river
Inn. Arnulf, duke of Bavaria, rebelled against the king and fled
with his wife and sons to the Hungarians. The king, bringing to
a close at one time his life and reign, died in the seventh year of
his reign. In accordance with advice he had given, Henry [70] the son
of Duke Otto was chosen to succeed him as king in the nine hundred
and twentieth year from the incarnation of the Lord.

17. From this point some reckon a kingdom of the Germans as
supplanting that of the Franks. Hence they say that Pope Leo,
in the decrees of the popes,[71] called Henry's son Otto the first king
of the Germans. For that Henry of whom we are speaking refused,
it is said, an honor offered him by the supreme pontiff.[72] But it

[67] See VI. 32 (beginning) below where Otto again takes up the line. The
work quoted in the next line below has probably been lost since Otto's day.

[68] Conrad I, duke of Franconia, king from 911 to 918.

[69] Defeated by Duke Arnulf on the Inn in 913, they yet continued to devastate Saxony, Thuringia and Swabia, and in 917 penetrated Alsace.

[70] Henry I (called the Fowler), 919-936, founder of the Saxon line. *Cf.*
C. M. H. 3. 179-186.

[71] The spurious privileges circulated under the name of Pope Leo VIII
(*MG. LL. Constit.* 1. 448 ff.).

[72] Otto evidently means the Pope, but Widukind (copied by Frutolf, p.
180. 15) refers to the Archbishop of Mainz, who may, however, have been the
Pope's emissary. The *dignitas* which Henry refused was doubtless the crown
of empire.

seems to me that the kingdom of the Germans — which today, as we see, has possession of Rome — is a part of the kingdom of the Franks. For, as is perfectly clear in what precedes,[73] at the time of Charles the boundaries of the kingdom of the Franks included the whole of Gaul — that is, Gallia Celtica, Gallia Belgica and Gallia Lugdunensis — and all Germany, from the Rhine to Illyricum. When the realm was divided between his son's sons, one part was called the eastern, the other the western, yet both together were called the Kingdom of the Franks.[74] So then in the eastern part, which is called the Kingdom of the Germans, Henry was the first of the race of the Saxons to succeed to the throne when the line of Charles failed. In West Francia, on the other hand, Charles, a king of the stock of Charles, still survived. Henry's son Otto, because he restored to the German East Franks the empire [75] which had been usurped by the Lombards, is called the first king of the Germans — not, perhaps, because he was the first to reign among the Germans but because he first, after those who were named after Charles Carlings or Carolingians (as the Merovingians were named after Merovech), was born of another line (that is, the Saxon) and restored the empire to the German Franks. But just as, when the Merovingians failed and the Carlings succeeded, the kingdom nevertheless remained Frankish — so also, when the Carlings ceased, the Ottos, though of another family and speech, yet came to the throne of a kingdom that kept its identity. Such changes, betraying the frailty of mortal estate, appear at intervals from the beginning of the world down to the present day. Thus in the kingdom of the Egyptians the Ptolemies succeeded the Pharaohs, and in the Roman Empire also the painstaking investigator will find after the families of the Caesars were exhausted repeated changes, pitiful in the extreme, in the royal succession. And as you read in the Book of the Kings, so in consequence of the sins (in part of the rulers, in part of the people) after the fourth or the fifth generation some vanished to be succeeded by others, who not only did not honor the sons of their predecessors but even afflicted them greatly and sought to destroy them. And in fact, scarcely ever do you find that the seed of any king endured for long in its own glory except in the case of David, to whom Christ was promised. All of which, as I have often said, reveals human wretchedness and the round of changes and points us to the state of eternal blessedness. But enough of this.

[73] V. 32. [74] *Cf*. V. 35 (end) above. [75] See VI. 22 below.

18. So then Henry the son of Duke Otto reigned in East Francia while Charles [76] held the western kingdom. Certain Celtic writers [77] assert that he was at first only duke of the Saxons and was subject to Charles but that afterwards (upon the advice of his son-in-law Gisilbert,[78] duke of Lorraine) he, together with all the eastern nobles, broke away from the sway of Charles and assumed the title of king. Others say that after Conrad's death Henry was chosen king in his stead by the eastern Franks, being elected by the nobles, and never received anything from the hand of Charles. Yet the authorities agree that he ruled mightily over the kingdom of Germany and had a controversy with Charles over Lorraine. These conflicting accounts of historians resulted, I think, from the fact that since men's intellectual abilities had begun to grow and to keep pace with the glory of empire, as a result, when the imperial authority was transferred to the Franks and men's sympathies were divided upon the physical division of the kingdom, the writers extolled each his own state as much as he could with the aid of his transcendent abilities. But I myself, keeping a middle course in these matters, and, so far as I am able and can conjecture from what they have said, holding fast the thread of truth,[79] will strive by God's grace to turn aside neither to the right hand nor to the left.

And so when Henry reigned on this side of the Rhine and was having a dispute with Charles about Lorraine (according to the statement in which, as we said, both sets of writers are in accord), with the consent of both a day was set to decide this disagreement in the town of Bonn.[80] Lorraine fell to Henry. Only Gallia Celtica, and Aquitania, and part of Gallia Lugdunensis remained in the possession of Charles (Burgundy had a king of its own). And so the kingdom which is called the Kingdom of the Franks lost of its ancestral heritage Belgic Gaul, including the palace at Aachen and the greater part of Francia.[81]

[76] Charles III, the Simple (898-929).

[77] See Frutolf, p. 182. 13: *Haec sunt verba illius Gallici hystoriographi.*

[78] Or Gilbert.

[79] Observe Bishop Otto's high ideal as historian.

[80] The two kings met on neutral territory, a boat moored in the middle of the Rhine at Bonn, Nov. 7, 921. But it was not until 925 that Henry finally secured Lorraine. *Cf.* Waitz, *Jahrbücher des deutschen Reichs unter König Heinrich I*, 83-86.

[81] It will be noted that Otto frequently follows his early sources, notably

About the same time Arnulf duke of Bavaria, upon learning of the death of King Conrad, returned from Hungary to his own land eager to rule there. He was, however, finally quieted by the king, who left him the churches of his own country. This is the Arnulf who cruelly destroyed the churches and the monasteries of Bavaria and distributed their possessions among his soldiers. When he was at first too weak, spending all his energies in efforts to become king, two swords were shown in a vision to the blessed Ulric, the bishop of Augsburg, the one of which lacked a hilt. He heard that the sword with a hilt was King Henry and that the sword without a hilt was Arnulf, who was without wisdom and justice. After this Henry defeated the Hungarians in Saxony, with incredible bloodshed, as they were trying to burst forth from their own land according to their custom. Henry had a picture of the victory painted in his palace at Merseburg, which is called also Martinopolis. He also extorted by threats from Rudolph,[82] the king of Gallia Lugdunensis (or Burgundy), the Holy Lance which our kings still possess.[83] After many valorous deeds Henry was smitten with disease while he was setting out for Rome to obtain the imperial title, and died in the seventeenth year of his reign.

19. In the nine hundred and thirty-sixth year from the incarnation of the Lord, Otto [84] the son of Henry succeeded his father on the throne — a worthy heir — and was crowned in the palace at Aachen by Hildebert archbishop of Mainz. He quieted the Slavs, who are called also Bohemians, when they resisted him; he put to flight the Belgians who were trying, at the advice of their duke Gilbert,[85] to keep him from crossing the Rhine and, after laying waste the entire land with sword and flame, invested a castle sit-

Orosius, in applying the Roman nomenclature for the divisions of Gaul (cf. VI. 30). The "Kingdom of the Franks" is here France; Gallia Belgica is, of course, Lorraine and has been regularly so rendered in this translation.

[82] Rudolph II, king of Upper Burgundy.

[83] Frutolf (p. 182. 40) says of this Holy Lance: eamque credimus esse, quae extunc hodieque in imperatorum tutela solet manere. Hofmeister has written a monograph, Die Heilige Lanze, ein Abzeichen des alten Reichs (Untersuchungen zur Deutschen Staats und Rechtsgeschichte, herausg. von O. Gierke, Heft 96, Breslau, 1908) to show that another lance, still preserved today at Vienna, was substituted, between the years 1035 and 1099, for the lance acquired by Henry.

[84] Otto I, the Great, 936-973; see C. M. H. 3. 187-203.

[85] Of Lorraine. He rebelled against Otto in 939 in company with a number of other dukes.

uated on Chèvremont. Louis [86] the son of Charles entered Alsace, since he was eager to take advantage of this opportunity to recover Lorraine which, as I have said before, his father had lost. Upon hearing of this the king raised the siege of Chèvremont and, after driving Louis out of Alsace, beleaguered Breisnach. Meanwhile Duke Gilbert, wishing to avenge this wrong, this disgrace, collected an army and moved as far as Andernach. When the Germans met him there a very bitter combat ensued: Duke Gilbert himself was drowned in the Rhine while he was trying to escape, and the rest were driven in flight after very many of them had been slain. Upon learning of this the people of Breisnach surrendered the city to the king. The king again invaded Lorraine and received the submission of the whole land; henceforth that province was in the undisputed possession of the kings of the Germans. Now King Louis married the sister of King Otto; she had been widowed by the death of Duke Gilbert. Not long afterwards, having been driven from his kingdom by his own subjects,[87] Louis came to Otto as a suppliant and having conquered his foes by Otto's aid regained his kingdom. After this a synod was celebrated at Ingelheim in the presence of both kings at which Marinus, a legate of the Apostolic See, presided. Otto, after many triumphs, prepared to add to his kingdom Italy also, which had for many years been alienated from the Franks and from the Germans. At this time Italy was being oppressed in many different ways by the tyrant Berengar, by whom also Adelaide the widow of the emperor Lothar (Otto's predecessor) was then held in captivity. Therefore the king entered Italy and, having freed the queen from captivity, took her to wife. After repulsing Berengar he celebrated the day of the Lord's nativity in Pavia. When he returned to his own land in the spring he left Duke Conrad [88] in Italy to pursue Berengar. By Conrad's advice Berengar went to the king, in Saxony, to gain his favor, with the aid of the duke and of the king's son Liudolf.[89] For three days he was not admitted to the king's presence; then finally, through the intercession of the aforesaid duke and of the king's son, he succeeded in having a day for an audience set for him in Augsburg, a city of Rhaetia.[90] To

[86] Louis IV (d'Outremer), king of West Francia, the son of Charles III (the Simple).

[87] Notably Hugh the Great, who was duke of the Franks and count of Paris.

[88] Conrad the Red, duke of Lorraine, who had married Otto's daughter Liutgard in 947.

[89] Duke of Swabia since 949.   [90] *I.e.,* Bavaria.

this place, where many of the vital parts of the empire had been united, Berengar came humbly with his son Albert and gave himself up to the king, and received from him the kingdom of Italy except the marches of Verona and Aquileia.[91] On his return to Italy Berengar did much harm to the nobles of the land, even as before, and aroused against himself universal hatred. At that time Liudolf, the king's son, upon the advice of certain men planned an insurrection against his father.[92] But he soon desisted from the undertaking and was received back into favor, in a truly fatherly way, by the king.

20. In the nine hundred and fifty-fifth year from the incarnation of the Lord, the Hungarians, a thoroughly savage race, burst forth in countless numbers, and, covering the whole land like a swarm of locusts, came as far as the Lech to the city of Augsburg, over which at that time the venerable priest Ulric — a priest who was fit servant of God — presided. At the exhortation of the aforesaid man of God, the most glorious king met the Hungarians. Protected by faith rather than by arms he defeated the barbarians [93] I have mentioned — aye, defeated them with such valor that thenceforth that most monstrous of all races not only did not dare invade his kingdom, but was even seized with such despair that they planned to defend their own kingdom against our countrymen by ramparts and palisades in swampy places. In that battle fell the illustrious Duke Conrad of Worms,[94] the son-in-law of the king. The barbarians however — although this seems beyond belief — are said to have been entirely destroyed, even to utter annihilation: only seven survived.[95] It is said that the man responsible for this great carnage was a certain Bavarian Count of Scheyern.[96] Yet he paid the penalty for his treachery, for, when he had exposed to death the Hungarians who had been recklessly led forth, he was killed by them as a traitor. Moreover his land is said to have been

91 These they were required to cede to Duke Henry of Bavaria.

92 The second rebellion of the German dukes against Otto, 953-954.

93 In the decisive battle in the Lechfeld (955).

94 He had lost his dukedom of Lorraine in consequence of his revolt in 953-954.

95 On the various stories about the seven Hungarians, see E. Dümmler, *Nachrichten von der Göttinger Ges. der Wiss.*, 1868, pp. 365-375; R. F. Kaindl in *Mittheil. d. Inst. f. Oesterreich. Geschichtsf.*, Erg.-Bd. 6. 209-219.

96 In Upper Bavaria. The author of the *Vita s. Oudalrici* (Gerh., c. *MGH. SS.* 4. 401) states that Berthold the son of Arnulf, count-palatine, conspired with the Hungarians against Otto.

confiscated by the state. Part of it was divided by the king among the churches; a part (which with the castle of Scheyern was left to his heirs) was placed under an everlasting curse by the bishops.[97] Out of his blood many tyrants have arisen hitherto, and Otto the count-palatine (heir not unlike his treacherous and iniquitous father and a man who surpasses in malice all his predecessors) even to the present day ceases not to persecute the Church of God.[98] For, strange to say, almost all of that Count's descendants — by what divine judgment I know not — were so delivered over "unto a reprobate mind" that none of them, or at least very few of them, of either sex can be found, of whatever calling or station in life, who did not either rage in open tyranny or else, utterly infatuated, prove themselves unworthy of every office, ecclesiastical or secular and, devoted to the practice of thievery and brigandage, pass a wretched existence in a state of beggary.

The king departed thence and made war upon the Slavs, who were rebelling against him;[99] since he proved victorious over them, as over the Hungarians, he was styled the Father of his Country.

21. In the nine hundred and sixtieth year from the incarnation of the Lord, while the king was moving his troops against the Slavs again, John the Deacon and the *scriniarius* Azo came to the king. They had been sent by the Apostolic See, both to make complaint about Berengar's tyranny and to invite the king himself to come to the defense of the holy Roman Church and in fact of all Italy. Walpert also, bishop of Milan, and Waldo, bishop of Como, together with other nobles of the kingdom of Italy came to the king as suppliants, making the same requests. Accordingly the king, after celebrating the day of the Lord's nativity at Regensburg, set out for Lorraine. Having there elevated his son Otto to the throne

[97] For an alternative passage at this point see Hofmeister's edition of the *Chronica*, pp. 282-283 (about 34 lines).

[98] In this interpolation Otto allows himself to evidence much personal animosity. Count Otto of Scheyern-Wittelsbach was *advocatus* of the bishopric of Freising. He was contemporary with our author and we know that their relations were not always of the friendliest. His "treacherous and iniquitous father" was Ekkehard, also *advocatus* of the bishopric of Freising. Count Otto is said to have been born of his union with a former nun whom he took from a convent in Regensburg. *Cf.* Hirsch, S., *Jahrbücher des deutschen Reichs unter Heinrich II*, pp. 422 *et seq.*, and a letter of Pope Eugenius III, listed in Jaffé, *Regesta pontificum*, Nos. 9412 and 9412a.

[99] The Wends. Their ally and leader Wichmann, nephew of Herman, duke of Saxony, was defeated by Otto in 958.

in his palace at Aachen, he returned to Saxony, raised an army there and entered Italy under arms by way of Bavaria and the Tridentine valley. After subjugating the entire land he celebrated the day of the Lord's nativity at Pavia and ordered the palace there, which had been destroyed by Berengar, to be rebuilt.

22. In the nine hundred and sixty-fourth year from the incarnation of the Lord the glorious king Otto, proceeding from Pavia to the City, was received with all honor by John the Supreme Pontiff and by all the people, and received the title of Emperor and Augustus [100] amid universal applause. According to those who place Arnulf in the list of emperors, but exclude from the list those who reigned in Italy in the interim, he is found to be the seventy-seventh emperor; but according to the Romans who, ignoring Arnulf, count in the number of previous emperors Louis, the two Berengars, Hugo, Berengar, Lothar and likewise Berengar and his son Albert (however obscure their reigns were), Arnulf is the eighty-fourth emperor. Thenceforth, after the rule of the Franks and the Lombards, sovereignty of the Romans was transferred to the Germans; or, as it seems to others, it was transferred back to the Franks, out of whose control it had in a measure slipped. In support of this belief seems to be the fact that the Roman Empire, according to our predecessors, is said to have an origin and a progress similar to those of the empire of the Babylonians. For just as that empire is known to have succumbed to two famous changes — namely the rule of the Medes and that of the Persians — so, men claim, Rome too ought to be subject to two other empires and only two: the rule of the Greeks and that of the Franks. For they have said that all other incursions of various nations upon Rome, as upon Babylon, involve an eclipse of Roman sway rather than really thoroughgoing change.

The emperor, returning from the City, celebrated the Lord's Easter Day at Pavia. But Berengar, fleeing from the emperor, lay hidden in a mountain called Mt. St. Leo.[101]

23. In the following year, when the emperor again celebrated the Lord's Easter Day at Pavia, and moving thence blockaded Berengar on Leo's mount, Albert, Berengar's son, at first avoided the emperor's wrath by entering Corsica; afterwards he approached Pope John and won him over to his side. Therefore the emperor

---

[100] Otto was crowned by Pope John XII, Feb. 2, 962.
[101] The strong castle of St. Leo in the Apennines.

abandoned the siege of the stronghold and directed his forces against the City. Some of the citizens, panic-stricken, fled together with their Pontiff; others gave hostages and submitted to the emperor. Otto, sending an embassy, summoned the pope to return and when he refused to come, gathered a synod of bishops and established Leo [102] in the pontificate in his stead. Seeing this Albert fled a second time to Corsica. Whether all these things were done lawfully or otherwise it is not the purpose of the present work to say, for we have undertaken to tell, in writing, what happened, not to pass judgment on what happened.[103] I have found, however, in certain chronicles (to be sure, of the Germans)[104] that the aforesaid John lived a disgraceful life and that there were frequent meetings of his bishops and other subordinates about his conduct. It seems difficult to put confidence in this statement, inasmuch as the Roman Church is accustomed to credit its bishops with this special prerogative that, through the merits of Peter, who was established upon a firm rock, no gate of Hell nor any disorder of the times involves them in ruinous destruction.

24. While the emperor was celebrating the day of the Lord's nativity at Rome he received in surrender Berengar, who had been besieged on Leo's mount, together with his castle, and sent him to Bavaria in exile under guard. See how the kingdom of the Germans has a beginning similar to that of the kingdom of the Franks and in a way related thereto. Among the Franks the first Charles bore the office of king, though he did not have the title of king. Among the Germans Otto the Great, duke of Saxony, exercised the supreme powers of the kingdom while kings of the stock of Charles survived.[105] Charles's son Pepin began to be king not only in fact but in name too, and to be called king. Otto's son Henry, in like manner, won the right to be honored by that name. Pepin's son, Charles the Great, was the first of the Franks to win not only a kingdom but the title of emperor, after he took Desiderius captive. Henry's son, Otto the Great, after many triumphs was the first of the Germans,[106] after the Carolingians, to rule over the Romans after he had taken Berengar captive.

[102] The *protoscriniarius*, a layman, was elected pope as Leo VIII.

[103] Note Bishop Otto's attitude toward history, and *cf.* VI. 31 below.

[104] *Cf.* Liudprand's *Historia Ottonis* 9; Sigebert on the year 963; Herimannus Contractus on the years 962-964.

[105] This was not, of course, the emperor Otto the Great, but Otto, father of Henry I. *Cf.* above, VI. 15 and 16.   [106] *Cf.* above, VI. 17.

While the emperor tarried in the City its inhabitants attempted
to kill him. In so doing they took into their councils members of
the neighboring nobility. The emperor, discovering the plot in time,
at first took precautions against the plot and afterwards destroyed
an enormously large number of the conspirators. On the following
day, upon pledge of good faith by an oath, he received a hundred hostages from them. After remaining near them for seven
days he departed to Spoleto and, at the request of Pope Leo, restored their hostages to the Romans. Upon his withdrawal the
Romans, driving out Leo, took back John. Without delay Leo went
to the emperor, while the latter was staying in the duchy of Cam-
erino, and celebrated Holy Easter with him. Presently John died
and Benedict was chosen by the Romans to fill his place. Augustus
therefore, aroused both by the expulsion of Leo and by the election
of Benedict, spurning the legates of the Romans whom they had
sent to calm his anger, led his army against the City. Having
hemmed in the City by a siege and exhausted it with famine beyond
belief, he finally compelled it to surrender. Thereupon the people
of the City were taken back by the emperor into favor — on the
condition that they were to open their gates to him and receive him
with all honor — and were to hand Benedict over to him. When
this was done the emperor reinstated Leo and, after celebrating at
Rome the nativity of St. John and the festival of Peter and Paul,
he departed from the City. On his journey he lost many of his men
because of the intense heat. Then, after celebrating the Lord's
nativity at Pavia, he returned to Cisalpine Gaul taking with him
Benedict, now deposed.

Not long after, when the Italians once more rebelled against him,
he crossed the Alps and, after celebrating the Lord's nativity at
Rome, he hanged on the gallows thirteen of the more prominent
inhabitants of the City in addition to the prefect, because they had
been responsible for the uprising against Pope Leo.[107] Then calling
into his presence his son Otto, he had him crowned by the Supreme
Pontiff and had him called Augustus.[108] He gave to him also in marriage Theophano the daughter of the emperor of Constantinople.
Having thus set all things duly in order he returned from Italy.
He celebrated the Lord's Easter Day at Quedlinburg, and later the

[107] The continuator of Regino has the correct name, John. Leo VIII
died early in 965, and was succeeded by Pope John XIII.
[108] Otto II was crowned as emperor at Christmas, 967.

Ascension at Merseburg, according to his custom. On the third day before Whitsunday he was taken sick and brought his days to a close in the thirty-seventh year of his reign and the thirteenth of his rule as emperor.[109] This is the Otto who, after the many victories which I have mentioned, conquered the Greeks too in Apulia and in Calabria,[110] and by his valor restored the rule of the Romans to the eastern Franks. He was the first to discover veins of silver and of copper near the city of Goslar in Saxony.[111] He also beautified with many adornments the metropolis of Magdeburg, where his body, buried in royal splendor, is yet to be seen. Berengar and his wife Willa died in exile at Bamberg. In that same year the blessed Ulric, bishop of Augsburg, also departed to the Lord.

25. In the nine hundred and seventy-fifth year from the incarnation of the Lord, Otto the Second,[112] the son of Otto the Great, who had been crowned by the Roman Pontiff during his father's lifetime, succeeded his father on the throne, ruling as the eighty-fifth in line from Augustus. While he was incautiously pursuing the Greeks in Calabria, he lost his army and himself escaped only by leaping overboard from a ship and swimming.[113] In the ninth year of his reign he died at Rome and was buried with all honor in a marble sarcophagus before the church of the blessed Peter. The Romans tell a story [114] about him to the effect that, when he had captured Benevento, he removed thence the bones of the blessed apostle Bartholomew and placed them in a porphyry sepulcher on the island in the Tiber at Rome; and that he had planned to transport them in the sarcophagus I have mentioned to his own land by way of the Tiber and the sea. Since, however, he was shortly afterwards himself taken from this life, that precious treasure remained there.

26. In the nine hundred and eighty-fourth year from the incarnation of the Lord, Otto the Third [115] as a mere boy succeeded his

[109] Otto the Great died on May 7, 973 at Memleben in the Harz mountains.

[110] Our chronicler is here in error, as Otto's campaigns in Apulia in 968 were unsuccessful.

[111] So also Sigebert on the year 968. The discovery of these metals in the Hartz Mts. was of much social and economic significance to Germany — more than Otto seems to realize from the space which he devotes to it.   [112] 973-983.

[113] The emperor, to avoid being captured, swam from shore to a Byzantine vessel and later escaped from it in turn by leaping overboard, as Otto says.

[114] But the tale was vigorously denied at Benevento. *Cf. Acta SS. Boll.* 25 Aug., V. 77.   [115] 983-1002.

father on the throne, the eighty-sixth in line from Augustus to secure the imperial power. In his time the blessed Albert,[116] bishop of Prague, was crowned with martyrdom while he was preaching to the Prussians. Otto died in the seventeenth year of his reign and was buried in the Church of St. Mary at Aachen. Although for the sake of brevity we have said little about the last two Ottos, these two were so high-spirited and so remarkable that the one was called "The Pale Death of the Saracens"[117] or "The Bloody," and the other "The Marvel of the World."[118]

27. In the one thousand and first year from the incarnation of the Lord, Otto died without an heir. Henry,[119] whose father was Hezilo,[120] a Bavarian by birth and duke of that same people, was chosen by all the nobles[121] of the kingdom as the eighty-seventh king in line from Augustus. After waging, bravely and successfully, many wars in Germany, Bohemia, Italy and Apulia, when rest was finally vouchsafed him by the Lord he then, since he was a most devout Christian, established the very famous bishopric in Bamberg and enriched it with many possessions and honors, even as we see today. Furthermore, having given his sister Gisela as wife to Stephen king of the Hungarians, he induced both King Stephen himself and his whole kingdom to accept the faith. The Hungarians, who still hold fast the Christian faith, regard this Stephen as the founder of their faith and so worthy to be worshipped among the saints. But the pious emperor Henry, having been removed from human affairs in the twenty-fourth year of his reign and the eleventh year of his rule as emperor, was buried in the church at Bamberg and, as that church bears witness, his sepulcher is regarded even to this day as famous for its many miracles.[122]

28. In the one thousand and twenty-fifth year from the incarnation of the Lord, since Henry died without an heir, Conrad,[123] a

116 St. Adalbert, second bishop of Prague (983), a Bohemian by birth.

117 The first time this cognomen is found; cf. Uhlirz, Otto II, p. 209, n. 63.

118 These nicknames occur in a catalog of kings and emperors of the eleventh century (apparently not much later than 1024) edited from a manuscript once at Freising. 119 Henry II, the Saint, 1002-1024.

120 Henry the Wrangler, second Duke of Bavaria, is meant. The catalog referred to in a preceding note [118] gives the name as Hezil.

121 Cf. C. M. H. 3. 215-217. The succession was disputed upon the death of Otto III.

122 On March 12, 1146 Henry was canonized by Pope Eugenius III.

123 Conrad II, 1024-1039. The Saxon dynasty (919-1024) came to an end

Frank by birth, was unanimously selected in accordance with the advice of his predecessor (he did not, however, enjoy Henry's favor while Henry was alive) and was the eighty-eighth in line from Augustus to obtain the throne. On his father's side he traced his ancestry to Conrad, the duke of Worms, who had fallen in the battle that had been fought under Otto with the Hungarians;[124] on his mother's side he traced his lineage to the most illustrious princes of Gaul, who were descended from the ancient stock of the Trojans and had been baptized by the blessed Remigius. He had a wife named Gisela who was sprung from the ancient and glorious blood of the Carolingians, as a certain writer [125] attests in these verses:

"When to the tenth generation a fourth generation is added,
From the great Charles is descended Gisela, known for her wisdom."

She was married first to Ernest duke of the Swabians, the brother of Albert margrave of Upper Pannonia, and bore him two children, Ernest and Herman. Upon the death of Ernest, she took as husband the Conrad of whom we are writing. This king was vigorous in war, prudent in counsel, endowed with tact as well as with sound wisdom, thoroughly devoted to the Christian religion and possessing that humility which is seemly for a monarch.

At the very beginning of his reign Boleslav,[126] duke of the Poles, who had recently been conquered by Conrad's predecessor Henry, laid his plans to break away from the kingdom and to be called king in his own right. He died, however, not long afterwards, leaving his son Mesco as his successor. Since Mesco was planning to imitate his father and besides had driven out his brother Otto, the king moved his army into Poland both to restore the exile to his native land and to punish the insolent ruler for the injury done to his realm. Mesco was not strong enough to withstand the king's attack and so, having broken certain insignia of the kingdom, he fled to Udalrich duke of Bohemia, who had himself at that time become an enemy to the kingdom. When Udalrich desired to deliver him up to the king and by such action to win back Conrad's favor, the

with Henry II. The Franconian line, started by Conrad II, endured until 1125. Otto's use of *Francus* (Frank) and *Francia* is confusing. Here *Francus* obviously means Franconian. Otto uses *Francia* to denote the kingdom of the Franks and also Franconia. 124 Lechfeld, VI. 20 above.

125 Wipo inserted these verses (taken from his *Tetralogus*, 159 *et seq.*) in the fourth chapter of his *Gesta Chuonradi*.

126 Known as "Chrobry" (the Mighty); he died in 1025.

latter, a very chivalrous man, refused to receive him in this way at the hands of the treacherous duke. Otto, having easily gained possession of the duchy of Poland, sent to the king the diadem which his father had unlawfully made, to the disgrace of the kingdom, and subjected himself in all things to the king's sway. Not long afterwards, however, he was robbed of his life by the treachery of his armor-bearer. Mesco, having become an exile instead of a king, went as a suppliant [127] to the emperor and, upon the intercession of the queen, his province was divided into three parts and he received one part for himself. Since that time, as is well known, that province has been subject to our kings and has paid tribute to them.

About the same time a kinsman of the king (Conrad by name, duke of Worms), and Ernest,[128] his [the King's] stepson, duke of the Swabians or the Alemanni, attempted with many others to rebel against the king. The king, after designating his son Henry, who was still a mere infant, as king to succeed him, entered Italy. Duke Ernest, upon the advice of his mother the queen, went to him and won his favor by her aid, promising that he would go with the king into Italy. Accordingly the king, moving his camp, celebrated Holy Easter at Vercelli. There he gave audience to the margrave Rainier [129] and the citizens of Lucca and, having received the submission of all those, directed his march toward the City.

29. In the one thousand and twenty-seventh year from the incarnation of the Lord, Conrad having reached Rome was crowned by the supreme pontiff John on the very day of the Easter Festival. At the coronation he walked in the position of honor between two kings, Knut of England [130] and Rodolph of Burgundy,[131] Queen Gisela's uncle. He obtained from all the people of Rome the titles of Emperor and Augustus. But in Easter week itself a riot broke

---

127 To Merseburg in 1033. He died the following year.

128 The Third. He rebelled against Conrad in 1025, in 1026, and again in 1030, each time unsuccessfully. Conrad (the Younger) joined him in his second rebellion. The latter is called by Otto *dux Vangionum*. The name comes from an early German tribe, the Vangiones, whose name still clung to the people of Worms. This Conrad was a great grandson of Conrad (the Red) of Lorraine, mentioned above (VI 20 and 28, beginning), as duke of Worms. He and his descendants were dukes in Western Franconia; hence the term duke of Worms. His son Otto was made duke of Carinthia. The younger Conrad was heir to this dukedom upon the death of his father in 1011, but he was deprived of it until 1036. He is regularly known in history as duke of Carinthia.

129 Rainier of Tuscany.   130 King Knut the Dane, 1017-1035.

131 Rodolph III, 993-1032.

out between the emperor's soldiers and the citizens; a desperate battle ensued. When many had been slain the Romans fled and the emperor gained the victory. After this he made peace with the citizens and withdrew from the City and, having captured a certain very notorious bandit named Tahselgart, he hanged him. Then as he was returning to Francia by way of the Pyrenees,[132] he heard that his stepson, Duke Ernest, was again endeavoring to rebel against him upon the advice of Count Werner.[133] By a just judgment and by the power of his royal majesty he banished him from land and sea and compelled him to take refuge in the forest. There he was afterwards killed by the king's loyal followers and his brother Herman received his duchy.

30. At that time Rodoph, king of Burgundy or Gallia Lugdunensis, died and by the terms of his will left to the king's son Henry, his nephew,[134] the kingdom together with the crown and other insignia. Certain writers declare that there are two Gauls, a Cisalpine and a Transalpine. One of these, they have said — namely Cisalpine Gaul or Gallia Togata — is in Italy between the Po and the Alps. The other, Transalpine Gaul or Gallia Comata, they have divided into three parts, namely Belgica, Lugdunensis and Celtica (they make Aquitaine a part of Gallia Celtica). Others likewise make three parts but they include Celtica in Belgica and set off Aquitaine as a third part by itself. Hence they make it out that three primates preside over these three Gauls, the Metropolitan of Trèves over Belgica, the Metropolitan of Bourges over Aquitaine and the Metropolitan of Lyons over the third. But Orosius seems to maintain that Celtica is included in Belgica, for in his division of the world he bounds Belgica by Britain and the province of Narbonensis, whereas, according to the division first given above, Belgica extended from the Rhine to the source of the Meuse or to the Argonne Forest. Orosius's statement runs as follows: "Gallia Belgica has these boundaries — on the east the river Rhine and Germany, on the southeast the Pennine Alps, on the south the pro-

---

[132] *I.e.*, of course, the Alps. See note 203 to Bk. II.

[133] Count Werner of Kiburg. Hofmeister points out that Otto has confused Ernest's second (1026) and third (1030) rebellions. The allusion in the following sentence is to the sentences of outlawry and excommunication pronounced against Ernest at a diet at Ingelheim in 1030.

[134] Rodolph originally willed his kingdom to Henry II. Upon the death of the latter, Conrad claimed the rights of his predecessor and forced Rodolph to acquiesce. In 1038 Conrad had his son Henry (III) crowned king of Burgundy.

vince of Narbonensis, on the northwest the British Channel, on the
north the island of Britain.''[135] He writes thus of Gallia Lugdunensis: ''Gallia Lugdunensis, a district long drawn out, narrow
and winding, half surrounds the province of Aquitaine. It has on
the east Belgica, on the south a part of the province of Narbonensis,
in which the city of Arles is situated and where the waters of the
Rhone are received by the Gallic Sea.''[136] Speaking of Aquitaine
not as of a third part of Gaul but as of a province of Gaul he says:
''The province of Aquitaine is encircled by the winding course of
the river Loire, which for the most part forms its boundary. It
has on the northwest that part of the ocean which is called the Bay
of Aquitaine, on the west the Spains; on the north and the east it
extends to Lugdunensis, on the southeast and the south to the
province of Narbonensis.''[137] According to this division there appear to be but two parts of Gallia Comata, namely Lugdunensis
and Belgica, so that Aquitaine is not a third part of Gaul but, as
has been said, a province of one or the other of two parts. And so
likewise there is found to be a threefold division of Gaul, if Gallia
Togata is counted in. So then, according to the first account there
are three divisions of Gallia Comata, if Gallia Togata is excluded;
according to the second, likewise three divisions of Gaul, if Gallia
Togata is included. Though, as I said above,[138] these all originally
were subject to the kingdom of the Franks, they began to have each
its own king when that kingdom was afterwards divided; and to that
part which is still called Francia there remained according to the
first division[139] only Celtica, according to the second Aquitaine
and part of Belgica.

31. Now when Rodolph handed over Gallia Lugdunensis to Henry, Odo[140] count of Gallia Celtica, because he was Rodolph's sister's
son, unreasonably claimed that the aforesaid kingdom belonged to
him by hereditary right and entered it with an armed force. This
happened at the time when the emperor was detained by the subjugation of the Poles,[141] as we said above by way of anticipation.
Augustus accordingly, upon hearing of the insolent conduct of Odo,

---

[135] Orosius 1. 2. 63. Hofmeister points out that Otto did not see that the
province of Lugdunensis was formed out of the middle and major part of
Celtica, only small portions being assigned to Aquitania and Belgica.

[136] *Op. cit.* 1. 2. 64. [137] *Op. cit.* 1. 2. 67. [138] VI. 17.

[139] Which Otto follows above, VI. 18; *cf.* below, VII. 12 and VII. 16.

[140] Odo II, Count of Blois, the son of Rodolph's sister Bertha and Odo I.

[141] Under Mesco II, who yielded late in the year 1032.

prepared an army at about the time of the Lord's Nativity to invade Burgundy. But since he could not set out for Burgundy because of the excessive cold he entered the Gauls again in the following summer, and after he had laid Odo's land waste with fire and sword for three weeks in succession, the latter was compelled to come to him as suppliant. When Odo had given assurance under oath that he would not in anywise harass further the aforesaid kingdom, the emperor went back home. In the following year the king entered Burgundy once more and accepted the submission of all the princes of that land, including the Metropolitan of Lyons, and taking them with him as hostages for the land he went back home in peace. Not long after he entered Italy to quell the insolence of the common rabble, which had almost overmastered the nobles. After celebrating the Lord's Nativity at Verona, he went by way of Brescia and Cremona to Milan, made the bishop of that city a prisoner because he was said to be guilty of forming a conspiracy against him, and entrusted him to the care of Poppo, patriarch of Aquileia. But the bishop secretly escaped and fled. Therefore the emperor, after celebrating the Lord's Easter Day at Ravenna, in the spring of the year laid waste the territory surrounding the aforesaid city, destroyed many strongholds which he had taken by force of arms and received the submission of many others. Then, going to Cremona, he met the Roman pontiff. Having graciously welcomed the pontiff and treated him with much respect, he sent him on his way and then, avoiding the heat, entered the mountainous country.

While this was taking place in Italy, Count Odo again broke his oath and rebelled in Gaul against the emperor. But when, to his disgrace, he had laid siege to a certain stronghold named Bar-le-Duc, he was killed by Gozelo duke of Lorraine, and by other faithful supporters of the kingdom, and his standard was sent to Italy to please the emperor as a token of victory. At that time the bishops of Piacenza, Vercelli and Cremona — whether properly or otherwise is a matter of dispute — were convicted of treason [142] and sent into exile. Soon after, while the emperor was celebrating the Nativity of the Lord at Parma, a disturbance arose and the king's Banquet Manager was killed. Aroused by this the emperor attacked the city with all energy. The citizens defended themselves valiantly but nevertheless, after many had been slain and they were no long-

[142] The three Lombard bishops were banished to Germany for complicity with Odo.

er able to withstand the king's assault, the wretched city was at last burned.

During these days the Roman pontiff excommunicated the archbishop of Milan because he wickedly rebelled against his lord the emperor. Conrad, crossing the Apennines after Italy on this side had been fully conquered, entered Apulia (the queen went on to Rome to pray and rejoined him later), and having passed through the cities of that land — Capua, Benevento and a great many others — planned to return home by way of the coast of the Adriatic Sea. But since his way took him through unhealthful regions he lost very many of his illustrious nobles and of his soldiers because of the pestilential air. Among those that died were Duke Herman son of the queen, Kunigunda [143] the bride of the king's son, Cono [144] duke of the Franconians and very many others. Hence a certain one of our number, deploring this catastrophe of our mortal state, composed a poem in simple style after the manner of a tragedy which begins as follows:

"Let him who has a voice that's clear
 Sing forth this dirge for all to hear." [145]

Not long after, the emperor, having returned from Italy, while he was celebrating Holy Pentecost in Utrecht, a city of Frisia, was taken sick in the very midst of the festival and brought his days to a close, in the seventeenth year of his reign and in the fourteenth year of his rule as emperor. His vital organs were buried there but the rest of his body was removed to the city of Speier and buried there in the Church of St. Mary.

32. In the one thousand and fortieth year from the incarnation of the Lord, Henry III [146] (the son of Gisela mentioned above), who had begun to reign during his father's lifetime, upon the latter's death reigned alone as the eighty-ninth in line from Augustus. In his person the imperial dignity, which for a long time no one of the seed of Charles had held, was restored to the noble and

[143] Or Gunnhild, a daughter of Knut, who had been married to Henry III in 1036. She died July 18, 1038.

[144] Or Conrad, duke of Carinthia. Otto has erred in adding his name here, probably because of Wipo's verses (*Gesta Chuonradi* 40); Conrad died July 20, 1039. On his relations with Franconia, *cf*. note 128.

[145] Wipo 40. But Wipo says that this poem was not composed until after the death of Conrad.

[146] 1039-1056.

ancient stock of Charles. He is said not only to have equalled his father in all respects but even to have surpassed him in good qualities. He governed the kingdom with great moderation. But in the beginning of his reign, while he was rashly making war on the Bohemians, who were offering opposition to him, he lost a great many of his soldiers in the hidden fastnesses of the woods. After he gave free rein to his righteous indignation caused by this mishap, and inflicted many disasters upon the aforesaid people, he finally accepted the submission of their duke.[147] He also pressed the Hungarians hard in many different battles, but when Peter their king was treacherously driven from his throne by Obo [148] he received the exile, upon the intercession of Margrave Albert (whose brother-in-law he was), entered Pannonia with an army and, small though his force was, fought a battle, defeated an incredible number of Hungarians and restored Peter to his throne. For this reason again, the following poem of Herman the Lame [149] was composed in honor of the aforesaid triumph. It begins thus:

"This voice of mine must sing a lay." [150]

Henry took to wife Agnes, the sister of a most renowned noble of Gaul, William duke of Poitou and Aquitaine. When according to royal custom he was celebrating the nuptials at Ingelheim, he let all the company of jesters and actors which, as was usual, had flocked together there, go away empty and lavishly distributed among the poor what he had taken from these limbs of Satan. But during the very wedding festival sadness was mixed with the rejoicing, for the youthful Leopold,[151] the most illustrious son of Margrave Albert, was carried off by a premature death. Mourned by all he was buried by his uncle Poppo, archbishop of Trèves, in the city of Trèves. This is the Leopold who, with his father Albert, took the Eastern March [152] from the Hungarians and among other valiant deeds al-

[147] Duke Břatislav yielded in 1041.

[148] He was crowned as king at Easter, 1042. Peter was restored (as Henry's vassal) in 1044. Otto has united the three expeditions made by Henry into Hungary (1042, 1043 and 1044).

[149] Herman of Reichenau, who wrote on the reigns of Conrad II and Henry III.

[150] Pertz is inclined to attribute this to Wipo rather than to Herman; cf. Wattenbach, Deutschlands Geschichtsquellen 2.13 (note 3), sixth edition.

[151] Leopold (II), the grandfather of Bishop Otto of Freising. He died Dec. 9, 1043.

[152] Or the East Mark, the region between the Leitha, Fischa, March and Thaya rivers.

most utterly destroyed with a few men the countless host of Obo
that had suddenly taken up arms and was unexpectedly laying
waste his borders. Such a procedure, however, is hazardous in any
conflict, even for the brave.

At about the same time there was a shameful confusion in the
Church of God in the city of Rome. Three usurpers,[153] one of whom
was called Benedict, were occupying the chair at the same time,
and as a crowning misfortune had divided the patriarchate together
with its revenues. One of them sat in St. Peter's, the second in
Santa Maria Maggiore, and the third (that is, Benedict) in the
Lateran Palace. All were living a disgraceful life, as I myself have
heard in the City from Roman informants. A certain devout man,
a priest named Gratian, seeing this most lamentable state of the
Church, and because of what he saw feeling compassion for his
Mother,[154] in the zeal of his piety approached the men [155] I have
mentioned and persuaded them by means of money to withdraw
from the Holy See, leaving to Benedict the revenues of England
because he seemed to be a man of more decided personality. Wherefore the citizens, deeming the aforesaid priest liberator of the
Church of God, chose him the highest pontiff and, changing his
name, called him Gregory VII [VI]. Hearing this the king moved
his forces against Italy. Gratian, meeting the king at Sutri,[156] is
said to have offered him a precious diadem to assuage his anger.
The king at first received him with due honor, as was fitting, but
afterwards assembled a synod of bishops and persuaded him to
withdraw from the pontificate because he had disgraced himself
by simony, and in his place substituted Suidger, bishop of Bamberg,
who is called also Clement. This he did with the consent of the
Church of Rome. Tradition has it that Hildebrand had followed
Gratian as he was crossing the Alps and that afterwards, when he
was made supreme pontiff, he expressed the desire to be called
Gregory VII out of love for him because Gratian, the original
Gregory VII [VI], had been removed from the list. And as you
read in Lucan,[157]

153 Benedict IX, Sylvester III, and Gregory VI.

154 *I.e.*, the Church just referred to.

155 Otto is confused here: Gratian (afterwards Pope Gregory VI) was one
of the three.

156 Not at Sutri but at Piacenza, as we learn from Herman of Reichenau
and others. It was at Sutri that a synod was held later (Dec. 20, 1046) and
Gregory VI and his rival Sylvester were both compelled to withdraw from the
papacy, as was Benedict at Rome.   157 *Pharsalia* 1. 128.

"Gods the victorious cause upheld, but Cato the vanquished,'

so to Hildebrand, who was ever most unyielding in zeal for the Church, that cause in which the opinion of the emperor and the bishops prevailed was always displeasing. Hereafter the Church of Rome, we find, was so greatly weakened in the canonical election of pontiffs that Clement and the next four pontiffs [158] are found in the list only because they were placed there by the emperor. How through the activity and the exertions of the aforesaid Hildebrand the Church regained her freedom — in part under the younger Leo, completely under Alexander — we shall relate hereafter as we have learned the story from the recital of trustworthy men.

33. In the one thousand and forty-seventh year from the incarnation of the Lord, the victorious king Henry was crowned by Clement at Rome on the day of the Lord's Nativity and obtained the title of Emperor and Augustus, the ninetieth in line from Augustus. From Rome he led his army through Apulia and returned with honor to his own land. In the same year, upon the death of Suidger, Poppo, the patriarch of Aquileia, was chosen in his stead.[159] Not long afterwards, Peter, king of the Hungarians, was deprived of his eyesight and of his kingdom by a certain client of his named Andrew. When Poppo, too — who is called also Damasus — was dead, Bruno, bishop of Toul — who is called also Leo [160] — received the charge of the Church of Rome. He was descended from a noble family of the Franks and had been designated for the chair of the blessed Peter [161] through the influence of His Royal Highness. When he had assumed the purple and was making a journey through Gaul it happened that he visited Cluny where, they say, Hildebrand (whom I mentioned above) was, as it chanced, at that time holding the office of prior.[162] Being filled with zeal for God he approached Leo and courageously rebuked him for what he had done, saying that it was unlawful for him, with the help of a layman, to enter by force as supreme pontiff upon the government of the entire Church. Hildebrand promised that if

[158] Damasus II; Leo IX; Victor II; Stephen IX.

[159] As Pope Damasus II. This is not the patriarch of Aquileia mentioned in VI. 31 above (as Otto supposes), but a German, Poppo of Brixen.

[160] Leo IX, 1048.

[161] Hofmeister gives the reading *beatri Petri,* a misprint.

[162] Critics agree that this is a myth. But it is agreed that Hildebrand did accompany Pope Leo IX to Rome.

Bruno would trust his plans he would bring it to pass that, on the one hand, His Imperial Majesty would not be angry at him, and that on the other the freedom of the Church in the matter of the canonical election would be restored. The pope, assenting to his suggestion, laid aside the purple and assuming the garb of a pilgrim started on his way taking Hildebrand with him. When they arrived at the City, Bruno was upon the advice of Hildebrand elected as supreme pontiff by clergy and people, and so the Church of Rome was in a measure put in possession again of the privilege of election. The emperor, invading Lorraine, forced Duke Godfrey and Duke Baldwin to surrender.[163] After this a synod was held at Mainz in the presence of Leo, the Supreme Pontiff, and the Emperor. The king again invaded Pannonia [164] to crush the arrogance of Andrew, who had deposed Peter and had usurped the throne of the Hungarians. But since the inhabitants of that country hid themselves everywhere and either concealed or destroyed the provisions necessary to support life, the king because he was unable to support his soldiers there, laid waste the whole country and then returned home. In the following year he again invaded Pannonia, taking Leo the Supreme Pontiff with him.

At that time Norsemen, that restless people, under the leadership of Duke Robert Guiscard (a man of lowly station but of very great energy), invaded Apulia and, by treachery and violence, afflicted the inhabitants of that country with many woes.[165] When Pope Leo, after he returned to the City with an army, wished to make them subject to the jurisdiction of the Church and the Empire, a battle was fought in which many were slain and Leo was obliged to flee to Benevento. The loss on both sides entailed in this battle was so great that to this day a heap composed of bones of the dead is pointed out there by the inhabitants. In the following year Pope Leo died. He lies buried in the church of the blessed Peter at Rome and is held in renown for his miracles. Gebhard of Eichstätt, who is called also Victor, succeeded him and Stephen, likewise a German by race, followed Gebhard. The emperor, again entering Italy, brought back with him his kinswoman Beatrice the mother of Mathilda, whose husband, Margrave Boniface,[166] had

---

[163] In 1049. [164] The Hungarian expeditions of 1051 and 1052.
[165] Pope Nicholas II conferred upon Robert the title of duke of Apulia and Calabria, and his dominion — a fief of the Holy See — lasted from 1059.
[166] Of Tuscany. 1077. The invasion here mentioned occurred in 1053.

died. But he himself was taken sick not long after in a place which is called Bodfeld, on the borders of Saxony and Thuringia, made public confession of his sins, brought the last day of his life to a close in the seventeenth year of his reign and in the eleventh of his rule as emperor, and was buried beside his father. Herman the Lame,[167] in a certain little book which he intended for the emperor, has discoursed clearly enough regarding Henry's acts and virtues as well as those of his father.

34. In the one thousand and fifty-seventh year from the incarnation of the Lord, Henry's son, Henry IV,[168] though he was still a very young boy, succeeded his father on the throne and began to reign as the ninety-first in line from Augustus. He was at first under the regency of his mother, the empress Agnes, who for some time ruled the kingdom with wisdom and with might. But afterwards he became estranged from his mother through the machinations of certain individuals [169] and reigned in his own person. This was the source of very violent dissension. The empress, a most noble woman, marking the uncertainties of life withdrew to the monastery of Fruttuaria where she lived a devout life. Thence she went to Rome and, having tarried there for some time, departed this life. She was buried with all honor in a marble tomb in the church of the blessed Petronella.

During these days [170] Alexander, at first bishop of Lucca, afterwards by general desire and election advanced to be supreme pontiff, restored the Church, which had long been in a state of servitude, to its ancient liberty and with great resolution checked Cadalus [171] bishop of Parma when he sought to seize the Roman see by armed force. Hence I have found written concerning him in the Lateran Palace this line:

"Alexander is pope; Cadalus falls and is conquered."

As I have often said, whenever the royal diadem had to be struck

---

[167] Hofmeister argues that there can be no doubt that some connection exists between this work by Herman of Reichenau and the *Gesta Chuonradi* of Wipo. See the Introduction to his edition of Otto's *Chronicle*, p. XCV.

[168] 1056-1106. He was a boy of six at the time of his accession.

[169] He was carried off to Cologne in 1062 by Archbishop Anno and came under the influence of the latter and his party.

[170] In 1061. This is Pope Alexander II.

[171] He had been elected pope in 1063 and took the name of Honorius II, but was driven out of Rome in the following year.

by the sacerdotal sword the kingdom was divided against itself,[172] and whenever the Saxons were plotting a revolt there were conspiracies, aspersions were cast upon the emperor and many disgraceful stories about him were carried to the ears of the supreme pontiff. When Anno bishop of Cologne, and Herman bishop of Bamberg were sent by the king to Rome in defence of the rights of the kingdom, after discharging their mission they returned and delivered to the king a letter from the Supreme Pontiff in which the latter called upon the king [173] to make explanation regarding the charge of simony and many other matters of which he had been accused. At that time the Saxons, no longer able to conceal the wickedness long since conceived in their hearts, openly rebelled against the king and destroyed strongholds and fortifications which he had built in their country.

In the following year Alexander, rounding out the years of his life and of his priesthood, died and left the see to his archdeacon Hildebrand, who was called Gregory VII. Hereupon a very violent dissension arose because he had been designated by election without the consent of the king. Hildebrand, who had for a long time labored in humble station to secure freedom for the Church, thought it wrong to cease from his efforts now that he had attained high priestly office, and so he labored much in the sweat of his brow both to achieve the purpose just mentioned and to stamp out simony and check the incontinence of the clergy. In a word, he not only frequently summoned the king to account before synods for offenses of this sort but also passed decrees [174] forbidding the clergy, from the subdiaconate upward, to marry anywhere in the entire Roman world. Making himself an example to his flock he set forth in practice what he taught in word; being in all respects a valiant champion he did not fear to interpose himself as a wall of defense before the house of the Lord. The king, gathering his troops from all the interior parts of his kingdom, waged war against the Saxons and in a battle that was fought near the river Unstrut,[175] after many had fallen on both sides, finally a bloody victory fell to the king. In this conflict fell Gebhard the father of Lothar, who was afterwards king, and Margrave Ernest,[176] the son of that Albert of whom mention was made above, and countless others.

[172] Cf. above, V. 35; V. 36; VI. 3.   [173] In 1073.
[174] In the Roman synods of 1074 and 1075; cf. Hauck 3. 774 (third edition).
[175] June 9, 1075. Cf. Gesta Friderici 1. 6.
[176] Bishop Otto's great-grandfather. See family tree, Introduction, p. 9.

35. In the one thousand and sixty-sixth year from the incarnation of the Lord, a star of the sort that is called a comet [177] is said to have been seen and failed not to have its effect. In the same year William count of Normandy conquered Greater Britain,[178] which is now called England, killing Harold its king and, after reducing the entire province to slavery and settling the Norsemen there, ruled there himself as king. In the following year the king [179] took to wife Bertha, the daughter of the Italian Margrave Otto,[180] celebrating the wedding at Tribur. The Roman pontiff excommunicated the king after frequently summoning him [to appear before him to do penance],[181] and upon the pontiff's advice and authority (so tradition says) Rudolf [182] duke of Alemannia was made king by certain nobles. Not long afterwards Rudolf was killed in open and public war [183] and Herman [184] prince of Lorraine was chosen in his stead; he too was killed not long afterwards by loyal supporters of the king. I have read and reread the history of the Roman kings and emperors, but I nowhere find that anyone of them was excommunicated by a Roman pontiff or deprived of his kingdom before this emperor — unless perchance one is to consider as equivalent to excommunication the fact that Philip was for a short time placed among the penitents by a bishop of Rome and that Theodosius was barred by the blessed Ambrose from the portals of the church on account of a bloody and murderous deed.

36. At this point I think I ought to relate what above I postponed,[185] the fact that the Roman Empire — compared in Daniel [186] to iron — had feet "part of iron and part of clay" till that it was struck and broken to pieces by a stone cut out of the mountain without hands. For, without the prejudgment of a better interpretation, how can I interpret "the stone cut out without hands" as anything other than the Church, the body of its Head, a body that was conceived by the Holy Spirit without carnal admixture,

---

[177] Subsequently known as Halley's Comet and visible most recently in 1910.

[178] John of Salisbury also writes of "Greater Britain." Cf. *Policraticus* 6. 17: *de maiori Britannia.*   [179] *I.e.,* Henry IV.

[180] Of Savoy. His wife was Adelaide the countess of Turin, the widow of Herman of Swabia, brother of the emperor Henry III.   [181] In 1076.

[182] Of Rheinfelden. This was in 1077. He was slain in 1080.

[183] For the manner of expression, *bellum publicum, cf.* above, VI. 14 and *Gesta Friderici* 1. 6. Otto seems to have in mind the contrast between this and mere private warfare between nobles.

[184] Of Luxemburg. He abdicated in 1088 and died the same year.

[185] II. 13.   [186] Dan. 2. 34 and 42.

was born of a virgin and reborn of the Spirit and of water —
a rebirth in which mortal man had no part. This most glorious
virgin, because she was born again without spot to be a new creature — like a young maid and therefore without a blemish — thus
daily, though she remains a virgin, mothers a new and glorious
people: even as the mother of its Head, though she remained a
virgin, yet contrary to the law of nature brought forth a new and
glorious birth, thus rejoicing in her virginity without remaining
barren. It was clearly the Church that smote the kingdom near its
end (that is the meaning of "the feet"). The kingdom was of
iron on account of its wars [187] and of clay on account of its condition. The Church smote the kingdom in its weak spot when the
Church decided not to reverence the king of the City as lord of the
earth but to strike him with the sword of excommunication as being
by his human condition made of clay. All can now see to what a
mountainous height the Church, at one time small and lowly, has
grown. What great calamities, how many wars and perils of wars
followed in consequence of the weakness of the kingdom; how often
unhappy Rome was besieged, captured, laid waste; and how pope
was placed over pope even as king over king, it is a weariness to
record. In a word, the turbulence of this period carried with it
so many disasters, so many schisms, so many dangers of soul and
of body that it alone would suffice to prove the unhappy lot of our
human wretchedness by reason of the cruelty of the persecution
and its long duration. The aforesaid Pope Gregory was driven out
of the City by the king and Gwibert, archbishop of Ravenna, was
thrust into his place. Gregory abode at Salerno and, as the time of
his summons drew near, he is said to have remarked, "I have loved
righteousness and hated wickedness; therefore I am dying in
exile." [188] Not only, then, was the kingdom severely smitten in the
case of its emperor, who had been cut off by the Church, but the
Church also suffered no little sorrow in being bereft of so great a
shepherd, who had been notable among all the priests and bishops
of Rome for his zeal and force of character. With so great a transformation, as the times were passing from perfection to overthrow,
let us put an end to the sixth book that, with God's guidance, we
may hasten on to the seventh and to that rest of souls which follows
the wretchedness of this present life.

HERE ENDS THE SIXTH BOOK

[187] Otto's word here is *Martem*.   [188] Ps. 45. 7; Heb. 1. 9.

THE PROLOGUE OF THE SEVENTH BOOK [1]

Every man is capable of reason, to the end that he may acknowledge God as his creator, and not overlook his own deeds because his heart is blind or fail to hear because his ears are deaf. In brief, the very form of man's body, not inclined towards the ground as the bodies of the other animals are, but upright that he may give heed to the heavens, proves that man was created for this end. Besides, the inner man, made after the likeness of his Creator, receives the means of investigating the truth not only in relation to other beautiful and great creatures outside himself but also in relation to himself, because he has "the light of the Lord's countenance set upon him as a seal." [2] Therefore from the fact that every wise and good man loves and cherishes his own good works, we are privileged to understand clearly that God does not neglect His world, as some claim, but rather that by His omnipotent majesty He created things that were not, by His all-wise providence guides His creatures and by His most kindly grace preserves what He guides and controls. But if man, though he is subject to mutability — wise only as he participates in wisdom, good only as he participates in

---

[1] In the seventh book of his *Chronicle*, the author brings his outline of universal history from the death of Pope Gregory VII, in 1085, down to the year of the composition of the work, 1146, and appends a list of kings of Italy, Roman emperors (including, of course, the rulers of the Holy Roman Empire) and popes. This part of his book possesses a special interest and value because of the chapters in which Otto is recounting contemporaneous events, particularly because of his own high station and his intimate connection with so many of the chief actors in the drama which he unfolds. In the first eleven chapters of Book VII, Otto is following Ekkehard's *Chronicle* (which, however, he never mentions by name; see Introduction, p. 25). At the close of this chapter, the year 1106 (which is also the date at which the second edition of the Frutolf-Ekkehard *Chronicle* ends) Otto says: *Hucusque tam ex Orosii quam Eusebii et eorum qui post ipsos usque ad nos scripserunt libris lecta posuimus. Ceterum quae secuntur, quia recentis memoriae sunt, a probabilibus viris tradita vel a nobis ipsis visa et audita ponemus.* There are, as usual, frequent citations from Scripture. Special acknowledgment should here be made of the full and valuable notes in Hofmeister's edition, which make up no small part of the Commentary which follows on Book VII. Hofmeister has left little for succeeding writers to do.   [2] Ps. 4. 6.

goodness (nay, only as he is *called* good) — loves and cherishes his own good works, how much more must we believe that God, the only Being not subject to change, who alone is wise of His own wisdom, who alone is good of His own goodness, and therefore the only good Being, does this! Hence we have the well-known statement of Augustine: "There are two reasons why God loves His creation: that it may come into being and that it may continue in being. That there might be something which should endure, 'the Spirit of God moved upon the face of the waters.' Moreover, that this something might endure, 'God saw all that he had made and it was very good'." [3] If therefore God loves what He created, and none of the things that come to pass can come to pass without His will, if He regulates all powers, much more does He permit the kingdoms through which He governs other smaller matters, and the changes in them to come into being. That all this comes to pass without hatred or envy is made evident not only by the fact that, to use Plato's phrase,[4] "Envy is far removed from the best," but also by this fact, that the Author and Creator of all things can hate none of the things which He has made. This is why in the Book of Wisdom it is beautifully said of Him, "Thou hast compassion upon all, O Lord, and abhorrest none of the things which thou didst make." [5] And again, "But thou, O Lord, judgest all things in gentleness." [6] Therefore that "the world passeth away," that it changes so pitifully, occurs — since, as I have said, nothing can come to pass without His nod — not from cruelty, for He "has compassion upon all," not from hatred, because "He hates none of the things which He made," not from wrath because "He judges in gentleness," but by His righteous judgment and for a reason which, although it be hidden from us, we yet believe to be most to our profit. For we must believe that the author of goodness and the fount of grace permits no evil save that which, however much it may in itself be hurtful, is yet of advantage to the whole. This truth may be seen in the downfall of the Jewish nation — because through the blinding of that people all nations received the light of truth. So let us leave it to God, under whose dispensation nothing can flow uselessly away, to see what advantage attends the changes in governments, and their final impairment.

[3] *De Genesi ad litteram* 1. 8. 14.

[4] *Timaeus, interpr. Chalcidio*, 29 E, *ed.* J. Wrobel, Leipsic, 1876, p. 26.

[5] Wisd. of Sol. 11. 24.   [6] *Ib.* 12. 18.

However, men are not lacking who say that God desired the state to be brought low that he might exalt the Church. Forsooth no one questions the fact that the Church was exalted and enriched by the strength of the state and the favor of kings, and it is quite evident that the Church could not have so deeply humiliated the state until the latter was enfeebled by its love of the priesthood, and so robbed of its strength that it was pierced and destroyed not only by the sword of the Church (that is, the spiritual weapon) but also by its own weapon, namely the material sword. To settle this point or even to discuss it is beyond our strength. However those priests seem altogether blameworthy who attempt to strike the state with its own sword, a sword which they hold by the king's favor — unless perchance they think to imitate David who by God's grace first struck the Philistine and afterwards slew him with his own sword. But because, as I have said, the Church, which is destined to obtain the glory of the eternal country and after the toil of this present life to attain rest, and at this very time is, besides, growing to mountainous proportions and has begun to reach great authority as the state declines, it remains for us in this work to relate the results that followed in consequence both of the failure of the temporal and of the advance of the spiritual, and which give rise to a feeling of contempt for the world (especially since we have come to our own times and to events still fresh in the memory).

But let no one because of these words suppose that we separate the Christian sovereignty from the Church, for there are, as is well known, two rôles in the Church of God — the sacerdotal and the royal. Let every one remember that, as I stated above, the history I have put together for the period extending from the time of Theodosius to our own day, is an account not of the Two Cities, but rather, I might almost say, of one — composite, to be sure — the Church.[7] I have made this qualification of my statement on account of such of the kings as were heretics or were excommunicated. For that, as matters now stand, the rest who profess the Christian faith must be numbered as members of the Church, even if they do not follow up their professions of faith, no one can doubt who knows that the net of the Lord contains both bad and good. For the good and the bad cannot be separated at present, inasmuch as the Church judges only the things which are on the surface [8] and

[7] *Cf.* above, Prol., V.
[8] Or "that are revealed," Deut. 29. 29.

God alone, Who knows who are His, "whose fan is in his hand," [9] weighs the merits of individuals. We have then, designated as the Church certain ecclesiastical personages — namely, the bishops of Christ and their attendants — both in accordance with the common usage of speech and out of regard for the finer element, though we are not ignorant of the fact that these ecclesiastical personages also, if they have lived an evil life, will not belong to the City of God in eternity.

HERE BEGINS THE SEVENTH BOOK

1. When Gregory, the Supreme Pontiff of blessed memory, died at Salerno and the Church was placed in the greatest peril because Gwibert, by the authority of the emperor, had seized the Roman see and the City, a few of the Romans elevated, against his will, Cardinal Desiderius,[10] abbot of Monte Cassino (who is called also Victor), to the eminence of the highest priesthood and after bribing the guards of the Leonine City, brought him into the Church of the blessed Peter to be consecrated there, by night, for fear of a schism. There he was smitten by dysentery. Presently leaving the City he departed this life not long afterwards, and left the rule of the Church to Otho bishop of Ostia, who is called also Urban.

2. At that time — while Henry IV still reigned at Rome, and Alexius [11] reigned at Constantinople — all over the world (in the words of the Gospel)[12] nation rose against nation and the Eastern Church suffered severe persecution at the hands of pagans. The Holy City was trampled under foot by the heathen and only the sepulcher of the Lord was held in great veneration by them — though, to be sure, it was for the sake of gain. And so the worshippers of Christ, who dragged out a wretched existence there subject to tribute, sent, along with Alexius the emperor of Constantinople, a letter to Pope Urban and asked him to help them. Moved by the affliction of the people of God, Urban undertook a wearisome journey into Gaul and held a council there.[13] By the word of his holy preaching he united about one hundred thousand men of various nations in the warfare of Christ, and set over them as leaders Godfrey of Lorraine,[14] Robert of Flanders, Raymond [15] count of St.

---

[9] Luke 3. 17.   [10] Victor III, 1086. He died in 1088.
[11] Alexius I, Comnenus, 1081-1118.   [12] Luke 21. 10.
[13] At Clermont, November 18-28, 1095. *Cf.* below, VII. 6 (beginning).
[14] Better known as Godfrey of Bouillon, duke of Lower Lorraine.
[15] Raymond IV, count of Toulouse.

Gilles, Hugh the brother of Philip king of France and other nobles and men of war. The charge over all these men he entrusted to the venerable bishop of Puy.[16] Reports of what Urban had done aroused various little-known peoples of Aquitaine, Normandy, England, Scotland, Ireland, Brittany, Galicia, Gascony, France, Flanders, Lorraine and the other peoples — not only those that lived on the continent but also those that dwelt in the islands of the sea and the farthest ocean. Among these were peoples who seemed so distinct in language, customs and resources that some, it was said, subsisted only on bread and water while others employed only silver for all utensils. All these men, coming from many nations and employing many different tongues, were united into one body. They wore the cross on their garments and promised that they would be in word and deed disciples of the Cross of Christ. Trusting in the efficacy of the Cross they set out on their journey to the East, with Godfrey as their leader, to fight in the name of the Lord against the enemies of the Cross. This expedition had less effect on the Eastern Franks, the Saxons, the Thuringians, the Bavarians and the Alemanni on account of the schism which existed at that time between the state and the Church. Yet there were some of these people who undertook that same warfare, falsely pretending to do so in the name of religion. Among these was a certain Emicho,[17] count of the Rhine country. Arrogating to himself the leadership of about twelve thousand men, he devoted himself to destroying Jews wherever he found them or else sought to bring them into union with the Church. But since the inhabitants of Pannonia opposed their passage in the narrow passes, they were compelled to return to their homes. But Godfrey and the other leaders I have mentioned above, having by God's favor passed through Bulgaria, although with difficulty, reached Constantinople. There they suffered much from the treachery of the emperor Alexius. When they had escaped the peril of death in an uprising that occurred, they stormed a bridge of the royal city and destroyed its suburbs. Then, numbering three hundred thousand warriors, without counting women or children, they proceeded to Nicaea — once a stronghold of the Catholic faith — and, after putting to flight Soliman the leader of the heathen, captured it and handed it over to the emperor. Moving forward they came to the maritime

16 The pope's legate was Ademar of Puy.
17 Count of Leiningen.

regions of the Scythians, where they found such abundance of supplies that a ram was sold for a denarius, a cow for twelve denarii, as Count Robert records. By God's help they also overcame the princes or kings of the Saracens who opposed them. Elated by these successes they besieged Antioch, the metropolis of Syria, but after remaining there for nine months, they were greatly weakened by the dwindling of their army and the failure of their supplies. Therefore the Lord, seeing the affliction of his people, gave over the city[18] together with the supplies of the Turks into their hands.

3. At about the same time, while the Christians were tarrying over the siege of Antioch and all the eastern peoples were filled with terror, ambassadors from the king of the Egyptians, who is commonly believed to be the king of the Babylonians, came to Duke Godfrey and treacherously promised him aid against the Turks — who then held Jerusalem, together with all Palestine, which they had taken from the Saracens. For, as we have ascertained from trustworthy men from beyond the seas,[19] a part of ancient Babylon, called Bagdad,[20] is still habitable; a part, however, as you read in the prophecy,[21] is "deserted and inaccessible," extending for ten miles, even to the Tower of Babel. The part which is inhabited and is called Bagdad is very large and densely populated and, although it is rightfully part of the empire of the Persians, has been bestowed by the kings of the Persians[22] upon their highest priest, whom they themselves call the Caliph, so that herein there is evident (as has frequently been said already) a certain resemblance between Babylonia and Rome,[23] because what was in our part of the world bestowed by a Christian Emperor upon our Supreme Pontiff in the city of Rome was there indulgently granted by the pagan kings of the Persians, to whom Babylon has long been subject, to their highest priest. Even as our own rulers have chosen a royal city, namely Aachen, so the kings of the Persians have established as the seat of their kingdom Ekbatana (which, as we read in the book of Judith, Arphaxad founded), a city called in their

18 June 3, 1098.

19 Hofmeister is of the opinion that we need not suppose that Otto inserted the following passage in his already completed work after he undertook to go on the Crusade of 1147, for we are told (VII. 32 et seq., below) that Otto saw in the Roman synod at Viterbo in 1145 the legates of the Armenian bishops and Hugo, the bishop of Djebele (in Syria).

20 Or Baghdad; the text has *Baldach*.   21 Jer. 50. 12.

22 The Seljūq Turks. See C. M. H. 4. 299-317.   23 VI. 22; IV. 21.

own tongue Hamadan,[24] which contained, so they maintain, a hundred thousand or more fighting men. This city they took as their royal seat, reserving for themselves nothing out of Babylon except the name of emperor. That city which, as I have said, is now generally called Babylon, is situated not on the Euphrates (as men suppose) but on the Nile, about six days' journey from Alexandria. It is in fact Memphis, once called Babylon by Cambyses the son of Cyrus. The king of the Egyptians dwells there, it is said, on account of the balsam garden, although the capital of his realm is Alexandria. This may also be inferred from the fact that whereas Christians dwell in both cities, though subject to tribute, the bishop of Memphis is by ecclesiastical law subject to the patriarch of Alexandria. We find [25] that, by the original arrangement, and by the authority of the Council of Nicaea, the patriarch was placed not over Assyrians or Babylonians but over Egyptians and Africans.

4. When the ambassadors of the aforesaid king presented themselves to Duke Godfrey, most carefully chosen nobles of the Franks — this is the name by which the Orientals are accustomed to call all western peoples, I suppose on account of the ancient glory of that race and because of its valor — were sent to Babylonia. The barbarians, marvelling at the strength, the stature, the attire, the gait and the refinement of the men, declared that they were gods, not human beings. After a council had been held the King of the Babylonians, taking the ambassadors of the Franks with him, besieged Jerusalem and, bringing forth to general view the aforesaid heroes, declared that he was their ally; and having in this way received the submission of the city — by reason of the terror inspired by them, rather than by any dread he caused — he drove out the Turks and settled the Saracens there.[26]

Meanwhile the Christians (having, as we said, captured Antioch) did not worthily give the glory to God, and so they were surrounded by so great a host of Saracens that the famine — which succeeded their former abundance — was so unendurable that they hardly refrained even from devouring human flesh. The compassionate Lord, beholding in mercy the contrition of His people, and viewing them with the eye of His grace, by a revelation from on high pointed out to His faithful followers the Holy Lance (up to this time un-

---

[24] *Hani* in the text.
[25] *Conc. Nic.*, c. 6, Rufinus, *Historia ecclesiastica* 10. 6; *cf.* III. 2 above.
[26] Jerusalem was taken from the Seljūqs by the Fatimites in August, 1098.

known) by which, as we read, the side of His Son, Christ, had been pierced at the crucifixion. The Christians, trusting in this spear, although they were weak from famine, went forth and routed the Saracens, not through any strength of their own but through the strength of Christ. Then, moving into Syria, they captured the cities of Kafar el-Bara and Maarrat-en-Numan.[27] While they were tarrying there they were afflicted again, it is said, by such grievous dearth of food that they even ate human bodies that were already decaying. Afterwards they directed their armies against the Holy City, now inhabited by the Saracens. Since they were unable to capture it by siege they held a conference and decided to imitate the Master's humility and to walk about the city with bare feet. Accordingly on the eighth day, namely that on which the dispersion of the Apostles is celebrated, the city was captured [28] and the enemy found there were cut down with such slaughter that in Solomon's Porch the blood of the slain reached even to the knees of the steeds of our warriors. And observe that after the self-abasement of the people of God, and the pouring out of their prayers to the Lord, the Holy City that had been trodden under foot by the Gentiles was on the eighth day gloriously recovered by our people. Even as Jericho was taken by an earlier people on the seventh day when the Sabbath was observed, so here the beleaguered city of Jerusalem was stormed by the Christian people on the eighth day (the resurrection day that followed the Sabbath), to indicate that the [Jewish] law and the seventh day had been supplanted. From this time forth Jerusalem and the Lord's sepulcher have been in our possession.[29]

5. The king of the people of Memphis, or Alexandria — called by pilgrims the Ammiraldus [30] of the Babylonians — who tarried at Ascalon, taking the ambassadors of the Franks with him [31] directed his march toward Antioch, in order to take it by the sort of trick

[27] Kafar el-Bara (*Barra* in the text) in September, and Maarrat-en-Numan (*Marra* in the text) in December.

[28] The Crusaders took Jerusalem on July 15, 1099.

[29] Jerusalem was taken by Saladin (Salāh-ad-Dīn) in 1187, regained for a short time in the Fifth Crusade, lost once more in 1244, and again regained by Allenby. [30] Perhaps equivalent to Emir.

[31] Otto appears to have confused Ekkehard's statement (p. 217. 26 *et seq.*): *nunciatum est eis* (*i.e.*, the Christians), *quod rex Babyloniorum Ascalonam venisset . . . ducturus Francos, qui Hierosolimis erant, in captivitatem et expugnaturus Antiochiam, sicut ipse dixerat.*

by which he had captured the Holy City. But the Christians, leaving their baggage and the sick in the city, led their force against the Saracens. When they had caught sight of the countless multitude of the foe they poured out prayers unto God and boldly assailed them with their small force. And strange to say, by the grace of God, who can do all things, though they had but five thousand horse and fifteen thousand foot they compelled a hundred thousand cavalrymen and three hundred thousand infantrymen to turn their backs and secured enormous spoils. In that battle more than a hundred thousand of the Saracens perished by the sword, two thousand also are said to have been suffocated at the city gate, and countless others are reported to have been drowned or impaled on thorns. After the victory was won [some of] the leaders returned to their homes, but Godfrey [remained and] most zealously exercised rule as duke over those who had stayed. He intervened also as mediator between the Romance Franks and the Germans, who have a habit of quarreling frequently, employing certain bitter and odious jests.[32] Godfrey was able to mediate between them because he had been reared on the borders of both races and so was acquainted with the language of each, and he taught them in many ways to be forbearing.

6. Urban, after his return from the Council of Clermont-Ferrand, by the aid of those whom he had fired to undertake the expedition to Jerusalem, expelled Gwibert from the City (though not from the Castle of Crescentius) and regained his own see. Then journeying through Apulia and Calabria to Sicily,[33] which at that time the Norsemen inhabited, he amassed a great sum of money. Then, having returned to the City, he bribed with gifts those who guarded the Castle of Crescentius and, having by such means driven Gwibert from the castle as well as from the City, gained full posses-

[32] This is a very interesting indication of the beginnings of national rivalry, based apparently upon differences of language. Otto speaks of *Franci Romani et Teutonici*, contrasting obviously those who spoke a language predominantly Latin with those who spoke the German. *Cf.* Du Cange on *Lingua Romana*, under *Romanus*. There are numerous similar references to this rivalry, on the basis of language, between peoples east and west of the Rhine. *Cf.* Paul Viollet, *Histoire des Institutions politiques et administratives de la France*, 2. 36 and the references there cited.

[33] Otto is his own authority for much of this statement regarding Urban's activities, and in the matter of the Urban's collecting a large sum of money with which he bribed the guards Otto is the sole authority. Urban gained full possession of Rome in 1098.

sion of the entire City.[34] But not long afterwards he departed this life and left his chair to Paschal.

7. In the one thousand and one hundredth year from the incarnation of the Lord, when the faithful were flocking from all parts of the world to the earthly Jerusalem (the counterpart of the heavenly) to pray, many died from the unwholesome climate. Godfrey too, that most glorious duke, was carried off by a lamentable death after he had been duke for but one year and was buried in a church near the Lord's sepulcher. His brother Baldwin was, by the authority of the supreme pontiff, honored by the name of king and appointed in his stead. As to the signs and portents seen in heaven and on earth about this time — signs that portended both a division of the kingdom and an expedition to Jerusalem — let it suffice that they have been recorded by others. At that time Gwibert died and so brought to an end a horrible schism that had enveloped us like the thick darkness of Egypt. In the following year Conrad, the most Christian son of the emperor Henry, to whom his father had entrusted Italy, was overtaken by a premature death in the ninth year from that in which he had parted from his father, and died and was buried with all honor in Florence, a city of Tuscany.

At the same time William, count of Poitou and duke of Aquitaine, Tiemo, archbishop of Salzburg, Welf, duke of Bavaria [35] (who in a war waged against the emperor had destroyed the cities of Freising and Augsburg), the margravine Itha, mother of Leopold [36] (who was the margrave of Austria), William and Stephen,[37] Italian barons — together with many from Italy, Aquitaine and Germany — set out for Jerusalem by way of Hungary and Greece. The emperor Alexius treacherously exposed them in narrow passes and cruelly killed almost all of them. The more illustrious of their number he took captive and presented to the king, or Ammiraldus, of Memphis. One of their number,[38] who testifies that he took part in the expedition, has recorded this story, clearly and pathetically, after the manner of a tragedy. The venerable bishop Tiemo, having been captured with the rest, was ordered, as they say, to worship

[34] Aug. 10, 1098.

[35] *Noricorum dux* in the text.

[36] Leopold III (IV), margrave of Austria, 1095-1136, Bishop Otto's father. He was canonized Jan. 6, 1485.

[37] William, count of Nevers, and Stephen, count of Blois or Mâcon (*Matisconensis*). Why Otto calls them ''Italian barons'' is not clear.

[38] Ekkehard, p. 220.

idols. Having asked for a respite [and secured it] he entered the shrine and, since he possessed most vigorous strength of mind and body, broke to pieces the idols which he was to have worshipped, showing thereby that they were not gods but the work of men's hands. For this he was led forth and, after suffering exquisite torments and all sorts of torture, was crowned with glorious martyrdom. That he suffered for his faith in Christ a most reliable tradition affirms, but that he demolished idols is difficult to believe [39] because, as is well known, the Saracens universally are worshippers of one God; they accept the Books of the Law and also the custom of circumcision and do not even reject Christ and the Apostles and the apostolic men; they are cut off from salvation by one thing alone, the fact that they deny that Jesus Christ, who brings salvation to the human race, is God or the Son of God, and hold in reverence and worship as a great prophet of the supreme God, Mahomet, a deceiver of whom mention was made above.[40] The beginning of his deception and — as he himself falsely calls it — his preaching is, according to their tradition, as follows: "The beginning of the gospel of Mahomet, the son of God, the prophet of the Most High: 'Wash you, make you clean'." [41] And the aforesaid race in its stupidity is accustomed to observe this precept by washing the secret parts of the body daily.

8. In the one thousand one hundred and third year from the incarnation of the Lord, the emperor Henry celebrated the Lord's Nativity at Mainz and there, having designated his son Henry as king [42] to succeed him, publicly announced that he would visit the sepulcher of the Lord and inspired many from various parts of his kingdom to the same resolve. In the following year, as he was observing the Lord's birthday at Regensburg, a strife arose and Count Sigehard was killed by that body of nobles who are called *ministeriales*,[43] because he was said to be infringing upon their rights. In the following year, while the emperor was again celebrating the Lord's birthday at Mainz, his son Henry, upon the advice

[39] Note Otto's critical tendency even with respect to legends of the Church.
[40] V. 9.
[41] Hofmeister states that he has searched in vain for the following quotation in the Latin version of the Koran (translated in Spain in 1143 at the bidding of Peter, abbot of Cluny).
[42] Henry V had already been crowned as king on Jan. 6, 1099.
[43] Unfree retainers of the emperor, who were drawn from the crown lands or from his patrimonial estates.

of Margrave Theobald and Count Berengar, plotted rebellion against his father in Bavaria. This he did under the cloak of religion on the ground that his father had been excommunicated by the Roman pontiffs. Associating with himself certain nobles from East Franconia, Alemannia and Bavaria he entered Saxony, a land and people easily aroused against the kingdom. There he was received with all honor. Remaining at Quedlinburg for the Lord's Easter [44] he won over all the leading men of that race to his will. In a council of bishops held in the royal city of Nordhausen, whose president was Rothard, archbishop of Mainz (who was long deposed by the emperor from his own see) Henry condemned simony and other practices contrary to the Church of Rome. Presently, after observing Whitsunday at Merseburg, he had Henry (who had been elected but was rejected by his father's loyal supporters) consecrated as archbishop of Magdeburg. Then having collected an army he directed his march toward Mainz in order to reinstate the archbishop, but since his father and many followers were awaiting his coming with an armed force within the walls, he was unable to carry his desire into effect. Thereupon he went to Würzburg and cast out Erlung and placed Robert over that church. This done he sent away the Saxons and with his Bavarians laid siege to Nürnberg. Within two or three months he captured it and then he moved on to Regensburg, the metropolis of the duchy of Bavaria. His father, following hard upon his steps, put Robert to flight and restored Erlung. Moving onward, with the help of the people of Regensburg he drove his son from the city, established a certain Ulric there as bishop and laid waste the margraviate of Theobald through the agency of the Bohemians.

9. After the kingdom had been thus pitifully divided against itself, all the soldiers its resources could supply brought together and the whole land cruelly laid waste with fire and sword, the two combatants, father and son, took up their positions on the banks of the river Regen. Their camps were already being marked out, their battle lines were already in process of formation, the father was already being inflamed by his supporters against his son and the son against his father in parricidal strife, but their unhallowed designs were frustrated by the channel of the stream. You might have seen the lamentable and pitiable preparations, you might have seen the world betraying by its deeds more clearly than the sun-

[44] April 9, 1105.

light its contempt for itself because, forsooth, contrary to the law
of nature a son was rising against his father, contrary to the standard of justice a soldier was preparing to do battle against his king,
a slave against his master, brother stood opposed to brother, kinsman to kinsman, and each was planning to shed the blood of the
sharer in his own blood.

Could this deed of the world — so unheard of, so inhuman — fail
to provoke us to contempt of itself? Does not the world itself, [so
lovely, so pure] (or rather, as Augustine termed it, "so unlovely,
so impure")[45] entice and cajole its lovers with false delights, does
it not impose deeds of this sort upon those who cleave to it and finally drag them to their doom? These are what Paul calls "the last
days" and therefore "grievous," in which men "seeking their own,
not the things of Jesus Christ,"[46] and for that reason becoming
"lovers of self . . . unholy, without natural affection, disobedient
to parents,"[47] are hurried into deeds of wicked daring and most
unholy acts as they wallow amid their various disgraceful pleasures.
And mark you this: these times of ours, which are with good reason
believed to be "the last" — because they are destined to set a limit
to the previous deeds of wickedness and are, so to speak, at once
threatening the approaching end of the world in consequence of
the enormity of its sinfulness, and indicating that the kingdom
of Christ is soon to come — these times of ours, I say, on the one
hand (as I have said) make some most evil and eager lovers of the
world, on the other cause some to be most fervid in zeal for God
and abundantly filled with longing for heaven. Hence just as the
spirit of wickedness, which now, "having but a short time" and
therefore raging all the more violently, entices some all the more
surely to vice, so the sweetness of the heavenly kingdom, as though
it were here already "even at the doors," the more surely attracts
others to love of itself. Accordingly, during these times when,
through the lust for power, the kingdom of the Romans was rent
not only by civil war but even by parricide, some, for Christ's
sake, despising their own interests and considering that it was not
for naught that they were wearing the girdle of knighthood, set out
for Jerusalem and there, undertaking a new kind of warfare, so
conducted themselves against the enemies of the Cross of Christ

[45] The pun on *mundus* and *inmundus* is difficult, if not impossible, to reproduce in English.

[46] Phil. 2. 21.   [47] II Tim. 3. 2 and 3.

that, continually bearing about in their bodies the death of the cross, they appeared by their life and conversation to be not soldiers but monks. Moreover, among both the monastic and the secular clergy austerity of life and conduct began to increase from that time even to the present day, so that by a great and righteous judgment of God, though the citizens of the world grew more unclean in their uncleanness, His own citizens attained more and more through His grace to the fulness of the virtues. But now let us return to the history.

When the two armies had taken up positions on the banks of the aforesaid river, and certain had met each other face to face in the very stream itself and been killed, Henry the Younger, considering that all his father's strength would lie in Bořivoi the duke of Bohemia and in Margrave Leopold (whose sister the duke had to wife), prevailed upon them by many inducements — he offered in marriage to the Margrave his own sister,[48] who had recently been left a widow by the death of Frederick, duke of Swabia — and persuaded them both to forsake his father. When they withdrew the emperor was compelled to retreat, and from this time on his strength began to diminish and his son's to increase. Rothard, at that time archbishop of Mainz, was restored by Henry the Younger to his see in the eighth year from the time at which he had been deposed.

10. Not long afterwards the son addressed his father in the town of Bingen on the Rhine and exhorted him to render obedience to the Roman See in accordance with the ban of excommunication. But the father asked that a council of nobles be assembled regarding this matter, and so, in response to his request, notice was given of an assembly at Mainz to be attended by all the princes of the realm on the next Christmas Day.[49]

At about the same time King Baldwin laid siege to Ascalon and made it tributary. He fought a battle also with the Saracens, and though he had but few men — that is, only four thousand — he put to flight fifty thousand by divine rather than by human might.

[48] Agnes, Bishop Otto's mother; cf. Otto's *Gesta Friderici* 1. 10.

[49] Hofmeister points out that Otto has here confused the sequence of events by failing to connect properly the letter of the emperor to Philip II with Ekkehard's narrative. For Ekkehard correctly states that the assembly at Mainz preceded the conference (at Coblenz as we learn from the letter, not Bingen, as Ekkehard says). The letter and Ekkehard both state that the father requested only a safe audience.

He captured one of their leaders and killed the other. But the emperor Alexius, arch-traitor, being no longer able to conceal the evil scheme long before conceived in his heart, most shamefully entered upon an alliance with the Turks, who were by this time almost in despair, and most impiously delivered over to them Nicaea, which had been won at the cost of the shedding of so much blood of our people. Mark the grievous times in which two emperors — one in the East, one in the West — were enemies to God.

11. In the one thousand one hundred and sixth year from the incarnation of the Lord, a very great assembly of nobles was held on the day of the Lord's Nativity at Mainz. To this assembly the legates of the Apostolic See came and publicly proclaimed to all who were present the decree of excommunication that had been pronounced against the emperor by the Roman pontiffs. Therefore when the emperor, who had been imprisoned in a certain castle under guard, demanded a hearing the nobles, fearing an insurrection of the people, met him at Ingelheim. There they prevailed upon him by manifold exhortations (or as others say, they tricked him) and forced him to resign the royal insignia and send them to his son, in the forty-third year [50] of his reign after the death of his father and the . . . [51] of his rule as emperor. To the latter dignity, however, he had after his capture of the City been elevated by Gwibert, more by might than by right. Whether all these things were done lawfully or otherwise we do not venture to determine; but there are those who believe that this test came to him near the end of his life to justify him, not to condemn him, and they affirm that, because of his almsgiving and his many deeds of mercy, he had earned mercy at the hands of the Lord, that his excesses and his wanton conduct in his exalted station on the throne should be punished in this wise in the present world. The nobles, returning to his son, bestowed upon him the royal insignia, and through the laying on of hands by the legates of the Apostolic See and by general election chose him as king (he had already been selected by his father), the ninety-second in line from Augustus, in the one thousand one hun-

---

[50] This is, of course, an error since Henry III died in 1056 and the assembly at Mainz convened Dec. 25, 1105. Hofmeister suggests that Otto may perhaps have based his estimate on Frutolf's words on the year 1057 (p. 198. 5): *Heinricus quartus . . . quando haec conscriptio facta est, anno 42 regnavit; cf.* Ekkehard on the year 1106, p. 231. 10.

[51] There is a *lacuna* in the text where the numeral should appear.

dred and sixth year from the incarnation of the Lord, as I have said.

Thus far [52] we have set down extracts from the books of Orosius, of Eusebius and of those who wrote after them, even to our own time. What follows, since it is still fresh in men's memories, we shall record as it has been related to us by credible men or seen and heard by ourselves.

12. After the royal insignia had been resigned by the emperor he himself, having now become a beggar instead of a wealthy and powerful king, thereby affording to mortals a pitiable example, withdrew to the regions of the lower Rhine (to Lorraine) and was there received by the people of Cologne, not as an exile but as a king, with royal pomp. This city, situated in Belgic Gaul on the Rhine, excels, as is well known, all the other cities of Gaul and Germany — since Trèves has begun to decline in wealth and in buildings, in size and in beauty. When he went from Cologne to Liège and was received by the people there in royal state, he declared to all to whom he could — whether they dwelt in his own kingdom or in other realms — that he had been over-reached by treachery and compelled by force to surrender the royal insignia. There is extant, among other letters of his, one on this subject which he sent to the king of Celtica,[53] who is called the king of the Franks, and to the duke of Aquitaine.[54] It contains the tragic story of his sorrows and might soften even hearts of stone, leading them to contemplate and to deplore the miseries of this changing world. It begins thus:

"Dearest Prince and most faithful of all those friends in whom, after God, we place our hope: I have chosen you first and particularly out of all to whom I have thought it necessary to lament and deplore all my misfortunes and my sorrows, and I even cast myself before your knees — if that were possible without violating the majesty of my imperial rank."[55]

His son, now king, collected an army and pursuing his father

[52] To the year 1106. On the statement contained in this paragraph, see the opening remarks in the Commentary on Book VII, and Introduction, p. 25. For a list of similar statements concerning individual sources used by Otto see III. 8, note 65.

[53] *Cf.* above, VI. 30 (end). The reference is to Philip I of France.

[54] William IX, his cousin. Hofmeister says that this statement — to his best knowledge — is found only in Otto.

[55] The entire letter may be found in Sigebert on the year 1106.

encamped near the Meuse. But, having been attacked there by Henry duke of Lorraine and others loyal to his father, at a bridge over the Meuse in a place which is called Visé,[56] he was obliged to retreat. Not long afterwards, while he was returning to the upper courses of the Rhine and again making ready an army, his father died at Liège. When this internal dissension had been brought to an end in this way, negotiations for peace were begun.

13. Henry V, reigning [57] without opposition upon the death of his father, besieged Cologne and finally compelled it to surrender after it had agreed to pay a heavy indemnity. When he had duly set in order all matters in Gaul and Germany he also reinstated the bishops who, during the course of the strife, had been driven from their sees. One of these bishops, the venerable Conrad, archbishop of the Church at Salzburg (who, as is well known, is still happily occupied [58] in the Church of God in fruitful labors), was restored to his see. This see, by permission of Henry the Elder, a certain Bertoldus had usurped after the death of the martyr Tiemo of blessed memory.

At that time Koloman, king of the Hungarians, persecuted his brother Almus because he suspected him of seeking to obtain a share in the government of the kingdom. Koloman went as a fugitive to Henry and, bewailing the injustice that had been done him,[59] sought his aid. And so the king, consenting to the undertaking, made war on the Hungarians but, since he heedlessly wasted his time at a stronghold called Pressburg,[60] he could accomplish little and so returned to his own domain leaving the matter unsettled.

14. In the third year after this he collected an enormous army from all parts of his kingdom with the intention of going to Rome. He crossed the Pyrenees [61] by the Great St. Bernard [62] and, halting in a plain of Italy near the Po, reviewed his troops. In his train were thirty thousand picked horsemen, not counting those who had flocked to him in Italy. Eyewitnesses, who are still alive, report that the circuit of his camp was so great that it could scarcely have been measured by the eye. After they had pitched their camp in the plain in Italy, every one of the soldiers kindled a light before

---

[56] Near Liège; *Guegesaz* in the text.   [57] 1106-1125.

[58] He was archbishop of Salzburg from Jan. 7, 1106 (consecrated Oct. 21), until his death in the year 1147.   [59] *Cf.* VII. 26 below.

[60] *Bosan* in the text. *Cf. Gesta Friderici* 1. 31.

[61] Otto says *Pyreneum transit.* The reference, of course, is to the Alps. See II. 36 and note 203.   [62] The text reads *per montem Iovis.*

his tent at night. This was done for the display of earthly glory.
What an astonishing spectacle it afforded the natives in so wide a
circuit there is no need to set forth in detail. Having moved his
camp and ascended the Apennines he besieged a town called Pon-
tremoli because it opposed his passage and, though it was defended
by the nature of the ground and by very lofty towers, he captured
it. After this, directing his course through Tuscany, he razed to
the ground Arezzo, though it trusted in the strength of its walls and
the height of its towers. He destroyed the city because its citizens
had destroyed the Church of St. Donatus outside its walls that
they might not have an episcopal see there. While he was marching
through Lombardy he had taken Novara, a city of Liguria, and set
it on fire. And so after many valiant achievements both in Farther
and in Nearer Italy, which are now called Lombardy and Tuscany,
he went on to the City. There he was received with the greatest
rejoicing by Pope Paschal and the clergy and the Roman populace,
who awaited his coming in the Leonine city, standing before the
doors of the blessed Peter with crosses and censers and other ecclesiastical or worldly insignia. But upon the advice of certain evil men
the king made the pontiff a prisoner, though he treated him with
the greatest respect, and entrusted him to the custody of Ulric the
patriarch of Aquileia. In this way then, since a tumult had arisen
and all the precious objects which had been exhibited to grace the
occasion and to do honor to his royal majesty had been most shamefully scattered, joy was turned to sorrow.

The reason for this disgraceful act was as follows. As the king
was hastening toward Rome a compact was made,[63] it is said, between him and the pope, and ratified by the giving of hostages, to
the effect that the king should hand over the investitures of the
bishops and that the pope should resign their regalia to him. And
so when he had reached Rome and had demanded that what the
pope had promised him should be performed, although the pope
was altogether innocent he was confined in prison as if he were
guilty, just because he could not fulfil what was requested (since
the bishops objected). Seeing this the venerable Conrad, archbishop
of the Church at Salzburg — who had come with the king — grieved
in his passion for righteousness on God's account and condemned
the deed. When one of the king's attendants, Henry Caput by

---

[63] On Feb. 4, 1111; see *MGH. LL. Constit.* 1. 137 *et seq.*, Numbers 83-86;
see also 87.

name, drew his sword and threatened him with death he bared his neck as though he craved death on behalf of the right. 'It was Conrad's wish to end his earthly life — if the other really was minded to carry his threats into effect — rather than shut his eyes to the commission of so great a sin. The Roman people arose in countless throngs, crossed the Tiber and caught the king almost off his guard before the steps of the Church of St. Peter, since many of the soldiers were staying in the City or in the country. The king, who was a man of great experience in warfare, charged the foe with the few whom he had there. After a long and fierce fight, since his men were now coming up, he slew many and put the rest to flight. In their flight the Romans were crowded together in a small place on a bridge near the fortress of Crescentius. They cast themselves into the Tiber and more, it is said, perished in its waters than fell by the sword. After perpetrating this cruel deed the king, suspicious of the narrow gates of the city, tore down the walls of the City and so made his way out, taking the pope with him as a captive. Albert, a Lotharingian by birth, was responsible (tradition says) for this evil deed. He was afterwards made archbishop of Mainz.[64] At this time, however, he was the king's Chancellor and was held in high esteem by him as the counsellor most dear to his heart. And yet the king, after his return, took him captive, put him in prison and tormented him with various tortures and pangs of hunger beyond belief. All this the king did because, by a divine judgment, he felt until the end of his life that Albert had become, instead of his best friend, his worst enemy and a dangerous foe to his kingdom. But enough of this.

When the supreme pontiff through such sacrilegious audacity had been for some time kept prisoner, a council was held [65] and the king was recalled by the citizens. After he had extorted by force from the pope the rights in the matter of investiture of bishops, the king released the pope and entered the City. Then, as though moved to repentance, he conciliated the citizens and the pope by gifts and, having been crowned by him amid universal favor, obtained the titles of Emperor and Augustus in the one thousand one hundred and eleventh year from the incarnation of the Lord, and in the fifth year of his own reign since his father's surrender of the royal in-

---

[64] Designated in 1109, he received the investiture on Aug. 15, 1111 and was consecrated Dec. 25, 1115.

[65] April 11, 1111.

signia. These privileges, which he extorted from the Roman pontiff by threats, afterwards the bishops assembled in a synod by an authoritative decision condemned as being merely mock privileges.[66]

15. Then the emperor, departing from the City, returned to the Transalpine country. Since not only his neighbors but even peoples outside trembled in terror for fear of him, and all bowed to his authority and to his will, he entered Lorraine and made war on Count Reinald [67] because he considered the Count his enemy. He besieged him in the fortress of Bar-le-Duc, situated on the frontier on his realm, and finally received him in surrender together with his castle, which he had carried by storm, and took him away a prisoner. Afterwards he united to himself in marriage Mathilda the daughter of Henry, king of England, and celebrated the wedding magnificently with royal pomp at Mainz. During the solemnization of nuptials Lothar, duke of Saxony,[68] came to him in the presence of all, barefooted and clad in a rough cloak, and surrendered to him. For so great a fear had seized all the nobles of the kingdom at this time that none dared to rebel, not one, if he had rebelled, but strove to regain his favor at greatest cost to himself or even at the risk of his life.

In this assembly, since almost all the princes of the realm had come together, there were conspiracies. And henceforth not only secret plans, but even public intrigues, were formed against the emperor. Accordingly the wretched empire, which for a few years had enjoyed peace — troubled, to be sure — was again rent and divided against itself in its Transalpine as well as in its Cisalpine regions. In consequence there arose civil wars which involved much shedding of blood, both while the emperor was in his own domain and when he travelled to Italy and entrusted the control of the state to his sister's sons, Conrad and Frederick.[69] A decree of excommunication was also pronounced against the emperor by Calixtus [70] (who succeeded Paschal and Gelasius), at the instigation of

---

[66] The play on words (*privilegium, pravilegium*) can scarcely be reproduced.   [67] Count of Bar and Mousson. This was in 1113.

[68] See VI. 34 (end) above. He succeeded Henry as emperor in 1125.

[69] The sons of Agnes by her first husband, Frederick, and hence Bishop Otto's half-brothers; see *Gesta Friderici* 1. 8 and 9. Conrad afterwards reigned as Conrad III (1138-1152). Frederick was the father of the emperor Frederick Barbarossa (1152-1190).

[70] Calixtus II. But Gelasius II had already excommunicated the emperor, April 7, 1118.

Albert of Mainz, Frederick of Cologne and Conrad of Salzburg. Since the schism was renewed the whole empire was thrown into confusion. The king moved his troops against the City and, by force of arms, established Bourdin [71] a Spanish bishop in the Roman See. Bourdin was taken captive by the Romans at Sutri not long afterwards, when the emperor had departed, and was imprisoned at La Cava. [72]

At about the same time a dreadful earthquake overthrew very many towns, temples, villages and mountains, as may be seen even today in the Tridentine Valley. At that time also Stephen, king of Hungary, the son of Koloman, with a great army unexpectedly invaded the frontier of the kingdom, laid waste its borders and carried off spoils. That illustrious man Margrave Leopold, [73] associating with himself the duke of the Bohemians, [74] followed Stephen as far as the limits of the kingdom, and after capturing and burning a stronghold which is called Eisenstadt, and laying waste with fire and sword all the country round about, returned home without loss.

16. Since the Roman Empire was in many ways divided against itself the emperor, seeing that his kingdom was falling away from him on account of the ban of excommunication, and fearing the lot of his father, assembled a full council of nobles near Worms. There he resigned the right of investiture of bishops to Lambert, a legate of the apostolic see, and was by him absolved from the bonds of the curse. Lambert subsequently became pope under the name Honorius. With respect to the investiture a guarantee in writing was given to the Church. On the other hand, assurance was given in writing to the emperor that those who should be elected as bishops, both on this side and on the other side of the Alps, should not be regarded as definitely settled as bishops until they received their regalia from his hand through the scepter. [75] The Romans claim that this concession was made to him, and to him alone, for the sake of peace — and not to his successors. After this, since the Church was now fully restored to freedom and peace was

[71] Bishop of Braga in Portugal; he took the name Gregory VIII.

[72] A monastery near Salerno; *Clava* in the text.

[73] Bishop Otto's father.

[74] Wladislao (*Vladivoi*) I, the brother of Boriwoio II mentioned above in VII. 9. He held the dukedom from 1109 to 1125.

[75] On this passage see Hofmeister in *Zeitschrift für Kirchengeschichte* 29 (1908), 71 *et seq*. Cf. Otto's *Gesta Friderici* 2. 6.

secured anew, we find that under Pope Calixtus II it "became a great mountain." [76] Hence it was written concerning him at Rome:

> See Calixtus, the pride of his country, the Empire's glory!
> Bourdin the Base he condemns, and peace once more he restores. [77]

After this the emperor, intending to set out for the Celtic country with an army, moved as far as Metz. When he learned there that the people of Worms had revolted against him and had destroyed his palace outside the walls, he retraced his journey and laid siege to the city. When on a certain day the citizens recklessly made a sally and planned to engage in battle with Augustus, they were shrewdly enticed away from the walls and very many of them were killed. A few escaped by flight and the rest were taken captive. To curb the insolence of the others they were sent back — some deprived of their noses, others of their eyes. Upon agreement to pay an enormous amount of money [78] they at last regained the emperor's favor. When everything had been thus satisfactorily settled, the emperor, upon the advice of his son-in-law [79] the king of England, planned to make his entire kingdom subject to a tax [80] and so incurred the bitter hatred of the nobles. While in relation to this purpose he was preparing to traverse the country of the lower Rhine he was taken sick at Utrecht, a city of Frisia, and ended his days in the nineteenth year of his reign as king and in the fourteenth of his imperial power. His body was transported through Cologne and buried in royal state in Speier, a city of Gaul, beside his father, his grandfather and his great-grandfather,[81] who had all been emperors.

17. In the one thousand one hundred and twenty-fifth year from the incarnation of the Lord, since Henry had died without an heir, the nobles assembled at Mainz and there deliberated with regard

[76] Dan. 2. 35. *Cf.* above, VI. 36.

[77] At this point in manuscript B₄ there is an additional paragraph in the text in the same hand and ink; see Hofmeister's text, p. 332, lines 18-36.

[78] Ekkehard says *quinque milibus talentorum*; in the Annals of Paderborn, a continuation of the *Annales Hildesheimenses*, we read *bina Marcarum milia*.

[79] This should be "father-in-law," as Wilmans has pointed out, for he had married Matilda the daughter of Henry I of England.

[80] *Cf.* G. Waitz, *Deutsche Verfassungsgeschichte* 8. 399 *et seq.*

[81] Henry IV, Henry III, Conrad II. The Franconian line came to an end upon the death of Henry V. *Cf.* Otto's *Gesta Friderici* 1. 15 and and also 1. 10, where we find practically the same things said about Henry IV as here about Henry V.

to his successor. Four princes of the realm — Lothar the duke of Saxony, Frederick [82] duke of Swabia, Leopold [83] margrave of Austria and Charles [84] the count of Flanders were considered for the throne. Finally Lothar, a Saxon by birth, the son of Gebhard, although he objected and protested vigorously was compelled by the prayers of all, in the presence of the legate of the apostolic see, to become king and he reigned as the ninety-second in line from Augustus. He humiliated the children of the emperor Henry in every possible way, so that by a righteous judgment of God, even as you read in the book of Kings,[85] their seed was plainly seen to be afflicted for the sins and the transgressions of their fathers. As a result, a serious dissension in the kingdom, which was prolonged for many years, brought very many into peril of soul and body. For when the aforesaid young men, Frederick and Conrad (sons of a sister of the emperor Henry), saw that they were being imposed upon [86] they tried to the best of their ability to retaliate. For this reason they were excommunicated by Pope Honorius, who had succeeded Calixtus. Conrad, having been made king [87] by his brother and others, crossed the Pyrenees [88] by the pass of Septimer — where the rivers Rhine and Inn have their source. He was received with all honor by the people of Milan, who at that time by capturing and destroying Como brought to a successful conclusion a war with that city which had been most pitiably protracted for ten years,[89] to the destruction of the people of both states, and was anointed as king by Anselm their archbishop at Monza,[90] the capital city of the Italian kingdom. For this and other reasons this archbishop was deposed [91] by the pope and another was put in his place.

[82] Frederick II, Bishop Otto's half-brother.   [83] Bishop Otto's father.

[84] There is no mention elsewhere of the count of Flanders being considered as emperor, and Otto is mistaken in saying that he was nominated at Mainz together with the other three.

[85] Otto says "kingdoms": *in libro Regnorum*. See I Kings 11. 39.

[86] Frederick was proscribed by a vote of the nobles at the Council of Strasbourg toward the end of 1125 or the beginning of the following year. The Goslar expedition directed against him soon after won universal approval.

[87] Dec. 18, 1127.

[88] *I.e.*, the Alps. *Cf.* II. 36 above and note 203.

[89] Como was taken by the citizens of Milan on Aug. 27, 1127. The warfare between Como and Milan began in 1118.

[90] In Lombardy; *Modoyci* in the text.

[91] He was excommunicated in 1129 by the synod of Pavia and finally deposed in 1135 under Pope Innocent II.

18. Not long afterwards, upon the death of Honorius, a very grievous schism arose in the Church of God, since Innocent was canonically elected whereas Peter,[92] the son of Pierleoni, was elevated to the papacy through the use of force by his friends [93] who were the strongest party in the City, and had too the support of Roger of Sicily. Since Innocent was not powerful enough to resist Peter he withdrew from the City, crossing the Alps into Gaul. There, within the realm of the French king, he held a council at Clermont in the region of Auvergne, at which he met Conrad bishop of Salzburg and Ekbert bishop of Münster, the messengers of King Lothar. After leaving that city he convoked a synod of bishops at Liège, a city of Lorraine, and summoned King Lothar [94] to the defense of the Holy Roman Church. Though Lothar at first set forth in restrained language how greatly the kingdom had been weakened by its love for the churches, and at how great cost to himself he had relinquished the investiture of their bishops, he nevertheless without delay promised his aid to the Roman Church. The supreme pontiff returned to Italy. In the following year the emperor renewed military preparations and collected an army, though on account of the dissension in his kingdom it was a small army.[95] This army he led into Italy by way of the Tridentine Valley. In many places he was mocked and held up to ridicule by those who dwelt in that country, both because of their love for Conrad and in consequence of the fewness of his troops. But, shortly before, Conrad, who had been established as king by the people of Milan, had lost almost all his men and returned at great risk to his home. The emperor, having more confidence in his own ability than in his soldiers, moved on as far as the City and there, having zealously done what he could with so few, was crowned by Pope Innocent in the Church of San Salvatore (which is called the Constantinian) and received the title of Augustus. At that time Peter had taken possession of the Church of the Blessed Peter, in which it was customary for the emperors to be crowned.

19. Returning from the City, the emperor entered Germany.[96] [In this land] not long afterwards, while he was conducting a gen-

[92] Called Anacletus II.

[93] But Hofmeister believes that on the contrary Innocent used fraud and violence, while Peter was duly elected by a majority of the cardinals.

[94] End of March, 1131.   [95] Only 1500 soldiers.

[96] He stopped at Freising on Aug. 23, 1133.

eral council at Bamberg (about the middle of Lent), he received
back into favor Dukes Frederick and Conrad upon the intercession
of Bernard, abbot of Clairvaux, and after peace had thus been
restored and all the affairs of Gaul and Germany duly set in order,
he again proclaimed an expedition to Italy. As he turned aside into
Saxony from this expedition he met the duke of Poland, who was
bringing to him many gifts. Yet he did not deign to admit him to
his presence until he had paid tribute for twelve years, five hundred
pounds per year, and had done homage to him on behalf of the
Pomeranians and the Rugians and affirmed upon oath that he
would be forever subject to the emperor. He also compelled the
king of Denmark to bring him, as a sign of subjection, his sword
under the crown, that he might thus enhance the glory of the imperial majesty. From the king of the Hungarians, whom he had
inspired with terror, he received many magnificent gifts.

After this Lothar again led into Italy through the Tridentine
Valley an army — not as before small, but consisting of a large
number of picked men. He took with him Conrad, who, as I said
above, had been made king by certain persons but had afterwards
recovered his senses. After capturing some very strongly fortified
castles in the passes, together with a certain chieftain who was making vigorous efforts to deny him access to a pass, he pitched his
camp in a plain of Italy near Garda. Upon his surrender the emperor moved on as far as the Po and captured Guastalla. There he
summoned before him men of Milan and of Cremona who were engaged in a protracted warfare against each other. After an investigation of the cases of the two cities, the people of Cremona were
adjudged enemies by the nobles of Italy and outlawed. When after
this decision they fled, the emperor pursued them and destroyed
their lands, their villages and their strongholds. Then, going to
Pavia, he received its citizens into favor upon their agreement to
pay a sum of money. The people of Bologna and those of Emilia,
who had held him in derision upon his former expedition, voluntarily met him as suppliants and made earnest protestations of
submission to him. Afterwards he went on as far as Turin and reduced all Northern Italy to a province. Then he crossed the Apennines [97] and making his way through the interior of Italy received
the submission of Ancona, Spoleto and other cities and fortified
towns. Next he directed his forces against Roger and marched

[97] Otto is here in error.

through Campania and Apulia. Henry, duke of Bavaria,[98] the king's son-in-law, leading an army through Tuscany gave the pope safe conduct to the emperor. Indeed Augustus performed such valiant deeds in Apulia and Campania that none of the kings of the Franks (from Charles the Great even down to the present time) is found to have accomplished so much in that country. In short he captured not only cities — as for example Capua,[99] Troja, Salerno, Barletta and Bari — but also very strongly fortified camps and inaccessible fortresses. Duke Henry, also, with his Bavarian soldiers, took Benevento and restored it to the Pope. At Alba he had captured and destroyed the suburbs of the city, which was striving to offer resistance to him.

20. While the emperor was tarrying in Italy, Roger, having failed in an attempt to bribe him by an enormous amount of gold and silver, assembled a far greater army and announced that he would meet him in open and public [100] war. The emperor, who was a very valiant warrior and unafraid, made his troops ready again, drew up a line of battle and encouraged them for the combat; assuring them that, by reason of their own natural courage and the cowardice innate in the enemy they could not be vanquished by any force of their foes, however great, particularly because, since they were now in this distant and remote region, they could not retreat to their native land, and because they had taken up arms in a righteous cause against a tyrant who was the enemy, not only of the kingdom but also of the Church, and so had been excommunicated. When the emperor was advancing to meet him in battle, Roger lost courage and fled to the mountains. But the emperor, after meeting with Pope Innocent, moved on as far as Bari where he was welcomed by the citizens with great joy. By the exercise of great skill the emperor captured a certain stronghold situated there, in which Roger had a garrison, and hanged upon the gallows the soldiers he found there, particularly the Saracens. But when Augustus, having driven Roger out of Campania and Apulia, was planning to pursue him to Calabria and into Sicily, too, he was prevented by his followers who, having long been absent from their native land, longed to return to their wives, their children and their friends.

[98] *Noricorum dux* in the text. This is Henry X, the Proud, duke of Bavaria and Saxony. He married Gertrude the daughter of the emperor Lothar.

[99] Capua and Troja were taken not by Lothar but by Duke Henry.

[100] *Cf.* VI. 35 and note 183 above.

Accordingly he declared Roger an enemy and handed over the Duchy of Apulia to Rainulf,[101] a brave and noble man, and left part of his troops with him. This done the victorious emperor laid plans for his return.

But we cannot pass over in silence the fact that, in the matter of the bestowal of the duchy, a controversy almost arose between him and the Roman Pontiff, since each affirmed that the Duchy of Apulia was under his jurisdiction. This dispute, it is said, was settled finally, after due deliberation, in the following way: in bestowing the standard upon the duke each was to lay his hand upon it.

As Lothar was returning from Italy he was taken sick at Trent, and there in the mountains, in a lowly hut, this mighty emperor died, full of days, in the thirteenth year of his reign and in the seventh [102] of his imperial power, leaving behind him a pitiable memory of our human estate. Had he not been forestalled by death he might have been the man to restore, by his ability and energy, the imperial crown to its ancient dignity. His son-in-law Duke Henry, in whose territory he had died, received the royal insignia. The king was transported through Augsburg and East Franconia into Saxony, to the monastery of Königslutter, which he himself had built, and was buried there with all due honor. That none of his deeds might be forgotten and obliterated they were recorded on leaden tablets [103] and buried by his side.

21. About this time many famous nobles either preceded their emperor or soon followed him in death. Bruno, the venerable archbishop of Cologne (an especially learned man), died in Apulia and was buried with all honor in the Church of St. Nicholas at Bari. His successor Hugo, terminating his life and his priestly duties within two months, was likewise laid to rest in Apulia, at Melfi. Of those who had survived, Albert bishop of Mainz (a man learned in secular matters, powerful and very wealthy) and Henry bishop of Freising,[104] the abbot of Fulda, Leopold [105] margrave of Austria, a most Christian man, father of the clergy and of the poor, together with many other noble and illustrious men came to

---

[101] King Roger's brother-in-law.　　[102] It was actually the fifth.

[103] Found when the emperor's tomb was opened in 1620 and preserved today in the museum at Brunswick.

[104] Upon his death on Oct. 9, 1137 he was succeeded by Otto.

[105] Bishop Otto's father died Nov. 15, 1136.

the end of their lives. Louis too, king of France, and Henry king of England, Reginald archbishop of Rheims and Gaufrid [106] count of Poitou died at the same time. From this time forth England, a land hitherto most prosperous, began to be subject to such great disasters that many, afflicted there by hunger and by want came, it is said, to a miserable end.

Upon the death of King Henry the nobles invited Stephen,[107] his sister's son, from Gaul to the throne. But the wife of the Count of Anjou,[108] Matilda (formerly the wife of the emperor Henry V, and the daughter of that King Henry),[109] demanded her father's kingdom as of hereditary right and even to the present day she ceases not to harass it, to such an extent that a few years ago the king I have mentioned fell into the hands of this woman and became her prisoner.[110] France too, after the loss of its king, suffered so many afflictions by ravagings and burnings under his son Louis [111] (who is still living) in consequence of the warfare between him and Theobald, count of Blois, that if peace had not recently been restored through the merits, the prayers and the counsel of the holy men who dwell there the land would, it is believed, have been utterly ruined.

Pannonia [112] was likewise afflicted by many calamities, since her king, Stephen the son of Koloman, died not long before this time; he too, all through his life, had had a prolonged conflict with the emperor of the Greeks. When Bela the son of Almo,[113] who together with his father Almo had been blinded by Koloman, was raised to the throne in Stephen's stead, Boris — who was himself, it was said, a son of Koloman, not by Stephen's mother, but by a daughter of the king of the Ruteni and of Kiev — laid claim to his

[106] Also known as William VIII (tenth Duke of Aquitaine). He died on April 9, 1137.

[107] Crowned Dec. 22, 1135. He was son of Adela, daughter of William I.

[108] Geoffrey Plantagenet, son of Fulk V, count of Anjou and king of Jerusalem.   [109] I.e., Henry I, of England.

[110] King Stephen was captured Feb. 2, 1141 at Lincoln by Matilda's men and dismissed from custody the following November. Upon his death, Oct. 25, 1154, in accordance with an agreement made the preceding year, Henry II, the son of Matilda by her second husband, succeeded Stephen as king of England.

[111] Louis VII king of France (1137-1180).

[112] I.e., Hungary.

[113] The brother of King Koloman.

father's kingdom. Accordingly Boris crossed·over to Greece and married there a relative of King Kaloiohannes.[114] Later he invaded Poland and inclined the duke of that land to his will. And so, aided by his army, at the invitation of certain Hungarian counts he invaded Pannonia,[115] passing through the forest which separates the Poles from the Hungarians. King Bela associated with himself Albert [116] the son of Margrave Leopold, who had Bela's sister to wife, and certain nobles of our kingdom and went to meet Boris. When the latter heard the tumult and the voices of those who were exhorting the host to battle, and realized from the idiom they were using that there would be a large number of Germans in the battle line, smitten with terror of them rather than of the Hungarians, he and the Duke of Poland fled, losing many men in the rout. In the very first engagement between the Hungarians and the Poles, before the Germans came up, many were slain on both sides and certain of those who were of Bela's party, but had treacherously delivered over their own friends to the enemy, were killed, by a just judgment paying the penalty of their treachery.

We know that these calamities are rife in our own day in neighboring kingdoms; but what we hear from day to day from remote kingdoms and lands across the sea we withhold, at present,[117] to save our reader from utter weariness. For they are so monstrous that, if the world did not stand upon the merits and the petitions of the saints — of whom by God's grace there is now a great company — we should be compelled to fear that it would soon perish utterly.

22. In the one thousand one hundred and thirty-eighth year from the incarnation of the Lord, since the emperor Lothar died in the autumn without sons, a general convention of nobles was appointed to meet at Mainz on the following Whitsunday. But certain of the nobles,[118] fearing that in this general assembly Duke Henry,[119] who was then a man of outstanding reputation and influence in the kingdom, might prevail by his might, took counsel together and held a convention at Coblenz, a town of Gaul,

114 I.e., "Good John," John II, Comnenus.

115 I.e., Hungary. This was in 1132.

116 Or Adalbert, Bishop Otto's eldest brother.

117 See below, VII. 28, 30 and 33.

118 Arnold and Albero, archbishops of.Cologne and of Trèves, Bucco bishop of Worms and Frederick duke of Swabia; cf. also Gesta Friderici 1. 23.

119 Henry the Proud, duke of Saxony and Bavaria.

about the middle of Lent. And there they elected as king, the ninety-third in line from Augustus, Conrad [120] the son of the emperor Henry's sister (we made mention of this emperor above),[121] in the presence of Theodewin, a cardinal bishop and legate of the Holy Roman Church, who promised to them the assent of the pope and of the entire Roman people and of the cities of Italy. Presently Conrad went to the palace at Aachen and was there anointed king by the aforesaid cardinal, assisted by the archbishops of Cologne and Trèves and the other bishops for the archbishop of Cologne, who ought by custom to have done this, had been but newly installed and was yet without the *pallium*. The king, after celebrating the ensuing Easter at Cologne, journeyed on to Mainz, which at that time chanced to be without a shepherd, and there by election of the clergy and the people established Albert,[122] a nephew of the former Albert, as archbishop. But the Saxons and Duke Henry and others [123] who had not been present at the election claimed that the king had not been chosen openly and lawfully but by stealth and trickery. A general assembly for them all was appointed to meet at Bamberg on the following Whitsunday.

It should be added that, after the departure of the emperor Lothar, Roger sought to regain Apulia but was put to flight in a battle with Duke Rainulf. The death of Pierleoni also brought to an end the disgraceful schism.

23. And so, as had been arranged, King Conrad held on Whitsunday, in the city I have mentioned, an assembly with the most regal magnificence. The assembly was attended by a very large gathering of nobles. The Saxons came all together, with their widowed empress Richenza, and voluntarily subjected themselves to his sway. Of the nobles Duke Henry,[124] who held possession of the royal insignia, alone was absent. A day was appointed for him to return the insignia, the day of the festival of the apostles Peter and Paul,[125] at Regensburg. He went to that city and did indeed deliver up the royal insignia; however he was not admitted to the king's presence and returned without the king's favor, and with

120 Conrad III of Hohenstaufen, 1138-1152, Bishop Otto's half-brother. He was the son of Agnes, the sister of Henry V, by her first husband, Frederick I.
121 VII. 17-19.
122 Albert II (1138-1141), brother-in-law of Frederick II, duke of Swabia. See *Gesta Friderici* 1. 23.
123 *E.g.*, Conrad archbishop of Salzburg.
124 The Proud.   125 June 29, 1138.

the matter of peace still unsettled. After this man, previously so proud and so haughty but now by the will of God humiliated, had sought in many ways for forgiveness and failed to obtain it, he was finally outlawed by a vote of the nobles at Würzburg; and on the following anniversary of the Lord's Nativity, in the palace at Goslar, his duchy was declared forfeited by him. Strange to say, a prince previously most powerful, whose authority extended, as he himself used to boast, "from sea to sea," that is, from Denmark even to Sicily, was so humbled within a short time that almost all his adherents and friends in Bavaria forsook him. Therefore, departing in secret from Bavaria he went to Saxony attended by only four companions.

At that time, upon the death of Rainulf, Roger entered Apulia, then without a ruler,[126] drove out Rainulf's brother, the prince of Capua, and many other nobles, and regained possession both of Apulia and of Campania. He visited its inhabitants with many afflictions and oppresses them even to this day.[127] He cruelly despoiled of its many ecclesiastical ornaments the monastery of the blessed Benedict, situated on Monte Cassino, an object of veneration to all the world. Report has it that in his first invasion, when he captured the city of Bari, he perpetrated a cruel and monstrous deed. When he had captured the city he not only persecuted the living with various kinds of torture but vented his fury even on the dead: he ordered the corpse of Duke Rainulf to be exhumed [128] and to be dragged through the streets. These and other works of cruelty, patterned upon the deeds of the ancient Sicilian tyrants [129] — acts told of him in uncountable numbers — we omit since they are [now] known to well nigh everyone. Yet there are those [130] who say he does these things in the interests of justice rather than of tyranny, and claim that he is more than all other rulers a lover of peace; and they assert that it is to preserve peace that he holds rebels in restraint with such severity. But others say that it is through his love of money, in which he has surpassed even all western kings, more than through love of justice that he follows peace.

[126] He came to Salerno on May 25, 1139. But he had fought with Rainulf on land the preceding year.

[127] Roger II died Feb. 26, 1154.

[128] This happened not at Bari but at Troja, where Rainulf died and was buried.

[129] II. 19 (end) above.

[130] Hofmeister thinks that Bernard of Clairvaux is meant.

King Conrad, having entered Bavaria, bestowed the duchy upon Leopold the Younger,[131] the son of the margrave Leopold and brother to Conrad on his mother's side. From that time our province began to be subject to many woes. In the following mid-Lent a very full council,[132] consisting of about a thousand bishops, was held at Rome under the presidency of Pope Innocent. After many salutary decrees had been promulgated in this council, the schismatics who had favored the party of Pierleoni were condemned.

24. At this point we may consider God's "terrible doing toward the children of men" [133] and the transitory nature of the world. For behold, upon the death of the emperor Henry his kinsmen — who at that time had great fame in the kingdom and stood, so to speak, at the very pinnacle of the realm and were therefore wholly secure from all anxiety — were not only not chosen to royal power but were even greatly afflicted and downtrodden by the king who was placed over them. After they had been so greatly humbled — whereas Duke Henry, by the high position of his father-in-law [134] the emperor and by his own might, had become so powerful that he despised all men and deigned to consult none on behalf of the kingdom — the Lord, who "hath . . . respect unto the lowly and knoweth the haughty from afar," [135] "but putteth down princes and exalteth them of low degree," [136] raised to the glory of empire him who had been humiliated and was almost in despair, and cast down from on high him who had boasted of his glory and his power. What else can we say here than that He first humbled Conrad when he was great in his own eyes and that, by reason of his piety, He exalted him again when he had been humbled. This mutability of our mortal lot, having its origin in the riches of the grace of God, ought to inspire us to shun pride and seek to attain lowliness of heart. What else does this wretched destiny of humanity, which drags a man now from poverty to a throne, now from a throne to poverty, and torments him — what else, I say, does it engender than contempt for this present life as it points to the abiding nature of things eternal, a nature which changes not and passes not away!

[131] Before July 25, 1139. This Leopold was the third son of Leopold III and Agnes; Bishop Otto was the fifth son. See Introduction p. 9, note 32.

[132] The Second Lateran Council, held early in April, 1139.

[133] Ps. 66. 5.

[134] Lothar II, whose daughter Gertrude he had married.

[135] Ps. 138. 6.

[136] Luke, I. 52.

What great misfortunes befell the whole realm, and particularly unhappy Bavaria, in consequence of all this we are realizing daily. The Saxons, who rebelled against the king because of his election, are being inclined to obedience more by his mercy than by his arms.[137] But Roger, sacrilegiously laying hands upon the anointed of the Lord, caught Pope Innocent in ambush, as he sought to enter Apulia with an armed force of Romans, and extorted from him both the prestige of the name of king in Sicily [138] and absolution from excommunication, together with the duchy of Apulia and Calabria and the principality of Capua.

25. While these things were taking place in Italy, the margrave Leopold,[139] having received from the king the duchy of Bavaria, first made subject to his jurisdiction Regensburg, the metropolis and seat of his dukedom, since almost all the barons were either attached to him by love or came to him, of their own accord, out of fear. Afterwards having collected a large force of soldiers, he marched through the whole of Bavaria and at its very bounds — near the river Lech, opposite the city of Augsburg — dealt with land matters for three days, proving himself a stern judge.

At that time Duke Henry, who had been banished from Bavaria, died in Saxony and was buried beside his father-in-law. After his death the Saxons rebelled anew against the king, out of love for Henry's little son [140] whom, while he was yet alive, Henry had commended to their keeping. Leopold, however, continued to hold the duchy of Bavaria under his power and governed it with a strong hand. While he was incautiously delaying at the siege of the Castle of Valley[141] — which belonged to two brothers [142] who alone of the Bavarian barons had taken their stand with the party of Duke Henry — Welf, Duke Henry's brother, came up unexpectedly and by his valiant fighting compelled the duke to retreat after many

---

[137] Through the intervention of Adalbero archbishop of Trèves, about the middle of August, 1139, a truce was granted until Pentecost 1140. *Cf.* also VII. 26 below.

[138] Hofmeister commends the precision of statement here. For while Anacletus had previously granted Roger *coronam regni Siciliae et Calabriae et Apuliae*, Innocent by his diploma of July 27, 1139 confirmed only *regnum Siciliae, ducatum Apuliae et principatum Capuae*.

[139] The Younger; see VII. 23 above.

[140] Henry the Lion, then a boy of ten.

[141] The text reads *castri Phalaia.*

[142] Conrad and Gebhard, sons of Otto I, count of the family of Wittelsbach.

had fallen on both sides. Elated at this success Welf attempted, not long afterwards, to attack the king also while he was delaying in the siege of the castle at Weinsberg; but he lost many men and fled with but few followers from the battle. Soon afterwards, while Duke Leopold was dispensing justice in the city of Regensburg, an uprising occurred in consequence of the insolence of Otto [143] count palatine. Because the people were surging about them on all sides, the duke with his followers took up arms and escaped from danger by setting fire to several quarters of the city, since the citizens dispersed in part through fear of a conflagration, in part through dread of an armed conflict. The duke then departed from the city and, after laying waste the country round about, withdrew for a time; but, having collected an army, he pitched camp not far from the city and finally, upon promise of payment in money, he received the submission of the citizens, now thoroughly frightened. Thereupon, deciding to avenge the disgrace put upon him by Welf at Valley, he moved with an armed force as far as the Lech and there destroyed the strongholds of certain of his personal enemies, laid waste all the surrounding country and returned through our territories, doing great damage to our church. Not long afterwards he took sick and died at Regensburg in the district of Passau. He was buried in the Monastery of the Holy Cross, which was founded by his father and which he himself had greatly enriched, and his brother Henry [144] succeeded him in the margraviate.

26. At that time Conrad count of Moravia, forming a conspiracy with the Bohemians and aspiring to the dukedom of that land, led an army from Moravia into Bohemia. When Duke Vladislav [145] prepared to meet him with his troops he was betrayed by his men and barely escaped death by taking to flight. And so he went to the king as an exile and bewailed his lot. The king, moved with compassion, escorted him back to Bohemia with an army and, after celebrating Whitsunday in the city of Prague (the metropolis of that province), defeated Conrad and restored Vladislav to his dukedom.

[143] It was against this same Otto as *Frisingensis ecclesiae advocatus* that Bishop Otto directed his invective in VI. 20 above.

[144] The second son of Leopold III and Agnes, Henry "Jasomirgott"; see Introduction p. 9, note 32.

[145] Or Wladislaus II; the text reads *Labezlaus*. He married Gertrude the sister of Bishop Otto and of King Conrad III, and in 1140 had succeeded his uncle Sobeslaus as duke; *cf.* below, VII. 34.

Not long afterwards the king entered Saxony [146] and gave the widow of Duke Henry, the daughter of the emperor Lothar, in marriage to the margrave Henry, his brother, and made peace with the Saxons. He bestowed upon this margrave the duchy of Bavaria which the son of Duke Henry,[147] upon the advice of his mother, had already resigned. This circumstance was the source of great discord in our land. For Prince Welf, falsely claiming that the aforesaid duchy had fallen to him by right of inheritance, entered Bavaria with an armed force under the very eyes of the duke; then, after laying waste part of the province, he retreated.[148] The duke, aroused at this, gathered about him an enormous army and invaded our borders, stripped many churches of their revenues and finally even destroyed the fortifications of our own city [149] on account of certain of its citizens who were said to be adherents of Welf. Welf came with his army to meet him but retreated when he heard that the king was to follow him. Thereupon the duke, in company with the king, invested with siege-works the castle of Count Conrad,[150] who had sided with Welf and, after laying waste everything round about, by the king's aid forced it to surrender and destroyed it by fire.

27. While such things were happening in Gaul and in Germany the Roman Pontiff, Innocent — who had long before excommunicated the people of Tivoli and had in other ways oppressed them — afflicted them still more till he forced them to submit to him. He received hostages from them and subjected them to an oath of fealty. Since the Roman people desired that he should force them by means of the hostages and the oath to agree to the most severe terms — namely that they should tear down their walls and all leave the country — they rose in rebellion because Innocent, that most noble and generous priest, was unwilling to assent to so unreasonable and so inhuman a request. The people impetuously stormed the

---

[146] It was early in 1143 that King Conrad entered Saxony and bestowed the duchy of Bavaria upon his brother Henry; peace had been made with the Saxons the previous year and it was then (1142) also that Gertrude was married at Frankfort.

[147] Henry the Lion.

[148] The *Chronica Regia Coloniensis* on the year 1143 states that he devastated Swabia also in company with his nephew, Frederick, afterwards emperor.

[149] Freising.

[150] This Conrad was cousin of the Counts of Valley mentioned above in VII. 25. See also *Gesta Friderici* 1. 26 and 4. 18.

capitol [151] and, in its eagerness to restore the ancient glory of the City, reëstablished the senatorial order, which had come to an end many generations before. It then renewed the war [152] with the people of Tivoli. The reason for such great cruelty was that during the previous year, while the people and the pope were besieging the aforesaid city, its inhabitants sallied forth and joined in hand-to-hand conflict with them; after losing much spoil the Romans had been disgracefully put to flight. Therefore they claim to this day that they can be appeased by no terms save by the terms we have mentioned.[153] But the pope, in his great wisdom and foresight, fearing that the Church of God, which for many years had vigorously maintained the secular power over the City handed down to it by Constantine, might lose it sooner or later in some such way as this, sought in many ways — by threats as well as by gifts — to prevent the execution of their design. But he could not accomplish his purpose since the populace was growing stronger. As he lay on his couch — some say after he had received a vision of things to come — he rested in peace and Celestine, a man endowed with piety and a knowledge of literature, succeeded him, having been chosen by general agreement.

About this time the people of Verona, who had long been at odds with the inhabitants of Padua and had turned aside from its course the river which flows past the city of Padua, fought a battle with them and won a bloody victory,[154] taking many captives.

28. In the one thousand one hundred and forty-third year from the incarnation of the Lord, Kaloiohannes,[155] the emperor of Constantinople (who had entered upon a treaty of friendship with the Roman king Conrad through a betrothal of his own son Manuel and the sister of Queen Gertrude), entered Syria with a very large army because Raymond prince of Antioch had sworn to give him that province, together with the city itself, in consideration of a sum of money but had not kept his promise.[156] But the venerable

[151] In his *Gesta Friderici* 2. 28, Otto mistakenly says that this took place at the instigation of Arnold of Brescia *circa principia pontificatus Eugenii*. Cf. also *ibid*. 1. 28. [152] Cf. below, VII. 31 (end).

[153] The Romans obtained their desire in 1146.

[154] A similar story is told of the relations between Venice and Padua. Hofmeister thinks Otto has confused the facts through a lapse of memory.

[155] John II, Comnenus, the son of Alexius I.

[156] In 1137. The emperor John, coming to Antioch with an army, had extorted the assent by force.

N. . . ,[157] bishop of Djebele, manfully resisted him to his face and fearlessly warned him, in the names of the Bishop of Rome and of the emperor, to desist from his attack upon the city I have mentioned because it was in the possession of Latins. But John, since he had been deceived by the prince, though he spared the city, ravaged the entire province with fire and sword and even drove out the hermits,[158] of whom there is a large number in that district, from their cells and treated them most cruelly. Herein he did not play the part of a "Kalo"[159]—that is to say, "Good"—John. Not long afterwards, while he was following the hunt and was using poisoned arrows; he was unexpectedly wounded by one of them. Thus this wealthy king died very wretchedly in the midst of his army and left the throne to his son Manuel.[160]

At the same time Fulk, king of Jerusalem, died and surrendered the helm of state to his son Fulk,[161] then a mere stripling. Manuel, on his elevation to the throne, sent messengers to King Conrad with precious gifts (even as his father had done before) and renewed the treaty.[162] And just as this custom was frequently observed between these two emperors, for various considerations, after transference of the imperial title to the Franks, so at this time also this compact was entered upon between John, the father of this emperor, and Conrad, against Roger who had invaded both empires.

29. During these days the cities of Italy waxed insolent on account of the king's absence. The Venetians waged fierce warfare against the people of Ravenna, the men of Verona and of Vicenza against the Paduans and the inhabitants of Treviso, the Pisans and the Florentines against the men of Lucca and Siena; they filled almost all Italy with bloodshed, rapine and fire. In addition to the injuries which, as we said above,[163] were inflicted upon the

[157] Hugo is meant. We may assume that Otto heard this from the bishop of Djebele himself; cf. below, VII. 33.

[158] Otto is the only one who speaks of the emperor's cruelty to the hermits.

[159] Otto translates καλός by the Latin equivalent bonus.

[160] Manuel I, Comnenus, Eastern Emperor, 1143-1180.

[161] This is a mistake. He was succeeded as king of Jerusalem by Baldwin III, then a boy of thirteen. He is called Fulk in Gesta Friderici 1. 35 (beginning) also.

[162] In 1145. Cf. Conrad's letter to Manuel in Gesta Friderici 1. 25. It was not until then that Manuel's betrothed, the sister of Queen Gertrude, was conducted to Greece where the wedding was celebrated in Jan., 1146. Cf. Gesta Friderici 1. 24.

[163] See note 154.

Paduans in the preceding year, the inhabitants of Verona and of Vicenza in the following year laid waste with fire and sword the castles, villages and fields of the people of Treviso. The Venetians and the people of Ravenna inflicted very great damage upon one another by land and sea. The inhabitants of Pisa and Lucca — because of the great opportunities for fight afforded by their nearness to one another — waged war with unwearied frenzy, involving all the strength of Tuscany in their own ruin. The Florentines together with Ulric [164] the margrave of the land, moving on to the very gates of Siena, burned its suburbs. The inhabitants of Siena, knowing themselves to be no match in numbers or in strength for the Florentines, asked the people of Lucca for aid. The people of Lucca, both on their behalf and on that of Count Guido Guerra — who had also appealed to them, since he was himself engaged in bitter warefare with the Florentines — declared the people of Florence their enemies. The latter, effecting a union with the Pisans, not only assailed the people of Lucca in war but also laid waste the castles, towns and fields of the aforesaid count, burning and plundering; furthermore they laid an ambush in the rear of the citizens of Siena, who had sallied forth to lay their fields waste, and captured them; only a bare handful escaped by flight. Moreover not only were very many of the people of Pisa and of Lucca slain by the sword, by a sudden and swift death terminating their misery, but countless numbers on both sides were taken captive and — as I myself have seen [165] — tormented by imprisonment, starvation and filth long continued, and thereby exhibited in their own persons to all passers-by a pitiable spectacle of our mortal lot.

30. Near the beginning of the one thousand one hundred and forty-fifth year from the incarnation of the Lord, during the very festival of the Holy Nativity of Christ, there befell in the East, in consequence of the sin of the Christian people, a sad and lamentable misfortune. For Zangi, prince of Aleppo in Syria and of Mesopotamia (excepting Antioch and Damascus), a vassal of the King or Sultan of the Persians and the Medes, with a countless horde of Saracens besieged Edessa (which is now called Urfa). [166] This city,

---

[164] Ulric de Attems, who held Tuscany from 1139 to 1152.

[165] On July 19, 1144 and again a little later the people of Lucca defeated the Pisans; on Oct. 16 of the same year the Pisans defeated the citizens of Lucca. In the autumn of 1145 Otto attended the Roman *curia* at Viterbo; *cf.* VII. 32 below.   [166] *Rohas* in the text.

because of its size and its wealth, has been the only refuge of the Church at Jerusalem. On the very day of the Lord's Nativity, as I said, Zangi having stormed the city slew at the edge of the sword all Christians in it together with the bishop of the city, or else reduced them to the terrible bondage of slavery. He foully polluted the churches of Christ, and particularly the basilica of the Blessed Mary (ever Virgin) and that where the body of the apostle Thomas is buried, "bringing inside things that were not befitting," [167] in mockery of our Saviour. Having utterly exterminated our people or made them subject to the payment of tribute, he stationed Saracens there to inhabit the city.

31. During the same period Pope Lucius, a man who by reason of his gentleness and humility was worthy of the priestly office and the successor of Celestine (who had been Pope for not quite six months), was subjected to severe persecution at the hands of the citizens. He therefore sent to King Conrad a humble letter,[168] which contained an account of his own affliction but expressed thanks to God for the emperor's safety and prosperity, and invited him to undertake the defense of the Roman Church. His words were as follows:

"The bishop Lucius, the servant of the servants of God, sends to his dear son Conrad, illustrious king of the Romans, greetings and the apostolic benediction. Every good gift," and so forth.

The Roman people, unwilling to set any bounds to their folly,[169] added to the senators whom they had previously appointed a Patrician and, having elected to this office Jordan the son of Pierleoni, subjected themselves to him as to a prince. Then they approached their pontiff and demanded that he surrender all his insignia, both those kept within the City and those without, to the jurisdiction of their patrician. They declared that according to the custom of the priests of old he ought to live by tithes and offerings alone, and they feared not "to afflict the soul of the righteous" [170] from day to day. The pope, exhausted by the daily annoyances and weary of life, died within the first year of his pontificate. His successor was Eugenius, a man notable for piety and holiness, who was elected by the unanimous vote of clergy and people. Immediately after his

---

[167] II Macc. 6. 4.

[168] Not extant. Otto unfortunately throws little light on its contents.

[169] Otto is here referring to the attempt to establish the Roman Commune, in 1143. See C. M. H. 5. 369-370.   [170] Prov. 10. 3.

assumption of office — inasmuch as the whole people sought to harry him, as they had his predecessor, into handing over his insignia to the City — he with his bishops and cardinals withdrew from the City. On the following Lord's Day he was consecrated as pontiff in the Monastery of Farfa. This involved a departure from custom — a departure due to the savage persecution of the pope. Then to escape the fury of the Roman people he withdrew to various fortified places, and finally, going to Viterbo, lived there for some time. But the Roman people, with its Patrician Jordan, giving full rein to madness abolished the office of prefect, forced all the great and noble citizens to subject themselves to the patrician and, having destroyed not only the fortified towers of certain illustrious laymen but also the homes of cardinals and of the clergy, carried off an enormous amount of booty. They did not even shrink from turning into a fortress, in sacrilegious and godless manner, the Church of the Blessed Peter, the head of all the churches. [171] In their eagerness for gain they exacted, by stripes and blows, offerings from pilgrims who came to pray. Indeed in their sinful daring they did not shrink from killing, in the very portico and vestibule of the temple, certain of those who were unwilling to make the offerings. The venerable pontiff, after first smiting Jordan and certain of his followers with the sword of anathema, checked them by uniting his military forces with those of the people of Tivoli, the ancient foe of the Romans, and finally forced them to seek peace.

32. At that time legates from the Armenian bishops and their metropolitan (whom they themselves call "The Catholic," that is to say "The Universal" bishop, because of the countless number of bishops he has under him) came to the supreme pontiff at Viterbo from almost the farthest Orient, completing the wearisome journey in a year and six months. After assuring him in their greetings, in the name of that church, of their entire submission they set forth at Vetralla [172] the reasons for their coming. At this meeting I myself was present [173] with many others. These reasons were as follows. In the administration of the Eucharistic rite they agree in certain

171 All this was done by the Romans in 1145 before Arnold of Brescia had entered the City.

172 Twelve kilometers south of Viterbo, where the Pope stayed on Dec. 1-16, 1145. It is evident from this passage that he had been there before, about the beginning of November.

173 Nothing is known of this journey of Bishop Otto to Italy except what he has himself written here, VII. 29 (end) above, and VII. 33 below.

respects with the Greeks, in certain other respects they differ from the Greeks. They take leavened bread, exactly as do the Greeks, but they do not mix water with the wine as we and the Greeks do. Furthermore they join together the Nativity of the Lord and the Epiphany, making those two festivals one.[174] Since they differed in these and in other matters they had chosen the Roman Church as arbiter and had come to consult it, asking that they be instructed in the form of the sacrifice according to the Roman custom. The Roman bishop, receiving them gladly, admitted them to the solemnization of the mass and the mystic rites of the sacrifice and admonished them to observe carefully all that took place there. As they did so and were standing, keenly alert, before the holy altar, one of them — who was endowed with the office of bishop — saw something which he afterwards related in a full assembly on the eighth day following the feast of the blessed Martin, when the dedication of the Church of the Blessed Peter is customarily celebrated.[175] What he saw, he said, was this: while the supreme pontiff was performing the holy mysteries a sunbeam flashed about his head in shining splendor, and in its light two doves ascended and descended. As he intently turned his eyes this way and that and yet found no opening through which the light was making its way, he realized that this was God's doing and so was the more inspired to obedience to the Roman See. He made known also to all what he had seen. But the venerable Father, refusing to attribute this to his own merits, declared that it was rather because of the bishop's faith that this vision had been revealed to him from heaven, in order that the church by which he had been sent might recognize, bathed in the light of truth, the power of the sacraments and thereby learn, also, with what reverence and in what form she should celebrate them.

The aforesaid bishop reported too that there were certain peoples near the confines of Armenia, who bore children with an offensive smell, and straightway took them to be bathed in the waters of Armenia. The Armenians, by sprinkling them with the waters of baptism, dispelled this natal odor; but presently on their return they reverted to their p.gan rites and their filthiness. They asked the advice of the Roman Church also as to whether this should be done.

[174] They celebrate the festival of the Lord's birth on the day of Epiphany.
[175] November 18.

33. At that time and place I saw, also, the aforesaid bishop of Djebele [176] in Syria — by whose efforts, in particular, Antioch began to be fully subject to the Roman See — making complaint both of his patriarch at Antioch and of the mother [177] of the Prince, the daughter of Baldwin — once king of Jerusalem — and demanding by ancient right, according to the example of Abraham [178] (for he gave a tithe of his spoils to Melchizedek, since he attributed his victory to God), a tithe of the spoils taken from the Saracens. He asked for the authorization of the Apostolic See in this matter. I heard him making pitiful lament concerning the peril of the Church beyond the sea since the capture of Edessa, and saying that he was minded on this account to cross the Alps to the king of the Romans and the Franks to ask for aid.

He related also that not many years before a certain John,[179] a king and priest who dwells beyond Persia and Armenia in the uttermost East and, with all his people, is a Christian but a Nestorian,[180] made war on the brother kings of the Persians and Medes, called Samiardi,[181] and stormed Ekbatana (the seat of their kingdom) of which mention has been made above.[182] When the aforesaid kings met him with an army composed of Persians, Medes and Assyrians a battle ensued which lasted for three days, since both parties were willing to die rather than turn in flight. Prester John, for so they are accustomed to call him, putting the Persians to flight with dreadful carnage finally emerged victorious.[183] He said that after this victory the aforesaid John moved his army to the aid of the Church in Jerusalem, but that when he had reached the river Tigris and was unable to transport his army across that river by any

---

[176] Hugo; cf. above, VII. 28 and note 157.

[177] Not the mother but the mother-in-law of Prince Raymond I of Antioch. She was the widow of Prince Bohemund II and the mother of Constantia, Raymond's bride.

[178] Gen. 14. 20.

[179] This is the first mention of the famous "Prester John." Cf. F. Zarncke, "Der Priester Johannes," in Abhandl. der königl. Sächsischen Gesellsch. der Wissensch., philol.-hist. Cl. 7 (1879), pp. 827 et seq.; 8 (1876) pp. 1 et seq.

[180] The Arab historian Ibn al-athīr calls him a Manichaean.

[181] Or Saniardi. At that time the Seljūqs held these regions and were ruled by the sultan Sanjar (died 1156), who governed the East, and Mas 'ūd (1131-1152), the son of his brother Mahmūd (died 1119), who dwelt in the West.

[182] VII. 3.

[183] On Sept. 9, 1141 Sanjar was defeated between the Oxus and the Jaxartes rivers.

device he turned toward the north where, he had learned, this stream was frozen over on account of the winter's cold. When he had tarried there for several years without, however, seeing his heart's desire realized (the continued mild weather prevented it), and lost many of his soldiers because of the unfamiliar climate he was forced to return home. It is said that he is a lineal descendant of the Magi, of whom mention is made in the Gospel,[184] and that, ruling over the same peoples which they governed, he enjoys such great glory and wealth that he uses no scepter save one of emerald. Inflamed by the example of his fathers who came to adore Christ in his manger, he had planned to go to Jerusalem but by the reason aforesaid he was prevented — so men say. But enough of this.

34. Eugenius made peace with the Romans on the understanding that they should abolish the office of patrician, should take back the prefect to his former authority and retain the senators by his authorization. Then, returning to the City, he celebrated the Lord's Nativity there at the beginning of the one thousand, one hundred and forty-sixth year from the incarnation of the Lord. There he was again so insistently urged by the people of Rome from day to day to destroy the people of Tivoli that he moved from the Lateran Palace to the region of Trastevere, being unable to endure their wickedness and confessing that his soul was weary of life.

The king, after observing the same Christmas in his palace at Aachen, entered Bavaria. There Vladislav, duke of Bohemia, came to him accompanied by Boris, whom I named above. In tearful and mournful tones Boris complained that he had been deprived of his ancestral kingdom and begged that he should be aided by that imperial authority to which the entire world looks for protection. Through the intercession of the aforesaid duke of Bohemia and his wife Gertrude, sister of the king, he obtained the king's promise regarding this matter, ratified by an honorable pledge. In consequence we not only are experiencing unrest at the present time but, in our alarm, we conjecture for these and other reasons that there is worse to follow. For behold! a great conflict is expected between our kingdom and that of the Hungarians,[185] for not only is Boris preparing an army but Vladislav is bribing many of our people with his money. In Poland, so we hear, there is a wretched struggle

---

[184] Matt. 2. 1 *et seq.*

[185] This was written before Sept. 11, 1146, when the Hungarians put the Germans to flight; *cf. Gesta Friderici* 1. 33.

between three brothers,[186] princes of that country; in Belgic Gaul there is endless strife among the powerful men. Among ourselves, moreover, the disturbance now seems so serious that not only do men throw everything into confusion by plundering and burning through all the rest of the year, but they do not shrink from committing violence contrary to divine and human law during the very season of Lent and the time for repentance. Finally we are oppressed by so poignant a memory of the past, so violent an onslaught of present woes and so great a fear of future perils that receiving "the sentence of death within ourselves we despair even of life,"[187] particularly since we think that the world could not long endure, both by reason of the multitude of our sins and the shameful unrighteousness of this most unsettled time, if it were not sustained by the merits of the saints, the true citizens of the City of God, companies of whom flourish all over the world in large numbers, and finely distinguished, in divers ways, one from the other.

But inasmuch as I have, to the best of my ability, passed under review the series of transient events from Adam to the present year — which is one thousand, one hundred and forty-sixth from the incarnation of the Lord, the one thousand, nine hundred and eighteenth[188] from the founding of the City, the ninth year of Conrad, ninety-third emperor in line from Augustus, and the second year of the Supreme Pontiff Eugenius III — and have set forth the manifold miseries of mortals, I think it unfitting to pass over in silence the various orders of holy men by reason of whose sanctity, as I have said, the wickedness of the world is still endured by a most merciful judge. Therefore I shall now set down the notable deeds of those great men that limit and restrain the disturbances caused by so great sinfulness.

35. So then, aside from such of the clergy and the laity as "in sober, godly, and righteous fashion" possess their own property "as not their own," compassionately ministering to the necessities of their brethren, there are various companies of the saints who, renouncing their desires, their possessions and even their parents

---

[186] Four, as Otto correctly states in *Gesta Friderici* 1. 30. Wladislaus II, the eldest son of Boleslav III (he died in 1138), who had married Otto's sister Agnes, was trying to subject his brothers to his overlordship or even to drive them from the country. *Cf.* also Rahewin's *Gesta Friderici* 3. 2.

[187] II Cor. 1. 9 and 8.

[188] *MDCCCCXVIII* of the text. Otto apparently intended to write *MDCCCXCVIII*; see above, III. 6.

in accordance with the command of the Gospel, continually bear the cross for the mortification of the flesh and, being filled with heavenly longings, follow Christ. Some of these, dwelling in cities, in castles, in villages and in the countryside, impart to their neighbors by word and by example the rule of right living; others — not, indeed, avoiding intercourse with men but rather making provision for their own peace — shun crowds, and, devoting themselves to God alone, withdraw to retreats in the woods and in secluded places. The former do not refuse to let their light shine before men to the glory of God; the latter, regarding themselves as dead to the world, for the present hide their lives with Christ in God and do not desire their own glory to shine forth until, through their lives, Christ shall appear in glorious form. Yet all alike spend their lives on earth in purity of living and conscience, and in holiness like that of the angels in heaven. Having but one heart and one soul they dwell together as one body in cloisters or in churches, they lay themselves down to sleep at the same time, they arise with one accord for prayer, partake of refreshment together in one house, devote themselves to prayer, to reading, to work by day and by night, with such unwearied watchfulness that they think it sinful to let any interval of time pass unoccupied by heavenly matters save only the brief period during which they consign their weary limbs to rest on a mean bed of osiers or a rough blanket; and they carry this so far that, at the very time of bodily refreshment, they are ever intent upon the reading of the Holy Scriptures, preferring to feed the spirit rather than the body. They all alike abstain from meat. Some, denying themselves all the more delicate foods and abstaining from wine, use for food sometimes pulse, sometimes only bread and water. Why should I speak of their celibacy? The custom of marriage, a custom common to the whole human race and everywhere permitted, they have so completely renounced that certain of them guard not only the inner but even the outer barriers with such care that they never admit any woman to their presence for any reason — not even for the purpose of prayer. All the workshops of the various artisans — the bakers, the smiths, the weavers and others — are located within, that no one of them may have occasion to wander outside. These workmen are very carefully secluded. The entrance door is situated in the outer court. There a devout and holy [189] brother is ever present, welcoming all who come as guests —

[189] The text reads *timoratus*.

pilgrims, the poor — with ready good-will, as though he were receiving Christ himself. Having washed their feet and then zealously bestowed upon them all the other services that human kindness suggests, he conducts them to the oratory and then assigns them to a guest room. But if a woman comes for the sake of receiving exhortation, or for any other duty, she is kept without and the father of the monastery or some one of the brothers speaks to her — not in the house, nor alone, but under the sky and in an open place that has only a roof to keep off the rain and, indeed, rarely has that. Others, even if they do not bar women from the oratory if they come to pray, yet do not permit them to enter the inner living rooms of the brothers. Furthermore, the brothers guard themselves with such anxious care that they not only shrink from the greater sins, but even so restrain their senses from the least and most trivial sins — those which through their very familiarity have become to us insignificant — that they very rarely speak, save to God alone and to the father of their congregation. The things that they need they seek from one another by gestures and signs rather than by words. If in consequence of human weakness (through carelessness or indiscretion) anyone of them has offended in aught, even a most trivial matter, the brothers assemble in a place set apart for this purpose, at about the first hour or the third hour, and there humbly confess their faults, after first invoking divine aid, and they mutually correct one another in love. An older brother sits and judges them in mild severity "without wrath and disputing," and often, with serene countenance and honey-sweet voice, instructs them by the Word of the Holy Scriptures, preparing them, thus cleansed and wholly purified, and so worthy recruits in the training ground of this present life, to take their place in the armies of heaven.

As the beauty of a house is made manifest by the very entrance hall, so the outward bearing of these brothers, in the presence of their fellowmen, declares from without how the inner man shines resplendent in the presence of God, the searcher of hearts. Just as they glow within with the varied splendors of the virtues, so without they employ garments of varied colors, according to the saying of the Psalmist: "The king's daughter is all glorious within, clad in broidered work with threads of gold." [190] Some, leading the apostolic life, show forth in their very garb the purity of innocence

[190] Ps. 45. 13.

since they wear a spotless linen robe; others of the same order, to mortify the flesh, cloth themselves more roughly in a woolen shirt; others, free from all outside occupations and portraying their angelic life in their garb, figuratively portray its sweetness by the form rather than by the soft texture of their dress. For they wear next to the skin very rough shirts and over these others, ampler, with hoods. These ampler shirts consist of six parts which resemble as many wings, in the likeness of the Seraphim. With two of these (the hood) they cover their heads; with two (the sleeves) they fly to the heavenly regions by directing every movement as though raising their hands to God; and with two they cover the rest of their bodies before and behind, and show that they are defended against all the cruel darts of the tempter by the divine grace which precedes and follows them. They differ however in this: some, to express their contempt for the world, wear the same dress, only black, whereas others, caring nothing for color or thickness, are accustomed to wear a robe that is white or gray or of some other color, but mean and rough. Being equipped thus within and without, and having multiplied beyond measure in a short time — both in merit and in numbers, throughout the entire circuit of the globe — with fruitful and abundant increase they shed abroad the light of their devices, they shine by their virtues, are often exalted by divine revelation and are frequently consoled, toward the end of their lives, by visions of the Lord and of angels. They heal the sick, cast out demons, sometimes through contemplation gain a foretaste of the sweetness of the heavenly country (so far as it is permissible in this present life) and because of this, although they are worn with toil, wearied by watching and weakened by fasting, yet, like the locusts that chirp the more shrilly when they are famished, the brothers spend almost the whole night in wakefulness singing psalms and hymns and spiritual songs. Whereas they dwelt once in greatest numbers in Egypt they are most numerous now in the regions of Gaul and Germany, so that one need not wonder at the transfer of power or of wisdom from the East to the West, since it is evident that the same transfer has been effected in matters of religion.

There is besides, dwelling in widely sundered places, a holy company of anchorites and hermits — men who are spiritually prepared for single combat in the best kind of warfare. They are indeed fewer in number but they are equal or superior to the preceding in austerity of life. Some of them, living subject to a prior in remote and secluded places, inhabit each his own little tomblike cell. They support themselves by the labor of their hands. Content with modest fare they receive on the sabbath a store of food for the whole week. They are utterly cut off from human consolation; indeed the one and only thing from which they do not withdraw is converse with God through prayer. On Sundays only they gather in the oratory, which is situated in a common meeting place and, being strengthened by the elder with the word of holy exhortation and wholesomely refreshed by the God-given mysteries, they go away again in all eagerness. Others, desiring to have God alone as witness of their life, shut themselves up in caves, in dens and by walls; and spend the sabbath, it is believed, the more ardently inclined toward heaven because, it is clear, they are cut off more completely from all human society. There are, besides, those who seek the desolation of the solitudes, who do not fear the company of wild beasts, who live on plants and use the skins of beasts for a covering. They are made as black as Ethiopians by the chill of the night and heat of the sun; their skin becomes stiff as a drumhead. Dwelling in a habitation in the earth they disdain to be shut in and use only the sky for a roof, making it evident that they are not so much men as comrades of the heavenly hierarchy.

All these, being secluded from all the piteous changes of the world about which I spoke above, after they complete six days of labor dwell in the peace of the true sabbath, gaining thereby a foretaste of eternal rest, the gracious and appropriate intercessors for our sin. They may well form the end of this seventh book, and may by their prayers make us able to relate what follows, namely, what consummation awaits the City of God, what destruction the reprobate City of Earth. AMEN.

HERE ENDS THE SEVENTH BOOK

These are the kings of Italy before the founding of the City: Italus,[191] Janus, Saturn, Picus and Faunus reigned in Laurentum.

In Latium or Alba, Latinus, Aeneas, Ascanius, Aeneas Silvius, Latinus Silvius, Alba Silvius, Egyptus Silvius, Capys Silvius, Capetus Silvius,[192] Tiberinus Silvius, Agrippa Silvius, Aremulus Sil-

---

[191] Hofmeister states that he cannot find Otto's source for this.

[192] *Carpentus Silvius* of the text. His name, omitted in I. 30 above, is found in Frutolf, *MGH. SS.* 6. 46. 70.

vius, Aventinus Silvius, Procas Silvius and Amulius Silvius reigned.

After the City was founded under Numitor, Remus and Romulus, the sons of Rhea Silvia, Numa, Tullus Hostilius, Ancus Marcius, Tarquinius Priscus, Servius, and Tarquinius Superbus reigned in the City.

After this there were consuls down to the time of the emperors.

EMPERORS [193]

Octavianus Augustus, Tiberius, Gaius Caligula, Claudius, Nero (the first persecution), Galba, Vespasian, Titus, Domitian (the second persecution), Nerva, Trajan (the third persecution), Hadrian, Antoninus Pius, and his sons Marcus Antoninus Verus with his brother Lucius Aurelius Commodus (the fourth persecution), Commodus, successor to Antoninus, Helvius Pertinax, Severus (the fifth persecution), Antoninus Caracalla, Macrinus, Antoninus, Alexander, Maximin (the sixth persecution), Gordian, Philip, the first Christian Emperor, with his son Philip, Decius (the seventh persecution), Gallus with Volusian, Valerian with his son Gallienus (the eighth persecution), Claudius, Aurelian (the ninth persecution), Probus, Tacitus, Carus with his sons Carinus and Numerian, Diocletian and Maximian (the tenth persecution), Caesars Constantius and Galerius and Licinius, Constantine, Constantine with his brothers Constantius and Constans, Julian, Jovian, Valentinian, Valens, Gratian with his brother Valentinian, Theodosius in association with the two preceding and in succession to them, Arcadius and Honorius, Theodosius with Valentinian, Valentinian with Marcian, Marcian succeeding Valentinian, Leo, Zeno, Anastasius, Justin, Justinian, Justin, Tiberius, Maurice, Phocas, Heraclius with his son Constantine, Constantine, Constantine, Justinian, Leo, Tiberius, Justinian, Philippicus, Anastasius, Theodosius, Leo with his son Constantine, Constantine with his son Leo (Pepin king of the Franks was then patrician of the Romans), Leo, after his father's death (Charles was king of the Franks and patrician of the Romans), Constantine with his mother Irene, Irene succeeding

---

[193] The careful reader will note in the following lists of emperors and popes certain omissions and discrepancies. Otto is here not always consistent with his text or with the sources that he follows. But it seems hardly worth while to point out all these discrepancies or errors in detail. They are all carefully noted by Hofmeister.

her son (the imperial power was now transferred to the Franks),
Charles, Louis with his son Lothar, Lothar succeeding his father,
likewise Lothar with his son Louis, Louis succeeding his father,
Charles, Charles, Arnulf, according to some authorities. The fol-
lowing, according to the Romans, were Lombards: Louis, Berengar,
Berengar, Hugo, Berengar, Lothar, Berengar with his son Albert.
The following were Germans: Otto with his son Otto, Otto succeed-
ing his father Otto, Henry I, Conrad I, Henry II,[194] Henry III.
Henry IV, Lothar, Conrad II, Frederick.

ROMAN PONTIFFS

Peter, Linus, Cletus, Clement, Anacletus, Evarestus, Alexander,
Sixtus, Telesphorus, Hyginus, Anicetus, Pius, Soter, Eleutherius,
Victor, Zephyrinus, Calixtus I, Urban I, Pontianus, Anteros, Fabianus, Cornelius, Lucius, Stephen, Sixtus II, Dionysius, Felix,
Eutychianus, Gaius, Marcellinus, Marcellus, Eusebius, Melchiades
(all these were martyrs). The following were confessors: Sylvester,
Marcus, Julius, Liberius, Felix (observe that Felix, who has been
placed in the list, was substituted for Liberius in the latter's lifetime by heretics; ask the Romans why he is in the list), Liberius
upon his return from exile, Damasus, Siricius, Anastasius, Innocent, Zosimus, Boniface, Celestine, Sixtus, Leo, Hilarius, Simplicius, Felix, Gelasius, Symmachus, Hormisdas, John, Felix, Boniface,
John Mercuris, Agapetus, Silverius, Vigilius, Pelagius, John,
Benedict, Pelagius, Gregory, Sabinianus, Boniface, Boniface, Deus-
dedit, Boniface, Honorius, Severinus, John, Theodorus, Martin,
Eugenius, Vitalianus, Adeodatus, Domnus, Agatho, Leo II, Bene-
dict, John, Conon, Sergius, John VI, John VII, Sisinnius, Constan-
tine, Gregory, Gregory, Zacharias, Stephen, Paul, Constantine,
Stephen, Hadrian, Leo, Stephen, Paschal, Eugenius II, Valentinus,
Gregory IV, Sergius, Leo, Benedict, Nicholas, Hadrian II, John,
Marinus,[195] Hadrian III, Stephen, Formosus, Boniface, Stephen,
Romanus, Theodore, John, Benedict, Leo, Christopher, Sergius,
Anastasius, Lando, John, Leo, Stephen, John, Leo, Stephen, Mari-
nus,[196] Agapetus, John, Benedict, Leo, John, Benedict, Domnus,

---

194 III in VI. 32 above. But Otto is here listing only those German kings
who were also crowned as emperors. Thus Henry IV and Henry V appear here
as Henry III and Henry IV respectively.

195 Martin.

196 Martin.

Boniface, Benedict, John, John, John, Gregory the German, John, Sylvester, John, John, Sergius Os Porci, Benedict, John, Benedict, Sylvester, Gregory, Clement the German, Damasus the German, Leo the German, Victor the German, Stephen the German, Benedict, Nicholas, Alexander, Gregory VII, Victor, Urban II, Paschal II, Gelasius II, Calixtus II, Honorius II, Innocent II, Celestine II, Lucius II, Eugenius III, Anastasius, Hadrian IV.[197]

[197] Anastasius IV, Hadrian IV, and Frederick I (in the list of emperors) were added by Otto in 1157; *cf.* above, VII. 34 and the Letter to Chancellor Reinald.

THE PROLOGUE OF THE EIGHTH BOOK [1]

This work of ours, which we have entitled THE TWO CITIES, is, plainly, divided into three parts. For, whereas the City of Christ, or the Kingdom of Christ with reference to its present or its future status, is called the Church, it exists in one form so long as it is seen to hold the good and the bad in one embrace;[2] it will exist in another at that time when it shall cherish only the good in the glory of the heavenly embrace; it existed in yet another while it lived subject to princes of the heathen before "the fulness of the Gentiles"[3] was come. In brief that the Church, not only when it reigns with Christ but even while it contains in its present granary both grain and chaff, is called the Kingdom of Christ, you find very clearly set forth in the Gospel [4] where it is said that all things that cause stumbling are to be removed from His Kingdom — for of course none of these will be able to exist in that calm and blessed heavenly country. And so, after the manner of speaking in which Christ, because they share the sacraments, calls both the bad and the good His Kingdom [5] (the latter have a faith that works through love, the former a faith without works which is dead),[6] in that manner of speaking, I say, we call this present state His City. In connection with this subject we do not imitate the subtlety of those who cleverly strive to determine whether the wicked who continue in the Church truly partake of the sacraments or merely receive them in outward appearance, or discuss most cunningly whether the evil likewise ought to be called the Church, which is the body of Christ, because they mingle with the Church in temporal matters and partake of the sacraments. Rather, looking with single eye upon the

---

[1] For a discussion of the relation of the eighth book to Otto's *Chronicle* as a whole and a general resumé of the contents of this book, see Introduction, pp. 75-79. Quotations from the Bible are here very frequent, as might be expected from the subject matter, and there are a few passages from Augustine (Book 22) and from Hugo of St. Victor (*In caelestem Dionysii hierarchiam* and *Summa Sententiarum*), but there are practically no literary sources such as used in the preceding books of the Chronicle. I have, as usual, given the references found in Hofmeister's admirable notes.

[2] *Cf.* above, Prol., V; Prol., VII.   [3] Rom. 11. 25.

[4] Matt. 13. 41.   [5] Matt. 13. 47 *et seq.*   [6] James 2. 20 and 26.

common practice of Holy Scripture, we call all those who in the
Church hold fast their Catholic faith The City of Christ, leaving
to God, who alone knows who are His, the judgment and the examination of individuals.

The evil city likewise, we find, has three states [7] or stages. Of
these the first was before the time of grace, the second was and is
during the time of grace, the third will be after this present life.
The first is wretched, the second more wretched, the third most
wretched. On the other hand the first condition of that other company (the people of the City of Christ) is abject, the second prosperous, the third blessed; or (to put it in other words) the first is
lowly, the second intermediate, the third perfect. Enough has been
said in the preceding books with regard to the twofold status of
each part. The one was at first lowly while it was in obscurity.
Afterwards, when not only inward blessings but outward prosperity
as well had been bestowed upon it, it was not to be sure abject as
before, nor was it as yet gloriously perfect and blessed as it is to
be hereafter; it was rather in a middle or intermediate condition.
The other, in part through the effects of infinite changes, in part
through its ignorance of true religion, was at first wretched, later,
after the revelation of light, so much the more wretched as it was
the more inexcusable after the truth had been made manifest. It
remains now to tell in this eighth book about the third state, namely,
how the one City is to attain to the highest blessedness, the other
to fail and to descend to the utmost misery, when the most righteous
Judge shall, at the last judgment, examine and shall decide the
case of each city. Because, as Solomon says, before destruction the
heart is constantly exalted, before honor is constantly humbled, I
think it appropriate to tell by way of preface what humiliation
precedes this glory of His City, what transient exaltation under
Antichrist goes before this downfall of the evil city — insofar as
it is possible to reach conclusions from the authoritative books. For
thus after the dense darkness of the persecutions the eternal day of
eternal peace will appear the more delightful, and after the ap-
proving smile of this world the grievous storm of punishments and
the eternal night will appear the more terrible, inasmuch as the
hope of that glory makes present troubles light, the fear of that
doom detracts from this temporal pleasure (if there be any such)
because it is fleeting.

[7] But see Introduction, p. 33.

I must now, I think, make answer to those who will perhaps at-
.tempt to belittle this labor of mine as without value by claiming
that I do not properly combine the deep and mystic proofs of the
Scriptures with the historical accounts of so many successive misfortunes. In the first place, although I defend myself of this charge
by the example of the blessed father Augustine, whom we have undertaken to imitate [8] (he does the same thing in his book *The City
of God*), yet I must assail my critics with the darts of reason and
authority. Is not day the more pleasing because it follows night,
rest sweeter after toil, sleep after weariness, food after hunger?
Why need I speak of the Heptateuch, of the Book of the Kingdoms,[9]
of the Chronicles? The time would fail me for the telling if I should
wish to run through all the pages of sacred Scripture — for example
Ruth, Judith, Esdras, Esther, Maccabees — which, though they are
full of mystical meaning and sacred wisdom, nevertheless portray
divers woes of mortals and tempests of war. I say nothing of the
prophets, who, amid the frequent miseries of changing events,
sometimes set forth the mysterious prophecies of the Holy Spirit.
I leave out of account the Apostles, who often inserted among the
most profound secrets of the divine mysteries the impious deeds of
this world. Even so Daniel, beginning with a historical narrative,
concluded his work with a profound vision. That notable preacher,[10]
while discoursing excellently of the most secret miracles of God,
being enabled to do this by the wisdom granted him beyond the
other apostles, did not blush to mention for our correction, at the
outset of his letters, by way of reproof certain evil works of darkness. Even the disciple that was beloved by Christ, in concluding
his narrative of the truth of the Gospel — which he had begun with
that lofty prologue — when he said, "Many other signs therefore
did Jesus in the presence of his disciples which are not written in
this book: but these are written," [11] and so forth, added thereto
a comparison of the Lord foreshadowing the state of the future life
in the draught of fishes and in the strength of the net and in the
sweetness of the food, saying, "Jesus manifested himself at the sea
of Tiberias." [12] So by placing at the very end of his book, in a

[8] Prol., I, above. Hofmeister urges a careful comparison of Augustine's
City of God 20-22 with the eighth book of Otto's *Chronicle*.

[9] Here, as always in the Chronicle, Otto uses the word *Regna* in referring
to the books we know as *Kings*.

[10] Paul.   [11] John 20. 30.   [12] John 21. 1.

place of honor, the narrative of this glorious incident, he made the entire compass of his preceding narrative a sort of introduction to his account of this incident. The Lord also in the beginning "creating the heaven and the earth" [13] produced matter that at first was invisible and without form, and afterwards reduced it to order and brought it into the light. We do not think therefore that we are doing amiss if, after enumerating the miseries of this present life, we attempt (in so far as God permits) to treat of the eternal rest of the saints as of light after darkness.

HERE BEGINS THE EIGHTH BOOK

1. As we learn from Holy Writ, the City of Christ suffered first a violent persecution at the hands of the city of this world under tyrants and unbelieving kings, secondly a treacherous persecution in the time of the heretics, and thirdly a persecution consisting of pretense in the time of the hypocrites. It is further to suffer its last persecution under Antichrist [14] — a persecution violent, treacherous, hypocritical and the most severe of all. From the fact that while falsely claiming to be Christ he will be altogether opposed to Christ in life and in doctrine, he is called Antichrist because he is wholly against Christ. The Greeks, you must know, use *anti* in the sense of "against." [15] Furthermore it is believed [16] that Antichrist is to spring from the tribe of Dan — that is, he is to be of servile state — on the authority of the saying,[17] "Dan shall be a serpent in the way, an adder in the path."

2. What signs are to precede his coming the Apostle intimates when he says in his letter to the Thessalonians, "And now ye know that which restraineth until he shall be revealed in his own season.

[13] Gen. 1. 1.

[14] On Antichrist, *cf.* W. Bousset, *Der Antichrist in der Überlieferung des Judentums, des neuen Testaments und der alten Kirche*, Göttingen, 1895. On the first seven chapters of Otto, Book VIII, see also *Adsonis epistolam de ortu et tempore Antichristi*, edited by E. Sackur in *Sibyllinische Texte und Forschungen* 105-113.

[15] The text reads *contra*. For a discussion of Otto's knowledge of Greek, see Introduction, pp. 39-41.

[16] *Cf. Quaestiones in epistolam II ad Thessalonicenses*, edited under the name of Hugo of St. Victor, Migne, *Patrologia Latina* 175, *col.* 591; Adso, *l.c.*, p. 106; Gregory, *Moralia* 31. 24 and 43; Haimo, bishop of Halberstadt, *Expositio in epistolam II ad Thessalonicenses* 2.

[17] Gen. 49. 17.

For the mystery of lawlessness doth already work, only let him that now restraineth restrain until he be taken out of the way."[18] And again he says: "Except the falling away come first and the son of lawlessness be revealed, the son of perdition,"[19] etc. Some interpret these words with reference to Nero in whose time Paul wrote — as I said above, I remember. But others think they were spoken of the devil, whose members are all they that belong to the false city, and they say that Paul meant that Zabulus, who by persecuting the saints through their members was then working "the mystery of iniquity," must be revealed "in his own season" — that is, at the end of the world — that iniquity might be uncovered, and that he was to pour forth through Antichrist the strength he has collected. This is why you read in the Apocalypse[20] that, after a thousand years (a number which, of course, indicates the fulness of the time),[21] Satan, who as is well known is at present fast bound, as in an abyss, in the minds of the wicked which contain malice within them, must be loosed — that is, will burst forth into manifest wickedness — and will pour forth all his strength. Observe that Paul calls all the malice of the present day not iniquity but "the mystery of iniquity" in order that every trial which the Church suffers from the beginning of time even to Antichrist may appear, in comparison with that which she is to suffer *then,* not to be iniquity but, as it were, the mystery — that is a mere appearance of iniquity. Or else he calls it "the mystery" as being hidden, for we habitually call secret things "mystic," and the meaning then is as follows: "at that time the tribulation will be so manifest, so perilous, so bloody that the Church will consider all that it is suffering now, or has suffered, as hidden in comparison with that future tribulation." What follows, saying "Let him that restraineth restrain until he be taken out of the way," is seen to be in keeping with the aforesaid interpretation, as meaning "Let him who now hideth his vices beneath an honorable sense of restraining shame hide them until in the course of time his deeds shall come with unabashed countenance into the midst," that is into public view. He seems moreover to indicate this by his prefatory statement: "Ye know that which restraineth until he shall be revealed in his own season," as though he said, he will not be revealed until the time shall come at which he must be made manifest, when the iniquity of

[18] II Thess. 2. 6-7.   [19] II Thess. 2. 3.   [20] Rev. 20. 7.
[21] Augustine 20. 7.

the Amorites [22] shall be fulfilled. Whence, he relates, this revelation of himself will precede the falling away. For the source of error will rightly appear when truth shall be forsaken by the author of truth and almost the whole world shall fall away. Some [23] apply "the falling away" to the kingdom, and this further statement, "Let him that restraineth restrain until he be taken out of the way," in the sense that when all shall be striving against justice in their love of sin and thereby shall be departing from the justice of the kingdom, he who holds the kingdom will become so dejected that, unreverenced, he will be removed from the midst — that is from the public view — as one of the rabble might be. Men say also that the apostle set these things down under a veil and wrapping of words to escape the appearance of having uttered calumny against the Roman Empire, which was believed by the Romans themselves to be eternal. For the same reason, they believe, this too was said, "Ye know that which restraineth," as though he were to say, "I wish those men of other races to know by manifest evidence what you know." But others [24] interpret these words, with respect to the priesthood and the Roman See, in the same sense in which we have spoken of the kingdom.

3. Having indicated what signs are to precede Antichrist let us now take up the subject of his actual coming and of that persecution which is then to take place. When the Lord preached to the Jews and was not heard by them he said,[25] among other things, "I am come in my Father's name, and ye have not received me; if another shall come in his own name, him ye will receive." And Paul said, "Because they received not the love of the truth, that they might be saved, for this cause shall God send them a working of error, that they may believe a lie." [26] Nor did Paul fear to say that the Lord is to send him. For the wicked, although they afflict the City of God in their zeal, not for justice but for lawlessness, can nevertheless do nothing save that which they are permitted to do and to the extent that they are permitted to do it. This is why it is said [27] that an evil spirit from God came mightily upon Saul —

---

[22] Gen. 15. 16.   [23] Cf., for example, Adso, l.c., p. 110.

[24] (Hugo of St. Victor), Quaestiones in ep. II ad Thess., quaestio 6: "Nisi venerit discessio primum" . . . Hoc quatuor modis potest intelligi, vel de terreno Romano imperio, vel de spirituali imperio Romanae ecclesiae, vel de fide, vel de Antichristo.

[25] John 5. 43.   [26] II Thess. 2. 10 et seq.   [27] I Sam. 18. 10.

"evil" because of its most sinful desire, and "of God" because it had received from Him a just power. Now if the Lord permits all the wicked to reign, how much the more true is it that the prince of all the wicked does not, without God's nod, receive warranty for temporal prosperity and for the practice of cruelty against His own people? The Lord therefore will send Antichrist, because he will be able to employ the malice conceived in his heart no longer and to no greater extent than He shall permit. We must ask why the Lord permits His City to be so cruelly afflicted, why He grants to His enemy so great power of wrongdoing. It is not surprising if the Lord should, before the crowning by final tribulation, with the most severe kind of training first chasten and discipline His Church, which was raised out of nothing and exalted, as we said above,[28] to the highest pinnacle on earth — chasten and discipline it, I mean, to keep it from being enervated by long peace and becoming lukewarm in its love for its Creator.

This persecution will be, as was said above,[29] violent and treacherous and will exercise deeds of violence: not of itself, it seems to me, but through a powerful personality. This is why the Psalmist says, "He sitteth in the lurking-places with the rich, in the secret places to murder the innocent," [30] that is, he will by secret devices incite the mighty of this world to inflict open persecution upon the saints. It is this, I think, that is called The Beast in the Apocalypse.[31] For in that same Scripture the writer calls Antichrist himself the false prophet, but the devil who urges him on he calls the dragon.[32] From this it may be inferred that the devil himself, coming altogether in hypocrisy, will deceive the world — not by personally bringing to bear outward [and visible] torments upon the saints but craftily by lying signs, and by a pretence of holiness and an appearance of reason — and that some powerful being associated with him for this purpose will inflict visible tortures upon the saints. If any claim that, to achieve this end, he associates with himself a powerful man (as for example the emperor of the Romans) and that this man is called the beast, I do not take exception.

[28] VI. 36; VII. 16.   [29] VIII. 1.

[30] Ps. 10. 8. But the American Revision reads "of the villages" for "with the rich."

[31] Rev. 11. 7; 13. 1 and elsewhere. For another interpretation, see Augustine 20. 9 (ed. Dombart 2. 431) and 14; also Otto himself in VIII. 20 below (p. 479).

[32] E.g., Rev. 16. 13.

4. But since as we testified above the life and the doctrine of
Antichrist are opposed to those of Christ, let us by God's aid set
forth how this comes to pass. Regarding His life, indeed, the facts
are self-evident. Christ, descending from His father's throne and
from the heavens above, humbled Himself in order to redeem the
human race; that other, striving to ascend from the world below
and exalting himself "above all that is called God or that is worshipped as God" [33] will rise up to deceive mankind. Christ, concealing the virtue and excellence of His deity, exposed to spitting
and to the scourge the flesh He had assumed; Antichrist, not considering his own frailty but vaunting himself above man as a god,
will expect from mankind glory and honor for qualities he does not
possess. How far his doctrine differs from Christ's is clearer than
light, inasmuch as the Lord shows Himself to be a teacher of humility, saying, "Learn of me, for I am meek and lowly in heart";[34]
Antichrist is a teacher of arrogance, declaring, "Mine are the rivers
and I have made them." [35] Observe that in two points in particular
Antichrist finds in our faith a chance spitefully to condemn it:
one forsooth he declares to be contrary to human reason, the other
contrary to the pleasures of the flesh. Contrary to human reason,
he declares, are Virgin Birth, the sacrament of the altar, the adora-
tion of the crucifix, the belief in a man as God [36] and other matters
of like sort. Contrary to pleasure he asserts are, "If any man
would come after me," [37] and so forth, and "Except a man renounce all that he hath, he cannot be my disciple," [38] and "Woe
unto you that are rich," [39] and "Blessed are the poor," [40] and others
of like sort. Accordingly, misleading the wise with arguments and
reasoning, and alluring the foolish by the delights of temporal
things, he will lead both astray with false promises. Wherefore the
Lord says in the Gospel that so great shall be the danger of that
time "that they shall lead astray, if possible, even the elect." [41]
And in Job you read that the food of Antichrist is the elect.[42] For
those who, employing human reasoning, philosophize regarding the
causes of things, are more readily led by reasoning and by argument

[33] II Thess. 2. 4.   [34] Matt. 11. 29.   [35] Ezek. 29. 3 and 9.

[36] Hofmeister points out that the argument here is an old one, citing
Minucius Felix, *Octavius, c.* 9 and *c.* 29.

[37] Matt. 16. 24; Luke 9. 23.   [38] Luke 14. 33.   [39] Luke 6. 24.

[40] Luke 6. 20.   [41] Matt. 24. 24.

[42] Hofmeister cites the Latin version of Hab. 1. 16: *et cibus eius electus.*
But the American Revision here reads: "and his food plenteous."

to the point of denying their faith than frightened into doing so by threats or enticed by the delights of the world. Let these words suffice concerning the life and the doctrine of Antichrist.

5. While Antichrist shall himself be preaching and leading astray the human race — and in particular the Jewish people — Enoch and Elijah, who still survive, will come, it is believed, in order that by the authority of these men — one of whom was before the law and the other under the law — the world which has been deceived by error may return to "the knowledge of the truth." And of Elijah indeed you read [43] that the Lord says through his prophet, "Behold I will send you Elijah the Tishbite,[44] who shall turn the heart of the fathers to the children and the heart of the children to their fathers, before the great and manifest day of the Lord shall come." You find mention of them both in the Apocalypse,[45] where we read that they are to be put to death by Antichrist, and that after this he himself is to set an end to his persecution, being slain by the breath of the mouth of the Lord, because the blood of Enoch and Elijah as well as of the other saints shall cry out to God.

6. Besides, that the time of persecution is to continue for three years and a half — just as long indeed, as the Lord's ministry — is indicated in veiled fashion by the fact that it is stated,[46] also by a prophet: "Until a time and times and half a time." It is more clearly declared on the authority of the Apocalypse: "the holy city shall they tread under foot forty and two months." [47] The Lord intimates that, by reason of the enormity of the persecution, this short time has been provided by a most merciful judge for the elect's sake, when He says, "Except those days had been shortened, no flesh would have been saved, but for the elect's sake those days shall be shortened." [48]

7. When the head of the impious city shall be smitten, the Jews, that unbelieving people, seeing that they have been deceived will, it is believed, be converted, in accordance with the following saying of the prophet: "If the number of the children of Israel be as the sand of the sea, it is the remnant that shall be saved." [49] After this

---

[43] Mal. 4. 5 *et seq.*

[44] So also Augustine 20. 29, but the rest of the quotation is more in accord with the Bible as we have it.

[45] Rev. 11.   [46] Dan. 7. 25.   [47] Rev. 11. 2.

[48] Matt. 24. 22.

[49] Isa. 10. 22; but Otto cites the passage in the form in which Paul quotes it in Romans 9. 27. *Cf.* Augustine 18. 33 (end).

a time for repentance remains — a time whose length is hidden from all mortals. Then when all those things which have been foretold shall have been brought to completion, and strange signs shall have been revealed in the sun, the moon, the stars and the sea — when all men shall be fainting for fear, and for expectation of the things which are to come upon the whole world — then the destruction of the evil city, and the increase of the City of Christ, and the day of the Lord are at hand, in accordance with the word of truth which, sweetly consoling God's own people, says: "When ye see these things coming to pass, know ye that the kingdom of God is nigh." [50] Without doubt, the Kingdom "cometh as a thief in the night" [51] (that is, unforeseen) while, once more according to the word of the Lord,[52] men shall be eating and drinking, marrying and giving in marriage. We must believe that these matters are so ordered not in cruelty but in wisdom, through the wise providence of the Creator, that we may ever be found in fear of the coming of the Judge, ever prepared to render an account.

[Insertion and Preface to the Eighth Chapter. On the Future Life.]

As I have been lulled by long quiet and was dropping off to sleep, because of manifold occupations, may the trumpet of salvation arouse me as I am about to speak of the final time. For who, even if he were sunk in the slumber of sloth, would not wake up after hearing this trumpet whereat even the dead arise? I confess that, since my understanding had long been distracted by many matters, I felt that I was too little qualified (nay was absolutely unfit) to discuss such lofty topics and so I placed my finger upon my lips, thinking it better to pass the evil days in silence than to argue rashly of great matters in perturbation of spirit. I know one who said, "Be still and know." [53] I know that perturbation of spirit is always ignorant of a plan, whereas wisdom, the friend of calm, rejects burdensome tasks. While I never earn the privilege of avoiding these completely, at times nevertheless I seem to gain some relief, however slight, and they press upon me less importunately. Accordingly at this Easter season,[54] resting not upon our own strength and might but upon the strength and might of Him "who died for

---

[50] Luke 21. 31.   [51] I Thess. 5. 2.   [52] Matt. 24. 38.   [53] Ps. 46. 10.

[54] March 31, 1146, as M. Büdinger points out in "Die Entstehung des achten Buches Ottos von Freising," *Sitzungsgerichte der Wiener Akad. d. Wiss., Phil.-hist. Cl.*, 98 (1881), p. 358.

our trespasses and was raised for our justification,'' [55] let us undertake to speak of the resurrection of the dead and of the end of the world, zealously calling upon Him to give us grace that, being raised from the death of the soul, we may speak worthily of such great mysteries.

8. ''When''— according to the Apostle —''they shall be saying 'Peace and safety,' then sudden destruction shall come upon them,'' [56] and all things shall be consumed by the terrible power of fire. Not only have our own people [57] with prophetic inspiration rightly foretold this destruction of the world by fire, but even certain of the heathen also, relying upon merely human reasoning powers, have had a vision through the aid of physical speculations. Plato, chief of philosophers, asserts in his *Timaeus* that in accordance with the secret plans of nature the world must be purified first by water, afterwards by fire.[58] A certain one of the poets speaks as follows on the same theme:

. . . . . remembers a time that is coming,
Wherein the sea and the land and the boundless expanse of the heavens,
Even the boundless mass of the world shall in fire be ended.[59]

The Sibyl too, in the prophecy she uttered concerning Christ,[60] makes a clear reference to this final conflagration and the last judgment. Josephus states that the first man, who could more subtly trace the causes of things in that he saw at closer range their primordial creation, predicted that there would be one destruction of all things by the power of fire, another by a multitude of waters.[61] One of our own writers, Peter, agreeing with him said, ''There were heavens from of old and an earth compacted out of water and through water, by the word of God, by whom the world that then was, being overflowed with water, perished: but the heavens that now are, and the earth, by the same word have been stored up for fire, being reserved against the day of judgment and destruction of ungodly men.'' [62] Later he says, ''The great day of the Lord will

[55] Rom. 4. 25.　　[56] I Thess. 5. 3.　　[57] *I.e.*, the Christians.

[58] Hofmeister points out that this is not found in the part of the *Timaeus* translated into Latin by Chalcidius nor in his commentary; he is inclined to believe that Otto was thinking of what is said to have been told to Solon by a certain Egyptian priest. Minucius Felix (*Octavius, c.* 34) refers to this passage also, but without referring to the *Timaeus*.

[59] Ovid, *Metamorphoses* 1. 256 *et seq.*　　[60] Augustine 18. 23 and 2. 4.

[61] *Antiquities* 1. 2. 3, a passage which Otto cites in fuller form in I. 2 above.

[62] II Pet. 3. 5-7.

come, in which the heavens shall pass away with a great noise.'' [63]
Some claim that by these words Peter meant that the flame of fire
must ascend just as far as, it appears, the waters of the flood fell
before with destructive power.[64] For he says ''heaven and earth,''
clearly indicating by heaven the ethereal sky. Hence we say that
the birds of the heavens perished before in the deluge of waters,
but that the birds that now are have, by the same word, been stored
up and reserved for fire, that is, they must be destroyed or changed
for the better by fire that shall match, in measure and power, the
water that was used of old.

9. Here one may not inappropriately inquire how, according to
this authority and the attestation of the Truth itself,[65] heaven and
earth are to pass away, or rather be utterly destroyed, since the
Psalmist says ''They shall perish, but thou shalt endure.'' [66] for
how shall the foremost works of creation, made in the beginning,
perish (seeing that, as men believe, no substance perishes), and
Sacred Scripture, having first listed all things that are fleeting and
transitory, says, ''But the earth abideth for ever''? [67] It surely cannot be, men ask, that while the earth endures, the sky, which is a
mightier work and a higher, shall perish. This difficulty is the more
easy of solution if we were to examine a little more carefully what
is said and in what connection. We use the expression ''pass away''
in various senses.[68] There is a transition from not-being to being,
or from being to not-being, or from being to other being, that is,
transition of *aliation* [69] — if I may invent a word — by making
something, or of alteration by making something different. This
transition by alteration is said in the sacred page to occur in
various ways, that is from good to bad, or from bad to good, or
from good to better, or from bad to worse. Lucifer's transition was
from good to bad; he was transformed from an angel into a devil
and turned from life to death. Paul's transition was from bad to
good, for he was transformed from a persecutor into an apostle and
passed from death to life. Herod's was from bad to worse, for he
departed from the torments of the body to the most violent tortures

[63] *Loc. cit.* 10.   [64] Augustine 20. 18.
[65] Matt. 5. 18, 24. 35; Mark 13. 31; Luke 21. 33; *cf.* VIII. 9 (end) below.
[66] Ps. 102. 26.   [67] Eccles. 1. 4.
[68] I. Schmidlin (*Philosoph. Jahrb. der Görres-Gesellschaft* 18. 420 *et seq.*)
points out that in what follows Otto agrees closely with the general opinion
of scholars of his time.
[69] The text reads *aliationis*.

of Gehenna. From good to better is the transition of every believer, who passes from the goodly fellowship of this life to the rewards [70] of eternal recompense. It is said of Christ that "he passed from this world unto the father." [71] Therefore, when it is said that heaven and earth "pass away," it is by no means asserted that they are changing from being to not-being, as though they must perish, which would be to pass into something; it is rather asserted that they must be changed and transfigured from this condition to a different existence — that is, to another state, more beautiful and far more excellent.[72] Hence Paul says, "the fashion of this world passeth away";[73] the fashion, he says, not the nature.[74] The Psalmist, too, to keep us from interpreting too literally his saying, "They shall perish," added, "shall wax old like a garment, as a vesture shalt thou change them, and they shall be changed," [75] as though he were saying, "When they decay and as it were grow old in consequence of long and manifold corruption, you will renew these elements, clothing them with a better state as with a more comely garment." And yet, if we duly consider what he said and to whom he said it, we shall not be surprised that he said that heaven and earth pass away. For he says even to God, "They shall perish, but thou shalt endure," and again, "As a vesture shalt thou change them, and they shall be changed; but thou art the same, and thy years shall have no end." [76] Consider, therefore, that to God it is said, "But thou art the same, and thy years shall have no end," and you will not be surprised that a thing which is most enduring, yet is after all but a creature, must of necessity perish, grow old, be changed, in contrast to the unchanging nature and identity of its Creator, in comparison with Whose purity the most clean things are judged to be unclean, even as it is written, "the stars are not clean in his sight." [77] Accordingly it is not through the destruction of the substance but by a change in the form that there will be a new heaven and a new earth, fittingly prepared by a new beauty and by new bodies for a new use, purified, by the removal of every inequality and of all uncleanness, to the likeness of the paradise of God.

There are those who say that two elements, air and water, as

---

[70] *Bravium* is the word here used by Otto.

[71] John 13. 1.   [72] *Cf.* Augustine 20. 16.   [73] I Cor. 7. 31.

[74] Augustine 20. 14 (*ed.* Dombart 2. 439); *cf.* (Hugo of St. Victor), *Quaestiones in epistolam I ad Corinthios, quaestio* 67.

[75] Ps. 102. 26.   [76] *Loc. cit.* 26 *et seq.*   [77] Job 15. 15.

being unnecessary after the resurrection, will not endure; the one will be changed into earth, the other into ether. Hence we read in the Apocalypse, "And the sea is no more."[78] The writer did not say that the sea passes away, as before he said that heaven and earth pass away, but that it is no more. Others believe that they will not perish completely so as to exist no longer, but that they will be changed for the better, even as the earth is changed, for John again bears witness in the Apocalypse that he saw "a sea of glass."[79] Yet it seems that this utterance must be interpreted allegorically rather than literally.[80] So much then regarding water. Whether the air is to pass over into the fineness of ether or, continuing in its own substance, is to exist refined and purified, there is no contradiction to what has been said: "Heaven and earth shall pass away."[81] If anyone discussing the matter more critically avers that the ether itself will be a partaker in this purification and will pass over into a greater clearness, and that "heaven shall pass away" applies to the ether, we do not find fault with such a saying.

10. When this shall have taken place there remain the true sabbath[82] and resurrection of the dead.[83] Accordingly all shall rise, but not all in like manner; "some," according to Daniel "will awake from the dust of the earth to everlasting life, some to shame and everlasting contempt."[84] Here of course it must be noted that there are two resurrections[85] (one of the soul, another of the body) of which, in accordance with His two natures, Christ, the Son of God, the firstborn from the dead, is the source. "For the life of the body is the soul, the life of the soul is God."[86] Accordingly, inasmuch as He is God, it follows that He, as the Word, the Son of God, raises souls dead through sin; inasmuch as he is man, He, as man the Son of Man, raises bodies. This He himself makes known, speaking in these words in the Gospel, "Verily, verily, I say unto you,

---

[78] Rev. 21. 1.   [79] Rev. 4. 6; 15. 2.   [80] *Cf.* Augustine 20. 16.
[81] Mark 13. 31.   [82] The text says *octava*.

[83] Augustine (20. 14 and 16), Hugo of St. Victor (*De sacramentis* 2, part 17 *et seq.*), and Honorius Augustodunenesis. (*Elucidarium*) place the resurrection and the last judgment before the conflagration of the world, whereas Robert Pullus (and of succeeding writers Thomas, for example) keep the same order as Otto. *Cf.* Schmidlin (*Zeitschr. für katholische Theologie* 29. 456).

[84] So the American Revision, but Otto's text (from Jerome's Vulgate) reads: *ut videant semper*. The quotation is from Dan. 12. 2.

[85] *Cf.* Augustine 20. 6; Honorius Augustodunensis, *Elucidarium* 3. 11.

[86] A common phrase in Augustine. See, *e.g.* 19. 26.

the hour cometh, and now is, when the dead shall hear the voice of the Son of God, and they that hear shall live."[87] That this was spoken of the first resurrection the expression "now is" suffers no man to question. Thereafter, in speaking of the second resurrection,[88] He says, "For as the Father hath life in himself, even so gave he to the Son also to have life in himself."[89] Now God alone has life in Himself. He, living of Himself, by Himself, in Himself, does not receive life from another source; for Him life is being, nor is being anything else than life, because He Himself is life, and life in such a sense that from Him comes all life. "For in him we live, and move, and have our being;"[90] without Him neither live nor move nor have any being, because the creature is life not in itself but in Him. Accordingly "he gave to the Son also to have life in himself," when He made it possible for man, after He had been absorbed into God, to have by grace what God the Son of God had by nature. Hence the writer continues, joining what follows to the thought that has preceded, "He gave him authority," also, "to execute judgment, because he is a Son of Man,"[91] as though he were saying, "He who gave him to have life in himself gave him authority also to execute judgment, not because he is the Son of God, but because he is a son of man." For not because He is the Son of God did the Father give Him anything, or did He receive any authority from the Father, with whom He was born from all eternity as co-omnipotent even as He is consubstantial with Him and co-eternal, unless perchance we are to say that He gave in that He begat. But let us hear in due order what more John says regarding the second resurrection. "Marvel not," he says, "at this: for the hour cometh."[92] Of course he means the last hour — not the hour which now is but the time when "they that are in the tombs shall hear his voice and shall come forth." He said before, "The hour cometh, and now is, when the dead shall hear the voice of the Son of God; and they that hear shall live,"[93] declaring that the first resurrection originates with Him in that He is God the Son of God. After he declared that the Father gave Him authority also to execute judgment, because He is a Son of Man, he added, "Marvel

[87] John 5. 25. With this and what follows, *cf.* Augustine's *Tractatus in evangelium Iohannis* 19-23.
[88] That is, of bodies.   [89] John 5. 26.   [90] Acts 17. 28.   [91] John 5. 27.
[92] Verses 28 *et seq.* Sometimes the language here is more in accord with Augustine (20. 6) than with the actual wording of the Vulgate.
[93] John 5. 25.

not . . . for the hour cometh" when they "that are in the tombs shall hear his voice and shall come forth," as though he were saying, "Marvel not if I, as a son of man, have received authority to execute judgment, since I have also received authority to recall to life out of the tombs bodies reduced to ashes." Whosoever therefore shall have been raised in the first resurrection from the death of the soul shall in the second be changed and pass from corruptible to incorruption. Hence we read, "Blessed . . . is he that hath part in the first resurrection: on such the second death hath no power." [94] It follows conversely that he who, dying in his sins, was not a partaker in the first resurrection, is accursed and must be eternally sentenced to the second death. [95]

11. That the dead will rise again is not only affirmed by the Gospel and the Apostles and the teachers of the new law, but the fathers of old also foretold it through their prophetic powers. Such is that witness of the lawgiver which the Lord adduced to confute the Sadducees, saying, "I am the God of Abraham, the God of Isaac, the God of Jacob," since He is "not the God of the dead but of the living." [96] And in the book of Job we read, "Think you that a man that has died shall live again? All the days of my warfare will I wait, till my change shall come." [97] I believe "that my Redeemer liveth, and on the last day I am to arise out of the earth." Note too the saying of Ezekiel, "O ye dry bones, hear the word of Jehovah. Thus saith the Lord, Behold, I will cause breath to enter into you, and ye shall live, and I will lay sinews upon you, and will bring up flesh upon you, and cover you with skin, and put breath in you, and ye shall live." [98] And presently he says, "And the bones came together, bone to its bone." [99] Also, "Behold, I will open your graves, and cause you to come up out of your graves, O my people." What, I ask you, what could be said more clearly and more plainly of a matter so mystical, so profound, so obscure? For he foretells that bones — and bones that are dry because they no longer have in them the power of life, but have physically lost their freshness — grow sinews, are clothed with flesh, are covered with skin, are spiritually reanimated and finally are by divine power led forth from their tombs. And yet by that argument of which Paul makes mention when he says, "that which thou . . . sowest

[94] Rev. 20. 6.   [95] *Cf.* Augustine 20. 6 (end); 19. 28.

[96] Exod. 3. 6; Matt. 22. 32; Mark 12. 26 *et seq.*   [97] Job 14. 14 and 19. 25.

[98] Ezek. 37. 4 *et seq.*   [99] Ezek. 37. 7 and 12.

is not quickened except it first die,''[100] we are also led to believe in
the resurrection, since every year we see the earth warmed by the
summer's heat and, after being so warmed, dried by the autumn's
drought, and thus dried, dying in the winter's cold, but aroused as
from the dead when its freshness is revived by the kindly moisture
of spring. How the Creator of all performs some things naturally,
in accordance with causes inherent in nature, and other things by
His might through causes invested in Himself alone, has been related elsewhere [101] and does not concern the present theme.

12. Having said what precedes we must now see in what manner,
with what age, sex and form the dead are to arise. Here we must
realize first of all that all human bodies, whether they have been
swallowed up by the waters, destroyed by flames, reduced to ashes
in the bowels of the earth, devoured by beasts and incorporated
with them or scattered and spread abroad over various regions of
the earth, do, according to the Apostle, without a doubt return to
the substance they had when they lived in the world — yea, return
thereto ''at the Lord's command uttered through the voice of the
archangel and the trump of God.''[102] Moreover, ''all shall rise
again,'' as Augustine says,[103] ''of the same stature as they had or
were to have in the period of their youth, although it will be of no
disadvantage even if the form of the body shall be that of an infant or of an old man, in a day when no infirmity of the mind or
of the body itself shall remain. Hence, even if anyone insists that
each man is to rise in that condition of body in which he died, one
need not argue with him with toilsome contradiction. Because of
certain expressions — such as ''Till we all attain . . . unto a full-
grown man, unto the measure of the stature of the fulness of
Christ,''[104] and ''conformed to the image of his Son''[105] — some
believe that women will not rise in the female sex, but all of them
in the male, inasmuch as God created man alone out of clay but
created woman out of man. But I find more wisdom in those who
do not doubt that both sexes will rise. For that carnal desire which
is the cause of confusion will not *then* exist. Accordingly all de-

---

[100] I Cor. 15. 36.

[101] Augustine 21. 7 *et seq.*; *De Genesi ad litteram liber* 9. 17. 32 and 18. 33;
cf. Hugo of St. Victor, *Summa sententiarum* 3. 3. Hofmeister believes that
Schmidlin (*Philosoph. Jahrbuch der Görres-Ges.* 18. 421 *et seq.*) is mistaken
in finding in this passage an allusion to a lost book by Otto of Freising.

[102] I Thess. 4. 16.   [103] 22. 16 and 17.

[104] Eph. 4. 13.   [105] Rom. 8. 29.

fects will be taken from bodies, but the natural state of the bodies will be preserved. Now the female sex is not a defect but a natural state. For the female members will not be adapted to the old use but to a new grace whereby the desire of the beholder will not be aroused; for there will be no desire, but God's mercy and wisdom will be praised, which created what was not and freed from corruption what it created.'' A little later [Augustine said], ''Woman, like man, is the creation of God, but their unity was commended, so that she was created from man. Since therefore He created both sexes, He will restore both.'' So writes Augustine.

It remains for us to discuss their form. We must not suppose that giants are brought back in such great stature, dwarfs in such extreme littleness, the lame or the weak in a state so feeble and afflicted, the Ethiopians in an affliction of color so disagreeable, the fat or the thin in their superabundance or their lack of flesh, to a life which ought to be free from every blemish and every spot. Hence Augustine says, ''All the beauty of a body consists in harmony of its parts together with a certain charm of coloring. But where there is no harmony of parts, a body offends either because it is deformed, that is, because there is a defect or because there is an excess. Accordingly there will be no deformity such as lack of harmony of the parts produced when those parts which are misshapen are corrected; and what is less than is seemly shall be supplied from a source known to the Creator, and that which is more than is comely shall be removed, though the integrity of the matter is preserved. Moreover, how great will be the charm of the coloring when the righteous shall shine as the sun in their Father's kingdom! We must believe that this brightness in Christ's body when He rose again was concealed from the eyes of the disciples, rather than suppose that it was lacking.'' [106] So much concerning the righteous. To consider the nature of the wicked is unnecessary.

Of monsters and of abortions we must, I believe, hold the view that everything to which the description ''a rational and mortal animal'' applies will rise either to life or to death. If therefore there are monstrous beings [107] that are rational and mortal, or abortions which have already begun to have a soul, [108] like those of which Moses speaks in Deuteronomy, saying, ''If any one shall have struck a woman and that shall have produced an abortion, if

[106] 22. 19.   [107] Augustine (16. 8) enumerates three kinds.
[108] *Cf.* Augustine 22. 13.

a child has been formed, he shall pay a life for a life,'' [109] they are subject to this law. All the others, creatures that lack reason, however nearly they approach to human form (as for example apes), or by whatever other form the ancient enemy mocks the human race (as for instance fauns), and all other creatures of this sort have, as is well known, no part in this resurrection. Regarding hermaphrodites, and two-headed creatures, whom a mistake of nature has badly joined or badly divided, it is not necessary to argue at length, especially as this question has been sufficiently elucidated by the fathers in other passages of Scripture.[110]

13. Regarding those who shall be found [at the resurrection] to be alive we must make inquiry whether they are to be swept from that state to judgment or are rather to die, as the others do, but are to rise again.[111] No one can rise who does not first die. Yet there is no lack of those who believe that such an interpretation must be put upon the saying ''to judge the living and the dead'' [112] that they call those who shall be found continuing in the flesh ''the living,'' but understand by ''the dead'' those who shall have fallen asleep but who shall awake from the dust of the earth. What we read in Paul seems to be in accord with this:[113] ''For we would not have you ignorant . . . concerning them that fall asleep; that ye sorrow not, even as the rest, who have no hope. For if we believe that Jesus died and rose again, even so them also that are fallen asleep will God through Jesus bring with him. For this we say unto you by the word of the Lord, that we that are alive, that are left at the coming of the Lord, shall not precede them that are fallen asleep. For the Lord himself shall descend from heaven in authority,[114] in the voice of the archangel and in the trump of God: and the dead that are in Christ shall rise first; then we that are alive, that are left, shall together with them be caught up in the clouds, to meet the Christ in the air: and so shall we ever be with the Lord.'' These words appear to mean that the saints, those that are still alive and that are rising from the dead, are to meet the Lord in the air as He is descending for the judgment. To make clear the suddenness of the resurrection Paul declares that the dead are not to be preceded by the living, but that they also in the same hour

---

109 *Cf.* Exod. 21. 22 *et seq.* The passage is not an exact quotation.
110 For this discussion *cf.* Augustine 15 and 16.
111 Augustine 20. 20.   112 I Pet. 4. 5. *Cf.* II Tim. 4. 1.
113 I Thess. 4. 13-17.   114 The text reads *in iussu.*

and at the same moment are caught up with them into the air to meet Christ. If in accordance with this interpretation those who shall have been found alive shall not die, how will there be a general resurrection? How will that which Paul says be fulfilled, "We shall all rise"?[115] Shall he be regarded then as contradicting himself? Far from it! Therefore, in accordance with the interpretation of our elders, it is true that they shall be caught up alive into the air together with those who are rising; and it is true that, in accordance with what is sung in the psalm, "What man is he that shall live and not see death?",[116] they shall not be absolved from the debt of all flesh, that debt which even the Lord, who had taken nothing away [i.e., who owed nothing], was willing to pay. The Omnipotent, Who created all things out of nothing, is able in the very act of catching them up to dissolve them in death with marvellous quickness and straightway to recall them to life. However, the living and the dead may not inaptly be interpreted by a figure, as the good and the bad. If anyone says that the bad must be consumed in that general conflagration and thus be recalled with the others, the saints, to life, we need not argue with him; only let him consider how he is to interpret the words of the Apostle in which it is declared that they are caught up into the air to meet Christ.

14. In that passage of Paul we must not casually pass over in our reading the meaning of "the voices of the archangel" and "the trump of God." Elsewhere too in speaking of the same mystery he says, "We shall all rise, but shall not all be changed in a moment, in the twinkling of an eye, at the last trump. For the trumpet shall sound, and the dead shall be raised incorruptible, and we shall be changed."[117] By calling it the last trump he intimates that other trumps have sounded before. And indeed you read in the Apocalypse, "And the seven angels that had the seven trumpets prepared themselves to sound. And the first sounded and the second, and the third,"[118] and so on even to the seventh. Which trump Paul called the last can be readily understood. There are those who understand by the six trumpets before the last the holy preachers who, in the course of the six ages of the world, appealed to sluggish hearts by the word of holy exhortation — now as it were sounding more mildly with promises of rewards, now thrilling them by

[115] I Cor. 15. 51. But the American Revision says, "we all shall not sleep, but we shall all be changed," etc.

[116] Ps. 89. 48.   [117] I Cor. 15. 51 et seq.   [118] Rev. 8. 6 et seq.

threats and the fear of punishment, as though sharply rebuking them. Such were in the first age Enoch, in the second Noah, in the third Abraham and the patriarchs, in the fourth Moses, in the fifth David and the prophets, in the sixth Christ and the Apostles and their followers.[119] The seventh voice, which is also the last, they call the voice sent forth to arouse those that sleep, so much the more terrible in its sound as it is the more instant, and as by its effect it more realistically brings to fulfillment the things which were foretold. Inasmuch as this sound is believed to be produced through the agency of angels it is not inappropriately called a voice on account of the fact, a trumpet on account of its significance. For if that angelic voice which sounded so gently when the Lord calmly and serenely ascended to the heavens, "He shall so come in like manner as ye beheld him going into heaven," [120] is compared to the voice of a trumpet in accordance with the statement, "God is gone up with a shout, and Jehovah with the sound of a trumpet,"[121] how much more rightly, when he shall descend in dread majesty and in sternness to judge the world, is that angelic voice which is fearfully to arouse the living and the dead for judgment to be called a trumpet! If the voice of those predicting the judgment to come was a trumpet, how much the more rightly shall the sound that announces realistically and immediately the judgment be a trumpet! Some with greater exactitude compare the seven trumpets to the seven gifts of the Holy Spirit and, assigning separate gifts to the separate ages in succession, call the last trump the spirit of fear.

15. After these things shall have come to pass the Lord will, beyond doubt, come for the judgment and for the final sifting of both cities. He will come to judge, moreover, in the form in which He previously came to be judged, that with even justice the world may find a severe judge in Him whom previously with haughty mind it despised when He came humbly in the flesh. Hence we have the prophetic saying, "They shall look on him whom they pierced." [122] For "the Father," judging not in His own person, "hath given all

119 Hofmeister points out that Berengaudus, *Expositio super 7 visiones libri Apocal.* (Migne, *Patrologia Latina* 17, *col.* 934 ff.) claims that entirely different personages are meant by these seven angels of the Apocalypse.

120 Acts 1. 11. 121 Ps. 47. 5.

122 John 19. 37. Hofmeister points out that the prophet's actual words, as found in Zech. 12. 10, are more at variance with Otto's interpretation than is the quotation in John.

judgment unto the Son," [123] in order that Him whom (though He was innocent) He had exposed to all manner of insult and to the cross, He may now make the Lord of "things in heaven and things on earth and things under the earth," [124] ordaining Him to be "the Judge of the living and the dead." [125] Yet, while to the just His human form will appear merciful, to the wicked He will be the more bright and terrible as He before seemed to them obscure and deserving of contempt. For His beauty and His strength, which in His former coming were not lost or ever diminished but only hidden from view, will be the more clearly revealed as they shall be the more vigorously employed for the punishment of His adversaries. Hence we have the saying of Malachi, "Who can abide the day of His coming?" Or "who shall stand to behold Him? For he is like a refiner's fire and like fullers' soap: and he will sit as a refiner and purifier of silver, and he will purify the sons of Levi." [126] That is to say, He will not merely condemn those who shall be consumed "like stubble" by the fire of His wrath. He will do more than that; those who, having no lot of inheritance on the earth are called the sons of Levi,[127] and those who, being compared to silver, have been found worthy to be stored away in the heavenly treasury, He will terrify with the surpassing excellence of the majesty of His goodness and, as the blessed Job says,[128] He will purge those whom He has dismayed. "For" even "the powers of the heavens shall be shaken." [129] I believe it was this severity and this glory of the judge that Daniel had in mind when he said, "His throne was fiery flames, and the wheels thereof burning fire. A fiery and consuming stream issued from his face." [130] With what surpassing excellence of glory and with what a gleaming company of the heavenly assembly He will appear, all glorious and awe-inspiring, the same prophet states in these further words: "Thousands of thousands ministered unto him, and ten thousand times ten thousand stood before him." [131]

16. And so, when both the cities shall have been presented before the throne of His majesty — the one set at the right hand (that is, the better part), the other at the left — the cause of each shall be decided by a most righteous judgment. When the judge shall have so great and so living a power of reading the consciences which

---

[123] John 5. 22.   [124] Phil. 2. 10.   [125] Acts 10. 42.
[126] Mal. 3. 2 *et seq.*   [127] *Cf.* Num. 18. 20 *et seq.*; Deut. 10. 9.
[128] *Cf.* Job 41. 25.   [129] Luke 21. 26.   [130] Dan 7. 9 *et seq.*   [131] Verse 10.

accuse and defend themselves, there will be no difficulty in reaching a decision. Hence Daniel, in the book of his vision, says, "the judgment sat, and the books were opened." [132] John speaks more clearly in his Apocalypse, "I saw a great white throne, and him that sat upon it, at whose appearance the heaven and the earth fled away; and no place was found by them. And I saw the dead, the great and the small, standing in sight of the throne; and books were opened: and another book was opened, which is the book of life: and the dead were judged according to their works." [133] What are these books which Daniel and John mentioned? What is that other book which John added, which he called also the book of life? Can it be that God, after the manner of men, wrote down the deeds of every man lest they should escape His memory, and that in accordance with this record He will judge each man? Does He not, since He is the Creator, know the conscience of each man and, since He is unchangeable, find it impossible to forget, and will He not render a decision as a judge true and penetrating from all eternity? The books, then, are books of men's consciences which condemn themselves to life or to death. The other book, which is called the book of life, is the foreknowledge of the Creator, Who from all eternity foresaw those that must be justly condemned and predestined those who were mercifully to be called and justified. The Psalmist prays that the wicked may be blotted out of this book when he says, "Let them be blotted out of the book of the living and not be written with the righteous." [134]

17. But what is the meaning of the words, "The judgment sat"? This question we must ask, because we are accustomed to say that one sits for judgment or in judgment, but not that judgment sits. The Psalmist also says, "For there sat thrones in judgment." [135] Do thrones sit? What are those thrones? What is that judgment? Let us ask, let us seek, let us knock; that we may find, that we may receive, that we may deserve to be admitted. Only *living* thrones can sit, only a *living* judgment can sit. There are then some thrones, *living* thrones, on which God sits. There is a judgment, and a *living* judgment, in which He distributes His decisions. This figure is frequently found in Holy Scripture. So even as in the writings of men "the painted Parthenopaeus" is spoken of by metonymy in-

---

[132] Dan. 7. 10.   [133] Rev. 20. 11 *et seq.*
[134] Ps. 69. 28.
[135] Ps. 122. 5. The text reads: *Quia illic sederunt sedes.*

stead of "the painted shield of Parthenopaeus," [136] so by the same figure is "the throne" instead of Him who sits upon it, "the judging." And yet by another interpretation they may here be called the judgment or thrones not only because they judge but also because God sits (that is, abides) upon them.[137] "Thou sittest," said the prophet, "in the throne judging righteousness." [138] Are we to suppose that this was said only concerning angels? Does it not refer also to the saints, who shall sit with Him, shall judge with Him, among whom He Himself shall sit and judge? For the saints do sit in judgment with Him even as He Himself promises them in the Gospel.[139] He Himself sits among the saints in judgment, guiding their minds by dwelling in them, lest by any confusion they may waver, filling them with life-giving power lest, through any frowardness, they swerve from the path of rectitude — even as it is written, "The soul of the righteous is the seat of wisdom." [140] The judgment therefore sitteth, the thrones sit, because the holy Apostles (that sacred council) and their imitators, in whom God dwells, in coming to judgment play the part not of those who must be judged but of those who judge.

Four groups will be there — two of the good, two of the bad. Of the good one will be judging, the other to be judged; of the bad likewise one will be awaiting judgment, the other will have been judged already. Those that are to judge consist of the perfect, who have followed Christ in renouncing their own wishes and powers; of them it has been said, "Ye also shall sit upon twelve thrones, judging the twelve tribes of Israel." [141] The company of those that are to be judged consists of men not so perfect but yet just, who, lawfully holding their own possessions, have by deeds of mercy earned the right to be placed at His right hand, and, after first being judged and examined, to hear His kindly words, "I was hungry, and ye gave me to eat," and "Come, ye blessed of my Father, inherit the kingdom" which has been "prepared for you from the foundation of the world." [142] Those that are to be judged and to be condemned consist of the bad, who through the sin of

---

[136] Statius, *Thebais* 4. 267 *et seq.*

[137] So Augustine, *Enarrationes in psalmos*, 121.

[138] Ps. 9. 4.   [139] Matt. 19. 28 and Luke 22. 30.

[140] *Cf.* Prov. 14. 33 and Wisd. of Sol. 1. 4.

[141] Matt. 19. 28. *Cf.*, for the passage, Hashagen, *Otto von Freising* 65, and above, II. 34.

[142] The same words are to be found in Augustine, *In Iohannis evangelium*,

avarice claimed for themselves the transitory goods bestowed by the Creator upon the human race for the common use of all, and withheld their compassion from the need of the poor. To them the saying applies "I was hungry, and ye did not give me to eat," and "Depart from me, ye cursed, into the eternal fire," and so forth.[143] Those who have already been judged and are to be condemned consist of the bad who, persisting in the obstinacy of unbelief, have not come "to the knowledge of the truth" and to the true worship of the true God, which the Greeks call *eusebia* and we call piety. To them the saying applies, "He that believeth not hath been judged already."[144] The Psalmist said of them, "Therefore the wicked do not stand in the judgment nor sinners in the congregation of the righteous."[145] For he did not say sinners do not stand. When he had said that the wicked (that is, unbelievers) were not to stand in the judgment to be placed on trial, he added concerning them, "Nor sinners in the congregation of the righteous," as though he meant, "They shall indeed stand in the judgment but not to fellowship with the just." Hence it appears that not only the avaricious but also whatsoever other guilty persons have died in their sins, though they bore the name of the Christian religion, belong to the company of those who are to be judged only to be condemned. I could never believe that any are more justly to be tried and condemned for heartlessness than those who, in their carelessness about their own lives, have not troubled themselves to have compassion upon, to aid, I will not say their neighbors but their own souls. For there is truth in the saying, "He that is unkind to himself, to whom is he kind?" and in that saying of the wise man: "Please God by showing mercy to thine own soul."

18. Next we must consider where the assizes of that last judgment are to be held. Some, in accordance with the prophecy which says, "In the valley of Jehoshaphat" will I judge them (which they interpret literally), think that the judgment will take place not far from the Holy City in the valley of Jehoshaphat, that the Lord, when he comes to judge, may come to the place in which he was judged. Hence certain simple-minded persons, on visiting the Lord's sepulcher in that valley for the purpose of prayer, set up

c. 3, *Tractactus* 14. 8. The quotation differs somewhat from the text of the Vulgate.

[143] Matt. 25. 42 and 41.   [144] John 3. 18.

[145] Ps. 1. 5. For "do not stand" the Latin has *non resurgunt*.

stones or some other mark as though they were selecting places for themselves against that hour.[146] This pious error, to use the words of Jerome,[147] since it arises from the devotion and the simplicity of their faith, we do not condemn nor yet do we give it the approval of our judgment. Others, interpreting the passage as an allegory — inasmuch as the Hebrew word Jehoshaphat signifies, in Latin, *judgment* — declare that the place in which the assizes may be held, be it where it may, is Jehoshaphat, that is, "Judgment." But others, on account of the words of the Apostle which were quoted above [148] (because, after he said that the saints must be caught up into the air to meet the Lord, he added, "and so shall we ever be with the Lord,") are of the opinion that the judgment will take place in the air. But to me the better view seems to be held by those who say that it will be held on earth. For it is more reasonable that bodies that were made of earth and that, because they were evil, were not changed to incorruption, should be placed on the earth for judgment than that they should be carried aloft to a rarer element with that weight by reason of which they ought rather to be borne downward. Nor is the testimony of the Apostle at variance with this view when he says that the saints, from the time that they meet Christ in the air, shall always be with Him, since they may also return with Him to the earth, to whatsoever place He appoints, without the burden of heaviness, and afterwards, when the wicked has been removed that he may not behold the majesty of God, may enter into the joy of their Lord, there to remain ever with Him.

19. It is needless to say how swiftly this judgment will be accomplished when all subterfuges and all sophistry, such as we are accustomed to endure in court trials in this world, shall be swept away by the clear perception of the judge and the keen insight of the searcher of reins and of hearts. In this world of ours where, in accordance with court procedure, in the case of an accused person the prosecutor brings suit, the advocate makes a defense, the witness endeavors to convince, the judge, since he is ignorant of the hearts of men, because he is but mortal, is often deceived and frequently a criminal who ought to be condemned is acquitted. Because this cannot happen in the court where each man's own conscience accuses

---

[146] Otto probably added this sentence from his own observation in the Holy Land.

[147] The words *pio . . . errore* are found in Jerome, but in another connection altogether.   [148] VIII. 13.

or defends him, we must believe that the judgment in that court is consummated with a swiftness beyond belief.

20. It remains to inquire concerning the end of both cities, the end which follows the resurrection and the judgment. As has been said, after the cause of each shall have been scrutinized in the judgment, the one will be crowned in accordance with its deserts and the other will be condemned to everlasting punishments, along with the devil, its head, and Antichrist, its prince and deceiver. John, forseeing this, says in the Apocalypse, "And the devil that deceived them was cast into the furnace of fire and brimstone, where are also the beast and the false prophet; and they shall be tormented day and night for ever and ever." [149] He set down three personages — the devil, the beast and the false prophet. The devil he indicated under his own name; by the beast he meant Babylon or the world;[150] and by the false prophet he meant Antichrist. These three, he said, "are to be cast into the furnace of fire and brimstone to be tormented day and night for ever and ever." By the fire and the brimstone he indicated the dreadful nature of the burning, by the furnace the horror of the place, by the words "day and night" and "for ever and ever" the unending persistence of the punishments. There will be therefore in that place fire without limit, a spot without cooling, continuous night without the light of day, unbroken misery of punishment without end. In speaking elsewhere of the condemnation of that city which he here calls the beast, he says, "One strong angel took up a stone as it were a great millstone and cast it into the sea, saying, 'Thus with a mighty fall shall Babylon, the great city, be cast down, and shall be found no more at all'." [151] Such language is called by the Greeks figurative — language, I mean, in which Holy Scripture, in speaking of an invisible matter (a spiritual matter), employing a simile uses material and visible symbols. So for example when we wish to indicate the swiftness of angels we describe them as having wings.[152] We need not believe that the angel cast a real stone into the sea. We should believe rather that by the aforesaid mode of speech the author made known the suddenness and the speed of damnation of the city, even as we read in the Psalm, "The remembrance of them has perished with

149 Rev. 20. 10 *et seq.*

150 So Augustine 20. 9 and 14; but Otto himself gives a different interpretation above, VIII. 3.

151 Rev. 18. 21.   152 Pseudo-Dionysius, *De coelesti hierarchia, c.* 15.

a crash." [153] Hence in the Apocalypse the destruction of the afore-said city is more fully described when it is said, "Fallen, fallen, is Babylon the great, and its habitation is become a habitation of demons, and a prison of every unclean spirit, and a prison of every unclean and hateful bird. For of the wrath of her fornication all the nations have drunk; and the kings of the earth committed fornication with her." [154]

Some hold that the Apocalypse of John is akin to the visions of the prophets of old, particularly Daniel and Ezekiel, and that the earlier prophecies were necessarily explained by it. In the final vision he describes — the vision of the temple and of Jerusalem — he is like Ezekiel; in that of the last judgment and of the kingdom of Christ he is like Daniel. Thus he makes it clear that Ezekiel spoke not concerning an earthly Jerusalem or temple, as the Jews perversely think he spoke,[155] but of a heavenly, and that Daniel likewise prophesied not, as the Jews believe, concerning a judgment of the Gentiles and an earthly kingdom of the Messiah, but of the true heavenly and eternal judgment and Kingdom of Christ. So also, inasmuch as many of the prophets uttered many things against Babylon, John, to keep us from imagining that they spoke only of that famous city which once oppressed the nations with its unjust dominion and so was destroyed, receiving the just reward of its iniquity — John, I say, declaring that under the figure of Babylon he had reference to the whole extent of the wicked city, indicates the final destruction of that city when he says, "Fallen, fallen is Babylon." This resembles the prophesies of Isaiah and Jeremiah, agreeing in its first part with Israel, at the end with Jeremiah. For in Isaiah we read, "Fallen, fallen is Babylon; and all the graven images of her gods are broken unto the ground," [156] and elsewhere more fully, "Babylon, the glory of kingdoms, renowned for the Chaldeans' pride, shall be as when the Lord overthrew Sodom and Gomorrah. It shall never be inhabited and shall be confounded from generation to generation : neither shall the Arabian pitch tent there, neither shall shepherds rest there, but wild beasts shall rest there ; and their houses shall be full of serpents, and ostriches shall dwell there, and wild goats shall dance there, and screech-owls shall cry in her castles, and strange birds in the pleasant palaces." [157] In

---

[153] Ps. 9. 6. But the American Revision reads, "The very remembrance of them is perished."   [154] Rev. 18. 2 et seq.
[155] See below, VIII. 26.   [156] Isa. 21. 9.   [157] 13. 19 et seq.

Jeremiah we read as follows, "Babylon hath been a golden cup in Jehovah's hand, that made all the earth drunken: all the nations have drunk of her wine, and therefore are mad. Babylon is suddenly fallen and destroyed," and so forth.[158]

First, let us see how these statements can literally apply to that Babylon which, as we have related in our history,[159] was destroyed by Cyrus. Let us make an assumption that is denied by many natives of the East:[160] that it was so utterly destroyed that it shall be uninhabited for ever, from generation to generation, that wild beasts shall rest there, that its houses shall be full of serpents and ostriches, that there shall be in its palaces of pleasure strange birds and the other monsters which are set down in the words of Isaiah. Even so, it was not destroyed as thoroughly as Sodom and Gomorrah were destroyed, was it? For we nowhere read that it was consumed by fire from heaven; we read, rather, that it was captured by the hand of man and fell in ruins, and was destroyed by the lapse of time. It follows that, even though certain parts of the prophecy were fulfilled to the letter, the remainder may be believed to be more completely and truly brought to consummation in a figurative sense. It might indeed be literally true that this city, previously "the glory of kingdoms," subdued the neighboring nations and kingdoms after making them drunken as with wine, and mad; and that afterwards she herself also, as if drunken, fell and was broken, becoming a lurking-place of monsters, not the habitation of men. But inasmuch as many things are true both in this wise as figures and literally — as, for example, it was true in fact that Abraham had two sons and it was none the less true that these sons are, figuratively, the two covenants — so we shall briefly indicate how what was said of Babylon applies to the world. "Fallen, fallen," says John, "is Babylon the great."[161] And likewise Isaiah says, "Fallen, fallen is Babylon; and all the graven images of her gods are broken unto the ground." And again, "Babylon, the glory of kingdoms, shall be as when the Lord overthrew Sodom and Gomorrah. It shall never be inhabited, and shall be confounded from generation even to generation." The city of wicked men which, flourishing here with temporal glory amid the pomp of demons was in those men's own eyes, so to say, glorious for the pride of the Chaldeans, will not only fall in ruins, having been

---

[158] Jer. 51. 7 *et seq.*   [159] II. 11.   [160] See above, VII. 3.
[161] Rev. 18. 2.

dragged down from its glory to the infernal regions but, overwhelmed by fire and brimstone as Sodom was, will never more return to its old-time delights — the delights it so sorely misses —
as to an ancient habitation, but will burn forever without hope of
restoration. What Isaiah says presently, "The Arabian shall not
pitch tent there, neither shall shepherds rest there, but wild beasts
shall rest there," and so forth, or according to John, "demons, unclean spirits, unclean birds" [162] (with the rest there) appears to
mean this, that by the Arabs and shepherds shall be understood
the elect, who nourish themselves and their neighbors well, who
inhabit this present world not as an abiding city but as a tent or
a tabernacle, and that by the beasts, the wild goats, the serpents,
the ostriches, the strange birds, the screech-owls, the unclean birds
we shall understand that manifold, diverse, foul company of unclean spirits. Therefore, let that false city justly hear that the
Arabian shall not pitch tent there, neither shall shepherds rest
there, but that wild beasts shall rest there and so forth, because
from the time when it is condemned to eternal punishment, together with the devil, its head, it is separated from the elect, whom
it previously oppressed, as the chaff presses about the wheat, not
only by a difference in spirit but also by an interval of space. For
by the words, "Fallen, fallen is Babylon, and all the graven images
of her gods are broken unto the ground," it is indicated that we
manufacture for ourselves as many graven images, so to speak, as
there are temporal things which we inordinately love and set before God. And so, when Babylon falls the graven images also are
swept to the ground, while in the passing of the world each is
snatched away for punishment, to be chastised the more severely
as he has the more wantonly followed his own desires, holding God
in contempt.

Therefore we may see in a figure how according to Jeremiah, and
likewise according to John, Babylon, a golden cup in Jehovah's
hand that makes mad and drunken with the wrath of her fornication all the earth and all the kings that commit fornication with
her, is herself to be finally dashed to pieces and destroyed. Babylon has her gold, she has her wisdom, whereby she allures all the
simple and the foolish with shrewd casuistries and clever sophistical
arguments, as though by displaying a cup. When they have been
lured on by false promises she entices them to drink and, when they

[162] Rev. 18. 2.

have been enticed, she leads them to the brink of the precipice in their drunkenness; and as you read in the Book of Wisdom [163] lures them — not only by her clamorousness but also by her harlot's attire and her bearing — to her unlawful embraces, as to fornication, and casts them down to destruction. For there is a spiritual fornication, whereby every soul that departs from the love of its Creator and embraces the various delusions wrought by demons plays the harlot, departing from his God, even as it is written, "Thou hast destroyed all them that play the harlot, departing from thee." [164] Because therefore the world, by vain wisdom, not only allures those who love her but also, after they have wallowed in various desires, subjects them in mad lust to as many fornications, as it were, of unclean spirits, it is appropriately said by these two chief prophets that Babylon by her golden cup makes drunken with the wrath of her fornication all the earth, all the kings and all the nations that commit fornication with her.

But we must see how that golden cup that maddens all the earth is said to be in Jehovah's hand. Surely it cannot be that it is by His will and consent that the world is so shaken, so deluded, and finally cast down to destruction with those who love the world. But although it does not take place of His good pleasure, yet we believe that it does not occur without the permission of His power, for, when He forms the light, the good is in such wise pleasing to Him that, unless He himself created the darkness, evil could not exist. Babylon is therefore a golden cup in Jehovah's hand because it is not only by His permission, as I have said, that it is overthrown, but it is by His gift also that it has the gold. Yet in its pride it shamefully abuses it, in accordance with the saying of the prophet, "I gave them silver and gold, but they sacrificed with it unto the Baalim." [165] Babylon, therefore, which had maddened all nations with her golden cup, will finally fall and be destroyed, because the world will find in the last judgment no advantage before the stern and righteous judge in its own power or in its wisdom, and the mighty, being delivered over to mighty torments, will be sent "into the eternal fire which is prepared for the devil and his angels." [166] Let us set that time before our eyes, as though it were at this very moment, and let us, viewing the whole series of emperors or kings of that city, say with Wisdom in the name of them

[163] Rather in Prov. 7. 10. [164] Ps. 73. 27.
[165] Hos. 2. 8 and 11. 2. [166] Matt. 25. 41.

all, "What did our arrogancy profit us? or what good have riches and vaunting brought us? Those things all passed away as a shadow, and as a message that runneth by — and as a ship passing through the billowy water, whereof, when it is gone by, there is no trace to be found, neither pathway of its keel in the billows; or as when a bird flieth through the air, no token of her passage is found," [167] and so forth, "So we also, as soon as we were born, ceased to be, and of virtue we had no sign to show, but in our wickedness we were utterly consumed." [168] I think enough has been said of the end of that city which, according to the blessed Job,[169] spending its days in prosperity and then in a moment going down to Sheol, will obtain everlasting death as the wages of its works. It remains for us to speak of the nature of its punishments.

21. So then, in accordance with the nature of its works and its desire for various pleasures, the measure of its punishments also is enlarged, it is believed, in agreement with that passage of the Apocalypse, "How much soever she glorified herself, and was luxurious, so much give her of torment and of mourning," [170] and in the book of Wisdom, "In that wherein a man sinneth, he is also punished." [171] Hence that rich man in the Gospel [172] who, while faring sumptuously, had sinned more with his tongue, kept begging that it might be cooled by a drop of water, thereby showing clearly that his tongue burned more in Hell than his other members. If any one wishes to know how various people are differently affected by one and the same fire, he will find this subject more fully discussed in Augustine's *City of God*.[173] There it is proved that the possibility of the damned living eternally in fire not only can be changed by the power of the omnipotent God into a reality but is not at variance with reason, as is shown by the example of certain animals which, in this present world, live in fire.

Some, on the authority of the verse, "Their worm shall not die, neither shall their fire be quenched," [174] believe that the wicked are not only burned in Hell by a material fire but are furthermore tormented by a worm. Others, interpreting the worm as the sting of conscience, likewise posit a twofold torture — the one spiritual and within, the other material and without. Others again, understanding both tortures in a spiritual sense, believe that the damned are

---

[167] Wisd. of Sol. 5. 8-11.   [168] *Ibid.* 5. 13.   [169] Job 21. 13.
[170] Rev. 18. 7.   [171] Wisd. of Sol. 11. 16.   [172] Luke 16. 24.
[173] 21. 1 *et seq.*   [174] Isa. 66. 24.

burned with fire in like manner as they are consumed by the worm. They adduce as their authority that well-known passage of Augustine, "The flame is of like nature as the tongue." [175] But the more reasonable belief seems to be the view of those who say that the body is tormented by real flame, the soul by conscience. Since therefore eternal death is to consume the conscience with respect to an ill-spent life, and unfailing fire is to burn without end both body and soul, the prophet well says, "Their worm shall not die, neither shall their fire be quenched."

There are even those who say that they are speedily hurried from unquenchable fire to intolerable cold, according to the statement of the book of Job, "They shall pass from the heat of flames to the waters of snows." [176] This too is what the Lord appears to mean in the Gospel when he says, "There shall be weeping and gnashing of teeth." [177] For weeping is wont to result from heat, gnashing of teeth from cold.[178] Nor are there lacking those who add an offensive smell to these evils, to heighten the misery, according to the word of the prophet, "And instead of a sweet smell there shall be noisesomeness." [179] Some add six other kinds of punishments to these three [180] and, to secure correspondence with the nine orders of the heavenly hierarchy, they assume as many divisions of the infernal house of correction for those who must be punished. With respect to all these matters we must not investigate too curiously, but rather be on our guard lest we experience them, since this alone is clear — that that most wretched and unhappy state will surpass the misery of all things external or internal, as much by the magnitude of the torments as by the unwearied persistence of that eternal death which itself avoids death.

22. The question is often raised, by what justice is eternal punishment the due reward for those who have sinned temporally? The question is asked because the Lord says, "With what measure ye mete it shall be measured to you again." [181] Hence some, led astray by a mistaken piety, denied that sinners are punished forever, and in proof of their false belief adduced the following words of the

[175] 21. 10.   [176] Job 24. 19, which Otto misquotes.

[177] Matt. 8. 12; 13. 42; 22. 13.

[178] Cf. Honorius Augustodunensis, *Elucidarium* 3. 4.

[179] Isa. 3. 24.

[180] Honorius Augustodunensis, in *Elucidarium* 3. 4, enumerates these nine forms of punishment.

[181] Luke 6. 38. Cf. Augustine 21. 11 et seq.

writer of Psalms,[182] "Shall God forget to be gracious or shall he
in his anger shut up his tender mercies?" and the verse, "How
great is the abundance of thy goodness, which thou hast concealed
from them that fear thee, but hast wrought for them that hope in
thee."[183] They thought that this was to be understood as follows,
that God in this life conceals the richness of His goodness and His
abundant mercy to increase the fear of sinners, and by uttering
threats to insure their correction through fear, but that in the
life to come works by revealing His grace to them that hope. Others
said heretically that all human kind (and the race of demons as
well) are to be freed from punishments after a thousand years, not
properly understanding a passage of Isaiah, "They shall be thrust
back into prison, and after many days shall they be visited."[184]
We, however, who follow the standard of Catholic truth in accordance with the testimony of the Lord himself — wherein He says,
"These shall go to eternal punishment"[185] — believe that the penalties of the damned are eternal. For if it was merely to terrify
the wicked that He said the punishments are eternal, we must believe also that it was merely to please that He said that the glory of
the good is eternal. That such a view can by no means be maintained
no one who recognizes Him as the truth and the life can doubt.
Nor are the authorities which have been cited at variance with this
interpretation, since "the merciful and gracious Jehovah," so long
as "it is time to have pity," bestows upon sinners abundant opportunity of repentance by waiting long and patiently, and in His
anger — that is, in the judgment — does not withhold His compassion, punishing them perhaps less than they had deserved, or
sometimes granting them in their punishments the alleviation of
coolness. This moreover is what that statement of Isaiah seems to
mean, which declares that, after they have been thrust back into
prison they are to be visited; doubtless by this visitation he indicates
some kind of alleviation. But that other passage which they adduce,
"How great is the abundance of thy goodness!", demands a far
different interpretation. For God conceals[186] the abundance of His
goodness from those that fear Him, because fear, which is not a
constituent of love, servilely seeking God does not succeed in tasting

---

182 The text reads *psalmigraphi*. See Ps. 77. 9.

183 Ps. 31. 19. *Cf.* Augustine 21. 18.   184 Isa. 24. 22.   185 Matt. 25. 46.

186 The familiar Biblical expressions which occur in this sentence and the
next are taken from I John 4. 18; Eph. 3. 17; Rom. 12. 12; I Pet. 4. 8.

His sweetness, which those who "being rooted in love, rejoicing in hope, patient in tribulation" find in consequence of their merits. For hope which exists without antecedent merit, or at least without that love which "covereth a multitude of sins," is to be called not hope but presumption. But surely God conceals His goodness in this life from those also who have a holy fear. Upon those that hope in the hereafter and wait for it He bestows this hope by showing Himself openly to them face to face,[187] so that they that fear and they that hope are the same. What then is the meaning of the saying "With what measure ye mete,"[188] and so forth, if the punishments for those that sin temporally are eternal? This knotty point is more easily solved if we regard God as the scrutinizer not only of deeds but also of hearts. With the same measure, therefore, with which men have meted will it be measured to them again when He imposes eternal punishments upon those who die in the eternal desire to do evil, having lacked only the opportunity, not the will, to sin.

23. Another question too must be raised, whether those who have been doomed to such great torments truly repent of the sins they have committed, or would have the wish to sin again if they were free from punishments. We read in the book of Wisdom, "When they see it, they shall be troubled with terrible fear, and shall be amazed at the suddenness of unhoped for salvation. They shall say within themselves, repenting. . . ."[189] In the Gospel parable the rich man is represented as troubled concerning the safety of his brothers, when he says, "I pray thee, therefore, father, that thou wouldst send him to my father's house; for I have five brethren; that he may testify unto them, lest they also come into this place of torment."[190] For if with affectionate solicitude he desires them to be warned that they may not come into the place of torment, how much more must it be supposed that he wishes that he himself had guarded against such a fate?

But it must be observed that the term "repentance" is understood in various ways. Sometimes it is understood in the sense in which also it is described in the words, "Repentance is to grieve for what has been done, and not to do things to be grieved over," even as Paul exults that certain have repented, to whom he says, "I rejoice that ye were made sorry, not that ye were made sorry,

---

[187] I Cor. 13. 12.   [188] Luke 6. 38.
[189] Wisd. of Sol. 5. 2 *et seq.*   [190] Luke 16. 27 *et seq.*

but that ye were made sorry unto repentance.'' [191] Of this the Lord speaks in the Gospel, ''Repent ye: for the kingdom of heaven will draw near.'' [192] That repentance is real, is fruitful, whereby we not only obtain the remission of sins but also win the right to reach the Kingdom of Heaven. Repentance is also used in the sense of regret, such as that of robbers and all evildoers who have been caught in their misdeeds and have been condemned to punishments. For they are sorry, not that they have committed a crime but that they have been condemned to punishment for their sin, nor would they desire through hatred of evil to be free from sin; they wish rather, if it were possible, to be free from due punishment after committing a crime. We may well believe that the wicked are affected by such sorrow in Hell, since they are deeply disturbed and tormented not merely by the immediate horror of their own punishment but by envy of the safety and happiness of others. So that wise man says, ''When they see'' — doubtless ''the righteous standing in great boldness of peace'' — ''they shall be troubled with terrible fear and shall be amazed at the suddenness of un-hoped for salvation.'' And then at last, by reason of these two things — namely the consideration of their own damnation and of the salvation of others — ''they shall say within themselves repent-ing, and for distress of spirit shall they groan, 'These are they whom aforetime we had in derision and made a parable of reproach!' '' Hence it is clear that the wise man spoke not of the true and fruit-ful penitence but of the false and forced sorrow, or rather grief and indignation. Let us see furthermore if that rich man we have men-tioned was moved by true penitence: ''I pray therefore, father,'' he said, ''that thou wouldst send him to my father's house; for I have five brethren; that he may testify unto them, lest they also come into this place of torment.'' He does not say that he may testify unto them to shun evil, but that he may warn them to avoid torment; nor does he say that he may warn them to do good (if ever they undertake good) through love of virtue but through slavish fear of punishment. Further, if anyone were to say that this passage, as being a parable, is not to be understood literally, we need not labor violently to elucidate its meaning. So then the wicked feel sorrowful at being in torments, but not so much so as to be willing to give up their sins if they were permitted to return to their former life. If anyone is so contentious as to believe that

191 II Cor. 7. 9.   192 Matt. 4. 17.

they truly repent there but that their penitence is without avail, in accordance with the saying of the Apostle, "Behold now"— not *then* — "is the acceptable time; behold, now is the day of salvation," [193] we need not ever argue with him. And yet there are not lacking those who say that, as the good who have perfectly become one spirit with God in eternal glory are neither able nor willing to desire anything save that which is good, so also the wicked in their punishment, being as it were fully incorporated with their head, the devil, are so conformed to his obstinacy that they are thereafter neither willing nor able to desire anything save what is evil. According to their opinion, not only are they not truly repentant of their past life but would even desire, if it were possible, to continue in their sins.

24. Now that all this has been said I think we should discuss the question whether after the judgment there is to remain, besides the lower infernal regions, a place for less severe punishments. Some assert that there is in Hell a place of cleansing in which those who are to be saved are punished only by darkness or are heated in the fire of expiation, in accordance with the statement of the Patriarch, "I will go down to Sheol mourning," [194] and the saying of the Apostle, "But he himself shall be saved, yet so as through fire." [195] If no one shall be cleansed any more after the cases of individuals have been decided in the judgment, and eternal punishments have been meted out to them in accordance with the nature of their deserts, how shall that upper place of cleansing remain? [196] If it does not remain, what will become of little children, to say nothing of others, who are stained only by original sin? Surely we cannot believe that they too will be thrust back into the depths of the lowest Sheol! Some affirm that they, as also the fathers of old, are punished only by the darkness, because they are found guilty in nothing save that they have not attained to the grace of baptism and the knowledge of the true light, interpreting the statement of Augustine that they are to be afflicted by the mildest penalty as implying darkness only. [197] Others, interpreting the aforesaid words of Augustine more strictly, say that they are to be punished by a real penalty but one that is very mild. But if that upper place shall be reserved, not as before for cleansing but for the punish-

[193] II Cor. 6. 2.   [194] Gen. 37. 35.   [195] I Cor. 3. 15.
[196] *Cf.* Augustine 21. 13 *et seq.*
[197] *De peccatorum meritis et remissione* 1. 16 and 21.

ment of such persons or of persons less wicked, this view will not be at variance with the belief that after the judgment no place of cleansing remains, since by changing not the place but its function that which was before a place of cleansing would then become a place of punishment. Still, even if that place were to be utterly abolished and they were to be consigned to the general place of punishments, this view is not beyond belief since the omnipotent hand of God can either preserve them untouched in that terrible place of burning or can afflict them less, even as he once preserved three young men unhurt in a furnace of fire.[198] We see that even by one and the same heat of the sun all are not equally burned or affected. Yet we leave to God's judgment the definite decision of this matter, as we do not yet find the matter settled on sure authority.

25. We must also discover regarding that eternal fire how it lacks light, since it is the nature of real fire not only to burn but also to shine to give brilliant light.[199] If it gives light, how is there outer darkness in that place — darkness which may be touched ?[200] In this matter we must consider that God, the Creator of nature, made her subject to certain causes and bestowed on her certain powers. If for certain reasons He, as being God, sometimes removes them, we ought not to be surprised, inasmuch as that fire in the furnace of the Chaldeans also had power to consume the chains of the young men but did not have power to injure their bodies. Of old in the bramble bush which He wished to burn and yet not to be consumed, there was burning but it was not consumed, because the fire had its natural power to give light but not power to consume.[201] So on the other hand, the infernal fire will lack its power to give light and will have in all fulness power to burn. There will be, therefore, in that place the torture of fire without the alleviation of light; burning, not illuminating; afflicting, not refreshing; so that it will have every kind of wretchedness in greater measure than can, I will not merely say be told, but even be imagined, and will lack every delight whereby the wretched creatures may be relieved.

26. Finally, having by laborious argument made our way through the fate of the wicked (as though we were swimming through a sluggish sea), let us, relying on Christ's grace, come to the sweet and joyous end of His City. Now that Babylon, the

198 Dan. 3. 23 *et seq.*   199 *Cf.* Gregory, *Moralia* 9. 65 and 97.
200 Exod. 10. 21.   201 Exod. 3. 2.

city of the world, has been miserably brought to destruction let us hear how the Holy Jerusalem, the City of Christ, is to be glorified. When John in the Apocalypse had said of the former city that with its seducer, the devil, and its false prophet, Antichrist, it had been cast into the furnace "of fire and brimstone, where they shall be tormented day and night for ever and ever,"[202] after a moment he added, "And I saw the holy city, new Jerusalem, coming down out of heaven, made ready by God as a bride adorned for her husband. And I heard a great voice out of the throne saying, Behold, the tabernacle of God is with men, and he shall dwell with them," and so forth. The Jews believe that, at the coming of their Messiah, the earthly Jerusalem will be restored with great glory and that there, amid the greatest abundance of all things, they will abound in the delights of all earthly glory in company with Him who is to reign. They interpret literally that house of Ezekiel[203] on the mountain, and also the prophecy of Isaiah, "Arise, shine, Jerusalem; for thy light is come, and the glory of Jehovah is risen upon thee," and "Then shalt thou see and be radiant, and thy heart shall thrill and be enlarged; because the abundance of the sea shall be turned unto thee, the wealth of the nations shall come unto thee. The multitude of camels shall cover thee," and so forth.[204] Certain persons who bear the *name* of Christians, following the mistaken belief of the Jews, have supposed that the kingdom of Christ is to be on earth and that there, in the earthly Jerusalem, when the saints shall have reigned in delight with Him, after a thousand years Satan must be loosed and then finally cast down and the saints received into the heavenly kingdom.[205] The sons of Zebedee, when they were not yet "clothed with power from on high," were not far from this belief when they asked (through their mother's intervention) that they might sit, in the Kingdom of Christ, one on Christ's right hand, the other on His left. John therefore, to overthrow all these mistaken views, first strove to narrate the condemnation of the wicked city and its descent into the final fire; and afterwards, when heaven and earth had been made new, he added — speaking of the glory of the

---

[202] Rev. 20. 9 *et seq.*, and 21. 2-3. *Cf.* above, VIII. 20 (beginning).

[203] Ezek. 43. 12.   [204] Isa. 60. 1; also 5-6.

[205] Rev. 20. 7. The other Biblical phrases used in this paragraph are from Luke 24. 49; Rev. 21. 2; Matt. 23. 37; Ps. 122. 3; Gal. 4. 26; Exod. 3. 14; I John 3. 2.

heavenly, not the earthly Jerusalem — "And I saw the holy city, new Jerusalem, coming down out of heaven." How could he call that city holy which he had previously called Babylon, which slew the prophets and stoned those who had been sent to her? How could he call that city new which still continues under the old law? How, finally, could he claim that the city which was ever of the earth, earthy, descends out of heaven? Hence the Apostle, well comparing that city which is on earth to Hagar, declares that she is in bondage with her children, bearing witness, however, that the Jerusalem which is above is our mother and is free. The Psalmist also, when he bore witness that he rejoiced over the fact that he was to go into the house of the Lord and within the gates of Jerusalem, said, "Jerusalem which is builded as a city." In saying, not that it is builded *a* city but builded *as* a city,[206] he declared that it must be builded not in our fashion nor of our stones but by divine power and out of living stones. If anyone is loath to believe let him hear what follows, "whose participation is in him, the abiding."[207] How does abiding belong to a city that is destined to fall and not destined to endure? The participation therefore of that city which is *our* mother and is above is in Him who said, "I am that I am," and "He that is hath sent me to you," in Him, I say, who abides forever — that is, in His own identity, eternally and unchangeably, ever in one and the same way. And since the city will then be truly and perfectly a partaker in His eternity and in His identity, when it shall see Him as He is, it is well said, "whose participation is in him, the abiding."

Accordingly let us, setting aside their mistake, examine further the words of the Apostle. "I saw," he says, "the holy city, new Jerusalem, coming down out of heaven"[208] — a statement mystical and profound, and utterly passing our comprehension. For why does he say that the Holy City, that is firmly established to be immutable — new, as having been freed from all corruption and mortal taint and so renewed — came down out of heaven? It cannot be that the reward which was promised us in heaven is to be on earth. For if, as Augustine says,[209] the reward of the saints is not laid up for them in these visible heavens, how much more surely

---

[206] On what follows, Hofmeister calls attention to Augustine, *Enarrationes in psalmos* 121, who cites (among other passages) I Pet. 2. 5 and Exod. 3. 14.

[207] The text reads *cuius participatio eius in id ipsum.*

[208] Rev. 21. 2. [209] *Cf.* Augustine, *l.c.*, 32.6.

must it not be placed lower than the heavens? What is the meaning then of the words "I saw the holy city, new Jerusalem, coming down out of heaven"? I, for my part, admit that I do not fully understand what he saw, although with due veneration I cherish his vision as a holy mystery, unless, perhaps, he meant by heaven the super-excellent nature of divinity itself, of which the Psalmist says, "His going forth is from the highest heaven," [210] so that the meaning would seem to be that the glory of that City, which was established from all eternity in its predestination by God alone and was known to Him only, shall then, and only then, finally descend to the full knowledge of the saints when "God shall be all in all and shall be seen even as he is." [211] For that in this life that super-inestimable blessedness cannot be fully comprehended even by the elect is proved by that well-known testimony of Prophet and Apostle: "Eye hath not seen and ear hath not heard, neither hath it entered into the heart of man, what things God hath prepared for them that love him." [212] The City, therefore, is said to come down out of heaven because, by a mysterious ordering of the divine plan, that incomparable crown is to come to the notice of the elect not only by knowledge but also by experience. "Made ready by God as a bride adorned for her husband." The prophet, foreseeing in the spirit this adornment and filled with boundless joy, said, "With rejoicing will I rejoice in Jehovah, and my soul shall be joyful in my God," [213] and, setting forth the reason for his gladness, said, "For he hath clothed me with the garments of salvation, and hath covered me with a robe of righteousness, as a bridegroom decketh himself with a garland, and as a bride adorneth herself with her jewels." The adornment of the City, therefore, will consist of a crown and jewels — a crown that fadeth not away, adorning her with the everlasting glory of immortality and incorruption, and jewels of ineffable purity of heart, whereby also God is seen beautifying her with virtue. In a word, that the Holy City is not only conducted, by her Creator, with power to her heavenly abode — as a creature eternally foreknown — but is also lovingly established in the chamber of His kingdom as a bride in her beauty, is well expressed in the statement that she descends out of heaven,

---

[210] Ps. 19. 6.

[211] I Cor. 15. 28. There are also, within the next few sentences, scriptural phrases and expressions from I John 3. 2; Rev. 21. 2.

[212] Isa. 64. 4 and I Cor. 2. 9.   [213] Isa. 61. 10.

made ready by God as a bride adorned. For through the marvelous and unspeakable abundance of his goodness the creation becomes a bride, when He more wonderfully fashions anew her whom He had wonderfully created out of nothing for His service [214] and welcomes her to the joyful embrace of the heavenly marriage chamber.

"And I heard a great voice out of the throne saying." [215] Let us hear what that voice says — that sweet voice, that voice of gladness, sounding from on high, delightfully calling from the sublime abode of divinity: "Behold, the tabernacle of God is with men, and he shall dwell with them." What is that tabernacle? Is it, perhaps, to be thought of as one of those of which it is said, "How goodly are thy tabernacles, O Jacob, thy tents, O Israel"?[216] Or rather as one of those which the Psalmist longed for when he said with a deep sigh: "How amiable are thy tabernacles, O Lord of virtues; my soul longeth, yea, even fainteth for the courts of Jehovah"?[217] For the tabernacles of Jacob are tabernacles of those that struggle in the warfare of this present life, burdened with conflict and strife but, by reason of the crown, fair to look upon, always good but not always pleasant. There are also the tabernacles of God, the tabernacles of them that rule in the assembly of the heavenly country, where all fear is trampled under foot: tabernacles filled with peace, delightful, completely happy at having received the crown, not only always good but without an admixture of sadness, always glad and joyous without the weariness of toil. The former therefore are well called goodly, the latter amiable. For what is better than in the hope of a crown to wrestle with our vices and desires? What more amiable than, after the victory is won, to rejoice over the crown we have received? The tabernacles of Jacob, therefore, are goodly; the tabernacles of God, amiable; because from the toil of striving we come to the satisfaction of garnering the reward. But because in the heavenly assembly the various companies of holy angels form one city in the bond of love, the tabernacles which the Psalmist spoke of are here well called "the tabernacle." When the united armies of the saints form with the angels the single abiding place of a single city, it is well said that the tabernacle of God has been joined with men for an eternal dwelling. What follows surpasses by its sweetness beyond belief all that has been said

---

[214] II Macc. 7. 28.   [215] Rev. 21. 3.   [216] Num. 24. 5.

[217] Ps. 84. 1; but for "O Lord of virtues" we read (in the American revision) "O Jehovah of hosts."

before: "And he shall dwell with them." For if the appearance of the tabernacles delights, how much more shall the sight and abiding company of their inhabitant be delectable — the sight and the company of Him who made them! So then God shall dwell in them, filling them with perfect and true joy, that they may never waver, bestowing upon them the full knowledge of His appearance and "becoming all things to all men," [218] giving them perfect blessedness. Hence is added the beautiful statement, "And they shall be his people, and God himself shall be with them, and be their God." For in this life where "the earthly frame lieth heavy on a mind that is full of cares," [219] as often as we give way to anxieties and to cares so often do we, as it were, forget that God, whom we ought to have placed before all fleeting and transitory things, is our God. But in that City where the contemplation of the divine, in this way uniting all forever with itself [the divine], makes them so happy that, being perfectly filled through and through with internal and eternal joy, they ought not to go out thence any more, "they shall be his people, and God himself shall be with them and be their God." Indeed it is afterwards declared that they shall there be so exhilarated with the wine of eternal joy and gladness that they shall be no more affected by the misery of all their past life, when it is said, further, "And God shall wipe away every tear from the eyes of the saints, and now there shall be no mourning, nor crying, nor pain, any more: the first things are passed away." [220]

Next we must note what is elsewhere stated [221] that the City itself is made of pure gold, its foundation of every sort of precious stones, its twelve gates each of one pearl, its streets of pure gold, as it were translucent glass. How great and how delightful an abode do these things promise us in that heavenly City? If such things are beautiful and comely when they are interpreted literally, how much the more are they found to be joyous and delightful far beyond compare when they are spiritually interpreted! If gold is precious, how much more precious is that which is signified by gold! For wisdom "being compared with light" [222] "is found to be before it."

We have told, to the best of our ability, how after the wicked

---

[218] But, as Hofmeister points out, Paul is speaking of himself in the passage (I Cor. 9. 22) where this phrase occurs.

[219] For the quotation see Wisd. of Sol. 9. 15.

[220] Rev. 21. 4.   [221] Rev. 21. 18-21.   [222] Wisd. of Sol. 7. 29.

shall have been removed, that he may not behold the majesty of Jehovah,[223] then the City of Christ, the Holy Jerusalem, shall be glorified, though we have passed over many things which might be said of such great gladness, because we are hastening on to those things which remain still to be set forth.

27. The question may be raised, what sort of bodies the saints, after the resurrection, are to have in that City. The Apostle says, "It is sown a natural body, it shall rise again a spiritual body,"[224] and again, "Flesh and blood shall not inherit the kingdom of God." Hence some [225] have thought that after the resurrection the bodies of the saints are transformed into spiritual substance. Others, although they said that the saints would be bodies, not spirits, yet believed that those bodies must be reduced to such fineness that they could neither be handled nor imagined. But inasmuch as we believe that our actual bodies shall rise in the actual substance of the flesh, after the likeness of our Lord, who said [226] to his disciples after the resurrection, "Handle me, and see; for a spirit hath not flesh and bones, as ye behold me having," let us see how the aforesaid words of the Apostle are to be understood. "It is sown," he says, "a natural body; it shall rise again a spiritual body." Let us consider in the light of what follows what he meant by "natural," what he meant by "spiritual." When he had said, "It is sown a natural body, it shall rise again a spiritual body," he added, "If there is a natural body, there is also a spiritual body. So also it is written, the first man Adam became a living soul. The last Adam became a life-giving spirit. Howbeit that is not first which is spiritual, but that which is natural; then that which is spiritual. The first man is of the earth, earthy: the second man is of heaven, heavenly. As is the earthy, such are they also that are earthy; and as is the heavenly, such are they also that are heavenly." Did he then in these words deny that the second man, Christ Jesus (whom he called spiritual and heavenly), has actual flesh? In calling Him spiritual or heavenly he did not mean that He is without flesh, but declared that He was in life and teaching hostile to the deeds of the flesh, by way of distinction from the first man who

---

[223] *Cf.* Isa. 26. 10 and see VIII. 18 (end) above.

[224] I Cor. 15. 44 and 50.

[225] Augustine 13. 20 and 22 *et seq.* refutes them, while in Otto's time Honorius Augustodunensis appears to have defended this belief; *cf.* I. A. Endres, *Honorius Augustudunensis,* Kempten and Munich, 1906, pp. 121 *et seq.*   [226] Luke 24. 39.

followed the will of the flesh and became a transgressor against the command of God. Hence he also says, "The first man is of the earth, earthy; the second man is of heaven, heavenly," as though he meant, "The first man destroyed us by earthy deeds, but the second restored us by a heavenly life." And so he adds, "Therefore as we have borne the image of the earthy, we shall also bear the image of the heavenly," [227] and "Now this I say, brethren, that flesh and blood cannot inherit the kingdom of God." The body, therefore, which is sown a natural body, shall rise again a spiritual body because its defective substance is taken away, its true nature left. For that is the meaning of what he then adds, "It is sown in corruption, it shall be raised in incorruption." For — being born through passion into this mortal life — we are sown as natural bodies, but being born again through grace to that immortal life we rise as spiritual bodies. There is perfect harmony between this view and the fact that, when he had said that flesh and blood shall not inherit the Kingdom of God, he added, to prevent anyone from thinking that this had been said regarding the substance of the flesh, "neither shall corruption inherit incorruption." The saints therefore shall have in that City real bodies of the actual substance of flesh, but cleansed of all corruption, not inferior to the spirits in the dignity of purity and the refinement of activity, and so harmoniously united with their spirits that they desire to be nowhere where they cannot be and are in no place they would not be. For there can be no lack of harmony in those whom the divine spirit, supporting them from within, binds together in the perfect harmony of true peace. Wherefore we ought not to ask *where* they are, since judging by the example of our Lord, who after the resurrection entered though the doors were shut, we may be sure that they have such boundless power of movement that, whether they desire to be in heaven or to be on earth, being now made new they have it in their power to be in either place now that their wills are not at variance with their ability nor their ability at variance with their wills.

28. We should now inquire, I think, whether they have in that blessed country memory or knowledge of their past lives. Isaiah, that prince of prophets, says, "They shall not remember the former things, nor shall they come into their minds." [228] But what is it

[227] I Cor. 15. 42, and afterwards verse 50.

[228] Isa. 65. 17. The quotation here is more in accord with Augustine 20. 21 and 22. 3 than with the Vulgate.

that he says elsewhere, "They shall go forth, and look upon the
bodies of the dead that have transgressed against me"?[229] Surely
it is not to be believed that they leave the abodes of blessedness and
go out to behold the torments of the wicked on the spot? Not so!
If then it is because they have knowledge that they do not depart
from the enjoyment of eternal good and go forth, how shall they
not remember the former things? Or are they to know the punishment of others but to give over to oblivion their own past miseries,
by reason of which they ought to be grateful to their Saviour? In
this matter you must know that there are two kinds of knowledge,
two kinds of forgetting. The sick man knows weakness in one way,
by experience, the doctor in another way, by his knowledge of his
art. So also we forget in one way those things which we have known
through experiment, in another way those which we comprehend
merely by skill in an art, but without having actually experienced
them. Accordingly, as the saints will have full memory of all
things which can cause delight, so nothing which would cause them
pain will touch their consciousness, that they may have full cause
to express their gratitude to their Redeemer, and may remember
nothing by reason of which they may grieve, sick at heart, at the
recollection of former things but, abounding in all sorts of delights
and rejoicing perfectly in "the peace of God which passeth all
understanding,"[230] they may on the one hand be assailed by no
tempter from without and, on the other, they may be affected by
no suffering within through the recollection of sad experiences.
Therefore, for the greater fulness of their happiness, as they recall
the abundant goodness of their Redeemer, they shall know both
their own deeds and the torments of the wicked among the dead —
though not as having experienced them — to the end that they may
not only rejoice at their own happy state but also may be grateful
to their God, who mercifully separated from the destruction of the
wicked those who were made from the selfsame lump.[231] They shall
know, I say, as has been stated, Him who fully knows both their
own deeds and the deeds of others — not through the misery of
experience but through the superabundant glory of internal and
eternal wisdom.

29. After this cursory discussion let us inquire how that heavenly hierarchy is arranged. It cannot be that they all in like manner
enjoy equally that eternal blessedness, in accordance with the

---

[229] Isa. 66. 24.   [230] Phil. 4. 7.   [231] Cf. Rom. 9. 21.

parable [232] in which all, though they did not exert themselves equally in the Lord's vineyard, are said to have received equal pay for their work, as it were every man a shilling? If so, how shall we understand the testimony of the Lord Himself, wherein He says, "In my Father's house are many mansions," [233] and that saying of the Apostle, "There is one glory of the sun, and another glory of the moon," and "star differeth from star in glory: so also shall be the resurrection of the dead"? [234] It is true therefore that they receive each a shilling, and it is true that dwelling in different mansions one is more glorious than another because, while all shall indeed be received into the same blessedness, yet there shall be alloted to them various mansions there in accordance with the nature of their deserts. For the Lord also in saying that this variety of mansions exists (not in houses but in one house) pointed out that the blessedness would be one, but that there are differences in the enjoyment of that blessedness. We see this even in the present life, where in one Church we behold in the varying grades of honors one more glorious than another, one superior to another. That this has been arranged after the likeness of that heavenly assembly the Lord made clear in speaking to Moses, when He said, "See that thou make all things after their pattern, which hath been showed thee in the mount." [235] There are, therefore, in that house various mansions to be occupied by various saints as one is more glorious than another, and one is holier than another, because so much the more closely and, as it were, more directly shall each saint be lighted by the splendor of the divine radiance as he is in this life the more ardently and earnestly inflamed by love for Him through the faith which worketh through love. And even as when many together flock to one fountain, and taste its waters together, he that is thirstier drinks the more, so they that hasten to God, the fount of life, are the more abundantly satisfied with the fatness of His house, with the river of His pleasure, as they wait for Him the more zealously and eagerly in the greater ardor of their thirst. Therefore, in accordance with the diversity and the capacity of individuals, the blessed glory of the saints will be varied and yet will be one.

30. Next because that City, compacted of two walls, consists of angels and of men,[236] let us consider what the relation between them

---

[232] Matt. 20.   [233] John 14. 2.   [234] I Cor. 15. 41 *et seq.*
[235] Exod. 25. 40; and *cf.* Heb. 8. 5.
[236] *Cf.* Gregory, *Homilia in evang.* 34. 11, copied by Hugo of St. Victor, *Summa Sententiarum* 2. 5 (end). *Cf.* below, VIII. 31.

is, what its nature is. Dionysius [237] that chief of theologians posits three hierarchies (that is, holy sovereignties) of angels and then, dividing each hierarchy into three orders, to complete nine orders of angels establishes three sets of three. In the first he places Seraphim, Cherubim, Thrones; in the second Dominions, Powers, Virtues; in the third Principalities, Archangels, Angels. He asserts moreover that the first hierarchy immediately surrounds the Trinity and is illumined by it alone, but that the second, being midway between the first and the last, is both illumined by the preceding hierarchy and in turn illumines the succeeding. To investigate the explanation of their mysterious nature, which transcends human understanding, is beyond us, nor does the present work demand it. The theologian I mentioned above says, ''How great indeed and of what nature the glories of the superheavenly beings are, and how the hierarchies are perfected in relation to them, I hold that only the speculative guardian [238] of their perfection knows thoroughly.'' Since in these words he declares that only divine wisdom — from which they have their beginning, that they may exist, and to which they look by contemplation, that they may be made perfect — knows their sacred and very glorious ordering, it seems rash to investigate their nature, inasmuch as he confesses that even the angels themselves are not able to comprehend of what nature they were made or how they were ordered. Therefore he says, ''I declare that even they are as yet ignorant of their own virtues and illuminations, and their holy and very glorious ordering.'' Hence he adds, ''For it is impossible for us to know the

---

[237] In his *De caelesti hierarchia*, which was translated into Latin by *Iohannes Scotus Eriugena* (Migne, *Patrologia Latina* 122). Hugo of St. Victor wrote an expository work entitled *Commentariorum in hierarchiam coelestem S. Dionysii Areopagitae libri decem* (Migne, *l.c.*, 175) and Hofmeister believes that Otto used the book of Dionysius only in this form. *Cf.* Hashagen, *Otto von Freising* 18 *et seq.* With chapters 30-32 of Book VIII *cf.* also Ios. Turmel, ''L'angélologie depuis le faux Denys l' Aréopagite,'' in *Revue d' histoire et de littérature religieuse* 4 (1899), 217-238; 289-309; 414-434; 537-562. As the text of Otto indicates, the work of the Pseudo-Dionysius had much influence in the Middle Ages. It was translated into English by Parker in 1894. It is to be noted that Otto (p. 501), in common with his contemporaries, doubted not at all that *The Celestial Hierarchy* was written by the friend and disciple of Paul. The work was probably written in the fifth century. Its authorship is unknown.

[238] *I.e.*, wisdom. Otto's text reads: *contemplativam eorum perfectionis principem.* Scotus uses the word *teletarchiam* instead of *perfectionis principem.*

mysteries of super-celestial souls and their very holy perfections, except someone there shall have told us whatever mysteries divinity has taught us, through them who know them well, as something peculiarly their own.'' It has also been said, ''We labor in vain to comprehend super-celestial mysteries, since we believe that not even those super-celestial spirits themselves, by whose revelation we ought to know such things, can fully comprehend them.'' What is the explanation of the fact that, though he asserts above that they do not know, he here says that divinity instructs us through them who know such matters well as peculiarly their own, unless the meaning is that they know mysteries peculiarly their own sufficiently for our instruction, but do not know them with full and perfect understanding? Therefore, although we may not be able of our own power to comprehend anything of their nature, let us unhesitatingly hold this view which inspired utterance and that great theologian both attest with respect to those holy hierarchies. So then, he says, ''All theology has called the nine celestial beings by perfectly intelligible names.'' Then he adds what he was taught by his master Paul, that notable teacher of the Gentiles who, having been caught up to the third heaven,[239] had heard the mysteries of God. Dionysius's words are, ''These [the nine celestial beings] our holy Perfecter divides into three groups of three each.'' Because we do not read this statement anywhere in Paul's writings it is assumed that Dionysius, who was a lover of divine wisdom, learned it from Paul in intimate conversation. Nor is the fact that the Apostle denies that it is lawful for a man to utter the mysteries which he heard at variance with this view,[240] since both he that taught and he that was taught was not a man but superman, being wholly dead to this life. Let him say, therefore: These our holy Perfecter divides into three groups of three each. The first indeed he declares to be round about God, always existing, and describes as united more immediately to God than the rest — the most holy Thrones and the orders of beings full of eyes and feathers, called in the tongue of the Hebrews Cherubim and Seraphim. For because the Seraphim are conceived of as kindling knowledge, the Cherubim as the very fulness of knowledge, he figuratively calls the Cherubim full of eyes on account of their power of contemplation, and describes the Seraphim as full of feathers on account of their fine love, born of a most ardent passion. But the Thrones on which God renders his

---

[239] II Cor. 12. 2.   [240] II Cor. 12. 4.

judgments, which he elsewhere calls firm and lofty seats, he here anagogically [241] calls most holy Thrones. Lofty are they because of their dignity, firm because of the truth of their judgments, holy because of the abiding eternity of their immutability. The characteristic of the Thrones therefore is discernment in judgment, of the Cherubim knowledge of the truth, of the Seraphim the perfect love of knowledge. Because in these three all perfection consists, therefore the members of the hierarchies, because they love rightly, because they know and judge as if they presided within and never went out from inward contemplation to duties outside, are said to be immediately united with God and before all others ever to dwell intent on Him alone. Dionysius testifies that the lowest three are either sent to the outer world, as the angels and the archangels are, or by their invisible might arrange for their sending, as the Principalities do. Moreover, he says that the intermediate hierarchies administer, according to their dignity and their functions, such commands as must be carried from the hierarchies above them to the hierarchies below them. Among these he puts Dominions in the first place, because they formulate whatever must be proclaimed solely by authority; in the second place he puts Virtues, because they pass on to the Powers the authority received from the Dominions; in the third place he puts the Powers, because they carry into accomplishment by means of the Archangels and Angels that are subject unto them for the work the mandate conceived among the Principalities. Those who place the Virtues after the Angels and the Archangels, and then Powers and Principalities, understand by Virtues those through whom signs and miracles are wrought, by Powers those who check the malign influence of spirits that they may not be able to do as much harm as they desire to work, by Principalities those who rule even good spirits. In so doing they follow the etymology of the names rather than a rational consideration of their duties. For, according to our usage, it is a greater thing to rule by authority than by virtue. Again, a Principality is greater than a Power — for not every Power is a Principality, but all Principalities are Powers. Moreover, no one denies that it is more honorable to have dominion in a Principality than to be subject to a prince, and so they have put Dominions in a more prominent place because they lord it over the Principalities.

Why is it that, whereas the supreme hierarchy is believed to stand

241 The text reads *anagogice*.

immediately about God, and always in such rapt devotion that it never goes forth from the most delightful presence of His majesty — why is it, I ask, that a Seraph is said to have gone forth to cleanse the lips of the prophet, in the words, "Then flew one of the seraphim unto me," [242] and so forth? There doubtless, according to the same Dionysius, it is indicated that though the being that was sent was of the inferior order he received, by reason of the office, the name belonging to the superior order. Since he was coming to cleanse the lips of the prophet and to kindle in his mind the love of the divine, he received the name Seraph, that is, "one who kindles." [243] And yet there are those who say that spirits of the very highest order are not improperly sent to work out exalted plans, inasmuch as even the Only Begotten Himself, being sent from the bosom of the Father to earth, was called "an angel of great counsel." [244] That all are sent the Apostle seems to testify when he says, "Are they not all ministering spirits, sent forth to do service?" [245] and so forth. Hence men believe that Michael, Gabriel and Raphael, whom the Church of God holds in reverence before all other spirits, are princes of those highest orders; and men say that they never depart from the intimate presence of divinity, because they wish them to be of such great fineness and such inestimable purity that they may go forth to the outer world in such a way as yet to stand ever before God in the heavens. Hence we have that well-known statement of Gabriel in the Gospel, "I am one of those that stand ever before God, and I was sent to announce these things to thee." [246] When he said this he had been sent to the earth and yet he said that he was standing in the presence of God.

That some are taught by their superiors, while others are enlightened immediately by God, is proved by the authority of the prophets. Certain persons who did not understand the mystery of the incarnation, when they beheld Jesus ascending in glory to the heavens, marvelled at the advent of a new king and inquired of their superiors, saying, "Who is this king of glory?" [247] Their superiors also — not altogether ignorant but desiring to learn immediately from Him, yet not daring to press forward in haste to question Him — first deliberate among themselves: "Who is this that cometh from Edom, with dyed garments from Bozrah"?[248]

242 Isa. 6. 6.   243 *Cf.* Dionysius, *l.c.*, 7; Hugo, *l.c.*, 5. 2 and 6.
244 Isa. 9. 6 in the Septuagint version.   245 Heb. 1. 14.
246 Luke 1. 19.   247 Ps. 24. 8 and 10.   248 Isa. 63. 1.

When He of His own accord presented Himself for their instruction saying, "I that speak in righteousness," then at length, gaining assurance, they put the question to Him, "Wherefore art thou red in thine apparel, and thy garments like him that treadeth in the winevat?" In that they ask they show that they seek enlightenment, and in that they deliberate, conferring with one another, they indicate that they dare not anticipate the divine progress toward them. Hence that theologian says, "They take counsel together before they ask, showing that they are learning and seeking sacred wisdom, yet not pressing forward toward the enlightenment granted by the divine progress." Be it observed that the question put by those spirits to God is nothing else than the fulness of effort to obtain enlightenment, and God's reply is nothing else than the bestowal of enlightenment. Because therefore they themselves do not anticipate the enlightenment by way of comprehension, but the divine grace anticipates them in giving it, it is not said that they inquire beforehand that they may learn, but it is said that the Giver and Teacher offers them instruction. What Dionysius says is this, "Not pressing forward toward the enlightenment granted by the divine progress." For they would be pressing forward toward the enlightenment granted if in human fashion they were to seek, by their eager questions, to come to the light of knowledge, and so there would be progress, not of God to them but of them to God. But as the divine progress — that is, the gift proceeding from God, coming of its own accord upon them — so illumines them that no eager questioning effects this enlightenment, it is well said that they do not press forward toward the enlightenment granted by the divine progress.

Let this suffice then regarding the nature of angels. It has been derived not from our own opinions but from Holy Writ. Herein, defining nothing rashly but holding in reverence what is hid, we believe firmly that, whether all are sent forth or not — whether all know all the secrets of super-celestial matters or not — yet all rejoice, with unfailing exultation, in the contemplation of their Creator. Hence Dionysius testifies that "they are all alike turned toward the beginning that is above all beginnings and to the beginning that itself creates the beginning." This also seems to be in favor of the view that the spirits of the supreme hierarchy always stand in the presence of God, without going forth for service abroad, and that God's secrets are sometimes hid from the lesser spirits until they learn them by revelation made by their superiors. Even if this is not so it does not diminish their blessedness because, since they behold Him who knows all things, they so know all in Him that they desire to know whatever it is advantageous for them to know, and do not desire to know anything which it is not to their profit for them to know.

31. Because we have spoken in passing regarding the hierarchies of celestial spirits, for the reason that it is believed that the elect must be received into their orders to make one City with them, it remains for us to inquire how they may be taken in varying degrees into fellowship with them. That excellent theologian whom I have so often mentioned says on this point, "To these," that is, to super-celestial beings, "in proportion to our several achievements and varying degrees of enlightenment we ascend by the steps of spiritual advance in ourselves or the difference of gifts that exists between us." [249] It has been said that, even as we are in this present life graded proportionally through gifts of graces and grades of hon-ors — that is, by differing and ordered participation in such graces and honors — so we are to be promoted in varying degrees to fellowship in the heavenly company. For, according to the testi-mony of the Lord Himself, he that is faithful in little will be set over many things, and he who serves well will gain a high station since faithful stewards of the Church are more splendidly crowned in the heavens in proportion as they have by word and example toiled upon earth, feeding the Lord's flock.[250] Hence he who gained the more from the talent which he received to be put out at interest received the recompense of the reward — in proportion to the pre-eminence of his deserts — since it was said [251] to one, "Be thou over five cities," and to the other, "Be thou over ten." The saints therefore shall ascend by differences of progress (that is, they shall go forward according as they have done well) and by increase of enlightenment (that is, in so far as they have well taught those placed under their care) through grades of spiritual advance. That is to say, [they shall go forward] from strength to strength, not of the feet but of the mind, to varying dignities or differences of gifts — the divine gifts of grace — through the various orders of the blessed spirits. Inasmuch as these qualities are in them and among them — according to the saying of the Psalmist, "Blessed is the man

[249] Hugo of St. Victor, *l.c.*, 2.
[250] *Cf.* I Pet. 5. 2.   [251] Luke 19. 19 and 17.

whose help is from thee; he hath set in his heart the ways of ascent" [252] — that famous theologian well declares that "in proportion to our several achievements and varying degrees of enlightenment we ascend by the steps of spiritual advance in ourselves or by the difference of gifts that exist between us" into fellowship with the angels. Moreover, how separate individuals are taken out of the elect into the separate orders of the blessed spirits — so that they become like unto the angels, not only in purity of mind and of body but in rank of advancement, and equal to them in blessedness — the blessed Gregory [253] has discussed in words flowing with honey, words based solely upon this text, "He set the bounds of the peoples according to the number of the angels of God," [254] clearly showing that the number of the elect in that state would be as great as the number of the sacred angels that remained with God.

32. But it may be asked, since the tenth piece of silver,[255] which represented a part of the angels, being lost must be replaced by men, how is the number of the elect to be made as great as the number of the angels that remained with God? In this connection we must, doubtless, observe that the words six, ten, one hundred and others of the sort on the sacred page do not always indicate a definite number but often the implications of number. For since the shilling in the Sacred Scripture is wont to indicate perfection,[256] the tenth piece of silver is said to have been lost when a company of that reprobate gathering turned aside from God and, departing from the fitting perfection of their created state to the exercise of their own will, fell through pride, so that it is said not that a tenth part fell in their fall, but that this part fell *tenth*. In a word then, *tenth* imparts its meaning or significance as a word to the verb, so that "tenth" is joined with "fell" not substantively but as a predicate adjective. As a result it does not indicate a number but is subject to a literary interpretation — though, in accordance with the meaning of the number, that sense is also a mystical one. Hence to say

[252] Ps. 84. 5.   [253] *Homilia in evang.* 34. 11.

[254] Deut. 32. 8. The Vulgate reading is *filiorum Israel,* whereas *statuit terminos gentium secundum numerum angelorum Dei* is found in Gregory, *l.c.,* and in Dionysius, *De caelesti hierarchia, c.* 9. *Cf.* below, VIII. 32 and P. Sabatier, *Bibliorum sacrorum Latinae versiones antiquae seu vetus Italica* 1 (Rheims, 1743), 386.

[255] The text gives *dragma.* See Luke 15. 8.

[256] Hofmeister gives as references Gregory, *Moralia* 35. 16 and 42; Isidore, *Liber numerorum qui in sanctis scripturis occurrunt, c.* 11.

"fell tenth" is exactly equivalent to saying "fell perfect," that is, wherein it was perfect. So we are wont to say, "I see you wise," joining the verb transitively to "you," substantively to "wise." Perhaps, however, the phrase is *corruit decimā*, that is, *perfectā*; that is to say, *from* the tenth or *from* perfection. In that case "tenth" or "perfect" is the ablative or has the meaning of the ablative. For just as, according to the grammarians, the subject nominative frequently hints at its significance, so the ablative or the nominative in the predicate always hints at the force of the noun. When I say "Martin is a man" I do not, according to the logicians, predicate this but *of* this, just as, conversely, when I say "The man runs" I set down as subject not the "of this" but the "this." Now, if we are obliged by this parable to believe that a tenth part of the angels fell and must be replaced by men, we shall equally be obliged on the basis of the parable of the hundred sheep,[257] to admit that only a hundreth part [of the angels] fell. The aforesaid words, *denarius* and *centenarius,* therefore, because, as has been said, they refer us not to a specific number but to the implications of a number, do not oblige us to believe that a tenth part or a hundredth part of the angels fell, nor do they compel us to admit that the number of those to be substituted will be just as large as the number of those that fell, but they indicate only this, that the misery of those who fell is counterbalanced by the joy of the others, the imperfection of the one group by the perfection of the other. Nor, because it is said that the tenth coin was lost, were there ever ten grades there, one of which fell; the truth is rather that those who fell from the nine separate orders made one disordered throng, one disordered array. And yet, if anyone were to say that Gregory did not set this down as an assertion, we need not exert ourselves greatly to settle the matter, provided that this alone be believed, that the elect are truly received into the ranks of the various angels — whether they are equal or unequal in number — to be equal in blessedness with them. For Gregory does not say that we *know*, but that we *believe* that so and so many will ascend to a like number. And it is clear that the text which he set down, "He set the bounds of the peoples according to the number of the angels," is not in harmony with this interpretation since it is there said afterwards, "For Jehovah's portion is His people." On the testimony of Dionysius it appears that the meaning intended by

[257] Matt. 18. 12 *et seq.*; Luke 15. 4 *et seq.*

this passage is as follows. All the other peoples, devoting themselves to the service of the angels, cherished the varied warfare of the heavens; the people of Israel alone, preserving the worship of one God, became peculiarly His as His portion and the lot of His inheritance. Hence comes the saying of the Psalmist, "In Judah is God known: His name is great in Israel." [258] But if, following another translation we read, "according to the number of the sons of God," it is indicated that we need a far different interpretation — unless we call those whom we also call angels sons of God, in accordance with that passage in Genesis [259] in which one translator states that "the sons of God," another that "the angels" approached the daughters of men. But if, in harmony with our interpretation, the reading is "according to the number of the sons of Israel," the passage will be far removed from that meaning. Accordingly, leaving to wiser men the decision concerning a matter that is very mysterious and wholly removed from our comprehension, let us go on to those things which remain, believing only this, that in the book of the perfectly wise foreknowledge of God, which no profundity escapes and from which no secret is hid, there is definitely fixed the number of the elect and there is a proper reward for the merits of each.

33. Now we must inquire what the blessedness of that country is. For we must not suppose that souls, after they have been stripped from the body, or after they have taken up spiritual bodies and are not inferior to the angelic spirits in purity and in rank, find delight in external things as men do in this life. Accordingly, whenever Holy Scripture says [260] that their spirits are refreshed and affected by flowering and verdant meadows, by pleasant places, by the singing of birds, by fragrant things (such as cinnamon and balsam), such expressions should, it is clear, be interpreted spiritually rather than carnally. And yet, for the sake of the simple — who must be nourished on milk, not on solid food, whose understanding is not yet exercised and who cannot as yet comprehend spiritual delights — these things are frequently set down by certain teachers that the simple may thus be directed through the visible to the understanding and discovery of the invisible. The blessedness of the saints then lies in beholding their Creator, in accordance with that saying of the Lord, "This is life eternal, that they should know thee the true God, and him whom thou didst send, even

[258] Ps. 76. 1.   [259] Gen. 6. 2, and see I. 2 above.   [260] Ezek. 34. 14.

Jesus Christ''; [261] of course we must understand the words ''with
the Holy Spirit'' who proceedeth from both [the Father and the
Son]. ''This,'' he says, ''is life eternal.'' For what else is life
eternal than purest blessedness? For if the life were temporary it
would not be blessed since it would be rendered anxious lest it come
to an end. Again, however long in duration, it could not be called
blessed unless it were free from the defect of misery of every kind
and abounded in every sort of happiness, or if it were marred by
any sort of blemish. That life therefore is eternal and blessed,
blessed and eternal, ''that they should know thee the true God,
and him whom thou didst send, even Jesus Christ.'' Observe that
he said that the enjoyment of blessedness is the knowledge of
divinity. Hence it is to no purpose that certain people strive in
this life to comprehend the divine nature, which is seen by saints
in this life only with difficulty as ''in a mirror'' and ''in a riddle,''
since it is promised that it is to be seen and fully understood by
them only in the life to come. The saints therefore find their delight
in the wholly ecstatic and eternally blessed vision of God, in accordance with the saying of the Psalmist, ''He who gave the law
shall give his benediction, they shall go from strength to strength,
the God of gods shall be seen in Zion.'' [262] What can be greater,
what more delightful, what more glorious? With what overwhelm-
ing longing do we, if we sit in darkness, yearn for the sun of our
world, with what great earnestness do we wish for that light! If
this light when missed by us is recovered again with joy and beheld with wonder when it has been received again, and if our
vision, when struck by it, frequently is aroused to look on it yet
again — and it does not grow common through familiarity, and
familiarity with it does not produce distaste for it — what delight,
think you, will the Light of Lights bestow upon those that behold
it, what admiration will it arouse without ever causing satiety!
If we look with admiration and with a certain pleasurable sensa-
tion upon earthly kings or emperors, in their fleeting and transitory glory, with what inestimable joy shall we count those to be
thrilled — with what unspeakable exultation of heart shall we believe them to be inspired who shall behold the King of Kings, the
Creator of the universe, in His incomparable and unfading grace
and glory, attended by His celestial host of angels and of men?
They shall not only behold Him but they shall love Him whom they

261 John 17. 3.   262 *Cf.* Ps. 84. 7.

have seen and shall glorify Him whom they have loved.[263] Hence
the Psalmist has beautifully said, "Blessed are they that dwell in
thy house; they shall praise thee for ever and ever." [264] Their
blessedness, therefore, consists in seeing God, upon whom the angels
long to gaze;[265] in seeing Him continually yet without weariness;
when they have seen Him, to love Him incessantly without satiety,
and when they have loved Him to praise Him untiringly without
exhaustion; and to rejoice over these things for ever and ever with
ineffable exaltation of heart and with joy beyond belief, without
any admixture of sadness. Because this blessedness cannot be fully
attained in this life, it is fittingly reserved for that heavenly City.
Hence the Psalmist says again, "The habitation of all is in thee,
as of those that rejoice." [266] In that he says, not "of those that rejoice," but "as of those that rejoice," he thus indicates that the joy
there far excels our joy in this life.

Since, therefore, they rejoice fully and perfectly, with a joy at
the sight of God which no one can take away from them, how can
we suppose they are to be delighted by more external things, seeing
that, even in this present life, where we have a bare foretaste of
that glory as "in a mirror" and "in a riddle," the saints are sometimes so exalted by the contemplation of the things that are above,
that all their senses lose their ordinary powers and they are sweetly
thrilled by a delight that is wholly internal? Therefore we must
not suppose that, even though in a new heaven and a new earth —
where all is changed for the better and everything shines resplendent with a charming loveliness — the saints, whose joy, as was
said above, lies in seeing and praising their Creator, will be so occupied with that loveliness that they will be won away from that
joy. For although, according to the prophet,[267] the light of the
moon shall there become as great as the light of the sun now is, and
the light of the sun shall be sevenfold as great as it is now, yet
elsewhere you read that the "city hath no need of the sun, neither
of the moon, to shine upon it: for the glory of God shall enlighten
it and the lamp thereof is the Lamb." [268] But if those who are illumined by the radiance of God and are ineffably bathed in the light of

---

[263] Cf. the closing section of Augustine's City of God, in which the sentence
occurs (22. 30): Ibi vacabimus et videbimus, videbimus et amabimus, amabimus
et laudabimus.

[264] Ps. 84. 4.   [265] Cf. I Pet. 1. 12.   [266] Cf. Ps. 87. 7.
[267] Isa. 30. 26.   [268] Rev. 21. 23.

the contemplation and actual vision of Him need no lights there above to increase their delight, much less shall they need for their pleasure these lesser luminaries whereby, as was said above, our bodily senses are wont to be affected. And yet there is no lack of those who say that there too that delight is not lacking. They say that those who are there have an abundance of all sorts of pleasures and that, although they do not miss the more external joys because they are completely happy in the vision of God, yet those external delights follow in the train of the vision, as its satellites, even as sometimes in the writings of the saints secular knowledge, although not the aim of the writer, is known to accompany divine wisdom as a handmaiden.[269] All these things therefore, if they are there, will be there as embellishment, not to meet a need.

34. It remains to consider whether God is seen there both with the eyes of the body and with the eyes of the spirit, or only with the eyes of the spirit in accordance with the saying, "Blessed are the pure in heart: for they shall see God."[270] Some interpret this in such a way as to assert that even there God is to be seen with the heart only, in the most perfect purity of its nature. Augustine appears to be so far in accord with such persons as to say in his book *The City of God*[271] that it is hard to believe that we cannot close our eyes there, still harder to believe that God is not seen there even when the eyes are closed. But it must be observed that the aforesaid father in that same work made many statements in anything but an authoritative fashion, as he himself bears witness, saying, "I do not wish everything that I have set down to be rashly believed, because some things are not so fully believed by me as though there were no doubt about them in my mind."[272] Hence when his opinion on this very matter was opposed by his fellow bishops, on the ground that he spoke in opposition to the text, "Whom I, even I, shall see and not a stranger, and mine eyes shall behold him,"[273] he replied that he had not erred in this, in saying that God was not to be seen with our present eyes, since either He will not be seen by them or, if He shall be seen by them, they will not be the same eyes as they now are, inasmuch as they shall be changed to a far different state. Wherefore there is no lack of those who claim that God is to be seen in both ways. They say that complete blessedness consists in seeing God and that, if the bodies were

[269] An interesting comment on Christian Latin literature.
[270] Matt. 5. 8.   [271] 22. 29.   [272] 21. 7.   [273] Job 19. 27.

then to be deprived of this vision, the saints would by no means enjoy supreme blessedness in both respects but·only in the spirit. Nor would that condition differ much from our present condition, since even now, when their bodies are mouldering in the ground, the spirits and the souls of the just behold God in Heaven. Nor is this at variance with the saying, "Blessed are the pure in heart: for they shall see God," for of course not the impure but only the pure in heart shall deserve to behold God. The statement is true. therefore, in the subject, "Only with a pure heart shall they behold God," not true in the predicate, "They shall see God with a pure heart only." For example this is true, "The Father is the only God," but this is not true, "Only the Father is God." In the former proposition it is stated that there is no God other than the Father, which is true; in the second it is stated that God is no other than the Father, which is false, because the Son is God and, though He is in person separate from the Father, He is not another God. Wherefore also it is denied by theologians that God can be spoken of separately or alone. Whether therefore the saints shall behold God with the soul only, or — to the greater increase of blessedness (as though clothed in a double mantle, namely the flesh and the spirit) — they shall look upon God with both kinds of vision, it is still certain that with unveiled faces they shall see Him as He is, they shall rejoice in Him and concerning Him, they shall praise Him forever and ever. This is that eighth day which not having an evening follows the Sabbath or rather continues the Sabbath. For this evening does not darken by merging into night but dawns toward the first day of the week, which is also the eighth, when the rest of souls is not terminated but is doubled by the receiving of bodies. This is the rest of rest, the sabbath of sabbaths, the month of months. This will be at the end without end.

Mark you how divine wisdom, ever conquering evil, "reacheth from one end of the world to the other with full strength," [274] how "she ordereth all things graciously." For how can any power show greater might than by first casting out the devil with all his members into the abyss of the nethermost pit and then leading its own members to the super-celestial joys? What is more gracious than to perform all these things without any disturbance? From one end to the other therefore, namely from the beginning even to the conclusion (whence He is called Alpha and Omega),[275] He reacheth

---

[274] Wisd. of Sol. 8. 1.   [275] Otto's text reads *Alfa et* ω; Rev. 1. 8.

with full strength — that is, He justly distributes to both [good and bad] the various rewards that they deserve. Or, if you will, He reacheth from the end of the good to the end of the bad. Hence the prophet says, "Who sittest above the cherubim, who beholdest the abodes of the dead."[276] For He sits as the unchanging one above the loftiest heights and, as a just judge, views the uttermost depths. He sits, because judging in gentleness He ordereth all things graciously; He shall gaze upon the abodes of the dead from above the Cherubim because He reacheth with full strength from one end to the other. He reacheth, by beholding and by justly ruling both, the end than which there is nothing lower from the end than which there is nothing higher, the end than which there is nothing more bitter from the end than which there is nothing sweeter, the end than which there is nothing more wretched from the end than which there is nothing more blessed. "This is the heritage of the servants of Jehovah."[277] "There," as Augustine says, "we shall be at leisure, we shall see, we shall love, we shall praise."[278] Moreover according to the prophet "the name of the city from that day shall be 'Jehovah is there'."[279]

35. Let it suffice to have said this much, in accordance with the capacity of our understanding, concerning the end of the City of Christ. Herein, to use the words of Dionysius, "Taking thought of the limitations of our powers of speech, we have passed over certain matters, at the same time also honoring with silence the mystery which is above our powers."[280] For "it is the glory of kings to conceal a matter,"[281] and so he who divulges mysteries disparages majesty. I am, of course, aware that great things ought to be spoken of in such a way that there shall always remain something to be investigated with care, lest if the whole matter be unfolded promiscuously it may appear of little value. Accordingly, though we devotedly offer to your love these matters which have been set forth, in however rude a style — not out of our own wisdom but in accordance with the teachings of the Scriptures — we do not bestow them upon those who are unwilling to receive or who scornfully reject them. For, as I have said above[282] of Augustine, some matters are set down in his writings not as assertions but only on the basis of opinion and investigation, and the decision of

---

[276] See Song of Three Children, 32.　[277] Isa. 54. 17.
[278] 22. 30 (end).　[279] Ezek. 48. 35.　[280] Chapter 15.
[281] Cf. Prov. 25. 2.　[282] VIII. 34.

a final judgment has been left to those who are wiser. It will be your task to supplement what has been said insufficiently, to correct what has been said imperfectly, to prune away the superfluous and as, laden with sins, I struggle in this wide sea of the world, to aid me by the solace of your prayers.

INDEX